ENVIRONMENTAL RIGHTS

Environmental rights, also known as the human rights or constitutional rights that are used for the protection of the environment, have proliferated over the last 45 years. However, the precise levels of protection that they represent has since been a major question associated with this phenomenon. *Environmental Rights: The Development of Standards* systematically investigates this question by analyzing the emerging standards of environmental protection that are associated with such rights and the way that those associations are becoming formalized. It covers all of the relevant human rights treaties, selected national constitutions and other developments to illustrate how environmental rights standards are emerging in this dynamic area. Bringing together an elite group of scholars, this book discusses significant new insights into the way that environmental rights are developing, the standards of protection that they confer, and the way that standards in the field of environmental rights can potentially be further developed in the future.

Stephen J. Turner is a Senior Lecturer at Lincoln University, United Kingdom.

Dinah L. Shelton is Manatt/Ahn Professor of International Law Emeritus at George Washington University.

Jona Razzaque is Professor of Environmental Law at Bristol Law School, University of the West of England.

Owen McIntyre is Professor and Director of the LL.M. at the University College Cork, School of Law.

James R. May is Distinguished Professor of Law at Widener University, Delaware Law School.

Environmental Rights

THE DEVELOPMENT OF STANDARDS

Edited by

STEPHEN J. TURNER
Lincoln University

DINAH L. SHELTON
George Washington University, Washington DC

JONA RAZZAQUE
University of the West of England, Bristol

OWEN MCINTYRE
University College Cork

JAMES R. MAY
Widener University, Delaware Law School

CAMBRIDGE
UNIVERSITY PRESS

CAMBRIDGE
UNIVERSITY PRESS

University Printing House, Cambridge CB2 8BS, United Kingdom

One Liberty Plaza, 20th Floor, New York, NY 10006, USA

477 Williamstown Road, Port Melbourne, VIC 3207, Australia

314–321, 3rd Floor, Plot 3, Splendor Forum, Jasola District Centre, New Delhi – 110025, India

79 Anson Road, #06–04/06, Singapore 079906

Cambridge University Press is part of the University of Cambridge.

It furthers the University's mission by disseminating knowledge in the pursuit of education, learning, and research at the highest international levels of excellence.

www.cambridge.org
Information on this title: www.cambridge.org/9781108482240
DOI: 10.1017/9781108612500

First published 2019

Printed and bound in Great Britain by Clays Ltd, Elcograf S.p.A.

A catalogue record for this publication is available from the British Library.

Library of Congress Cataloging-in-Publication Data
NAMES: Turner, Stephen J. (Stephen James), editor.
TITLE: Environmental rights : the development of standards / Edited by Stephen J. Turner, Lincoln University, Dinah L. Shelton, George Washington University, Washington DC, Jona Razzaque, University of the West of England, Bristol, Owen McIntyre, University College Cork, James R. May, Widener University School of Law, Delaware.
DESCRIPTION: New York, NY : Cambridge University Press, 2019. | Includes index.
IDENTIFIERS: LCCN 2018048313 | ISBN 9781108482240
SUBJECTS: LCSH: Environmental law, International. | Environmental law – International cooperation. | International and municipal law.
CLASSIFICATION: LCC K3585 .E653 2019 | DDC 344.04/6–dc23
LC record available at https://lccn.loc.gov/2018048313

ISBN 978-1-108-48224-0 Hardback

Contents

Contributors

Alexandra Aragão is Professor at the Faculty of Law of the University of Coimbra (Portugal), where she teaches environmental law, EU law, risk governance and food law. She is vice director of the Portuguese journal *Planning, Urban and Environmental Law Review*. Professor Aragão is a member of several European observatories, research groups and academic organizations related to environmental law. Her present areas of research in environmental law are justice, impact assessment, ecosystem services, waste law, fundamental principles and the Anthropocene.

Sumundu Atapattu PhD (Cambridge), is Director of Research Centers and International Programs at the University of Wisconsin Law School (United States), Executive Director of the Human Rights Program at the University of Wisconsin-Madison and Lead Counsel for Human Rights at the Center for International Sustainable Development Law (Montreal, Canada). She is the author of *Human Rights Approaches to Climate Change: Challenges and Opportunities* (2016), co-editor of *International Environmental Law and the Global South* (Cambridge University Press, 2015), co-author with Andrea Schapper of *Human Rights and the Environment: Key Issues* (2019) and co-editor of the *Cambridge Handbook on Environmental Justice and Sustainable Development* (forthcoming).

Nathan J. Cooper is Associate Professor at Te Piringa – Faculty of Law, University of Waikato (New Zealand). His research relates primarily to water governance and to the interface of human rights and environmental protection in relation to fresh water resources, addressing the challenge of realizing sustainable and equitable water for everyone.

Erin Daly is Professor of Law at Delaware Law School, Widener University, USA. She has written extensively on comparative constitutional law and transitional justice issues, including *Dignity Rights: Courts, Constitutions, and the Worth of the Human Person* (2012) and *Reconciliation in Divided Societies: Finding Common Ground* (2006). She and James R. May co-authored *Global Environmental Constitutionalism* (Cambridge University Press, 2013) and have co-edited other volumes on environmental constitutional law, including *Implementing Environmental Constitutionalism* (Cambridge University Press, 2018). She serves as the Director of the Global Network for Human Rights and the Environment and as the United States representative to the Centre internationale de droit comparé de l'environnement.

Anél du Plessis is Professor of Law at the Faculty of Law, North-West University (South Africa). Professor du Plessis' field of specialization is the intersection between environmental rights, environmental law and local governance. She heads the NWU LLM Environmental Law and Governance Programme and is the co-project leader of an Alexander von Humboldt-funded research project on 'Legal Perspectives on Safe and Sustainable Cities'. She is member of the Secretariat of the Environmental Law Association of South Africa, the teaching committee of the IUCN Academy of Environmental Law and the South African Young Academy of Science.

Gitanjali N. Gill is Professor of Environmental Law at the Law School, Northumbria University, Newcastle upon Tyne (United Kingdom). Her research interests and expertise focus on social and environmental justice issues, human rights, public interest litigation and sustainable development with emphasis on India. She is widely published on environmental law in India and has articles in the *Environmental Law Journal*, *Environmental Law Review*, *Transnational Environmental Law*, *Northern Ireland Legal Quarterly*, *Public Law* and has authored chapters in several books. In 2017, her book *Environmental Justice in India: The National Green Tribunal* was published.

Evadné Grant is Associate Head in the Department of Law at the University of the West of England, Bristol (United Kingdom). Her research covers a variety of issues in international human rights law, including human dignity, the interface between human rights and the environment and social, economic and cultural rights. She co-edits the *Journal of Human Rights and the Environment* and is a series editor for *Critical Reflections on Human Rights and the Environment*.

Angela Kariuki is an environment officer in the International Environmental Law unit of the Law Division at the United Nations Environment Programme. She holds degrees and postgraduate qualifications in international relations, law, human rights and environmental policy. Following her graduate studies, Angela worked at a national human rights institution on issues related to environment, natural resource management and rural development. In this role, her work focused specifically on the environmental and human rights impacts of the extractive industry, particularly mining operations. She is currently reading for her PhD in environment and society at the University of Pretoria (South Africa).

Craig M. Kauffman is Associate Professor of Political Science at the University of Oregon (United States), where he specializes in environmental politics. His book *Grassroots Global Governance: Local Watershed Management Experiments and the*

Evolution of Sustainable Development (2017) won the 2017 Sprout award for best book in environmental studies. He has also authored numerous publications in *Global Environmental Politics, World Development, Environmental Research Letters, Latin America Research Review, Agricultural Water Management, Peace Review* and other sources. His current research analyses the politics surrounding efforts to implement Earth-centered laws and explains why some efforts succeed while others fail.

John H. Knox is the Henry C. Lauerman Professor of International Law at Wake Forest University (United States). He is an internationally recognized expert on human rights law and international environmental law. In 2012, the United Nations Human Rights Council appointed him to a three-year mandate as its first Independent Expert on the issue of human rights obligations relating to the enjoyment of a safe, clean, healthy and sustainable environment. In 2015, his mandate was extended for another three years and his title changed to Special Rapporteur. In that position, he reported to the Council on the relationship of human rights and environmental protection.

Louis J. Kotzé is Research Professor of Law at the Faculty of Law, North-West University (South Africa). He is a visiting professor at the University of Lincoln (United Kingdom) and a Fellow of the Sustainability College Bruges (Belgium). His research focuses on the Anthropocene, environmental constitutionalism, human rights and global environmental governance. In 2016, he obtained a second PhD at Tilburg University (the Netherlands), and has been awarded the prestigious European Commission Horizon 2020 Marie Curie Individual Fellowship to lead a research project during 2018–19 at the University of Lincoln entitled "Global Ecological Custodianship – Innovative International Environmental Law for the Anthropocene."

David Marrani PhD, MA, Maîtrise, Licence, LAP, studied law, philosophy and psychoanalysis in France and at the University of Essex (United Kingdom). He is Dean and Professor of Law at the Institute of Law, Jersey (United Kingdom), where he teaches jurisprudence and French public law. He previously was a senior lecturer at the University of Essex. He is Visiting Professor at the University of Turin (Italy), the Universitat Autònoma de Barcelona (Spain) and the Catholic University of Lille in Paris (France). His research relates to the intersections between law, philosophy and psychoanalysis. He also works on comparative constitutional law and has published numerous articles on the French Charter for the Environment.

James R. May is a distinguished professor of Law, Director of the Global Environmental and Natural Resources Law Institute, Co-director of the Environmental Law Center and Adjunct Professor of Graduate Engineering at Widener University, Delaware Law School (United States), where he also founded and co-chairs a program on marine policy. He is the author of six books and more than eighty articles and book chapters relating to environmental, water quality or constitutional law. May is a Member of Faculty to the National Judicial College and a Fellow of the American College of Environmental Lawyers, for whom he has served as a delegate to China regarding environmental law.

Owen McIntyre is a professor at the School of Law, University College Cork (Ireland), where he is the Director of the LLM (Environmental and Natural Resources Law) Programme and Co-director of the Centre for Law and the Environment. He serves as Chair of the IUCN World Commission on Environmental Law, Specialist Group on Water and Wetlands, as a member of the Project Complaints Mechanism of the European Bank for Reconstruction and Development (EBRD) and is a former member of the Scientific Committee of the European Environment Agency.

Karen Morrow has been professor of Environmental Law at Swansea University (United Kingdom) since 2007. Her research focuses on theoretical and practical aspects of public participation in environmental law and policy, and on gender and the environment. She has published extensively in these areas. She is on the editorial boards of the *Journal of Human Rights and the Environment*, the *Environmental Law Review* and the *University of Western Australia Law Review*. She is a series editor for *Critical Reflections on Human Rights and the Environment* and a member of the International Advisory Board for the *Gender and Environment* book series.

Silvia Nonna is Professor of Environmental Law in the School of Law at the University of Buenos Aires (UBA, Argentina), from which she has received a law degree, a PhD and a postdoctoral degree. She also holds a post-graduate degree in International Commerce of Hydrocarbons from the School of Engineering at UBA. She has been the Secretary of Academic Affairs at the School of Law at UBA since 2010, and is also Vice President of the Centre for Judicial Capacitating at the Supreme Court City of Buenos Aires. She is the director of research for numerous programs and projects.

Lara Ognibene joined the United Nations Environment Programme (UN Environment) in 2009. She is a legal officer in the Law Division of the UN Environment headquarters in Nairobi. Her main areas of work are human rights and the environment, climate change and international water law. Before joining UN Environment, she worked as an international lawyer at DLA Piper. In 2006, she was granted a law fellowship at the Center for International Environmental Law in Washington, DC. She holds degrees from the University of Milan (Italy) and the University of San Sebastian (Spain), and an LLM in international law from the University of Edinburgh (United Kingdom).

Jona Razzaque Professor of Environmental Law at Bristol Law School, University of the West of England (UWE, Bristol, United Kingdom), is a barrister and holds a PhD in law from the University of London (United Kingdom). Prior to joining the

UWE, she worked as a staff lawyer with the Foundation for International Environmental Law and Development. She is a member of the Advisory Board of the Journal of Environmental Law and serves as a member of the IUCN World Commission on Environmental Law. She has researched and published widely on access to justice and participatory rights in environmental matters.

Áine Ryall is a senior lecturer at the School of Law, University College Cork (Ireland), where she specializes in environmental law, EU law and tort law. A qualified barrister called to the Irish Bar in 1995, she is Vice Chair of the Aarhus Convention Compliance Committee and a member of the Avosetta Expert Group on EU environmental law. She is a member of the statutory Advisory Committee to the Irish Environmental Protection Agency, the board of the Irish Centre for European Law and the Royal Irish Academy Climate Change and Environmental Sciences Committee.

Linda Sheehan is Senior Counsel at the Leonardo DiCaprio Foundation, where she advances climate change solutions and provides legal direction. She formerly ran the Earth Law Center, where she advocated for nature's rights, and directed the California Coastkeeper Alliance and Ocean Conservancy's Pacific Region. For her efforts "fight[ing] pollution of the Pacific and the streams and rivers that flow into it" she was recognized as a California Coastal Hero. She holds a BS in Chemical Engineering from MIT, MPP from the UC Berkeley Goldman School of Public Policy, and a JD from Berkeley Law School. She developed and taught Earth Law for the Vermont Law School (United States).

Dinah L. Shelton joined the law school at George Washington University (Washington, DC) in 2004. She is the author or editor of three prize-winning books. In 2006, she was awarded the Elizabeth Haub Prize in Environmental Law. She has served as a legal consultant to the United Nations Environment Programme, UNITAR, World Health Organization, European Union, Council of Europe, and the Organization of American States. In 2009, she became the first woman nominated by the United States to become a member of the Inter-American Commission on Human Rights. She served a four-year term, during which she went on to become President of the Commission.

Stephen J. Turner is a senior lecturer at Lincoln University (United Kingdom). He specializes in the areas of international environmental law, global environmental governance and corporate law. He has written two books that relate to rights-based approaches to global environmental governance: *A Substantive Environmental Right* (2009) and *A Global Environmental Right* (2014). He has also held academic positions at Winchester and Kingston universities. In 2003 he was awarded a PhD scholarship from London University (Queen Mary), and in 2013 was named Researcher of the Year at Kingston University (Law School).

Foreword

John H. Knox

The concept of environmental human rights is a relative latecomer to human rights law. The Universal Declaration of Human Rights does not mention the environment at all, much less include a human right to a healthy environment. After the modern environmental movement began in the late 1960s, references to environmental rights did start to appear, especially in national constitutions, but it was not until the 1990s that national and international tribunals began to seriously explore what human rights law has to say about environmental protection.

Over the past two decades, the breadth and depth of rights-based environmental law have greatly accelerated. Many more countries have amended their constitutions to include a right to a healthy environment, and national courts have applied the right to a variety of environmental challenges and forged innovative and far-reaching remedies. At the international level, however, the right to a healthy environment has still not been recognized in a global agreement. While many regional human rights treaties have incorporated environmental rights, in one form or another, only the African Charter on Human and Peoples' Rights has provided for it to be applied by an oversight mechanism. In the absence of a justiciable, globally recognized right to a healthy environment, international human rights tribunals and quasi-tribunals have brought human rights norms to bear on environmental issues by "greening" well-established human rights such as the rights to life and health. Human rights bodies have described how environmental harm interferes with the enjoyment of these and other rights, and have held that governments have obligations under human rights law to protect against such harm.

In 2012, the United Nations Human Rights Council decided to appoint an independent expert to review these developments and clarify the obligations under human rights law relating to the enjoyment of a safe, clean, healthy and sustainable environment. I had the honor to receive this mandate, and I spent the next two years issuing a series of reports reviewing the extensive jurisprudence applying human rights law to environmental issues. Regional tribunals, UN human rights treaty bodies, Special Rapporteurs and other authoritative sources had issued dozens of opinions, statements and reports on environmental issues. Despite addressing different rights, different environmental threats and different legal sources, they had reached very similar conclusions. Moreover, governments and international organizations were engaging in a broad range of good practices in the implementation of a rights-based approach to environmental protection.

I described the human rights obligations relating to the environment in a "mapping" report to the Human Rights Council, which I presented in 2014, and the following year presented a report identifying more than one hundred good practices in the use of these obligations. At the March 2015 session of the Council, it decided to renew the mandate for another three years, change my title to Special Rapporteur and request me to promote implementation of the obligations. The Council decision was adopted by consensus, illustrating the increasing acceptance of States that the human rights obligations relating to the environment are clear enough that it is reasonable to expect States to comply with them.

One of my goals over the next three years was to provide a clear, succinct statement of the obligations. To that end, I presented the Framework Principles on Human Rights and the Environment in March 2018, in my last report to the Council. These sixteen principles, with their accompanying commentary, set out the principal human rights obligations relating to the enjoyment of a safe, clean, healthy and sustainable environment. I used the term "framework" to emphasize that while the Principles should provide a sturdy basis for further development, they are certainly not the final word. I expect that our understanding of environmental rights will continue to grow and deepen in coming years.

The Framework Principles show both how far human rights law has come in relation to environmental protection and how far it still has to go. Many of the obligations that human rights bodies have found it easiest to apply are essentially procedural obligations, including duties of States to provide environmental information, undertake environmental assessments of proposed projects and policies and to facilitate public participation. Nor is there much dispute that States have obligations to respect and protect rights to freedom of expression, peaceful assembly and association in the environmental context, to take steps to protect those who receive threats or suffer violence or harassment because of their exercise of their rights or to provide effective remedies for violations of rights.

Other areas remain less settled. While it is inarguable that obligations of non-discrimination apply to environmental law and policy, much more needs to be done to clarify what steps States must take to protect those who are most at risk from environmental harm. Treaty bodies with jurisdiction over the rights of women and children, for example, have only recently begun to start addressing environmental issues. Even when standards are clearly defined, of course, implementation often lags far behind. The obligations of States towards indigenous peoples, for example, are set out in international instruments, but they seem to be violated on a virtually continual basis. Nevertheless, the adoption of clear standards is critically important because they at least provide a basis for criticism, legal proceedings and even, in some cases, sanctions.

Substantive environmental standards continue to resist clear definition. While it is clear that States have obligations to take steps to protect against harmful environmental interference with human rights, international human rights bodies have generally not set specific substantive standards. Instead, they have typically applied an indeterminate list of factors, including whether the standard is nonretrogressive and whether it takes into account relevant international or domestic standards. This differential treatment of substantive versus procedural standards may, to some extent, be unavoidable. Perhaps human rights bodies are simply better suited to police compliance with procedural standards and States should receive more discretion in setting substantive standards. At the same time, some national courts are showing a greater willingness to hold governments to specific substantive as well as procedural standards.

This volume provides an invaluable contribution to the ongoing clarification of the issues surrounding rights-based environmental standards. It includes essays by an extraordinary group of scholars, who address the topic from many different angles. They provide fascinating case studies of the growth of environmental rights in many countries around the world, including Argentina, Bhutan, France, India, Portugal and South Africa. The contributions also address regional developments, including in Africa, the Americas and Europe, as well as global multilateral environmental agreements and the United Nations human rights mechanisms. They also tackle the question from different cross-cutting thematic perspectives, including by focusing on obligations owed to indigenous peoples, rights to water and sanitation and rights of nature.

The scholarly and political discussion of these issues is far from over – indeed, it may be still in its early stages – so this book will not be the final word. But it will provide lasting guidance for all of those who work for a healthy environment that can and does support the full enjoyment of our human rights.

Preface and Acknowledgements

In April 2016, Lincoln University (UK) held a one-day symposium related to the development of "standards" in the field of environmental rights. The symposium focused on the actual standards of protection associated with particular environmental rights. A number of the contributors to this volume took part, including Alexandra Aragão, Gitanjali Gill, Evadné Grant, Louis Kotzé, James May, Áine Ryall and Stephen Turner. John Knox, the Special Rapporteur for Human Rights and the Environment, gave a pre-recorded video message for the delegates and Silvia Nonna delivered a keynote address.

The conceptual basis for the symposium had in part been prompted by some of the debates that took place at a conference held at Yale University in September 2014. That conference, the Yale/UNITAR Conference on Human Rights, Environmental Sustainability, Post-2015 Development, and the Future of Climate Change, involved many discussions, but some of them centered on the "vagueness" of the content of many environmental rights and the effect that such a lack of clarity can have. Later in 2015, Stephen Turner visited Buenos Aires University, which resulted in a discussion with Silvia Nonna related to standards in the Argentine constitution. This led to Silvia Nonna visiting Lincoln University to speak on the subject the following April, and this provided a good opportunity to hold a symposium at which experts could consider the way that standards are evolving within the field of environmental rights.

The symposium itself started the process of unpacking and analyzing the different types of standards emerging within the field of environmental rights. It resulted in a consensus from those attending that the subject deserved more detailed attention, and it was suggested that the group continue to work together with a view to developing a body of knowledge and analysis relating to the subject.

Following this, other leading academics in the field agreed to lend their skills, knowledge and experience to what loosely became known as the "Standards in Environmental Rights Project." Therefore, at that juncture we welcomed Dinah Shelton, Linda Sheehan, Jona Razzaque, Anél du Plessis, Lara Ognibene, Karen

Morrow, Owen McIntyre, David Marrani, Craig Kauffman, Angela Kariuki, Erin Daly and Sumudu Atapattu. While this group are diverse in viewpoints, backgrounds and areas of expertise, they share an interest in furthering the understanding and development of the field. It was the combined efforts of all of the above-named academics that has led to this book coming to fruition.

A debt of gratitude is owed to numerous organizations and individuals for their support during different stages of this project.

Wilkin Chapman Solicitors LLP generously sponsored the symposium in April 2016, we therefore wish to thank them, and in particular Ruth Brewin, Peter Hanson and Alison Mitchell.

Lincoln Council also supported the 2016 symposium and facilitated a private viewing of the Magna Carta at Lincoln Castle that was much appreciated.

Thanks are also due to Santander plc for the travel bursary for Stephen Turner's visit to Buenos Aires mentioned above.

We wish to thank John Knox in his role as the United Nations Special Rapporteur for Human Rights and the Environment. We thank him for his leadership, encouragement and advice, and for writing the Foreword for this book.

There are other colleagues that either supported or took part in the original symposium in April 2016 whom we wish to thank. These are Duncan French, Matthew Hall, Sam Adelman, Ole Pedersen and also Ben Standing of Browne Jacobson LLP.

We thank John Berger and the editorial and production staff at Cambridge University Press who have been extremely patient and helpful in all aspects of the writing, editing and production process.

At the World Health Organization, we wish to thank Steven Solomon for helpful advice and also Rebecca Halbach for research assistance.

At Lincoln University, we wish to thank Helen Williams for her expert technical assistance with certain chapters. Additionally, we thank Cristina Cherino Munoz for assistance with Spanish language translations.

We would also like to thank the following student research assistants for their hard work, Kathryn Henry, Olivia Jacobsen, Daniel Jeffrey, Esther McGillivray, Andy Poole, Tom Welch and Megan Wilgress.

Finally, we thank our families and friends for all of their love, kindness and support.

Stephen Turner
Dinah Shelton
Jona Razzaque
Owen McIntyre
James May
August 2018

Abbreviations

ACHR	1969 American Convention on Human Rights
ACHPR	1981 African Charter on Human Rights and Peoples Rights
ACommHPR	African Commission on Human and People's Rights
ACUMAR	Matanza-Riachuelo Basin Authority
ANC	African National Congress
AQI	Air Quality Initiative
AU	African Union
BAT	Best Available Technology
BIS	Bureau of Indian Standards
BPJ	Best Professional Judgement
CAG	Comptroller and Auditor General
CBD	1992 Convention on Biological Diversity
CEDAW	1979 Convention on the Elimination of All Forms of Discrimination against Women
CERD	Committee for the Elimination of Racial Discrimination
CESCR	United Nations Committee on Economic Social and Cultural Rights
CESR	Centre for Economic and Social Rights
CJEU	Court of Justice of the European Union
COFEMA	Federal Council of Environment
CPCB	Central Pollution Control Board
CMA	Catchment Management Agencies
CRC	1989 Convention on the Rights of the Child
DWA	Department of Water Affairs
DWAF	Department of Water Affairs and Forestry
EBRD	European Bank for Reconstruction and Development
ECHR	1950 European Convention on Human Rights

ECOSOC	United Nations Economic and Social Council
ECtHR	European Court of Human Rights
EIA	Environmental Impact Assessment
ENGO	Environmental Non-Governmental Organization
EPA	Environmental Protection Agency
ESIA	Environmental and Social Impact Assessment
EU	European Union
FAO	United Nations Food and Agriculture Organisation
FCPF	The Forest Carbon Partnership Facility
FMU	Forest Management Unit
FNCA	1995 Forest and Nature Conservation Act
FPIC	Free Prior and Informed Consent
GDP	Gross Domestic Product
GIS	Geographic Information System
GNP	Gross National Product
GNH	Gross National Happiness
HRC	Human Rights Committee
IACHR	Inter-American Commission on Human Rights
IACtHR	Inter-American Court of Human Rights
IBRD	International Bank for Reconstruction and Development
ICCPR	1966 International Covenant on Civil and Political Rights
ICESCR	1966 International Covenant on Economic Social and Cultural Rights
ICJ	International Court of Justice
IFAD	International Fund for Agricultural Development
IFC	International Finance Corporation
IFI	International Financial Institution
IHP	International Hydrological Programme
ILA	International Law Association
ILO	International Labour Organization
IPPC	Integrated Pollution Prevention and Control
ISO	International Organization for Standardization
MDB	Multilateral Development Bank
MEA	Multilateral Environmental Agreement
MHI	Median Household Income
MOEFCC	Ministry of Environment, Forest and Climate Change
MOP	Meeting of the Parties
NAP	National Action Programme
NAPA	National Academy of Public Administration
NAP	National Action Plan

NEMA	1998 National Environmental Management Act
NFP	National Forest Policy
NGO	Non-Governmental Organization
NGT	National Green Tribunal
NNPC	Nigerian National Petroleum Company
NWA	1998 National Water Act
OAS	The Organization of American States
PEDF	Pennsylvania Environmental Defense Foundation
PCB	Polychlorinated Biphenyl
PIC	Prior Informed Consent
PIL	Public Interest Litigation
PNI	Projects of National Interest
P&CGC	Peer and Core Group Committee
REDD+	Reducing Emissions from Deforestation and Forest Degradation
RGOB	Royal Government of Bhutan
SAARC	South Asian Association for Regional Cooperation
SERAC	Social and Economic Rights Action Center
SDG	Sustainable Development Goals
SPCB	State Pollution Control Boards
SRO	Sustainability Rights Ordinance
TFEU	2007 Treaty on the Functioning of the European Union
UDHR	1948 Universal Declaration of Human Rights
UN	United Nations
UNCED	United Nations Conference on Environment and Development
UNCCD	1994 United Nations Convention to Combat Desertification in those Countries Experiencing Serious Drought and/or Desertification, particularly in Africa
UNCHE	United Nations Conference on Human Rights and the Environment
UNCLOS	1982 United Nations Convention on the Law of the Sea
UNDP	United Nations Development Programme
UNDRIP	2007 United Nations Declaration on the Rights of Indigenous Peoples
UNECE	United Nations Economic Commission for Europe
UNEP	United Nations Environment Programme
UNESCO	The United Nations Educational, Scientific and Cultural Organization
UNFCCC	1992 United Nations Framework Convention on Climate Change
UNGA	General Assembly of the United Nations
UNICEF	The United Nations International Children's Emergency Fund

USEPA	United States Environmental Protection Agency
VAT	Value Added Tax
WHO	World Health Organization
WINS	Water Information Network System
WMA	Water Management Area
WSA	1997 Water Services Act
WWF	World Wide Fund for Nature

Table of Cases, Communications and Advisory Opinions

Aarhus Convention Compliance Committee

ACCC/S/2004/1 Romania
ACCC/C/2008/23 United Kingdom
ACCC/C/2008/24 Spain
ACCC/C/2008/27 United Kingdom
ACCC/C/2008/32 (Part II) European Union
ACCC/C/2008/33 United Kingdom
ACCC/C/2011/57 Denmark
ACCC/C/2012/77 United Kingdom
ACCC/C/2013/85 and ACCC/C/2013/86 United Kingdom
ACCC/C/2014/111 Belgium
ACCC/C/2014/112 Ireland
ACCC/C/2014/113 Ireland
ACCC/S2015/2 Lithuania
ACCC/C/2016/139 United Kingdom
ACCC/C/2016/142 United Kingdom
ACCC/S/2016/3 Albania

African Commission on Human and Peoples' Rights

African Commission on Human and Peoples' Rights *v.* the Republic of Kenya, Application 006/2012 (May 26, 2017)

Centre for Minority Rights Development (Kenya) and Minority Rights Group International on behalf of Enderois Welfare Council *v.* Kenya, Communication 276/2003 (May 2009, approved by the African Union in January 2010)

Communication Nos. 25/89, 47/90, 56/91, 100/93, Decision taken at the 18th Ordinary Session (1995)

Social and Economic Rights Action Center and the Center for Economic and Social Rights *v.* Federal Republic of Nigeria, Communication. No. 155/96 (2001)

European Court of Human Rights

Asselbourg and others *v.* Luxembourg, Application No. 29121/95 (June 29, 1999)
Ashworth and others *v.* The United Kingdom, Application no. 39561/98 (January 20, 2004)
Băcilă *v.* Romania, Application No. 19234/04 (March 30, 2010)
Borysiewicz *v.* Poland, Application No. 71146/01 (July 1, 2008)
Brânduşe *v.* Romania, Application no. 39951/08 (October 27, 2015)
Brincat and Others *v.* Malta, Application Nos. 60908/11, 62110/11, 62129/11, 62312/11 and 62338/11 (July 24, 2014)
Demir and Baykara *v.* Turkey, ECHR 1345 (2008)
Di Sarno and others *v.* Italy, 30765/08 (January 10, 2012)
Dubetska and Others *v.* Ukraine, Application No. 42488/02 (September 4, 2014)
Dzemyuk *v.* Ukraine, ECHR 1130 (2014)
Fadeyeva *v.* Russia, ECHR 376 (2005)
Fägerskiöld *v.* Sweden, Application No. 37664/04 (February 26, 2008)
Flamenbaum and others *v.* France, Application nos. 3675/04, 23264/04 (December 13, 2012)
Giacomelli *v.* Italy, Application no. 59909/00 (November 2, 2006)
Guerra and Others *v.* Italy 26, EHRR 357 (1998)
Hamer *v.* Belgium, Application no. 21861/03 (November 27, 2007)
Hatton and Others *v.* the United Kingdom, Application No. 36022/97 (July 8, 2003)
Kyrtatos *v.* Greece, ECHR 242 (2003)
Leon and Agnieszka Kania *v.* Poland, Application no. 12605/03 (October 21, 2009)
L'Erablière A.S.B.L. *v.* Belgium, Application No. 49230/07 (February 24, 2009)
Loizidou *v.* Turkey (Preliminary Objections) 20 EHRR 99 (1995)
Lopez Ostra *v.* Spain, 303 ECHR 38 (1994).
Moreno Gómez *v.* Spain, Application no. 4143/02 (November 16, 2004)
Mileva and others *v.* Bulgaria, Applications Nos. 43449/02 and 21475/04 (November 25, 2010)
Powell *v.* the United Kingdom, ECHR 703 (2000)
Pretty *v.* the United Kingdom, ECHR 427 (2002)
S *v.* France, 65 DR 250 (1990)
Taşkın *v.* Turkey, ECHR 62 (2004)
Tatar *v.* Romania, Application No. 67021/01 (January 27, 2009)
Tyrer *v.* the United Kingdom, Series A no. 26 (1978)
Vearncombe and others *v.* the Federal Republic of Germany and the United Kingdom, 59 DR 186 (1989)
Zander *v.* Sweden 18 EHRR 175 (1992)

European Court of Justice

Case C-115/09 Bund für Umwelt und Naturschutz Deutschland, Landesverband Nordrhein Westfalen ev *v.* Bezirksregierung Arnsberg, Trianel Kohlekraftwerk Lünen GmbH & Co KG EU:C:2011:289

Case C-427/07 Commission *v.* Ireland EU:C:2009:457

Case C-530/11 Commission *v.* United Kingdom EU:C:2014:67

Case C-71/14 East Sussex County Council *v.* Information Commissioner, Property Search Group and Local Government Association EU:C:2015:656

Case C-222/84 Johnston *v.* Chief Constable of the Royal Ulster Constabulary EU:C:1986:206

Case C-240/09 Lesoochranárske zoskupenie VLK *v.* Ministerstvo životného prostredia Slovenskej republiky EU:C:2011:125

Case C-470/16 North East Pylon Pressure Campaign Ltd *v.* An Bord Pleanála EU:C:2018:18

Case C 182/10 Solvay *v.* Région Wallonne EU:C:2012:82

Case C-260/11 R (Edwards) *v.* Environment Agency EU:C:2013:221

Inter-American Commission / Court of Human Rights

Acevedo Buendía *v.* Peru, IACtHR Series C No. 198 (July 1, 2009)

Advisory Opinion: The Environment and Human Rights (State obligations in relation to the environment in the context of the protection and guarantee of the rights to life and to personal integrity – interpretation and scope of Articles 4(1) and 5(1) of the American Convention on Human Rights), IACtHR Series A No. 23, Advisory Opinion OC-23/17 (November 15, 2017)

Awas Tingni Mayagna (Sumo) Indigenous Community *v.* Nicaragua, IACHR Series C No. 79 (August 31, 2001)

Claude-Reyes *v.* Chile (Merits, Reparations and Costs), IACtHR Series C No. 151 (September 19, 2006)

Five Pensioners *v.* Peru (Merits, Reparations and Costs), IACtHR Series C No. 98 (February 28, 2003)

García Fajardo *v.* Nicaragua (Merits), IACHR Report No 100/01 Case 11.381 (October 11, 2000)

Kaliña and Lokono Peoples *v.* Suriname (Merits, Reparations and Costs), IACtHR Series C No. 309 (November 25, 2015)

Kawas-Fernández *v.* Honduras (Merits, Reparations and Costs), IACtHR Series C No. 196 (April 3, 2009)

Kichwa Indigenous People of Sarayaku *v.* Ecuador, IACtHR Series C No. 245 (2012)

Maya Indigenous Community of the Toledo District *v.* Belize, Case 12.053, Report No. 40/04, OEA/Ser.L/V/II.122, doc. 5 rev. 1 (2004)

Mayagna (Sumo) Awas Tingni Community *v.* Nicaragua (Merits, Reparations and Costs), IACtHR Series C No. 79 (August 31, 2001)

Miranda Cortez *v.* El Salvador (Merits) Report No 27/09, Case 12.249 (March 20, 2009)
Moiwana Community *v.* Suriname (Preliminary Objections, Merits, Reparations and Costs), IACtHR Series C No. 124 (June 15, 2005)
Saramaka People *v.* Suriname (Preliminary Objections, Merits, Reparations, and Costs), IACtHR Series C No. 172 (November 28, 2007)
Sawhoyamaxa Indigenous Community *v.* Paraguay (Merits, Reparations and Costs), IACtHR Series C No. 146 (March 29, 2006)
Villagrán-Morales *v.* Guatamala (Merits), IACtHR Series C No. 63 (November 19, 1999)
Xákmok Kásek Indigenous Community *v.* Paraguay (Merits, Reparations and Costs), IACtHR Series C No. 214 (August 24, 2010)
Yakye Axa Indigenous Community *v.* Paraguay (Merits, Reparations and Costs), IACtHR Series C No. 125 (June 17, 2005)

International Centre for Settlement of Investment Disputes

ICSID Case No. ARB/03/19 Aguas Argentinas S.A., Suez, Sociedad General de Aguas de Barcelona S.A. and Vivendi Universal S.A. *v.* The Argentine Republic, Order in Response to a Petition for Transparency and Participation as Amicus Curiae (2005)
ICSID Case No. ARB/03/17 Aguas Provinciales de Santa Fe S.A., Suez, Sociedad General de Aguas de Barcelona S.A. and InterAguas Servicios Integrales del Agua S.A. *v.* The Argentine Republic, Order in Response to a Petition for Participation as Amicus Curiae (2006)
ICSID Case No. ARB/05/22 Biwater Gauff (Tanzania) Ltd. *v.* United Republic of Tanzania, Procedural Order No. 5 (2007)
ICSID Case No. ARB/03/19 Suez, Sociedad General de Aguas de Barcelona S.A. and Vivendi Universal S.A. *v.* The Argentine Republic, Order in Response to a Petition by Five Non-Governmental Organizations for Permission to Make an Amicus Curiae Submission (2007)

International Court of Justice

Advisory Opinion: Western Sahara, ICJ Reports 12 (October 16, 1975)
Pulp Mills on the River Uruguay (Argentina *v.* Uruguay), ICJ Reports 18 (Judgment 2010)

United Nations Human Rights Committee

Andre Brun *v.* France, Communication No. 1453/2006, CCPR/C/88/D/1453/2006.
Angela Poma Poma *v.* Peru, Communication No. 1457/2006.
E. H. P. *v.* Canada, Communication No. 67/1980, UN Doc CCPR/C/OP/1 (1984)
E.P. et al. *v.* Colombia, Communication No. 318/1988, UN Doc CCPR/C/39/D/318/1988.

Ilmari Lansman et al. *v.* Finland, UN Doc CCPR/C/52/D/511/1992 (October 26, 1994)
Jouni Lasnman et al. *v.* Finland, UN Doc CCPR/C/587/D/671/1995 (October 30, 1996)
Lubicon Lake Band *v.* Canada, Communication No. 167/1984, UN Doc Supp. No. 40 (A/45/40) (March 26, 1990)
Mahuika *v.* New Zealand, UN Doc CCPR/C/70/D/547/1993 (October 26, 2000)
Susila Malani Dahanayake and 41 other Sri Lankan citizens *v.* Sri Lanka, UN Doc CCPR/C/87/D/1331/2004 (July 25, 2006)
Vaihere Bordes and John Temeharo *v.* France, Communication No. 645/1995, UN Doc CCPR/C/57/D/645/1995

NATIONAL CASES

Argentina
Asociación Argentina de Abogados Ambientalistas de la Patagonia *v.* Santa Cruz, Provincia de y Otro s/Amparo Ambiental (Corte Suprema de Justicia de la Nación, December 21, 2016)
Bustos and Others *v.* Fabricaciones Militares (Juzgado Federla de Primera Instancia de La Plata, December 30, 1986)
Fundación Ciudadanos Independientes *v.* San Juan, Provincia de, Estado Nacional y Otros s/Acción Ambiental Meramente Declarativa (Corte Suprema de Justicia de la Nación, September 20, 2016)
Kattan, Alberto E y otro *v.* Gobierno Nacional – Poder Ejecutivo (Juzgado Nacional de la Instancia en lo Contencioso-Administrativo Federal Nro 2 (J N Fed Contencioso Administrativo) (No. 2, May 10, 1983)
Mendoza Beatriz Silvia and Others *v.* Estado Nacional and Others (M 1569 XL) (Corte Suprema de Justicia de la Nación, June 20, 2006)
Quevedo Miguel Ángel y otros *v.* Aguas Cordobesas SA Amparo (Sentence 260) (Juzgado de 1ª Inst. y 51 Nom Civil y Com de Córdoba, April 5, 2002)
Saladeristas Podestá, Bertam, Anderson, Ferrer y otros *v.* Provincia de Buenos Aires (La Corte Suprema de Justicis de la Nación, May 14, 1887)

Bhutan
The Government of Bhutan *v.* Opposition Party, No. SC (Hung 11–1) (Judgment 2011)

Botswana
Matsipane Mosetlhanyane and Gakenyatsiwe Matsipane *v.* The Attorney General, CA (Lobatse) CACLB07410 (2011)

Columbia

Re: The Atrato River 2016, Constitutional Court, Case T-622 (2016), Proceeding T-5.016.242 (2016)

Re: Deforestation in the Amazon rainforest, Supreme Court, Case STC-4360–2018, Filing no. 11001–22-03–000-2018–00319-01 (2018)

Ecuador

Judgment No. 09171–2015-0004, Ninth Court of Criminal Guarantees, Guayas Province (April 23, 2015)

Judgment No. 0567–08-RA, Constitutional Court (December 8, 2009)

Judgement No. 11121–2011-0010, Provincial Court of Justice, Loja Province (March 30, 2011)

Judgment No. 166–15-SEP-CC, Case No. 0507–12-EP, Constitutional Court (May 20, 2015)

Judgment No. 1711120130317, Case No. 3160, Provincial Court of Pichincha (June 20, 2013)

Judgment No. 2003–2014 – C.T., National Court of Justice, Specialized Chamber of Criminal, Military Criminal, Criminal Police and Transit Cases (September 7, 2014)

Judgment No. 269 – 2012, Civil and Mercantile Court, Galápagos Province (June 28, 2012).

France – Constitutional Council

Decision No. 2005–514 DC of April 28, 2005, JORF May 4, 2005

Decision No. 2009–599 DC of December 29, 2009

Decision No. 2012–262 QPC of July 13, 2012

Decision No. 2012–269 QPC of July 27, 2012

Decision No. 2012–270 QPC of July 27, 2012

Decision No. 2012–282 QPC of November 23, 2012

Decision No. 2012–283 QPC of November 23, 2012, M. Antoine de M., JORF November 24, 2012, 18547

Decision No. 2013–308 QPC of April 26, 2013

Decision No. 2013–316 QPC of May 24, 2013

Decision No. 2013–317 QPC of May 24, 2013

Decision No. 2013–666 DC of April 11, 2013

Decision No. 2014–394 QPC of May 7, 2014, Société Casuca, JORF May 10, 2014

Decision No. 2014–694 DC of May 28, 2014

Hungary

Magyar Közlöny case 1994/No. 55 (May 20, 1994).

India

Almrita Patel *v.* Union of India, Writ Petition No. 888 (1996)

Amit Maru *v.* MoEF (October 1, 2014)

M. C. Mehta *v.* Union of India (2004) 12 SCC 118
M. K. Balakrishnan (1) *v.* Union of India (2009) 5 SCC 507
Municipal Corporation of Greater Mumbai *v.* Kohinoor CTNL Infrastructure (2014) 4 SCC 538;
Narmada Khand Swabhiman Sewa *v.* State of Madhya Pradesh (National Green Tribunal, Central Zone Bench, Bhopal, October 1, 2014)
Occupational Health and Safety Association *v.* Union of India (2014) 3 SCC 547
re Judges Transfer Case AIR (1982) SC 149
re Noise Pollution AIR (2005) SC 3136.
S.Jagannath *v.* Union of India (1997) 2 SCC 87
Sher Singh *v.* State of Himachal Pradesh (Judgment, February 4, 2014)
State of Uttranchal *v.* Balwant Singh Chaufal (2010) 3 SCC 40
Subhash Kumar *v.* State of Bihar (1991) 1 SCC 598
Sudeip Shrivastava *v.* State of Chattisgarh (Judgment, March 24, 2014)
Swaraj Abhiyan *v.* Union of India (2016) 7 SCC 498
TN Godavaraman Thirumulpad (87) *v.* Union of India (2006) 1 SCC 1
Tribunal on its Own Motion *v.* Secretary of State (National Green Tribunal, Central Zone Bench, Bhopal, April 4, 2014)
Unnikrishnan, J P *v.* State of AP (1993) 1 SCC 645
Vellore Citizen Welfare Forum *v.* Union of India AIR (1996) SC 2715
Virender Gaur *v.* State of Haryana (1995) 2 SCC 577
Vincent Panikulangara *v.* Union of India (1987) 2 SCC 165
Vardhman Kaushik *v.* Union of India (National Green Tribunal, Principle Bench, New Delhi, November 10, 2016)

Portugal
Case 8199/11 Judgment of June 2015
Case 1362/12 Judgment of January 2016

South Africa
BP Southern Africa (Pty) Ltd *v.* MEC for Agriculture, Conservation and Land Affairs 2004 (5) SA 124 (WLD)
Certification of the Constitution of the Republic of South Africa, 1996 (CCT 23/96) (1996) ZACC 26
City of Johannesburg & others *v.* Mazibuko & Others (Centre on Housing Rights & Evictions as amicus curiae) (2009) JOL 23337 (SCA)
Earthlife Africa Johannesburg *v.* Minister of Environmental Affairs and Others (65662/16) (2017) ZAGPPHC 58
Government of the Republic of South Africa *v.* Grootboom & Others 2001 (1) SA 46 (CC)
HTF Developers (Pty) Ltd *v.* Minister of Environmental Affairs and Tourism and Others 2006 (5) SA 512 (T).

Mazibuko and Others *v.* City of Johannesburg and others (Centre on Housing Rights & Evictions as amicus curiae) (2008) JOL 21829 (W)
Mazibuko and others *v.* City of Johannesburg and Others (2009) JOL 24351 (CC)
Mazibuko and Others *v.* City of Johannesburg and Others (2010) (3) BCLR 239 (CC)
Minister of Health and Others *v.* Treatment Action Campaign and Others (2002) ZACC 15
Pheko *v.* Ekurhuleni Metropolitan Municipality 2012 2 SA 598 (CC) (2013) 28 SAPL 448

United States of America
Commonwealth *v.* Blair 805 NE 2d 1011 1018 (MASS App Ct 2004)
Commonwealth *v.* National Gettysburg Battlefield Tower Inc 454 Pa 193 205 311 A2d 588 594–95 (PA 1973)
Community College of Delaware County *v.* Fox 342 A2d 468 482 (PA Commonwealth Ct 1975)
Davis *v.* Burke 179 US 399 (1900)
Glisson *v.* City of Marion 720 NE 2d 1034 1042 (Ill 1999)
Laurien Enos & others *v.* Secretary of Environmental Affairs 731 NE 2d 525 (MASS 2000)
Lujan *v.* Defenders of Wildlife 504 US 555, 560–561 (1992)
Montana Environmental Information Center *v.* Department of Environmental Quality 988 P2d 1236 (MONT 1999)
New State Ice Co *v.* Liebmann 285 US 262 311 (1932)
Northern Plains Resource Council *v.* Montana Board of Land Commissioners 288 P3d 169 (MONT 2012)
Payne *v.* Kassab 312 A.2d 86 (PA Commw Ct 1973), aff'd 361 A.2d 263 (PA 1976)
Pennsylvania Environmental Legal Defense Foundation *v.* Commonwealth of Pennsylvania 161 A.3d 844 (PA 2017)
Pennsylvania General Energy Company, LLC *v.* Grant Township, No. 14-209ERIE, Judgment, Western District Court of Pennsylvania (14 October 2015)
Robinson Township *v.* Commonwealth 83 A3d 901 999–1000 (PA 2013)
Re Application of Maui Electric Company (Sierra Club) *v.* Public Utility Commission of Hawai'I, SCWC-15–0000640 (Supreme Court of Hawai'i 2017)
Sierra Club *v.* Department of Transport 167 P3d 292, 313 n28 (HAW 2007)
State *v.* General Development Corp 448 So 2d 1074 (FLA Dist Ct App), aff'd, 469 So 2d 1381 (Fla. 1985)
Sullivan *v.* Resisting Environmental Destruction on Indigenous Lands 311 P3d 625 (AK 2013)

Table of Treaties

1945

Charter of the United Nations (June 26, 1945, entered into force October 24, 1945) 1 UNTS XVI

1948

Charter of the Organization of American States (1948) 119 UNTS 3

1949

Geneva Convention (III) on the Treatment of Prisoners of War (1949, entered into force 1950) 75 UNTS 135 (Geneva Convention III)

Geneva Convention (IV) on the Treatment of Civilian Persons in Time of War (1949, entered into force 1950) 75 UNTS 287 (Geneva Convention IV)

1950

European Convention for the Protection of Human Rights and Fundamental Freedoms (Rome) (November 4, 1950, entered into force September 3, 1953) 213 UNTS 221 (ECHR)

1965

International Convention on the Elimination of All Forms of Racial Discrimination (March 7, 1966, entered into force January 4, 1969) 660 UNTS 195 (CERD)

1966

International Covenant on Economic Social and Cultural Rights (December 16, 1966, entered into force January 3, 1976) Annex to UNGA Res. 2200 (XXI) 6 ILM 360 (1967) (ICESCR)

International Covenant on International Civil and Political Rights (December 16, 1966, entered into force March 23, 1976) Annex to UNGA Res. 2200 (XXI) 6 ILM 368 (1967) (ICCPR)

Optional Protocol to the International Covenant on Civil and Political Rights (December 16, 1966, entered into force March 23, 1976) Regn. 14668 999 UNTS 171

1969

American Convention on Human Rights (1969, entered into force July 18, 1978) OAS Treaty Series No 36, 1144 UNTS 123 (ACHR)

Convention on the Law of Treaties (Vienna) (May 23, 1969, entered into force January 27, 1980) 8 ILM 679 (1969) 1155 UNTS 331 (VCLT)

International Convention on Civil Liability for Oil Pollution Damage (November 29, 1969, entered into force June 19,1975) 973 UNTS 3 (amended by 1992 CLC Protocol) (Civil Liability Convention)

1971

Convention on Wetlands of International Importance Especially as Waterfowl Habitat (February 2, 1971, entered into force December 21, 1975) 996 UNTS 245 (Ramsar Convention)

Convention on the Establishment of an International Fund for Compensation for Oil Pollution Damage (December 18, 1971, entered into force October 16, 1978) 1110 UNTS 57 (superseded by Protocol, November 27, 1992, entered into force May 30, 1996)

1972

Convention on the Prevention of Marine Pollution by Dumping of Wastes and other Matter (December 29, 1972, entered into force August 30, 1975 (modified by Protocol, November 7, 1996) 1046 UNTS 484 (London Convention)

1973

Convention on International Trade in Endangered Species of Wild Fauna and Flora (March 3, 1973, entered into force July 1, 1975) 993 UNTS 243 (CITES)

International Convention for the Prevention of Pollution from Ships (November 2, 1973, amended by Protocol, February 17, 1978, entered into force October 2, 1983) 1340 UNTS 61 (MARPOL 73/78)

1974

Nordic Convention on the Protection of the Environment (Stockholm) (February 19, 1974, entered into force October 5, 1976) 13 ILM 511 (1974) (Nordic Convention)

1977

Additional Protocol to the Geneva Conventions Relating to the Protection of Victims of International Armed Conflicts (Protocol I) (June 8, 1977, entered into force December 7, 1978) 1125 UNTS 3

Additional Protocol to the Geneva Conventions Relating to the Protection of Victims of Non-International Armed Conflicts (Protocol II) (June 8, 1977, entered into force December 7, 1978) 1125 UNTS 609

1979

Convention on the Elimination of All Forms of Discrimination Against Women (December 18, 1979, entered into force September 3, 1981) 1249 UNTS 13 (CEDAW)

Statute of the Inter-American Commission on Human Rights (La Paz) (October 1, 1979, entered into force November 1, 1979) OAS Res. 447 (IX-0/79) OAS Off. Rec. OEA/Ser P/IX.0.2/80

1981

African Charter on Human and Peoples' Rights (June 27, 1981, entered into force October 21, 1986) 21 ILM 58 (1982) (African Charter)

1982

United Nations Convention on the Law of the Sea (December 10, 1982, entered into force November 16, 1994) 1833 UNTS 3, 21 ILM 1261 (1982) (UNCLOS)

1984

Convention Against Torture and Other Cruel, Inhuman or Degrading Treatment or Punishment (December 10, 1984, entered into force June 26, 1987) 1465 UNTS 85

1985

Vienna Convention for the Protection of the Ozone Layer (March 22, 1985, entered into force September 22, 1988) 1513 UNTS 293 (Ozone Convention)

1987

Montreal Protocol on Substances that Deplete the Ozone Layer (September 16, 1987, entered into force January 1, 1989) 1522 UNTS 28 (Montreal Protocol)

1988

Additional Protocol to the American Convention of Human Rights in the Area of Economic, Social and Cultural Rights (November 17, 1988, entered into force November 16, 1999) OAS Treaty Series No. 69, 28 ILM. 156 (Protocol of San Salvador)

1989

Basel Convention on the Control of Transboundary Movements of Hazardous Wastes and their Disposal (March 22, 1989, entered into force May 5, 1992) 1673 UNTS 57, 28 ILM 657 (Basel Convention)

Convention (No. 169) concerning Indigenous and Tribal Peoples in Independent Countries (June 27, 1989, entered into force September 5, 1991) 28 ILM 1382 (1989) (ILO Convention 169)

Convention on the Rights of the Child (November 20, 1989, entered into force September 2, 1990) 1577 UNTS 3 (CRC)

1990

African Charter on the Rights and Welfare of the Child (July 11, 1990, entered into November 29, 1999) OAU Doc. CAB/LEG/24.9/49

1991

Convention on Environmental Impact Assessment in a Transboundary Context (February 25, 1991, entered into force September 10, 1997) 1989 UNTS 309 (Espoo Convention).

Protocol on the Antarctic Treaty on Environmental Protection (October 4, 1991, entered into force January 14, 1998) 30 ILM 1455 (Madrid Protocol).

1992

Convention on Biological Diversity (June 5, 1992, entered into force September 29, 1993) 1760 UNTS 79 (CBD)

Convention on the Protection and Use of Transboundary Watercourses and International Lakes (March 18, 1992, entered into force October 6, 1996) 1936 UNTS 269 (UNECE Water Convention or Helsinki Convention)

Convention on the Transboundary Effects of Industrial Accidents (March 17, 1992, entered into force April 19, 2000) 2105 UNTS 457, 31 ILM 1333 (1992) (Convention on Industrial Accidents)

United Nations Framework Convention on Climate Change (May 9, 1992, entered into force March 21, 1994) 1771 UNTS 107 (UNFCCC)

Protocol to amend the International Convention on Civil Liability for Oil Pollution Damage of 1969, November 27, 1992, entered into force May 3, 1996, 1956 UNTS 255 (Civil Liability Convention)

1993

Convention on Civil Liability for Damage Resulting from Activities Dangerous to the Environment (June 21, 1993, not in force) 32 ILM 1228 (Lugano Convention)

1994

United Nations Convention to Combat Desertification in those Countries Experiencing Serious Drought and/or Desertification, particularly in Africa (June 17, 1994, entered into force December 26, 1996) 1954 UNTS 3, 33 ILM 1328 (1994) (UNCCD)

1997

Convention on the Law of the Non-Navigational Uses of International Watercourses (May 21, 1997, entered into force August 17, 2014) 36 ILM 700 (1997) (UN Convention on Watercourses)

Protocol to amend the 1963 Convention on Civil Liability for Nuclear International Atomic Energy Agency (September 12, 1997, entered into force October 4, 2003) 2241 UNTS 270

Protocol to the United Nations Framework Convention on Climate Change (December 11, 1997, entered into force February 16, 2005) 2303 UNTS 148, 37 ILM 22 (1997) (Kyoto Protocol)

1998

Convention on Access to Information, Public Participation and Decision-Making and Access to Justice in Environmental Matters (June 25, 1998, entered into force on October 30, 2001) 2161 UNTS 447, 38 ILM 517 (1999) (Aarhus Convention)

Protocol to the African Charter on Human and Peoples' Rights on the Establishment of an African Court on Human and Peoples' Rights (June 10, 1998, entered into force January 25, 2004) (Replaced by the Protocol on the Statute of the African Court of Justice and Human Rights on July 1, 2008)

1999

Protocol on Water and Health to the 1992 Convention on the Protection and Use of Transboundary Watercourses and International Lakes (June 17, 1999, entered into force August 4, 2005) 2331 UNTS 202 (Protocol on Water and Health)

Rotterdam Convention on the Prior Informed Consent Procedure for Certain Hazardous Chemicals and Pesticides in International Trade (September 10, 1998, entered into force February 24, 2004) 2244 UNTS 337, 38 ILM 1 (1999) (Rotterdam Convention or PIC Convention)

2000

Protocol on Biosafety to the Convention on Biological Diversity (January 29, 2000, entered into force September 11, 2003) 2226 UNTS 208, 39 ILM 1027 (2000) (Cartagena Protocol).

2001

Convention on Persistent Organic Pollutants (May 22, 2001, entered into force May 17, 2004) 2256 UNTS 119, 40 ILM 532 (2001) (Stockholm Convention or POPS Convention)

2003

African Convention on the Conservation of Nature and Natural Resources (Revised Version) (July 11, 2003, entered into force July 23, 2016) (2003 Revised African Nature Convention)

Protocol on Civil Liability and Compensation for Damage caused by the Transboundary Effects of Industrial Accidents on Transboundary Waters to the 1992 Convention on the Protection and Use of Transboundary Watercourses and International Lakes and to the 1992 Convention on the Transboundary Effects of Industrial Accidents (adopted May 21, 2003, not in force) (UNTC: CTC XXVII 16) (UNECE Protocol on Civil Liability)

Protocol on Strategic Environmental Assessment to the Convention on Environmental Impact Assessment in a Transboundary Context (May 21, 2003, entered into force July 11, 2010) 2685 UNTS 140 (SEA Protocol)

The Protocol to the International Convention on the Establishment of an International Fund for Compensation for Oil Pollution Damage (May 16, 2003, entered into force March 3, 2005) <www.imo.org> (Supplementary Fund)

2004

Arab Charter on Human Rights (League of Arab States) (September 15, 1994, entered into force March 16, 2008) (reprinted: 12 Int'l Hum Rts Rep 893) (2005)

2007

Treaty on the Functioning of the European Union (December 13, 2007, entered into force December 1, 2009) 2008/C 115/01 (TFEU)

2010

Protocol on Access to Genetic Resources and the Fair and Equitable Sharing of Benefits Arising from Their Utilization to the Convention on Biological Diversity (October 29, 2010, entered into force October 12, 2014) UN Doc UNEP/CBD/COP/DEC/X/I (29 October 2010) (Nagoya Protocol)

2013

Minamata Convention on Mercury (October 10, 2013, entered into force August 16, 2017) (UNTC: CTC-XXVII-17) (Minamata Convention)

2015

Paris Agreement (April 22, 2015, entered into force November 4, 2016) (UNTC: CTC-XXVII-7) (Paris Agreement)

2018

Regional Agreement on Access to Information, Public Participation and Justice in Environmental Matters in Latin America and the Caribbean (March 4, 2018, not in force) UN ECLAC, UNTC C.N.195.2018.TREATIES-XXVII.18 (Escazú Agreement)

Table of International Declarations, Resolutions, Guidelines and Standard Setting Instruments

UNITED NATIONS

1948

Universal Declaration of Human Rights (1948) GA Res. 217 UN GAOR 3rd Sess. UN Doc A/810

American Declaration on the Rights and Duties of Man (Bogota 1948) OAS Res XXX adopted by the Ninth International Conference of American States

1972

Declaration of the United Nations Conference on the Human Environment (New York 1972) UN Doc A/CONF 48/14/Rev 1 (Stockholm Declaration)

1982

CCPR "General Comment No. 6 The Right to Life" (April 30, 1982) UN Doc HRI/GEN/1/Rev

World Charter for Nature (October 28, 1982) UN Doc A/RES/37/7

1984

CCPR "General Comment No. 14: Article 6 (Right to Life) Nuclear Weapons and the Right to Life" (November 9, 1984) UN Doc HRI/GEN/1/Rev.9 (Vol I)

1990

CESCR "General Comment No. 3: The Nature of States Parties' Obligations" (1990) UN Doc E/1991/23

1991

CESCR "General Comment 4, The Right to Adequate Housing" (Article 11(1)) (December 13, 1991) UN Doc E/1992/23

1992

Rio Declaration on Environment and Development (June 13, 1992) UN Doc A/CONF.151/26. Rev.1 (Rio Declaration)

1993

UN General Assembly, Vienna Declaration and Programme of Action (July 12, 1993) UN Doc A/CONF.157/23

1994

CCPR "General Comment No. 23: Article 27" (Rights of Minorities) (April 8, 1994) UN Doc CCPR/C/21/Rev.1/Add.5

1997

CERD General Recommendation XXIII on the Rights of Indigenous Peoples (1997) UN Doc A/52/18

1998

CESCR "General Comment No. 7: The Right to Adequate Housing (Art 11.1): Forced Evictions" (May 20, 1997) UN Doc E/1998/22

1999

CESCR "General Comment No. 12: The Right to Adequate Food" (Art 11) (May 12, 1999) UN Doc E/C.12/1999/5

2000

CESCR "General Comment No. 14: The Right to the Highest Attainable Standard of Health" (Article 12) (August 11, 2000) UN Doc E/C.12/2000/4

The Aarhus Convention: An Implementation Guide (2000) UN Sales No. E.13. II.E.3

2001

UNCHR, Human Rights and Indigenous Issues (April 24, 2001) 57 Sess., Res. 2001/57

2002

CESCR "General Comment No. 15, The Right to Water" (Articles 11 and 12) (November 26, 2002) UN Doc E/C.12/2002/11

UNCHR The Right to Health (April 22, 2002), 58th Sess., Res. 2002/31

UN "Report on the World Summit of Sustainable Development" (September 20, 2002) UNGA A.Conf/199/20 (Johannesburg Declaration on Sustainable Development)

Secretariat of the Convention on Biological Diversity, "Bonn Guidelines on Access to Genetic Resources and Fair and Equitable Sharing of the Benefits Arising out of their Utilization" (2002) CBD Decision VI/24

2004

Secretariat of the Convention on Biological Diversity, "Akwé Kon Voluntary Guidelines for the Conduct of Cultural, Environmental and Social Impact Assessment regarding Developments Proposed to Take Place on, or Which are Likely to Impact on, Sacred Sites and on Lands and Waters Traditionally

Occupied or Used by Indigenous and Local Communities" (2004) CBD Decision VII/16 F

UNECE Aarhus Convention "Report of the First Meeting of the Parties" (2004) ECE/MP.PP/2/Add.8

2007

UNGA Declaration on the Rights of Indigenous Peoples (September 13, 2007) UN Doc A/RES/61/295

2008

UN Human Rights Council "Mandate of the Special Rapporteur on the Situation of Human Rights Defenders" (March 28, 2008) 40th Meeting Res. 7/8

UN Human Rights Council "Human Rights and Access to Safe Drinking Water and Sanitation" (March 28, 2008) 41st Meeting UN HRC Res. 7/22

2009

CESCR "General Comment No. 21: Right of Everyone to take part in Cultural Life" (December 21, 2009) 43rd Session UN Doc E/C.12/GC/21

2010

UN GA Resolution 64/294 "The Human Right to Water and Sanitation" (July 26, 2010) UN Doc A/64/L.63/Rev.1

UNEP "Guidelines for the Development of National Legislation on Access to Information, Public Participation, and Access to Justice in Environmental Matters" (February 26, 2010) Decision SS/XI/5 Part A

2011

UN Human Rights Council "The Human Right to Safe Drinking Water and Sanitation" (April 8, 2011) 16th Session A/HRC/Res./16/2

2012

UN GA Resolution "The Future We Want" (July 27, 2012) UN Doc. A/Res/66/288

Joint FCPF/UN-REDD Programme "Guidelines on Stakeholder Engagement for REDD+ Readiness with a Focus on the Participation of Indigenous Peoples and Other Forest-Dependent Communities" (April 20, 2012)

2013

UN-REDD Programme "Guidelines on Free, Prior Informed Consent" (January 2013)

2014

UNECE "The Aarhus Convention: An Implementation Guide" (2nd edn, 2014)

2015

UN Human Rights Council "Human Rights and the Environment" (April 7, 2015), UN Doc A/HRC/28/11

UN GA Resolution "Transforming Our World: the 2030 Agenda for Sustainable Development" (September 25, 2015) UN Doc A/RES/70/1

UN GA Resolution "Harmony with Nature" (December 22, 2015) UN Doc A/RES/70/208

UNEP "Putting Principle 10 into Action: An Implementation Guide" (2015)

2016

UN GA Resolution "The Human Right to Safe Drinking Water and Sanitation" (February 22, 2016) UN Doc A/RES/70/169

UN Human Rights Council Resolution "The Human Right to Safe Drinking Water and Sanitation" (September 27, 2016) UN Doc A/HRC/33/L.19

OAS General Assembly "American Declaration on the Rights of Indigenous Peoples" (June 15, 2016) AG/RES. 2888 (XLVI-O/16)d

2018

CCPR "General Comment No. 36: Article 6 (Right to Life)" (30th October, 2018) UN Doc CCPR/C/GC/36

WORLD HEALTH ORGANIZATION

1993

WHO "Guidelines for Drinking Water Quality" (2nd edn, 1993)

2005

WHO "Air Quality Guidelines for Particulate Matter, Ozone, Nitrogen Dioxide and Sulphur Dioxide: Global Update – Summary of Risk Assessment" (2005) WHO/SDE/PHE/OEH/06.02

2009

WHO and UN FAO "International Code of Conduct on the Distribution and Use of Pesticides – Guidelines on Developing a Reporting System for Health and Environmental Incidents Resulting from Exposure to Pesticide" (2009)

2011

WHO "Guidelines for Drinking Water Quality" (4th edn, 2011)

2017

WHO "Guidelines for Drinking-Water Quality – Fourth Edition Including the First Addendum" (4th edn Incorporating the First Addendum, 2017)

INTERNATIONAL LAW ASSOCIATION

1966

ILA "Helsinki Rules on the Uses of Waters of International Rivers" Report of the Fifty-Second ILA Conference (Helsinki, 1966)

2004

ILA "Berlin Rules on Water Resources" Adopted at the 71st Conference of the ILA (2004)

INTERNATIONAL ORGANIZATION FOR STANDARDIZATION

2007

ISO 24510:2007 "Activities Relating to Drinking Water and Wastewater Services – Guidelines for the Assessment and for the improvement of the Service to Users"

ISO 24511:2007 "Activities Relating to Drinking Water and Wastewater Services – Guidelines for the Management of Wastewater Utilities and for the Assessment of Wastewater Services"

ISO 24512:2007 "Activities Relating to Drinking Water and Wastewater Services – Guidelines for the Management of Drinking Water Utilities and for the Assessment of Drinking Water Services"

2015

ISO 24518:2015 "Activities Relating to Drinking Water and Wastewater Services – Crisis Management of Water Utilities"

2016

ISO 24516–1:2016 "Guidelines for the Management of Assets of Water Supply and Wastewater Systems – Part 1: Drinking Water Distribution Networks"

2017

ISO 24523: 2017 "Service Activities Relating to Drinking Water Supply Systems and Wastewater Systems – Guidelines for Benchmarking of Water Utilities"

ORGANISATION FOR ECONOMIC CO-OPERATION AND DEVELOPMENT

2008

OECD "OECD Guidelines for Multinational Enterprises" (OECD Publishing, 2011)

2018

OECD "OECD Due Diligence Guidance for Responsible Business Conduct" (2018)

WORLD BANK

2004

World Bank "Striking a Better Balance: The World Bank Group and Extractive Industries – The final Report of the Extractive Industries Review" (Washington, DC: World Bank 2004)

2005

World Bank "Operational Manual, OP 4.10 Indigenous Peoples" (July 2005, revised April 2013)

2012

International Finance Corporation "Performance Standards on Environmental and Social Sustainability" (IFC – World Bank Group, January 1, 2012)

AFRICAN COMMISSION ON HUMAN AND PEOPLES RIGHTS

2009

AfCmHPR "Resolution on Climate Change and Human Rights and the Need to Study its Impact in Africa" (November 25, 2009) Res. 153

2010

AfCmHPR "Principles and Guidelines on the Implementation of Economic, Social and Cultural Rights in the African Charter on Human and Peoples Rights" (2010)

AFRICAN DEVELOPMENT BANK

2010

African Development Bank "Guidelines for User Fees and Cost Recovery for Urban Water and Sanitation" (AfDB 2010)

Table of European Union Directives

1976

Directive 76/464/EEC of May 18, 1976 on pollution caused by certain dangerous substances discharged into the aquatic environment of the Community [1976] OJ L129/23

1980

Directive 80/778/EEC of July 15, 1980 relating to the quality of water intended for human consumption [1980] OJ L229 30.8.80

1982

Directive 82/176/EEC of March 27, 1982 concerning the discharge of mercury by the chlor-alkali electrolysis industry [1982] OJ L81

1983

Directive 83/513/EEC of October 24, 1983 concerning the discharge of cadmium [1983] OJ L291/1

1984

Directive 84/156/EEC of March 17, 1984 concerning the discharge of mercury by the chlor-alkali electrolysis industry [1984] OJ L74

Directive 84/491/EEC of October 9, 1984 on limit values and quality objectives for discharges of hexachlorocyclohexane [1984] OJ L274/11

1985

Directive 85/337/EEC of June 27, 1985 on the assessment of the effects of certain public and private projects on the environment [1985] OJ L175/40

1986

Directive 86/280/EEC of June 12, 1986 on limit values and quality objectives for discharges of certain dangerous substances included in List I of the Annex to Directive 76/464/EEC, including carbon tetrachloride, DDT and pentachlorophenol [1986] OJ L181/16

1988

Directive 88/347/EEC of June 25, 1988 on limit values and quality objectives relating to aldrin, dieldrin, endrin, isodrin, hexachlorobenzene, hexachlorobutadine, and chloroform (1988) OJ L158/35

1989

Council Directive 89/552/EEC of October 3, 1989 on the coordination of certain provisions laid down by law, regulation or administrative action in Member States concerning the pursuit of television broadcasting activities [1989] OJ L298/23

1990

Directive 90/313/EEC of June 7, 1990 on the freedom of access to information on the environment [1990] OJ L158/56

1992

Directive 92/43/EEC of May 21, 1992 on the conservation of natural habitats and wild fauna and flora [1992] OJ L206/7 (Habitats Directive)

1996

Directive 96/61/EC of September 24, 1996 concerning integrated pollution prevention and control [1996] OJ L257/26

1998

Directive 98/83/EC of November 3, 1998 on the quality of water intended for human consumption [1998] OJ L330/32

2000

Directive 2000/60/EC of October 23 establishing a framework for Community action in the field of water policy [2000] OJ L327/1.

2001

Directive 2001/42/EC of June 27, 2001 on the assessment of the effects of certain plans and programmes on the environment [2001] OJ L197/30

2003

Directive 2003/4/EC of January 28, 2003 on public access to environmental information [2003] OJ L41/26

Directive 2003/35/EC of May 26, 2003 providing for public participation in respect of the drawing up of certain plans and programmes relating to the environment and amending with regard to public participation and access to justice Council Directives 85/337/EEC and 96/61/EC [2003] OJ L156/17

2005

Directive 2005/29/EC of May 11, 2005 concerning unfair business-to-consumer commercial practices in the internal market and amending Council Directive 84/450/EEC [2005] OJ L149/22

2006

Directive 2006/7/EC of February 15, 2006 concerning the management of bathing water quality and repealing Directive 76/160/EEC [2006] OJ L64/37

2008

Directive 2008/50/EC of May 21, 2008 on ambient air quality and cleaner air for Europe [2008] OJ L152/1

2009

Directive 2009/29/EC of April 23, 2009 amending Directive 2003/87/EC so as to improve and extend the greenhouse gas emission allowance trading scheme of the Community [2009] OJ L140/63

2010

Directive 2010/75/EU of November 24, 2010 on industrial emissions (integrated pollution prevention and control) (Recast) [2010] OJ L334/17

2011

Directive 2011/92/EU of December 13, 2011 on the assessment of the effects of certain public and private projects on the environment (codification) [2011] OJ L26/1

2012

Directive 2012/18/EU of July 4, 2012 on the control of major-accident hazards involving dangerous substances, amending and subsequently repealing Council Directive 96/82/EC Text with EEA Relevance [2012] OJ L197/1

2014

Directive 2014/52/EU of April 16, 2014 amending Directive 2011/92/EU on the assessment of the effects of certain public and private projects on the environment [2014] OJ L124/1

2015

Directive (EU) 2015/412 of March 11, 2015 amending Directive 2001/18/EC as regards the possibility for the Member States to restrict or prohibit the cultivation of genetically modified organisms (GMOs) in their territory [2015] OJ L68/1

1

Introduction: A Brief History of Environmental Rights and the Development of Standards

Stephen J. Turner

1.1 INTRODUCTION

Environmental law and human rights law have developed rapidly in recent decades. Human rights in the contemporary sense have developed in theory and in practice since the Universal Declaration of Human Rights (UDHR) 1948.[1] Environmental law has been a relative latecomer, but since 1972, triggered by the United Nations Conference on Human Rights and the Environment (UNCHE),[2] has developed exponentially. Both fields have largely developed independently and therefore lawyers in these respective areas have generally operated separately from one another. For example experts on issues such as the right to a fair trial and the right to be free from torture exercise a different range of knowledge and skills to those focussing their attention on issues such as climate change, waste management and pollution control. However, it has long been recognised that there are aspects of human rights and environmental law that overlap.[3] This has been evident in the way that the right to life and the right to health can be negatively affected through the pollution of air and drinking water, for example.[4] Also the civil and political rights that entitle people to engage meaningfully in decision-making processes can be of crucial importance in protecting the environment. It is from these broad connections that much of the theory and practice relating to 'environmental rights' has emerged.

1 Universal Declaration of Human Rights (1948) GA Res 217, UN GAOR, 3rd Sess, UN Doc A/810 (1948).

2 Report of the United Nations Conference on the Human Environment (New York, 1973) UN Doc A/Conf.48/14/Rev.1 (1972), adopted in GA Res 2997 UN GAOR, 27th Sess, Supp No 30 at UN Doc A/8901 (1972) (UNCHE).

3 See for example Louis B Sohn, 'The Stockholm Declaration on the Human Environment' (1973) 14 Harv Int'l L J 423, 451–55.

4 See Stephen J Turner, A *Global Environmental Right* (Earthscan by Routledge 2014) Chapter 2 (*The State of Degradation of the Planet's Environment, the Impact upon Human Rights and the Current Status of the Development of Environmental Rights*).

The development of the discourse, drafting and practice relating to those human rights used for environmental protection has not been an uncontested journey.[5] One of the questions raised has been whether the rights that were being created for the protection of the environment could be effective as legal mechanisms owing to the fact that they were often drafted in extremely vague terms.[6] Another argument was whether human rights are appropriate legal mechanisms to be used for the protection of the environment, when other legal tools are available which could possibly be more effective.[7] While recent decades have shown that there is definitely a role for environmental rights to play, there are still questions relating to their content and the manner in which they should be used.

It is certainly true that many environmental rights are expressed in broad terms. The type of language that is used in human rights treaties and constitutions will often confer on rights holders the right to live in an environment that is, for example, 'healthy', 'safe' or 'clean'.[8] Such terminology places an obligation upon states to realise certain objectives but often leaves judges, lawyers and citizens wondering precisely what is meant by them.[9] Similarly, in terms of civil and political rights, the rights to information, to participate in decision-making and to have access to justice relating to environmental issues leave many questions relating to the precise levels of disclosure, involvement and remedy that citizens are entitled to.

It is here that this book positions itself as it seeks to explore the standards of environmental protection that have emerged within the field of environmental rights. It does this from a number of perspectives. Each of the chapters considers the law itself that is provided for under a particular regime, or in the cases of the right to water, free prior and informed consent (FPIC), multilateral environmental agreements (MEA) and the rights of nature, from the perspective of those type of rights that have emerged through a number of different regimes. It then considers the extent to which specific standards of environmental protection have emerged as a result of that law. Such standards can manifest themselves in a variety of different ways. For example, some constitutionally granted rights have very strong

5 Sohn (n 3); see generally Alan Boyle and Michael Anderson (eds), *Human Rights Approaches to Environmental Protection* (OUP 1996); Donald K Anton and Dinah L Shelton, *Environmental Protection and Human Rights* (CUP 2011) 131–50; also Stephen J Turner, *A Substantive Environmental Right* (Kluwer Law International, 2009) 45–72.

6 Sionaidh Douglas-Scott, 'Environmental Rights: Taking the Environment Seriously', in Conor Gearty and Adam Tomkins (eds), *Understanding Human Rights* (Mansell 1996) 424.

7 Alan Boyle, 'The Role of International Human Rights Law in the Protection of the Environment' in Boyle and Anderson (eds), (n 4) 54; Günther Handl, 'Human Rights and Protection of the Environment' in Eide, Krause and Rosas (eds) *Economic, Social and Cultural Rights* (2nd revised edn, Martinus Nijhoff Publishers 2001) 303, 327.

8 See Turner (n 5) 44–48; David R Boyd, *The Environmental Rights Revolution – A Global Study of Constitutions, Human Rights, and the Environment* (UBC Press, 2012) 47.

9 John Lee, 'The Underlying Legal Theory to Support a Well Defined Human Right to a Healthy Environment' (2000) 25 Colum J Envtl L 283, 339.

relationships with national legislation that sets specific standards; in other instances the judiciary may take on the role of developing standards, and sometimes agencies that are autonomous or quasi-autonomous of the state are relied upon for the creation and development of associated standards. In certain instances, national constitutions expressly provide for specific standards or expressly create an obligation that requires standards to be developed; sometimes international institutions such as the World Health Organisation and the United Nations play key roles in the development and determination of so called 'international standards' that are then used by tribunals as the standard applicable under a particular regime.

As well as considering the different types of standards that are emerging, the book also considers those factors that affect their development or recognition. As such it considers the extent to which standards are desirable or even possible in certain contexts. Therefore, it analyses those instances where human rights regimes have been reluctant to associate very specific standards with environmental rights and why in many cases this can be founded on logic and pragmatism.[10] Where precise standards of protection are emerging, it is often the case that they are in nascent stages of development. From this perspective, the book seeks to provide guidance on the possible ways that such standards can be further developed and the options that are available to states and the international community to do this.

To pave the way for the analyses carried out in this book, this opening chapter sets out the historical context from which all of the other chapters can be viewed. It maps the history of environmental rights, and in doing so highlights how each of the chapters in this book have a place in telling the story of the development of standards within the field. As well as mapping the history of the philosophical and legislative developments that have shaped environmental rights, this chapter also considers the instrumental role that the United Nations has played and continues to play in the development of human rights that are used for the protection of the environment.

1.2 EARLY SCHOLARLY CONCEPTIONS OF ENVIRONMENTAL RIGHTS

The earliest conceptions of environmental rights are difficult to ascribe. However some authorities refer to Aldo Leopold, who identified a relationship between ethics and nature at a time when human rights as we now think of them were still in their infancy. In 1949 he stated that

[10] See for example the discussions in this volume by Karen Morrow relating to the European Convention of Human Rights (Chapter 3) and Àine Ryall relating to the Aarhus Convention (Chapter 6).

> the extension of ethics to this third element in human environment is, if I read the evidence correctly, an evolutionary possibility and an ecological necessity ... the land ethic simply enlarges the boundaries of the community to include soils, waters, plants, and animals, or collectively: the land.[11]

It was not, however, until the 1960s and 1970s that specific conceptions of environmental rights began to emerge. In 1962, the scientist and pioneer in the field of advocacy for environmental protection, Rachel Carson, argued that the US Constitution's Bill of Rights should contain a provision that guarantees citizens freedom from lethal poisons.[12] In 1972, Christopher Stone put forward the argument that natural objects such as trees could have rights.[13] Subsequently, in 1974, the Nobel Prize-winning human rights lawyer, René Cassin, observed that over the previous twenty years the notion of an environmental right had emerged.[14] And in 1976, Professor W. P. Gormley asserted the existence of a new human right that guaranteed a 'minimum decent environment'.[15]

These early conceptions of the possibilities of extending human rights protection to environmental issues created fertile ground for thought, understanding and discussion from which more tangible developments in the law have emerged.

1.3 LEGAL DEVELOPMENTS IN THE FIELD OF ENVIRONMENTAL RIGHTS

The earliest global international human rights treaties that provided the potential bases for the protection of the environment are the International Covenant on Civil and Political Rights (ICCPR)[16] and the International Covenant on Economic, Social and Cultural Rights (ICESCR).[17] These were established in the mid 1960s, and as such predate most early conversations about environmental rights. However, contained within them are the rights to life,[18] health[19] and an adequate standard of

[11] Aldo Leopold, A *Sand County Almanac – and Sketches Here and There* (OUP 1949) 203–04.

[12] Rachel Carson, *Silent Spring* (Penguin Books – Houghton Mifflin 1962) 29.

[13] Christopher Stone, *Should Trees Have Standing – Towards Legal Rights for Natural Objects* (William Kaufman 1972).

[14] René Cassin, 'Les Droits de L'Homme' in IV Recueil des Cours (Sitjhoff 1974) at 327 states 'Dans les vingt dernière années est née la notion du droit á l'environment, impossible à classer purement et simplement comme droit politique ou économique et dont il vous sera sûrement parlé'.

[15] WP Gormley, *Human Rights and the Environment: The Need for International Cooperation* (Sitjhoff 1976) 1.

[16] 16 December 1966, in force 23 March 1976, Annex to UNGA Res 2200 (XXI), 6 ILM 368 (1967) (ICCPR).

[17] 16 December 1966, in force 3 January 1976, Annex to UNGA Res 2200 (XXI), 6 ILM 360 (1967) (ICESCR).

[18] ICCPR (n 16) art 6.

[19] ICESCR (n 17) art 12.

living,[20] all of which have a relationship with the quality of the environment. It is here that the analysis in this book begins.

In Chapter 2 Sumudu Atapattu explores the instances where those particular rights have subsequently been developed or interpreted to encompass environmental protection. This has meant considering relevant complaints heard by the UN Human Rights Committee[21] and the UN Committee on Economic, Social and Cultural Rights,[22] and the effect of the Concluding Observations that these committees have made in their oversight roles. It also considers the way that 'General Comments' along with state reports have provided an evolutionary understanding of specific rights. Within this analysis, Prof. Atapattu considers the extent to which 'standards' can be said to have emerged, if at all.

In 1972, the United Nations Conference on the Human Environment was held in Stockholm. This was the first time that such a conference had been convened and is regarded by many lawyers as the starting point of contemporary international environmental law. The outcome was the 'Stockholm Declaration' that contained a set of principles.[23] Principle 1 stated that 'man has the fundamental right to freedom, equality and adequate conditions of life in an environment of a quality that permits a life of dignity and well-being, and he bears a solemn responsibility to protect and improve the environment for present and future generations'.[24] While the Stockholm Declaration represented 'soft law', and the language used fell short of declaring the existence of a fundamental environmental right per se, its authority and influence resonated with governments and the international community. One of the ways that it influenced governments was through the manner in which they proceeded to consider the rights and obligations included in their national constitutions.

Indeed, from then on many states, when amending their national constitutions decided to include provisions relating to environmental protection.[25] The first country to do so was Portugal in 1974, following its peaceful revolution.[26] The environmental provisions of the Portuguese constitution are now extensive, which means that they are of particular interest in an analysis to determine the relationship that they have with standards. Additionally, as Portugal is a member of the European Union (EU), analysis can reveal interesting insights into the relationship between those national standards that relate to EU law and those which can be

20 ibid art 11.
21 One of the functions of the UN Human Rights Committee is to hear complaints related to alleged violations of the ICCPR.
22 One of the functions of the UN Committee on Economic, Social and Cultural Rights is to hear complaints related to alleged violations of the ICESCR.
23 UNCHE (n 2).
24 ibid.
25 See generally Boyd (n 5); also James R May and Erin Daly, *Global Environmental Constitutionalism* (CUP 2015).
26 The Constitution of the Republic of Portugal (2005, 7th Revision).

linked directly to provisions found in the constitution. Alexandra Arágao explores these issues in depth in Chapter 11.

While many countries have integrated environmental provisions into their national constitutions, the lack of such a provision did not necessarily constrain states from using constitutional rights for the purposes of environmental protection. India to this day does not have a specific actionable environmental provision within its national constitution.[27] However, its right to life provision has been relied upon for the protection of the environment and is now interpreted as incorporating a right to a healthy environment.[28] In the early 1980s lawyers began relying on the right to life in the Indian constitution for the protection of the environment.[29] This led to a significant number of cases and a proactive stance from the judiciary, which has used its authority to order government departments in a range of different types of measures to take action to protect the environment.[30] Gitanjali Gill in Chapter 10 focuses on the way that this tradition has now developed through the function of the National Green Tribunal (NGT) and the relationship that this has with the development of environmental standards.

The 1980s also saw significant developments taking place at the regional level. In 1981, the African Charter on Human and Peoples' Rights (ACHPR) was promulgated.[31] This treaty includes a provision that entitles people to live in 'a general satisfactory environment favourable to their development'.[32] Insights related to this article of the ACHPR are provided by Louis Kotzé and Anél du Plessis in Chapter 5, which as well as providing an analysis of the inherent limitations relating to the development of rights-orientated standards in the region, considers the broader issue of some of the different types of standards that can be identified within the field of environmental rights.

In 1988, a significant development took place in South America through the Additional Protocol in the Area of Economic, Social and Cultural Rights (the Protocol of San Salvador)[33] which includes a provision for the protection of the environment,[34] that added to the treaty obligations under the American Convention of Human Rights.[35] Until recently, the environmental provision in the Protocol of

27 The Constitution of India (1950).

28 ibid art 21.

29 See generally Jona Razzaque, *Public Interest Environmental Litigation in India, Pakistan and Bangladesh* (Kluwer Law International 2004).

30 ibid.

31 African Charter on Human and Peoples' Rights (Banjul) art 4, 27 June 1981, in force 21 October 1986, 21 ILM 59 (1982) (AFCHPR).

32 ibid art 24.

33 Additional Protocol to the ACHR on Economic, Social and Cultural Rights (San Salvador) 17 November 1988, in force 16 November 1999; 28 ILM 156 (1989).

34 Article 11 states that 'everyone shall have the right to live in a healthy environment and to have access to basic public services'. It also states that 'the state parties shall promote the protection, preservation and improvement of the environment'.

35 American Convention on Human Rights (1969) OAS Treaty Series No 36; 1144 UNTS 123.

San Salvador had not been considered to be actionable. Nevertheless, the right to property and the right to life had in certain cases been successfully argued before the Inter-American Court of Human Rights (IACtHR) to protect aspects of the environment in the context of claims brought by indigenous communities. Evadné Grant in Chapter 4 considers these provisions and provides an analysis of the manner in which judgments assist in our understanding of the standard of environmental protection that they afford to rights holders. She also analyses a 2017 Advisory Opinion in which the IACtHR clarified and extended state obligations relating to the environment under the convention, and in doing so has gone some way to further clarifying the standards of protection that they entail.[36]

By the early 1990s considerable momentum had been achieved at the national and international levels relating to environmental protection. This led to the United Nations Conference on Environment and Development (UNCED), which had a number of outcomes, one of them being the Rio Declaration.[37] Whereas a relatively strong reference to human rights and the environment had been provided in the Stockholm Declaration,[38] the Rio Declaration did not assert that a human right to a certain substantive quality of environment existed; instead it states that 'human beings are at the centre of concerns for sustainable development. They are entitled to a healthy and productive life harmony with nature.'[39] While this appeared to downplay the role that substantive environmental rights might play in future of environmental law and policy,[40] the Rio Declaration made clear that procedural rights should play a major role.[41]

This role was set out in Principle 10, which affirmed that states should ensure that citizens are able to access information, participate in decision-making and access justice in environmental matters.[42] Such participatory rights are now widely accepted to the point that they can possibly be regarded as customary in many regions of the world, even if their acceptance in theory is not always matched by the quality of governmental implementation. Such is the normative acceptance of procedural rights by states that they are also incorporated in numerous MEAs. As MEAs are not designed to act as human rights instruments, this inclusion is a very interesting development and has the potential to provide further valuable insights. In Chapter 8, Lara Ognibene and Angela Kariuki focus on the way that procedural rights within MEAs have developed their own relationship with

36 The Environment and Human Rights (State Obligations in Relation to the Environment in the Context of the Protection and Guarantee of the Rights to Life and Personal Integrity – Interpretation and Scope of Articles 4(1) and 5(1) in relation to Articles 1.1 and 2 of the American Convention on Human Rights). Advisory Opinion OC-23/17, Inter-Am Ct HR (ser A) No 23 (15 November 2017).

37 Report of the United Nations Conference on Environment and Development (Rio de Janeiro), 14 June 1992, UN Doc A/CONF 151/5/Rev.1 (UNCED).

38 UNCHE (n 2).

39 UNCED (n 37) Principle 1.

40 Dinah L Shelton, 'What Happened in Rio to Human Rights?' (1995) 3(3) YB Int'l Envt'l L 75.

41 UNCED (n 37) Principle 10.

42 ibid.

'standards' of environmental protection. This relationship includes the association that specialised standard-setting institutions have with MEAs and the way that they can assist in developing and clarifying the standards of protection applicable.

An aspect of procedural rights that is of particular significance to rural communities in developing countries is the concept of 'free prior and informed consent' (FPIC). This relates to the obligation that states (and in turn non-state actors) have to consult adequately with communities prior to any significant developments that may affect them or their environment. In certain instances, where relocation might occur, it is possible that the consent of communities is necessary; however, in most instances adequate consultation processes are required to pave the way for some form of consensus as to the manner in which the development will take place. Various international instruments have recognised FPIC, and significantly it was given particular recognition in the 2007 UN Declaration on the Rights of Indigenous Peoples.[43] While it is doubtful that FPIC can be regarded as a stand-alone human right, it is grounded in the principles and duties that are derived from both human rights law and multilateral environmental agreements. Jona Razzaque analyses FPIC in Chapter 9 and considers what standards of protection are associated with it and the sources from which they are derived.

Naturally, the history and background to environmental rights have in part been shaped by national and global politics. The end of the Second World War led to the advent of the United Nations and the promulgation of the international human rights covenants which ultimately have influenced this field enormously. Other major events on the national level include the end of the apartheid era in South Africa in 1993, which led to a new national constitution.[44] The new constitution included both a specific environmental right[45] and a right to water.[46] One of the major issues facing South Africa was and continues to be the limited supply and distribution of potable water. This has led to the expression 'water apartheid' owing to the disparities of distribution between traditionally rich and poor or black and white areas.[47] This raises particular questions relating to 'standards' in terms of both the quality and quantity of water that people are entitled to under the constitution. Nathan Cooper analyses these issues in Chapter 13.

While the Rio Declaration appeared to play down the future role of substantive environmental rights, countries continued to adopt them and incorporate them into

43 Arts 10, 11(2), 19, 28(1), 29(2), 32(2). The UN Declaration on the Rights of Indigenous Peoples adopted by General Assembly Resolution 61/295 (13 September 2007).

44 Constitution of the Republic of South Africa (10 December 1996).

45 s 24.

46 s 27.

47 See Larry A Swatuk, 'The State and Water Resources Development through the Lens of History: A South African Case Study' (2010) 3 3 Water Alternatives 521; the issue of 'environmental racism' and the maltreatement of vulnerable groups was also highlighted in the 'Ksentini Report', see: UN Commision on Human Rights, Sub-Commission on Prevention of Discrimination and Protection of Minorities, Human Rights and the Environment, *Final Report of the Special Rapporteur.* UN Doc E/CN.4/Sub.2/1994/9 74 (6 July 1994) paras 86 and 125–36.

their constitutions. One particularly interesting example for the purposes of this volume is that of Argentina, because in adopting an environmental right in its revised constitution of 1994,[48] it also incorporated a provision which required the government to develop minimum standards of environmental protection.[49] This created a special type of environmental right; one which ultimately would be linked to legislation specifying the standards of environmental protection that are required under it. Silvia Nonna explains in Chapter 12 how this right has evolved and the range of different sectors for which associated legislation has been passed. She also analyses the role of the Supreme Court in attempting to give effect to standards of environmental protection.

Meanwhile in Europe the 1990s also bore witness to significant developments within the field of environmental rights. While the European Convention on Human Rights (1950) (ECHR)[50] had not included a provision for the protection of the environment, a number of rights such as the right to life,[51] the right to property[52] and the right to private and family life[53] gradually became grounds upon which aspects of the environment could be protected. The first case in which this type of claim was successfully argued was that of *Lopez Ostra* v. *Spain* (1994).[54] Since then the ECHR has proved fertile territory for such claims, which has led to an interesting body of jurisprudence. As the ECHR is one of the most, if not the most, developed of the regional human rights systems, this is of particular importance in the context of standards of environmental protection. In Chapter 3 Karen Morrow analyses the range of issues that the European Court of Human Rights must take into account in such cases, and as such illustrates the complicated relationship that exists between those treaty provisions that are relied upon and the standards of protection that they ultimately confer.

Another significant development occurred in Europe in 1998 with the signing of the Aarhus Convention, which came into force in 2001.[55] It is a ground-breaking treaty which solely addresses procedural environmental rights, and as such is a far-reaching manifestation of Principle 10 of the Rio Declaration. As well as representing a major development in terms of environmental rights, it has influenced Latin America and the Caribbean region in the adoption of the 2018 Escazú Agremeent which is also dedicated solely to procedural environmental rights.[56] The treaty's

48 The Constitution of the Argentine Nation (as amended 1994) Seciton 41.

49 ibid.

50 European Convention for the Protection of Human Rights and Fundamental Freedoms (Rome) 4 November 1950, in force 3 September 1953; 213 UNTS 221 (ECHR).

51 art 2.

52 art 1 of Protocol 1 to the ECHR (Paris, 20 March 1952).

53 art 8.

54 303 Eur Ct HR 38 (1994).

55 UN ECE Convention on Access to Information, Public Participation and Decision-Making and Access to Justice in Environmental Matters (Aarhus) 25 June 1998, in force 30 October 2001. UN Doc ECE/CEP43 ('Aarhus Convention').

56 UN ECLAC Regional Agreement on Access to Information, Public Participation and Justice in Environmental Matters in Latin America and the Caribbean (adopted 4 March 2018, not in force) UNTC C.N.195.2018.TREATIES-XXVII.18 (Escazú Agreement)

Compliance Committee plays a significant part in articulating the expectations that states must comply with in relation to the convention provisions. In Chapter 6 Aine Ryall focuses on the way that the Compliance Committee treats the right of access to justice, and she also considers the crucial interface that the convention has with EU law. The analysis illustrates the way that broad standards are gradually emerging.

This period demonstrates quite starkly the general disparity of living conditions between developed and developing countries. Access to water and sanitation in many parts of the world, but most notably in sub-Saharan Africa, was (and still is) a critical issue. In 2003, the UN issued General Comment No. 15 which states that Art. 11 of the ICESCR[57] could be interpreted to mean that all citizens have a right to water, and it detailed a set of general obligations relating to it.[58] Owen Mcintyre in Chapter 7 maps out the range of other developments that have reinforced the international recognition of that right. He then explains the different standards of protection that can be associated with the right to water and sanitation and the wide range of sources from which they are derived.

In the 2000s a number of other major developments took place in the field of environmental rights. One of them occurred in 2005 when the French Government incorporated its Charter for the Environment (Charter)[59] into the national constitution.[60] One of the most interesting aspects of this development was the way that the government could use a constitutional mechanism whereby the Charter could be deployed to challenge bills or actual legislation. This raises questions relating to the criteria or standards that legislation must comply with if it is to be deemed consistent with the constitution. David Marrani and Stephen Turner consider the use of the Charter for the protection of the environment in Chapter 14.

By the 2000s, as climate change became more prominent as an issue, the relationship that it has with human rights also became part of scholarly debate.[61] In practice, however, although several states have now included mention of climate change within their national constitutions,[62] human rights obligations relating to climate change are in their very early stages of development, and for this reason this volume does not provide an associated analysis relating to possible standards.

Some of the most significant developments that took place during the 2000s within the field of standards in environmental rights have been through national

57 ICESCR (n 17). Article 11(1) recognises 'the right of everyone to an adequate standard of living for himself and his family, including adequate food, clothing and housing, and to the continuous improvement of living conditions'.

58 Committee on Economic, Social and Cultural Rights, General Comment No. 15, The Right to Water (arts 11 and 12 of the International Covenant on Economic, Social and Cultural Rights) UN Doc E/C.12/2002/11, 26 November 2002.

59 Loi constitutionnelle 2005–205, 1 March 2005 (Loi constitutionnelle relative à la Charte de l'environnement (1)), JORF 2 March 2005, 3697.

60 The Constitution of the Republic of France (4 October 1958).

61 Stephen Humphreys (ed), *Human Rights and Climate Change* (CUP 2009).

62 See Constitution of Tunisia (26 January 2014) art 45; Constitution of the Dominican Republic (13 June 2015) art 194; Constitution of Ecuador (28 September 2008) art 414.

constitutions. Bhutan provides just such an example. The promulgation of Bhutan's first national constitution in 2008 included an environmental provision which provided that the government has a responsibility to maintain at least sixty percent of the country under forest cover for all time.[63] As the usual type of standard that is found within environmental rights is qualitative rather than quantitative in nature, this provision is remarkable. Stephen Turner analyses this provision in Chapter 15 to understand the reason for its existence, its justiciabliity and the potential wider significance that it could have.

In South America another significant development that occurred at the national level quite independently in 2008 was the inclusion within the Ecuadorian constitution of the 'right of nature' to exist.[64] Whereas Christopher Stone many years previously had contemplated the possibility of natural objects themselves potentially having rights,[65] the Ecuadorian government actually introduced such a right in a bid to change the way that the country treated the environment and to attempt to inculcate approaches to development that recognised the intrinsic importance of all aspects of nature. Bolivia then replicated this progressive step legislatively shortly afterwards.[66] Other countries such as New Zealand have also developed laws based on the same principle.[67] In Chapter 16 Craig Kauffman and Linda Sheehan explore the nascent development of standards within this field and provide a discussion of the scientific challenges that accompany those processes.

To a certain extent, developments that have taken place within national constitutions have been mirrored at the sub-national level within republican systems where provincial states have incorporated environmental rights within their own constitutions. In Chapter 17, Daly and May discuss examples where this has taken place. While experience at the sub-national level is growing and cannot be said to be consistent across all countries, certain developments are of particular note. For example, the concept that natural resources are held on trust for the public has developed at the sub-national level in certain jurisdictions.[68] Additionally, in a similar manner to that noted in relation to the French constitution, there is evidence of a willingness to invalidate state laws where they are found to violate the environmental provisions of the constitution.[69]

Throughout all of the developments that have been described, whether at the international, regional or national levels, the influence, of the UN has been ever present. Therefore the next section will consider the role that it has played in the

63 Constitution of Bhutan (18 July 2008) art 5(3).
64 Constitution of Ecuador (n 61) arts 71–72.
65 Christopher Stone (n 13).
66 Ley de Derechos de la Madre Tierra, Law No. 071 (21 December 2010).
67 Te Awa Tupua (Whanganui River Claims Settlement) Act 2017; Te Urewera Act 2014.
68 *Pennsylvania Environmental Legal Defense Foundation v Commonwealth of Pennsylvania* 161 A.3d 844 (PA 2017).
69 *Robinson Township et al. v Commonwealth of Pennsylvania*, Pa Sup Ct, No J-127A-D-2012 (decided 19 December 2013).

development of environmental rights; this assists in understanding the processes that have led to the development of associated standards.

1.4 THE ROLE OF THE UNITED NATIONS

Although at the UN level there have been varied positions adopted by different governments related to the desirability of developing human rights for the protection of the environment,[70] the organisation has nonetheless played a significant role in many of the developments that have taken place in this field. In particular, the UN has facilitated a number of the international instruments that have represented milestones in the establishment of environmental rights such as UNCHE,[71] UNCED[72] and the Aarhus Convention.[73] It also promoted the recognition of the right to water and sanitation through a General Assembly resolution in 2010.[74] Its human rights treaty bodies have responded to certain complaints that relate to environmental matters and extended the understanding of existing human rights through 'General Comments' to incorporate environmental protection.[75] There have also been numerous initiatives that have been developed by its charter-based bodies, and these have increased in intensity as the field has emerged.[76]

In 1989, the UN Commission on Human Rights appointed a Special Rapporteur, Ms Fatma Zohra Ksentini, to undertake a five-year examination of the linkages between human rights and the environment.[77] The result of her final report included a draft declaration of principles on human rights and the environment.[78] Although this was not adopted formally by the UN, it reinforced the linkages between human rights and the environment and provided a foundation for further work. The UN Commission on Human Rights appointed other Special Rapporteurs to cover areas that included environmental matters such as the enjoyment of the highest attainable standard of physical and mental health,[79] the right to food[80] and issues facing indigenous people.[81] After the Human Rights Commission was

70 See, for example, Dinah L Shelton, 'Human Rights Bodies: Decisions and Actions' (2004) 34(2) Envt'l Pol'y & L 66.

71 Report of UNCHE (n 2).

72 Report of UNCED (n 37).

73 Aarhus Convention (n 55).

74 UNGA Res A/Res/64/292, July 2010.

75 ibid; see in particular Chapter 2 of this volume by Sumudu Attapatu.

76 Anton and Shelton (n 5) 280–334.

77 Human Rights and the Environment: Preliminary Report, UN Doc E/CN.4/Sub.2/1991/8, 2 August 1992; First Progress Report, UN Doc E/CN.4/Sub.2/1992/7, 2 July 1992; Second Progress Report, UN Doc E/CN.4/Sub.2/1993/7, 26 July 1993.

78 The UN Commision on Human Rights, Sub-Commission on Prevention of Discrimination and Protection of Minorities, Human Rights and the Environment, *Final Report of the Special Rapporteur* UN Doc E/CN.4/Sub.2/1994/9 74 (6 July 1994).

79 UN HRC Res 2002/31, 58th Sess (22 April 2002).

80 UN HRC Res 2000/10, 56th Sess (17 April 2000).

81 UN HRC Res 2001/57, 57th Sess (24 April 2001).

replaced by the Human Rights Council in 2006, further Special Rapporteurs were appointed in areas that included the right to safe drinking water and sanitation,[82] and the situation of human rights defenders.[83]

In 2011, the Human Rights Council made the decision to appoint an Independent Expert in the field of human rights and the environment. This mandate was given to Prof. John Knox in 2012. In 2015, the mandate was extended for a further three years and changed to that of Special Rapporteur.[84] This move by the UN and the work carried out under the mandate resulted in increased attention to the issue of human rights and the environment. In particular, it catalysed further work in the field through the facilitation of multi-level meetings and dialogues. Over the period of Prof. Knox's tenure, his work focussed on mapping existing human rights obligations that affect the protection of the environment,[85] surveying different practices within different countries to identify 'good practices',[86] working with state and non-state partners on the development of implementation of human rights obligations relating to the environment,[87] analysing and making representations relating to the relationship between human rights and climate change,[88] surveying and reporting on the relationship between biodiversity and human rights[89] and reporting on the responsibilities relating to children in the context of human rights and the environment.[90]

The mandate highlighted certain aspects of the developments in the field of human rights and the environment. Firstly, the appointment itself in 2012 was an indication of the relative seriousness with which environmental rights were being considered by the international community and an acknowledgement that many forms of environmental degradation can impact upon and be affected by human rights. Secondly, the breadth of the work that the Special Rapporteur undertook illustrates how debates relating to human rights and the environment, and in some cases the law too, had moved on to encompass issues such as climate change, biodiversity, vulnerable groups and human rights defenders. In fact, one of the individual achievements of Prof. Knox's tenure was the increased recognition and attention given to the plight of human rights defenders, which hitherto had rarely been formally included in debates and practice relating to human rights and the environment. Finally, his work highlighted the level of sophistication that had started to infiltrate the field. The experience of judges, legislators, academics, civil

82 UN HRC Res 7/22, 41st Meeting (28 March 2008); A/HRC/Res./16/2 (8 April 2011).
83 UN HRC Res 7/8, 40th Meeting (28 March 2008).
84 March 2015, Res 28/11.
85 March 2014 (A/HRC/25/53).
86 March 2015 (A/HRC/28/61).
87 March 2106 (A/HRC/31/53).
88 March 2016 (A/HRC/31/52).
89 March 2017 (A/HRC/34/49).
90 2018 (A/HRC/37/58).

society and communities were beginning to coalesce in ways which have paved the way towards a more concrete understanding of what the international community expects of states and also non-state actors vis à vis human rights as they relate to the protection of the environment.

Prof. Knox's final report to the Human Rights Council in 2018 included a set of sixteen 'Framework Principles' that were drafted to 'set out basic obligations of States under human rights law as they relate to the enjoyment of a safe, clean, healthy and sustainable environment'.[91] These 'Framework Principles' detail a number of human rights obligations that are broadly recognised by the international community. Therefore, as a document it is not drafted to create new obligations, but equally it acknowledges that not all states have formally accepted all of the norms that it contains.[92] The evidence upon which the Framework Principles are based is founded 'in certain instances on treaties but also on the statements of human rights bodies that have the authority to interpret human rights but not necessarily to issue binding decisions'.[93]

The sixteen Framework Principles themselves relate to key aspects of the ways that human rights intersect with the protection of the environment. The full titles of each of the Framework Principle are lengthy, and therefore for the purposes of brevity abbreviated forms of those titles are given here to capture their general scope. They are as follows:

Principle 1. To protect the environment that can affect human rights.
Principle 2. To protect those human rights that are required to ensure the protection of the environment.
Principle 3. To prohibit discrimination
Principle 4. To ensure that human rights defenders remain safe
Principle 5. To allow freedom of expression.
Principle 6. To facilitate education relating to the environment.
Principle 7. To facilitate access to information.
Principle 8. To ensure that Environmental Impact Assessments (EIA) are carried out where necessary.
Principle 9. To facilitate public participation in decision-making.
Principle 10. To provide effective remedies.
Principle 11. To establish substantive environmental standards.
Principle 12. To enforce environmental standards.
Principle 13. To cooperate with other states in relation to transboundary environmental harm.
Principle 14. To protect vulnerable individuals and groups.

[91] United Nations Human Rights Council, *Report of the Special Rapporteur on the Issue of Human Rights Obligations Relating to the Enjoyment of a Safe, Clean, Healthy and Sustainable Environment* 37th Sess, 19 January 2018, A/HRC/37/59 para 8.

[92] ibid Main report para 8.

[93] ibid.

Principle 15. To protect indigenous peoples.
Principle 16. To protect human rights in the processes of sustainable development.[94]

It is too early to say precisely what influence they will have on the development of environmental rights as the international community moves forward. It has been suggested by Prof. Knox that the UN could issue a General Resolution that expresses recognition of the right to live in a 'safe, clean, healthy and sustainable environment'.[95]

For the purposes of this book a number of the Framework Principles relate directly to aspects that chapters of this book go on to consider. However, of particular relevance are Principles 11 and 12 that refer directly to environmental standards. Therefore, for the purposes of clarity their full titles are provided below:

> Framework Principle 11 says that 'states should establish and maintain substantive environmental standards that are non-discriminatory, non-retrogressive and otherwise respect, protect and fulfil human rights'.[96]
>
> Framework Principle 12 says that 'states should ensure the effective enforcement of their environmental standards against public and private actors'.[97]

These references to 'standards' within the field of environmental rights are part of the process of translating human rights obligations that are generally written in broad qualitative terms into practical directions for states, businesses, industry, communities and individuals alike. They express important principles such as 'non-discrimination'[98] and 'non-regression',[99] which characterise contemporary expectations of such standards. Importantly, they also specifically iterate the need for states to effectively enforce the standards that they introduce. In this respect the Framework Principles interface directly with the purposes of this book, which is ultimately about understanding with greater precision the standards of protection that are expected as a result of, or represented within, different types of environmental rights.

Whatever comment can be made in relation to the development of environmental rights, one factor appears to be certain, and that is that, at the time of writing, the process of development of 'environmental rights' is still underway and is likely to

94 ibid Annex paras 3–55.
95 ibid Main report para 14.
96 ibid Annex paras 31–33.
97 ibid Annex paras 34–35.
98 The UN Commision on Human Rights, *Final Report of the Special Rapporteur* (1994) (n 77). Paragraph 248 states: 'Environmental damage has direct effects on the enjoyment of a series of human rights, such as the right to life, to health, to a satisfactory standard of living, to sufficient food, to housing, to education, to work, to culture, to non-discrimination, to dignity and the harmonious development of one's personality.'
99 Michel Prieur and Gonzalo Sozzo, *Le Principe de Non Régression en Droit de l'Environnement* (Bruylant 2012).

continue long into the future. As Prof. Knox states in his final report as Special Rapporteur,

> the framework principles and commentary provide a sturdy basis for environment, but they are in no sense the final word. The relationship between human rights and the environment has countless facets, and our understanding of it will continue to grow for many years to come.[100]

This point indicates the difficulty of making generalisations relating to the scope of future developments in the field. However, there is little doubt that greater understanding of all of the different aspects of environmental rights can facilitate the improvement of their application in practice.

1.5 CONCLUSION

This book focuses on specific legal instruments that have developed environmental rights such as the international human rights covenants, regional human rights treaties, national and sub-national constitutions, and in certain instances rights that have emerged not through single legal instruments but through a culmination of different instruments and initiatives such as the right to water, FPIC, MEAs and the rights of nature.

The brief historical narrative provided in this chapter demonstrates that the development of environmental rights has been highly fragmented. However, that fragmentation can sometimes belie the influence that states have on each other, the catalytic influence that international instruments such as the UN's Rio Declaration can have on states and the international consensus that has coalesced around certain developments such as procedural rights.

In terms of the development of standards, this introduction has given an indication of the different types of standards that have emerged within the field. These standards are discussed throughout the chapters of this book, which provides not only an understanding of the relevant law, legal principles and obligations from which they are derived, but also an indication of the processes through which they are emerging. The concluding chapter will focus on how these different types and sources of standards could potentially be classified, what further work could be done to develop a deeper understanding of the field, and how the understanding of these developments can potentially be put to use in the theory and practice of environmental rights in the future.

100 UNHRC Report A/HRC/37/59 (n 91), para 10.

2

Environmental Rights and International Human Rights Covenants: What Standards Are Relevant?

Sumudu Atapattu

2.1 INTRODUCTION

During the last two decades, victims of environmental abuse have resorted to the human rights machinery to seek redress.[1] While none of the global human rights treaties embody a distinct right to a healthy environment, human rights institutions have used existing rights to articulate environmental rights. Although the link between environmental degradation and human rights is no longer in doubt, it is not clear what standards these institutions use when deciding whether there has

[1] There is considerable literature on this topic. See generally, Michael Burger, "Bipolar and Polycentric Approaches to Human Rights and the Environment" (2003) 28 Columbia Journal of Environmental Law 371; Sumudu Atapattu, "The Right to a Healthy Life or The Right to Die Polluted? The Emergence of a Right to a Healthy Environment under International Law" (2002) 16 Tul Envtl LJ 65; Alan Boyle, Michael R Anderson, *Human Rights Approaches to Environmental Protection* (Clarendon Press 1999); Carmen G Gonzalez, "Environmental Justice, Human Rights, and the Global South" (2015) 13 Santa Clara Journal of International Law 151; Burns H Weston, David Bollier, "Toward a Recalibrated Human Right to a Clean and Healthy Environment: Making the Conceptual Transition" (2013) 4 2 Journal of Human Rights and the Environment 116; Bridget Lewis, "Environmental Rights or Right to the Environment? Exploring the Nexus between Human Rights and Environmental Protection" (2012) 8 1 Macquarie Journal of International and Comparative Environmental Law 36; Earthjustice, "Environmental Rights Report 2008: Human Rights and the Environment" (2008) <https://earthjustice.org/sites/default/files/library/reports/2008-environmental-rights-report.pdf> accessed December 18, 2017; (Various Authors) *Symposium: The Confluence of Human Rights and the Environment* (2009) 11 2 Oregon Review of International Law, 225–461; United Nations General Assembly, "Analytical study on the relationship between human rights and the environment" Human Rights Council (2011) UN Doc A-HRC-19–34; Barry E Hill, Steve Wolfson and Nicholas Targ, "Human Rights and the Environment: A Synopsis and Some Predictions" (2004) 17 Georgetown International Environmental Law Review 359; Conor Gearty, "Do Human Rights help or Hinder Environmental Protection?" (2010) 1 1 Journal of Human Rights and the Environment 7; Dinah Shelton, "Developing Substantive Environmental Rights" (2010) 1 J. of Hum. Rights and the Environment 89; Prudence E Taylor, "From Environmental to Ecological Human Rights: A New Dynamic in International Law?" (1998) 10 Georgetown International Environmental Law Review 309; Council of Europe, "Manual on Human Rights and the Environment" (2012) <www.echr.coe.int/LibraryDocs/DH_DEV_Manual_Environment_Eng.pdf> accessed December 18, 2017; Ole W Pedersen, "European Environmental Human Rights and Environmental Rights: A Long Time Coming?" (2008) 21 Georgetown International Environmental Law Review 73.

been an infringement of environmental rights. Many of these cases require scientific knowledge. Lawyers and judges do not necessarily have the expertise in science needed in such cases. This points to the need to use experts' testimony to help the court to decide whether a violation of standards amounts to a violation of protected rights.

Shelton points out the importance of standards:

> Both national and international courts have used environmental law and science to give content to the level of environmental protection required by human rights law. This approach can involve reference to World Health Organization standards on acceptable emission levels, incorporation of the precautionary principle to judge the adequacy of measures taken by a government, or reference to environmental treaties and declarations. The breadth of the search for standards depends in part on whether or not there is a textual guarantee of environmental quality and if there is on the descriptions of that quality.[2]

She also notes that environmental quality standards, precaution and principles of sustainability can establish the limits of environmental decision-making and continue to give specific content to environmental rights in law.[3]

This chapter seeks to discuss how two UN treaty bodies – the Human Rights Committee, and the Committee on Economic, Social and Cultural Rights – have developed environmental rights by interpreting existing rights creatively. In so doing, it discusses whether these two committees have applied any standards to ascertain whether the rights protected under the two treaties have been violated. If so, are there any emerging principles about standards that may be useful for other human rights bodies that have to adjudicate environmental rights disputes? This chapter proceeds in four parts. Section 2.2 will discuss the relevant provisions of the treaties that have been used by these treaty bodies to develop environmental rights. It will also look at General Comments adopted by these two treaty bodies to see whether they refer to any standards that might be useful in articulating environmental rights. It will briefly discuss the emergence of environmental rights under the two treaty bodies in question, but will not discuss the emergence of the right to a healthy environment under international law as this has been the subject of intense scholarship during the past decade.[4] Where relevant, reference will be made to Concluding Observations by the treaty bodies with regard to environmental degradation affecting protected rights. Next, section 2.3 will extrapolate standards, if any, that have been applied by these two treaty bodies in relation to environmental rights in an effort to understand what standards are relevant, whether any principles have

2 Dinah Shelton, "Whiplash and Backlash – Reflections on a Human Rights Approach to Environmental Protection" (2015) 13 Santa Clara Journal of International Law 11.

3 ibid 29.

4 See Donald K Anton and Dinah Shelton, *Environmental Protection and Human Rights* (Cambridge 2011); Svirtlana Krevchenko and John E Bonine, *Human Rights and the Environment: Cases, Law and Policy* (Carolina Academic Press 2008); and the authorities cited in (n. 1).

emerged in relation to standards, and whether these standards can be used by other treaty bodies in similar cases. Finally, section 2.4 will conclude with some recommendations and observations.

2.2 THE LAW

Neither the International Covenant on Civil and Political Rights (ICCPR)[5] nor the International Covenant on Economic, Social and Cultural Rights (ICESCR)[6] contain a distinct right to a healthy environment. Thus, the articulation of environmental rights at the international level has taken place mainly by interpreting existing rights in an expansive manner – i.e. by "greening" existing rights.[7] An early attempt at examining the relationship between environmental issues and human rights by the United Nations was the appointment of a Special Rapporteur in 1989 to study this relationship.[8] Although a set of draft articles on the topic was developed and several reports submitted, the UN General Assembly merely took note of them.[9] A more recent (and positive) development is the appointment of an Independent Expert by the UN Human Rights Council in 2012. This mandate was later converted to a Special Rapporteur position,[10] which points to a renewed interest by the Council to develop environmental rights.

Regional human rights institutions, on the other hand, have been much more forthcoming. Three regional instruments specifically embody a right to a healthy environment,[11] although the African Charter on Human and Peoples' Rights remains the only human rights treaty to expressly include a justiciable right to a healthy environment.[12] Environmental rights are twofold – *substantive rights*, including the right to a healthy environment and related rights such as the rights

5 International Covenant on Civil and Political Rights (adopted December 16, 1966, entered into force March 23, 1976) 999 UNTS 171.

6 International Covenant on Economic, Social and Cultural Rights (adopted December 16, 1966, entered into force January 3, 1979) 993 UNTS 3.

7 Dinah Shelton, "Human Rights and the Environment: What Specific Rights have been Recognized?" (2006) 35 Denver Journal of International Law & Policy 129.

8 Zohra Ksentini was appointed in 1989 as the Special Rapporteur, see United Nations Economic and Social Council, "Review of further developments in fields with which the sub-commission has been concerned human rights and the environment" (July 6, 1994) E/CN.4/Sub.2/1994/9.

9 "Draft principles on human rights and environment" appended to the final report of Ksentini, ibid.

10 See UN Human Rights Council Resolution 28/11 A/HRC/RES/28/22 (April 7, 2015).

11 Two regional human rights treaties recognize this right: African Charter on Human and Peoples' Rights (adopted June 27, 1981, entered into force October 21, 1986) (1982) 21 ILM 58 (African Charter) and the Additional Protocol to the American Convention on Human Rights in the Area of Economic, Social and Cultural Rights (Protocol of San Salvador) (entered into force November 16, 1999) OAS Treaty Series No 69 (1988). In addition, one regional environmental treaty recognizes a right to a healthy environment in the context of procedural rights. See Convention on Access to Information, Public Participation in Decision-Making and Access to Justice in Environmental Matters (Aarhus Convention) 2161 UNTS 447 (25AD).

12 Article 24 of the African Charter provides: "All peoples shall have the right to a general satisfactory environment favourable to their development." In *The Social and Economic Rights Action Center and*

to food, water, an adequate standard of living and housing and sanitation; and *procedural rights*, consisting of the rights to access to information, participation in decision-making processes, and access to remedies and environmental impact assessments (which include procedural rights).[13] Moreover, human rights law imposes additional obligations to protect vulnerable communities such as women, children, indigenous peoples and displaced persons.[14]

Contemporary concern for human rights emerged after World War II, when the international community vowed never to allow such atrocities to be committed again.[15] One of the purposes of the United Nations is to protect human rights and fundamental freedoms.[16] The UN Charter was closely followed by the Universal Declaration of Human Rights (UDHR),[17] which affirmed both civil and political rights and economic, social and cultural rights. This founding document, adopted in less than two years, was to be followed by a binding document.[18] However, the Cold War intervened, and it took the international community almost two decades to adopt binding obligations. In the end, the obligations in the UDHR were bifurcated along civil and political rights, and economic, social and cultural rights, and two covenants – the ICCPR[19] and the ICESCR[20] – were opened for signature in 1966 embodying each set of rights. Despite the official UN position that all rights are indivisible, interrelated and interdependent,[21] this bifurcation has unfortunately given rise to continuing arguments that only civil and political rights are justiciable.

Because the International Bill of Human Rights[22] predates the emergence of international environmental law, these treaties do not include a distinct right to a healthy environment. However, even later human rights treaties, such as the Convention on the Rights of the Child, make only a passing reference to environmental pollution[23] and do not include a right to be free from pollution or a right to live in a healthy environment. The former Special Rapporteur on Human Rights

the Center for Economic and Social Rights v Nigeria, African Commission on Human and Peoples' Rights, Comm. No. 155/96 (2001), where there was severe environmental pollution caused by oil spills, toxic waste disposed in open pits, gas flaring etc. the African Commission elaborated on, *inter alia*, Article 24 and what duties that right imposed on the Nigerian Government.

13 See John H Knox, "Report of the Independent Expert on the issue of human rights obligations relating to the enjoyment of a safe, clean, healthy and sustainable environment (Mapping Report)" (December 2013) UN Doc A/HRC/25/53.

14 ibid.

15 Charter of the United Nations (signed June 26, 1945, entered into force October 24, 1945) 1 UNTS XVI.

16 ibid art 1(3).

17 Universal Declaration of Human Rights (1948) GA Res 217, UN GAOR, 3rd Sess, UN Doc A/810.

18 Olivier De Schutter, *International Human Rights Law* (Cambridge 2012) 20.

19 ICCPR (n 5).

20 ICESCR (n 6).

21 UN General Assembly, Vienna Declaration and Programme of Action (July 12, 1993) A/CONF.157/23.

22 UDHR (n 17), ICCPR (n 5), ICESCR (n 6). See "Fact Sheet No.2 (Rev.1), The International Bill of Human Rights" <https://www.ohchr.org/Documents/Publications/FactSheet2Rev.1en.pdf> accessed April 26, 2018.

23 See Convention on the Rights of the Child (November 20, 1989, entered into force September 2, 1980) 1577 UNTS 3, art 24(c), which enjoys near universal acceptance.

and the Environment, John Knox, believes that if these human rights treaties were to be drafted today, there is no doubt that they would include a right to a healthy environment.[24] That said, the international community has not rushed to amend these treaties to *include* a right to a healthy environment or to adopt a protocol to recognize such a right. On the contrary, there seems to be a general reluctance by states to recognize a distinct right to a healthy environment, despite positive developments at regional[25] and national[26] levels. In this respect, international law seems to be lagging behind. At best, what we have is a greening of existing human rights by international human rights institutions.[27] This section will look at these developments with specific reference to the Human Rights Committee and the Committee on Economic, Social and Cultural Rights.[28]

The treaty bodies that have been established under human rights treaties[29] have, over the years, interpreted and elaborated on the content of rights embodied in these treaties[30] In addition to interpreting the rights, these treaty bodies supervise states parties' compliance with their obligations, monitor progress, and offer Concluding Observations on the country reports that are submitted to them. Moreover, they issue general comments[31] and receive complaints from individual victims where the treaty bodies are authorized to receive such complaints.[32] This is one of the most remarkable achievements of international human rights law. Giving individuals direct

24 John H Knox, "Preliminary Report of the Independent Expert on the issue of human rights obligations relating to the enjoyment of a safe, clean, healthy and sustainable environment" (December 24, 2012) A/HRC/22/43.

25 (n 11).

26 Domestic courts have made an enormous contribution to the development of environmental rights – the Supreme Court of India and the South African courts are good examples. In addition, over 100 constitutions embody environmental rights. See David Boyd, *The Environmental Rights Revolution: A Global Study of Constitutions, Human Rights, and the Environment* (UBC Press 2012), Varun Gauri and Daniel Brinks (eds), *Courting Social Justice: Judicial Enforcement of Social and Economic Rights in the Developing World* (Cambridge University Press 2010); Sumudu Atapattu, "The Role of Human Rights Law in Protecting Environmental Rights in South Asia" in LaDawn Haglund and Robin Stryker (eds), *Closing the Rights Gap: From Human Rights to Social Transformation* (University of California Press 2015) 105.

27 See Anton and Shelton (n 4), ch 7.

28 The Human Rights Committee is a body of independent experts and was established under Article 28 of the ICCPR to monitor the implementation of the ICCPR. Its functions include evaluating country reports submitted by member states and issuing Concluding Observations, receiving communications by individuals seeking redress for rights violated and issuing General Comments on various provisions of the ICCPR. Similarly, the Committee on Economic, Social and Cultural Rights is a body of independent experts appointed to monitor the implementation of the ICESCR. It was established under ECOSOC Resolution 1985/17 of May 28, 1985.

29 Currently, there are ten treaty bodies. See United Nations Human Rights Office of the High Commissioner, "Human Rights Bodies" <www.ohchr.org/EN/HRBodies/Pages/HumanRightsBodies.aspx> accessed December 18, 2018.

30 See Kerstin Mechlem, "Treaty Bodies and the Interpretation of Human Rights" (2009) 42 Vanderbilt Journal of Transnational Law 905.

31 See Anton & Shelton (n 4) 236, 237.

32 See de Schutter (n 18) 805.

access to bring a complaint in an international forum against their own state is unprecedented in international law.[33] While the methods of interpretation used by various treaty bodies have been subject to criticism,[34] the important role played by them interpreting the provisions of the treaty cannot be understated as they play a quasi-judicial role in relation to the complaints they receive. Given the proliferation of treaty bodies and the multitude of functions they perform, achieving some level of coherence is necessary for the development of international law. In this regard, adopting uniform standards to evaluate state conduct in relation to environmental issues becomes important but remains under-studied. What is the relationship between these various treaty bodies?[35] Does the interpretation adopted by one treaty body have any bearing on another? A careful analysis of these interpretations and standards adopted is necessary to avoid fragmentation and to ensure coherence. However, as the discussion below suggests, there does not seem to be an indication that this is a paramount consideration of the two treaty bodies discussed here.

2.2.1 *ICCPR and the Human Rights Committee*

The UN Human Rights Committee was established under Article 28 of the ICCPR. Its main tasks are to (a) formulate Concluding Observations; (b) develop general comments; and (c) adjudicate individual communications.[36] These tasks have a clear legal mandate although the Committee itself may comprise non-legal experts. Under Article 41, states parties can declare that they recognize the competence of the Committee to receive and consider communications by individuals.[37]

The Human Rights Committee is the oldest human rights treaty body and possibly the most active vis-à-vis the number of communications received. Since its establishment in 1977, it has received 2,759 communications concerning ninety-two states parties.[38] Despite this large number of communications, cases involving environmental issues are few and far between. As the ICCPR does not contain a specific provision on the right to a healthy environment, the communications that

33 Indeed, according to Article 38(1) of the ICJ statute, only states may be parties to a dispute before the Court. Individuals have no standing.

34 See Kerstin Mechlem (n 30), who criticizes these bodies for not basing their interpretations on appropriate and accepted methods to make them rational and legitimate.

35 See Michael Bowman, "Beyond the 'Keystone' CoPs: The Ecology of Institutional Governance in Conservation Treaty Regimes" in Malgosia Fitzmaurice and Duncan French (eds), *International Environmental Law and Governance* (Brill/Nijhoff 2015).

36 See de Schutter (n 18) 805.

37 First Optional Protocol to the ICCPR gives individuals the right to bring petitions directly to the Human Rights Committee, provided local remedies have been exhausted, see Optional Protocol to the International Covenant on Civil and Political Rights (adopted December 16, 1966, entered into force March 23, 1976) Regn 14668 999 UNTS 171.

38 Human Rights Committee, Consideration by the Human Rights Committee at its 114th, 115th and 116th sessions of communications received under the Optional Protocol to the ICCPR (October 7, 2016) CCPR/C/116/3.

were submitted to the Committee that related to environmental issues were based on rights that are recognized in the Covenant, such as the right to life. Even the handful of cases that were in fact submitted did not reach the merits phase. Thus, jurisprudence of the Committee on environmental rights is rather sparse and does not provide us with much guidance. We will discuss briefly the emergence of environmental rights under the ICCPR.

The rights embodied in the ICCPR are generally formulated in negative terms (hence the reference to negative rights) to prevent states' interference with citizen's rights. Thus, the objective of the right to life was to prevent arbitrary killings by states: "Every human being has the inherent right to life. This right shall be protected by law. No one shall be arbitrarily deprived of his life."[39]

Right to life is one of the few rights from which no derogation is allowed even in times of an emergency.[40] While this is formulated in negative terms, in General Comment No. 6, the Human Rights Committee recognized that positive obligations emanated from it:

> The Committee noted that the right to life has been too often narrowly interpreted. The expression "inherent right to life" cannot properly be understood in a restrictive manner, and the protection of this right requires that States adopt positive measures. In this connection, the Committee considers that it would be desirable for States parties to take all possible measures to reduce infant mortality and to increase life expectancy, especially in adopting measures to eliminate malnutrition and epidemics.[41]

Anton and Shelton believe that the "reference to malnutrition and epidemics seems to extend article 6 into matters perhaps more appropriately considered under the right to health, including environmental conditions that might give rise to famine and epidemics."[42] Is this sufficient to extend the obligation under Article 6 to protect life from environmental degradation? The Committee seems to be open to this possibility, as indicated in the Port Hope case, discussed next. Three decades later, the Committee specifically acknowledged this link in General Comment 36.

In one of the early cases – the case of *EHP et al.* v. *Canada* – Port Hope Environmental Group submitted a communication against Canada on behalf of present and future generations of Port Hope, Ontario, Canada, including 129 Port Hope residents who had specifically authorized the author to act on their behalf.[43]

39 See Article 6 ICCPR (n 5).

40 General Comment 6, The Right to Life, adopted April 30, 1982 UN Doc HRI/GEN/1/Rev.7, at 128; see Human Rights Committee, General Comment 6, Article 6 (Sixteenth session 1982), Compilation of General Comments and General Recommendations Adopted by Human Rights Treaty Bodies UN Doc HRI/GEN/1/Rev.1 at 6 (May 27, 2008).

41 ibid; see General Comment 36, The Right to Life, (30th Oct. 2018) UN Doc CCPR/c/GC/36. This replaces General Comments 6 and 14. At the time of writing, General Comment 36 was being finalized.

42 Anton and Shelton (n 4) 437.

43 University of Minnesota Human Rights Library (1984) "E. H. P. v. Canada, Communication No. 67/1980, UN Doc CCPR/C/OP/1 at 20" <http://hrlibrary.umn.edu/undocs/html/67-1980.htm> accessed December 18, 2017.

It alleged the violation of the right to life of the residents, including future generations, due to the radioactive waste remains in Port Hope. The author claimed that "the current state of affairs is a threat to the life of present and future generations of Port Hope, considering that excessive exposure to radioactivity is known to cause cancer and genetic defects."[44] Although the petition was deemed inadmissible for nonexhaustion of local remedies, the Committee recognized that the right to life could be impacted as a result of an environmental harm.[45] It observed that the present communication raised serious issues with regard to the obligation of states to protect human life under Article 6 of the Covenant. It also considered that the author had standing to submit the communication on her behalf and on behalf of those who had expressly authorized her to do so. However, with regard to the reference to "future generations," the Committee treated it as "an expression of concern purporting to put into due perspective the importance of the matter raised in the communication."[46] While this is the first step in recognizing the link between environmental issues and protected rights, more guidance as to the standards that should apply would be welcome. Some scholars argue that "there is a strict duty upon States, as well as upon the international community as a whole, to take effective measures to prevent and safeguard against the occurrence of environmental hazards which threaten the lives of human beings."[47] Threatening the life of human beings seems a high threshold to establish. It is also vague, and some guidance as to what this means would be helpful.

The case of *Vaihere Bordes and John Temeharo* v. *France*[48] involved the announcement by France that it intended to conduct a series of underground nuclear tests on the atolls of Mururoa and Frangataufa in the South Pacific. The authors of the communication – Bordes, Tauira (who later withdrew his communication) and Temeharo – were all French citizens living in Papeete, Tahiti, French Polynesia. They claimed that the tests represented a threat to their right to life and the right not to be subjected to arbitrary interference with their privacy and family life. The authors relied on General Comment No. 6 on the Right to Life[49] as well as General Comment No. 14 on Nuclear Weapons and the Right to Life.[50] General Comment No. 14 notes that "designing, testing, manufacture,

44 ibid.

45 ibid.

46 ibid.

47 Bertrand G Ramcharan, *The Right to Life in International Law* (1985) 310–11 referred to in David Hunter, James Salzman and Durwood Zaelke, *International Environmental Law and Policy* (5th edn, Foundation Press 2015), 1347–48. See also Richard L Herz, "Litigating Environmental Abuses under the Alien Tort Claims Act: A Practical Assessment" (2000) 40 Va J IL L 545, 577, who argues that under international law environmental harms presenting grave risks to life also violate the right to life – for example, in the Port Hope case, the Human Rights Committee found that the complainant made out a *prima facie* case based on the threat to life the waste dump presented.

48 Communication 645/1995, UN Doc CCPR/C/57/D/645/1995.

49 Right to Life (n 40).

50 UN Human Rights Committee (HRC), CCPR General Comment No. 14: Article 6 (Right to Life) Nuclear weapons and the Right to Life, November 9, 1984.

possession and deployment of nuclear weapons are among the greatest threat to the right to life which confront mankind today"[51] and urged the international community to prohibit the production of nuclear weapons and to recognize it as a crime against humanity.[52] They further alleged that the French authorities had failed to take sufficient measures to protect their life and security and did not show that underground nuclear tests do not constitute a danger to the health of inhabitants of the South Pacific and the environment.

The authors relied on studies that showed the danger to life caused by nuclear tests due to their effects on the health of people living in the vicinity as well as the indirect risk through contamination of the food chain. France argued, *inter alia*, that the authors did not qualify as "victims" within the meaning of Article 1 of the Optional Protocol because there had been neither a violation nor a real threat. The Committee noted that the issue here is whether the conduct of underground nuclear tests by France on these atolls amounted to a violation of their rights to life and family life. The Committee noted, based on the information presented by the parties, that the authors had not substantiated their claim that the conduct of nuclear tests entitled them to be considered "victims" within the meaning of the ICCPR.[53] Referring to the authors' assertion that nuclear tests would further deteriorate the geological structure of the atolls and increase the likelihood of an accident with catastrophic consequences, the Committee noted that it was highly controversial even in scientific circles, and it was not possible for the Committee to ascertain its validity.[54] The Committee stressed, however, relying on its General Comment No. 14, that although the authors did not show that they were victims, nuclear weapons present a great threat to the right to life.[55]

The decision here is intriguing given the Committee's position that activities involving nuclear weapons *including testing* pose a great threat to the right to life of people. It was no secret that France was engaged in nuclear testing. It was also clear that the complainants were living in the vicinity of these tests. The reasoning suggests that the Committee considered the threat of harm in question to be rather remote and hence the authors did not fall within the definition of a victim. Nonetheless, this case is important because it recognized that there is a clear link between nuclear tests and the right to life. However, while it recognized that the threat of harm should not be too remote, it was unclear why it was held to be so in this case because clearly the complainants were living in close proximity to the nuclear test sites. It is not clear what "standards" if any, the Committee took into consideration when evaluating this application. This case also raises questions about how the Committee would evaluate scientific evidence. Had there been scientific

51 ibid para 4.
52 ibid para 6.
53 (n 48) para 5.7.
54 ibid para 5.6.
55 ibid para 5.9.

consensus about the danger nuclear testing posed to the environment of these atolls, would the Committee have taken a different position? Clearly, the Committee is not a scientific body, but from time to time it will be called upon to evaluate scientific evidence in order to decide whether a complainant is a "victim." Having clear standards would be beneficial in this regard.

In the submission in *Susila Malani Dahanayake*[56] the authors also invoked Article 6, claiming that:

> The right to life guaranteed by Article 6 of the Covenant has been interpreted by other treaty bodies, also by the Human Rights Committee, in a broad manner, and consequently claim a violation of their right to life, which includes a right to a healthy environment.[57]

The subject matter of this communication related to the proposed southern expressway by the Road Development Authority of Sri Lanka. Two possible routes were examined by the proponent in the EIA, but a third route – the "final trace" – which was not examined in any EIA report was ultimately selected for implementation. This route affected the authors' property and no new approval from the Central Environmental Authority was sought. When the authors complained about this in a fundamental rights case before the Supreme Court of Sri Lanka, the Court, while recognizing that the authors' fundamental right to equality under Article 12(1) of the Constitution and principles of natural justice were infringed, did not order the project to be halted. The authors then brought this submission before the UN Human Rights Committee claiming that no new EIA was prepared for the third route and no opportunity was given to the authors to be heard as required under the law. The state party responded that it did not intend to interfere with the authors' right to live in a healthy environment,[58] indicating that it accepted that the right to life included a right to live in a healthy environment. While the Committee concluded that the authors had not sufficiently substantiated their claim that they were victims of a violation of their right to life under Article 6 because they were deprived of a healthy environment, both parties seemed to have accepted the link between right to life and the right to a healthy environment. Because they received compensation and costs for the violation of a fundamental right by the Supreme Court of Sri Lanka, the Committee was of the view that they are no longer "victims" within the meaning of Article 1 of the Optional Protocol. While this case did not deal with standards *per se*, it gives us some direction as to who a victim is for the purposes of the Optional Protocol which has ramifications for standing.

Interestingly, many of the communications under the ICCPR that relate to the environment have arisen under Article 27 on minority rights, mostly

[56] *Susila Malani Dahanayake and 41 other Sri Lankan citizens v Sri Lanka* (July 25, 2006) UN Doc CCPR/C/87/D/1331/2004, referred to in John H Knox, Mapping Report (n 13).

[57] ibid para 3.2.

[58] ibid para 4.7.

involving indigenous groups and their right to culture. In the submission of *EP et al.* v. *Colombia*,[59] the authors invoked Article 27 on the basis that they had been dispossessed of their lands; that the Colombian government had encouraged massive development of the islands that caused severe environmental damage that affected the water table, making farming impossible, and destroyed their traditional livelihoods; the government had permitted destruction of mangrove swamps by allowing electric power plants to freely dump hot, polluted water; and the government had granted fishing rights to Honduras without regard to native interests, depriving them of their traditional means of survival. They alleged that government policies and other development activities resulted in damage to the environment of the outlying islands on which the authors lived, "making farming impossible and depleting other traditional sources of sustenance such as fish and shellfish from mangrove swamps, and were also depriving them of fishing rights."[60] The Committee found that the communication was inadmissible because local remedies had not been exhausted. Where there is a ruling of inadmissibility, the Committee does not go into the merits of the claim to ascertain whether the standards of protection afforded by the rights in the Covenant are infringed.

The communication of *Lubicon Lake Band* v. *Canada*[61] also involved an indigenous group whose rights had been violated due to oil and gas development on lands traditionally used by the Band leading to environmental destruction and, in the process, violated a number of rights protected by the ICCPR. The author claimed that oil development in its traditional lands had destroyed the subsistence livelihood of its people and that the delay in litigation would cause it irreparable harm. It further claimed that a permanent injunction would not constitute an effective remedy:

> The recognition of aboriginal rights or even treaty rights by a final determination of the courts will not undo the irreparable damage to the society of the Lubicon Lake Bank, will not bring back the animals, will not restore the environment, will not restore the Band's traditional economy, will not replace the destruction of their traditional way of life and will not repair the damages to the spiritual and cultural ties to the land.[62]

Moreover, the author alleged that the state party, through actions affecting the Band's livelihood, had led to the deaths of twenty-one persons and that the ability of the community to survive was in serious doubt as the number of miscarriages and stillbirths had skyrocketed, constituting a violation of Article 6. Furthermore, it was claimed that "the appropriation of the Band's traditional lands, the destruction of its

59 *E P et al. v Colombia*, Communication (1990) No 318/1988 UN Doc CCPR/C/39/D/318/1988.
60 ibid 8.
61 Communication No. 167/1984 (March 26, 1990) UN Doc Supp No 40 (A/45/40) at 1 (1990).
62 ibid para 11.2.

way of life and livelihood and the devastation wrought to the community constituted cruel, inhuman and degrading treatment within the meaning of Article 7."[63] Canada contested many of the claims: it argued that even in areas that were covered by timber leases the forest remained intact and sustained sufficient animal population to satisfy those who wished to engage in traditional activities. The allegations in this case were serious to the extent of casting doubts on the community's ability to survive. The case provides an indication of the level of seriousness of the harm suffered by this community. In holding that a violation of Article 27 had occurred, the Committee was mindful of the historic inequities that had contributed to the violation of rights enshrined in Article 27, and the violations here were serious enough as to question the ability of the community to survive:

> Historical inequities, to which the State party refers, and certain more recent developments threaten the way of life and culture of the Lubicon Lake Band, and constitute a violation of Article 27 so long as they continue.[64]

In several other communications where the Committee did not find a violation of Article 27, it nonetheless acknowledged the link between the right to culture and environmental degradation.[65] In many of these cases, it was difficult to attribute action to government authorities, pointing to the uphill battle these communities face when taking their claim to an international body.

The case of *Andre Brun* v. *France*[66] involved the alleged contamination of the complainant's crops by the dissemination of genetically modified products by a private company, Biogemma, and the consequent destruction of transgenic crops by the author to protect his crops. The complainant, relying on the jurisprudence of the European Court of Human Rights, argued that the Committee should proceed by analogy and adopt an extensive interpretation of Article 17 of the ICCPR[67] to encompass the right to live in a healthy environment under the ambit of private and family life.[68] He also invoked the precautionary principle and contended that the medium and long-term risk of genetically modified organisms (GMOs) on health and the environment should be taken into account.[69] He argued that Article 6 on the right to life was violated and that the promotion of a healthy environment contributed to the protection of the right to life. He cited the *Port Hope*

[63] ibid para 16.2.
[64] ibid para 33.
[65] *Ilmari Lansman et al. v Finland* (26 Oct 1994) UN Doc CCPR/C/52/D/511/1992; *Jouni Lasnman et al. v Finland* (October 30, 1996) UN Doc CCPR/C/587/D/671/1995 and (March 17, 2005) UN Doc CCPR/C/83/D/1023/2001; *Mahuika v New Zealand* (October 27, 2000) UN Doc CCPR/C/70/D/547/1993 and *Angela Poma Poma*, discussed below.
[66] Communication No. 1453/2006, CCPR/C/88/D/1453/2006.
[67] Article 17 of the ICCPR embodies the right to privacy, family, home and correspondence (n 5).
[68] Communication No. 1453/2006 (n 66) para 3.
[69] ibid para 3.2.

case[70] to support the link between the right to life and the right to a healthy environment. In conclusion, the author argued that planting of transgenic crops in open fields resulted in the destruction of conventional crops and that the minimum distance between genetically modified fields and non-GM fields was ineffective. Therefore, the destruction of transgenic crops became necessary and he had acted out of the necessity to protect the environment.

The complainant also contended that the interference with private and family life protected under Article 17 "must be justified and proportionate in the light of the provisions, aims and objectives of the Covenant."[71] The interference in this case consisted of the government's failure to take the necessary measures to prevent the threats to his health and the environment associated with the dissemination of GMOs in open fields. He relied on the extensive jurisprudence of the European Court of Human Rights relating to pollution cases, and contended that the Committee should proceed by analogy and adopt an extensive interpretation of Article 17 under which "private and family life encompasses the right to live in a healthy environment."[72] The Committee was of the view that there was no actual violation or an imminent threat of violation of his rights to life and privacy, family and home and, therefore, the complainant could not claim to be a victim within the meaning of Article 1 of the Optional Protocol. Therefore, the communication was deemed inadmissible. The Committee pointed out that Article 2(3)(b) of the Covenant guarantees protection to alleged victims if their complaints are "sufficiently well-founded to be arguable" under the Covenant. "Sufficiently well-founded" seems to be the standard that the Committee applied in relation to admissibility. What is more interesting in this communication is the fact that the complainant relied on the extensive jurisprudence of the European Court of Human Rights to substantiate his claim under the ICCPR. While the Committee did not decide on the merits of the communication, the potential for cross-fertilization of jurisprudence is significant.

In the communication in *Angela Poma Poma* v. *Peru*[73] the complainant brought a claim under Article 1(2),[74] Article 2(3)(a),[75] Article 14(1)[76] and Article 17[77] of the ICCPR. The complainant claimed that the diversion of the course of the river Uchusuma by the government and the subsequent drilling of wells considerably reduced the water supply to pastures and to areas where water was drawn for human and animal consumption. She further claimed "that this caused the gradual drying

70 *Port Hope case* (n 43).
71 Communication No. 1453/2006 (n 66) para 5.2.
72 ibid para 3.1.
73 Communication No. 1457/2006.
74 Article 1(2) deals with the right of all peoples to freely dispose of their natural wealth and resources and provides that in no case may a people be deprived of its own means of subsistence.
75 Article 2(3)(a) deals with the right to an effective remedy.
76 Article 14 embodies the right to equality before courts and tribunals.
77 Article 17 embodies the right to privacy, family, home or correspondence.

out of the wetlands where llama-raising is practiced in accordance with the traditional customs of the affected families, who are descendants of the Aymara people, and which has been part of their way of life for thousands of years."[78]

The complainant claimed that the state party violated Article 1(2), because the diversion of groundwater from her land had destroyed the ecosystem of the Altiplano and caused the degradation of the land and the drying of wetlands. As a result, thousands of livestock had died and the community's only means of survival had collapsed, leaving it in poverty and depriving it of its livelihood.[79] Further, she claimed that it constituted an interference in the life and activities of her family in violation of Article 17, as the lack of water had seriously affected their only means of subsistence.

The Committee, recalling its General Comment No. 23 on Rights of Minorities,[80] noted that the right to culture under Article 27 manifests itself in many forms, including a particular way of life associated with the use of land and resources, especially in the case of indigenous peoples: "That right [right to culture] may include such traditional activities as fishing or hunting and the right to live in reserves protected by law."[81] In this case, the Committee evaluated the question of whether the consequences of the water diversion were such as to have substantive negative impacts on the complainant's enjoyment of her right to culture. The Committee noted that thousands of livestock died because of the degradation of 10,000 hectares of Aymara pastureland as a direct result of a project implemented by the government.

The Committee stated:

> The admissibility of measures which substantially compromise or interfere with the culturally significant economic activities of a minority or indigenous community depends on whether the members of the community in question have had the opportunity to participate in the decision-making process in relation to these measures and whether they will continue to benefit from the traditional economy. The Committee considers that participation in the decision-making process must be effective, which requires not mere consultation but the free, prior and informed consent of the members of the community. *In addition, the measures must respect the principle of proportionality so as not to endanger the very survival of the community and its members.*[82]

The Committee observed that neither the complainant nor the community was consulted at any time by the state regarding the construction of the wells. The state had not requested studies to be undertaken by a competent body. Moreover, it

78 Communication No. 1457/2006 (n 73) para 2.2.
79 ibid para 3.1.
80 ICCPR General Comment No. 23: Article 27 (Rights of Minorities) (April 8, 1994) CCPR/C/21/Rev.1/Add.5.
81 Communication No. 1457/2006 (n. 73) para 7.2.
82 ibid para 7.6 (emphasis added).

observed that the she could not benefit from her traditional economic activity and, therefore, concluded that the state's action had substantively compromised the her way of life and culture as a member of her community.[83] Thus, the principle of proportionality was used as the yardstick to measure whether the activities endangered the very survival of the community. Here too, the Committee seems to be using two "standards": (a) that the participation of the community must be "effective";[84] and (b) that measures taken by the state party must respect the principle of proportionality. According to the Committee, the test here is whether the proposed activity endangers the survival of the community in question. This seems a high threshold to establish, as most measures will not endanger the survival of the community, although they could have a considerable impact on the lives of its people.

In several Concluding Observations, the Committee has noted that environmental degradation can affect the enjoyment of protected rights. Thus, for example, in its Concluding Observations on Colombia's report, the Committee pointed out that it wished to receive information on measures taken to address the ecological deterioration of the Amazon region and whether Colombia "had encountered any problems in reconciling development of its oil reserves with the maintenance of a balanced ecosystem."[85] Similarly observations that were made with respect to Ecuador, it requested information on how ecological deterioration of the Amazon region was affecting indigenous communities and the measures taken to address that situation.[86] Similar in observations have been made with regard to Mexico,[87] Guyana,[88] Argentina,[89] Belize[90] and Sweden.[91] While these observations do not relate to standards per se, they do provide the reader with guidance as to how to balance economic development (i.e. exploiting oil reserves) with environmental protection. They also recognize the importance of providing affected communities with relevant information and giving them an opportunity to participate in the decision-

83 ibid para 7.7.

84 See also Chapter 9 of this volume by Jona Razzaque relating to "free, prior and informed consent."

85 "Mapping Human Rights Obligations," Report No. 2 Individual Report on the International Covenant on Civil and Political Rights, Report of the Human Rights Committee for the forty-seventh session, Consideration of reports submitted by State parties under Article 40 of the Covenant: Colombia (October 9, 1992) UN Doc CCPR/A/47/40 paras 378–79.

86 ibid 16. Report of the Human Rights Committee for the forty-seventh session, Consideration of reports submitted by State parties under Article 40 of the Covenant: Ecuador (October 9, 1992) UN Doc A/47/40 paras 257–58.

87 Concluding Observations of the Human Rights Committee for the sixty-sixth session: Mexico (July 27, 1999) UN Doc CCPR/C/79/Add.109, 19.

88 Concluding Observations of the Human Rights Committee: Guyana (March 24 and 27, 2000) UN Doc CCPR/C/79/Add.121, 21.

89 Concluding Observations of the Human Rights Committee for the ninety-eighth session: Argentina (March 31, 2010) UN Doc CCPR/C/ARG/CO/4, 25.

90 List of Issues Prepared in the Absence of the Initial Report of Belize (November 23, 2012) UN Doc CCPR/C/BLZ/Q/1, 28.

91 Concluding Observations of the Human Rights Committee for the seventy-fourth session: Sweden (April 24, 2002) UN Doc CCPR/CO/74/SWE, 15.

making process. That a human rights institution is referring to the need to maintain a balanced ecosystem is itself a major step forward.

2.2.2 *ICESCR and the Committee*

As the ICESCR does not contain a distinct right to a healthy environment, the most relevant rights under the ICESCR with regard to environmental protection are: the right to an adequate standard of living (Article 11), which includes the right to food and water, and the right to health (Article 12). The right to culture (Article 15) is also relevant. ICESCR does not recognize a separate right to water, although it specifically mentions the right to food. This *lacuna* was addressed in 2002 with the adoption of General Comment No. 15, which recognized the right to water as being included in Articles 11 and 12.[92] It asserted: "Water is a limited natural resource and a public good fundamental for life and health. The human right to water is indispensable for leading a life in human dignity. It is a prerequisite for the realization of other human rights."[93] The General Comment elaborates on the normative content of the right to water under three headings:

(a) Availability – the quantity of water available for each person should correspond to WHO guidelines.
(b) Quality – "the water required for each personal or domestic use must be safe, therefore free from micro-organisms, chemical substances and radiological hazards that constitute a threat to a person's health."[94] In this regard the Committee refers states parties to WHO guidelines for drinking water quality that are "intended to be used as a basis for development of national standards."[95]
(c) Accessibility – water facilities and services have to be accessible to everyone without discrimination. This comprises physical accessibility, economic accessibility, non-discrimination and information accessibility.

With regard to both quantity and quality of water, the General Comment relies on WHO guidelines. This clearly links water with health and well-being. The WHO Guidelines for Drinking Water Quality are very detailed and contain indicators relating, *inter alia*, to health-based targets, water safety plans and those applicable in specific circumstances such as during climate changes, during disasters and in instances of temporary water supply.[96] Given the detailed nature of these guidelines, it is not clear how the committee determines whether they have been breached in a given case. The General Comment calls upon states parties to develop

92 See Chapter 7 of this volume by Owen McIntyre relating to the right to water and sanitation.
93 General Comment No. 15 (November 26, 2002) Committee on Economic, Social and Cultural Rights UN Doc E/C.12/2002/11.
94 ibid.
95 ibid.
96 World Health Organisation, Guidelines for Drinking Water Quality, 4th edition (2011) <http://apps.who.int/iris/bitstream/10665/44584/1/9789241548151_eng.pdf> accessed December 18, 2017.

right-to-water indicators to be included in their national water strategies or plans of action. These indicators should be designed to monitor states parties' obligations under Article 11 and should address different components of adequate water (such as sufficiency, safety and acceptability, affordability and physical accessibility), drawing on appropriate indicators from the work of the WHO, FAO, United Nations Centre for Human Settlements, UNEP and UNDP.[97] Thus, while the General Comment itself does not adopt standards, it makes it clear that states should be guided by the standards and indicators developed by specialized agencies with expert knowledge on the subject in question. This is a good strategy to adopt.

General Comment No. 12 on the Right to Adequate Food similarly recognizes that it is indispensable for the fulfilment of other human rights and is indivisibly linked to the inherent dignity of the human person.[98] It notes that "it is also inseparable from social justice, requiring the adoption of appropriate economic, environmental and social policies."[99] The General Comment notes that the right to adequate food shall not be interpreted narrowly, equating it with "a minimum package of calories, proteins and other specific nutrients."[100] It elaborates on the normative content of Article 11 and considers that the core content of the right to adequate food implies:

> The availability of food in a quantity and quality sufficient to satisfy the dietary needs of individuals, free from adverse substances, and acceptable within a given culture;
>
> The accessibility of such food in ways that are sustainable and that do not interfere with the enjoyment of other human rights.[101]

The General Comment further notes that "free from adverse substances" sets requirements for food safety and for measures to prevent contamination of foodstuffs through adulteration and/or through bad environmental hygiene or inappropriate handling at different stages throughout the food chain. States are required to adopt targets and goals and a timeframe to achieve them, develop a national strategy to ensure food and nutritious security and to develop benchmarks and framework legislation with help from UN specialized agencies such as the FAO and UNICEF. It notes that these organizations have developed expertise in their fields and, if requested, they should assist in drafting and reviewing legislation. Unlike the General Comment on the Right to Water, the General Comment on the Right to Food does not refer specifically to standards or guidelines adopted by specialized agencies, but encourages states to make use of their expertise.

97 General Comment No. 15 (n 93) para 53.
98 Committee on Economic, Social and Cultural Rights, General Comment No. 12 (1999) UN Doc E/C/12/1999/5.
99 ibid para 4.
100 ibid para 6.
101 ibid para 8.

General Comment No. 14 on the Right to Health, on the other hand, refers specifically to health policies and programs developed by the WHO. It also recognizes the link to a healthy environment:

> The Committee interprets the right to health, as defined in article 12.1 as an inclusive right extending not only to timely and appropriate health care but also to the underlying determinants of health, such as access to safe and potable water and adequate sanitation, an adequate supply of safe food, nutrition and housing, healthy occupational and environmental conditions.[102]

The General Comment elaborates on the normative content of the right to health under (a) availability; (b) accessibility; (c) acceptability; and (d) quality. In this regard, the General Comment notes: "As well as being culturally acceptable, health facilities, goods and services must also be scientifically and medically appropriate and good quality. This requires, *inter alia,* skilled medical personnel, scientifically approved and unexpired drugs and hospital equipment, safe and potable water, and adequate sanitation."[103] States parties are encouraged to adopt a framework law, a national health strategy and plan of action and identify appropriate health indicators and benchmarks, targets to be achieved, and the timeframe for achieving them. In this regard, they are encouraged to obtain guidance from the work of the WHO and UNICEF with regard to the right to health as they can provide good benchmarks. The General Comment provides:

> The indicators should be designed to monitor, at the national and international levels, the state party's obligations under article 12. States may obtain guidance on appropriate right to health indicators, which should address different aspects of the right to health, from the ongoing work of WHO and the United Nations Children's Fund (UNICEF) in this field. Right to health indicators require disaggregation on the prohibited grounds of discrimination.[104]

Once these indicators have been set, states parties are invited to set appropriate national benchmarks in relation to each indicator. These national benchmarks should inform the state party in its implementation of Article 12. In their reports to the Committee, the state party should indicate whether the benchmarks have been achieved and whether there were difficulties in achieving them. Here benchmarks seem to be used synonymously with standards and provide an important yardstick to measure compliance.

Just as Concluding Observations have a role to play in the understanding and development of civil and political rights (as seen in Section 2.2.1), Concluding Observations of the Committee on Economic, Social and Cultural Rights on reports submitted by countries pursuant to Article 16 of the Covenant are relevant

[102] Committee on Economic, Social and Cultural Rights, General Comment No. 14 para 11 (August 11, 2000) UN Doc E/C.12/2000/4.

[103] ibid para 12(d).

[104] ibid para 57.

here.[105] These documents can also be helpful with regard to standards that states have to comply with when fulfilling their obligations under the Covenant. Thus, for example, in its Concluding Observations on the second periodic report of Ecuador, the Committee on Economic, Social and Cultural Rights "voiced concerns about the negative health and environmental impacts of natural resource extracting companies' activities on the exercise of land and cultural rights by the affected indigenous communities and the equilibrium of the eco-system."[106] In response to Ecuador's 2012 report, the Committee again referred to the environmental impacts of mining and agribusiness projects and their effects on the people's ability to exercise their right to water.[107] Similarly, in its Concluding Observations on Honduras, the Committee referred to the state party's failure to address the problem of excessive deforestation, which was negatively impacting the habitat of indigenous peoples.[108] On Paraguay's report the Committee noted that the impact of indiscriminate use of toxic agrochemicals related to the expansion of soybean cultivation was leading to deaths and illnesses among people (including children), the contamination of water supplies and the disappearance of ecosystems, which meant the loss of traditional food resources for affected communities.[109]

Australia was informed of the Committee's concern regarding the negative impact of climate change on the right to an adequate standard of living, including the rights to food and water particularly of indigenous communities.[110] The Committee reiterated its recommendations with regard to climate change in its Concluding Observations on the 5th period report of Australia. It called upon Australia to revise its climate change and energy policies, to take immediate steps to reduce its greenhouse gas emissions and to pursue alternative and renewable energy production.[111] The Committee further recommended that Australia addressed the impact of climate change on indigenous peoples more effectively "while fully engaging indigenous peoples in related policy and programme design and implementation."[112] The fact that a human rights institution is calling upon states to reduce their greenhouse gas emissions and to explore renewable sources of energy is by itself a significant development.

The Committee also discussed the effects on the right to food caused by the depletion of natural resources of the rainforest traditionally used by indigenous

105 Under art 16, states parties have undertaken "to submit reports on the measures which they have adopted and the progress made in in achieving observance of the rights recognized herein."
106 Anton and Shelton (n 4) 439, referring to the Concluding Observations on Ecuador (May 14, 2004) UN Doc E/C.12/1/Add.100, para 12.
107 John H Knox, Mapping Report (n 13) 12.
108 ibid 11.
109 ibid 12.
110 ibid 14.
111 Committee on Economic Social and Cultural Rights, Concluding Observations on the Fifth Period Report of Australia (June 23, 2017) UN Doc E/C.12/AUS/CO/5.
112 ibid para 12.

communities in Cameroon.[113] Similarly, the Committee expressed its concern regarding the situation of indigenous peoples in the Russian Federation, many of whom live in poverty and "whose food supply is based on fishing and an adequate stock of reindeer and who are witnessing the destruction of their environment by widespread pollution."[114] The reference here to the need to have "an adequate stock of reindeer" gives an indication of the standard that the Committee had applied. "Adequate" here presumably means a supply of reindeer adequate to sustain the indigenous community in question. Terms such as "adequate" and "sufficient" give flexibility to the state party, and their meaning would depend on the circumstances of each case, but they can also be abused or narrowly interpreted. Moreover, what the state party considers adequate may not be what the community considers adequate for its members. Hence, safeguards such as those requiring "consultation with the community" become important.

Concluding observations by the Committee that link the violation of protected rights with environmental degradation, pollution and resource depletion are numerous.[115] In addition, the Committee has made statements and reports recognizing the impact of climate change on protected rights,[116] rights of future generations[117] and the rights of indigenous peoples.[118] The Committee has also recognized procedural rights, especially the right to participate in the decision making process and the right to a remedy.[119] Thus, while the body of decisions of the Committee recognizing environmental rights is not very extensive, the Committee has explicitly recognized the link between environmental degradation and protected rights, especially rights to food, water, health, housing and an adequate standard of living in its Concluding Observations. It has used general phrases such as "all appropriate measures," "all necessary measures" and "taking immediate steps" with regard to protecting rights in its comments on country reports. These phrases do not refer to any standards but seem to give some guidance as what is required of states to effectively comply with their obligations under the Covenant.

113 ibid 15.

114 ibid 16.

115 For a compilation of these Concluding Observations (n 87) and (n 109).

116 For example, General Comment No. 15 on the Right to Water (January 20, 2003) E/C.12/2002/11, and Report of the Committee on Economic, Social and Cultural Rights for the forty-second session, Consideration of reports of States parties: Australia (May 22, 2009) UN Doc E/C.12/AUS/CO/4, para 27.

117 See General Comment No. 15, ibid.

118 See statement in the context of the Rio+20 Conference on "the green economy in the context of sustainable development and poverty eradication," adopted by the Committee at its Forty-eighth session, April 30–May 18, 2012 (June 4, 2012) UN Doc E/C.12/2012/1, para 6(g); and Report of the Committee on Economic, Social and Cultural Rights for the fortieth and forty-first sessions, Consideration of reports of States parties: The Philippines, April 28–May 16, 2008 (November 3–21, 2008) UN Doc E/C.12/2008/3 para 484.

119 See General Comment No. 7: The right to adequate housing (Art. 11.1): forced evictions (May 20, 1997) UN Doc E/1998/22 para 13 and General Comment No. 12: The right to adequate food (May 12, 1999) UN Doc E/C.12/1999/5 art 11 para 32.

2.3 COMMENT AND ANALYSIS ON THE DEVELOPMENT OF STANDARDS

Despite the recognition of the link between environmental degradation and human rights by the two treaty bodies discussed in this chapter, explicit application of standards by them is another story. This section will rely on the salient cases discussed in Section 2.2 to ascertain whether we can extrapolate some general standards that could provide guidance in similar cases in the future.

As the above discussion reveals, the two Committees that were the subject of this chapter have not engaged in a wide-ranging discussion of relevant standards except in a handful of cases. While many cases that implicated environmental issues were presented before these two Committees, many of the communications did not succeed for various reasons, although the two institutions were open to the idea that environmental factors could lead to a violation of rights protected under the two Covenants. This recognition is important. It opens the door to the victims of environmental abuse to seek redress under these two covenants. It also allows the Committees to scrutinize environmental issues that lead to the violation of rights protected under the two covenants under country reports and Concluding Observations. Concluding Observations have been the main vehicle through which the Committee on Economic, Social and Cultural Rights has made its mark recognizing the link between environmental degradation and human rights. Individual communications under this covenant are still at the nascent stage as the Optional Protocol under the ICESCR came into force in 2013.

The principle of proportionality seems to be the main yardstick used by the Human Rights Committee when evaluating whether a violation of rights has taken place. While this gives flexibility to the decision-maker, it is also quite vague and what proportionality means would depend on the circumstances of each case. The question arises as to whether a "principle" can also be a standard. The principle of proportionality has played an important role in many areas of international law,[120] especially humanitarian law,[121] and is considered a customary international law principle.[122] It provides the decision-maker with an important guideline that punishment must be commensurate with the crime and that a response to an action should

[120] See James Crawford, *Brownlie's Principles of Public International Law* (8th edn, Oxford 2012); the proportionality principle has been applied in relation to countermeasures (587–88), delimitation of the continental shelf (290–91), human rights enforcement (665) and state jurisdiction (486). It has also been described as a doctrine. The principle of proportionality has also played an important role in relation to remedies. See James Crawford, *State Responsibility: The General Part, Cambridge Studies in International and Comparative Law* (Cambridge University Press 2013) 482, 697–99 (proportionality in relation to countermeasures).

[121] See Jonathan Crowe and Kylie Weston-Scheuber, *Principles of International Humanitarian Law* (Edward Elgar 2013), who point out that an attack on a legitimate military objective may sometimes become wrongful if the principle of proportionality is not respected. They cite art 51(5)(b) of the Additional Protocol 1 which prohibits attacks "which may be expected to cause incidental loss of civilian life, injury to civilians ... which would be excessive in relation to the concrete and direct military advantage anticipated" (55).

[122] See Crawford (n 120) 585.

be proportionate to the action. It is also an important principle in the jurisprudence of the European Court of Human Rights, where the court seeks to strike a balance between the general interests of society and the rights of the individual.[123] Thus, in the absence of specific standards, the principle of proportionality can play an important role in a multitude of situations. It could also help us decide whether a restriction of rights in a given situation is justified.[124]

Moreover, the Committees seem to be content to apply standards such as "effective," "adequate" or "sufficient." While these terms give flexibility, they are also vague and subjective. These standards have been applied to decide on both the admissibility and the merits of the claim. Apart from these general and rather vague terms, the communications referred to the Committees do not provide much guidance with regard to standards in relation to environmental rights. The General Comments, on the other hand, are more helpful. The General Comment on the Right to Water refers to WHO guidelines on drinking water quality which the Committee recommends that states should use for developing national standards. The General Comment on the Right to Food, on the other hand, does not refer to any standards but encourages states to tap into the expertise of specialized agencies in developing benchmarks and framework legislation. With regard to food safety and meeting the nutritional needs of the population, standards play an important role. The General Comment on the Right to Health refers to the importance of healthy environmental conditions and encourages states parties to obtain guidance from the work of the WHO and UNICEF with regard to their guidelines on the right to health. While these General Comments provide guidance to states with regard to the adoption of standards, the Committees themselves do not seem to have followed that advice in the communications referred to them.

2.4 CONCLUSION

While the convergence between environmental issues and human rights can be seen in the decisions on the communications referred to the Human Rights Committee and the Committee on Economic, Social and Cultural Rights, these two Committees have not contributed to the development of environmental rights in the way that the regional human rights institutions have. Their most significant contribution to environmental rights seems to be through the Concluding Observations, where these two bodies have consistently linked environmental

123 ibid 665.

124 ibid. In *Dudgeon* (1981) 67 ILR 395, 414, 416–17, the European Court said: "In Article 8 . . . the notion of 'necessity' is linked to that of a 'democratic society.' A restriction on the Convention right cannot be regarded as 'necessary in a democratic society' – unless, amongst other things, it is proportionate to the legitimate aims pursued" (665). Crawford (n 120) notes, "Notwithstanding the margin of appreciation left to the national authorities, the question of proportionality is ultimately one for the Court" (665). It has also played an important role in jurisprudence of the Inter-American system and the African system (665).

degradation, exploitation of natural resources and environmental pollution with protected rights. The Human Rights Committee has also developed some jurisprudence relating to the rights of indigenous peoples to enjoy their culture through Article 27 of the ICCPR. It has additionally taken a stand against nuclear weapons, including their testing, on the ground that it poses a threat to the right to life. Moreover, it has moved away from the negative formulation in Article 6 to encompass positive obligations to protect the right to life. Protecting against damage caused by environmental degradation clearly comes within this duty. The UN Human Rights Committee recognized, in General Comment 36 adopted in 2018 (which now replaces General Comments 6 and 14), that the duty to protect life implies that states should take appropriate measures to address situations that pose a threat to the right to life. This includes environmental degradation. It specifically acknowledged that environmental degradation, climate change and unsustainable development are among the most serious threats to the right to life of the present and future generations. It should be emphasized that both the ICESCR[125] and the ICCPR[126] require states parties to take steps to give effect to the provisions in the two covenants, including the adoption of legislative and other measures "as may be necessary to give effect to the rights recognized in the present Covenant."[127] To give effect to this obligation, states parties must adopt not only legislation but also relevant standards and indicators to provide guidance to public officials and dispute resolution bodies, including the judiciary.

The two Committees have also become increasingly concerned about the impact of climate change on the enjoyment of rights, complementing the work done by the Human Rights Council and the Office of the High Commissioner for Human Rights.[128] While petitions relating to climate change have been filed before regional human rights bodies, treaty bodies are yet to be faced with communications relating to the threat posed to protected rights by climate change.

With regard to developing standards, however, these two bodies have a long way to go. In this regard, the two committees discussed here as well as other treaty bodies can draw from the rich jurisprudence developed by the regional human rights bodies relating to environmental rights promoting coherence and consistency of international law. Such standards would be helpful to better articulate environmental rights and assist these human rights bodies with deciding on whether a violation of rights has taken place.

If international human rights law were to recognize a distinct right to a healthy environment either by amending the existing treaties or by adding a protocol to

125 Article 2 ICESCR (n 6).
126 Article 2 ICCPR (n 5).
127 ibid.
128 Report of the Office of the United Nations High Commissioner for Human Rights on the relationship between climate change and human rights (January 15, 2009) UN Doc A/HRC/10/61 <https://documents-dds-ny.un.org/doc/UNDOC/GEN/G09/103/44/PDF/G0910344.pdf?OpenElement> accessed December 18, 2017.

them, the situation could change significantly. States would be required to report on their environmental laws and the state of environment in their country reports, rather than link environmental damage to protected rights or even in the absence of a direct link to other rights. Thus, for example, states might have to provide an explanation of significant deforestation in their countries despite the fact that no rights had been immediately violated. Although the political will to adopt a distinct right to a healthy environment may be lacking and some scholars have cautioned against it in the past,[129] due, *inter alia*, to the important contribution made by the Special Rapporteur on Human Rights and the Environment, the Human Rights Council may be slowly becoming amenable to such a recognition.[130] Given that a healthy environment is necessary for the enjoyment of many of the protected rights, and with the adverse consequences of climate change looming large, the time may be ripe for the recognition of a right to a healthy environment under international human rights law. This would require judiciaries to articulate the standards necessary to give it effect.

129 See Phillip Alston, "Conjuring Up New Human Rights: A Proposal for Quality Control" (1984) 28 American Journal of International Law 607.

130 In addition to extending the mandate of the independent expert, the Human Rights Council has adopted many resolutions on the link between climate change and human rights. See <www.ohchr.org/EN/Issues/Environment/SREnvironment/Pages/ClimateChange.aspx> accessed December 18, 2017.

3

The ECHR, Environment-Based Human Rights Claims and the Search for Standards

Karen Morrow

3.1 INTRODUCTION

This chapter investigates the peculiar challenges in developing coverage for environmental concerns and the standards necessary to support them, in the context of the European Convention on Human Rights (ECHR), a treaty regime that has no specific coverage for environmental matters. By way of context, brief reference will be made to the jurisprudential climate and adjudicational strategies adopted to lay claim to regime competence in this area in the first place. The door having been opened to human rights claims founded on matters of environmental concern (not, strictly speaking environmental human rights, the distinction being a significant one), the chapter will survey developments in two main areas. First, in Sections 3.2 and 3.3, it will investigate how the European Court of Human Rights (ECtHR) addressed the initial task of setting a threshold – the most basic, yet fundamental, standard – for triggering judicial intervention in the context of what remains a fundamentally supervisory regime, a particularly challenging task in the absence of environment-related content in the Convention texts. The chapter will go on, in Section 3.4, to consider the development of the Court's subsequent jurisprudence, elaborating ever more detailed and demanding standards for evaluating signatory States' behaviour. In so doing, it will examine the search for content and legitimacy in standard setting through deploying various 'proxies' rooted in domestic and international (including EU) law and policy, to supply the obvious criteria deficit in the regime texts. The chapter will conclude, in Section 3.5, by briefly discussing the fact that, however desirable such a development may be in principle, political constraints indicate that adopting a more coherent approach to environment-based human rights claims through agreeing applicable standards in a new Protocol to the ECHR is unlikely. This being the case, as the ECtHR seems destined to remain the prime driver of engagement with such claims for the foreseeable future, a final reflection is offered on the pros and cons of this approach.

3.2 THE ECHR AND THE ENVIRONMENT – OPERATING IN A LACUNA

While it is undoubtedly true that employing human rights law, with its typically anthropocentric, individualistic focus,[1] is in some respects a poor fit for addressing environmental issues,[2] it nonetheless is increasingly recognised as having a significant contribution to make in this regard.[3] However, the regime established by the ECHR does not contain an 'environmental human right' or indeed any sort of coverage of environmental issues in the body text of the Convention instrument or its protocols.[4] While there has been ample opportunity for the signatory States to act on this, and expand the regime's reach, they have not chosen to do so, even though applicants have long raised environmental concerns in their applications to vindicate their Convention rights.[5] Nonetheless, a will emerged within the Convention's adjudicatory institutions to accommodate environment-based claims, though given this constraint, finding a way to do so required a certain amount of judicial creativity.[6] This task has been undertaken with aplomb, however, and development has been both comparatively swift and broad.[7]

3.2.1 *Extending a Conducive Jurisprudential Climate to Embrace Environmental Concerns*

The Convention regime first showed willingness to consider an environment-based claim in the 1990 opinion issued by the now defunct European Commission on

1 Exceptions to this aspect of the general position are beginning to emerge, notably in the United Nations Declaration on the Rights of Indigenous Peoples (UNDRIP), United Nations General Assembly (2007) Resolution 61/295 'Declaration on the Rights of Indigenous Peoples' <www.un.org/esa/socdev/unpfii/documents/DRIPS_en.pdf> accessed 19 July 2017.

2 See, for example, RG Lee, 'Resources, Rights and Environmental Regulation' (2005) 32(1) JLS 111. Exceptions to the general position are beginning to emerge, notably in the UNDRIP.

3 See, for example, Donald K Anton and Dinah L Shelton, *Environmental Protection and Human Rights* (CUP 2011); and A Boyle, 'Human Rights and the Environment: Where Next?' (2012) 23(3) EJIL 613.

4 Council of Europe, European Convention for the Protection of Human Rights and Fundamental Freedoms (4 November 1950, in force 3 September 1953) ETS 5.

5 The initial absence of coverage for environmental issues in the Convention is explicable given the vintage of the instrument, which emerged long before environmental concerns became mainstream societal concerns. Its continued absence, which has been confirmed, on many occasions, for example in *Moreno Gómez v Spain* no. 4143/02 (Nov 16, 2004), is less easy to justify. The position is expressed with particular clarity in *Kyrtatos v Greece* ECHR (2003) 242 which states in para 52 that: 'Neither Article 8 nor any of the other Articles of the Convention are specifically designed to provide general protection of the environment as such; to that effect, other international instruments and domestic legislation are more pertinent in dealing with this particular aspect.'

6 Discussed in Karen Morrow, 'After the Honeymoon: The Uneasy Marriage of Human Rights and the Environment Under the European Convention on Human Rights and in UK Law Under the Human Rights Act 1998' (2013) 43 Revue Générale de Droit 317.

7 The considerable corpus of case law that has developed is evident in the Council of Europe, 'Manual on human rights and the environment' (2nd edition) Council of Europe, Strasbourg (2012) (hereafter CoE 'Manual') <www.echr.coe.int/LibraryDocs/DH_DEV_Manual_Environment_Eng.pdf> accessed 19 July 2017.

Human Rights in *S* v. *France* (1990).[8] While this claim ultimately failed on its facts, it signalled that the regime's door had been opened to such litigation. The ECtHR followed this lead in *Lopez Ostra* v. *Spain*(1994),[9] which in many ways provided the template for the Court's subsequent approach, and to which we will return later in this section. The Court's willingness to extend the interpretative flexibility spawned by its general and established teleological, 'living instrument' approach to interpreting the Convention, to allow established rights to be invoked to address environment-based claims, is, given the absence of textual coverage for environmental rights referred to above, born of necessity. The tendency of at least some of the Court's judicial complement towards activism doubtless assisted in this.[10] That said, this was a far from straightforward process, as the Convention primarily comprises 'first generation' civil and political rights. The subsidiary coverage which it offers for 'second generation' social and economic rights does not sit particularly comfortably with its main thrust; still less environmental rights claims, which are regarded as falling into the category of 'third generation'[11] rights.

Over the years, various Convention articles have, however, been pressed into service to advance environment-based claims.[12] The Court has progressed its approach on the rationale that the enjoyment of a variety of Convention rights can potentially be compromised by adverse environmental factors,[13] and in response has developed what may be termed a 'patchwork approach'[14] that enables it to accommodate a considerable, but not unlimited, range of environmentally founded claims. As discussed below, Article 8, which invokes the right to privacy and family life, is the most frequently pursued and arguably the most significant[15] of the

8 *S v France*, 65 DR 250 (1990); The European Commission on Human Rights operated between 1953 and 1998 and decided on the admissibility of applications. It was abolished when the Court was restructured on the entry into force of Protocol No. 11 to the Convention for the Protection of Human Rights and Fundamental Freedoms.

9 *Lopez Ostra v Spain*, 303 ECHR 38 (1994) Series A No. 303-C, 20 EHRR 277.

10 Although broad judicial activism tends to be assumed by legal commentators, the actual picture that emerges from political science analysis is more nuanced, see Erik Voeten, 'The Politics of International Judicial Appointments: Evidence fom the European Court of Human Rights' (2007) 61(4) International Organisation 669; the term 'living instrument' appeared in Tyrer v the United Kingdom, (1978) Series A no. 26, para 31: 'The Court must also recall that the Convention is a living instrument which… must be interpreted in the light of present-day conditions.' Its established credentials were referred to in Loizidou v Turkey (Preliminary Objections) (1995) 20 EHRR 99 para 71; See also Alistair Mowbray, 'The Creativity of the European Court of Human Rights (2005) 5(1) Human Rights Law Review 57.

11 After Karel Vasak, 'A 30-Year Struggle: The Sustained Efforts to Give Force of Law to the Universal Declaration of Human Rights' (1977) 30(11) UNESCO Courier 28.

12 Most commonly: procedural rights under Article 6 – the right to a fair hearing, and Article 13 – the right to a remedy in domestic law; and substantive rights under Article 2 – the right to life, Article 8 – the right to privacy and family life, Article 10 – freedom of expression, and Article 1 to the First Protocol – the right to enjoyment of property, ECHR (n 4).

13 See, for example, Malgosia Fitzmaurice, 'Environmental Degradation' in Daniel Moeckli, Sangeeta Shah and Sandesh Sivakumaran (eds), *International Human Rights Law* (OUP 2010) 622.

14 Morrow (n 6).

15 See, for example, CoE 'Manual' (n 7) and 'Human Rights and Environment: The Case Law of the European Court of Human Rights in Environmental Cases – Legal Analysis' (2011) <www.justicean

Convention rights thus deployed, not least due to the Court's broad and expansive interpretation of its provision.[16] For reasons of space, key claims brought under this head will provide the prime, but not exclusive, focus for discussion here.[17] It is worth pointing out that, from the very first, the Court has taken a generous approach to interpreting the applicability of Article 8 in environment-based claims. For example, in *Lopez Ostra*, it determined that hydrogen sulphide emissions from a waste treatment plant located close to the applicant's home constituted both tangible (in the form of chemical pollution) and intangible (by creating an unpleasant smell) interference which could form the basis of a claim.[18]

From the outset, once it indicated a willingness to entertain environment-based human rights claims, it was clear that the ECtHR took the view that States could be implicated in human rights claims in their capacity as actors, i.e. where state activity impinged on an individual's human rights without justification, which was entirely predictable given that, as Convention signatories, they are the direct subjects of the regime and its requirements. The Court also took the view that States could be subject to human rights claims founded on the indirect consequences of their acts or omissions in respect of their regulatory role. In this guise, the State is obliged to ensure that it exercises its powers in such a way as to ensure that individuals (both legal and natural) subject to its control do not impose unwarranted adverse impacts on the protected rights of other individuals. In light of this, States are subject to negative obligations requiring them to refrain from arbitrary interference with individual's Convention rights, and positive obligations requiring them to ensure respect for Convention rights.[19] This two-pronged approach to finding State behaviour wanting and falling below acceptable standards under the Convention has proved decisive in laying the foundation for judicial

denvironment.org/_files/file/2011%20ECHR.pdf> accessed 18 July 2017; See also Malgosia Fitzmaurice, 'The European Court of Human Rights, Environmental Damage and the Applicability of Article 8 of the European Convention on Human Rights and Fundamental Freedoms' (2011) 13(2) Environmental Law Review 107.

16 Underlined in *Pretty v the United Kingdom* (2002) ECHR 427.

17 For an excellent overview of the operation of the range of environment-based human rights claims under the ECHR see Universite de Geneve, Global Studies Institute: 'Mapping Human Rights Obligations Relating to the Enjoyment of a Safe, Clean, Healthy and Sustainable Environment, Individual Report on the European Convention on Human Rights and the European Union', Report No. 14, Prepared for the Independent Expert on the Issue of Human Rights Obligations Relating to the Enjoyment of a Safe, Clean, Healthy, and Sustainable Environment (December 2013) <www.ohchr. org/EN/Issues/Environment/ SREnvironment/Pages/MappingReport.aspx> accessed 19 July 2017 (hereafter Universite de Geneve Global Studies Institute Report).

18 *Lopez Ostra* (n 9).

19 *Guerra and Others v Italy* (1998) 26 EHRR 357, para 58; See also F Akandji-Kombe, 'A Guide to the Implementation of the European Convention on Human Rights: Positive Obligations Under the European Convention on Human Rights' 47–48. <www.echr.coe.int/LibraryDocs/DG2/HRHAND/DG2-EN-HRHAND-07(2007).pdf > accessed 18 July 2017.

intervention in environment-based cases. This is highly apparent in regard to Article 8 claims, where positive obligations have been found to encapsulate such things as: poor enforcement of/failure to comply with domestic law; failure to provide the public with the information necessary to allow them to enjoy their Convention rights; and failure to regulate.[20] On occasion, as in *Lopez Ostra*, both negative and positive obligations may be in question – here the State part-funded the offending facility and had a regulatory role concerning it, authorizing its siting and operation. Negative obligations may arise, for example, in regard to the operation of state-owned industries, as in *Dubetska and Others* v. *Ukraine* (2011).[21] More typically, as for example in *Hatton and Others* v. *the United Kingdom* (2003) (considered further in Section 3.3.1),[22] claims focus only on positive obligations and the State's regulatory role.

3.3 SETTING A THRESHOLD FOR INTERVENTION

3.3.1 *The Limitations Inherent in a Supervisory Jurisdiction: Fair Balance and the Margin of Appreciation*

The ECHR, like other international human rights law regimes, has limited legal reach and subsidiarity-style considerations[23] constrain both the role that it plays and how it is played. Accordingly, the ECtHR in superintending the functioning of the Convention operates a supervisory jurisdiction. *Lopez Ostra* was, as indicated above, the case that saw the ECtHR seize the initiative in entertaining environment-based human rights claims and features the main ingredients of the approach that continues to be adopted by the Court. In essence it demonstrates the fundamental underpinnings of the ECtHR's involvement in this area. The case concerned the applicant's claim that her rights under Article 8 had been violated by severe pollution attributable to a series of regulatory failures concerning a poorly performing waste treatment works serving the needs of the wider community that was located adjacent to her family home. The case, as has proved typical of many of the subsequent environment-based claims litigated under the convention, saw individual rights on the one hand set against the State's capacity to

[20] As for example in *Brânduse v Romania*, no. 6586/03 (ECHR 7 April 2009), where a waste tip was allowed to operate without an authorization.

[21] *Dubetska and Others v Ukraine*, No. 30499/03 (ECHR 10. February 2011).

[22] *Hatton and Others v the United Kingdom* ECHR 2003-VIII 189.

[23] For a broad contextual consideration of this approach, see Paolo G Carozza, 'Subsidiarity as a Structural Principle of International Human Rights Law' (2003) 97(1) American Journal of International Law 38; Carozza offers brief specific discussion of practice under the ECHR as raising this issue, at 74–76, drawing on LR Heifer and Anne-Marie Slaughter, 'Toward a Theory of Effective Supranational Adjudication' (1997) 107 Yale LJ 273.

interfere with/curtail these rights in the public interest on the other. The goal of the Court is to consider

> the fair balance that has to be struck between the competing interests of the individual and of the community as a whole, and in any case the State enjoys a certain margin of appreciation.[24]

In *Lopez Ostra*, the margin of appreciation notwithstanding, the State was found to have failed to arrive at such an accommodation.

The issue of fair balance, always a fraught issue, is further complicated by the fact that most rights under the ECHR, and certainly those invoked in environment-based claims, are qualified. Article 8 is in many respects typical of the Convention approach, stating:

1. Everyone has the right to respect for his private and family life, his home and his correspondence.
2. There shall be no interference by a public authority with the exercise of this right except such as is in accordance with the law and is necessary in a democratic society in the interests of national security, public safety or the economic well-being of the country, for the prevention of disorder or crime, for the protection of health or morals, or for the protection of the rights and freedoms of others.[25]

Thus, the individual rights guaranteed in Article 8.1 are not absolute and may, subject to the qualifications of legality and necessity in a democratic society imposed in Article 8.2, be subject to legitimate interference/qualification. The concepts of fair balance and the margin of appreciation (MoA) mentioned in *Lopez Ostra* are therefore central to the Court's adjudicatory role. The MoA serves a dual function in the Convention regime, allowing States a considerable degree of latitude in running their own affairs, according deference to their superior knowledge of conditions on the ground (arguably a particularly significant matter in situated environment-based claims), and at the same time giving expression to the fundamentally supervisory nature of the jurisdiction of the Court.[26] As Carozza expresses it:

> Whether at the level of national law or the decisions of international institutions like the European Court of Human Rights, effective action on behalf of human rights depends on their integration with local knowledge.[27]

State recognition of and consequent action to ameliorate[28] the imposition of adverse impacts on individuals' rights by the environmental consequences of

[24] *Lopez Ostra* (n 9) para 51.
[25] ECHR (n 4).
[26] See Heifer and Slaughter (n 23).
[27] Carozza (n 23) 76.
[28] In this case, noise controls had been put in place and compensation paid to affected individuals.

State-sanctioned activities, as in *Powell and Rayner v United Kingdom* (1990),[29] will go a long way to satisfying the Court that the MoA has not been exceeded. Under the MoA, the Court accords States considerable room to manoeuvre before it will intervene; it will do so if not satisfied that procedures have been adopted to ensure that a fair balance has been arrived at between the public interest on the one hand and the Convention rights of affected individuals on the other. The MoA and the latitude allowed to the State in determining what constitutes a fair balance between the public interest and that of the individual was to also prove central in *Hatton*. Here unusually,[30] a majority of five to two in the Chamber found that the UK government had exceeded the MoA and thus failed in its positive obligations to provide adequate protection for the applicants against noise from night flights at Heathrow airport. This position was subsequently reversed in a further majority decision (twelve to five) on appeal to the Grand Chamber, which stated succinctly, reiterating the approach in earlier cases, that:

> The national authorities have direct democratic legitimation and are, as the Court has held on many occasions, in principle better placed than an international court to evaluate local needs and conditions ... In matters of general policy, on which opinions within a democratic society may reasonably differ widely, the role of the domestic policy-maker should be given special weight ... where the Court found it natural that the margin of appreciation 'available to the legislature in implementing social and economic policies should be a wide one'.[31]

While many claims under the ECHR see an individual's rights claim pitted against the broader public interest (for example, raising resource allocation issues), in environment-based claims this juxtaposition is arguably particularly present and acute.[32] The ensuing conflict may take a variety of forms: notably, an individual may be exposed to adverse environmental impacts resulting from economic activity that is beneficial to society more widely (as is often the case in Article 8 claims relating to tangible and/or intangible pollution);[33] alternatively, an individual's activities may be curtailed to serve the broader public interest in environmental matters (as is often the case in claims bought under Article 1 to the First Protocol). While most of the cases that arise and which form the basis for discussion in this chapter concern the former, we will now

[29] *Powell and Rayner v United Kingdom* ECHR Series A no. 172; (1990 12 EHRR 355); see also, *Ashworth and Others v the United Kingdom* no. 39561/98 (ECHR 20 January 2004).

[30] This is rare, but does happen occasionally, as for example in the asbestos exposure cases of *Brincat and Others v Malta* (2014) ECHR 900 in which the margin of appreciation was held to be exceeded and violations of Articles 2 and 8 were found.

[31] *Hatton* others (n 22) para 97. See also *Flamenbaum and Others v France* (2012) ECHR 2069.

[32] See, for example, Lee (n 2).

[33] See, for example, *Lopez Ostra* (n 9); *Hatton* (n 22).

consider an example of the latter, in which the Court reveals a great deal about its thinking on the individual rights/public interest nexus: *Hamer* v. *Belgium* (2007).[34] This case, brought under Article 6 and Article 1 to the First Protocol, concerned an order for the forced demolition of a holiday home which had been constructed in 1967 in a protected forest area, in which building was prohibited. Interestingly, in adjudicating on the proportionality of the State's enforcement actions, which had been initiated many years later, the Court stated that the environment constituted a 'valuable cause' and that:

> Public authorities therefore assumed a responsibility which should in practice result in their intervention at the appropriate time in order to ensure that the statutory provisions enacted with the purpose of protecting the environment were not entirely ineffective.[35]

The Court added that:

> Even certain fundamental rights ... should not be afforded priority over environmental protection considerations, in particular where the State had legislated in that regard.[36]

The State's actions were found not to have a disproportionate impact on the individual's rights. The Court's approach here was essentially founded on the importance that it was prepared to accord to the need for States to protect what it termed the 'general interest' in the environment – in this case embodied in keeping forest areas free of development. This approach serves to elucidate the nature of the MoA by articulating the public interest in environmental protection, which provides the counterweight to the individual's competing rights claim in determining whether or not a fair balance has been arrived at. This is a constant consideration in environment-based human rights claims under the ECHR (and indeed more generally),[37] but it is rarely clearly articulated, and even here, while it is alluded to, the concepts involved are less than fully developed.

3.3.2 *The 'Serious Harm' Threshold*

The factors considered above prompted the Court's adoption of a 'serious harm'/'des atteintes graves' threshold for admissibility of claims from the outset, as indicated in

34 Only extracts of the judgement are available in English, European Court of Human Rights: Reports of Judgments and Decisions, 2007-V , 75. <www.echr.coe.int/Documents/Reports_Recueil_2007-V.pdf> accessed 19 July 2017.

35 ibid 76–77.

36 ibid 76.

37 See Francesco Francioni, 'International Human Rights in an Environmental Horizon' (2010) 21(1) European Journal of International Law 41 for a discussion of the difficulties that ensue with the application of the prevailing individualistic models of rights in an environmental context.

Lopez Ostra.[38] The level that the threshold requirement is set at in environment-based claims requires that interference with a protected human right exceed a 'minimum level of severity' to merit a claim. However, given the nature of the rights arguments involved, it is crucial to note that the serious harm threshold pertains not to the damage wrought on the environment as such, but rather to a failure of due process in taking proper account of adverse impacts on the applicant's protected private life/home/family life. In consequence, the decision arrived at stands to fail to deliver a 'fair balance' between the latter and the public interest in regulatory processes.[39]

In *Fägerskiöld* v. *Sweden* (2008) a case involving noise interference caused by wind turbines, the Court, drawing on previous case law, summed up its approach to the minimum level of severity, stating that:

> To raise an issue under Article 8, the interference must directly affect the applicant's home, family or private life and the adverse effects of the environmental pollution must attain a certain minimum level of severity. The assessment of that minimum is relative and depends on all the circumstances of the case, such as the intensity and duration of the nuisance, and its physical or mental effects. The general context of the environment should also be taken into account.[40]

The fact that the issue of seriousness is context dependant makes evidencing the claims made crucial in convincing the Court firstly, that a causal link is established between the environmental interference and the protected Convention right; and secondly, that the threshold for admissibility has therefore been exceeded. This causal link, which can be challenging in the context of environment-based litigation, will normally fall to be established by the applicant, but evidence gathered by the State in its regulatory role can also serve this purpose.[41] Demonstrating general environmental harm or deterioration will not, however, suffice.[42]

While it was established early on that is not necessary to do so for the purposes of establishing 'direct and serious harm' under the Convention,[43] many applications under Article 8 are founded on claims relating to the alleged impact of the interference on the applicant's health. Such claims implicate a wide range of pollutants and various forms of tangible and intangible environmental degradation. *Băcilă* v. *Romania* (2010),[44] is illustrative; here the applicant's health was harmed by lead poisoning attributable to emissions from the ill-regulated industrial plant whose operations formed the basis of the claim. The *Fägerskiöld* case demonstrates how the

38 *Lopez Ostra* (n 9) paras 40 and 51.
39 Discussed in R Desgagne, 'Lopez Ostra v Spain' (1995) 89(4) AJIL 788.
40 *Fägerskiöld v Sweden*, no. 37664/04 (ECHR 26 February 2008) 16.
41 See *Tatar v Romania* no. 67021/01 (ECHR 27 January 2009).
42 See, for example *Kyrtatos* (n 5); *Fadeyeva v Russia* (2005) ECHR 376; and *Dubetska and others v Ukraine*, no. 30499/03 (ECHR 10 February 2011).
43 *Lopez Ostra* (n 9) para 51.
44 *Băcilă v Romania* no. 19234/04 (ECHR 30 March 2010).

courts go about engaging the serious harm threshold where less straightforward impacts on health are concerned. Here, the interference complained of centred on alleged adverse health impacts created by noise and light reflection from a neighbouring windfarm. The applicants failed to establish that their health claims were supported by the evidence garnered in the case, and the impacts that they raised were therefore not deemed sufficiently serious for the case to proceed.[45]

Brânduşe v. *Romania* (2009)[46] represents an expansive approach to health-based claims. The case involved a claim regarding nuisance caused by strong odours emanating from a poorly regulated waste dump. The interference in question was demonstrated to have affected the applicant's quality of life and well-being, though not his health, but was nonetheless, due to its severity and duration, deemed sufficiently serious to meet the Convention's harm-based threshold requirement. Furthermore, it appears from *Vearncombe and others* v. *the Federal Republic of Germany and the United Kingdom* (1989)[47] that in determining whether the serious harm threshold has been breached, the nature of the interference (which must be intense and sustained, and not merely concerned with risk) is significant, in addition to considerations pertaining to its impact.[48]

In addition, or in the alterative to health-based claims, Article 8 applications can also focus on arguments based on 'quality of life' or 'quality of home'. The concept of 'home', while discussed in *Lopez Ostra*, took centre-stage in *Moreno Gómez* v. *Spain*,[49] in which the Court stated that 'the right to respect for the home does not only include the right to the actual physical area, but also to the quiet enjoyment of this area within reasonable limits'.[50]

The Court also elaborated on the extent of the protection that was to be accorded to the home, stating that:

> Breaches of the right to respect for the home are not confined to concrete or physical breaches, such as unauthorised entry into a person's home, but also include those that are not concrete or physical, such as noise, emissions, smells or other forms of interference. A serious breach may result in the breach of a person's right to respect for his home if it prevents him from enjoying the amenities of his home.[51]

[45] *Fagerskiold* (n 40); the interference did not exceed WHO guidelines and was not of the same magnitude as that complained of in cases like *Moreno Gómez* (n 5), *Hatton* [GC] (n 22) or *Ashworth* (n 29). The claim relating to light reflection was not supported by any evidence.

[46] Brânduşe Romania no. 6586/03 (ECHR 7 April 2009); the judgment is not available in English, material is therefore drawn from ECtHR Information Note on the Court's case-law No. 118, <http://hudoc.echr.coe.int/eng#{"itemid":["002-1567"]}> accessed 20 July 2017.

[47] Vearncombe and others v the Federal Republic of Germany and the United Kingdom (1989) 59 DR 186.

[48] See also *Asselbourg and others*, no. 29121/95 (ECHR 29 June 1999).

[49] *Moreno Gómez* (n 5).

[50] ibid para 53.

[51] ibid. Note that the use of the term 'emissions' here as examples of non-concrete interferences would only apply to gaseous atmospheric emissions; some emissions to air, for example, particulates, constitute physical interference, as would emissions to water or land (soil).

This expansive interpretation has been further developed in subsequent case law. In *Brânduşe*, for example, the Court allowed a claim under Article 8 by a long-term prisoner who was subjected to nuisance in his cell, which while not his 'home' as such, did constitute his living space and was therefore deemed ripe for protection under the Convention.

For both health-based and quality of life/home-based claims, failure to provide supporting evidence establishing that the seriousness threshold has been breached will cause applications to be deemed inadmissible, as, for example, in *Borysiewicz* v. *Poland* (2008).[52] In this case, the applicant failed to provide the Court with the noise assessments that had been carried out regarding her complaint about a neighbouring property, and additionally provided no evidence of adverse impact on her health caused by the noise complained of.

3.3.3 The 'Direct Harm' Requirement

The judgment in *Kyrtatos* v. *Greece* (2003),[53] reaffirms that the harm complained of must involve direct impact on the applicant's rights to be actionable, and significantly, clearly indicates that harm to the environment alone will not suffice to found an action under the Convention. The application concerned an invasive tourist development that the applicants alleged had destroyed a swamp area, eroding its scenic nature and its value as a habitat for protected species. The applicants argued that this adversely affected their private life. The claim under Article 8 failed on the basis that the applicants were deemed not to have shown that they were directly affected by these environmental changes. This approach exhibits a narrow view of the ability of environmental degradation to directly affect human health and well-being. The Court has been happy to accept that adverse impacts/threats to physical well-being can be raised (*Hatton*, *Băcilă*, etc.); and to consider extending coverage to mental well-being (*Fägerskiöld*); and even to apply well-being more broadly as a concept (*Brânduşe*). In line with this expansive approach, it would have been plausible for the Court in *Kyrtatos* to consider that the tourist development, in interfering with the applicant's access to the natural world as an adjunct to enjoying his home, detracting from the positive impacts on mental health and well-being that such access is increasingly viewed to provide,[54] could constitute a basis for action. The interference in question was not,

52 *Borysiewicz v Poland* no. 71146/01 (1st July 2008) paras 53 and 54.

53 Kyrtatos (n 5).

54 See, for example, J. Africa, A. Logan, R. Mitchell, K. Korpela, D. Allen, L. Tyrväinen, L., E. Nisbet, Q. Li, Y. Tsunetsugu, Y. Miyazaki, and J. Spengler, on behalf of the NEI Working Group: The Natural Environments Initiative: Illustrative Review and Workshop Statement, Center for Health and the Global Environment at the Harvard School of Public Health (2014) <www.chgeharvard.org/sites/default/files/resources/Paper-NaturalEnvironmentsInitiative_0.pdf> accessed 1 August 2017; For general discussion of the health/environment nexus and Natural England Commissioned Report NECR204 see 'A Review of Nature-Based Interventions for Mental Health Care, Natural England'

however, regarded as raising a justiciable conception of well-being under the ECHR regime. This suggests that there are limits to the Court's conception of human well-being and in conjunction with previous case law indicates that, currently, while the Court will intervene if environmental factors manifest negative impacts on mental health or well-being, it will not do so to preserve or promote positive influences.

While the notion of direct harm may have been treated narrowly in *Kyrtatos*, the application of the concept has, of late, been interpreted more expansively in other respects. This was the case in *L'Erablière A.S.B.L.* v. *Belgium* (2009)[55] which saw a procedure-based Article 6 – right to a fair hearing – claim by a regionally focussed environmental NGO succeed. The Court held that, rather than constituting an *actio popularis* (which is not available under the ECHR), the group had been entitled to challenge plans to expand a waste collection site as they could directly affect the private lives of its (exclusively local) members. This stands in contrast to an early NGO-initiated Article 6 application that raised Article 8 issues, *Asselbourg* v. *Luxembourg*.[56] Here, the applicant NGO was held not to be a victim of harm complained of (as required under Article 34 – individual applications) and was viewed as being unable to make a claim in its own right – its role being limited to acting as a representative of its members/employees. The distinction is subtle but significant, and it may be argued that *L'Erablière*, as the more recent authority, reflects a now established, broadly accommodating judicial approach towards entertaining environment-based claims that now extends, in certain circumstances, to actions by NGOs. This development potentially suggests a nascent accommodation of environment-based rights claims that are not expressed solely in terms of individual rights, but which is also capable of embracing more collective dimensions, and airing a plurality of views of the public interest. In any event, the case law makes it apparent that the concepts of serious harm and fair balance have proved foundational thresholds that must be met for successful environment-based human rights claims under the ECHR.

3.4 DEVELOPING STANDARDS

In the continuing absence of an environmental right or coverage of environmental matters in the Convention regime, in addition applying general Convention jurisprudence and the thresholds considered above to environment-based claims, the Court also needs to be able to have recourse to standards in order to

(2016) <http://publications.naturalengland.org.uk/publication/4513819616346112> accessed 19 July 2017 with reference to vulnerable groups.

55 *L'Erablière A.S.B.L v Belgium* no. 49230/07, ECHR 2009 II 365 (extracts) see also Chapter 11 in this volume by Alexandra Aragao relating to the Portuguese Constitution, which discusses the use of *actio popularis*.

56 *Asselbourg and others* (n 48).

determine whether the said thresholds have been crossed. These standards provide the Court with tools that can support and secure consistency in the evaluation of signatory states' performance regarding environment-based human rights infringement claims. The standards prayed in aid come from a variety of sources, the main examples of which will now be considered, and in effect provide proxy content to fill the *lacuna* in the regime texts' coverage and serve to underpin the Court's consideration of environmental issues pertaining to Convention rights.

3.4.1 *Domestic Law and/or Standards*

Consideration of domestic law necessarily forms the starting point for the ECtHR's consideration of any application to it, as the content and observance of domestic provision, drawn from both general constitutional and administrative law[57] and subject-specific sources – notably but not exclusively in the current context, town and country planning and environmental law – must be addressed in the adjudicatory process. Domestic provision specifies the procedural processes to be followed by States, which will be evaluated to see if their execution satisfies Convention requirements under, for example, Article 6 and Article 13 – right to an effective remedy. Domestic law may also provide substantive coverage that is relevant to evaluating Article 8 and other claims. However, even if domestic laws and standards are complied with, this is not necessarily decisive, as the question of compliance with Convention rights goes not only to adherence to them but also to their adequacy in the first place. As stated in *Lopez Ostra*, the Court 'need only establish whether the national authorities took the measures necessary for protecting the applicant's right to respect for her home and for her private and family life under Article 8', which encapsulates both making necessary provision and applying it.[58] Equally, a breach of domestic law is not necessarily definitive;[59] though failure to comply with domestic environmental standards without securing protection of the interests of the affected population tends to weigh heavily against a state.[60]

As considered in *Taşkın* v. *Turkey* (2004), Article 8 claims raise both procedural[61] and substantive[62] elements that may be scrutinised by the Court. While Article 8 does not itself contain explicit procedural elements, the court infers that procedures adopted by States in this area must be 'fair and such as to afford due respect for the interests of the individual'.[63] Substantive infringement likewise is not defined in

57 Particularly significant in cases involving procedural rights, notably Article 6 – right to a fair hearing and Article 13 – right to an effective remedy.
58 *Lopez Ostra* (n 9) para 55.
59 *Mileva* and others v Bulgaria. no. 37857/05 (ECHR 25 February 2011) para 91.
60 See, for example, *Fadeyeva v Russia* (2005) ECHR 376 and *Dzemyuk v Ukraine* (2014) ECHR 1130.
61 *Taşkın v Turkey*, no. 71913/01, 13 September 2005, paras 118–25.
62 ibid paras 116–17.
63 ibid para 118.

Article 8, but can be fleshed out by reference to other legal provision from a variety of sources. The instant case related to the State's failure to comply with the rulings of the domestic courts.[64] In *Taşkın*, in evaluating the State's compliance with the Convention, reference was made to several aspects of the applicable domestic legal landscape: constitutional provision;[65] environmental law;[66] administrative law;[67] environmental impact assessment provision;[68] and the law of obligations.[69] The ECtHR will, however, often wish to look wider to contextualise and inform its approach to assessing the adequacy or otherwise of the State's provision and actions, and we shall now consider some of the other sources that it may draw upon.

3.4.2 *International (including EU) Law and/or Standards*

Taşkın saw the ECtHR refer not only to domestic law, but also to a considerable range of what it termed 'relevant' international law provisions, specifically: the procedure-focussed (soft law/non-binding) Article 10 of the Rio Declaration on the Environment and Development (1992);[70] and the (hard law/binding on signatories)[71] Convention on Access to Information, Public Participation in Decision-Making and Access to Justice in Environmental Matters (1998) (Aarhus Convention).[72] The Court also referred to the non-binding Parliamentary Assembly of the Council of Europe Recommendation 1614 on environment and human rights (2003),[73] which relates directly to the ECHR and covers both procedural and substantive issues.[74] All of these instruments speak to the

64 ibid para 123.

65 ibid para 90, which refers to Article 56 of the Turkish Constitution, which provides a 'right to live in a healthy, balanced environment'.

66 Environment Act (Law No 2872), published in the Official Gazette on 11 August 1983, ibid paras 91 and 92; Environmental Impact Assessment Law, para 94.

67 ibid para 93.

68 ibid.

69 ibid.

70 ibid para 98.

71 Notably though, Turkey was not among them, see ibid paras 99 and 119 for reference to the importance of access to information and access to justice.

72 *Taşkın* (n 61) para 99; See also, for example, *Demir and Baykara v Turkey* (2008) ECHR 1345 para 83; See also Chapter 6 in this volume by Áine Ryall relating to the Aarhus Convention.

73 *Taşkın* (n 61) para 100.

74 ibid, citing para 9: 'The Assembly recommends that the Governments of member States:

> i. ensure appropriate protection of the life, health, family and private life, physical integrity and private property of persons in accordance with Articles 2, 3 and 8 of the European Convention on Human Rights and by Article 1 of its Additional Protocol, by also taking particular account of the need for environmental protection;
>
> ii. recognise a human right to a healthy, viable and decent environment which includes the objective obligation for states to protect the environment, in national laws, preferably at constitutional level;
>
> iii. safeguard the individual procedural rights to access to information, public participation in decision making and access to justice in environmental matters set out in the Aarhus Convention.'

growing, varied, international law coverage of human rights and the environment, and act as indicators of state practice, and perhaps of fledgling *opinio juris*, though the broader rationale for referencing them is not explicitly stated in the rather terse judgment. Nonetheless, it appears that the ECtHR is using such developments as a species of yardstick against which to gauge State action by drawing a notion of generally acceptable standards of behaviour from them.

Other examples such as *Giacomelli* v. *Italy* (2006) see EU law (in this case, environmental impact assessment provision) drawn into play.[75] In *Tatar* the Court also looked at a range of relevant EU provisions, including a number of Directives in its consideration of the evidence supporting the claim.[76] Indeed, there has until quite recently been an active and broadly productive, if not altogether comfortable, judicial dialogue on rights issues between the ECHR and the European Union, more generally, though its future status is uncertain at best.[77]

3.4.3 *General Principles and Concepts*

While general concepts and principles were inferred in cases such as *Taşkın*, they came explicitly to the fore in *Tatar*, which engaged specifically with risk assessment and the precautionary principle. This case involved the escape of waste water contaminated with cyanide used in extraction processes from a breached dam at a gold mine, flooding the local area. In finding a breach of Article 8, the Court held that the State had failed to carry out an adequate risk assessment, i.e. for present purposes, one that took due account of the rights of the local population. The Court also referred to the State's breach of the precautionary principle in allowing the plant to continue to operate after the accident, the absence of scientific and technical certainty prevailing with regard to the situation not being regarded as sufficient grounds to justify inaction.[78]

75 *Giacomelli v Italy* ECHR 2006–XII 345.

76 Tatar (n 41) is only available in French. Coverage of the facts and legal context is therefore drawn from the Third Section Decision as to the Admissibility of No. 67021/01 Section C: European law paras 44–45 <http://echr.ketse.com/doc/67021.01-en-20070705/view/> accessed 18 July 2017.

77 See, for example, Nicolas de Sadeleer, 'Enforcing EUCHR Principles and Fundamental Rights in Environmental Cases' (2012) 81 Nordic Journal of International Law 39. However, CJEU Opinion 2/13 18 December 2014, at <http://curia.europa.eu/juris/document/document.jsf?text=&docid=160882&pageIndex=0&doclang=en&mode=lst&dir=&occ=first&part=1&cid=40247> accessed 17 July 2017, ruling that the Draft Agreement on EU accession to the ECHR is incompatible with EU law, renders the prospects of substantial further progress in this regard unlikely, at least at present.

78 *Tatar* (n 41); see also Nicolas de Sadeleer, *Environmental Principles: From Political Slogans to Legal Rules* (OUP 2005) and Eloise Scotford, *Environmental Principles and the Evolution of Environmental Law* (Hart 2016).

3.4.4 *Other Standards*

The Court may also draw on other sources to supply standards to evaluate the efficacy of State activity in protecting individual rights. For example, in *Hatton* reference was made to WHO noise guidelines.[79] Likewise, the evidence base of the decision in *Tatar* drew on a United Nations study of the incident,[80] that detected pollutants around the applicants home, at levels exceeding 'international norms' (the report explicitly drew on WHO and EU provisions in reaching its conclusions.)[81]

3.4.5 *The (Variously Framed) 'Right to Environment'?*

The ECtHR occasionally makes reference in its judgments to an 'environmental right',[82] though this is framed in a variety of ways,[83] which makes pinning down its exact scope problematic. In any event, in legal terms, the value to be attached to this environmental rights talk must be considered in the context of its appearance in claims founded on rights that are already established in the Convention regime, rather than as a free-standing concept. *Băcilă*,[84] for example, saw the Court bring consideration of environmental rights under the Convention centre-stage. The case concerned an applicant who lived close to a large plant producing lead and zinc, which was a long-term source of pollution by heavy metals that a variety of evidence showed significantly exceeded permitted levels and had adverse impacts on the health of the local population through lead poisoning. The applicant made repeated attempts to get the State to act to curb the plant's emissions, but the problems were not effectively addressed, and ultimately her own health was adversely affected.

79 At para 112 of the majority judgment and para 14 of the joint dissenting judgement of Zupancic and Steiner in the Grand Chamber. See also RKM Smith, 'Hatton v UK' (2002) 96(3) AJIL 692; Such reference is quite frequent in noise cases, see for example Fägerskiöld (n 40).

80 United Nations Environment Programme, UNEP/Office for the Co-ordination of Humanitarian Affairs, OCHA Report: 'Spill of Liquid and Suspended Waste at the Arul S.A. Retreatment Plant in Baia Mare' (2000) <http://reliefweb.int/sites/reliefweb.int/files/resources/43CD1D010F030359C12568CD00635880-baiamare.pdf> accessed 17 July 2017.

81 ibid, reference to WHO guidelines, at 9; and WHO and EU water quality standards, at 57; see also Chapter 7 of this volume by Owen McIntyre relating to the right to water and the influence of WHO guidelines.

82 See, for example, Aurelija Puraite and Ieva Deviatnikovaite, 'The Right to a Healthy and Safe Environment in the Case-Law of the European Court of Human Rights (2013) 1 *Internal Security* 17, suggesting a developmental trajectory in this regard, albeit one rather lacking in clarity at the time.

83 This reflects the considerable variance in the language used to describe environmental rights more generally, see for example, David R Boyd, *The Environmental Rights Revolution: A Global Study of Constitutions, Human Rights and the Environment* (University of British Columbia Press 2012) and Chris Jeffords, 'Constitutional Environmental Human Rights: A Descriptive Analysis of 142 National Constitutions' (2013) <www.christopherjeffords.com/Constitutions_Jeffords.pdf> accessed 19 July 2017.

84 *Băcilă* (n 44); the judgment is not available in English, commentary is drawn from COE 'Manual' (n 7) at para 44 and Universite de Geneve, Global Studies Institute Report (n 17).

A violation of Article 8 was found based on the State's relative inaction in response to complaints; this was prompted in large part by the economic need to keep the plant, which was the largest employer in the area, open. Significantly, the Court explicitly stated that the economic arguments should not have been allowed to prevail over the locals' 'right to enjoy a healthy environment'.[85] This went further than statements in earlier cases – such as the rather generic approach in *Hatton*, which also considered the need to achieve a fair balance between the States' economic goals and the rights of others.[86]

Subsequent cases have seen the Court return to the environmental rights issue – for example, in *Di Sarno and others* v. *Italy* (2012).[87] This application was rooted in the notorious Campania waste crisis, and in considering the substantive Article 8 aspect of the application, the Court described the State's infringement on protected rights as relating to failures in:

> The collection, treatment and disposal of waste are without a doubt dangerous activities [thus attracting particular scrutiny] . . . That being so, *the State was under a positive obligation to take reasonable and adequate steps to protect the right of the people concerned to respect for their homes and their private life and, more generally, to live in a safe and healthy environment.*[88]

The application succeeded on the substantive aspect of Article 8.[89] Though the 'environmental right' terminology employed by the Court in the *Băcilă* and *Di Sarno* cases is, somewhat unhelpfully, not identical, it does share a strong core focus on the importance of protecting human health that draws on the ECtHR's more general approach to environment-based claims.

3.5 THE ONGOING QUESTION: HOW TO ADVANCE THE DEVELOPMENT OF STANDARDS IN ENVIRONMENT-BASED CLAIMS IN THE ECHR REGIME

Ultimately, the most legally expedient way of dealing with the question of standards under the ECHR would be by altering the text of the Convention, either extending its coverage by amendment or (more likely given past regime practice of the regime in the past) through the adoption of a new protocol, to include an environmental human right. While this is appealing in principle and could do much to clarify provision in the area, it is highly unlikely to eventuate in practice. This is in part because of profound, though perhaps not insurmountable disagreement about how

85 ibid drawing from Universite de Geneve, Global Studies Institute Report (n 17) ibid, quoting the French versions of paras 70–71 of the judgment.
86 *Hatton* (n 22) para 86.
87 *Di Sarno and others v Italy* no. 30765/08 (ECHR 10, January 2012) para 113.
88 ibid para 110 (emphasis added).
89 ibid para 112.

such a right might be framed[90] – what standard(s) would be invoked by such an environmental human right if it was agreed remains a contentious matter of conjecture, even among a relatively homogenous regional grouping of states. Jurisprudential complexity aside, more decisive in real terms is the entrenched political resistance to such a step within powerful parts of the Convention regime,[91] reflecting consistent reluctance by State signatories to move in this direction.[92] So, while other options are possible,[93] for now, the established approach adopted by the ECtHR in developing the Convention jurisprudence, applying the living instrument approach to allow for the accommodation of environment-based rights, claims seems set to continue to dominate. Broadly, the Court has carefully trodden the difficult path necessitated by its supervisory jurisdiction and the need to reconcile the interests of signatory States on the one hand, and the rights of applicants on the other, to good effect. The Court has been active across a wide range of claims variously invoking: substantive Convention rights; their secondary procedural aspects; purely procedural rights; and combinations thereof, taking a pragmatic approach to their interpretation in order to effectively embrace a new area of societal concern. In disposing of environment-based claims, the Court's developing jurisprudence has supplied some of the most significant deficiencies of Convention coverage by invoking standards drawn from international, regional and domestic environmental law and policy provision that apply to the intersection between human rights and the environment. This is a shrewd move, as in many, if not most cases, the Convention's signatory States have subscribed to the regimes invoked, and even where this is not the case, their content and broad acceptance speaks to their normativity. In either case, being seen to diverge from broadly accepted norms would be politically awkward for States. In any case, tacit support for the current approach indicated by State acceptance of a marked level of judicial activity in this regard indicates that, even if there is disagreement on creating an

90 See Anton and Shelton (n 3). This hurdle has been surmounted in many domestic laws, see Boyd (n 83) and Jeffords (n 83). More compellingly, environmental rights feature in the texts of other regional human rights regimes: see art 24 of the African Charter of Human and People's Rights (1981) <http://www1.umn.edu/humanrts/instree/z1afchar.htm> accessed 23 March 2016, art 11 of the Additional Protocol to the American Convention on Human Rights in the Area of Economic, Social and Cultural Rights (1988) <www.oas.org/juridico/english/treaties/a-52.html> accessed 23 March 2016; art 38 of the Arab Charter on Human Rights (2004) <www.whatconvention.org/en/convention/1582> accessed 13 July 2017; and art 28 of the ASEAN Human Rights Declaration (2012) <http://asean.org/asean-human-rights-declaration/> accessed 13 July 2017.

91 See Morrow 2013 (n 6).

92 Boyle (n 3) at 615 goes so far as to assert a causal link between 'the rapid development of environmental jurisprudence in Europe' and recurrent rejections of variously drafted proposals for adding an environmental protocol to the ECHR.

93 See, for example, Karen Morrow, 'New Frontiers: Europe, Human Rights, and the Environment – The Continuing Need for Innovation' in E Daly, L Kotze, J May, C Soyapi, A Kreilhuber, L Ognibene and A Kariuki (eds), *New Frontiers in Environmental Constitutionalism* (UNEP 2017) 36 <www.unep.org/environmentalgovernance/erl/resources/publications/new-frontiers-environmental-constitutionalism> accessed 15 May 2018.

environmental right within the regime among signatory States, sufficient political consensus exists to support the Court's approach to adjudicating environment-based Convention rights claims.

Case law-led coverage is, however, vulnerable in some respects, not least to the happenstance of sufficient and appropriate cases arising, and being channelled into the system, to allow it to flex its jurisprudential muscles. In the context of the ECHR this has not in fact been lacking, and there has been a sustained stream of relevant applications ever since the regime indicated its willingness to engage with environment-based claims. Indeed, it can be argued that the current approach, being application driven, is responsive to those issues where citizens are most concerned about environmental issues impinging on their protected Convention rights. There are, however, other constraints on a case law-led approach to developing coverage for environment-based claims that are more problematic. Central to these is that a case law-led system is unlikely to achieve the consistency and conceptual coherence that an explicit base in the Convention texts in a new protocol would. That said, as this is scarcely a realistic option, the ECtHR will likely continue to respond to the applications that come before it and press ahead, continuing to offer evolutionary, if not revolutionary, coverage to environment-based claims. It could also be argued that this type of incremental approach sits well with the regime's essentially supervisory jurisdictional character. It may also be said that the efficacy of the current approach in addressing claims obviates the need for undertaking what would doubtless prove a fraught negotiating process to add an environmental right to the regime. It is also that case that while such a development would have considerable symbolic significance and potentially offer greater coherence,[94] it may not, given the constraints under which the ECHR regime operates, deliver much more of substance on the ground than has already been achieved. The Court's approach arguably adequately reflects and propagates the current level of consensus among the Convention's signatories, acknowledging environmental issues as established core concerns of both modern Statecraft and, relatedly, human rights law, while sidestepping the conceptual and practical difficulties of crafting an environmental right that is both effectual for citizens and acceptable to States.

94 See, for example, Boyle (n 3) 616.

4

The American Convention on Human Rights and Environmental Rights Standards

Evadné Grant

4.1 INTRODUCTION

International human rights instruments usually articulate human rights norms at a very high level of generality, making it necessary for more specific requirements for implementation to be developed in the process of application. These more specific standards are expressed at varying levels of detail, likely to be more exact if specified by a national authority than if laid down by regional or international institutions.[1] This chapter focuses on environmental standards that have been established under the American Convention on Human Rights (ACHR)[2] by the Inter-American Commission on Human Rights (the Commission)[3] and the Inter-American Court of Human Rights (the Court).[4] Designed to apply across different jurisdictions with diverse constitutional, legislative and administrative arrangements, these standards are expressed at a relatively high level of abstraction.

Adopted in 1969, the ACHR protects a wide range of civil and political rights, together with a single article devoted to social and economic rights.[5] The 1988 Protocol of San Salvador makes separate provision for a variety of social, economic and cultural rights, including the right to a healthy environment.[6] However, the

[1] The term 'standards' is often used in different ways by courts and commentators, sometimes interchangeably with obligation or duty and sometimes in the more specific sense used in this collection.

[2] American Convention on Human Rights (1969) OAS Treaty Series No 36; 1144 UNTS 123.

[3] Statute of the Inter-American Commission on Human Rights (1979) OAS Res 447 (IX-0/79) OAS Off Rec OEA/Ser P/IX.0.2/80, Vol 1 at 88, Annual Report of the Inter-American Commission on Human Rights, OEA/Ser L/V/11.50 Doc 13 rev 1 at 10 (1980), reprinted in Basic Documents Pertaining to Human Rights in the Inter-American System, OEA/Ser L V/II.82 Doc 6 rev 1 at 93 (1992).

[4] Statute of the Inter-American Court of Human Rights (1979) OAS Res 448 (IX-O.79) OAS Off Rec OEA/Ser P/IX.0.2/80, Vol 1 at 98; Annual Report of the Inter- American Court on Human Rights, OEA/Ser L/V.III.3 Doc 13 corr 1 at 16 (1980), reprinted in Basic Documents Pertaining to Human Rights in the Inter-American System, OEA/Ser L V/II.82 doc 6 rev 1 at 133 (1992).

[5] Article 26 ACHR.

[6] Additional Protocol to the American Convention on Human Rights in the Area of Economic, Social and Cultural Rights (Protocol of San Salvador) (1988) OAS Treaty Series No 69, art 11; see CS de Windt and MA Orellana, 'Introduction to Environmental Law in the Americas' in W Scholtz and

jurisdiction of the Commission and Court over the Protocol is limited.[7] Until recently, this meant that the right to a healthy environment did not enjoy direct protection in the Inter-American human rights system. In the absence of direct protection, the Inter-American institutions have, through creative interpretation, progressively extended the reach of a number of other ACHR rights, including particularly the right to property (Article 21) and the right to life (Article 4), to encompass a measure of environmental protection. This indirect approach to environmental protection has been elaborated mainly in the context of mining and other industrial development activities on land claimed or occupied by indigenous and tribal communities,[8] activities that have often had disastrous consequences for the environment.[9]

However, the *Advisory Opinion on the Environment and Human Rights* (2017 Advisory Opinion) delivered by the Inter-American Court in November 2017 is set to change the approach to environmental protection under the ACHR in radical ways.[10] In it, the Court, for the first time, recognises the right to a healthy environment as one of the social and economic rights that enjoys direct protection under Article 26, the lone social and economic rights provision of the ACHR.[11] At the same time, the Court reinforces and elaborates its existing indirect approach to environmental protection by clarifying the extent of the positive obligations to protect the environment that states must comply with in order to respect and guarantee the rights to life and personal integrity (Articles 4 and 5) under the ACHR.[12] What is particularly noteworthy is that while the Court's established environmental jurisprudence has been developed, as noted above, mainly in the context of protection of the rights of indigenous peoples, the 2017 Advisory Opinion is not confined to the rights of indigenous peoples.

J Verschuuren (eds), *Regional Environmental Law: Transregional Comparative Lessons in Pursuit of Sustainable Development* (Edward Elgar 2015) 131, 154–56.

7 The Inter-American Commission and Court are not authorised to receive individual petitions in relation to most of the rights protected under the Protocol, including the right to a healthy environment; see OR Ruiz-Chiriboga, 'The American Convention and the Protocol of San Salvador: Two Intertwined Treaties – Non-Enforceability of Economic, Social and Cultural Rights in the Inter-American System' (2013) 31 NQHR 159.

8 The terms 'tribal peoples/communities' refer to communities or groups that are not indigenous to the region but, like indigenous communities, have a particular connection with their territory and identify with specific shared traditions that distinguish them from the rest of the population. This is consistent with the usage of the Inter-American institutions; see Inter-American Commission of Human Rights, *Indigenous Peoples, Afro-Descendent Communities and Natural Resources: Human Rights Protection in the Context of Extraction, Exploitation and Development Activities* OEA/Ser L/V/II, Doc 47/15 (31 December 2015) 20.

9 ibid 16.

10 *The Environment and Human Rights (State obligations in relation to the environment in the context of the protection and guarantee of the rights to life and to personal integrity – interpretation and scope of Articles 4(1) and 5(1) of the American Convention on Human Rights)* Advisory Opinion OC-23/17, IACtHR Ser A No 23 (15 November 2017).

11 ibid para 57.

12 ibid paras 108–14.

The full implications of the 2017 Advisory Opinion will take time to crystallise. Clearly, the Court's approach to indirect protection of the environment will build on existing jurisprudence, while recognition of a justiciable substantive environmental right requires further clarification and development. This analysis therefore considers human rights standards that have been developed under the established approach of protecting the environment via other rights, particularly in the context of the rights of indigenous communities as well as the implications for environmental standards of the 2017 Advisory Opinion.

4.2 THE LAW

The Organization of American States (OAS) was established in 1948 with the declared aim of promoting peace and security, democracy, economic, social and cultural development and the elimination of poverty in the region.[13] The American Declaration on the Rights and Duties of Man (American Declaration) was adopted at the same time as the OAS Charter, predating the Universal Declaration of Human Rights.[14] Although the American Declaration is not legally binding, it remains an important milestone in codifying human rights in the region, especially since it protects not only civil and political rights but also social, economic and cultural rights. The Inter-American Commission on Human Rights was established by the OAS in 1959 to act as an advisory body, to prepare reports and studies to promote and support the protection of human rights based on the American Declaration.[15] Its powers were increased in 1965 when it was authorised to examine individual communications.[16] The ACHR is now the primary regional human rights treaty,[17] and the remit of the Commission encompasses compliance with its provisions by states parties. The ACHR created the Inter-American Court and provided it with both advisory and contentious jurisdiction.[18]

The roles of the Commission and Court are crucial in the development of human rights standards under the ACHR. The Commission has a dual mandate, 'to promote respect for and defense of human rights'.[19] In implementing its mandate, the Commission employs a range of mechanisms to hold states

13 Charter of the Organisation of American States (1948) 119 UNTS 3, Articles 2–3.

14 American Declaration on the Rights and Duties of Man, adopted by the Ninth International Conference of American States (1948) reprinted in Basic Documents Pertaining to Human Rights in the Inter-American System OEA/Ser L V/II.82 Doc 6 rev 1 at 17 (1992).

15 Statute of the IACHR (n 3).

16 ibid Article 1. This mandate remains important as it allows the Commission to investigate violations of the American Declaration by OAS Member States who are not parties to the ACHR.

17 The number of ratifications or accessions currently stands at twenty-three states. The USA and Canada are not parties, while Venezuela and Trinidad and Tobago have denounced the Convention, see ACHR Signatories and Ratifications <www.oas.org/dil/treaties_b-32_american_convention_on_human_rights_sign.htm> accessed 15 February 2017.

18 ACHR (n 2) arts 52–64.

19 ACHR (n 2) art 41.

accountable for human rights violations and to promote human rights standards. The Commission receives and examines individual petitions, holds public hearings, undertakes on-site visits, prepares country and thematic reports, issues guidelines and general recommendations and often provides a platform for civil society organisations.[20]

The Court has jurisdiction to issue binding decisions on claims of violation of the ACHR submitted to it by the Commission or states parties,[21] as well as advisory opinions.[22] While the Court and Commission are mandated to respond to individual claims by determining whether domestic legislation, policies and actions violate state commitments under the ACHR, the institutions have gradually broadened their focus. Rather than concentrating exclusively on individual contentious cases, they are increasingly concerned with the promotion of broader policy and institutional changes though their jurisprudence. For example, the Commission increasingly makes use of thematic reports to disseminate information and create awareness of rights such as the rights of indigenous peoples in the region, and to clarify and develop the applicable law.[23] The development of specific human rights standards is part of this shift in focus to a more general promotion of standards throughout the region.

As noted above, while the ACHR focuses primarily on civil and political rights, Article 26 makes general provision for the protection of social and economic rights, stating:[24]

> The States Parties undertake to adopt measures, both internally and through international cooperation, especially those of an economic and technical nature, with a view to achieving progressively, by legislation of other appropriate means, the full realization of the rights implicit in the economic, social, educational, scientific and cultural standards set forth in the Charter of the Organization of American States.[25]

The Court has indicated that it is the American Declaration 'that defines the human rights referred to in the [OAS] Charter', thereby providing scope for recognition of the social and economic rights protected under the American Declaration to be

20 See TM Antkowiak and A Gonza, *The American Convention on Human Rights: Essential Rights* (OUP 2017); C Sandoval, 'The Inter-American System of Human Rights and approach' in S Sheeran and N Rodley, *Routledge Handbook of International Human Rights Law* (Routledge 2013) 427;

21 Decisions are binding on states who have recognised the contentious jurisdiction of the Inter-American Court, see ACHR (n 2) Article 62.

22 ACHR (n 2) Article 64.

23 Sandoval (n 20) 436; see discussion of IACHR, *Indigenous Peoples, Afro-Descendant Communities and Natural Resources* in Section 4.3.1.

24 T Antkowiak, 'Social, Economic and Cultural Rights: The Inter-American Court at a Crossroads' in Y Haeck et al. (eds), *The Inter-American Court of Human Rights: Theory and Practice, Present and Future* (Intersentia 2015) 259.

25 The Preamble of the ACHR also recognises social, economic and cultural rights as necessary for 'free men' to enjoy 'freedom from fear and want'.

incorporated into Article 26.[26] However, in implementing this, the Inter-American institutions have, to date, recognised a very limited number of socioeconomic rights,[27] and environmental rights had not been specifically considered under Article 26 until the Court's 2017 Advisory Opinion.[28]

Together with the provisions of the OAS Charter, the American Declaration and the Protocol of San Salvador, Article 26 also provides the context for the development of indirect protection for social, economic and cultural rights by the Inter-American institutions. Indirect protection of the right to a healthy environment has been elaborated mainly in dealing with complaints of violation of the right to life (Article 4) and the right to property (Article 21), although it has also been recognised that other rights such as the right to freedom of thought and expression (Article 13)[29] and the right to due process of law (Article 8)[30] have environmental dimensions.[31]

Expansive interpretation of ACHR rights to provide indirect protection for social and economic rights is supported and influenced not only by the explicit provisions of the ACHR, but also by a number of principles of interpretation. First, the Court has reiterated that the ACHR is a 'living instrument, the interpretation of which must evolve over time and reflect current living conditions'.[32] Responding to the environmental challenges posed by the enormous increase in extraction and exploitation of natural resources as well as infrastructure and other developments in the region is thus an essential aspect of the role in interpreting the ACHR.[33] The Court's ability to interpret the ACHR in light of current problems and priorities is supported by Article 29, which precludes restrictive interpretation of ACHR rights or interpretation that limits the enjoyment of rights recognised in the domestic law of state parties or other

26 *Interpretation of the American Declaration of the Rights and Duties of Man within the Framework of Article 64 of the American Convention on Human Rights*, Advisory Opinion OC-10/89, IACtHR Series A No 10 (14 July 1989) para 45.

27 *García Fajardo v Nicaragua* (Merits) IACHR Report No 100/01 Case 11.381 (11 October 2000) (workers' rights); *Miranda Cortez v El Salvador* (Merits) Report No 27/09 Case 12.249 (20 March 2009) (right to health); *Five Pensioners v Peru* (Merits, Reparations and Costs) IACtHR Series C No 98 (28 February 2003); *Acevedo Buendía v Peru* (Preliminary Objection, Merits, Reparations and Costs) IACtHR Series C No 198 (1 July 2009) (right to social security); see Antkowiak (n 24) 264–65.

28 (n 10).

29 *Claude-Reyes v Chile* (Merits, Reparations and Costs) IACtHR Series C No 151 (19 September 2006) paras 75–103.

30 ibid, paras 114–23; *Yakye Axa Indigenous Community v Paraguay* (Merits, Reparations and Costs) IACtHR Series C No 125 (17 June 2005) paras 96–98.

31 S Thériault, 'Environmental Justice and the Inter-American Court of Human Rights' in A Grear and LJ Kotzé (eds), *Research Handbook on Human Rights and the Environment* (Edward Elgar 2015) 309, 318–21.

32 *Kichwa Indigenous People of Sarayaku v Ecuador* (Merits and Reparations) IACtHR Series C No 245 (27 June 2012) para 40; *Mayagna (Sumo) Awas Tingni Community v Nicaragua* (Merits, Reparations and Costs) IACtHR Series C No 79 (31 August 2001) para 146; 2017 Advisory Opinion (n 10) para 43.

33 IACHR, *Indigenous Peoples, Afro-Descendent Communities and Natural Resources* (n 8) para 17; 2017 Advisory Opinion (n 10) para 22.

international instruments.[34] The effect of this provision is to mandate interpretation of the ACHR to provide the best possible protection of human rights,[35] as well as to draw on relevant national and international law in interpreting ACHR rights, including international environmental law principles.[36] The discussion of environmental standards in Section 4.3 provides ample evidence of the operation of these imperatives in practice, the Court drawing on diverse legal instruments, from UN human rights and environmental law instruments to the constitutional provisions of relevant states to ensure that rights are protected to their fullest extent.

The primary context in which the development of environmental standards has taken place to date has been through petitions filed by indigenous peoples. The 'unique' vulnerability of indigenous communities to environmental harm is widely recognised.[37] It is estimated that there are between 250–375 million indigenous people worldwide, with high numbers living in environmentally sensitive areas such as forests, mountains and other ecologically vulnerable places.[38] These territories are often remote and difficult to access, but rich in natural resources. Recent years have seen a huge increase in mining, oil extraction, timber logging and other development activities in these areas, resulting in environmental destruction, often on a massive scale, as well as other damaging impacts on the lives of indigenous peoples.[39]

Indigenous peoples are also especially vulnerable because, as John Knox, the former Special Rapporteur on Human Rights and the Environment, emphasised in his report on 'Biodiversity and Human Rights', they often depend very directly on the forests, rivers, lakes and other natural resources found on their native land for food, medicine, fuel and shelter.[40] Many such communities have no alternative sources of subsistence or income, and environmental harm may thus have particularly disastrous consequences for

34 L Lixinski, 'Treaty Interpretation by the Inter-American Court of Human Rights: Expansionism at the Service of the Unity of International Law' (2010) 21 EJIL 385, 587; AD Fisher and M Lundberg, 'Human Rights' Legitimacy in the Face of the Global Ecological Crisis – Indigenous Peoples, Ecological Rights Claims and the Inter-American Human Rights System' (2015) 6 JHRE 177, 186–87; A Meijknecht, 'The Contribution of the Inter-American Human Rights System to Sustainable Development' in W Scholtz and J Verschuuren (n 6) 177, 184.

35 Lixinski ibid 588; 2017 Advisory Opinion (n 10) paras 41–42.

36 2017 Advisory Opinion ibid para 44.

37 DK Anton and DL Shelton, *Environmental Protection and Human Rights* (CUP 2011) 545.

38 LF Duchicela et al., *Indigenous Peoples Development in World Bank-Financed Projects: Our People, Our Resources* (World Bank Group 2015) 3.

39 Human Rights Council (HRC), *Report of the Special Rapporteur on the rights of indigenous peoples, James Anaya: Extractive industries operating within or near indigenous territories* A/HRC/18/35, paras 30–35; IACHR, *Indigenous Peoples, Afro-Descendant Communities and Natural Resources* (n 8) paras 16–18.

40 HRC, *Report of the Special Rapporteur on the issue of human rights obligations relating to the enjoyment of a safe, clean healthy and sustainable environment*, A/HRC/34/49, 19 January 2017 (Biodiversity and Human Rights report) para 22.

them.[41] But the relationship of indigenous peoples with their native territory encompasses more than economic dependence, as highlighted by the Inter-American Court:

> The culture of the members of the indigenous communities directly relates to a specific way of being, seeing, and acting in the world, developed on the basis of their close relationship with their traditional territories and the resources therein, not only because they are their main means of subsistence, but also because they are part of their worldview, their religiosity, and therefore, of their cultural identity.[42]

Preservation of their environment is thus fundamental to both physical and cultural survival of indigenous peoples. The vulnerability of indigenous peoples is heightened by poverty and marginalization.[43] Poor and marginalised communities often lack opportunities to participate in decision making that may affect their lives and livelihoods, and their interests are often overlooked when development projects that have the potential to damage the environment on which they depend are planned and approved.[44]

The analysis of environmental standards begins by focusing on Articles 21 and 4 ACHR as applied to claims of indigenous peoples, as this has long been the most important context for the development of environmental protection under the ACHR. However, this analysis is supplemented by discussion of the 2017 Advisory Opinion, considering in particular the implications for the development of environmental standards in the context of the rights to life and physical integrity (Articles 4 and 5).[45] This jurisprudence is not yet embedded and the full implications will take time to become apparent, but the assessment provided here highlights some of the important implications for the development of environmental standards.

Article 21 of the ACHR expresses the right to property in expansive terms, including a strong formulation of the requirement of compensation for deprivation of property that has supported the development of environmental standards. A number of other facets of the right to property in the context of claims of indigenous peoples under the ACHR are also significant for the development of standards. The first is the recognition and protection of *collective* land tenure of indigenous and tribal communities.[46] A second and related aspect is the acknowledgment of the

41 ibid.

42 *Yakye Axa* (n 30) para 135; IACHR, *Indigenous and Tribal Peoples' Rights over Their Ancestral Lands and Natural Resources: Norms and Jurisprudence of the Inter-American Human Rights System*, OEA/Ser.L/V/II. Doc 56/09 (30 December 2009) paras 55–57.

43 GH Hall and HA Patrinos (eds), *Indigenous Peoples, Poverty, and Development* (CUP 2014); World Bank, *Indigenous Peoples: Still among the poorest of the poor* (World Bank Policy Brief 64760) <www.worldbank.org/en/topic/indigenouspeoples > accessed 28 February 2017.

44 ibid; Duchicela (n 38) 8.

45 2017 Advisory Opinion (n 10) ch VIII.

46 *Mayagna (Sumo) Awas Tingni Community* (n 32) para 148. See B Saul, Indigenous Peoples and Human Rights (Bloomsbury 2016) ch 4; Antkowiak and Gonza (n 20) 269.

distinctive relationship between indigenous communities and their territory.[47] This has, in turn, led to the association of the right to property with a number of other rights including rights to cultural identity, political participation and a healthy environment, in spite of the absence of direct protection of those rights under the ACHR.[48]

The Inter-American institutions have similarly interpreted the right to life under Article 4 ACHR broadly, embracing the idea of a dignified life (*vida digna*).[49] Within this understanding, a dignified life encompasses a number of particular socioeconomic rights, including the right to health, food, water and environment, rights that did not or do not enjoy direct protection under the ACHR.[50] This interpretation of the right to life is confirmed by the Court in its 2017 Advisory Opinion in relation to both indigenous and non-indigenous communities, emphasizing in particular that a healthy environment is essential for a dignified life.[51]

We now turn to more detailed consideration of the standards developed in implementing Articles 21 and 4 ACHR.

4.3 THE DEVELOPMENT OF STANDARDS

4.3.1 *Standards Relating to the Right to Property of Indigenous Peoples under Article 21 ACHR*

As already noted, the development of specific environment-related standards under Article 21 is closely bound up with the recognition of property rights of indigenous and tribal communities as collective rights and with the acknowledgement of the close ties between such communities and their territory. It is therefore necessary to briefly consider the meaning of the right to property of indigenous peoples.

In a series of cases the Court has established that traditional possession of their native lands by indigenous and tribal peoples has equivalent effect to full property title and that indigenous communities therefore have the right to demand official recognition and registration of their collective property title.[52] The right endures for

47 IACHR (n 42); *Mayagna (Sumo) Awas Tingni Community* ibid 149.

48 T M Antkowiak, 'Rights, Resources, and Rhetoric: Indigenous Peoples and the Inter-American Court' (2013) 35 University of Pennsylvania Journal of International Law 113, 120.

49 *Yakye Axa* (n 30) paras 161–64; *Sawhoyamaxa Indigenous Community v Paraguay* (Merits, Reparations and Costs) IACtHR Ser C No 146 (29 March 2006) para 153.

50 JM Pasqualucci, 'The Right to a Dignified Life (Vida Digna): The Integration of Economic and Social Rights with Civil and Political Rights in the Inter-American Human Rights System' (2008) 31 Hastings International and Comparative Law Review 1, 2. Antkowiak (n 48) 176.

51 2017 Advisory Opinion (n 10) paras 108–14.

52 Summarised in *Sawhoyamaxa* (n 49) para 128; see also *Xákmok Kásek Indigenous Community v Paraguay* (Merits, Reparations and Costs) IACtHR Ser C No 214 (24 August 2010) para 109; *Kaliña and Lokono Peoples v Suriname* (Merits, Reparations and Costs) IACtHR Ser C No 309 (25 November 2015) para 131. In *Moiwana Community v Suriname* (Preliminary Objections, Merits, Reparations and Costs) IACtHR Ser C No 124 (15 June 2005) 131–34 the same protection was extended

as long as the community maintains its unique relationship with the land, as demonstrated, for example, by the holding of traditional ceremonies, seasonal gathering, hunting, fishing and other use of natural resources associated with traditional customs.[53] The aim of recognition and protection of collective property rights of indigenous and tribal peoples is to ensure their survival and the survival of their way of life, their distinct cultural identity, social structures, economic system, customs, beliefs and traditions.[54] The Court has therefore expanded the reach of Article 21 to specifically encompass both the right of indigenous peoples to freely determine their own development and also, as a necessary corollary, the right to the natural resources on their lands.[55] This expansive interpretation is justified by the Court by reference to Article 29 ACHR referring to both domestic legislation relating to indigenous peoples in the states concerned and other international instruments, including the International Labour Organisation's (ILO) Convention No. 169 concerning Indigenous and Tribal Peoples.[56]

In the seminal case of *Saramaka People* v. *Suriname*, the Court held, first, that the protection afforded by Article 21 includes a range of rights associated with the ability of indigenous peoples to 'freely determine and enjoy their own social, cultural and economic development'.[57] Secondly, the Court confirmed that the right to property under Article 21 encompasses the right to control and use the natural resources on and within the land, limited, however to resources that are necessary for the survival and development of the culture and way of life of indigenous communities.[58] When considering whether Article 21 has been breached, it is therefore necessary to determine which natural resources are 'essential' for the survival of the community and its way of life.[59] The case of *Saramaka* concerned mining and logging concessions on traditional territory granted by the state to third parties.[60] The Court held that because the community traditionally used and traded timber

to non-indigenous communities descended from African slaves who have the same cultural, spiritual and material relationship to their territory as indigenous communities. See also IACHR, *Indigenous and Tribal Peoples' Rights over Their Ancestral Lands and Natural Resources* (n 47) paras 78–106; Saul (n 46) 144–58.

53 *Sawhoyamaxa* ibid paras 131–32.

54 *Saramaka People v Suriname* (Preliminary Objections, Merits, Reparations and Costs) IACtHR Ser C No 172 (28 November 2007) para 122. See IACHR, *Indigenous and Tribal Peoples' Rights over Their Ancestral Lands and Natural Resources* (n 47) para 55.

55 *Saramaka* ibid.

56 International Labour Organization Convention concerning Indigenous and Tribal Peoples in Independent Countries No 169 (1989) 28 ILM1382 (ILO Convention No. 169). Other instruments referred to include the International Covenant on Economic Social and Cultural Rights (1966) 993 UNTS 3 (ICESCR) and the International Covenant on Civil and Political Rights (1966) 999 UNTS 172 (ICCPR). See *Saramaka* (n 55) paras 92–95; IACHR, *Indigenous Peoples, Afro-Descendent Communities and Natural Resources* (n 8) paras 157–59.

57 *Saramaka* (n 55) para 95.

58 ibid para 122; *Kichwa Indigenous People of Sarayaku* (n 32) para 146; *Sawhoyamaxa* (n 49) para 143.

59 *Saramaka* (n 55) para 123. See IACHR, *Indigenous and Tribal Peoples' Rights over Their Ancestral Lands and Natural Resources* (n 42) paras 179–89.

60 *Saramaka* ibid para 124.

and other forest products, this use was protected under Article 21.[61] With regard to gold mining concessions, however, the Court concluded that since gold was not traditionally used or traded by the Saramaka people, Article 21 protection did not necessarily extend to gold mining. However, gold mining activities would clearly affect other natural resources such as forests and rivers that are essential for the physical and cultural survival of the community.[62] Based on this understanding of the right to property of indigenous peoples, the Court held that any restriction of the right must comply with specific 'safeguards' that must be implemented by the state before granting concessions such as those for logging and mining in the *Saramaka* case.[63] Elaboration of these safeguards has allowed the Court to identify and develop particular standards that apply in the implementation of Article 21 – standards that play an especially important role in protecting the environment.

The safeguards identified in *Saramaka* are highlighted and commented on in a report focusing on the impact of extractive industries on the rights of indigenous peoples, published in December 2015 by the Commission. In this report, the Commission outlines a range of general state obligations under the ACHR applicable to extractive and development activities, as well as specific obligations that apply where extractive and development activities involve indigenous communities.[64] The general human rights obligations that apply to extractive and other resource exploitation and development activities include: the duty to design, implement and effectively enforce an adequate legal framework; the duty to prevent, mitigate and eradicate the negative impacts on human rights; the duty to supervise development and extractive activities; the duty to guarantee effective participation and access to information; the duty to prevent illegal activities and forms of violence against populations affected by extractive and development activities; and the duty to guarantee access to justice, including investigation, sanction and reparations for human rights violations.[65]

Regarding the specific obligations that apply to natural resource exploitation and development activities involving indigenous communities,[66] the Commission notes that these obligations have been articulated in order to address historical discrimination against such communities and to safeguard their physical and cultural survival, which, in turn depends on protecting the environment.[67] The Court has elaborated on these obligations in a number of cases, developing specific standards for their implementation – described by the

61 ibid para 146.
62 ibid para 155.
63 ibid para 143.
64 IACHR, *Indigenous Peoples, Afro-Descendent Communities and Natural Resources* (n 8).
65 ibid ch 2.
66 ibid ch 3.
67 ibid para 149.

Court as internationally recognised standards that must be implemented by states parties to the ACHR.[68] The specific obligations and the standards applicable to them are articulated in *Saramaka* as follows:

> First, the State must ensure the *effective participation* of the members of the Saramaka people, in conformity with their customs and traditions, regarding any development, investment, exploration or extraction plan (hereinafter 'development or investment plan') within Saramaka territory. Second, the State must guarantee that the Saramakas will receive a *reasonable benefit* from any such plan within their territory. Thirdly, the State must ensure that no concession will be issued within Saramaka territory unless and until independent and technically capable entities, with the State's supervision, perform a *prior environmental and social impact assessment*. These safeguards are intended to preserve, protect and guarantee the special relationship that the members of the Saramaka community have with their territory, which in turn ensures their survival as a tribal people.[69]

Although the three specific obligations applicable to indigenous communities identified in *Saramaka* and the detailed standards for their implementation imposed by the Court relate specifically to the right to property of indigenous peoples, in light of the close relationship between indigenous communities and their territory, they also function to protect the environment as discussed in Section 4.3.1.1.

4.3.1.1 Participation

The first and most extensive of the obligations relating to the right to property of indigenous communities is the requirement of participation or, as rephrased in *Kichwa Indigenous People of Sarayaku* v. *Ecuador*, 'rights to consultation and participation'.[70] In developing this requirement, the Inter-American Court refers to requirements imposed by the ICCPR, ILO Convention No. 169 and UNDRIP,[71] as well as to domestic legislation of participating states.[72]

The link between participation and protection of the environment is specifically highlighted by the Inter-American Commission in its Report on Indigenous Peoples, Afro-Descendent Communities and Natural Resources.[73] The Commission stresses that participation is necessary to ensure that specific rights of indigenous peoples are protected, including 'life, integrity, health, participation, territory and

68 *Kichwa Indigenous People of Sarayaku* (n 32) para 166.

69 *Saramaka* (n 55) para 129 (emphasis added). See also *Kichwa Indigenous People of Sarayaku* ibid para 157; *Kaliña and Lokono* (n 52) para 201.

70 *Kichwa Indigenous People of Sarayaku* ibid para 167.

71 UN Declaration on the Rights of Indigenous Peoples, GA Res 61/295, A/RES/61/295 (13 September 2007); see *Saramaka* (n 55) paras 130–31.

72 *Kichwa Indigenous People of Sarayaku* (n 32) parass 159–65; *Saramaka* (n 55) paras 130–31.

73 IACHR, *Indigenous Peoples, Afro-Descendent Communities and Natural Resources* (n 8) para 176.

environment'.[74] In the view of the Commission, 'these rights must guide the procedural guarantees'.[75] Ensuring that the environment is protected is thus clearly recognised as one of the specific objectives of the requirement of participation, and it is therefore reasonable to expect that the standards applied to implementation of this obligation should reflect this.

What, then, are the standards that apply to implementation of the obligation of participation? First, it is arguable that reference to 'effective' participation in *Saramaka* establishes 'effectiveness' as a standard for implementation. Although 'effective' is not specifically defined by the Court, it does elaborate a number of further requirements that begin to clarify what 'effective' participation involves. First, reflecting that the right to participation and consultation is very closely associated with recognition of the rights of indigenous communities to their own culture and cultural identity,[76] the Court specifies that participation and consultation must be conducted in accordance with the particular community's traditional decision-making processes and that what this entails is to be decided by the community itself.[77]

Secondly, the Court specifies that participation and consultation must commence at the earliest stages of planning, including 'early notice'[78] and continue throughout the project cycle.[79] This standard was breached in the case of *Kichwa Indigenous People of Sarayaku*, for example, as there had been no consultation with the affected community prior to the state signing a contract with a private company for oil exploration and exploitation on their traditional lands.[80] It is notable that the need for early and continuing consultation extends to the other safeguards relating to developments on indigenous land, namely benefit sharing and impact assessments, as will be discussed below. In cases where environmental damage had been caused, for example, communities must be consulted about clean-up operations to ensure that these are implemented in ways that respect the culture, way of life and environment of the communities affected.[81]

Thirdly, 'effective' participation requires states to share information on the proposed project and its implications and to accept information provided by the community.[82] The Inter-American Commission has interpreted this to require 'the sharing of full and precise information on the nature and consequences of the

74 ibid.
75 ibid.
76 *Saramaka* ibid para 129; *Kichwa Indigenous People of Sarayaku* (n 61) para 159.
77 *Saramaka* ibid para 133; *Kichwa Indigenous People of Sarayaku* ibid para 165; IACHR, *Indigenous Peoples, Afro-Descendent Communities and Natural Resources* (n 8) para 210.
78 *Saramaka* ibid.
79 *Saramaka* (n 55) para 133; *Kichwa Indigenous People of Sarayaku* (n 61) paras 180–81; *Kaliña and Lokono* (n 52) para 207.
80 *Kichwa Indigenous People of Sarayaku* ibid para 184.
81 ibid para 293.
82 *Saramaka* (n 55) para 133.

process on the peoples and communities consulted'.[83] The processes for sharing of information must, according to the Court, be culturally appropriate.[84] The shared information must, furthermore, be 'accessible' and 'timely'.[85] The requirement of timeliness is linked to the requirement already noted of 'early notice'. Accessibility requires that indigenous communities should be able to understand the information provided. In complex cases, it may be necessary for the state to provide technical assistance or interpretation services in order to comply with this standard.[86] The overall standard by which the sharing of information is to be judged is, according to the Court in *Saramaka*, that the state must ensure that members of the community are made aware of any risks associated with the project, including environmental and health risks, 'in order that the proposed development or extraction plan is accepted knowingly and voluntarily'.[87]

Fourthly, consultations must be carried out in good faith.[88] This requires that the parties engage positively in building mutual trust and respect. Any attempts on the part of the state to undermine community leaders or coerce members of the community, such as intervention by the police or security forces or attempting to bribe leaders or members of the community, are incompatible with this requirement.[89]

The fifth standard elaborated by the Inter-American Court in relation to participation is perhaps the most controversial, namely that the objective of participation and consultation must be to reach agreement or consensus.[90] In principle, this means that the outcome of consultations must not be predetermined and that the state must remain open-minded and willing to accommodate the perspectives and proposals of the community and to address their concerns.[91] What is controversial is whether 'effective' participation ultimately demands that the *consent* of the affected community be obtained in order for the project to go ahead. Can the community withhold consent altogether or impose conditions to mitigate any potential harm? Or, more broadly, is free, prior and informed consent (FPIC) a requirement for compliance with Article 21?[92]

FPIC is a common technique through which 'issues of environmental justice and the links between human rights and environmental protection' are addressed,[93] but

83 IACHR, *Indigenous Peoples, Afro-Descendent Communities and Natural Resources* (n 8) para 198.
84 *Saramaka* (n 55) para 133.
85 IACHR, *Indigenous Peoples, Afro-Descendent Communities and Natural Resources* (n 8) para 198.
86 ibid para 199.
87 *Saramaka* (n 55) para 133.
88 *Kichwa Indigenous People of Sarayaku* (n 61) para 185.
89 ibid paras 185–206.
90 *Saramaka* ibid; *Kichwa Indigenous People of Sarayaku* (n 61) para 186.
91 *Kichwa Indigenous People of Sarayaku* (n 61) paras 179–82.
92 As required for example by UNDRIP Article 32. Consent is not an independent requirement under ILO Convention No. 169 Article 6.
93 Anton and Shelton (n 37) 431; see also Chapter 9 by Jona Razzaque, which focuses on the standards that have developed in accordance with the principle of FPIC.

there is no internationally recognised definition or universal implementation method. The question of whether FPIC is required is examined in *Saramaka*, the Court drawing specific attention to the difference between 'consultation' and 'consent'.[94] The Court concludes that consent is only required for 'large-scale development or investment projects that would have a major impact' on the property rights of the members of the community in relation to a large part of their territory.[95] The subsequent decision of the Inter-American Court in *Kichwa Indigenous People of Sarayaku* is, unfortunately, silent on this issue, leaving this aspect of 'effective' participation unclear.[96]

If community consent is required only for 'large-scale development projects' with 'major' impacts, clarification of these terms is essential. In the absence of clarification, there is concern that small-scale projects that could significantly affect a community, due to their devastating effects on, for example, religious sites or places where medicinal plants grow, will be excluded from the requirement of FPIC.[97] As Thériault suggests:

> The duty to obtain the free, prior and informed consent of indigenous communities, I would argue, should not hinge on the relative scale of the project, but rather on the intensity of its ecological, social and cultural impacts as assessed by the concerned communities and their members.[98]

While the elaboration of the standards that apply to consultation have been broadly welcomed,[99] concerns have been raised about the standard of 'culturally appropriate' participation and consultation. Implementation of this standard demands that participation must be in accordance with the traditional decision-making processes of the community concerned, as decided by the community itself. Some scholars have questioned whether the implicit approval of the decision-making structures and processes of indigenous communities without consideration of their inclusiveness is appropriate and consistent with other rights protected under the ACHR.[100] It is arguable that additional safeguards for women and vulnerable groups within indigenous communities should be investigated in order to ensure that consultation processes allow for their views to be expressed and taken into account. Indeed, in its Report on Indigenous Peoples, Afro-Descendent Communities and Natural

94 *Saramaka* (n 55) para 134.

95 *Saramaka* ibid; see TM Antkowiak, 'Nicaragua's Canal Initiative Endangers the Rights of Indigenous and Afro-Caribbean Communities' (2015) 47 University of the Pacific Law Review 233, 238.

96 In *Maya Indigenous Communities of the Toledo District v Belize* (Merits) IACHR, Report No 40/04 Case 12.053 (12 October 2004) para 142 the Commission expresses support for FPIC.

97 Thériault (n 31) 327; Antkowiak (n 48) 170.

98 Thériault, ibid.

99 See S J Anaya, 'Indigenous Peoples' Participatory Rights in Relation to Decisions about Natural Resource Extraction: The More Fundamental Issue of What Rights Indigenous Peoples Have in Lands and Resources' (2004) 22 Arizona Journal of International and Comparative Law 7, 16.

100 ibid 190; D Shelton, 'The Inter-American Human Rights Law of Indigenous Peoples' (2013) 35 University of Hawaii Law Review, 937, 977.

Resources, the Inter-American Commission draws attention to states' obligations to ensure that indigenous women are able to participate in decision-making institutions and processes in the course of consultation about development activities on indigenous land.[101] Ensuring that all voices are heard has important implications for environmental protection.

Overall, it can be said that the Inter-American Court has established a detailed, yet far from comprehensive, set of standards in relation to participation of indigenous communities in decisions relating to their communal right to property. The right to participation and consultation is described in *Kichwa Indigenous People of Sarayaku* as being not only a norm derived from the ACHR, but as 'a general principle of international law'.[102] Moreover, the applicability of the standards for 'effective' participation is expressed in broader terms in *Kichwa Indigenous People of Sarayaku* than previously in *Saramaka*, to encompass not only extraction and development activities on indigenous land, but 'any administrative and legislative measure that may affect their rights, as recognised under domestic and international law'.[103] It is arguable, therefore, that the right to participation and consultation, as human rights, and the developing standards applicable to their implementation, extend beyond Article 21 and beyond the rights of indigenous peoples. As discussed below, the Court has recently confirmed in its 2017 Advisory Opinion that public participation and consultation in relation to environmental matters are required for compliance, not only with Articles 4 and 5, but also with a wide range of other rights.[104]

4.3.1.2 Benefit Sharing

The second specific state obligation applicable to indigenous communities identified in *Saramaka* is that the community concerned should receive a 'reasonable benefit' from any resource exploitation or development activities on their traditional lands.[105] Benefit sharing is a requirement found in a variety of international instruments, including those concerned with the environment and the rights of indigenous peoples.[106] The standard applicable to benefit sharing, as expressed by

101 IACHR, *Indigenous Peoples, Afro-Descendent Communities and Natural Resources* (n 8) paras 211–12.
102 *Kichwa Indigenous People of Sarayaku* (n 61) para 164.
103 ibid para 166.
104 2017 Advisory Opinion (n 10) paras 124–25; 211–12.
105 *Saramaka* (n 55) para 129; see also Chapter 9 by Jona Razzaque, which considers access and benefit sharing within the context of FPIC and in particular the CBD.
106 See eg ILO Convention No. 169 (n 57) Article 15; Convention on Biological Diversity (CBD) 1992, 1760 UNTS 79 Article 1, 15; Nagoya Protocol on Access to Genetic Resources and the Fair and Equitable Sharing of Benefits Arising from Their Utilization (ABS) to the CBD, UN Doc UNEP/CBD/COP/DEC/X/I (29 October 2010); United Nations Convention on the Law of the Sea (UNCLOS) 1982, 1833 UNTS 3 Article 82, 140; UN, Report of the Special Rapporteur on the Right to Food, Olivier De Schutter, *Large Scale Land Acquisitions and Leases: A Set of Minimum Principles and Measures to Address the Human Rights Challenges*, UN Doc A/HRC/13/33/Add 2 (28 December 2009) para 33.

the Court is 'reasonable benefit sharing'[107] or 'fair and equitable benefit sharing'.[108]

As discussed in Section 4.3.1, the facts that gave rise to the claim in *Saramaka* were the granting of logging concessions and the removal of a large amount of timber from Saramaka territory, resulting in extensive environmental destruction and a range of consequent social problems.[109] There had been no prior consultation or negotiation about benefit sharing at all, and the primary concern of the Court in dealing with the case is to ensure that the community is compensated for deprivation of property and damage.[110] The Court thus defines benefit sharing as 'a form of reasonable equitable compensation resulting from the exploitation of traditionally owned lands and of those natural resources necessary for the survival of the Saramaka people',[111] and it specifically links benefit sharing to the right to obtain compensation under Article 21(2).[112] Thus, in relation to the specific facts of the *Saramaka* case, the standard applicable to benefit sharing is that of compensation for dispossession and damage. The Court therefore awarded monetary compensation for both material and immaterial damages.[113] Although the Court does refer to 'mutually acceptable benefit sharing'[114] which implies prior consultation and agreement, and specifically invokes UNDRIP and ILO Convention No. 169,[115] both of which emphasise the need for prior consultation on benefit sharing, this aspect is not explored in the case because the facts of the case raise only the issue of *ex post facto* compensation.

That the requirement of benefit sharing goes beyond payment of compensation for damage after the event to encompass the obligation to reach agreement about benefit sharing before any exploitation of resources takes place, is clearly the view of the Commission in its Report on Indigenous Peoples, Afro-Descendent Communities and Natural Resources. The standards that the Commission sets for benefit sharing based on advance agreement include: prior consultation; consultation in accordance with the traditional decision-making procedures of affected communities; identification of beneficiaries by affected communities;

[107] *Saramaka* (n 55) para 138.
[108] E Morgera, 'The Need for an International Legal Concept of Fair and Equitable Benefit Sharing' (2016) 27 EJIL 353.
[109] *Saramaka* (n 55) paras 149–52.
[110] ibid 139.
[111] ibid 140.
[112] ibid paras 138–39; *Kaliña and Lokono* (n 52) para 227.
[113] *Saramaka* ibid paras 198–202.
[114] ibid para 140 citing Rodolfo Stavenhagen, *Report of the UN Special Rapporteur on the situation of human rights and fundamental freedoms of indigenous peoples*, UN Doc E/CN.4/2003/90, 21 January 2003 para 21.
[115] ibid para 138.

agreement with affected communities and implementation of such agreements.[116] The Commission also emphasises that benefit sharing has nothing to do with charity or implementation of voluntary corporate social responsibility policies, and that the possibility of receiving benefits should not be used to induce communities to agree to developments on their territories. Benefit sharing is, in the view of the Commission, a mandatory requirement, and participation of indigenous peoples themselves in determining the benefits is an integral part thereof.[117]

Although the Court focuses primarily on *ex post facto* compensation in *Saramaka*, the need for prior consultation about benefit sharing is in fact indirectly raised by the Court in ordering the state to 'adopt legislative, administrative and other measures necessary to recognise and ensure the right of the Saramaka people to ... reasonably share the benefits of projects'.[118] A consistent approach would require prior consultation about benefit sharing to comply with all the standards relating to 'effective' consultation discussed under Section 4.3.1.1 above, including that consultation should take place in advance, that it should be based on provision of adequate information, be undertaken in good faith, in order to reach an agreement and be conducted according to the customs and traditions of the community concerned.

4.3.1.3 Environmental and Social Impact Assessments (ESIAs)

The third obligation identified by the Court relating to resource exploitation on indigenous land is the need for prior environmental and social impact assessments to be carried out.[119] The standards set for ESIAs in *Saramaka* are that assessments are to be carried out before permission is granted for developments on traditional territory, by 'technically capable entities' and supervised by the state.[120] These standards are not, however, discussed in any detail. No environmental or social impact assessments had been carried out in *Saramaka*, so apart from the finding that ESIAs should have been carried out, further elaboration was not needed for the purposes of the case. Elaboration and further guidance is, however, provided in a subsequent 'Interpretation of Judgement' by the Court[121] and in the later case of *Kaliña and Lokono Peoples* v. *Suriname*[122] as well as by the Commission in its

116 IACHR, *Indigenous Peoples, Afro-Descendent Communities and Natural Resources* (n 8) paras 219–24.
117 ibid 223; see Morgera (n 111) 354.
118 *Saramaka* (n 55) para 194(d); *Saramaka People v Suriname* (Interpretation of the Judgment on Preliminary Objects, Merits, Reparations and Costs) IACtHR Ser C No 185 (12 August 2008) paras 24–25.
119 *Saramaka* (n 55) para 129.
120 ibid.
121 *Saramaka* (Interpretation of the Judgment) (n 121); see also *Kichwa Indigenous People of Sarayaku* (n 61) paras 204–07.
122 *Kaliña and Lokono* (n 52) para 214.

Report on Indigenous Peoples, Afro-Descendent Communities and Natural Resources.[123]

The additional guidance provided by the Court emphasises that impact assessments must cover both social and environmental impacts of the proposed development. In particular, the Court identifies an additional standard for the implementation of ESIAs, namely that the implications of the proposal for the traditions and way of life of the affected community must be fully investigated in order to ensure its cultural and physical survival, and in particular to protect the special relationship between the community and its traditional territory.[124] It also clarifies that the aim of ESIAs is twofold: to provide an 'objective measure' of the potential impact of the proposed development on the land and the people, and to enable the community to take informed decisions about the proposed developments by providing them with full details of possible environmental, health and other risks.[125] Thus, the obligation to provide for ESIAs interrelates and overlaps with the obligation of participation discussed above: the conduct of ESIAs must involve indigenous communities who must be given opportunities to provide inputs,[126] and ESIAs form part of the sharing of information required for effective participation. The Court also provides further clarification of the standard relating to timing of ESIAs. In order for ESIAs to play a role in informing decision making, they must be concluded before concessions are granted by the state. And the Court elaborates additional standards for ESIAs, namely that they must respect and take into account the culture, traditions and way of life of the indigenous community involved,[127] and that they must specifically consider the cumulative impact of past, current and proposed projects in order to properly inform the affected communities.[128]

Finally, the Court stipulates that to provide an 'objective measure', ESIAs must be conducted in accordance with relevant international standards and best practice.[129] The Court cites the Akwé: Kon (Guidelines), adopted by the Conference of the Parties of the Convention on Biological Diversity (CBD), as an example of international best practice.[130] *Akwé: Kon* is a Mohawk term that means 'everything in

[123] IACHR, *Indigenous Peoples, Afro-Descendent Communities and Natural Resources* (n 8) paras 213–18.

[124] ibid paras 213–14.

[125] *Saramaka* (Interpretation of the Judgment) (n 119) para 40; *Kaliña and Lokono* (n 52) para 214.

[126] IACHR, *Indigenous Peoples, Afro-Descendent Communities and Natural Resources* (n 8) para 215; *Kaliña and Lokono* ibid para 215.

[127] *Saramaka* (Interpretation of the Judgment) (n 121) para 41; *Kaliña and Lokono* ibid.

[128] *Saramaka* (Interpretation of the Judgment) ibid.

[129] ibid.

[130] ibid; *Akwé: Kon Guidelines for the Conduct of Cultural, Environmental and Social Impact Assessments, regarding Developments Proposed to Take Place on, or which are Likely to Impact on, Sacred Sites and on Lands and Waters Traditionally Occupied or Used by Indigenous and Local Communities* <www.cbd.int/doc/publications/akwe-brochure-en.pdf>; Use of the Akwé: Kon Guidelines is also recommended by the former Special Rapporteur on Human Rights and the Environment, John Knox, in his Report on Biodiversity and Human Rights (n 40) para 72; see also Chapter 9 of this volume by Jona Razzaque, which provides more discussion relating to the significance of the Akwé: Kon Guidelines.

creation'.[131] The full title of the Guidelines is 'Voluntary guidelines for the conduct of cultural, environmental and social impact assessments regarding developments proposed to take place on, or which are likely to impact on, sacred sites and on lands and waters traditionally occupied or used by indigenous and local communities'. The name signals the aspiration of the drafters of the Guidelines to provide a holistic framework for social, environmental and cultural impact assessment that provides for full involvement of indigenous and local communities in considering the implications of development proposals for their culture, way of life and the environment.[132] The objectives of the Guidelines expressly include: ensuring effective participation of communities from the earliest stages of proposed projects; ensuring that the concerns of communities are 'properly' taken into account, in particular that the concerns of women are considered; ensuring that traditional knowledge and practices are taken into account and protected; prevention and mitigation of harmful effects of developments; and ensuring that the connection between cultural, environmental and social aspects affected by the proposed development is taken into account.[133] The Guidelines outline detailed procedures for implementing 'an integrated assessment' including screening and scoping, consideration of damage prevention and mitigation measures, reporting, decision making, management planning, monitoring and auditing. Many of these processes are similar to the standards required for 'effective participation' articulated by the Court in *Saramaka*, as discussed above, but they are defined in much more detail in the Guidelines and expressly relate to all aspects of development from consultation on initial proposals to management of implementation, monitoring and dispute resolution.[134] While the Guidelines provide a helpful model, the importance of a holistic framework needs to be more clearly acknowledged and the requisite standards need to be elaborated much more explicitly by the Court. Moreover, if it is the Court's intention that the detailed standards identified in the Guidelines should be adopted, this should be incorporated explicitly into the jurisprudence to establish the standards with the necessary clarity and authority.

Overall, it can be said that while the standards set for ESIAs appear to require the implementation of mainly technical processes, elaboration of the standards by the Court and Commission makes it clear that the standards required for ESIAs cannot be understood or implemented in isolation from the standards relating to participation and benefit sharing under Article 21. There is a significant overlap between the three obligations related to the implementation of Article 21. Both benefit sharing and the implementation of ESIAs require participation, including all the aspects outlined in Section 4.3.1.1 above. Moreover, all three overarching obligations are

131 Akwé: Kon Guidelines ibid 1.
132 ibid.
133 ibid 5–6.
134 ibid 8–13.

shaped by the overall imperative to guarantee to indigenous communities 'the collective right to survival as an organised people, with control over their habitat as a necessary condition for reproduction of their culture, for their own development and to carry out their life aspirations'.[135] This means that the detailed standards for implementation of the obligations of participation, benefit sharing and ESIAs must be considered together and demand an integrated approach as exemplified by the Akwé: Kon Guidelines.

4.3.2 *Overall Assessment of Standards under Article 21*

The willingness of the Court to step outside the confines of conventional legal paradigms and to recognise and extend protection of the right to property based on indigenous notions of territoriality rather than on a Western conception of private property centred on individual ownership and commercial circulation[136] has been crucial to the development of environmental standards.[137] The elaboration of that protection to include social and cultural aspects is a significant step forward in incorporating a 'richer, more relational' conception of property into the jurisprudence, and establishing an approach to property rights that is sensitive to the way of life of different communities and more capable of advancing environmental justice.[138] The acceptance of a conception of the right to property that explicitly recognises the dependence of humans on the environment is the foundation of many of the specific standards supporting environmental protection under Article 21 and informs their development.

However, one of the concerns that have been raised in relation to development of environmental protection in the context of property rights is that the text of Article 21 specifically permits states to interfere with or limit the right to property in the 'interest of society'[139] or 'for reasons of public utility or social interest'.[140] The usual tests that apply to restriction of the right to property are those of 'legality, necessity, proportionality and fulfilment of a lawful purpose in a democratic society (public benefit and public interest)'.[141] These tests are, where indigenous territory is affected, supplemented by the requirement that restrictions should not result in

[135] *Yakye Axa* (n 30) para 146. See IACHR, *Indigenous Peoples, Afro-Descendent Communities and Natural Resources* (n 8) para 151.

[136] The imposition of Western concepts of property and inheritance was a feature of colonialism in many countries, see E Grant, 'Customary Law and Human Rights' in S Sheeran and N Rodley (n 20) 303, 307.

[137] See S Coyle and K Morrow, *The Philosophical Foundations of Environmental Law – Property, Rights and Nature* (Hart 2004) 157–58; A Grear, 'Human Rights, Property and the Search for "Worlds Other"' (2012) 3 JHRE 173, 188–89.

[138] Grear, ibid 189; see K Birrell, L Godden and M Tehan, 'Climate Change and REDD+: Property as a Prism for Conceiving Indigenous Peoples' Engagement' (2012) 3 JHRE 196, 205–10.

[139] Article 21(1).

[140] Article 21(2).

[141] *Sawhoyamaxa* (n 49) para 138: *Yakye-Axa* (n 30) para 144; *Saramaka* (n 55) para 127.

endangering the physical and cultural survival of the indigenous community concerned.[142] Antkowiak argues that the Court has increasingly shown deference to states in relation to the application of the tests for public interest, signalling weakening protection of the property rights of indigenous peoples.[143] Moreover, the additional 'survival' test elaborated in *Saramaka* is arguably very narrow, taking a 'conservative view of cultural integrity' and implying a concern with mere subsistence rather than quality of life.[144] The applicability of the environmental standards discussed above may be of limited use in response to public interest arguments of states more concerned with economic development than with the maintenance of environmental integrity.[145]

In spite of the gaps and ambiguities identified in the Article 21 jurisprudence, the Court has succeeded in establishing important procedural standards that have the potential to put environmental protection firmly on the agenda in planning and implementation of development projects on indigenous territory. Further elaboration of these standards is, however, necessary to address the uncertainties and to ensure that both the broad state obligations and the detailed standards required are defined as comprehensively as possible, to facilitate the effective implementation of existing legislative and administrative frameworks protecting the environment or the development of such frameworks where these are not already in place.

4.3.3 *Standards Relating to the Right to Life under Article 4 ACHR*

As noted in section 4.2, in carrying out its mandate of promoting compliance with human rights obligations and holding states to account for human rights abuses, the Inter-American Commission issues both country and thematic reports.[146] One of the Commission's country reports that has been particularly influential in the context of the environment is its 1997 Report on the Situation of Human Rights in Ecuador.[147] In this report, the Commission describes the relationship between the environment and the right to life as follows:

> Respect for the inherent dignity of the person is the principle which underlies the fundamental protections of the right to life and to preservation of physical well-being. Conditions of severe environmental pollution, which may cause serious physical illness, impairment and suffering . . . are inconsistent with the right to be respected as a human being.[148]

142 *Saramaka* ibid para 128.
143 Antkowiak (n 48) 163–64.
144 ibid 154–55; Shelton (n 102) 975; Fisher and Lundberg (n 34) 192.
145 Fisher and Lundberg ibid 193.
146 Sandoval (n 20) 434–36.
147 OEA/Ser.L/V/II.96, doc 10 rev 1 (24 April 1997); see Anton and Shelton (n 37) 577.
148 ibid chapter VIII Conclusions.

The concept of human dignity is central to international human rights law, and is widely considered to be the foundation of all human rights.[149] The preamble to the American Declaration states in terms almost identical to those used in Article 1 UDHR that 'all men are born free and equal, in dignity and in rights'.[150] Dignity as a foundational value and as a right is also recognised in constitutions around the world, including those of a number of OAS member states.[151] The Court has followed the lead of the Commission in making the connection between human dignity and the right to life explicit. The right to life, in the view of the Court, encompasses more than mere physical existence: it includes the right to live a 'dignified life'.[152] Accordingly, in addition to negative obligations to ensure that individuals are not deprived of their lives and that states do not impede access to the conditions that make a dignified life possible, states also have positive obligations to take steps to generate 'minimum living conditions that are compatible with the dignity of the human person'.[153] In the words of Judge Sergio García-Ramírez in *Sawhoyamaxa Indigenous Community* v. *Paraguay*:

> In such framework, a single right with a double dimension is set, like the two-faced god Janus: one side, with a first-generation legal concept of the right to life; the other side, with the concept of a requirement to provide conditions for a feasible and full existence, that is to say a concept among the ones considered 'second-generation rights'.[154]

In relation to indigenous communities, in particular, the Court emphasises that compliance with the minimum standards necessary for a dignified life requires states to take into account the culture and way of life of the community affected, including the close and distinctive relationship of the community with its ancestral territory, and the 'life aspirations'[155] and 'right to self-development'[156] of individual members of the community and the community as a whole. Creating appropriate conditions in the indigenous context therefore requires protection of the environment necessary for traditional practices such as fishing, hunting, gathering and use of specific places for religious practices to continue. In other words, the state has a positive duty

149 E Grant, 'Dignity and Equality' (2007) 7 HRLR 299, 302–06; A Barak, *Human Dignity: The Constitutional Value and the Constitutional Right* (Cambridge 2015) 37–48; D Townsend, 'Taking Dignity Seriously? A Dignity Approach to Environmental Disputes before Human Rights Courts' (2015) 6 JHRE 204, 205–07.

150 American Declaration (n 14).

151 See E Grant, 'Human Dignity and Socio-Economic Rights' (2012) 33 Liverpool Law Review 235; Barak (153) 59–62; E Daly, *Dignity Rights: Courts, Constitutions, and the Worth of the Human Person* (Penn 2013); E Daly and JR May, 'Bridging Constitutional Dignity and Environmental Rights Jurisprudence' (2016) 7 JHRE 218, 222–26.

152 *Villagrán-Morales v Guatemala* (Merits) IACtHR Ser C No 63 (19 November 1999) para 144; *Yakye Axa* (n 30) para 162; 2017 Advisory Opinion (n 10) para 109; see Antkowiak and Gonza (n 20) 97.

153 *Yakye Axa* (n 30) para 162; see also 2017 Advisory Opinion (n 10) para 108.

154 *Sawhoyamaxa* (n 49) separate concurring opinion of Judge Sergio García-Ramírez, para 18.

155 *Yakye Axa* (n 30) para 163.

156 *Sawhoyamaxa* (n 49) separate concurring opinion of Judge Sergio García-Ramírez, paras 18, 20.

to ensure that the environmental conditions necessary for cultural expression and 'self-development' of indigenous communities are both maintained and not damaged by industrial or other developments.

What, then, are the minimum living conditions that must be generated if states are to meet their obligations under Article 4? The Court has begun to answer this question, initially specifically in relation to indigenous peoples and other vulnerable communities,[157] establishing, as a starting point, that the requirements of *vida digna* must be interpreted in light of the social and economic rights provided for in Article 26 ACHR and in the San Salvador Protocol.[158] In *Yake Axa* the Court refers to a range of social and economic rights, including the right to health, the right to a healthy environment, the right to food and water and the right to the benefits of culture, that must be implemented in order for the right to a dignified life to be fulfilled.[159] In relation to each of these social and economic rights, the Court has begun to elaborate minimum standards relating to, for example, the essential quality of water and food and requirements for access.[160] Although the Court refers to 'international standards' that apply to implementation of the rights concerned, it does not provide a detailed account of the applicable standards, but references general comments issued by the UN Committee on Economic Social and Cultural Rights (CESCR) in which requirements for implementation of rights to food and water are elaborated,[161] as well as World Health Organisation (WHO) guidance in relation to water.[162] In relation to the right to a healthy environment, which has also been explicitly identified as one of the social and economic rights relevant to implementation of the right to a dignified life, further elaboration of standards has, however, been lacking. This *lacuna* has now been filled by the Court in its 2017 Advisory Opinion.

4.3.4 *The 2017 Advisory Opinion and the Rights to Life and Personal Integrity under Articles 4 and 5 ACHR*

As noted above, the 2017 Advisory Opinion is particularly important because of its recognition of the right to a healthy environment as one of the social and economic rights that enjoys direct protection under Article 26 ACHR. But the Opinion is also significant for its explicit endorsement of the continuing

157 *Yakye Axa* (n 30) para 162; *Villagrán-Morales v Guatamala* (Merits) IACtHR Ser C No 63 (19 November 1999) (*Street Children Case*) para 139; Pasqualucci (n 50) 3.

158 *Yakye Axa* ibid para 163; *Kaliña and Lokono* (n 52) para 172.

159 *Yakye Axa* ibid; see also *Kaliña and Lokono* ibid.

160 See, for example, *Xákmok Kásek* (n 52) paras 195–98; see also other chapters that consider the right to water, in particular, Chapter 2 by Sumudu Attapatu, Chapter 7 by Owen McIntyre and Chapter 13 by Nathan Cooper.

161 *Xákmok Kásek* (n 52) para 195 and 198, 200. In relation to the right to water, the Court cites UN CESCR General Comment No. 15: The Right to Water (arts 11 and 12 of the Covenant) UN Doc E/C.12/2002/11 (20 January 2003). In relation to the right to food, the Court cites the UN CESCR General Comment No 12: The Right to Adequate Food (art 11) UN Doc E/C.12/1999/5 (12 May 1999).

162 G Howard and J Bartram, *Domestic Water Quality, Service Level and Health* WHO/SDE/WSH/03.02

relevance of a healthy environment to the right to life. A substantial part of the 2017 Advisory Opinion is thus devoted to delineating the environmental standards that states must apply in carrying out their obligations under Article 4, as well as Article 5, the right to physical integrity.[163]

While environmental standards are discussed in the 2017 Advisory Opinion in the context of the rights to life and to physical integrity (Articles 4 and 5 ACHR) to address the specific questions raised by Columbia (the state requesting the Opinion), it is important to note a number of significant aspects of the Court's response that have the potential to substantially broaden the reach of environmental standards beyond the indigenous context and beyond Articles 4 and 5. First, while the Court maintains that indigenous peoples need additional protection due to their extreme vulnerability, the environmental standards outlined in the 2017 Advisory Opinion in relation to the right to life are clearly not confined to indigenous communities, but are generally applicable.[164] Secondly, the 2017 Advisory Opinion explicitly recognises the interrelationship between environmental standards and other social and economic rights necessary to fulfil the right to life. This means that environmental standards apply not only directly to implementation of the right to life, but also indirectly, via state obligations in relation to other aspects of the right to life such as food, water and health, in light of the potential detrimental impact of environmental harm on those rights.[165] Thirdly, and relatedly, the environmental standards developed by the Court in the context of the right to life also apply to the newly recognised substantive right to a healthy environment, and arguably other rights as well, which means that the scope of application is potentially very broad.[166] And fourthly, the Court indicates that states must comply with environmental standards not only to prevent environmental harm occurring within their territory, but also to prevent cross-border damage, while at the same time broadening the test for the applicability of cross-border obligations.[167]

Having established that preventing and addressing environmental damage is an integral aspect of a state's obligations to respect and guarantee the right to life,[168] the Court first invokes the concept of due diligence to explain the obligations of conduct that arise under the ACHR in general and the right to life in particular, and then identifies the specific obligation that states must comply with in relation to environmental matters.[169] The specific environmental obligations identified are the obligation to prevent environmental damage, the obligation to implement the precautionary principle, the obligation to co-operate with other states as well as

163 2017 Advisory Opinion (n 10) para 114. The same standards applicable to the right to life also apply to the right to physical integrity.
164 ibid para 113.
165 ibid paras 110–11; 117.
166 ibid paras 124–25.
167 ibid para 125.
168 ibid paras 117–18.
169 ibid para 124.

particular procedural obligations.[170] It is in relation to each of these specific obligations that environmental standards are elaborated in the case.

4.3.4.1 Obligation to Prevent

The obligation to prevent is limited to the prevention of *significant* environmental damage, and significant damage is defined as damage that may lead to a violation of the right to life or personal integrity and, importantly, also relates to rights that form part of the content of the right to life, such as the right to food and health.[171] The scope of the obligation is therefore potentially wide, in spite of the ostensive limitation. The specific measures that states are required to adopt in order to comply with the obligation to prevent include: first, regulatory measures; second, monitoring and supervision; third, carrying out environmental impact assessments (EIAs); and fourth, contingency planning and implementing mitigation measures.[172]

The requisite standard set by the Court for implementing regulation is that it must reduce the risk to life and personal integrity. Further elaboration of this standard is, however, limited to establishing particular requirements for regulating EIAs. The standards laid down for regulating EIAs include the need for regulation to clearly establish the areas and the relevant impacts to be assessed, the procedures to be followed, who is to be responsible, the decision-making process and compliance mechanisms.[173] The obligation to implement EIAs is also identified as a separate element of the obligation to prevent, and specific standards for EIAs are elaborated as discussed below. Apart from the focus on EIAs, the 2017 Advisory Opinion therefore provides little development of standards for regulation. It is also disappointing that while the Court notes, with approval, recommendations by the UN CESCR and Committee for the Elimination of Racial Discrimination that home states should be required to regulate the operation of transnational companies to prevent extraterritorial breaches of human rights, it does not impose any specific obligation on states in this regard, so environmental standards are not considered in this context.[174]

In relation to the duty of monitoring and supervision, the Court directs that states must design and implement measures to monitor, prevent, investigate and sanction activities that have the potential to damage the environment. The standards that such measures must meet are very succinctly expressed as 'appropriate', 'adequate' and 'independent', but the Court indicates that the required standards will vary from case to case depending on the risks involved.[175]

170 ibid paras 77–82.
171 ibid para 140.
172 ibid para 145.
173 ibid para 150.
174 ibid para 151.
175 ibid para 154.

As noted above, the obligation to carry out EIAs is identified by the Court as a separate mandatory requirement. In relation to the standards required for EIAs, the Court refers back to its previous decisions under Article 21,[176] in specifying that EIAs must comply with international standards and best practice.[177] The Court further notes the need for EIAs to respect and protect the traditions and culture of indigenous peoples,[178] and it also specifies that EIAs should include assessment of social impacts. Unlike the Court's discussion of ESIAs in the context of Article 21, where the overriding concern is to guarantee the collective physical and cultural survival of indigenous communities, the requirement to assess social impacts under Article 4 is derived from states' general obligation to assess the impact of proposed developments on their international human rights obligations. This potentially broadens the obligation to consider social impacts well beyond the concerns highlighted under Article 21.[179] It is therefore puzzling that the Court refers to EIAs in its discussion of state obligations under Article 4, rather than drawing attention to the social aspect by using the term ESIAs as it does in relation to Article 21.

The standards for EIAs under Article 4 are outlined without much further elaboration. They include the requirement that EIAs should be carried out by independent and technically competent persons or organisations under supervision of the state,[180] that they should be conducted prior to permission being granted for development or at least before implementation commences,[181] and that the cumulative effects of all related projects should be considered.[182] However, participation of the general public in EIAs is not required under Article 4, although the requirement to involve indigenous communities in EIAs through consultation applies to both Article 4 and Article 21.[183] The Court does not seem to think that it is necessary to make specific provision for participation of the interested public in EIAs, referring only to the more general right to public participation elaborated under states' procedural environmental obligations as discussed in Section 4.3.4.4 below. Thus, while the standards in relation to EIAs under Article 4 are similar to those discussed under Article 21, no additional detail is provided in the 2017 Advisory Opinion.

Finally, the obligation to prevent requires that states develop detailed contingency plans to enable them to respond to environmental disasters, and that they implement appropriate measures to mitigate the effects of environmental damage. The Court elaborates a number of specific standards for such measures, including that they must make use of the best technology and science available and be implemented

176 *Saramaka* (Interpretation of the Judgment) (n 121) para 41; *Kaliña and Lokono* (n 52) para 216.
177 2017 Advisory Opinion (n 10) paras 161–65.
178 ibid para 169.
179 ibid para 164.
180 ibid para 163.
181 ibid para 162.
182 ibid para 165
183 ibid para 166.

without delay.[184] But, as with the other aspects of the obligation to prevent, the standards outlined in the 2017 Advisory Opinion provide mere starting points, and further elaboration will no doubt follow in due course.

4.3.4.2 Obligation to Observe the Precautionary Principle

Although the Court specifically asserts that, to protect the right to life and personal integrity, states have an obligation to act in accordance with the precautionary principle even in the absence of scientific certainty, it is disappointing that the applicable standards are not elaborated beyond stating that *effective* measures must be adopted to prevent harm to the environment. Moreover, while the Court identifies the level of harm that is required in order to trigger the overall obligation to prevent as 'significant harm', the obligation to observe the precautionary principle arises only where there is a risk of 'serious and irreversible' damage.[185] The question therefore arises whether the threshold for implementation of the precautionary principle is higher than the general obligation to prevent. A heightened threshold, if this is indeed the intention, will arguably limit the utility of the obligation to observe the precautionary principle, and clarification of the meaning of 'serious and irreversible' damage is urgently needed.

4.3.4.3 Obligation of International Co-Operation

According to the Court, the obligation of international co-operation in relation to environmental damage is an aspect of the general obligation to co-operate internationally in order to develop social, economic and cultural rights, provided for under Article 26 ACHR. The obligation includes co-operation to prevent environmental damage, and is particularly significant in the case of shared resources. The obligation applies between states and comprises a duty to notify other states of environmental damage that may affect them and the duty to consult potentially affected states.[186] Although an obligation to exchange information is also identified by the Court, this is not recognised as a binding obligation.[187]

The duty to notify relates to activities that have the potential to cause significant cross-border environmental damage, whether planned by the state or other parties over whom the state has jurisdiction. Notification is necessary to initiate co-operation and is also linked to the obligation to prevent, as discussed in the preceding paragraph. Notification must take place timeously, which means as soon as the state of origin becomes aware that an activity planned or carried out within its jurisdiction has the potential to cause significant transboundary environmental harm. In some

184 ibid para 172.
185 ibid para 180.
186 ibid para 186.
187 ibid para 208.

cases, awareness may arise from a preliminary assessment by the state of origin before an EIA is conducted, while in other cases awareness may arise based on an EIA.[188] The information provided in the notification must be sufficient to enable the potentially affected state to make an informed assessment of the likely impact of the planned activity.

The duty of international consultation is intended to facilitate cooperation between states to avoid or mitigate transboundary environmental damage and must take place in good faith and timeously.[189] Good faith requires that states engage seriously in consultation and negotiation with a view to reconciling the interests of all parties concerned. It also requires the state of origin not to proceed with the proposed project while the parties are in the process of consultation. However, it does not mean that states are obliged to reach an agreement or that the consent of states likely to be affected is necessary before a state of origin is able to authorise the project in question. If no agreement is reached during the consultation period, the state of origin may proceed or make use of available dispute resolution mechanisms, including mechanisms provided by the Inter-American human rights system, if appropriate.[190]

4.3.4.4 Procedural Obligations

The final part of the 2017 Advisory Opinion is devoted to consideration of procedural obligations that arise in the context of the rights to life and personal integrity. The procedural obligations identified by the Court under Articles 4 and 5 are the widely recognised trilogy of procedural environmental rights, namely access to information, public participation and access to justice.[191] Although aspects of these rights have been recognised under Article 21 as discussed in Section 4.3.1, and under other ACHR rights, such as the right to freedom of information (Article 13), the right to participate in government (Article 23) and the right to judicial protection (Article 25), this is the first time that these rights have gained specific recognition in the Inter-American system as environmental rights.

ACCESS TO INFORMATION. The Court has previously recognised that there is a public interest in making available information about development projects that may affect the environment. In the case of *Claude-Reyes* v. *Chile* the Court recognised a right of access to environmental information held by the state under Article 13 ACHR that provides for protection of the right to freedom of thought and expression.[192] The case arose from the denial of access to information about

188 ibid para 193.
189 ibid para 205.
190 ibid paras 204–05.
191 ibid para 212.
192 *Claude-Reyes* (n 29) paras 75–103.

a contentious deforestation project approved by the Chilean Foreign Investment Committee, a public body.[193] The right of access to information has also been established under Article 21 ACHR, relating to proposed projects on indigenous land, as discussed in Section 4.3.1.1.[194] In outlining the scope and content of the right of access to information under Article 4, the Court incorporates the standards that have been set for access to information under Article 13. Information must be made available without the need for individuals to show a direct interest in the information, and access must be *affordable*, *effective* and *timely*.[195] Moreover, the Court highlights that the obligation to provide information is an obligation of 'active transparency'.[196] This entails an array of standards, including that states have a duty to provide the maximum amount of information that is necessary for individuals to exercise other rights, such as the right to life or personal integrity. It also requires states to provide environmental information in an informal manner, that the information must be comprehensive, comprehensible, up-to date and that it must be provided in a language that is accessible and in a manner that conveys the information effectively to different communities. The obligation of 'active transparency' also requires states to collect and actively disseminate environmental information relevant to rights under the ACHR, including information on environmental quality, environmental factors that impact health, information on environmental legislation and policies and information on access to information.[197] The Court has thus specified quite specific standards for access to information, but the standards are not yet well developed and there is considerable scope for elaboration and further clarification.

PUBLIC PARTICIPATION. Public participation in environmental matters has previously been recognised by the Court as essential to democratic decision making and protected under Article 23 (right to participate in government) as well as under Article 21 in relation to indigenous communities.[198] The 2017 Advisory Opinion now also recognises the applicability of the right to public participation to the right to life.[199] The standards that apply are that states must secure the right, *without discrimination*, in an *equitable*, *meaningful* and *transparent* way based on *access to relevant information* that has been provided by the state. States must make opportunities for participation available from early on in the process of decision making, they must ensure that the public is informed of the right and they must secure *effective* participation. Relevant implementation mechanisms include notification, public hearings, consultations, participation in activities leading to the formulation

[193] ibid para 3.
[194] *Kichwa Indigenous People of Sarayaku* (n 61) para 230.
[195] 2017 Advisory Opinion (n 10) paras 219–20.
[196] ibid para 221.
[197] ibid paras 219–23.
[198] *Kaliña and Lokono* (n 52) 196–98; 203; 230.
[199] 2017 Advisory Opinion (n 10) para 231.

and application of laws as well as judicial review processes.[200] While some of these standards have already been identified in relation to Articles 21 and 23, the 2017 Advisory Opinion has provided the Court with an opportunity to provide a clearer enumeration in the environmental context with a view to further development.

ACCESS TO JUSTICE. In its 2017 Advisory Opinion, the Court commences discussion of access to justice by emphasizing that the right is recognised as a *jus cogens* norm and by recalling its own previous decisions establishing that states are obliged to provide effective judicial remedies in terms of Articles 25 and 8 read with Article 1.1 ACHR.[201] The relevant standards that apply to the obligation to provide access to justice in the context of Article 4 include access to resources and a due process framework to enable individuals to challenge decisions, rules, acts or omissions of public authorities and to secure the right of access to information and public participation. The obligation to secure access to justice extends to all individuals who may be affected by transboundary environmental harm that originates in the state's territory and must be implemented without discrimination.[202] As with the other procedural environmental rights, the applicable standards are outlined very briefly, providing a skeletal framework awaiting further elaboration in practice. This does not detract from the importance of the specific recognition given to procedural environmental rights within the context of Article 4.

4.3.5 *Overall Assessment of Standards under Articles 4 and 5 ACHR*

Although the 2017 Advisory Opinion has provided a very important extension and some clarification of state obligations in relation to the environment under Article 4, together with identification of some specific standards for implementation of those obligations, a number of challenges remain, not least the challenge of elaboration and elucidation of environmental standards. The outline provided by the Court is an important starting point, but environmental protection will not be achieved unless the 2017 Advisory Opinion is followed up with much more detailed discussion of standards in practice.

One of the limitations of the 2017 Advisory Opinion is that standards are conceived of as primarily procedural in nature. However, the Court's specific recognition of the concept of *vida digna* provides scope for the Court to give further consideration to development of substantive standards for environmental protection. The Article 4 jurisprudence developed in the indigenous context provides some examples of how this could be done. As noted above, in elaborating what the requirements for a dignified life are in relation to rights to food and water, the Court has invoked 'international standards' derived from sources such as CESCR

200 ibid para 232.
201 ibid para 233.
202 ibid para 237.

General Comments, among others. In considering the right to food in the case of *Xákmok Kásek*, for example, the Court describes its role as being

> to assess the accessibility, availability and sustainability of the food given to the members of the community and determine whether the assistance provided satisfied the basic requirements of an adequate diet.[203]

The identified standards of 'accessibility', 'availability', 'sustainability' and 'sufficiency' are specifically based on CESCR General Comment No. 12.[204] Similarly, in assessing implementation of the right to water, the Court uses the standard of 'sufficient quantity' and 'adequate quality'[205] derived from CESCR General Comment No. 15[206] and WHO guidelines.[207]

It is also important that the development of substantive standards be undertaken with careful consideration of context. Commenting on the elaboration of standards for a dignified life in the indigenous context, Schettini raises concerns about the imposition of Western standards of 'well-being' on indigenous communities. Although, as noted in Section 4.3.3, in elaborating the 'minimum living conditions' required under Article 4 in the indigenous context the Court has stated the need to take into account the culture and way of life of affected communities, this is not given detailed consideration in elaborating the social and economic rights that are identified as being necessary for compliance with Article 4.[208] Such considerations are also absent from the 2017 Advisory Opinion. Schettini proposes the incorporation of the idea of 'living well' into the Article 4 jurisprudence. 'Living well', she suggests, is a concept that is being developed in discussion with indigenous communities and reflects a community-based worldview in which the interconnection and co-existence of humans and nature is fundamental. A paradigm shift is necessary, she contends, that challenges current models of development based on the idea of the 'commercialization of nature',[209] gives indigenous communities a voice, and promotes a sustainable economic strategy and 'a commitment to restoring the relationship between quality of life and nature.'[210] The Court has yet to recognise the need for dialogue, not only with indigenous peoples but with all communities, in order to develop substantive environmental standards that challenge unsustainable practices and incorporate an understanding of the fundamental interrelationship between environmental integrity and quality of life. A holistic approach rather than one that

203 *Xákmok Kásek* (n 52) para 198.
204 (n 170) paras 6–8.
205 *Xákmok Kásek* (n 52) para 196.
206 (n 170) para 12.
207 G Howard and J Bartram (n 162).
208 *Yakye Axa* (n 30) para 163.
209 A Schettini, 'Towards a New Paradigm of Human Rights Protection for Indigenous Peoples: A Critical Analysis of the Parameters Established by the Inter-American Court of Human Rights' (2012) 17 SUR 59, 65.
210 ibid 66.

addresses problems on an ad hoc basis is more likely to be successful in achieving the changes in attitudes and practice necessary to protect the environment in the long term. While the Court has made important progress in developing procedural environmental standards in its 2017 Advisory Opinion, more attention needs to be focused on the development of substantive environmental standards in order to achieve the goal of constructing a holistic framework that will foster meaningful change in practice.

4.4 CONCLUSION

The analysis above provides ample evidence of an ecologically literate reading of the ACHR by the Inter-American Commission and Court.[211] The recognition of collective property rights of indigenous peoples and the acknowledgement of the distinctive relationship between indigenous communities and their ancestral land are particularly important in demonstrating that different approaches to property are possible. This opens the way for an understanding of the interconnectedness of humans and the environment and of the collective interest of whole communities in a sustainable environment becoming integral to human rights thinking. The development of standards relating to a dignified life likewise demonstrates a sophisticated understanding of the indivisibility and interdependence of human rights and the particular importance of a healthy and sustainable environment for all human rights.[212]

The 2017 Advisory Opinion has added significant breadth and depth to the existing analysis of the importance of a healthy environment for all the rights protected under the ACHR. The elucidation in the 2017 Advisory Opinion of a wide range of environmental obligations and associated standards in the context of the rights to life and physical integrity, not confined to indigenous communities, has begun to provide a general framework for the holistic development of environmental standards. And the Court has provided a clear signal that the standards elucidated in the 2017 Advisory Opinion are not exclusive to implementation of the right to life and personal integrity, but apply to multiple rights, including the newly recognised substantive right to a healthy environment.[213] However, as noted in section 4.3.5, while procedural environmental standards provide an important layer of protection, a holistic approach to standards incorporating substantive environmental standards is needed to safeguard the environment more effectively in the long term.

[211] See LM Collins, 'An Ecologically Literate Reading of the Canadian Charter of Rights and Freedoms' (2009) 26 Windsor Review of Legal and Social Issues 7, 8.

[212] See E Grant, 'Re-Imagining Adjudication: Human Rights Courts and the Environment' in A Grear and E Grant (eds), *Thought, Law, Rights and Action in the Age of Environmental Crisis* (Elgar 2015) 155, 157; 2017 Advisory Opinion (n 10) paras 47–55.

[213] 2017 Advisory Opinion ibid paras 124–25.

The 2017 Advisory Opinion's recognition of the right to a healthy environment as a substantive right under Article 26 holds out great promise for further development of both procedural and substantive environmental standards, particularly in light of the important statement by the Court that the right to a healthy environment is not solely focused on protection of the environment to protect human interests; the right to a healthy environment protects all aspects of the environment for the benefit of all life.[214] The challenge is to ensure that future development of both procedural and substantive environmental standards under the ACHR fully incorporates this understanding.

214 ibid para 62.

5

The African Charter on Human and Peoples' Rights and Environmental Rights Standards

Louis J. Kotzé and Anél du Plessis

5.1 INTRODUCTION

It is unsurprising that the notion of standards has found a foothold in the human rights discourse and normatively in human rights law. Law, after all, is the ideal regulatory institution to set agreed standards for social behaviour; law uses standards to set a threshold for transgression and/or to determine the scope of whatever entitlement 'a law' creates or obligations a particular law imposes. It stands to reason that standards will also find expression in law's apex paradigm of constitutionalism and its associated constructs of human rights, which is arguably the highest juridical level at which to regulate a polity.

Constitutionally entrenching standards relating to various societal concerns in human rights could either be a symbolic or a concrete attempt to elevate juridical guarantees of certain entitlements and duties of performance, to protect these entitlements and ensure the performance of these duties as of right, and to ensure compliance with the duty to realise these entitlements; in other words, to create and enforce 'obligations of conduct and obligations of result'.[1] Human rights standards may be created to fill normative gaps; to address application gaps; and/or to address supervisory gaps where monitoring, enforcement and compliance arrangements are deficient.[2] Human rights standards may, however, also be engineered through judicial interpretation or construction to the extent that rights are often formulated in relative indeterminate language and then given more concrete meaning by the judiciary. The judiciary further upholds human rights standards and guards against hegemonic decision making in the checks and balances arrangement of politicised government systems. Considering the present worrying state of global socio-ecological (in)security and the need to augment environmental protection the world over, and considering the potential regulatory benefits human rights hold out

[1] Helen Young et al., 'Linking Rights and Standards: The Process of Developing "Rights-based" Minimum Standards on Food Security, Nutrition and Food Aid' (2004) 28 Disasters 142, 145.

[2] International Council on Human Rights Policy, *Human Rights Standards: Learning from Experience* (ICHRP 2006) 7–9; see in the environmental context, Loretta Feris, 'Constitutional Environmnetal Rights: An Under-Utilised Resource' (2008) 24 SAJHR 29.

in this respect, it is unsurprising that the notion of human rights standards has found its way into the environmental rights domain; an idea that this volume seeks to explore.

In this chapter, we investigate African regional human rights law, with specific reference to the environmental right in the 1981 African Charter on Human and Peoples Rights (ACHPR) and corresponding jurisprudence that might reveal the manifestation of standards related on the one hand to the environment envisaged in this right,[3] and on the other to the manner in which this right must be respected, protected, promoted and fulfilled.[4] Where appropriate, we also refer to domestic environment-related rights provisions in some African countries in order to contextualise the analysis of African regional law and to illustrate, briefly, how it plays out at the domestic level.

The analysis commences in Section 5.2 with a brief discussion of what we understand 'environmental rights standards' to mean and a view on the functions that such standards may possibly serve. We do this with reference to some domestic examples from African countries. In Section 5.3 we explore article 24 of the ACHPR with a view to determining if this right provides for standards or not. The subsequent discussion in Section 5.4 analyses the extent to which the African Commission on Human and Peoples' Rights (ACommHPR) and the African Court on Human and Peoples' Rights (ACourtHPR) have interpreted article 24 and related rights in the ACHPR, and whether these judicial institutions have contributed to identifying, clarifying and applying any standards related to the environment envisaged and/or the manner in which the environmental and related rights must be respected, protected, promoted and fulfilled. In Section 5.5 we offer a critical appraisal and commentary on the existence and viability of environmental rights standards emanating from the ACHPR, and we conclude the discussion in Section 5.6 with brief views on the way forward.

5.2 ENVIRONMENTAL RIGHTS STANDARDS

While there may be other approaches, we believe human rights standards could manifest in at least three ways (often simultaneously), i.e.: (a) in a qualitative abstract sense that is aspirational in relation to the interest protected, (b) in a quantitative concrete sense that determines a specific quantity or measured or measurable value in relation to the interest protected, and (c) in a directive sense that establishes a specific minimum obligation of required performance.

In an abstract qualitative sense, human rights are higher order standards in and of themselves in the sense that they provide a minimum threshold expressing shared values and guiding principles of a social order to which the majority of people are

[3] See the Charter's art 24.
[4] As per the Charter's art 25 and otherwise.

taken to consent.[5] This abstract genesis of human rights standards historically derives from the so-called International Bill of Rights which includes the 1948 Universal Declaration of Human Rights (UDHR);[6] the 1966 International Covenant on Civil and Political Rights (ICCPR);[7] and the 1966 International Covenant on Economic, Social and Cultural Rights (ICESCR).[8] With reference to these and other international and regional human rights instruments, the International Council on Human Rights says:

> [Human rights] Standards are defined as internationally negotiated or endorsed human rights documents (instruments), whether these are binding or not binding. Binding documents codify or create legal obligations or duties ('hard law'), while nonbinding documents make recommendations about norms of conduct and policy ('soft law').[9]

In their abstract manifestation, human rights are part of the ideal of constitutionalism and the rule of 'good' law, and they fulfil a symbolic, but nevertheless crucially important, role by providing an abstract qualitative minimum threshold of protection that revolves on (often esoteric) conceptions such as natural law, freedom of the person, democracy, justice and legitimacy. Examples of typical qualitative formulations of human rights standards in international law include: 'All human beings are born free and equal in dignity and rights'; 'Everyone has the right to life, liberty and security of person'; and 'No one shall be subjected to torture or to cruel, inhuman or degrading treatment or punishment'.[10] The minimum standards set out in these rights are expressed at a 'relatively high level of principle'.[11]

In a concrete quantitative sense, rights could explicitly provide quantifiable standards within the right itself, for example, minimum standards of levels of harm that amount to violations of a right. None of the three instruments in the International Bill of Rights provides for quantifiable standards of this kind. The closest any of these come to providing a concrete standard is in a subsequent interpretative instrument, namely General Comment No. 15 that elaborates the right to water,[12] which is implied in articles 11 and 12 of the

[5] Bosselmann explains that a constitution provides the clearest manifestation and evidence of a social order's values and guiding principles. This is because a constitution most comprehensively embodies the shared consensus of a pluralistic society. Klaus Bosselmann, Im Namen der Natur: Der Weg zum ökologischen Rechtsstaat (Scherz 1992) 190.

[6] United Nations General Assembly Resolution 217A of 10 December 1948; see also Chapter 2 of this volume by Sumudu Atapattu, which relates specifically to the international covenants.

[7] United Nations General Assembly Resolution 2200A (XXI) of 16 December 1966.

[8] United Nations General Assembly Resolution 2200A (XXI) of 16 December 1966. For a detailed treatment of these instruments, see Chapter 2 in this volume by Sumudu Atapattu.

[9] International Council on Human Rights Policy (n 2) 4.

[10] Articles 1, 3 and 5 of the Universal Declaration of Human Rights, 1948.

[11] Young et al. (n 1) 145.

[12] ICESCR General Comment No. 15, The Right to Water (Twenty-ninth Session, 2003), UN Doc E/C.12/2002/11 (2002); see also Sumudu Atapattu and Owen McIntyre in Chapters 2 and 7 of this volume respectively.

ICESCR.[13] While the ICESCR refers to the right to water in abstract qualitative terms, its General Comment No. 15, in setting out the quantity of water every person should be entitled to per day, references scholarship that indicates this to be fifty litres per person per day.[14] Still, in this instance, it cannot be said that the right to water provides for quantitative standards in the right itself. It rather does so by reference to subordinate instruments. The paucity in international human rights instruments to provide quantifiable standards in the rights themselves is arguably not surprising when one considers that States will usually be reluctant to ratify international conventions that set out binding quantifiable standards that they need to adhere to in explicit and concrete terms. A case in point is the Kyoto Protocol of 1997,[15] which is not a human rights instrument, but which clearly illustrates the disdain States have for binding themselves to minimum standards in international environmental law. While States have been far more receptive to the vaguer type or more indeterminate commitments they incur under the 2015 Paris Climate Agreement,[16] it is unlikely that they will commit themselves to binding quantifiable standards which create absolute obligations in international human, and for that matter environmental, rights instruments.

In their more common directive sense, human rights standards may surface as a specific obligation of required performance on the part of those responsible for the actualisation and protection of a right. Rights may set direct obligations to take measures to achieve outcomes, most often expressed as duties to 'respect', 'protect', 'promote' and 'fulfil', as we shall see in further sections of this chapter. In other words, rights may include standards that govern the planning and execution of activities and the making of decisions by duty bearers, including, for example, State governments. However, the language of such standards often falls into the category of indeterminacy through the use of nouns expressing outcomes such as 'protection', 'conservation' and 'preservation' and through the use of adjectives such as 'reasonable', 'equitable', 'optimal', 'adequate', 'necessary' and 'sustainable'.[17]

[13] Article 11 of the ICESCR provides in abstract qualitative terms: 'The States Parties to the present Covenant recognize the right of everyone to an adequate standard of living for himself and his family, including adequate food, clothing and housing, and to the continuous improvement of living conditions.' Article 12 states in similar terms: 'The States Parties to the present Covenant recognize the right of everyone to the enjoyment of the highest attainable standard of physical and mental health.'

[14] General Comment No. 15 (n 12) para 12. See specifically the reference in the Comment's fn 14 to Jamie Bartram and Guy Howard, Domestic Water Quantity, Service Level and Health: What Should Be the Goal for Water and Health Sectors (WHO 2002); Peter Gleick, 'Basic Water Requirements for Human Activities: Meeting Basic Needs' (1996) 21 Water Int 83. See also Owen McIntyre in Chapter 7 of this volume.

[15] UN Doc FCCC/CP/1997/7/Add.1 (10 December 1997) 37 ILM 22 (1998).

[16] UN Doc FCCC/CP/2015/L.9/Rev.1 (12 December 2015).

[17] See the discussion by Douglas Fisher, *Legal Reasoning in Environmental Law* (Edward Elgar 2013) 167.

Domestic environment-related rights in African jurisdictions largely mirror standards that are of an abstract qualitative and a directive nature in terms of obligations they create. They most often provide for qualitative instead of quantitative standards, and where quantitative standards are provided, this is usually in terms of subordinate legislation and not in the rights provisions themselves. One example is the right of access to water in section 27 of the Constitution of the Republic of South Africa, 1996 which employs terms such as 'sufficient' and 'reasonableness' and a reference to 'adequate' in the section 26 housing right. Another is this constitution's environmental right, which embraces terms such as 'not harmful to health or well-being'.[18]

But there are exceptions to this general trend in the African context. An example is the environmental right entrenched in the Constitution of Kenya of 2010. Article 42 provides 'every person has the right to a clean and healthy environment which includes the right to have the environment protected for the benefit of present and future generations through legislative and other measures'.[19] A selection of required legislative and other measures are subsequently set out in more detail in article 69, including the obligation on the State to 'work to achieve and maintain a tree cover of at least ten per cent of the land area of Kenya'.[20] This novel provision is indicative of the fact that (a) it is possible for constitutional rights to refer to measurable standards of quality or required action that one would usually find in environmental legislation,[21] and that (b) in African countries where industry has not developed yet to the extent that it can fully compete with its Northern counterparts, industrial pollution will not necessarily be the main concern as far as the scope of rights-based protection is concerned. The focus of environmental rights may at this point be directed at human and environmental security threats such as deforestation, thus explaining why a matter such as 'tree cover' is used in the Kenyan context as a minimum standard to concretise the obligations flowing from the country's constitutional environmental right.[22] Yet, this example seems to be an exception to the general rule, rather than it being indicative of a trend in African constitutions to provide for concrete, quantifiable standards in environmental rights themselves. One of the more recent national constitutions in Africa, that of Zimbabwe,[23] for example merely provides in section 73 that:

18 See Nathan Cooper in Chapter 13 of this volume for a comprehensive discussion.

19 Robert Kibugi, 'Development and the Balancing of Interests in Kenya' in Michael Faure and Willemien du Plessis (eds), *The Balancing of Interests in Environmental Law in Africa* (PULP 2012) 173.

20 ibid 171–74.

21 See also Stephen Turner's discussion of the Constitution of Bhutan in Chapter 15 of this volume.

22 Michael Faure and Willemien du Plessis, 'Introduction' in Michael Faure and Willemien du Plessis (eds) (n 19) xxi.

23 Constitution of Zimbabwe 2013.

Everyone has the right –

1. (a) to an environment that is not harmful to their health or well-being; and
   (b) to have the environment protected, for the benefit of present and future generations, through reasonable legislative and other measures that -
      (i) prevent pollution and ecological degradation;
      (ii) promote conservation; and
      (iii) secure ecologically sustainable development and use of natural resources while promoting economic and social development.
2. The State must take reasonable legislative and other measures within the limits of the resources available to it, to achieve the progressive realisation of the rights set out in this section.

The wording of this right is verbatim that of section 24 in the South African Constitution, save for the addition in the Zimbabwean Constitution of an internal limitation clause in section 73(2). The closest one gets to a standard in this instance is arguably that of 'harmfulness' and 'reasonability'.

Consequent on the foregoing analysis, and in line with most environmental rights formulations the world over, we conclude that the general trend in African environmental rights seems to be to provide for abstract and vague quantifiable standards (e.g. 'sufficiency', 'harmfulness' and 'reasonable measures') that are used as the basis upon which the legislative and executive authorities will set detailed quantifiable standards in subsequent legislation. The environmental rights in combination with any such legislation eventually become the tools for judicial declarations on the violation of relevant rights-based interests. It follows that the rights mostly include standards that are supposed to regulate activities and inform decisions in aspirational and abstract terms.

5.3 THE ACHPR'S ENVIRONMENTAL AND RELATED RIGHTS

Moving from the nature of standards as perceived through the lens of domestic environmental rights to a regional perspective, the ACHPR is Africa's central regional human rights instrument. It was unanimously adopted in 1981 under the aegis of the Organisation of African Unity (which has since been replaced by the African Union (AU)), and it came into effect in 1986. The ACHPR was the first regional human rights instrument in the world to provide an environmental right, which reads 'all peoples shall have the right to a general satisfactory environment favorable to their development'.[24] Today, the wording of this

[24] Article 24 of the ACHPR. See for a more general discussion, Werner Scholtz, 'Human Rights and the Environment in the African Union Context' in Werner Scholtz and Jonathan Verschuuren (eds), *Regional Environmental Law: Transregional Comparative Lessons in Pursuit of Sustainable Development* (Edward Elgar 2015) 102.

right largely mirrors that of other regional human rights instruments. For example, the 1969 American Convention on Human Rights, with its San Salvador Protocol of 1988, states that 'everyone shall have the right to live in a healthy environment and to have access to basic public services'.[25] The 2004 Arab Charter on Human Rights provides that 'every person has the right to an adequate standard of living for himself and his family, which ensures their well-being and a decent life, including food, clothing, housing, services and the right to a healthy environment'.[26]

The ACHPR's environmental right is complemented in its scope of protection by articles 13(3) and 16(1), which respectively provides for access to public services (e.g. water, waste and sanitation services) and entrenches the right of every individual to 'enjoy the best attainable state of physical and mental health'.[27] The right further functions alongside the environmental provision in the Constitutive Act of the African Union of 2000, which lists as one of the objectives of the AU to 'promote sustainable development at the economic, social and cultural levels as well as the integration of African economies';[28] and more specifically, to 'promote and protect human and people's rights in accordance with the African Charter on Human and People's Rights and other relevant human rights instruments'.[29] The link between human rights and environmental concerns has been explicitly recognised by the ACommHPR as well in its 2009 Resolution 153: Human Rights and Climate Change and the Need to Study its Impact in Africa.[30] The Revised African Convention on the Conservation of Nature and Natural Resources of 2003, which acts as an environmental framework convention for AU Member States, also explicitly recognises the centrality of a rights-based approach to the achievement of the Convention's objectives.[31] Clearly then, the AU and its Member States recognise the central importance, and fully support the use, of environment-related rights provisions in the

[25] Article 11(1); see further Chapter 4 by Evadne Grant in this volume.

[26] Article 38.

[27] See for a review of the development and interpretation of the so-called health right (art 16) Ebenezer Durojaye, 'The Approaches of the African Commission to the Right to Health under the African Charter' (2013) 7 LDD 393.

[28] Article 3(j). See more generally, Hennie Strydom, 'Introduction to Regional Environmental Law of the African Union' in Werner Scholtz and Jonathan Verschuuren (eds) (n 24) 21.

[29] Article 3(h). For additional background, see Anél du Plessis, 'The Balance of Sustainability Interests from the Perspective of the African Charter on Human and Peoples' Rights' in Michael Faure and Willemien du Plessis (eds) (n 19) 36–38; Erika de Wet and Anél du Plessis, 'The Meaning of Certain Substantive Obligations Distilled from International Human Rights Instruments for Constitutional Environmental Rights in South Africa' (2010) 10 AHRLJ 350–51.

[30] The African Commission on Human Rights and Peoples' Rights (African Commission), meeting at its Forty-sixth Ordinary Session held from 11 to 25 November in Banjul, The Gambia. <www.achpr.org/sessions/46th/resolutions/153/> accessed 21 July 2018.

[31] See, among others, art III of the Convention which explicitly refers to art 24 of the ACHPR.

achievement of environmental protection and sustainable development on the African continent.

Similar to the domestic constitutions of some African countries, the wording of the ACHPR's environmental right at most meets the criteria for it to provide qualitative standards of a directive nature. It is unlikely that the right provides for quantifiable, concrete standards when considering wording to the effect that the environment must be 'general satisfactory' and 'favourable' to development. Scholtz has remarked that the meaning of these terms is 'vague' and that 'it is evident that this substantive environmental right includes the promotion of a threshold of environmental quality, but it is unclear what the level entails'.[32] Van der Linde and Louw agree:

> The right as phrased in the African Charter is vague and ambiguous. No clear indication is given by the African Charter as to what the terms 'satisfactory' and 'environment' entail. This allowed for different interpretations as to the exact meaning of this right by human rights scholars and environmentalists. This lack of clarity has initiated both positive and negative aspects of the interpretation. In a positive sense, the vagueness in itself can allow for a wider and more accommodating interpretation of the right to a satisfactory environment. On the other hand, the impact also tolerates a narrower and more restricted sense of interpretation, not giving this right the full recognition it deserves.[33]

Presumably, a 'general satisfactory environment' could mean that environmental quality must be such that it allows people to fully realise their potential to develop 'favourably'. This means that the issue of human development is central to both the environmental right and any possible standard it seeks to impose.[34] To this end, article 22 of the ACHPR sets out the right to development:

1. All peoples shall have the right to their economic, social and cultural development with due regard to their freedom and identity and in the equal enjoyment of the common heritage of mankind.
2. States shall have the duty, individually or collectively, to ensure the exercise of the right to development.

The wording of article 24 implies that the issue of development is an integral part of the environmental right to the extent that 'favourable development' is contingent upon a 'general satisfactory environment'. This would not only mean that the core genesis of the environmental right is entirely anthropocentric, but also that any standards set out by the environmental right must be such that it ensures the 'favourable development' of people, including to ensure their right to development

32 Scholtz (n 24) 108.

33 Morné van der Linde and Lirette Louw, 'Considering the Interpretation and Implementation of Article 24 of the African Charter on Human and Peoples' Rights in Light of the SERAC Communication' (2003) 3 AHRLJ 167, 174.

34 See also du Plessis (n 29) 48.

under article 22. The one right is thus conditional on the other; a notion which is reaffirmed by the ACHPR in its preamble.[35] The wording of the right to development suggests that the standard it sets is entirely cast in abstract qualitative terms, and it is accordingly of little value to clarifying any quantitative standards that could flow from the environmental right.

That said, the reference in the environmental right to a 'general satisfactory environment' may have to be interpreted in the spirit of article 16 enunciating the right of everyone to 'the best attainable state of physical and mental health' and the duty of State parties to 'take the necessary measures to protect the health of their people'. Read together, articles 16 and 24 suggest that the environment to which people are entitled must be generally satisfactory to the extent that it will not impede the physical or mental health of humans. While this understanding gives some sense of direction in terms of an abstractive qualitative environmental rights standard, it remains wanting of specific and more general application as the physical and mental health risk profile of every person is different and context specific.[36]

The extent to which the ACommHPR and the ACourtHPR have endeavoured to provide greater clarity to the environmental right's threshold of a 'general satisfactory environment favorable [to the development of people]', as well as the latter's interlinkage with other rights, is investigated hereafter.

5.4 JUDICIAL INTERPRETATION

In the African regional context, the ACommHPR and the ACourtHPR fulfil the role of judicial oversight in respect of the ACHPR. The ACommHPR is a quasi-judicial institution and its decisions are nonbinding. It mostly serves to promote and protect human rights through documentation, studies, seminars, symposiums and conferences to disseminate information; to support other human rights institutions; and to make recommendations to governments through its communications.[37] The ACourtHPR, on the other hand, operates as a classic regional court which could deliver binding decisions. To date the ACourtHPR has, however, not decided any cases involving the ACHPR's environmental right.

The ACommHPR did, however, provide a comprehensive interpretation of the regional environmental right in the well-known SERAC Communication of 2002.[38]

35 The preamble states, among others, that 'it is henceforth essential to pay a [sic] particular attention to the right to development and that civil and political rights cannot be dissociated from economic, social and cultural rights in their conception as well as universality and that the satisfaction of economic, social and cultural rights is a guarantee for the enjoyment of civil and political rights'.

36 See, for example, the World Health Organisation, *Children's Environmental Health* (2018) <www.who.int/ceh/risks/en/> accessed 24 April 2018.

37 U Oji Umozurike, 'The African Charter on Human and Peoples' Rights' (1983) 77 AJIL 902, 908.

38 ACommHPR, 'Communication 155/96: Social and Economic Rights Action Center (SERAC) and Center for Economic and Social Rights (CESR) / Nigeria' <www.achpr.org/files/sessions/30th/comunications/155.96/achpr30_155_96_eng.pdf> accessed 24 April 2018. See for a detailed

The Communication was brought to the ACommHPR as an *actio popularis* by the Social and Economic Rights Action Center (SERAC) and the Centre for Economic and Social Rights (CESR).[39] According to the Communication, the military government of Nigeria had been directly involved in oil production through the State-owned Nigerian National Petroleum Company, and those operations caused environmental contamination which led to health problems among the Ogoni people (an indigenous community).[40] It was alleged that a number of avoidable oil spills had occurred with resultant pollution of water, common soil and air. In its Communication, the ACommHPR held that the ACHPR imposes on African governments positive (working towards purposive obligations to realise) and negative (working protectively against infringements and towards the limitation of government power) obligations to respect, protect, promote and fulfil the entire range of human rights contained in the Charter.[41] The Communication alleged the violation of, among others, article 16 (the right to health),[42] article 21 (the right to free disposal of wealth and resources),[43] and more importantly for present purposes, article 24 (the environmental right) of the ACHPR.[44] These, and all the other rights of the Charter, are binding on the Nigerian government because it has explicitly incorporated the provisions of the Charter into domestic law through the African Charter on Human and Peoples' Rights (Ratification and Enforcement) Act on 17 March 1983.[45] All the alleged violations, the Commission believed, must further be considered in light of the numerous concomitant human rights obligations imposed on the Nigerian government flowing from a range of international human rights instruments to which it is a party.[46] The ACommHPR ultimately

discussion, Van der Linde and Louw (n 33) 167–87; Dinah Shelton, 'Decision regarding Communication 155/96 (Social and Economic Action Center/Center for Economic and Social Rights v. Nigeria). Case No. ACHPR/COMM/A044/1' (2002) 96 AJIL 937, 942. Kaniye Ebeku, 'The Right to a Satisfactory Environment and the African Commission' (2003) 3 AHRLJ 149; C Nwobike, 'The African Commission on Human and Peoples' Rights and the Demystification of Second and Third Generation Rights under the African Charter: Social and Economic Rights Action Center (SERAC) and the Center for Economic and Social Rights (CESR) v Nigeria' (2005) 2 Afr J Leg Stud 129.

39 For an outline of the procedure, see *Social and Economic Rights Action Centre (SERAC) and Another v Nigeria* (2001) AHRLR 60 (ACHPR 2001).

40 Communication para 10.

41 ibid paras 43–48.

42 As mentioned earlier, art 16 states, *inter alia*, 'every individual shall have the right to enjoy the best attainable state of physical and mental health . . . States Parties . . . shall take the necessary measures to protect the health of their people'.

43 Article 21 provides 'all peoples shall freely dispose of their wealth and natural resources . . . States parties . . . shall undertake to eliminate all forms of foreign economic exploitation particularly that practiced by international monopolies so as to enable their peoples to fully benefit from the advantages derived from their national resources'.

44 The others were arts 2 (non-discrimination), 4 (respect of life and personal integrity), 14 (property right) and 18 (rights of the family).

45 Nwobike (n 38) 132–33.

46 Including the ICCPR, the ICESCR, the Convention on the Elimination of All Forms of Racial Discrimination, the Convention against Torture and Other Cruel, Inhuman or Degrading Treatment

found that the Nigerian government had failed to uphold the myriad duties it derives from the ACHPR, including the duties flowing from the environmental right. Regrettably, significant as it was, this finding is nonbinding as a result of the Commission's judicial status. It is at most 'a moral victory',[47] but we believe nevertheless an important one providing a solid judicial foundation which could be built upon by the ACourtHPR (and other courts the world over) in the future, a matter to which we return in this section.

A major hallmark of the Communication is the Commission's elaboration of a range of qualitative standards of obligation (or standards of duty) that article 24 creates. These are both negative and positive and they manifest at 'four levels of duties for a State that undertakes to adhere to a rights regime, namely the duty to respect, protect, promote, and fulfil these rights'.[48] The negative duty to 'respect' entails 'that the State should refrain from interfering in the enjoyment of all fundamental rights; it should respect right-holders, their freedoms, autonomy, resources, and liberty of their action'.[49] This duty also requires of the State to respect the free use of resources owned or at the disposal of the individual alone or in any form of association with others.[50] The second negative duty of the State is to 'protect' rights holders, including the obligation 'to take measures to protect beneficiaries of the protected rights against political, economic and social interferences'.[51] To this end, protection specifically entails the creation and maintenance of a 'framework by an effective interplay of laws and regulations so that individuals will be able to freely realize their rights and freedoms'.[52] The environmental right therefore in a 'negative' way obliges governments to desist from threatening the health and environment of their citizens, and it asks of governments to respect the environmental right through noninterventionist conduct. It further obliges governments not to condone practices, policies or legal measures that violate individual integrity.[53]

The positive obligation to 'promote' the enjoyment of the environmental right requires of the State to 'make sure that individuals are able to exercise their rights and freedoms, for example, by promoting tolerance, raising awareness, and even building infrastructures';[54] whereas the positive duty to 'fulfill' 'requires the State to fulfil the rights and freedoms it freely undertook under the various human rights regimes. It is more of a positive expectation on the part of the State to move

or Punishment, the Convention on the Elimination of All Forms of Discrimination Against Women and the Convention on the Rights of the Child.

47 Ebeku (n 38) 164.

48 Communication para 44.

49 ibid para 45.

50 ibid.

51 Communication para 46.

52 ibid.

53 ibid para 52.

54 Communication para 46.

its machinery towards the actual realisation of the rights'.[55] Juxtaposed against the environmental right, the Commission held that this right 'imposes clear obligations upon a government. It requires the State to take reasonable and other measures to prevent pollution and ecological degradation, to promote conservation, and to secure an ecologically sustainable development and use of natural resources.'[56] The ACommHPR further stated that in order for governments to comply with article 24, they must facilitate independent scientific monitoring of threatened environments; require and publish environmental and social impact studies prior to any major industrial development; undertake appropriate monitoring; provide information to those communities exposed to hazardous materials and activities; and provide meaningful opportunities for individuals to be heard and to participate in the development decisions affecting their communities.[57] These 'subsidiary' obligations[58] relate to some of the actions required to fulfil the foregoing substantive elements of the environmental right, i.e. obligations to ensure the right is realised in practice, which could point to the existence of standards of obligation in a procedural sense. The Nigerian government actually undertook positive measures by adopting some environmental laws and by creating suitable governance institutions to apply these laws with a view to giving effect to the environmental right, but:

> Despite these laws, the government of Nigeria failed to apply them to regulate the exploration of oil in Ogoniland . . . The lack of health facilities and infrastructure in the area in addition to an absence of health-related information on the effects of oil exploration amounted to a failure to fulfill Nigeria's obligations under the African Charter.[59]

All the foregoing positive and negative obligations relate to the substantive elements of the environmental right, namely maintaining a 'general satisfactory environment favorable to . . . development'. The environmental right, in the words of the ACommHPR, also 'recognize[s] the importance of a clean and safe environment'.[60] Despite these proclamations and the potential opportunity to clarify what is specifically meant by a 'general satisfactory environment favorable to . . . development' and 'a clean and safe environment', the Commission did not offer any further explanation, thus shying away from an attempt to elaborate any possible quantifiable standards of environmental quality that might be created by the right. It was only prepared to state that there are qualitative standards

55 ibid para 47.

56 ibid para 52. Arguably, the ACommHPR meant to use the phrase 'reasonable *legislative* and other measures'; a more common formulation as is exemplified by s 24 of the Constitution of the Republic of South Africa (1996).

57 Communication para 53.

58 See Fisher (n 17) 256.

59 Nwobike (n 38) 138.

60 Communication para 51.

of obligation (expressed as minimum duties) which the Nigerian government had to respect, protect, promote and fulfil.

Collectively considered, nothing in the Commission's decision suggests that article 24 provides quantitative human rights standards. To the extent that it sets out and creates a range of minimum obligations on government to respect, protect, promote and fulfil the right in question, it is argued that the Commission at most pronounced on standards of a directive nature, or standards of obligation. In other words, the Commission may have set standards in the form of specific performance obligations (actions) on the part of the Nigerian authorities. The Commission formulated detailed actions (subsidiary obligations) to achieve the outcomes envisaged by article 24, for example: independent scientific monitoring of threatened environments; environmental and social impact studies; appropriate monitoring; provision of information; and provision of meaningful opportunities for individuals to be heard and to participate in decision making.[61] However, the language of these directive 'standards' is still largely indeterminate as a result of the Commission's use of imprecise adjectives such as 'appropriate' and 'meaningful'.

Less celebrated, but nevertheless useful for the present discussion, are two further cases before the ACommHPR and the ACourtHPR . These cases have not directly dealt with the application of article 24 of the ACHPR, but they do provide some insights in relation to the notion of environmental standards in terms of the more general body of African human rights law. The case of *African Commission on Human and Peoples' Rights* v. *the Republic of Kenya*[62] concerned a notice of eviction which the Kenyan Government issued in 2009 to the Ogiek indigenous minority community of the Mau Forest. The community comprises about 20,000 members, approximately 15,000 of whom inhabit the greater Mau Forest area, a land mass of some 400,000 hectares.[63] In this matter the Ogiek argued before the ACommHPR that their eviction by the Kenyan Government would have far-reaching implications for the political, social and

61 Notably, in November 2016 a delegation of the ACommHPR is reported to have undertaken a Promotion Mission in Nigeria with the objective to promote human rights protection in the country. With respect to the environment the delegation observed the following positive developments: the Ogoniland clean-up and restoration programme; the Petroleum Industry Roadmap, with its seven key areas called 7 Big Wins; and efforts for achieving transparency in the extractive industries, including through the Nigerian Extractive Industries Transparency Initiative. The delegation, however, also raised the following concerns: continuing problems of oil spillage and gas flare-ups; a dated policy and regulatory regime governing the extractive industries, including weak regulations which do not hold the operation of the oil and gas industry to a high standard and ensure that revenues are used for development purposes; and the lack of effective implementation and delivery of various initiatives meant to resolve the problems of the Niger Delta. See ACHPR, 'Press Statement at the Conclusion of the Promotion Mission of the ACHPR to the Federal Republic of Nigeria' (2016) <www.achpr.org/press/2016/12/d335/> accessed 24 April 2018.

62 *Application 006/2012: African Commission on Human and Peoples' Rights v the Republic of Kenya* <www.african-court.org/en/index.php/56-pending-cases-details/864-app-no-006–2012-african-commission-on-human-and-peoples-rights-v-republic-of-kenya-details> accessed 21 July 2018.

63 ibid Order of Provisional Measures para 3.

economic survival of the community, even though the rationale behind the government's decision was the protection of the Mau Forest, which is a valuable water catchment area.[64] The Ogiek also demanded compensation for the loss they suffered, *inter alia*, through the loss of their natural resources. After the ACommHPR received the communication for the Ogiek community, they issued provisional measures requiring the government of Kenya to stop any further evictions or change of status of land in the Mau Forest that could prejudice the Ogiek. Due to the government's failure to comply with the provisional measures, the case was subsequently referred to the ACourtHPR by the ACommHPR. The *Ogiek* case was scheduled to be heard before the Court in March 2014, but the Kenyan Government requested an extension in order to submit their merits. In 2013, however, the Court issued an 'Order of Provisional Measures' in which it stated with reference to articles 2, 17, 3, 4, 14 and 22 of the ACHPR that:

> There exists a situation of extreme gravity and urgency, as well as a risk of irreparable harm to the Ogiek Community with regard to violation of their rights guaranteed under the Charter.[65]

On 27 and 28 November 2014, the ACourtHPR heard arguments from the ACommHPR's legal team as well as two Ogiek witnesses, an expert witness and an intervention by Minority Rights Group International on behalf of the original complainants.[66] The case was finally decided on 27 May 2017, and the Court declared that the Republic of Kenya had violated articles 1, 2, 8, 14, 17(2) and (3), 21 and 22 of the Charter.[67] The Court ordered the Kenyan government in an indeterminate yet directive manner to 'take all appropriate measures within a reasonable time frame to remedy all the violations established and to inform the Court of the measures taken within six (6) months from the date of this Judgment'. This became one of the first cases brought originally by non-governmental organisations to have been referred to the ACourtHPR by the ACommHPR, and is the first case to have reached the hearing stage.[68] While a violation of the article 24 environmental right has not been argued in this instance, it is relevant for present purposes that in the context of the ACHPR, abstract qualitative 'environmental' standards may arise from the collective protection of rights other than the environmental right, such as the rights of cultural minorities and the right of access to ancestral land. The protection of the cultural and livelihood-related rights of the Ogiek people was at the heart of the matter decided by the ACourtHPR . While the Court did not elaborate on this fact, it explicitly confirmed that the protection of these rights

64 ibid para 4.
65 ibid para 20.
66 See Minority Rights Group International, 'Kenya: Guaranteeing Ogiek Rights' (2016) <http://minorityrights.org/law-and-legal-cases/the-ogiek-case/> accessed 24 April 2018.
67 *Application 006/2012* (n 62).
68 ibid.

depends on the preservation of the natural resource base offered by the Mau Forest. The Court stated:

> The most salient feature of most indigenous populations is their strong attachment with nature, particularly, land and the natural environment. Their survival in a particular way depends on unhindered access to and use of their traditional land and the natural resources thereon. In this regard, the Ogieks, as a hunter-gatherer community, have for centuries dependend [sic] on the Mau Forest for their residence and as a source of their livelihood.[69]

And further that:

> the Respondent's public interest justification for evicting the Ogieks from the Mau Forest has been the preservation of the natural ecosystem. Nevertheless, it has not provided any evidence to the effect that the Ogieks' continued presence in the area is the main cause for the depletion of the natural environment in the area. Different reports prepared by or in collaboration with the Respondent on the situation of the Mau Forest also reveal that the main causes of the environmental degradation are encroachments upon the land by other groups and government excisions for settlements and ill-advised logging concessions ... the Court is of the view that the continued denial of access to and eviction from the Mau Forest of the Ogiek population cannot be necessary or proportionate to achieve the purported justification of preserving the natural ecosystem of the Mau Forest.[70]

Following its view on the rights that have been violated in this matter, the ACourtHPR continued to emphasise the general duties of State parties arising from article 1 of the ACHPR stating that parties shall 'undertake to adopt legislative or other measures' to give effect to the rights, duties and freedoms enshrined in the ACHPR.[71] It follows that to a large extent the *development* of any quantifiable or qualitative standards applicable in this matter was judicially deferred by the ACourtHPR to the Kenyan legislature and the executive, with a report-back duty which reserves a future position for the Court as a monitoring agent.

In the case of *Centre for Minority Rights Development, Minority Rights Group International and Endorois Welfare Council (on behalf of the Endorois Community)* v. *Kenya*,[72] the matter of land and the linkages between the natural environment and the livelihoods (right to development) of indigenous peoples were under consideration. In 2003, the Endorois Community lodged a complaint before the ACommHPR.[73] The case challenged the lack of consultation and compensation for the forced displacement of this community and lack of protection afforded to the

69 *Application* 006/2012 (n 62) para 109.

70 ibid para 130.

71 ibid para 214.

72 *Application 276/03: Centre for Minority Rights Development (Kenya) and Minority Rights Group (on behalf of Endorois Welfare Council) / Kenya.*

73 ibid.

Endorois' traditional way of life.[74] It claimed violations of the Endorois' rights to non-discrimination, property, access to natural resources on their land, religious and cultural life, and to development.[75] In this case, the ACommHPR declared the expulsion of the Endorois from their ancestral lands for purposes of the declaration and operation of a State game reserve illegal. The Commission found that the Kenyan government had failed to recognise and protect the Endorois' ancestral land rights and failed to provide sufficient compensation or alternative grazing land following their eviction, or to grant restitution of their land, and similarly failed to include the community within the relevant development processes. It also made a series of far-reaching recommendations for the Kenyan government to follow, including that it should ensure that the Endorois community had unrestricted access to Lake Bogoria and surrounding sites for religious and cultural rites, and for grazing their cattle.[76]

In affirming the Endorois' collective right to ancestral lands, the ACommHPR's decision has not only awarded a remedy to the Endorois community, but also significantly contributed to a better understanding and greater acceptance of various indigenous rights in Africa. According to Minority Rights International, this decision represents 'the first case globally in which a ruling has been made on a regional right to development'.[77] In our view, the Endorois decision serves to show that even in the absence of a claim based on the article 24 environmental right, it is possible in the context of other rights in the ACHPR for procedural abstract qualitative environmental standards to be set (i.e. derivative environmental access rights). It is also clear from the decision that different kinds of sustainability interests (such as nature conservation and cultural heritage protection) require careful judicial balancing as part of the protection of the right to development, which collectively provide for a broad range of qualitative standards that could improve the human condition. More importantly perhaps, where these qualitative human rights standards are transgressed, African judicial institutions have not hesitated to clarify the range of intertwined obligations that rest on governments to respect, protect, promote and fulfil the rights in question, including the myriad interests these rights envelope.

5.5 A CRITICAL APPRAISAL

Human rights, possibly more than any other juridical expression of constitutionalism, properly postulate the idea that people have certain universal (belonging to everyone everywhere); inborn (the fact of being human bestows a right); inalienable

74 ibid.

75 ibid.

76 ibid.

77 Minority Rights International, 'Kenya: Protecting the Endoroi's Right to Land' (2016) <http://minorityrights.org/law-and-legal-cases/centre-for-minority-rights-development-minority-rights-group-international-and-endorois-welfare-council-on-behalf-of-the-endorois-community-v-kenya-the-endorois-case/> accessed 24 April 2018.

and imprescriptible claims (rights cannot be transferred, forfeited, waived or lost due to them not being claimed) that may not be infringed upon by governments or by other persons.[78] Borne by the ideals of equality, humanism and liberalism and deriving their special status from the dignity that is inherent in every human being (*dignitas humana*), rights are considered to be the foundation of every society, the source of regime legitimisation and the point of departure of social ordering.[79] To this end, rights are considered 'primary, anchoring principles'[80] that are morally and normatively superior to subordinate legislation and other laws. The foregoing mostly reflects on the positive attributes of and virtuous perceptions associated with rights, but considerable criticism has been leveled against rights. One such criticism is that because the socio-economic, political and legal change that rights seek to achieve in constitutional orders is not always immediately apparent, rights have also understandably been described as 'all rhetoric and exhortation',[81] and as being too vague and abstract, often leading to insignificant concrete improvements of the myriad vulnerabilities they have been designed to address in the first place. This is possibly one of the reasons that we are having the debate about (environmental) human rights standards: standards are seen as a concrete way to increase the effectiveness of human rights, to set measurable targets and indicators of achievement and performance. It is a debate that lawyers intuitively pursue in our efforts to flesh out the abstract, esoteric and vague promise of human rights.

Yet, writing from the African regional perspective, we suggest that this debate must also consider that human rights, acting as abstract but powerful apex 'primary anchoring principles' are not always the ideal juridical medium to provide for quantitative standards. While human rights are ideally suited to entrench qualitative standards that are formulated in broad terms, detailed, measurable quantitative standards may have to rather be entrenched in subsequent legislation. Human rights jurisprudence and practice suggest that this is in fact the preferred approach. The additional role of the judiciary should also not be underestimated in this respect. Whereas constitutional law and regional human rights instruments may not necessarily lay down concrete quantitative environmental standards, it is not to say that case-specific circumstances will not require of the courts to set down specific standards fitting a specific case at a specific point in time. The courts are ideally situated to develop and pass on case specific standards regarding *what* must be done to advance people's environmental right interests and *how* things must be done to actively respect, protect, promote and fulfil the said interests. The courts are further responsible to balance the interests protected in terms of human rights – a task that may become exceptionally technical and even impossible when constitutions and

78 Francois Venter, *Constitutional Comparison: Japan, Germany, Canada and South Africa as Constitutional States* (Juta 2000) 127.

79 Udo di Fabio, 'Verfassungsstaat und Weltrecht' (2008) 39 Rechtstheorie 399, 408.

80 Lorraine Weinrib, 'Constitutionalism in the Age of Rights: A Prolegomenon' (2004) 121 SALJ 278, 285.

81 Louis Henkin, *The Age of Rights* (Columbia University Press 1990) 27.

other human rights instruments provide for specified quantifiable standards to be met. The ACommHPR, and to a lesser extent the ACourtHPR, have already gone a long way in emulating specific types of qualitative standards of obligation and procedure in relation to the environmental and related rights in the ACHPR. It might nevertheless be in the interest of both ensuring legal certainty and consistency with respect to the application of these rights, if the AU were to develop an accompanying commentary to the ACHPR, possibly similar to General Comment No. 15 to the ICESCR that further elaborates and concretises the environmental right. It is hoped, however, that despite its approach to settling the *Ogiek* case by way of judicial deference, that the ACourtHPR will step into the fray as it starts to adjudicate environmental rights-related cases. One particular advantage is that these decisions will be binding. If the Court is able to creatively elaborate the full spectrum of qualitative standards that the environmental and related rights provide, it could meaningfully contribute to setting a minimum regional threshold of compliance by governments to the dictates of these rights.[82] Such a development could at once also create important judicial precedents, not only in Africa at a regional level and in domestic jurisdictions where such precedents will inevitably filter down, but also for other judicial bodies the world over that engage with environmental rights jurisprudence. Especially with respect to the last point, the ACommHPR's creative interpretation of the ACHPR's environmental right in the SERAC Communication is not significant only because it was the first international judicial forum to elaborate this right (even though it did not develop quantifiable human rights standards), but also because it counters the perception that African judicial institutions are somehow less progressive than their American or European counterparts. As Murray, convincingly in our view, argues:

> African institutions offer some examples of progressive developments in international human rights law. Without feeling constrained by the traditional views of human rights, taking on their own backgrounds and also having to accommodate existing standards, African institutions illustrate a mixture of a variety of experiences and are therefore excellent fora in which human rights can be developed within existing frameworks. Through these systems, some challenges to international human rights law could enlighten and refocus principles as they are presently formulated.[83]

It is further clear from our analysis that African regional human rights law shows a limited manifestation of quantitative standards related to environmental

82 As Nwobike says: 'The African regional human rights system has come of age. The recent coming into force of the Protocol on the Establishment of an African Court on Human and Peoples' Rights marks a turning point in the system. Its contribution to the promotion and protection of human rights on the continent lies fundamentally in its ability to hand down declaratory and enforceable judgments.' Nwobike (n 38) 146.

83 Rachel Murray, 'International Human Rights: Neglect of Perspectives from African Institutions' (2006) 55 ICLQ 193, 197.

protection. From the African context we can see that measurable quantitative environmental standards entrenched in rights potentially run the risk of overlooking technical context-specific mediating needs and the kind of 'conclusiveness' in law that changing times demand. The overall emphasis is on adhering to qualitative standards of procedure and obligation in relation to the manner in which environmental rights must be respected, protected, promoted and fulfilled. Why is there such a hesitance to detail quantitative standards in addition to the general qualitative standards that human rights create, and is it justified? There may be several reasons and justifications.

First, the drafters of human rights instruments will arguably seek to provide sufficient content to realise as many specific obligations of conduct and obligations of result as one could reasonably expect from a modern-day constitutional State, but only within available financial and human capacity means and time constraints. A clear example is the panoply of socio-economic rights that the 1996 Constitution of the Republic of South Africa provides.[84] While it is desirable that human rights protection is as comprehensive, encompassing and effective as possible, it is also understandable that certain rights in some instances allow some leeway for governments (especially those operating in poor, developing country contexts such as in Africa) when it comes to the realisation of the objectives and content of those rights. Considering that environmental rights are often characterised as being inextricably linked to socio-economic rights and the issues the latter seek to protect, it is understandable that there would be equal reluctance on the part of a government to bind itself to quantitative apex constitutional standards that must be met. It appears in the African regional and domestic law context that there is rather a tendency towards standards that are of an abstract qualitative and a directive nature in terms of the various obligations they create. This approach may also be more conducive to the often highly intricate judicial balancing acts necessary to preside over a conflict of rights issue.[85] Specific environmental rights standards have the potential to excessively complicate the interpretational manoeuvring that the courts need to do in their weighing of competing rights-based interest, and more often trigger limitation, derogation or reservation clauses[86] where specific circumstances (e.g. states of emergency, public emergencies or natural disasters) make it impossible for authorities to comply with specified environmental standards.

84 Sections 26 and 27 of the Constitution; see also Nathan Cooper in Chapter 13 of this volume.

85 See for a discussion of an example where the access to housing right and the environmental right clashed in the local disaster management context in South Africa, Anél du Plessis and Angela van der Berg, 'Some Perspectives on Constitutional Conflict in Local Disaster Management through the Lens of *Pheko v Ekurhuleni Metropolitan Municipality*' 2012 2 SA 598 (CC)' (2013) 28 SAPL 448.

86 Article 27(2) of the ACHPR, for example, determines that: 'The rights and freedoms of each individual shall be exercised with due regard to the rights of others, collective security, morality and common interest'. See further, Laurent Serment, 'The Absence of a Derogation Clause from the African Charter on Human and Peoples' Rights: A Critical Discussion' (2007) 17 AHRLJ 142.

Second, constitutions and international human rights instruments generally, and by implication the human rights they entrench, are arguably not well suited to provide measurable quantitative standards. They are arguably best geared towards expressing aspirational or broadly idealistic qualitative standards of constitutionalism that seek to guarantee a stable and legitimate law and governance order that enables and regulates interaction between a polity's citizens *inter se* and between citizens and the State. Human rights instruments do so by providing restrictions on power and the provision of legal limits;[87] the provision of certain guarantees through the recognition and protection of rights; the separation of powers; an independent judiciary that has the power of judicial review and the possibility to review the constitutionality of laws and actions (be they actions by the State or by non-State parties); strict control over amendments to the constitution; and the rule of law.[88] It would appear from the wording of article 66 of the African Charter[89] that in the African regional context more measurable quantitative standards are left for 'special protocols or agreements', among others.

Third, quantitative environmental rights standards and the associated technicalisation of environmental rights may have unintended consequences. It has the potential to result in increased judicial deference due to the specialised nature of adjudicating on adherence to technical quantifiable standards. Some courts have not hesitated to express their concern for their capacity – 'both with respect to the ability to process the volumes of information at issue' and with respect to 'technical expertise to engage with choices under scrutiny'[90] – to analyse, evaluate and decide complex rights-based questions. With reference to South Africa, Brand explains that the courts have 'voiced concern for the threat to their institutional integrity that might arise from them reaching decisions and issuing orders that, for reasons out of their control, prove to be impossible to implement'.[91] At the domestic level this approach may follow from the *trias politica*, while at the African regional level, adjudicating bodies reaching decisions on environmental rights violations that do not heed the ability of a State to actually implement or provide may open up other questions. We should, however, avoid a situation where environmental rights standards result in courts or adjudicating institutions adopting a 'cautious' approach suggesting (in the parlance of judicial deference) that engaging with the issues

87 ***Restrictions on power are realised through constitutions, by them establishing separate sets of distinctions, both hierarchically (right–good or law–religion/morality; federal–state–municipality; and citizen–state) and horizontally (law–politics or legislative–executive–judiciary).*** Fábio Almeida, *The Emergence of Constitutionalism as an Evolutionary Adaptation* (ExpressO 2014).

88 See the discussion below.

89 Article 66 determines that: 'Special protocols or agreements may, if necessary, supplement the provisions of the present Charter.' See also ACHPR, 'Subsequent Standards Supplementing the African Charter' (2018) <www.achpr.org/instruments/achpr/subsequent-standards/> accessed 24 April 2018.

90 Danie Brand, 'Judicial Deference and Democracy in Socio-Economic Rights Cases in South Africa' (2011) 3 Stell LR 616.

91 ibid.

arising from such rights is 'simply not our business'.[92] Conversely, affected communities or individuals may encounter difficulties with the burden of proof following from environmental rights standards. The burden of proof to establish *prima facie* contravention of an environmental right standard may be very difficult or even at times impossible to discharge, because an individual or community may, for example, not have access to sufficient information, since the type of technical information needed to build a solid case is in the hands of industry or the State. Having said that, it may also be that one of the reasons behind the pursuit of environmental rights standards is a high burden of justification placed on the State (and others) in cases involving a deprivation of environmental rights.

Fourth, the concept of 'minimum core', in the interpretation of the rights in the African Charter specifically, focuses on peoples' most basic ***human*** needs *vis-à-vis* the ability of the State to provide the means to satisfy these needs. It has been stated before that within the context of the African regional human rights system, the African Court has embraced the notion of the minimum core obligation in its interpretation of State parties' obligations in terms of the ACHPR.[93] According to the ACommHPR, State parties have an obligation at least to ensure the satisfaction of the minimum essential levels of each of the socio-economic rights guaranteed in the Charter.[94] This obligation requires State parties to ensure that no significant number of individuals is deprived of the essential elements of a particular socio-economic right.[95] According to the ACommHPR, the minimum core obligation exists regardless of the availability of resources, and this obligation is non-derogable.[96]

In the 2010 Principles and Guidelines on the Implementation of Economic, Social and Cultural Rights in the African Charter on Human and Peoples Rights, the concept of minimum core intersects with the article 24 environmental right only with reference to a derivative right to water and sanitation, and only to the extent that State parties should in terms of para 92:

> (a) Ensure access to the minimum essential amount of water, that is sufficient and safe for personal and domestic use, including preventing disease, together with access to adequate sanitation; (b) Ensure safe physical access to water facilities or services that provide sufficient, safe and regular water; that have an adequate number of water outlets to avoid prohibitive waiting times; and that are at

92 See for a more extensive discussion in relation to socioeconomic rights adjudication and deference generally, Brand (n 90) 624–30.

93 Oliver Fuo and Anél du Plessis, 'In the Face of Judicial Deference: Taking the Minimum Core of Socio-Economic Right to the Local Government Sphere' (2015) 19 LDD 6. See further ACommHPR, 'Principles and Guidelines on the Implementation of Economic, Social and Cultural Rights in the African Charter on Human and Peoples Rights' (2010) <www.achpr.org/files/instruments/economic-social-cultural/achpr_instr_guide_draft_esc_rights_eng.pdf> accessed 24 April 2018, 13.

94 ACommHPR (ibid) 13.

95 ibid.

96 ibid.

a reasonable distance from the household; education institution, workplace or health institution; and (c) Refrain from using access to water as a political tool.[97]

The ACommHPR has stressed that where a State party suffers from demonstrable resource constraints, it remains under the obligation to implement the minimum essential levels of each right for vulnerable and disadvantaged groups by prioritising them in all legislative and policy interventions.[98] Vulnerable and disadvantaged groups in this context are people who have faced and/or continue to face significant obstacles to their enjoyment of socio-economic amenities.[99] The obligation to realise the minimum core content of socio-economic rights means that 'the state should prioritise the realisation of the rights for the poorest and most vulnerable in society' while progressively seeking to realise the rights of all.[100] The poorest segment of society could in this context refer to those living in extreme social deprivation. The position taken by the ACommHPR appears to create an almost absolute right for the poorest people in society to receive minimum essential services under the rights provided for in the ACHPR. The focus is not on any explicit (environmental) rights standard(s), and even less so on a minimum core in relation to a standard, for example, in relation to the protection of biodiversity or fresh water resources. Instead, the 'access' rights of the most vulnerable in society are emphasised. This is not to say, though, that standards emanating from international environmental rights may not find interpretive application on the basis of articles 60 and 61 of the ACHPR.[101]

5.6 CONCLUSION

Notwithstanding their distinctive functions within the legal system, legal rules and principles as well as human rights collectively constitute the 'standards' and 'criteria' according to which human activity and human decision making take place.[102] It is generally accepted in the literature and in practice that human rights mostly provide for abstract qualitative standards. Our analysis above suggests that this is also the case in terms of domestic and regional environmental rights in Africa.

Yet there seems to be a growing desire, rightly or wrongly, to develop and pronounce more explicit quantifiable or computable standards for human rights. As this volume suggests, the discussion on standards in human rights is particularly pronounced in the

97 ibid 51.
98 ibid 13.
99 ibid 8–9. There is a long list of people classified as disadvantaged and vulnerable.
100 ibid 13.
101 These articles oblige the AComHPR to take into consideration the principles and provisions of other African and international law instruments as well as international legal precedents and doctrine.
102 Fisher (n 17) 56.

context of environmental rights, especially insofar as lawyers continuously attempt to give clearer substantive meaning to rights-based environmental claims, seek to visibly improve the impact and protective guarantees environmental rights potentially offer, and generally to extend the real impact of these rights. This is an important discussion that is borne out in scholarly debates, and one that will arguably gain increased traction in legislative, executive and judicial institutions as a response to the increasingly critical need to devise and augment solutions to the many deepening socio-ecological challenges facing humanity today.

6

The Aarhus Convention: Standards for Access to Justice in Environmental Matters

*Áine Ryall**

6.1 INTRODUCTION

The Aarhus Convention[1] (the Convention) is an international treaty under the auspices of the United Nations Economic Commission for Europe (UNECE). It guarantees three interconnected procedural rights: the right to information; the right to participate in decision making; and the right of access to justice in environmental matters. The Convention is groundbreaking in linking environmental rights and human rights. Its overarching objective is to contribute to the right of every person of present and future generations to live in an environment adequate to their health and well-being.[2] The Convention aims to strengthen environmental governance by providing opportunities for an informed public to express concerns about activities which may have a significant effect on the environment and insisting that public authorities take account of those concerns. Transparency and accountability in decision making is advanced by improving public access to environmental information and providing accessible, affordable and effective review mechanisms to ensure that the law is applied correctly and enforced by the courts where necessary. The Convention places special emphasis on the role played by non-governmental organisations (NGOs) in environmental protection, in particular by enabling them to enforce the law in the public interest.

This chapter examines the development of standards within the context of the rights guaranteed under the Convention and the obligations undertaken by State Parties (i.e. States that have ratified, and are therefore bound by, the Convention as a matter of international law). It focuses on how the Aarhus Convention Compliance Committee

* School of Law, University College Cork, Ireland and Vice-Chair of the Aarhus Convention Compliance Committee. The views expressed here are those of the author alone. I thank the participants at the symposium on Standards in Environmental Rights held at Lincoln Law School on 10 May 2016 and Dr Stephen Turner and Dr Jona Razaque for their comments on the draft paper on which this chapter is based.

1 United Nations Economic Commission for Europe (UNECE) Convention on Access to Information, Public Participation in Decision-Making and Access to Justice in Environmental Matters, 28 June 1998, 2161 UNTS 447 (Aarhus Convention).

2 ibid Preamble art 1 and Recitals 6 to 8.

(the Compliance Committee) and the Court of Justice of the European Union (CJEU) have developed these standards over time. Of course, courts and tribunals at national level are also involved intensively in interpreting, applying and enforcing Convention obligations. In order to provide a detailed account, this chapter focuses exclusively on the role of the Compliance Committee and the CJEU in developing standards within the framework of the Convention.

As is common in international instruments, certain obligations articulated in the Convention are drafted in general terms and leave a measure of flexibility to the Parties. This can lead to genuine disputes as to the scope and meaning of these obligations and their practical implications. In drafting international instruments such as the Convention, the fundamental challenge is to create obligations, and set standards associated with those obligations, that provide clear, workable and enforceable benchmarks while, at the same time, leaving an appropriate measure of flexibility to Parties to accommodate the specific legal, administrative, social and cultural conditions operating in a particular State.

Sharp tensions can arise where obligations set at international level do not fit neatly with well-established law and practice at local level. Parties can be resistant to change in such circumstances, particularly when there may be significant resource implications associated with full implementation of Convention obligations. For example, delivering timely access to environmental information and affordable and timely access to justice in environmental matters may prove challenging in States where resources are limited and public authorities and the courts are under pressure due to heavy workloads. Where disputes arise over implementation, the Compliance Committee and the CJEU play a vital role in interpreting Convention obligations and identifying the standards that must be met to deliver compliance.

The chapter begins by introducing the Convention and explaining the institutional framework in which it operates, including its innovative compliance mechanism (Section 6.2). It then traces how standards have evolved as the Compliance Committee and the CJEU have interpreted Convention provisions in the context of specific cases that have come before them (Section 6.3). Based on the jurisprudence developed by the Compliance Committee and the CJEU to date, three particular areas emerge as potential case studies on the development of standards within the framework of the Convention: the interpretation of the concept of a 'reasonable' charge for the supply of environmental information (Article 4(8));[3] the obligation to deliver 'early' and 'effective' public participation (Article 6(3) and (4));[4] and the obligation to deliver access to justice in environmental matters that is not 'prohibitively expensive' (Article 9(4)).[5]

This chapter selects the obligation in Article 9(4) to deliver affordable access to justice for detailed treatment. This sharp focus is necessary in order to provide a full

[3] See further UNECE, *The Aarhus Convention: An Implementation Guide* (2nd edn, UNECE 2014) 94.
[4] ibid 142–46.
[5] ibid 203–04.

account of the gradual evolution of standards and to explain the role of the Compliance Committee and the CJEU in promoting common standards for the enforcement of environmental rights across the UNECE region and in the European Union (EU) respectively. This account is followed by a critical appraisal of the evolution of standards within the framework of the Convention (section 6.4). The chapter concludes by assessing the current position and considers likely future developments.

6.2 THE AARHUS CONVENTION

The Convention opened for signature in June 1998 and entered into force on 30 October 2001. There are now forty-seven Parties to the Convention, including the EU and the twenty-eight Member States.[6] NGOs played a very significant role in the negotiations that led to the Convention text as adopted.[7] The recitals in the Preamble recall the Convention's origins.[8] A series of well-known international declarations, resolutions and other instruments played a major role in the creation of the Convention and influenced its content significantly.[9] Among the most important influences were: the Stockholm Declaration;[10] the World Charter for Nature;[11] the Environmental Impact Assessment (EIA) Directive;[12] the Brundtland Report;[13] the Directive on the Freedom of Access to Information on the Environment;[14] the Espoo Convention;[15] the Rio Declaration;[16] and the UNECE Guidelines on Access to

6 Notwithstanding the outcome of the referendum on EU membership held in the United Kingdom on 23 June 2016, where a majority voted to leave the EU ('Brexit'), the United Kingdom remains a Member State of the EU until the formal withdrawal process is completed in accordance with the EU Treaties. It is anticipated that the United Kingdom will remain a Party to the Aarhus Convention post-Brexit.

7 The reports of the sessions of the Ad Hoc Working Group for the preparation of a draft Convention on Access to Information and Public Participation in Environmental Decision-Making (1996–98) record the negotiations leading up to the adoption of the Convention. These reports are available at: <www.unece.org/env/pp/adwg.html> accessed 25 May 2018.

8 Aarhus Convention (n 1) Recitals 1–4, 22 and 23.

9 For a concise overview of the origins and development of the Convention see *The Aarhus Convention: An Implementation Guide* (n 3) 16–17.

10 Declaration of the United Nations Conference on the Human Environment, UN Doc A/CONF 48/14/Rev 1 (New York, 1972) (Stockholm Declaration).

11 World Charter for Nature (28 October 1982) UN DOC A/RES/37/7.

12 Directive 85/337/EEC on the assessment of the effects of certain public and private projects on the environment [1985] OJ L175/40.

13 Report of the World Commission on Environment and Development, *Our Common Future*, 10 March 1987, Annex to UN Doc A/42/427 (Brundtland Report).

14 Directive 90/313/EEC on the Freedom of Access to Information on the Environment [1990] OJ L158/56.

15 Convention on Environmental Impact Assessment in a Transboundary Context, 25 February 1991, 1989 UNTS 309 (Espoo Convention).

16 Rio Declaration on Environment and Development (13 June 1992) UN Doc A/CONF 151/26 Rev 1 (Rio Declaration).

Environmental Information and Public Participation in Environmental Decision-making.[17]

Reflecting principle 10 of the Rio Declaration,[18] the Convention is built around three core procedural environmental rights: the right to information; the right to participate in decision making; and the right of access to justice in environmental matters. The overarching objective is articulated in Article 1, which adopts a rights-based approach and also echoes elements found in principle 1 of the Stockholm Declaration:[19]

> In order to contribute to the protection of the right of every person of present and future generations to live in an environment adequate to his or her health and well-being, each Party shall guarantee the rights of access to information, public participation in decision-making and access to justice in environmental matters in accordance with the provisions of this Convention.

The three procedural rights are presented in Article 1 as underpinning the right to an environment 'adequate' to a person's health and well-being. Recital 6 in the Preamble recognises that 'adequate' environmental protection 'is essential to human well-being and the enjoyment of basic human rights, including the right to life itself'. The Convention is groundbreaking in linking environmental rights and human rights, and Article 1 has been described as 'one of the clearest statements in international law of a fundamental right to a healthy environment'.[20] The following statement from the Aarhus Convention Implementation Guide is instructive as to the ambitious intention behind the Convention as articulated in Article 1:

> The Aarhus Convention provides a set of minimum standards to Parties to guide them on how to protect the right to a healthy environment. The obligations of the Convention must be considered in this light – not as commitments among nations for the promotion of good-neighbourly relations, but as important benchmarks for contributing to the basic welfare of the public.
>
> Authorities should not look to the Convention as a set of strict and burdensome obligations to be minimized – if not avoided altogether – but rather as a valuable

17 *UNECE Guidelines on Access to Environmental Information and Public Participation in Environmental Decision-Making*, Third Ministerial Conference, Environment for Europe, 25 October 1995.

18 Rio Declaration (n 16) Principle 10 provides that:

> Environmental issues are best handled with participation of all concerned citizens, at the relevant level. At the national level, each individual shall have appropriate access to information concerning the environment that is held by public authorities, including information on hazardous materials and activities in their communities, and the opportunity to participate in decision-making processes. States shall facilitate and encourage public awareness and participation by making information widely available. Effective access to judicial and administrative proceedings, including redress and remedy, shall be provided.

19 Stockholm Declaration (n 10).

20 *The Aarhus Convention: An Implementation Guide* (n 3) 42.

tool to support them in discharging their responsibility to help the public to overcome the challenges of the times.[21]

The objective is to support the right to a healthy environment and to encourage Parties to push the boundaries and build on the minimum guarantees established in the Convention text. Section 6.2.1 explains the specific environmental rights guaranteed in the Convention and the institutional framework in which they reside.

6.2.1 *Aarhus Convention: Structure, Content and Compliance Mechanism*

The Convention is structured around three procedural environmental rights. With a view to supporting the practical implementation of these rights, Article 3 establishes a set of overarching 'general provisions' which create the following obligations on Parties: to establish and maintain a clear, transparent and consistent framework to implement Convention provisions;[22] to endeavour to ensure that officials and authorities assist and provide guidance to the public on their Convention rights;[23] to promote environmental education and awareness among the public;[24] and to provide appropriate recognition and support to environmental NGOs.[25] These obligations are essential to support the delivery of the Convention rights in practice. Article 3(5) confirms that the Convention sets a minimum standard; there is nothing to prevent Parties from providing broader access to information, more extensive participation and wider access to justice than that mandated by the terms of the Convention. A Party may decide, for example, not to include all of the exceptions to the right of access to environmental information provided for in Article 4(4) of the Convention in its domestic legal framework, or a Party may opt to extend participation rights to a wider range of decisions than those specified in Article 6(1).

6.2.1.1 The Right of Access to Environmental Information

Article 4 provides for the right of access to environmental information held by public authorities, on request and without having to state an interest, subject to certain exceptions.[26] It sets out the formalities and procedures by which the right is to be delivered in practice, including time limits governing the release of information. Recital 17 in the Preamble to the Convention acknowledges explicitly that public authorities hold environmental information in the public interest. This provision is important when it comes to applying the exceptions to the right of access set out in Article 4(4). These exceptions must

21 ibid 42–43.
22 Aarhus Convention (n 1) art 3(1).
23 ibid art 3(2).
24 ibid art 3(3).
25 ibid art 3(4).
26 'Public authority' and 'environmental information' are defined in broad terms in the Aarhus Convention (n 1) arts 2(2) and (3).

always be interpreted restrictively, taking into account the public interest served by disclosure. The Convention therefore creates a strong presumption in favour of information disclosure.

Article 4(2) sets a timeframe within which public authorities must respond to requests for access. It demands that, unless exempt from disclosure, the information must be released 'as soon as possible' and, at the latest, within one month after the request has been submitted by the applicant.[27] As regards the possibility of charges in the context of environmental information requests, Article 4(8) grants public authorities a discretion to levy a charge for supplying information, but any such charge must not exceed a 'reasonable' amount. Both the Compliance Committee and the CJEU have been called on to examine the concept of a reasonable charge and have clarified how to interpret this standard and to employ it as a benchmark in particular cases.[28] The overarching principle that has emerged from the jurisprudence to date is that a charge cannot be set at such a level that it may deter individuals and NGOs wishing to obtain environmental information or restrict their right of access to such information;[29] in other words, a purposive approach is adopted to the concept of a reasonable charge.

Article 5 governs the proactive collection and dissemination of environmental information by public authorities. Essentially, authorities must possess and update environmental information relevant to their functions and put practical arrangements in place to support the right of access.[30] There is a specific obligation to ensure that environmental information is made available progressively in easily accessible electronic databases.[31]

A close study of the text of Articles 4 and 5 of the Convention confirms the strong influence of Directive 90/313/EEC on the Freedom of Access to Information on the Environment.[32] However, the Convention provisions improve considerably on the relatively weak access regime created in that early directive. Whereas the 1990 directive merely provided for 'freedom' of access, Article 4 of the Convention guarantees a 'right' of access to environmental information and goes much further to restrict the situations in which a public authority may lawfully withhold

[27] ibid Article 4(2) makes provision for this period to be extended, up to a maximum period of two months after the request has been submitted, in circumstances where the volume and complexity of the information requested justify an extension. The applicant must be informed of any extension to the time period for the public authority's response and of the reasons justifying it.

[28] Consider, for example, ACCC/C/2008/24 Spain ECE/MP.PP/C.1/2009/8/Add.1 paras 75–79 where the Compliance Committee determined that the charge levied by the public authority in this case (€2.05 per one-sided page for a photocopy) was unreasonable. Spain had therefore failed to comply with the obligation in art 4(8). For the most recent CJEU jurisprudence on this point see Case C-71/14 *East Sussex County Council v Information Commissioner, Property Search Group and Local Government Association* EU:C:2015:656 paras 27–45.

[29] ibid para 42.

[30] Aarhus Convention (n 1) arts 5(1) and (2).

[31] ibid art 5(3).

[32] Directive 90/313/EEC on the freedom of access to information on the environment [1990] OJ L158/56.

information.[33] Prior to its ratification of the Convention in 2005, the EU adopted a revised directive on public access to environmental information (Directive 2003/4/EC)[34] with the aim of implementing the Aarhus access to information obligations in the Member States.

6.2.1.2 The Right to Participate in Decision Making

Article 6 guarantees 'the public concerned'[35] the right to participate in decisions on whether to permit certain proposed activities. The public concerned must be informed of specified matters at an early stage in the decision-making procedure and in an 'adequate, timely and effective manner'.[36] The procedures governing participation must include 'reasonable' timeframes for the different stages of the decision-making process, allowing sufficient time to inform the public and to enable them to prepare and participate effectively.[37] Parties must provide for 'early' public participation, when all options are open and 'effective' participation can take place.[38] The public is entitled to submit comments, information, analyses or opinions that it considers relevant to the proposed activity and the decision-maker must take 'due account' of the outcome of the public participation process.[39] The decision taken by the public authority, together with the reasons and considerations on which it is based, must be accessible to the public.[40]

A close reading of Article 6 reveals the strong influence of the original EIA Directive which was adopted in 1985.[41] The Convention provisions build on the participation obligations found in that early directive and are more specific as regards the quality of participation that must be delivered. In particular, Article 6(4) of the Convention obliges Parties to provide for early public participation when

33 Aarhus Convention (n 1) arts 4(1), 4(3) and 4(4).

34 Directive 2003/4/EC on public access to environmental information [2003] OJ L41/26.

35 The 'public concerned' is defined in the Aarhus Convention (n 1) art 2(5) as 'the public affected or likely to be affected by, or having an interest in, the environmental decision-making; for the purposes of this definition [NGOs] promoting environmental protection and meeting any requirements under national law shall be deemed to have an interest'.

36 Aarhus Convention (n 1) art 6(2).

37 ibid art 6(3).

38 ibid art 6(4).

39 ibid arts 6(7) and (8). See *The Aarhus Convention: An Implementation Guide* (n 3) 144–46 for selected examples of Compliance Committee jurisprudence on this point. See generally the *Maastricht Recommendations on Promoting Effective Public Participation in Decision-Making in Environmental Matters* (prepared under the Aarhus Convention) (UNECE 2014). On the 'early' and 'effective' opportunities for participation point in the context of the Strategic Environmental Assessment (SEA) Directive (Directive 2001/42/EC on the assessment of the effects of certain plans and programmes on the environment [2001] OJ L 197/30) see the CJEU judgment in Case C-474/10 *Department of the Environment for Northern Ireland v Seaport Investments (NI) Ltd & Others* EU:C:2011:681 paras 44–50.

40 Aarhus Convention (n 1) art 6(9).

41 Directive 85/337/EEC on the Assessment of the Effects of Certain Public and Private Projects on the Environment [1985] OJ L175/40.

all options are still open[42] and effective participation can take place. Prior to its ratification of the Convention, the EU adopted significant amendments to the EIA Directive, and a number of other environmental directives, to give effect to the enhanced public participation rights mandated by the Convention.[43]

Article 7 of the Convention governs public participation during the preparation of plans, programmes and policies relating to the environment, while Article 8 obliges Parties to strive to promote effective participation during the preparation of executive regulations and other generally applicable legally binding normative instruments. The specific participation obligations arising under Articles 7 and 8 are significant, although less onerous on Parties than those mandated in the case of specific activities falling within the scope of Article 6.

6.2.1.3 The Right of Access to Justice

A very specific concept of justice lies at the heart of the Convention. It centres around the goal of effective enforcement of environmental law. This goal is to be achieved by guaranteeing a right of access to robust review procedures, either before a court or another independent tribunal established by law, that may be invoked by the public and NGOs. The rights guaranteed in the Convention, and environmental protection laws generally, are at risk of being undermined in practice in the absence of accessible, affordable and effective enforcement mechanisms.[44]

Article 9(1) governs remedies where a public authority fails to deal with a request for access to information in accordance with Article 4 of the Convention. Essentially, in this situation, Parties must provide for review of a public authority's decision before a court of law or another independent body.[45] As regards enforcement of the right to participate in decision making, Article 9(2) provides that qualified members of the public concerned[46] must have access to a review procedure to challenge the substantive and procedural legality of any decision, act or omission that is subject to the participation obligations in Article 6. At a minimum, the Convention requires that members of the public concerned who can establish either 'a sufficient interest' or impairment of a right (where national administrative law or procedural rules set this as a requirement) have standing to invoke the review procedure. National standing rules must deliver 'wide' access to justice in this

42 Essentially, this means that 'the public authority must still be in the information gathering and processing stage and must be open to persuasion by members of the public to change its position or opinion': *The Aarhus Convention: An Implementation Guide* (n 3) 144.

43 Directive 2003/35/EC providing for public participation in respect of the drawing up of certain plans and programmes relating to the environment and amending with regard to public participation and access to justice Council Directives 85/337/EEC and 96/61/EC [2003] OJ L156/17.

44 Aarhus Convention (n 1) Recital 18 in the Preamble to the Convention confirms that 'effective judicial mechanisms' must be available to ensure that the law is enforced.

45 ibid Article 9(1) insists that where a Party opts for review before a court, it must ensure that there is also access to an expeditious, non-judicial procedure that is either free of charge or inexpensive.

46 Defined in ibid art 2(5).

context. This is an important benchmark which limits Parties' discretion to set restrictive standing rules.

Under Article 9(2), it is clear that NGOs which: (1) promote environmental protection and (2) meet any criteria set in national law[47] enjoy standing to invoke the review procedure.[48] In other words, NGOs that satisfy these two requirements do not have to demonstrate a 'sufficient interest' or impairment of a right; their interest is, to use the wording of Article 9(2), 'deemed' to be sufficient and they are also 'deemed' to have rights capable of being impaired. This generous approach to standing for environmental NGOs confirms the importance the Convention attaches to such organisations and the significant role that they play in enforcing environmental law in the public interest.[49]

Article 9(3) supplements Article 9(1) and (2) by providing the public with a general right of access to justice to enforce environmental law.[50] It envisages that members of the public who meet the requirements (if any) set down in national law may take action to enforce environmental law directly, such as by initiating a case before a court to have the law enforced, or in an indirect manner, for example by triggering enforcement action by the relevant national authorities.[51]

Article 9(4) sets down minimum standards for the review procedures required under Article 9(1), (2) and (3).[52] These review procedures must provide 'adequate and effective remedies', including injunctive relief as appropriate, and must be 'fair, equitable, timely and not prohibitively expensive'.[53] Decisions taken under Article 9 must be given or recorded in writing and decisions of courts must be publicly accessible.[54]

Article 9(5) creates a number of important practical obligations aimed at furthering the effectiveness of the access to justice provisions in the Convention. It requires Parties to 'consider' establishing 'appropriate assistance mechanisms to remove or reduce financial and other barriers to access to justice',[55] and to provide information to the public on access to administrative and judicial review procedures.[56]

47 There is no requirement in the Convention that Parties must actually set such criteria. Should they choose to do so, the criteria that Parties could potentially consider putting in place in this context might include, for example, a requirement that an NGO has been active for a minimum period of time and that it operates on a not-for-profit basis.

48 On the narrow scope of the discretion vested in Parties under art 2(5) of the Convention to set criteria at the national level that NGOs must meet, see *The Aarhus Convention: An Implementation Guide* (n 3) 57–58.

49 See further on this point *The Aarhus Convention: An Implementation Guide* (n 3) 58.

50 The obligation in art 9(3) is stated expressly to be 'in addition and without prejudice to' the review procedures referred to in arts 9(1) and (2).

51 See further *The Aarhus Convention: An Implementation Guide* (n 3) 197–99.

52 The requirements in art 9(4) are stated expressly to be 'in addition to, and without prejudice to' the procedures referred to in arts 9(1), (2) and (3).

53 Aarhus Convention (n 1) art 9(4).

54 Decisions of bodies other than courts are required to be publicly accessible only 'whenever possible'.

55 Examples of potential assistance mechanisms include legal aid, cost-capping arrangements and arrangements for protective (or pre-emptive) costs orders.

56 See further *The Aarhus Convention: An Implementation Guide* (n 3) 205–07.

Overall, Article 9 addresses a wide range of important practical matters concerning access to justice. It limits Parties' discretion to set restrictive standing requirements. It requires timely review procedures that deliver appropriate and effective remedies, including injunctive relief. It demands that the costs involved in engaging and participating in the review procedure must be affordable ('not prohibitively expensive'), although courts may still award 'reasonable costs'.[57]

On a first reading, therefore, Article 9 impresses as a strong provision that sets a high standard for Parties as regards access to justice in environmental matters. On closer examination, however, it becomes clear that the general nature of the language used in Article 9, and indeed in other provisions of the Convention, creates problems for implementation and enforcement. Important elements of the obligations created in Article 9, such as 'wide' access to justice, 'timely' review procedures and costs that are 'not prohibitively expensive', do not articulate specifically the precise standards that Parties must meet. Authoritative interpretation of Convention obligations is needed to distil their meaning and impact in practice. Even more significantly, the text of Article 9 makes multiple references to 'national legislation' and 'national law'. This explicit deference to national arrangements means that practical implementation of the access to justice obligations will be influenced, to a considerable extent, by the existing national legal frameworks. The deliberate reference to national legal systems also results in an inevitable diversity of approaches to implementation of Convention obligations across the forty-seven State Parties.

Section 6.3 examines the process by which the standards inherent in particular aspects of Article 9 of the Convention have emerged and crystallised over time through decisions of the Compliance Committee and the CJEU. Before moving to that analysis, it is necessary to introduce the specific compliance mechanism provided for under the Convention and to explain how the Convention interacts with EU law.

6.2.1.4 Aarhus Convention Compliance Committee

Article 15 requires the Meeting of the Parties (MoP) to the Convention to establish, on a consensual basis, 'optional arrangements of a non-confrontational, non-judicial and consultative nature' for reviewing compliance with Convention obligations. Such arrangements must allow for public involvement, and may include the option of considering communications from the public on matters relating to the Convention. In October 2002, pursuant to Article 15, the MoP adopted Decision I/7 on Review of Compliance and established the Compliance Committee.[58] Together with the MoP,

57 Aarhus Convention (n 1) art 3(8) confirms that national courts retain the power to award 'reasonable costs' in judicial proceedings.

58 Decision I/7 Review of Compliance ECE/MP PP/2/Add 8 para 1, <www.unece.org/fileadmin/DAM/env/pp/documents/mop1/ece.mp.pp.2.add.8.e.pdf> accessed 28 May 2018; For a fascinating account of the Compliance Committee's work in its early years see Fiona Marshall, 'Two Years in the Life:

this Committee (which comprises nine members made up of practising lawyers and academics with recognised expertise in environmental law)[59] oversees how Parties implement their Convention obligations. Its core functions involve: considering submissions by Parties,[60] referrals by the Secretariat[61] or communications from the public concerning compliance, and monitoring, assessing and facilitating the implementation of the Parties' reporting obligations.[62] It may also examine compliance issues of its own initiative and make recommendations if and as appropriate.[63] Having considered a submission, referral or communication (as the case may be), the Compliance Committee proceeds to makes findings. In the cases where it finds non-compliance with Convention obligations it will normally also make recommendations as to what the Party in question should do in order to address the non-compliance.[64]

The Compliance Committee reports on its activities directly to the MoP and makes such recommendations to the MoP as it considers appropriate.[65] Having considered a report and any recommendations from the Compliance Committee, the MoP may decide on 'appropriate measures' to bring about full compliance by a Party. Such measures may include, for example: issuing a declaration of non-compliance; providing advice regarding implementation of the Convention; making recommendations to the Party on specific measures to address the non-compliance at issue; issuing a caution; and suspending a Party's special rights and privileges under the Convention.[66]

Communications from the public, including NGOs, alleging non-compliance with Convention obligations by a particular Party are the mainstay of the Compliance Committee's work. Since its establishment in 2002, it has received over 150 communications from the public, including a significant number from NGOs.[67] It has delivered significant findings and recommendations across a wide range of issues, including access to justice to enforce the rights guaranteed under the

The Pioneering Aarhus Convention Compliance Committee 2004–2006' (2006) 8 International Community Law Review 123.

59 Compliance Committee members are elected by the MoP by consensus or, failing consensus, by secret ballot: Decision I/7 ibid para 7. The members serve in their personal capacity and do not represent the States of which they are nationals: Decision I/7 ibid para 1.

60 The Compliance Committee has received three submissions from Parties to date: ACCC/S/2004/1 from Romania concerning compliance by Ukraine; ACCC/S/2015/2 from Lithuania concerning compliance by Belarus; and ACCC/S/2016/3 from Albania concerning its own compliance with the Convention.

61 No referrals have been made to the Compliance Committee by the Secretariat to date.

62 Decision I/7 (n 58) para 13.

63 ibid para 14.

64 ibid para 35.

65 ibid para 36 for the Compliance Committee's limited powers to address compliance issues during the intersessional period (i.e. pending consideration of its report by the MoP).

66 ibid para 37.

67 Details of communications from the public are published on the Compliance Committee's website <www.unece.org/env/pp/cc/com.html> accessed 28 May 2018.

Convention. The Compliance Committee's approach to its mandate is geared primarily towards assisting Parties to comply with their obligations. As Koester (a former Chair of the Compliance Committee) has observed, the compliance mechanism under the Aarhus Convention 'is a forward-looking mechanism, not a redress mechanism'.[68] As such, the Compliance Committee does not provide a formal legal remedy in a particular case.

In practice, the normative force of the Compliance Committee's findings and recommendations is considerable, and the vast majority of Parties do strive diligently to implement its recommendations. Moving into a position of full compliance tends to occur gradually, and can sometimes take a considerable amount of time depending on the cause and degree of non-compliance and whether the situation can be remedied easily. It can involve substantial and often resource-intensive efforts by Parties – which usually go far beyond simply introducing new legislative measures or amending existing measures with a view to compliance.

While Decision I/7 does not explicitly mandate the Compliance Committee to provide authoritative interpretations of the Convention, it is clear that in order to fulfil its role in reviewing compliance the committee must 'justify its findings by a correct understanding of what is required of the parties'.[69] Notwithstanding the fundamental non-confrontational, non-judicial and consultative nature of the compliance mechanism, the consistent view presented in the literature is that when the Compliance Committee's findings are endorsed by the MoP, the normative value of its interpretations of the Convention's provisions increases in accordance with Article 31(3) of the Vienna Convention on the Law of Treaties.[70]

The MoP has endorsed all but one of the Compliance Committee's findings of non-compliance by individual Parties to date. This state of affairs confirms the high esteem in which the Compliance Committee is held. At the most recent (sixth) MoP held in Budva, Montenegro in September 2017, the Parties failed to reach consensus on the adoption of draft decision VI/8f concerning compliance by the EU with its obligations under the Convention.[71] Prior to the sixth MoP, the Compliance

68 Veit Koester, 'The Aarhus Convention Compliance Mechanism and Proceedings before its Compliance Committee' in Charles Banner (ed), *The Aarhus Convention: A Guide for UK Lawyers* (Hart/Bloomsbury 2015) 204.

69 Jonas Ebbesson, 'Access to Justice at the National Level: Impact of the Aarhus Convention and European Union Law' in Marc Pallemaerts (ed), *The Aarhus Convention at Ten: Interactions and Tensions between Conventional International Law and EU Environmental Law* (Europa Law Publishing 2011) 251.

70 Vienna Convention on the Law of Treaties 1969, 1155 UNTS 331. See further on this point: Veit Koester, 'The Aarhus Convention Compliance Mechanism and Proceedings before its Compliance Committee' in Banner (ed) (n 68) 205; Jonas Ebbesson, ibid 251 and Attila Tanzi and Cesare Pieta, 'The Interplay between EU Law and International Law Procedures in Controlling Compliance with the Aarhus Convention by the EU Member States' 380, both contributions ibid Marc Pallemaerts (ed), The Aarhus Convention at Ten.

71 Draft decision VI/8f concerning compliance by the European Union with its obligations under the Convention ECE/MP.PP/2017/25.

Committee, in a particularly complex and long-running case (ACCC/C/2008/32 EU), had determined that the EU was in breach of Article 9(3) and (4) of the Convention.[72] The essential basis for this finding was that neither Regulation 1367/2006 (which applies the Aarhus Convention to the EU's own institutions and bodies) [73] nor the jurisprudence of the EU Courts ensured that the public and NGOs had access to justice in environmental matters at EU level (i.e. in the context of direct actions before the EU Courts).[74] The main issue here is the restrictive standing requirements that apply to natural or legal persons who seek to bring a direct action before the EU Courts under Article 263(4) of the Treaty on the Functioning of the European Union (TFEU).[75] It fell to the MoP, to whom the Compliance Committee had reported, to endorse the committee's finding of non-compliance in respect of the EU. However, in an unprecedented development, the MoP failed to reach consensus on this matter. Following intense discussion, the MoP agreed eventually, as an exceptional measure, to postpone the discussion on this particular matter until the next MoP in 2021.[76]

It is, of course, extremely disappointing that the MoP could not reach consensus in this important case involving the EU and that the MoP's well-established practice of endorsing the Compliance Committee's findings has come to an abrupt end. However, it is heartening in terms of the Compliance Committee's authority that the MoP succeeded in reaching a compromise solution by agreeing to postpone its decision in this particular case until its next meeting. Meanwhile, it will be interesting to see how the EU proceeds to address the Compliance Committee's findings and recommendations in ACCC/C/2008/32 (Part II) EU, and when and how this long-running controversy over direct access to the EU Courts for individuals and NGOs to enforce environmental law will ultimately be resolved.

6.2.1.5 Interaction between the Aarhus Convention and EU Law

The Aarhus Convention is a mixed agreement to which the EU itself and the twenty-eight Member States are Parties. The Convention is therefore an integral part of the EU legal order.[77] In the specific context of the EU and its Member States, implementation of Convention obligations is overseen not only by the

72 ACCC/C/2008/32 (Part II) EU ECE/MP.PP/C.1/2017/7.

73 Regulation 1367/2006/EC on the application of the provisions of the Aarhus Convention on Access to Information, Public Participation in Decision-Making and Access to Justice in Environmental Matters to Community institutions and bodies [2006] OJ L264/13. For an overview see Suzanne Kingston, Veerle Heyvaert and Aleksandra Čavoški, *European Environmental Law* (Cambridge University Press 2017) 251–54.

74 ACCC/C/2008/32 (Part II) EU, ECE/MP.PP/C.1/2017/7 paras 121–22.

75 On this point see *European Environmental Law* (n 73) 246–51 and Ludwig Krämer, 'The Aarhus Convention and the European Union' in Charles Banner (ed), (n 68) 93–95.

76 Report of the Sixth Session of the Meeting of the Parties ECE/MP PP/2017/2 para 62.

77 Case C-240/09 *Lesoochranárske zoskupenie VLK v Ministerstvo životného prostredia Slovenskej republiky* EU:C:2011:125 para 30.

Compliance Committee (as a matter of international law), but also by the CJEU (which is tasked specifically with the enforcement of EU law, which includes the Convention) and by the national courts (in their capacity as 'EU courts' operating at local level). The existence of multiple legal avenues by which to enforce Convention obligations creates an obvious challenge for the coherent development of standards for effective environmental governance. A multilevel compliance/enforcement system involving the Compliance Committee, the CJEU and the national courts leads (inevitably) to a situation where it is difficult to keep track of rapid, parallel developments in the jurisprudence. This state of affairs creates a risk of fragmentation in the evolution of principles, a problem which is considered later in Section 6.4. With this complex, multilayered legal milieu in mind, Section 6.3 considers how the Compliance Committee and the CJEU have developed the standards that must be met in order to comply with particular aspects of the access to justice obligations in Article 9 of the Convention.

6.3 THE DEVELOPMENT OF STANDARDS GOVERNING ACCESS TO JUSTICE IN ENVIRONMENTAL MATTERS

Article 9 specifies the minimum qualitative standards that administrative and judicial review procedures must meet in order to comply with the Convention. It will be recalled from Section 6.2 of this chapter that Article 9(4) demands that review procedures must provide 'adequate' and 'effective' remedies (including injunctive relief, where appropriate) and must be 'fair, equitable, timely and not prohibitively expensive'. The main focus in this section of the chapter is to explore how the Compliance Committee and the CJEU have interpreted and clarified what is required in order to comply with the ban on prohibitive costs. This particular aspect is selected as a case study for a number of reasons. First, affordable access to justice is fundamental to the rule of law and to environmental law enforcement; the rights guaranteed in the Convention are at serious risk of being undermined if the public and NGOs cannot afford to bring review proceedings to enforce their rights. Second, access to judicial review is essential if Convention provisions are to be interpreted authoritatively so as to enable the law to develop and to provide legal certainty. Third, the ban on prohibitive costs has generated an interesting body of jurisprudence from the Compliance Committee and the CJEU that merits examination. It is useful to begin by introducing an important official source of guidance on the standards that apply under the Convention.

6.3.1 *Aarhus Convention Implementation Guide*

The UNECE publication, *The Aarhus Convention: An Implementation Guide*,[78] now in its second edition, is intended to provide 'a convenient non-legally binding

[78] *The Aarhus Convention: An Implementation Guide* (n 3).

and user-friendly reference tool to assist policymakers, legislators and public authorities in their daily work of implementing the Convention and of realizing [Rio] Principle 10 in practice'.[79] It is also intended to assist the public and NGOs to exercise their Convention rights. The guide is acknowledged widely as an important reference point and it provides helpful, practical insights into the standards that apply in the context of implementation of specific Convention obligations. In the case of the obligation in Article 9(4) to provide 'adequate' and 'effective' remedies, the guide explains that 'adequacy' requires that the remedy provided by the administrative or judicial review procedure 'must ensure the intended effect of the review procedure'.[80] This may, for example, involve compensation for past damage, the prevention of future damage and/or providing for restoration. As regards the 'effectiveness' requirement, the guide states that the remedies available 'should be capable of real and efficient enforcement'.[81]

Turning to the ban on prohibitive costs, the guide explains that 'the cost of bringing a challenge under the Convention or to enforce national environmental law must not be so expensive that it prevents the public, whether individuals or NGOs, from doing so'.[82] This clear explanation captures the essence of the ban on prohibitive costs and serves to clarify the essential meaning of this aspect of Article 9(4) for Parties, the public and NGOs. The guide is therefore an invaluable resource in demystifying the Convention provisions and relating them to practice. In *Solvay*,[83] the CJEU clarified that the guide may be regarded as 'an explanatory document' which can be taken into consideration when interpreting the Convention.[84] However, the observations presented in the guide 'have no binding force and do not have the normative effect of the provisions of the Aarhus Convention'.[85] As will be seen below, the CJEU has, on occasion, drawn on the guide when called on to interpret Article 9(4) and (5) of the Convention.

Before turning to an analysis of the jurisprudence of the Compliance Committee and of the CJEU concerning the ban on prohibitive costs, it is necessary to provide a brief account of the measures that the EU, as a Party to the Convention, has adopted in order to give effect to the access to justice obligations in the Member States. This is important because the CJEU interprets not only the provisions of the Convention (which, as explained earlier, are an integral part of the EU legal order), but also, of course, the EU legislative measures adopted to give effect to Convention obligations.

79 ibid 9.
80 ibid 200.
81 ibid.
82 ibid 203.
83 Case C-182/10 *Solvay v Région wallonne* EU:C:2012:82.
84 ibid para 27.
85 ibid.

6.3.2 *EU Measures Aimed at Giving Effect to the Aarhus Convention Access to Justice Obligations in the Member States*

Prior to its ratification of the Convention in 2005, the EU adopted secondary legislation to implement the Convention in the Member States, including the Article 9 access to justice obligations.[86] Directive 2003/4/EC[87] governs the right of access to environmental information. Article 6 of this directive provides for 'access to justice' and is based on Article 9(1) of the Convention. As regards the participation rights guaranteed in Article 6 of the Convention, Directive 2003/35/EC[88] (known as 'the public participation directive') amended a number of existing directives to take account of the participation and access to justice obligations mandated by the Convention. Of particular significance here are the amendments made to the EIA directive[89] and the integrated pollution prevention and control (IPPC) directive[90] – now repealed and replaced by the industrial emissions directive.[91] Directive 2003/35/EC inserted explicit access to justice provisions into the text of the EIA directive and the IPPC directive in order to implement Article 9(2) and (4) of the Convention. These access to justice provisions are modelled on the text of Article 9(2) and (4) and include the obligation to ensure that the cost of review procedures 'is not prohibitively expensive'. Prior to these amendments, both directives were silent on enforcement. As will be seen in the analysis presented below, the access to justice provisions in the EIA directive have featured prominently in the CJEU jurisprudence on matters relating to implementation of the Aarhus Convention. This is not surprising given the frequency with which the EIA directive is invoked by the public and NGOs to challenge environmental decisions in their Member States.

As regards the general right of access to justice in Article 9(3), the Commission had proposed a directive on access to justice in environmental matters as far back as 2003.[92] This proposal failed to progress due to resistance from certain Member

86 In addition to the secondary legislation adopted to implement Aarhus obligations in the Member States, Regulation 1367/2006/EC (n 73) was adopted with the aim of giving effect to Aarhus obligations in the specific context of the EU institutions and bodies (n 73). An analysis of the provisions of Regulation 1367/2006/EC lies beyond the scope of this particular chapter. See generally Kingston, Heyvaert and Čavoški (n 73); Krämer, 'The Aarhus Convention and the European Union' (n 75); also Martin Hedemann-Robinson, *Enforcement of European Union Environmental Law: Legal Issues and Challenges* (2nd edn, Routledge 2015) 459–69.

87 Directive 2003/4/EC on public access to environmental information [2003] OJ L41/26.

88 Directive 2003/35/EC providing for public participation in respect of the drawing up of certain plans and programmes relating to the environment and amending with regard to public participation and access to justice Council Directives 85/337/EEC and 96/61/EC [2003] OJ L156/17.

89 The current EU EIA rules are found in Directive 2011/92/EU on the assessment of the effects of certain public and private projects on the environment (codification) [2011] OJ L26/1 as amended by Directive 2014/52/EU [2014] OJ L124/1.

90 Directive 96/61/EC concerning integrated pollution prevention and control [1996] OJ L257/26.

91 Directive 2010/75/EU on industrial emissions (integrated pollution prevention and control) (Recast) [2010] OJ L334/17.

92 European Commission, *Proposal for a Directive on Access to Justice in Environmental Matters* COM (2003) 624 final, 24 October 2003.

States, and it was ultimately withdrawn in 2014 with the expectation that the Commission would bring forward a fresh proposal.

As it transpired, however, rather than bringing forward a new legislative proposal the Commission developed and, in April 2017, adopted a *Notice on Access to Justice in Environmental Matters*.[93] Essentially, this notice summarises the dynamic body of CJEU jurisprudence on access to justice in environmental matters before the national courts. The notice, described as an 'Interpretative Communication',[94] aims to communicate the Commission's view of the minimum requirements that it expects the Member States to deliver in the context of access to justice at national level.[95] The Commission's decision to proceed by way of a soft law measure, in the form of the Interpretative Communication, rather than legislation as anticipated, is considered a significant disappointment by NGOs and others who have long campaigned for a directive on access to environmental justice.

In the absence of a legislative measure implementing Article 9(3) of the Convention in the Member States, the CJEU has been called on to consider the impact of Article 9(3) in the national legal orders and whether it has direct effect. In *Lesoochranárske zoskupenie*,[96] the CJEU determined that the provisions of Article 9(3) 'do not contain any clear and precise obligation capable of directly regulating the legal position of individuals'.[97] Only members of the public who meet the criteria (if any) set down in national law would have standing to invoke the review procedure. It followed, in the CJEU's view, that implementation of Article 9(3) depends on the adoption of a subsequent (national) measure, and so Article 9(3) does not have direct effect in EU law.[98] The CJEU went on to emphasise, however, that Article 9(3), although drafted in broad terms, is intended to ensure effective environmental protection.[99] It is the Member States' responsibility to ensure that EU rights (in this particular case the rights arising under the Habitats Directive[100]) are protected effectively.[101] The CJEU insisted that if the 'effective protection' of EU environmental law is to be delivered, Article 9(3) could not be interpreted by a national court in such a way as to make it impossible in practice or excessively difficult to exercise rights conferred by EU law.[102] Where, as in this case, a species protected under the Habitats Directive was at issue, the principle of effective judicial

93 European Commission, *Notice on Access to Justice in Environmental Matters* [2017] OJ C275/1.

94 ibid para 9.

95 For commentary on the Commission Notice see Jan Darpö, 'On the Bright Side (of the EU's Janus Face): The EU Commission's Notice on Access to Justice in Environmental Matters' (2017) 14 Journal for European Environmental and Planning Law 373.

96 Case C-240/09 (n 77).

97 ibid para 45.

98 ibid.

99 ibid para 46.

100 Directive 92/43/EEC on the Conservation of Natural Habitats and Wild Fauna and Flora [1992] OJ L206/7 (Habitats Directive).

101 Case C-240/09 (n 77) paras 47–48.

102 ibid paras 48–49.

protection demanded that the national court interpret domestic law, 'to the fullest extent possible', consistently with the objectives in Article 9(3) of the Aarhus Convention[103] to enable an NGO to challenge a decision likely to be contrary to EU environmental law.[104]

This powerful ruling demonstrates the significant role played by the doctrine of consistent interpretation in aligning national law with Convention and EU requirements. It also serves to confirm the CJEU's unwavering commitment to ensuring effective access to justice in environmental matters in the Member States. This overarching goal permeates the jurisprudence, including the cases, considered below, where the CJEU has been called on to consider the ban on prohibitive costs.

6.3.3 *Jurisprudence of the Compliance Committee and of the CJEU on the Requirement that Costs Must Not Be 'Prohibitively Expensive'*

The Compliance Committee and the CJEU operate autonomously in parallel. The following sections examine how both have interpreted and clarified what is required in order to comply with the ban on prohibitive costs. It is helpful in the first instance to explain briefly the different mechanisms by which issues concerning access to justice come before the Compliance Committee and the CJEU.

Members of the public and NGOs bring access to justice issues before the Compliance Committee in situations where they consider that the relevant domestic legal framework fails to comply with any of the requirements of Article 9 of the Convention, either generally, in the systemic sense, and/or in relation to a specific case. It may be alleged before the Compliance Committee, for example, that arrangements for access to justice at local level are too slow or otherwise ineffective, or are inaccessible due to allegedly unreasonable standing requirements or prohibitive costs.[105]

There are two avenues by which issues relating to access to justice may come before the CJEU. The first is by way of infringement proceedings under Article 258 TFEU where the EU Commission brings a Member State before the Court alleging breach of EU law.[106] Such infringement proceedings might allege a failure to transpose and/or to implement correctly the Aarhus-inspired access to justice obligations set down in EU environmental legislation, for example, the EIA Directive[107] or

103 ibid para 50.

104 ibid para 51.

105 On the important practical question of exhaustion of domestic remedies in the context of admissibility of communications from the public, Decision I/7 (n 58) para 21 states that the Compliance Committee should take into account any available domestic remedy, unless the remedy in question 'is unreasonably prolonged or obviously does not provide an effective and sufficient means of redress'.

106 For an overview of the infringement procedure under art 258 TFEU see Kingston, Heyvaert and Čavoški, (n 86) 186–200; and Hedemann-Robinson (n 86) 40–50.

107 Directive 2011/92/EU on the assessment of the effects of certain public and private projects on the environment (codification) [2011] OJ L26/1 as amended by Directive 2014/52/EU [2014] OJ L124/1.

Directive 2003/4/EC on public access to environmental information.[108] The second avenue arises under the preliminary ruling procedure.[109] Essentially, Article 267 TFEU provides that a national court or tribunal may request the CJEU to give a preliminary ruling concerning the correct interpretation of the Treaties or the validity and interpretation of acts of the EU institutions including, for example, EU environmental directives. In *Lesoochranárske zoskupenie* the CJEU confirmed that, because the Aarhus Convention is an integral part of the EU legal order, it has jurisdiction to give preliminary rulings concerning the interpretation of the Convention.[110]

Before turning to consider the relevant jurisprudence, it is important to recall that there is a clear link between the obligation in Article 9(4) that the review procedures must not be 'prohibitively expensive' and the obligation imposed on Parties under Article 9(5) to consider the establishment of appropriate assistance mechanisms (for example, legal aid) to remove or reduce financial and other barriers to access to justice. Both provisions will therefore be examined in tandem. The sharp focus on Article 9(4) and (5) adopted here facilitates analysis of the processes by which the standards articulated in those provisions are developed and refined over time by the Compliance Committee and the CJEU. The Compliance Committee's jurisprudence on Article 9(4) and (5) is considered first. This is followed by an analysis of the judgments where the CJEU has interpreted these particular Convention provisions and the equivalent provisions in EU secondary legislation designed to implement Article 9 (4) and (5) in the Member States.

6.3.3.1 Minimum Standards for Review Procedures: the Compliance Committee's Approach to the Requirement that Costs Must Not Be 'Prohibitively Expensive'

As explained in Section 6.2.1.4, the Compliance Committee operates on a non-confrontational, non-judicial and consultative nature. It reviews Parties' compliance with Convention obligations and makes findings and recommendations to the MoP. The Compliance Committee has been called on to consider the ban on prohibitive costs in Article 9(4) on a number of occasions. Its analysis and findings clarify the scope of the obligation created here and set useful benchmarks to determine whether it has been met in a particular case.

In ACCC/C/2008/27 United Kingdom,[111] a costs order for £39,454 was (not surprisingly) found to be prohibitive. A similar conclusion was reached – in the specific circumstances of the case – in ACCC/C/2012/77 United Kingdom[112] as

[108] Directive 2003/4/EC on public access to environmental information [2003] OJ L41/26.

[109] For an overview of the preliminary ruling mechanism see Kingston, Heyvaert and Čavoški (n 86) 446–50.

[110] Case C-240/09 (n 77) para 30.

[111] ECE/MP.PP/C.1/2010/6/Add.2.

[112] ECE/MP.PP/C.1/2015/3.

regards an order for costs of £8,000 against an NGO.[113] In ACCC/C/2011/57 Denmark,[114] the Compliance Committee concluded that a fee of DKK3,000 (€400 approx.) for NGOs to bring an appeal before the Danish Nature and Environmental Appeal Board was prohibitive within the meaning of Article 9(4). Whether or not a particular sum of costs or a particular fee is compatible with Article 9(4) will depend, of course, on the facts of each case and must also be assessed in context by reference to the particular characteristics of the domestic legal system.

Beyond the cases where specific amounts of costs have been examined against the standard set in Article 9(4), a number of principles governing the cost of review proceedings have emerged from the Compliance Committee's jurisprudence that clarify how the 'not prohibitively expensive' standard is to be measured. In ACCC/C/2008/24 Spain,[115] the Compliance Committee confirmed that Article 9(4) extends to situations where a member of the public seeks to appeal an unfavourable court decision on a matter that falls within the scope of the Convention.[116] It insisted that Parties must ensure that Article 9(4) is implemented in such a way as to prevent unfair, inequitable or prohibitively expensive costs orders against members of the public who bring such appeals.[117] In order to achieve this requirement, judicial decisions concerning the costs of an appeal must take full account of the minimum requirements set down in Article 9(4).[118]

In ACCC/C/2008/27[119] United Kingdom, the Compliance Committee emphasised that the fairness requirement in Article 9(4) refers to what is fair for the claimant and not the respondent (a public authority).[120] It insisted that where a member of the public is litigating environmental matters in the public interest, and is unsuccessful in the proceedings, the allocation of liability for costs must take account of the public interest at stake.[121] It found that the manner in which costs of £39,454 were allocated in this particular case was unfair within the meaning of Article 9(4), and therefore amounted to non-compliance.[122]

113 Greenpeace Ltd had sought judicial review of the designation by the Secretary of State for Energy and Climate of a National Nuclear Policy. The application for judicial review was unsuccessful and Greenpeace Ltd was ordered to pay the respondent's (the State Party) costs of £11,813, which were reduced subsequently to £8,000. In ACCC/C/2008/23 (United Kingdom), the committee found that a costs order in the sum of £5,130, plus interest, was not prohibitively expensive. It is important to note, however, that in this case the communicant accepted that the costs were not prohibitive: ECE/MP.PP/C.1/2010/6/Add.1.

114 ECE/MP.PP/C.1/2012/7.

115 ECE/MP.PP/C.1/2009/8/Add.1.

116 ibid para 108.

117 ibid.

118 ibid para 110.

119 ECE/MP.PP/C.1/2010/6/Add.2.

120 ibid para 45.

121 ibid. See also ACCC/C/2014/111 Belgium ECE/MP.PP/C.1/2017/20 para 75.

122 ACCC/C/2008/27 United Kingdom ECE/MP.PP/C.1/2010/6/Add.2. On the facts here, the applicant, a resident's association, had been ordered to pay the full costs of the respondent (the Department of

In ACCC/C/2008/33 United Kingdom,[123] the Compliance Committee explained that when it is assessing costs in light of the standard set in Article 9(4), it considers the Party's cost system as a whole and in a systemic manner.[124] It took the view that the 'costs follow the event rule' was 'not inherently objectionable' under the Convention.[125] However, the rule's compatibility with Article 9(4) depended on the outcome in each specific case and 'the existence of a clear rule that prevents prohibitively expensive procedures'.[126] The Compliance Committee considered that the impact of the costs follow the event rule could be modified by other aspects of the domestic legal system such as legal aid, conditional fee agreements and protective costs orders.[127] However, it identified a number of problems with the rules governing protective costs orders that applied at that particular point in time in England and Wales. For example, when determining the allocation of costs in a specific case, the public interest nature of environmental litigation was not given sufficient consideration by the national courts.[128] The Compliance Committee also insisted that it is essential that there is 'equality of arms' between the parties to litigation where costs are concerned.[129] Furthermore, there would be non-compliance with Article 9(4) in a situation where the requirement for a cross-undertaking in damages, as a condition to injunctive relief, entails a risk of high costs in a case where a litigant is legitimately pursuing environmental concerns that involve the public interest.[130] The Compliance Committee concluded that, notwithstanding the availability of certain measures with the potential to address prohibitive costs (i.e. legal aid, protective costs orders, etc.), taken as a whole they did not ensure that costs remained at a level that met the standard set in Article 9(4).[131] More specifically, it found that the degree of judicial discretion concerning costs, and the absence of a clear, legally binding direction from the legislature or judiciary to ensure that costs are not prohibitive, resulted in considerable uncertainty for people legitimately pursuing environmental concerns in the public interest.[132] It followed that the United Kingdom had not adequately implemented its obligations under Article 9(4) to ensure that costs were not prohibitive.[133] The Compliance Committee also determined that the system as a whole operating in the United Kingdom was not

the Environment for Northern Ireland) following the dismissal of its application for judicial review challenging the decision-making process relating to the proposed expansion of Belfast City airport.

123 ECE/MP.PP/C.1/2010/6/Add.3.

124 ibid para 128. See also ACCC/C/2014/111 Belgium ECE/MP.PP/C.1/2017/20 para 65.

125 ACCC/C/2008/33 United Kingdom ECE/MP.PP/C.1/2010/6/Add.3. para 129.

126 ibid.

127 ibid.

128 ibid and also para 134.

129 ibid para 132.

130 ibid para 133.

131 ibid.

132 ibid para 135.

133 ibid para 136.

such as to remove or reduce financial barriers to access to justice as required under Article 9(5).[134]

In ACCC/C/2012/77 United Kingdom,[135] the Compliance Committee explained that in determining whether the cost of judicial review proceedings is prohibitively expensive the costs borne by the claimant 'as a whole' must be assessed,[136] and that this assessment 'should involve both objective and subjective elements'.[137] It took the opportunity to reiterate that, with respect to costs, 'fairness' in Article 9(4) refers to what is fair for the claimant, not the respondent.[138]

In ACCC/C/2013/85 and ACCC/C/2013/86 United Kingdom,[139] the Compliance Committee confirmed the general principles it had established in ACCC/C/2008/33 United Kingdom[140] (considered above) and found, on the facts here, that there was an absence of any clear, legally binding directions from the legislature or judiciary to ensure that the costs of actions for private nuisance were not prohibitively expensive.[141]

In ACCC/C/2014/111 Belgium,[142] the Compliance Committee explained that when assessing whether the costs associated with a review procedure are prohibitively expensive in a particular case, it first evaluates whether, taking account of the claimant's financial situation, the total amount of costs would prevent them from invoking the review procedure.[143]

Pulling together the various threads in the Compliance Committee's jurisprudence on costs to date, the essential elements that must be considered when assessing compliance with Article 9(4) and (5) are: whether a clear, legally binding direction from the legislature or judiciary is in place to ensure costs are not prohibitively expensive; taking account of the claimant's financial situation, whether the amount of costs involved would prevent them from invoking the relevant review procedure; whether there is 'equality of arms' between the parties to the litigation concerning costs; whether the public interest nature of environmental litigation is taken into account when determining costs liability; the costs borne by the claimant as a whole must be assessed and this should involve objective and subjective elements; and, finally, the overarching requirement that when assessing costs in light of the standards set in Article 9(4) and (5), the cost system of the Party as a whole must be taken into consideration. It is interesting to find that broadly similar principles have emerged in the jurisprudence of the CJEU concerning the

134 ibid.
135 ECE.MP.PP/C.1/2015/3.
136 ibid para 72.
137 ibid.
138 ibid.
139 ECE.MP.PP/C.1/2016/10.
140 ECE/MP.PP/C.1/2010/6/Add.3 paras 106–07.
141 ACCC/C/2013/85 and ACCC/C/2013/86 United Kingdom ECE.MP.PP/C.1/2016/10 para 108.
142 ECE/MP.PP/C.1/2017/20.
143 ibid para 74.

requirement that the cost of review procedures must not be prohibitively expensive. This jurisprudence is considered next in Section 6.3.3.2.

6.3.3.2 Minimum Standards for Review Procedures: the CJEU Jurisprudence on the Requirement that Costs Must Not Be 'Prohibitively Expensive'

This section begins by setting out a number of overarching principles in order to place the analysis of the CJEU jurisprudence in context. First, as explained in section 6.2.1.5, the Aarhus Convention is an integral part of the EU legal order.[144] Second, the CJEU has ruled that the access to justice provisions in EU environmental directives which give effect to Article 9 of the Convention must be interpreted in the light of, and having regard to, the objectives of the Convention.[145] It is also important to recall that long before the Convention ever formed part of EU law, the CJEU had championed the right to invoke EU (environmental) law before the national courts and developed the principle of effective judicial protection.[146] This principle is now enshrined in Article 19 of the Treaty on European Union, and Article 47 of the Charter of Fundamental Rights of the EU (the EU Charter) guarantees the right to an effective remedy for breach of EU law rights, including the right to legal aid where necessary to ensure effective access to justice.

When implementing Article 9 of the Convention and the related access to justice obligations in the EU directives, Member States enjoy a significant measure of discretion under the principle of national procedural autonomy. More specifically, it is for the Member States to determine which court (or other independent body established by law, as appropriate) has jurisdiction to provide the review procedure and to set the applicable procedural rules. However, the Member States' discretion in this regard is subject to compliance with the well-established EU law principles of equivalence and effectiveness.[147] The extent to which Member States can lawfully restrict access to justice under their local procedural rules is a significant theme in the CJEU jurisprudence concerning the Aarhus Convention. In light of the fact that the access to justice provisions in the Convention and the implementing EU

144 Case C-240/09 (n 77) para 30.

145 Case C-115/09 *Bund für Umwelt und Naturschutz Deutschland, Landesverband Nordrhein-Westfalen eV v Bezirksregierung Arnsberg, Trianel Kohlekraftwerk Lünen GmbH & Co KG* EU:C:2011:289 para 41.

146 Case C-222/84 *Johnston v Chief Constable of the Royal Ulster Constabulary* EU:C:1986:206 paras 18–19. On the evolution of this principle in the post-*Johnston* jurisprudence, see Áine Ryall, *Effective Judicial Protection and the Environmental Impact Assessment Directive in Ireland* (Hart Publishing 2009) 82–91 and Anthony Arnull, 'The Principle of Effective Judicial Protection in EU Law: An Unruly Horse?' (2011) 36 European Law Review 51.

147 Case C-240/09 (n 77) 47–48. Under the principle of equivalence, claims based on EU law may not be treated less favourably than those based on national law. The principle of effectiveness demands that national procedural rules must not be impossible in practice or excessively difficult to enforce EU law before the national courts. See Koen Lenaerts, 'National Remedies for Private Parties in the Light of the EU Principles of Equivalence and Effectiveness' (2011) 46 *Irish Jurist* 13.

directives are drafted in broad terms, it is not surprising to find that the CJEU has been called on regularly to determine their meaning and to provide guidance to the national courts on a range of issues, including the scope and meaning of the ban on prohibitive costs.[148] As explained in section 6.1, the ban on prohibitive costs, and how the CJEU has interpreted this obligation in its jurisprudence to date, is selected as the specific focus of analysis in this section. Four judgments are relevant here: two involved infringement proceedings under Article 258 TFEU, and two were references for preliminary rulings under Article 267 TFEU.

In infringement proceedings brought against Ireland by the Commission, the Court confirmed that the prohibition on excessive costs did not prevent national courts from making an order for costs, provided the amount of costs involved complied with the 'not prohibitively expensive' standard.[149] The Court determined, however, that a mere 'discretionary practice', whereby the Irish courts could decline to order an unsuccessful litigant to pay the other side's costs, could not be regarded as adequate transposition.[150] Such a practice did not satisfy the requirement for legal certainty.[151] This approach is similar to that adopted by the Compliance Committee in its jurisprudence on Article 9(4) considered in section 6.3.3.1. It will be recalled that the Compliance Committee insists that Parties put in place a clear, legally binding rule that prevents prohibitively expensive procedures.[152] As the infringement proceedings in *Commission* v. *Ireland* were concerned solely with alleged failure in transposition, the Court did not engage in any analysis of the substance of the concept of 'prohibitive' costs on this occasion.

In *Edwards*,[153] a reference for a preliminary ruling from the Supreme Court of the United Kingdom, the CJEU was presented with a series of questions on how a national court should approach the ban on prohibitive costs in the EIA and IPPC directives. As explained above, the access to justice provisions in these directives are modelled closely on Article 9 of the Convention, and include the requirement in Article 9(4) that costs must not be prohibitively expensive. The CJEU began by observing that the overarching objective of delivering 'wide access to justice' for 'the public concerned' reflected the desire of the EU legislature 'to preserve, protect and improve the quality of the environment and to ensure that,

148 For detailed analysis of the CJEU jurisprudence on the impact of the Aarhus Convention in the Member States see Áine Ryall, 'Access to Justice in Environmental Matters in the Member States of the EU: the Impact of the Aarhus Convention' Jean Monnet Working Paper 5/16, New York University School of Law (2016).

149 Case C-427/07 *Commission v Ireland* EU:C:2009:457 para 92.

150 ibid paras 93–94.

151 ibid para 94. In infringement proceedings in Case C-530/11 *Commission v United Kingdom* EU:C:2014:67, which also concerned implementation of the ban on prohibitive costs, the CJEU clarified that not every judicial practice is uncertain and inherently incapable of meeting the requirements of clarity and precision necessary in order to be regarded as valid implementation of obligations arising under a directive (para 36).

152 ACCC/C/2008/33 United Kingdom ECE/MP.PP/C.1/2010/6/Add.3 para 135.

153 Case C-260/11 *R (Edwards) v Environment Agency* EU:C:2013:221.

to that end, the public plays an active role'.[154] It linked the ban on prohibitive costs with the observance of the right to an effective remedy guaranteed under Article 47 of the EU Charter and to the principle of effectiveness of EU law.[155] Drawing on the Aarhus Convention Implementation Guide,[156] the CJEU concluded that the ban on prohibitive costs means that the public concerned should not be prevented from seeking a review by the courts 'by reason of the financial burden that might arise as a result'.[157] This approach is similar to that adopted by the Compliance Committee in ACCC/C/2014/111 Belgium.[158] It follows from this line of reasoning that where a national court is asked to make an order for costs against a member of the public who has been unsuccessful in judicial proceedings or, where it is required to make a protective costs order, it must be satisfied that the costs are not prohibitively expensive.[159] In determining this issue, the national court must take into account both the interest of individuals wishing to defend their rights and 'the public interest in environmental protection'.[160] Here, again, the CJEU's approach resonates with the Compliance Committee's insistence that the public interest in environmental protection must be taken into consideration when assessing whether costs are prohibitive.

As to the assessment criteria to be applied in order to ensure compliance with the ban on prohibitive costs, the United Kingdom Supreme Court had enquired whether this assessment was objective or subjective in nature and the extent to which national law must be taken into account. The CJEU recalled the well-established principle that where EU law lacks precision, it is for the Member States to ensure that it is transposed effectively, although they retain a broad discretion as to the choice of methods that may be used to implement the obligation in question.[161] It then considered the methods likely to secure the objective of ensuring effective judicial protection without excessive cost in the field of environmental law. It confirmed that all the relevant provisions of national law and, in particular, any national legal aid scheme and/or costs protection regime must be taken into consideration.[162] It is also necessary to take account of the 'significant differences' which exist between national laws in this area.[163] The CJEU concluded that the assessment of whether costs are prohibitive or not cannot be carried out solely on the basis of the

[154] ibid paras 31–32.
[155] ibid para 33.
[156] In *Edwards*, the Court of Justice referred to the original (1st) edition of the implementation guide published by the UNECE in 2010.
[157] Case C-260/11 *R (Edwards) v Environment Agency* EU:C:2013:221 para 35.
[158] ECE/MP.PP/C.1/2017/20 para 74.
[159] Case C-260/11 *R (Edwards) v Environment Agency* EU:C:2013:221 para 35.
[160] ibid. See also Advocate General Kokott's Opinion in *Edwards* EU:C:2012:645 paras 39–47 for detailed analysis of the importance of the public interest in environmental protection when examining whether costs are prohibitively expensive.
[161] Case C-260/11 *R (Edwards) v Environment Agency* EU:C:2013:221 para 37.
[162] ibid para 38.
[163] ibid.

litigant's specific financial situation. It must also be based on an objective analysis of the amount of costs involved. This is because members of the public and NGOs 'are naturally required to play an active role in defending the environment'.[164] Overall, the cost of proceedings 'must neither exceed the financial resources of the person concerned nor appear, in any event, to be objectively unreasonable'.[165]

As regards the analysis of the financial situation of the claimant, the assessment undertaken by the national court cannot be based exclusively on the estimated financial resources of the 'average' claimant.[166] This is because that information may have little connection with the actual situation of the claimant. An objective analysis of the amount of the costs must be made in every case. The national court may also take the following factors into account: the claimant's financial situation; whether the claimant has a reasonable prospect of success; the importance of what is at stake for the claimant and for the protection of the environment; the complexity of the relevant law and procedure; and the potentially frivolous nature of the claim at its various stages.[167] Furthermore, the fact that a claimant has not, in practice, been deterred from bringing proceedings is not in itself sufficient to establish that the proceedings are not prohibitively expensive in so far as that particular claimant is concerned.[168] The CJEU clarified that the requirement that judicial proceedings must not be prohibitively expensive cannot be assessed differently by a national court depending on whether it is adjudicating at the conclusion of first instance proceedings, an appeal or a second appeal.[169] No such distinction is envisaged in the access to justice provisions in the EIA and IPPC directives and such an interpretation would be unlikely to comply fully with the EU legislature's objective to ensure wide access to justice and to contribute to the improvement of environmental protection.[170]

In subsequent infringement proceedings in *Commission* v. *United Kingdom*,[171] where it was alleged that the United Kingdom had failed to transpose correctly the requirement that judicial proceedings must not be prohibitively expensive, the Court followed the approach it had adopted in *Edwards*.[172] It clarified on this occasion that when assessing costs the national court may take account of any costs already incurred at earlier levels in the same dispute.[173] The Commission had also alleged that the system of cross-undertakings in damages in respect of the grant of interim relief also infringed the ban on prohibitive costs. The CJEU took the

164 ibid para 40.
165 ibid.
166 ibid para 41.
167 ibid para 42.
168 ibid para 43.
169 ibid para 45.
170 ibid para 44.
171 Case C-530/11 *Commission v United Kingdom* EU:C:2014:67.
172 Case C-260/11 *R (Edwards) v Environment Agency* EU:C:2013:221.
173 Case C-530/11 *Commission v United Kingdom* EU:C:2014:67 para 49.

view that the requirement that proceedings must not be prohibitively expensive is not to be interpreted as *automatically* precluding an undertaking in damages as a condition to the grant of interim relief where this is provided for under national law.[174] The situation is the same as regards any financial consequences which might arise under national law where an action is found to be an abuse of the process of the court.[175] However, the national court must ensure that the resulting financial risk for the claimant is also included among the various costs generated by the case when it assesses whether or not the proceedings are prohibitively expensive.[176] On the basis of the documents submitted to the CJEU, it was not clear that the requirement that proceedings are not prohibitively expensive was imposed on the national courts in the United Kingdom 'with all the requisite clarity and precision'.[177] Consequently, the Court upheld the Commission's argument that the system of cross-undertakings in damages in respect of the grant of interim relief constituted an additional element of uncertainty and imprecision in the national measures aimed at ensuring compliance with the ban on prohibitive costs.[178]

Most recently, in *North East Pylon Pressure Campaign Ltd* v. *An Bord Pleanála*,[179] a reference for a preliminary ruling from the High Court of Ireland, the CJEU was required to consider *inter alia* whether a Member State could derogate from the ban on prohibitive costs in circumstances where a court determines that a challenge is frivolous or vexatious or where there is no link between the alleged breach of national environmental law and damage to the environment. The CJEU began by recalling that Article 9(4) of the Aarhus Convention 'in no way prevents' a national court from ordering a claimant to pay costs (Article 3(8) expressly provides that the power of national courts to award 'reasonable' costs is not impacted by the 'not prohibitively expensive' costs rule under Article 9(4)).[180] It is therefore open to a national court to take account of factors 'such as, in particular, whether the challenge has a reasonable chance of success, or whether it is frivolous or vexatious'.[181] However, the amount of costs actually imposed on the claimant cannot be 'unreasonably high'.[182] It followed, therefore, that there was no scope for a derogation from the ban on prohibitive costs in these particular circumstances.[183]

Having examined the wording of Article 9(3) and (4) of the Convention, the CJEU concluded that Member States are not permitted to insist on a link between the alleged breach of national environmental law and damage to the environment as

174 ibid para 67.
175 ibid.
176 ibid para 68.
177 ibid para 69.
178 ibid para 71.
179 Case C-470/16 *North East Pylon Pressure Campaign Ltd v An Bord Pleanála* EU:C:2018:18.
180 ibid para 60.
181 ibid para 61.
182 ibid.
183 ibid para 65.

a precondition for protection from prohibitive costs.[184] It is clear from the relevant provisions of the Convention that the State Parties had sought to apply the ban on prohibitive costs 'to challenges aimed at enforcing environmental law in the abstract', without any requirement to demonstrate a link with existing or potential damage to the environment.[185] The CJEU's ruling on these two points provides welcome and important clarifications on how the ban on prohibitive costs is to be applied in practice. It is not surprising to see the CJEU adopting an expansive approach here given the fundamental importance of access to the courts to enable law enforcement in the interests of environmental protection.

In *Commission* v. *Ireland*,[186] and again in *Edwards*,[187] Advocate General Kokott engaged in an interesting analysis of the role of legal aid and the impact of Article 9(5) of the Convention on the obligation to provide affordable review procedures. In the Irish case, the Advocate General noted that, although it is not reflected explicitly in the text of Directive 2003/35/EC, Article 9(5) must be taken into account when interpreting Article 9(4) and the corresponding access to justice provisions in the EIA and IPPC directives.[188] She observed that Article 9(5) demonstrates that the Parties to the Convention had the need for assistance mechanisms 'entirely in mind' when they determined that review procedures must not be 'prohibitively expensive'.[189] The Advocate General also referred to Article 47(3) of the EU Charter, which requires legal aid to be granted in so far as such aid is necessary to ensure effective access to justice.[190]

As regards the role of legal aid, in *Edwards*, the Advocate General recalled the principle of effective judicial protection under Article 47 of the EU Charter and, in particular, Article 47(3) which demands that legal aid must be made available to those who lack sufficient resources where such aid is necessary to ensure effective access to justice.[191] Acknowledging that Article 9(5) 'does not absolutely require' the introduction of assistance mechanisms such as legal aid, the Advocate General highlighted that 'legal aid makes it possible to prevent risks in terms of prohibitive costs in certain cases'.[192] She went on to argue that:

> In so far as the enforcement of provisions of EU law is concerned, legal aid may even be absolutely necessary if the risks in terms of costs, which are acceptable in principle, constitute an insurmountable obstacle to access to justice on account of the limited capacity to pay of the person concerned.[193]

184 ibid.
185 ibid para 64.
186 Case C-427/07 *Commission v Ireland* EU:C:2009:457.
187 Case C-260/11 *R (Edwards) v Environment Agency* EU:C:2013:221.
188 Case C-427/07 *Commission v Ireland* EU:C:2009:9 para 91 of the Opinion.
189 ibid.
190 ibid para 92 of the Opinion.
191 Case C-260/11 *R (Edwards) v Environment Agency* EU:C:2012:645 para 38 of the Opinion.
192 ibid.
193 ibid footnote omitted.

The CJEU has not, as yet, considered in any detail whether legal aid may be necessary in particular circumstances in order to ensure that costs are affordable.

6.4 ANALYSIS OF DEVELOPMENT OF STANDARDS FOR AFFORDABLE ACCESS TO JUSTICE IN ENVIRONMENTAL MATTERS

Article 9(4) of the Convention sets minimum standards governing the review procedures that Parties must provide to ensure effective access to environmental justice. These minimum standards include a requirement that the cost of accessing and participating in the review procedure must not be 'prohibitively expensive'. The Convention text does not set out any criteria by which to determine whether costs are prohibitive in a particular case. The award of 'reasonable costs' is permissible under Article 3(8), but the text does not elaborate on the meaning of 'reasonable' or how it is to be measured. The access to justice provisions in the EU environmental directives designed to implement Article 9 replicate the 'not prohibitively expensive' requirement without further elaboration.

The question therefore arises: what precisely does this standard demand in practical terms? The analysis presented in Section 6.3 of this chapter traced how the Compliance Committee and the CJEU have gradually developed a number of general principles governing the obligation to provide affordable access to justice, including a requirement to take account of the public interest in environmental protection. It also explained how, in *Edwards*[194] and *Commission* v. *United Kingdom*[195], the CJEU developed a set of criteria that national courts must apply in assessing whether costs are prohibitive in a specific case. Neither Article 9(4) of the Convention nor the access to justice provisions in the EIA Directive and the Industrial Emissions Directive (formerly the IPCC Directive) contain any such criteria. The elaboration of criteria is therefore an important step in facilitating a consistent approach to Article 9(4) across the Member States of the EU. In setting these criteria, the CJEU is alert to the significant differences that exist between the twenty-eight national legal systems operating in the EU. It is not surprising, therefore, to find that these criteria are pitched at a fairly general level and leave Member States with an important measure of flexibility to design an Aarhus-compliant costs regime in light of their particular legal system. However, this flexibility, and the lack of more specific guidance, inevitably leaves scope for further disputes as to the precise implications of the ban on prohibitive costs for national legal systems.

The jurisprudence will, no doubt, continue to develop and mature as new disputes bring new issues before the Compliance Committee and the CJEU for resolution. A number of communications are currently pending before the Compliance Committee in which it is alleged that certain State Parties are non-

194 Case C-260/11 (n 187).

195 Case C-530/11 *Commission v United Kingdom* EU:C:2014:67.

compliant as regards the ban on prohibitive costs under Article 9(4).[196] These cases may provide the committee with an opportunity to provide further clarification on its understanding of what affordable access to justice entails in practice. In a similar vein, more references for preliminary rulings are likely to arise as national courts seek further guidance on the interpretation of the 'not prohibitively expensive' standard and its impact on local costs rules.

It is important to appreciate fully that the process by which more precise requirements in relation to affordable access to justice are articulated is *ad hoc* and gradual. The development of authoritative principles depends on cases coming before the Compliance Committee and the CJEU and, ultimately, the national courts. Precise requirements will emerge only as and when new cases are decided and published. This state of affairs is not conducive to legal certainty, but it is the direct consequence of the general manner in which the access to justice obligations are articulated in the Convention and in the related EU implementing measures.

A further issue to be considered in the context of legal certainty is the fact that the Compliance Committee, the CJEU and the national courts are all involved in interpreting and applying the access to justice obligations within their own particular jurisdictional remit. The parallel operation of three dispute resolution processes creates a risk of fragmentation – and potential conflict – in the development of principle. It also complicates the overarching legal framework because it is necessary to consider the three sources of legal authority (Aarhus Convention, EU law and national law) in tandem in order to form a complete picture of the relevant legal principles. Thus far, it appears that the Compliance Committee and the CJEU adopt a broadly similar approach to the standard set in Article 9(4), although the Court has gone further than the committee by setting down general criteria by which to assess whether costs are prohibitive. The availability of the preliminary ruling procedure should eliminate, or at least reduce, the scope for divergent interpretations by the CJEU and the national courts. In any event, we are likely to see interesting future developments as new issues arise for consideration before the Compliance Committee, the CJEU and the national courts.

As regards the development of standards and their refinement over time, it is vital that effective access to justice is available to the public and NGOs to ensure that any disputes over interpretation and implementation of those standards can be addressed definitively. This confirms the importance and the urgency of precise standards governing access to justice being settled authoritatively so that these standards can then be applied in practice and come to be recognised widely as the norm. It is incumbent on the judiciary at national level to fold international and EU standards into the national system. To this end, it is vital that national judges engage proactively with arguments based on international and EU law, and take care when

196 For example, ACCC/C/2014/112 Ireland, ACCC/C/2014/113 Ireland, ACCC/C/2016/142 United Kingdom and ACCC/C/2016/157 United Kingdom.

crafting their judgments to provide the degree of clarity needed to embed international and EU principles into the local legal and administrative system.

6.5 CONCLUSION

The analysis presented in this chapter demonstrates the practical difficulties involved in developing precise standards when environmental obligations are articulated in vague terms in international environmental instruments. In the case of the Aarhus Convention, we have seen how the Compliance Committee and the CJEU each play a vital role in interpreting the content of environmental obligations and articulating criteria by which to assess compliance. The process by which standards are clarified by means of jurisprudence unfolds gradually as new cases bring new issues that must be resolved authoritatively. This process can be frustrating for the public and NGOs when it takes a significant period of time for cases to work through the system and for clear principles to emerge.

In the absence of clear principles and specific assessment criteria, some governments may be inclined to take a minimalist approach to Convention obligations, particularly when a more proactive stance would involve significant investment of resources. Lack of political will to deliver fully the procedural rights guaranteed in the Convention is the main obstacle to timely implementation. This state of affairs confirms the importance of accessible and effective enforcement mechanisms to address any uncertainty over the scope of Convention obligations and to ensure that the law is applied correctly and in a timely fashion. Informing the public and NGOs of their rights under the Convention and educating them on how to use those rights – including the potentially powerful role of public interest litigation – is essential if standards are to evolve progressively and become embedded more deeply in local legal and administrative systems.

The Aarhus Convention aims to improve environmental governance by empowering the public and NGOs to participate more effectively in decision making and to enforce the law in the public interest. The analysis presented in this chapter confirms that the Convention continues to gain momentum and to have a sharper legal impact at national level as the jurisprudence interpreting and applying its provisions matures.

7

The Emergence of Standards regarding the Right of Access to Water and Sanitation

Owen McIntyre

7.1 INTRODUCTION

Despite continuing uncertainty over the precise legal status of the putative human right(s) of access to water and sanitation in international law, and also within the domestic legal frameworks of many national jurisdictions, the elaboration continues apace of a rich montage of water services standards by a diverse cast of formal and informal global, regional, State and transnational actors. In addition to emerging standards regarding the physical safety and adequacy of water supplied for domestic purposes, notably including the WHO Guidelines for Drinking-water Quality, standards are also being adopted by bodies such as the International Organisation for Standardisation (ISO), which set down more general service quality guidelines for utilities providing domestic water and sanitation services. Also, certain institutions providing finance for major water services projects, such as multilateral development banks (MDBs), are developing sophisticated standards for cost recovery which seek to adopt elements of a human rights-based approach by taking account of the affordability of water and sanitation services and providing safeguards for poor and vulnerable people, including restrictions on service disconnection for non-payment of charges. At every level of decision-making regarding water and sanitation services, standards of governance informed by the practice of human rights, including standards concerned with transparency, participation, reviewability and accountability, have become pervasive.

The question of which standards attend the recent emergence in international human rights discourse of a right of access to water and sanitation is absolutely central to understanding this right's role in creating a novel normative paradigm to further universal access. Though the precise legal status, justiciability and normative implications of a right to water and sanitation in international human rights law remain the subject of debate,[1] the proliferation of substantive and procedural

[1] For example, United Nations Development Report (UNDP) 'Human Development Report 2006 – Beyond Scarcity: Power, Poverty and the Global Water Crisis' (2006) concedes at 60 that 'the recognition that water is a basic human right' can merely be understood as 'establishing a non-legally

standards in support of such a right testifies to the practical impact of such a rights discourse in this area. Myriad aspects of the various steps required to implement a human right to water and sanitation have come to be defined by diverse types of standards, both formal and informal, adopted at the international and transnational levels. These include technical environmental and health-related standards, such as those pertaining to the quality of drinking water, service standards for utility companies providing water and sanitation services, social and economic standards for the protection of vulnerable people and governance standards designed to ensure the meaningful participation of stakeholders and the public in decision making concerning all aspects of water services provision and water resources management.

Though a human right to water and sanitation might arise in either international law or domestic law, this chapter will focus on standards emerging at the international or transnational levels, as reference to the right to water or sanitation in national constitutions or legislation tend to be fleeting and lacking in detail. National rules therefore come to rely heavily on widely accepted standards developed at the international and transnational levels, as indicative of international 'best practice'.[2] Such standards inevitably inform and facilitate the practical application of domestic rules. However, this chapter does not confine itself to an analysis of formal standards developed and adopted by State-led and officially mandated international bodies. It also takes account of voluntary codes and other informal performance standards relevant to realisation of different aspects of the human right to water and sanitation, which might in certain situations have a greater influence on the conduct of key actors than formal legal frameworks, even where such frameworks exist. Lack of international consensus regarding the formal legal status of the human right to water and sanitation, along with wide disparities in the right's formal incorporation into national legal systems, illustrate the inherent inadequacies of traditional State-centred mechanisms for elaborating and enforcing economic, social and cultural rights.[3] In response, a range of novel, and often informal, standards are emerging which serve incrementally to normativise the values promoted within the human right to water and sanitation.

binding normative framework for the "progressive realisation" of the human right to water and sanitation'.

[2] See, for example, the Botswana case of *Matsipane Mosetlhanyane and Gakenyatsiwe Matsipane v The Attorney General* [2011] CA (Lobatse) CACLB07410, summarised in WaterLex/WASH United, The Human Rights to Water and Sanitation in Courts Worldwide: A Selection of National, Regional and International Case Law (WaterLex/WASH United 2014) 34.

[3] Walker describes Twining's point of departure in his examination of the new conception of legal order embodied in 'global law' as 'the inadequacy of the received model of modern law – the state-centred law-world – to our circumstances of intensifying "global" interdependence'; See N Walker, *Intimations of Global Law* (CUP 2014) 9, referring to W Twining, *General Jurisprudence: Understanding Law from a Global Perspective* (CUP 2009) Chapter 1.

7.2 DEVELOPMENT OF THE HUMAN RIGHT(S) TO WATER AND SANITATION

A degree of international consensus has now been achieved as regards the origins of the human right of access to water in international law and its broad normative content with the 2002 adoption of General Comment No. 15[4] by the UN Committee on Economic, Social and Cultural Rights (CESCR). General Comment No. 15 represents the CESCR's definitive position on the subject and 'is the first recognition by a United Nations human rights body of an independent and generally applicable human right to water'.[5] Though CESCR general comments do not formally impose legal obligations on States parties to the 1966 International Covenant on Economic, Social and Cultural Rights (ICESCR),[6] let alone other States, General Comment No. 15 constitutes a nonbinding but 'highly authoritative interpretation of the Covenant' and of the legal implications which flow from key relevant Covenant provisions.[7] As a nonbinding interpretation, General Comment No. 15 may be used to determine whether States have met their treaty obligations.[8] However, McCaffrey characterises General Comment No. 15 as being 'more in the nature of a statement *de lege ferenda* rather than *lex lata*' and cautions that the interpretation of Articles 11 and 12 of the 1966 Covenant contained therein 'must be accepted by the States parties to the Covenant in order to be binding upon them'.[9] Though McCaffrey noted in 2005 that 'it may take some time for countries to react, one way or another, to the Committee's views, and thus for observers to have evidence on which to base a judgment as to whether an independent human right to water truly forms part of international law', it is today possible to identify a reasonably significant body of recent State practice supporting the existence of this right.[10]

4 Committee on Economic, Social and Cultural Rights 'General Comment No. 15, The Right to Water (Articles 11 and 12 of the International Covenant on Economic, Social and Cultural Rights)' UN Doc E/C.12/2002/11 (26 November 2002); see also Chapters 2, 5 and 13 in this volume by Sumudu Attapatu, Louis Kotzé and Anel du Plessis, and Nathan Cooper, respectively, which also refer to the evolution of the right to water.

5 SC McCaffrey, 'The Human Right to Water' in E Brown Weiss, L Boisson de Chazournes and N Bernasconi-Osterwalder (eds), *Fresh Water and International Economic Law* (OUP 2005) 93 101.

6 UNGA Res 2200, 21 UN GAOR, 22nd Sess, Supp 49, UN Doc A/6316 (1967), (1967) 6 ILM 360

7 McCaffrey (n 5) 94.

8 M Williams, 'Privatization and the Human Right to Water: Challenges for the New Century' (2007) 28 Michigan Journal of International Law 469, 475; See also, EB Bluemel, 'The Implications of Formulating a Human Right to Water' (2004) 31 Ecology Law Quarterly 957, 972.

9 McCaffrey (n 5) 103.

10 For examples of relevant State practice, particularly judicial or official policy statements alluding to the human right to water or to General Comment No. 15, see WaterLex/WASH United (n 2); Bluemel (n 8) 977; R Pejan, 'The Right to Water: The Road to Justiciability' (2004) 36 George Washington International Law Review 1181, at 1194–96 and 1203–08; PH Gleick, 'The Human Right To Water' (1998) 1(5) Water Policy 487, 494.

While it has been suggested that a human right to water can be inferred from the 1948 Universal Declaration of Human Rights,[11] and the 1966 Covenant on Civil and Political Rights,[12] the CESCR contends that the emergence of the human right to water in general international law can primarily be traced to Articles 11 and 12 of the 1966 ICESCR.[13] Article 11(1) of the Covenant, which provides for the right to an adequate standard of living, sets out a non-exhaustive, indicative list of related entitlements which are indispensable for the realisation of that right, 'including adequate food, clothing and housing'. The CESCR concludes that 'the right to water clearly falls within the category of guarantees essential for securing an adequate standard of living, particularly since it is one of the most fundamental conditions for survival'.[14] One view suggests that water is such a fundamental requirement for an adequate standard of living that its formal inclusion under Article 11 was unnecessary.[15] In this context, General Comment No. 15 'notes the importance of ensuring sustainable access to water resources for agriculture to realize the right to adequate food', and also takes note of the duty in Article 1(2) of the Covenant, which provides that a people may not 'be deprived of its means of subsistence'.[16] The CESCR had earlier determined that the right to adequate housing should include 'sustainable access' to safe drinking water, site drainage, sanitation and washing facilities.[17] The Committee has also found that the right to water is inextricably linked to the right to the highest attainable standard of health, enshrined under Article 12(1) of the Covenant. General Comment No. 15 acknowledges the significance of clean, safe water for hygiene and health, stating that 'environmental hygiene, as an aspect of the right to health under article 12, paragraph 2(b), of the Covenant, encompasses taking steps on a non-discriminatory basis to prevent threats to health from unsafe and toxic water conditions'.[18] Gleick insists that access to

[11] Universal Declaration of Human Rights, UNGA Res 217A (III) (New York, 10 December 1948), UN GAOR, 3rd Sess, UN Doc A/64 (1948), notably art 25(1) on the right to an adequate standard of living; see further A Hardberger, 'Life, Liberty and the Pursuit of Water: Evaluating Water as a Human Right and the Duties and Obligations it Creates' (2005) 4(2) Northwestern Journal of International Human Rights 331, 337; and SMA Salman and S McInerney-Lankford, *The Human Right to Water: Legal and Policy Dimensions* (World Bank 2004); Gleick, ibid 491.

[12] UNGA Res 2200, 21 UN GAOR, 22nd Sess, Supp 52, UN Doc A/6316 (1967), (1967) 6 ILM 368. See General Comment No. 15 (n 4), para 3, notably Article 6 on the right to life; see Williams (n 8) 474.

[13] Williams (n 8) 476. See further, J Razzaque 'Trading Water: The Human Factor' (2004) 13(1) Review of European Community and International Environmental Law 15, 17.

[14] General Comment No. 15 (n 4) para 3.

[15] Gleick (n 10) 487. See further, SR Tully, 'The Contribution of Human Rights to Freshwater Resource Management' (2004) Yearbook of International Environmental Law 101,108.

[16] General Comment 15 (n 4) para 7; See further, Tully ibid 110.

[17] CESCR, General Comment 4, The Right to Adequate Housing (Article 11(1)), UN Doc E/1992/23, para 8(b).

[18] General Comment No. 15 (n 4) para 8. See also, CESCR 'General Comment No. 14, The Right to the Highest Attainable Standard of Health (Article 12)' UN Doc E/C.12/2000/4 (2000), at paras 11, 12, 15, 34, 36, 40, 43, 51 and 65.

water can readily be inferred as a derivative right necessary to meet both the explicit rights to health and an adequate standard of living.[19]

Therefore, though General Comment No. 15 effectively extends the scope of the right to water from a previously restricted understanding encompassing only a right to drinking water[20] to one including basic sanitation and water required to produce adequate food,[21] it strongly suggests that the right is ancillary to and must be implied from other economic, social and cultural rights rather than an independent right under the ICESCR.[22] This issue is of considerable practical significance because the normative content of a right to water that is ancillary to, and instrumental in the realisation of, other established rights will necessarily be determined by reference to the particular established right invoked. Noting that 'various connected rights may implicate different state obligations', Williams explains that a right to water derived from the right to life, and merely requiring the provision of drinking water, would impose lesser State obligations than a right to water derived from the right to health, requiring the provision of water for both drinking and sanitation.[23] Uncertainty also remains as to the true normative status and content of several economic, social and cultural rights listed under the ICESCR from which the right to water may be derived, leading to further confusion as to its precise legal implications.[24] For example, though some commentators describe the right to food as well established,[25] it might be argued that it raises many questions regarding the enforceability of such welfare rights under the ICESCR. At any rate, though proponents of an independent right to water argue that it would result in greater interpretive consistency, State compliance, enforcement and remedies for violations,[26]

19 Gleick (n 10) 492 citing a 1999 review of human rights progress over the past fifty years, Y Danieli, E Stamatopoulou and CJ Diaz, *The Universal Declaration of Human Rights: Fifty Years and Beyond* (Baywood Publishing Co. 1999).

20 See Salman and McInerney-Lankford (n 11) 65; M Mahayni, 'The Human Right to Water: is the State's Capacity to Fulfil its Obligations Hindered under Public-Private Partnerships?' (2006) 17(3) Water Law 100, 101; For example, under art 14(2)(h) of the 1981 Convention on the Elimination of All Forms of Discrimination against Women (CEDAW) 1249 UNTS 13 (30 September 1981), the right is expressed as a right of 'water supply', and under art 24 of the 1989 Convention on the Rights of the Child (CRC) 1577 UNTS 3 (20 November 1989), as a State obligation to ensure 'provision of . . . clean drinking water'. See further, Williams (n 8) 472–73.

21 The Committee's understanding of the scope of the right to water appears to have expanded between 2000 and 2002, as General Comment No. 14 (n 18) had only included at para 4, 'access to safe and potable water' within the rubric of the right to health.

22 UN General Assembly Resolution 70/16 (22 February 2016) UN Doc A/RES/70/169, recalls that 'the human rights to safe drinking water and sanitation are derived from the right to an adequate standard of living and are inextricably related to the right to the highest attainable standard of physical and mental health, as well as to the right to life and human dignity'. See also, Human Rights Council Resolution 33/10 (27 September 2016) UN Doc A/HRC/33/L 19

23 Williams (n 8) 477. Williams also concludes that both CEDAW and CRC (n 20) suggest that 'the right to water merits protection because of its connection to other rights'. See further, Bluemel (n 8) 963.

24 Bluemel ibid 971.

25 Williams (n 8) 479.

26 Bluemel (n 8) 968–72; Hardberger (n 11) 360–62; see Williams ibid 478; see also Gleick (n 10) as an example of a commentator who argues, at 490 and 501, that an independent right to water exists in customary international law.

such an independent right could only arise in international law by means of a dedicated treaty instrument or through customary international law.[27] There does not currently exist any such treaty instrument, nor any proposal therefor, by which States might bind themselves in this regard. Also, despite the sustained declaratory support of international conferences and UN agencies, as well as some legislative and constitutional State recognition, there is as yet insufficient generalised State practice to establish a right to water under customary international law that would bind those States that have not actively and formally recognised the right.[28] Williams therefore concludes that 'at best, this seems to give the independent right the current status of a normative ideal'.[29] Such legal uncertainty highlights the practical utility of the broad range of technical and performance standards currently emerging in relation to realisation of the right to water.

If the formal normative status and justiciability in international law of the human right to water remains in doubt, then even greater uncertainty bedevils the emergence and recognition of the closely related human right of access to sanitation.[30] As a leading proponent pointed out in 2010:

> As yet, there is no single resolution of the UN General Assembly on the right to sanitation and no worldwide agreement supporting this right. There is no agreed description of core obligations on sanitation and no definition of the content of the right to sanitation.[31]

Though the UN General Assembly has since adopted a 2010 Resolution on 'The Human Right to Water *and Sanitation*',[32] Smets' observation that States 'in particular have not adopted a General Comment on the Right to Sanitation' remains valid.[33] Where it does include express mention of sanitation, General Comment No. 15 states that 'ensuring that everyone has access to adequate sanitation is not only fundamental for human dignity and privacy, but is one of the principal mechanisms for protecting the quality of drinking water supplies and resources'.[34] This suggests that it focuses primarily on problems of access to drinking water rather than the issue of access to sanitation, largely viewing the universal provision of adequate sanitation as necessary for, and ancillary to, provision of safe drinking water. More recently, commentators have noted that Sustainable Development Goal 6 (SDG 6), adopted in 2015 under the auspices of the 2030 Agenda for Sustainable Development,[35] includes Target 6.2

27 See Hardberger ibid 361–62.
28 DJ Bederman, International Law Frameworks (2001) at 15, cited by Williams (n 8) 478.
29 ibid.
30 See generally H Smets (ed), L'Accès à l'assainissement, un Droit Fondamental (2010 Editions Johanet).
31 H Smets, 'The Right to Sanitation: A New Human Right in Developed Countries' (2010) 40(2) and (3) *Environmental Policy and Law* 112 (at 3 of on-line version).
32 UNGA Res 64/294 (26 July 2010), UN Doc A/64/L.63/Rev.1 (emphasis added).
33 Smets (n 31) (at 3 of on-line version).
34 Para 29. See also paras 1 and 28.
35 UNGA 'Transforming our world: the 2030 Agenda for Sustainable Development' UNGA Res 70/1 (25 September 2015) UN Doc A/RES/70/1. The SDGs are available at <www.undp.org/content/

committing the international community to 'achieve access to adequate and equitable sanitation and hygiene for all and to end open defecation', which may play a formative role in crystalizing the commitment of States to the right to sanitation.[36]

Overshadowing any discussion of whether the human right to water and sanitation might exist as an ancillary or independent right is the fact that the ICESCR, and any rights derived therefrom, suffers from a clear lack of immediate enforceability, with Article 2(1) merely requiring each State party 'to take steps ... to the maximum of its available resources, with a view to achieving progressively the full realization of the rights recognized in the present Covenant'. Thus, 'the principal challenge is therefore linking the expectations of individuals as rights-holders with the duties owed by others'.[37] Regarding the justiciability of the obligations set out under the ICESCR, McCaffrey suggests the language of Article 2(1) would provide a lawyer acting for a State accused of breaching its obligations with 'ample bases for a defense'.[38] However, in relation to the package of obligations set out in General Comment No. 15 as inherent to the right to water, Tully argues that 'several obligations – namely non-discrimination and undertaking deliberate, concrete and targeted steps – are amenable to immediate implementation'.[39] The CESCR has earlier characterised a number of such 'core obligations', expressly identified in General Comment No. 15 as applying to the right to water,[40] as being non-derogable and of 'immediate effect'.[41] The obligation upon a State to 'take steps ... to the maximum of its available resources' has been characterised as one of 'due diligence',[42] and Hardberger hints at the role of the due diligence concept in the elaboration of practicable standards for realisation of the right:

> Although due diligence has the disadvantage of being an undefined standard, it provides an adjustable criterion that depends on a particular government's capabilities and resources. The flexibility of the due diligence standard could also be its downfall in implementation. It raises several questions regarding who gets to determine a state's capabilities and who determines what diligence is sufficient. In spite of its drawbacks, the usefulness outweighs the uncertainty by providing a start that, in theory, can incorporate all countries.[43]

undp/en/home/sustainable-development-goals/goal-6-clean-water-and-sanitation.html> accessed 11 June 2018.

36 See O McIntyre, 'International Water Law and SDG 6: Mutually Reinforcing Regimes' in D French and L Kotze (eds), *Global Goals: Law, Theory and Implementation* (Edward Elgar 2018) 173, 179–182.

37 Tully (n 15) 104.

38 McCaffrey (n 5) 97.

39 Gleick (n 10) 104. Indeed, any State measure affecting access to water or sanitation which might be regarded as inherently discriminatory might fall foul of Article 2(2) of the ICESCR.

40 General Comment No. 15 (n 4), para 37. However, an examination of the 'core obligations' identified under para 37 would lead one to conclude that only those obligations listed under para 37(a), (b) and (f) might plausibly be considered capable of requiring immediate effect. See Mahayni (n 20) 102.

41 CESCR 'General Comment No. 3: The Nature of States Parties' Obligations (Article 2(1))' (1990) UN Doc E/1991/23.

42 See SC McCaffrey, 'A Human Right to Water: Domestic and International Implications' (1992) 5 Georgetown International Environmental Law Review 1, 13.

43 Hardberger (n 11) 336.

Regardless, however, of the formal legal status of the right to water and sanitation, the frenetic discourse launched by General Comment No. 15 has clearly had a significant impact on the practice of States and myriad other actors concerned, directly or indirectly, in the provision of water services or management of water resources. General Comment No. 15 correctly points out, at least insofar as it might apply in certain specific contexts, that 'the right to water has been recognized in a wide range of international documents, including treaties, declarations and other standards'.[44] Of greatest significance are several specialised binding instruments, including the 1979 CEDAW,[45] Article 14(2) of which requires that States parties ensure to women the right to 'enjoy adequate living conditions, particularly in relation to . . . water supply', and the 1989 CRC,[46] Article 24(2)(c) of which requires States parties to combat childhood disease and malnutrition 'through the provision of adequate nutritious foods and clean drinking water'. Williams points out that, in framing concluding observations in response to country reports submitted under the CRC and CEDAW, the respective monitoring bodies for each convention have tended to use language resonant of a right of access to water and sanitation.[47] Other relevant binding treaty instruments include the 1949 Geneva Convention (III) on the Treatment of Prisoners of War[48] and the 1949 Geneva Convention (IV) on the Treatment of Civilian Persons in Time of War.[49] While some commentators remain sceptical,[50] the significance of such clear treaty obligations for the development of the human right to water in general international law should not be underestimated. These obligations are set out in very widely ratified[51] and formally binding conventional instruments, with rigorous reporting and monitoring procedures and institutional monitoring machinery with the mandate and capacity to issue persuasive interpretations of the State obligations contained therein. Also, while water entitlements set out under these conventions extend only to women and children, it would be difficult at a practical level to compel provision of basic water and sanitation services to children or women to the exclusion of other members of families or

44 General Comment No. 15 (n 4) para 4.

45 UNGA (n 20). See also relevant declarations of intent, including the 1995 Beijing Declaration and Platform for Action, UN Doc A/CONF 177/20 (1995) and UN Doc A/CONF.177/20/Add.1 (1995), 'Women and Health' paras 92 and 106(x), cited in Tully (n 15) 105.

46 CRC (n 20).

47 Williams (n. 8) 482–85.

48 Articles 20, 26, 29 and 46 (1949) 75 UNTS 135. Entered into force 1950.

49 Articles 23, 55, 59, 85, 89 and 127 (1949) 75 UNTS 287. See also Additional Protocol to the Geneva Conventions Relating to the Protection of Victims of International Armed Conflicts (Protocol I), (1977) 1125 UNTS 3, at Articles 54 and 68–71, and Additional Protocol to the Geneva Conventions Relating to the Protection of Victims of Non-International Armed Conflicts (Protocol II) (1977) 1125 UNTS 609, at arts 5 and 18.

50 See, for example, McCaffrey (n 5) 98 and 107.

51 For example, Smets notes that CEDAW has 170 ratifications, while the CRC is 'the most widely accepted human rights treaty ever' with 191 ratifications. See H Smets, 'Economics of Water Services and the Right to Water' in E Brown Weiss, L Boisson de Chazournes and N Bernasconi-Osterwalder (eds), *Freshwater and International Economic Law* (OUP 2005); McCaffrey (n 5) 173 and 174.

communities. Other instruments lend further support for core elements of the right to water. For example, ILO Convention 169[52] aims to protect the rights of indigenous and tribal peoples and includes clear obligations for member States.[53]

A number of regional human rights instruments support the existence of a right to water. Article 14 of the 1990 African Charter on the Rights and Welfare of the Child, expressly requires States to ensure the availability of safe drinking water for the 'best attainable state of health',[54] while Article 11 of the 1988 Additional Protocol to the American Convention of Human Rights in the area of economic, social and cultural rights provides that 'everyone shall have the right to live in a healthy environment and to have access to basic public services'.[55] Regional bodies responsible for monitoring compliance with human rights obligations have also inferred the existence of a right to water from core obligations of States under general regional human rights instruments. For example, the African Commission on Human and Peoples' Rights found in 1995 that Zaire (Democratic Republic of Congo) had violated the right to health under Article 16 of the 1981 African Charter on Human and Peoples Rights[56] by failing 'to provide basic services such as safe drinking water'.[57] Similarly, the Inter-American Commission on Human Rights 1997 report on Ecuador found that the 'considerable risk posed to human life and health by oil exploration activities ... through, *inter alia*, contamination of water supplies'[58] could impact upon the right to life and the duty to protect the physical integrity of the individual under the 1969 American Convention on Human Rights.[59]

Quite apart from international human rights law, values inherent to the right to water and sanitation are reflected in other fields of international law. For example, regarding those elements of the right which relate to the environmental protection of freshwater resources,[60] Williams concludes that 'principles and texts of international

52 Convention concerning Indigenous and Tribal Peoples in Independent Countries, 27 June 1989, 28 ILM 1382 (1989). Notably, art 15(1) on the rights of indigenous peoples to use and management of natural resources.

53 See generally P Cullet and A Gowlland-Gaultieri, 'Local Communities and Water Investments' in E Brown Weiss, L Boisson de Chazournes, and N Bernasconi-Osterwalder (eds), (n 51); McCaffrey (n 5) 303, 323–25.

54 OAU Doc CAB/LEG/24.9/49 (1990) in force 1999.

55 Organization of American States (OAS), Additional Protocol to the American Convention on Human Rights in the Area of Economic, Social and Cultural Rights ("Protocol of San Salvador"), 17 November 1988. OAS Treaty Series No. 69; 28 ILM 156 (1989). <www.oas.org/juridico/english/Treaties/a-52.html> accessed 11 June 2018.

56 African Charter on Human and Peoples Rights (1981) 21 ILM 58.

57 African Commission on Human and Peoples' Rights, Comm No 25/89, 47/90, 56/91, 100/93, Decision taken at the 18th Ordinary Session, 1995; See McCaffrey (n 5) 99.

58 Inter-American Commission on Human Rights, 'Report on the Situation of Human Rights in Ecuador' OEA/Ser.L/V/II.96, Doc. 10 rev. 1 (24 April 1997); see McCaffrey ibid.

59 1144 UNTS 123; (1969) 9 ILM 673; (1971) 65 AJIL 679 (22 November 1969)

60 See General Comment 15(n 4), paras 8, 10, 11, 12(b), 16(c) and (d), 21, 23, 28(b) and (e), 29, 44(a)(iii) and (b)(i).

environmental law, while perhaps not sufficient to establish a right to water independently, do offer additional support for the right'.[61] More significantly, in the area of international water law the 1997 UN Watercourses Convention,[62] a general framework agreement widely regarded as a seminal codification of customary international law applying to shared international water resources,[63] qualifies the general position that 'no use of an international watercourse enjoys inherent priority over other uses' by providing that States must give 'special regard … to the requirements of vital human needs'.[64] Clearly, one would expect the 'requirements of vital human needs' to correspond closely with the obligations of States and the entitlements of individuals under the human right to water,[65] and as McCaffrey points out:

> While this language falls short of an explicit recognition of a human right to water, it expresses a fundamental idea behind such a right, namely, that in making allocation decisions governments must not forget basic needs of humans for water.[66]

Similarly, the 1992 UNECE Convention on the Protection and Use of Transboundary Watercourses and International Lakes[67] has given rise to a 1999 Protocol on Water and Health,[68] which expressly requires the parties to take 'all appropriate measures for the purpose of ensuring … adequate supplies of wholesome drinking water'[69] and further provides that the parties 'shall pursue the aims of … access to drinking water for everyone'.[70] In addition, the International Law Association's 2004 Berlin Rules on Water Resources Law,[71] which revise and update the ILA's seminal 1966 Helsinki Rules,[72] give clear and formal priority to vital human needs,[73] which the ILA defines to mean 'waters used for immediate

61 Williams (n 8) 476–77.

62 United Nations Convention on the Law of Non-Navigational Uses of International Watercourses (1997) 36 ILM 719 (21 May 1997).

63 See further O McIntyre, *Environmental Protection of International Watercourses under International Law* (Ashgate 2007) 2.

64 Article 10.

65 A statement of understanding on art 10(2) of the UN Watercourses Convention was inserted into the Report of the Working Group on the UN Convention to the General Assembly, which provided that 'in determining "vital human needs", special attention is to be paid to providing sufficient water to sustain human life, including both drinking water and water required for production of food in order to prevent starvation'. See the oral report of the coordinator of the informal consultations on Article 10(2), UN Doc A/C.6/51/SR.57 (1997) 3; See further A Tanzi and M Arcari, *The United Nations Convention on the Law of International Watercourses* (Kluwer Law International 2001) 139.

66 McCaffrey (n 5) 100–01.

67 (1992) 31 ILM 1312.

68 UN Doc MP.WAT/AC.1/1991/1 (17 June 1999).

69 Article 4(2)(a).

70 Article 6(1)(a).

71 ILA, Berlin Rules on Water Resources Law (2004) <www.asil.org/ilib/WaterReport2004.pdf> accessed 8 January 2018.

72 ILA, Helsinki Rules on the Uses of Waters of International Rivers 'Report of the Fifty-Second Conference' (Helsinki, 1966).

73 Article 14(1) provides: 'In determining an equitable and reasonable use, States shall first allocate waters to satisfy vital human needs.'

human survival, including drinking, cooking, and sanitary needs, as well as water needed for the immediate sustenance of a household'.[74] In conjunction with this formal priority for vital human needs in inter-State allocation of waters, the Berlin Rules include Article 17 on 'The Right of Access to Water', which provides, *inter alia*, that 'every individual has a right of access to sufficient, safe, acceptable, physically accessible, and affordable water to meet that individual's vital human needs'.

7.3 THE EMERGENCE OF STANDARDS

The CESCR presciently suggests the kind of standards required to realise the right to water by explaining that it consists of both freedoms and entitlements, the former including 'the right to be free from interference, such as the right to be free from arbitrary disconnections or contamination of water supplies', the latter including 'the right to a system of water supply and management that provides equality of opportunity for people to enjoy the right to water'.[75] Essentially, the various elements of the right to water 'must be *adequate* for human dignity, life and health, in accordance with articles 11, paragraph 1, and 12',[76] and General Comment No. 15 elaborates further, stating that the relevant factors in determining such adequacy include availability, quality and accessibility.[77] The requirement of availability stipulates that States ensure a sufficient and continuous supply of water for such personal and domestic uses as drinking, personal sanitation, washing of clothes, food preparation and personal and household hygiene, in a quantity which corresponds to World Health Organisation (WHO) guidelines.[78] Quality refers to the safety of water, in terms of the absence of micro-organisms, chemical substances and radiological hazards potentially dangerous to human health, and to available water being of an acceptable colour, odour and taste for each personal and domestic use.[79] The requirement of accessibility stipulates that water facilities and services should be accessible to everyone without discrimination[80] and has regard to physical accessibility,

74 Article 3(20).
75 General Comment No. 15 (n 4) para 10.
76 ibid para 11.
77 ibid para 12.
78 ibid para 12(a). As regards the minimum quantity of water required by individuals, the WHO suggests an absolute minimum of 7.5 litres per capita per day: <www.who.int/water_sanitation_health/emergencies/qa/emergencies_qa5/en/> accessed 11 June 2018. However, more in-depth WHO guidance recognises the need to distinguish between peoples' short-term, medium-term and long-term water needs. See WHO-WEDC, 'Technical Notes on Drinking-Water, Sanitation, and Hygiene in Emergencies' (July 2013) <www.who.int/water_sanitation_health/publications/2011/WHO_TN_09_How_much_water_is_needed.pdf?ua=1> accessed 11 June 2018.
79 General Comment No. 15 (n 4) para 12(b).
80 The ICESCR gives special priority to non-discrimination, with art 2(2) of the Covenant providing that 'the States Parties to the present Covenant undertake to guarantee that the rights enunciated in the present Covenant will be exercised without discrimination of any kind as to race, colour, sex, language, religion, political or other opinion, national or social origin, property, birth or other status'.

including physical security, gender and cultural factors and proximity to households, educational institutions and workplaces;[81] to economic accessibility, including the issue of affordability;[82] to non-discrimination, including accessibility to the most vulnerable and marginalised sections of the population;[83] and to information accessibility, including the right to seek, receive and impart information on water issues.[84] The CESCR places special emphasis on the issues of non-discrimination and equality of access,[85] and makes particular mention of a number of 'individuals and groups who have traditionally faced difficulties in exercising this right', including women; children; rural and deprived urban areas; indigenous peoples; nomadic and traveller communities; refugees, asylum seekers, internally displaced persons and returnees; prisoners and detainees; and groups facing difficulties with physical access, such as older persons and persons with disabilities.[86] In connection with the 'core obligation' of States 'to adopt and implement a national water strategy and plan of action', General Comment No. 15 stipulates that 'it should include methods, such as right to water indicators and benchmarks, by which progress can be closely monitored'.[87] Paragraph 53 advises that 'States parties may obtain guidance on appropriate indicators' from such intergovernmental bodies as WHO, FAO, ILO and UNEP, though such guidance is increasingly supplemented by standards established at the initiative of business and civil society actors.[88]

7.3.1 *Health Standards*

Regarding the quality of water required for personal or domestic use, General Comment No. 15 expressly refers to 1993 WHO guidelines[89] that are

> intended to be used as a basis for the development of national standards that, if properly implemented, will ensure the safety of drinking water supplies through the elimination of, or reduction to a minimum concentration, of constituents of water that are known to be hazardous to health.[90]

81 General Comment No. 15 (n 4), para 12(c)(i).
82 ibid para 12(c)(ii). See further below.
83 ibid para 12(c)(iii).
84 ibid para 12(c)(iv).
85 ibid paras 13–16.
86 ibid para 16.
87 ibid para 37(f). See also para 47(d) and (e).
88 See, for example, the Corporate Water Disclosure Guidelines (2014) adopted by the CEO Water Mandate, a network of business leaders established under the auspices of the UN Global Compact, the world's largest corporate sustainability initiative. See further, <https://ceowatermandate.org/disclosure/> accessed 11 June 2018.
89 WHO, Guidelines for Drinking Water Quality (2nd edn, WHO 1993) Vols 1–3.
90 General Comment No. 15 (n 4) para 12(b). WHO is also included among those organisations from whom 'State parties may obtain guidance on appropriate indicators', pursuant to General Comment No. 15, para 53.

The current 2017 edition of the relevant WHO guidelines[91] runs to 631 pages and provides a great deal of detail on the microbial, chemical and radiological aspects of drinking water quality standards, as well as on 'acceptability' aspects regarding taste, odour and appearance. In addition to specific technical parameters for an extensive list of commonly occurring waterborne pollutants, the guidelines advise on their application in a range of conditions and circumstances, including water scarcity and heavy rainfall, rainwater harvesting, vended water, desalination systems, emergencies and disasters, buildings and health care facilities, drinking water for travellers, and aircraft and ships. Further, the guidelines also elaborate upon such issues as the respective roles of various actors involved in drinking water supply, water safety plans, and drinking water quality surveillance. Whereas the third step of progressive monitoring for SDG Indicator 6.1.1 requires 'inclusion of water quality testing for faecal contamination and priority chemicals (arsenic and fluoride) by utilities and/or in household survey instruments',[92] it seems reasonable to assume that the results of such testing would be assessed against the values set down in the current WHO guidelines. Such specificity regarding the technical standards to be achieved, as well as the methodologies to be employed to that end, is centrally important in establishing the normative character of the core requirements of the human right to water.

7.3.2 *Environmental Standards*

It is clear that the right to water must encompass entitlements and obligations relating to protection of the natural environment, and aquatic ecosystems in particular, as the latter are increasingly understood to play a pivotal role in the provision of water-related ecosystem services. General Comment No. 15 declares that the right to water involves both the right of the individual to be free 'from unsafe and toxic water conditions'[93] and from 'contamination of water supplies',[94] and the obligation of States to refrain from 'unlawfully diminishing or polluting water'[95] and to adopt legislative and other measures to restrain third parties from polluting water sources.[96] In addition, it stipulates that States parties should adopt strategies and programmes aimed at 'reducing and eliminating contamination of watersheds and water-related ecosystems' and 'assessing the impacts of actions that may impinge upon water availability and natural ecosystems watersheds, such as climate change, desertification and increased soil salinity, deforestation and loss of biodiversity'.[97]

91 WHO, Guidelines for Drinking Water Quality (4th edn, Incorporating the First Addendum, WHO 2017) <http://apps.who.int/iris/bitstream/10665/254637/1/9789241549950-eng.pdf?ua=1> accessed 11 June 2018.

92 UN-Water, 'Integrated Monitoring Guide for SDG 6: Targets and Global Indicators' (19 July 2016) 5.

93 General Comment No. 15 (n 4) para 8.

94 ibid para 10.

95 ibid para 21.

96 ibid para 23.

97 ibid para 28(b) and (e).

As regards the environmental standards to be applied pursuant to the right to water, General Comment No. 15 expressly lists UNEP[98] among the organisations from whom 'States parties may obtain guidance on appropriate indicators',[99] thereby stressing the direct relevance of UN Environment's work on water and freshwater ecosystems. This connection once again highlights the strong interlinkages between the right to water and SDG 6 as UN Environment's new Freshwater Strategy 2017–2021 focuses on those SDG targets that relate to freshwater ecosystems, water quality and pollution, integrated water resources management (IWRM) and water-related conflict and disasters.[100]

Official guidance on implementation of SDG 6 emphasises the use of existing environmental standards set out under relevant multilateral environmental agreements (MEAs), wherever available. For example, UN-Water guidelines relating to Target 6.3 on water quality and wastewater,[101] which aim to protect both ecosystem health and human health by eliminating, minimising and significantly reducing different streams of pollution into water bodies, advocate doing so in a manner consistent with the Basel Convention on the Control of Transboundary Movements of Hazardous Wastes and their Disposal,[102] the Rotterdam Convention on the Prior Informed Consent Procedure for Certain Hazardous Chemicals and Pesticides in International Trade[103] and the Stockholm Convention on Persistent Organic Pollutants.[104] Regarding standards stipulated thereunder, the latter Convention has established a Persistent Organic Pollutants Review Committee comprising thirty-one experts nominated by the States parties, which reviews chemicals nominated for listing and control under the Convention having regard to detailed criteria relating to their persistence, bioaccumulation, potential for long-range environmental transport and toxicity (Annex D), to the likelihood of these chemicals leading to significant adverse effects on human health or the environment (Annex E) and to socioeconomic considerations associated with possible control measures (Annex F). Similarly, regarding SDG Target 6.5 on water resources management and SDG Target 6.6 on water-related ecosystems, the same guidance refers,[105] respectively, to the 1992 UNECE Convention on the Protection and Use of Transboundary Watercourses and International Lakes[106] and the 1997 UN Convention on the Law of the Non-Navigational Uses of International Watercourses,[107] as well as to

98 Now UN Environment, see <www.unep.org> accessed 11 June 2018.
99 General Comment No. 15 (n 4) para 53.
100 Specifically SDG Targets 6.3, 6.5, 6.6, 11.5 and 16.1. See UN Environment, 'Freshwater Strategy 2017–2021' (2017) 6 <https://wedocs.unep.org/bitstream/handle/20.500.11822/19528/UNEP-full_report-170502.pdf?sequence=3&isAllowed=y> accessed 11 June 2018.
101 UN-Water, 'Integrated Monitoring Guide for SDG 6: Targets and Global Indicators' (n 92) 8.
102 1673 UNTS 126; (1989) 28 ILM 657.
103 2244 UNTS 337; (1999) 38 ILM 1.
104 2256 UNTS 119; (2001) 40 ILM 532.
105 UN-Water (n 101) 16–20.
106 1936 UNTS 269; (1992) 31 ILM 1312.
107 (1997) 36 ILM 700.

the Ramsar Convention on Wetlands of International Importance[108] and the highly specific Aichi Biodiversity Targets adopted under the Convention for Biological Diversity Strategic Plan for Biodiversity 2011–2020.[109] The UNECE Water Convention, which is supported by a Secretariat, has been a very important source of technical guidance on all aspects of transboundary water resources management,[110] while the Ramsar Convention's Scientific and Technical Review Panel (STRP), established to provide objective and high-quality scientific and technical guidance to the Convention Parties and Secretariat, has over decades elaborated and refined the concept of 'wise use of wetlands' as a key standard of ecosystems protection.[111]

Therefore, the wealth of standards and practice developed under the auspices of established MEAs assists in informing the precise normative implications of the human right to water and sanitation. The relatively highly developed domestic legal frameworks for environmental protection of water resources also provide a rich source of environmental standards which function to assist realisation of the right to water. Notably, the European Union (EU) has long legislated for the management and protection of water resources, prescribing detailed standards such as the limit values introduced for List I substances under the 1976 EU Directive on Pollution Caused by Certain Dangerous Substances Discharged into the Aquatic Environment.[112] Such limit values were not to be exceeded by EU Member States when setting national emission standards for discharges into the aquatic environment. Over time, the EU adopted a comprehensive suite of Directives establishing limit values and water quality objectives relating to all List I substances.[113] The relevance of such a diversity of legal and nonlegal environmental standards for understanding the precise normative implications of the right to water provides an illustration of the phenomenon of growing normative convergence in

108 996 UNTS 245; (1972) 11 ILM 963.

109 CBD 'Strategic Plan for Biodiversity 2011–2020' <www.cbd.int/doc/strategic-plan/2011-2020/Aichi-Targets-EN.pdf> accessed 11 June 2018.

110 Including, notably, 1993 'Guidelines on the Ecosystem Approach in Water Management' (UN Doc ECE/ENV/WA/31 1993) and UNECE 'Recommendations on Payments for Ecosystems Services in Integrated Water Resources Management' (2007).

111 See Ramsar Convention, *Handbooks for the Wise Use of Wetlands* (4th edn, 2010) <www.ramsar.org/resources/ramsar-handbooks> accessed 11 June 2018.

112 Directive 76/464/EEC of 18 May [1976] OJ L129/23.

113 Including: Directive 82/176/EEC of 27 March 1982 concerning the Discharge of Mercury by the Chlor-Alkali Electrolysis Industry [1982] OJ L81; Directive 84/156/EEC of 17 March 1984 concerning the Discharge of Mercury by the Chlor-Alkali Electrolysis Industry [1984] OJ L74; Directive 83/513/EEC of 24 October 1983 concerning the Discharge of Cadmium [1983] OJ L291/1; Directive 84/491/EEC of 9 October 1984 on Limit Values and Quality Objectives for Discharges of Hexachlorocyclohexane [1984] OJ L274/11; Directive 86/280/EEC of 12 June 1986 on Limit Values and Quality Objectives for Discharges of Certain Dangerous Substances Included in List I of the Annex to Directive 76/464/EEC, including Carbon Tetrachloride, DDT and Pentachlorophenol, [1986] OJ L181/16; Directive 88/347/EEC of 25 June 1988 on Limit Values and Quality Objectives relating to Aldrin, Dieldrin, Endrin, Isodrin, Hexachlorobenzene, Hexachlorobutadine, and Chloroform (1988) OJ L158/35.

environmental regulation at all levels commonly referred to as 'global environmental law'[114] or 'global administrative law'.[115]

7.3.3 *Service Standards*

As this human right is largely concerned with equitable access to adequate water and sanitation services, the emergence of performance standards for utilities charged with provision of such services is centrally relevant. Since 2007, ISO Technical Committee 224 has been busy developing a range of general service quality standards covering various aspects of the work of water and sanitation services utilities, whether public or private. Standards adopted thus far include those for the quality of water supply and sanitation services provided to users,[116] for the management of wastewater utilities and the assessment of wastewater services,[117] for the management of drinking water utilities and the assessment of drinking water services,[118] for the management of drinking water distribution networks,[119] for crisis management of water utilities[120] and for benchmarking of water utilities.[121] A host of additional standards are currently under development relating to, *inter alia*, stormwater management, use of performance indicators, the management of water supply and wastewater system assets, water quality event detection processes, technical specifications for flushable products and water loss reduction and management projects.[122] Development of the ISO standards by Technical Committee 224 involves thirty-five participating States and seventeen observer States, in liaison with a range of interested international organisations, including the WHO, the World Bank and the International Water Association, along with leading industry interests. These

114 See further T Yang and R Percival, 'The Emergence of Global Environmental Law' (2009) 36 Ecology Law Quarterly 615–64.

115 See further O McIntyre, 'The Human Right to Water as a Creature of Global Administrative Law' (2012) 37(6) Water International 654–69.

116 ISO 24510:2007 'Activities relating to drinking water and wastewater services – Guidelines for the assessment and for the improvement of the service to users'. <www.iso.org/standard/37246.html?browse=tc> accessed 11 June 2018.

117 ISO 24511:2007 'Activities relating to drinking water and wastewater services – Guidelines for the management of wastewater utilities and for the assessment of wastewater services' <www.iso.org/standard/37247.html?browse=tc> accessed 11 June 2018.

118 ISO 24512:2007 'Activities relating to drinking water and wastewater services – Guidelines for the management of drinking water utilities and for the assessment of drinking water services' <www.iso.org/standard/37248.html?browse=tc> accessed 11 June 2018.

119 ISO 24516-1:2016 'Guidelines for the management of assets of water supply and wastewater systems – Part 1: Drinking water distribution networks' <www.iso.org/standard/64117.html?browse=tc> accessed 11 June 2018.

120 ISO 24518:2015 'Activities relating to drinking water and wastewater services – Crisis management of water utilities' <www.iso.org/standard/64118.html?browse=tc> accessed 11 June 2018.

121 ISO 24523: 2017 'Service activities relating to drinking water supply systems and wastewater systems – Guidelines for benchmarking of water utilities' <www.iso.org/standard/59814.html?browse=tc> accessed 11 June 2018.

122 See <www.iso.org/committee/299764/x/catalogue/> accessed 11 June 2018.

standards even attempt to deal with the difficult issue of the 'cost' or 'price' of water services under the rubric of the 'standard of service' to be provided. Clearly the ongoing elaboration and adoption of such globally applicable practice standards, though essentially voluntary, will prove influential in determining an acceptable level of service provision and will help to clarify the nature of due diligence obligations owed by States pursuant to the human right to water and sanitation,[123] whether themselves acting as public service providers or as regulators of public or private-sector service providers.[124] Commentators have cited this elaboration of quasi-normative standards by a body such as the ISO as an example of the 'global administrative law' phenomenon, which describes arrangements comprising 'hybrid blends of public and private actors linked in routines of both formal and informal participation at multiple levels of governance',[125] where the adoption of informal transnational regulatory standards is facilitated by the application of good governance standards reminiscent of national systems of administrative law.[126]

Consistent with this inclusive view of the processes of transnational, globalised regulatory activity, and with the broad relevance and applicability of regulatory norms and standards developed thereunder, the implications of the human right to water and sanitation for the service obligations of water services utilities has already emerged as a central issue of contention in a number of investor-State arbitrations. Several decisions of tribunals acting under the auspices of the International Centre for the Settlement of Investment Dispute (ICSID)[127] would appear to have recognised the key relevance of human rights concerns to contracts for the provision of water and sanitation services.[128] The ISO standards introduced

123 On the 'due diligence' nature of the key obligations imposed under the human right to water and sanitation, see McCaffrey (n 42) 13; and Hardberger (n 11) 336.

124 For a discussion of the significance of the adoption of ISO standards, see B Morgan, 'The Regulatory Face of the Human Right to Water' (2004) 15(5) Water Law 179, 182–83.

125 B Morgan, 'Turning Off the Tap: Urban Water Service Delivery and the Social Construction of Global Administrative Law' (2006) 17(1) European Journal of International Law 215, 216 and 224–27.

126 See further McIntyre (n 115).

127 See, for example, ICSID Case No. ARB/03/19 *Aguas Argentinas S.A., Suez, Sociedad General de Aguas de Barcelona S.A. and Vivendi Universal S.A. v The Argentine Republic, Order in Response to a Petition for Transparency and Participation as Amicus Curiae* [2005]; ICSID Case No. ARB/03/17 *Aguas Provinciales de Santa Fe S.A., Suez, Sociedad General de Aguas de Barcelona S.A. and InterAguas Servicios Integrales del Agua S.A. v The Argentine Republic, Order in Response to a Petition for Participation as Amicus Curiae* [2006]; ICSID Case No. ARB/03/19 *Suez, Sociedad General de Aguas de Barcelona S.A. and Vivendi Universal S.A. v The Argentine Republic, Order in Response to a Petition by Five Non-Governmental Organizations for Permission to Make an Amicus Curiae Submission* [2007]; and ICSID Case No. ARB/05/22 *Biwater Gauff (Tanzania) Ltd. v United Republic of Tanzania*, Procedural Order No. 5 [2007]. See further, B Farrugia, 'The Human Right to Water: Defences to Investment Treaty Violations' (2015) 31 Arbitration International 261–82; O McIntyre, 'The Emergence of the Human Right to Water in an Era of Globalization and its Implications for International Investment Law' in JF Addicott, MJH Bhuiyan and T Chowdhury (eds), *Globalization, International Law and Human Rights* (Oxford University Press 2011) 147–76.

128 Morgan (n 125) 216 notes that 'private sector participation from outside national borders in the provision of basic goods makes urban water services a fascinating case study for exploring the potential ambit of what scholars have provocatively called "global administrative law"'.

above might in time prove helpful in clarifying the nature of any human rights obligations relevant to international investors in utilities providing water and sanitation services.

Of course, ISO service standards are also likely to inform the behaviour expected under voluntary codes of corporate conduct[129] where water utility companies refer to human rights commitments in their own corporate social responsibility policies.[130] This may also be true where they sign up to global codes such as the UN Global Compact, which requires that participating companies should comply with international human rights norms,[131] or the OECD Guidelines for Multinational Enterprises, which consist of voluntary principles and standards for responsible business conduct in such areas of relevance to implementation of the right to water as human rights, environment, information disclosure, the combating of bribery and consumer interests.[132]

7.3.4 *Affordability*

It has long been clear that the difficult and contentious issue of economic accessibility is absolutely central to realisation of the human right to water and sanitation, and so, in addition to technical health and environmental standards and service standards for utilities, standards are also beginning to emerge in respect of the affordability of water services. The requirement of ensuring affordability[133] with a view to protecting vulnerable people[134] has found its way into the governance frameworks of a range of actors concerned with water services, such as MDBs, which are commonly called upon to finance water supply and sanitation system upgrades.[135] Typically, Paragraph 11 of the 2014 Environmental and Social Policy

129 See further SD Murphy, 'Taking Multinational Corporate Codes to the Next Level' (2005) 43 Columbia Journal of Transnational Law 388–433.

130 For example, Suez commits its support to the right to water and sanitation, declaring that 'Suez fully assumes its role in promoting and implementing the right to water and sanitation. Thanks to its expertise, it is able to offer a full range of solutions in response to all issues faced by both developed and developing countries.' See <www.suez.com/en/Who-we-are/A-commited-group/Support-the-right-to-water-and-sanitation> accessed 8 January 2018.

131 UN Global Compact. <www.unglobalcompact.org/what-is-gc/mission/principles> accessed 8 January 2018; see further Williams (n 8) 488–91. See also the water stewardship standards promoted by the CEO Water Mandate (n 88).

132 OECD Guidelines for Multinational Enterprises <www.oecd.org/corporate/mne/1922428.pdf> accessed 8 January 2018; See further McIntyre (n 115) 665.

133 General Comment No. 15 (n 4) para 12(c)(ii) provides: '*Economic accessibility*: Water, and water facilities and services, must be affordable for all. The direct and indirect costs and charges associated with securing water must be affordable, and must not compromise or threaten the realization of other Covenant rights.' (original emphasis)

134 See General Comment No. 15 (n 4), para 12(c)(iii).

135 See, for example, the 2004 World Bank 'Water Resources Sector Strategy' <http://siteresources.worldbank.org/INTINFNETWORK/Resources/water.pdf> accessed 11 June 2018, at 2, which emphasises 'poverty-targeted water service interventions (such as water and sanitation and irrigation services for the unserved poor)'.

adopted by the European Bank for Reconstruction and Development (EBRD), stipulates that:

> The EBRD will assess to what extent tariff changes caused by projects may create problems of affordability of basic levels of services for disadvantaged and/or vulnerable groups of the population, and satisfy itself that effective schemes to address this issue are developed and put in place.[136]

Highly specific guidance has been developed by MDBs on the nature of the actions required to ensure economic accessibility to water and sanitation services. For example, since 2010 the African Development Bank has published such guidelines, which helpfully distinguish between cost recovery in respect of urban, networked and rural, non-networked water supply and sanitation services.[137]

Difficulties in ensuring compliance with the requirement of affordability in the face of austerity measures were highlighted in a 2013 report submitted to the Human Rights Council by the former UN Special Rapporteur on the human right to safe drinking water and sanitation.[138] The report focuses on the aggravated risks to realisation of the right to water arising in times of economic and financial crisis by virtue of retrogressive austerity measures, and spells out the action necessary to ensure compliance with the non-derogable core obligations arising thereunder. It highlights the problem of 'increased prices and unaffordability-related disconnections',[139] including disconnections in the case of private service provision,[140] and recommends, *inter alia*, 'a social protection floor, especially for disadvantaged and marginalized groups and individuals'.[141] For the purpose of measuring affordability, the former Special Rapporteur recommended 'comparing per capita incomes against water and sanitation indicators among countries with comparable levels of development [which] provides a more objective benchmark'.[142] Thus, she provides

136 EBRD, 'Environmental and Social Policy' (May 2014) <www.ebrd.com/news/publications/policies/environmental-and-social-policy.html> accessed 11 June 2018.

137 See, for example, African Development Bank, 'Guidelines for User Fees and Cost Recovery for Urban Water and Sanitation' (AfDB 2010) <www.afdb.org/fileadmin/uploads/afdb/Documents/Project-and-Operations/brochure%20cost%20recouvry%20urban%203_11_2010.pdf> accessed 11 June 2018; African Development Bank, 'Guidelines for User Fees and Cost Recovery for Rural, Non-Networked, Water and Sanitation Delivery' (AfDB 2010) <www.afdb.org/fileadmin/uploads/afdb/Documents/Project-and-Operations/2011_03%20Guidelines%20for%20User%20Fees%20Cost%20Recovery_Rural.pdf> accessed 11 June 2018.

138 C de Alburquerque, 'Report of the Special Rapporteur on the Human right to Safe Drinking Water and Sanitation' (11 July 2013) UN Doc A/HRC/24/44 <www.ohchr.org/EN/HRBodies/HRC/RegularSessions/Session24/Documents/A-HRC-24-44_en.pdf> accessed 8 January 2018. The link between fiscal austerity and States' commitments to economic, social and cultural rights has also been recognised by civil society organisations in the Vienna+20 CSO Declaration, adopted on 26 June 2013. See further O McIntyre, 'The Human Right to Water and Reform of the Irish Water Sector' (2014) 5(1) Journal of Human Rights and the Environment 74–101 at 75–76.

139 de Alburquerque ibid para 32.

140 ibid para 44.

141 ibid paras 15(b) and 73–74.

142 ibid para 61.

a useful analysis of the human right to water and sanitation affordability benchmarks against which a national regime can be measured in a time of austerity.

However, the level of affordability which should guide service providers, or public welfare interventions, is essentially a question of policy to be determined by the national authorities charged with water services governance, and the methodologies that such actors might employ to assess affordability continue to evolve. For example, most agencies in the United States have for the past twenty years relied on an influential methodology developed in 1997 by the Environmental Protection Agency (EPA), which compares median household income (MHI) for the utility's service area to the area's average water and sewage bills.[143] As a general rule of thumb, the average sewage bill should not exceed 2 percent of MHI, while the average drinking water bill should not exceed 2.5 percent of MHI.[144] However, critics of this methodology point out that it is quite rudimentary and arbitrary. For example, by only looking at average demand across the community, it fails to take account of greater water consumption by rich households, which inflates estimates of essential household needs. Also, by using median income it obscures severe financial pressure on poorer households. Further, the EPA measure ignores the local cost of living, which might exacerbate financial pressure on poor households. Recently, the US Congress has instructed the National Academy of Public Administration (NAPA) to study alternative ways of measuring household water affordability with a view to assisting the EPA in revising its outdated community affordability guidelines, with the resulting report presented to Congress in October 2017.[145] US scholars have been busy developing alternative approaches, including one that links water bills to workers' wages by estimating the number of hours at the local minimum wage that a person would need to work in order pay their water bill, and another, called the affordability ratio, which compares a water bill to disposable income for households at the twentieth percentile (lower fifth) of the income distribution.[146] In each case, a monthly water bill would be based on consumption of fifty gallons (roughly 190 litres) per person per day, which is an estimate of water needed for basic hygiene, drinking and cooking.

143 See generally EPA, 'Pricing and Affordability of Water Services' <www.epa.gov/sustainable-water-infrastructure/pricing-and-affordability-water-services> accessed 11 June 2018.

144 See generally B Walton, 'When It Comes to Water Service How Expensive Is Too Expensive?' *Circle of Blue* (24 August 2017) <www.circleofblue.org/2017/water-management/comes-water-service-expensive-expensive/> accessed 11 June 2018.

145 National Academy of Public Administration, 'Developing a New Framework for Community Affordability of Clean Water Services' (5 October 2017) <www.napawash.org/uploads/Academy_Studies/NAPA_EPA_FINAL_REPORT_110117.pdf> accessed 11 June 2018.

146 See MP Teodoro, 'Measuring Water and Sewer Utility Affordability' – (Texas A&M University Working Paper August 2017) <http://mannyteodoro.com/wp-content/uploads/2017/08/mteodoro_affordability-method-working-paper-aug2017.pdf> accessed 11 June 2018.

7.3.5 Monitoring Standards

Acutely aware that monitoring compliance with the various facets of the right to water and sanitation is both complex and essential to realisation, General Comment No. 15 expressly stipulates that the strategy and plan of action to be adopted and implemented by States as a core obligation arising under the right to water 'should include methods, such as right to water indicators and benchmarks, by which progress can be closely monitored'.[147]

Accordingly, the former UN Special Rapporteur published detailed guidance on monitoring in 2014.[148] In addition to setting out clearly the international framework for monitoring compliance with human rights, it details the respective roles of State bodies, service providers and civil society. The guidance advises States on defining structural, process and outcome indicators of progress towards realisation of the right[149] and addresses in detail the monitoring of water and sanitation availability, accessibility, quality, affordability, acceptability and sustainability. For example, in relation to monitoring the quality of sanitation provision, the guidance explains that 'to safeguard the health benefits of access to sanitation and protect water resources, the full cycle of sanitation provision must be monitored, from collection to transport, treatment and disposal of waste', though it also readily acknowledges that 'at present, there is no agreed global indicator for monitoring this full provision'.[150] Therefore, though real progress has been made to date, it is clear that in several respects monitoring standards for compliance with the right to water and sanitation are at an early stage in their evolution.

However, it is likely to prove significant that a global programme for monitoring implementation of SDG 6 on water and sanitation was launched in 2017 following the development, testing and evaluation of methodologies for monitoring the indicators identified under each target set out thereunder.[151] As Target 6.1, concerning 'universal and equitable access to safe and affordable drinking water', and Target 6.2, concerning 'access to adequate and equitable sanitation and hygiene for all and to end open defecation', closely reflect the core values enshrined in the human right to water and sanitation, the

147 General Comment No. 15 (n 4) para 37(f). See further paras 47, 53 and 54.

148 C de Albuquerque, 'Monitoring Compliance with the Human Rights to Water and Sanitation' (OHCHR 2014) <www.ohchr.org/Documents/Issues/Water/Handbook/Book5_Monitoring.pdf> accessed 8 January 2018.

149 ibid at 7. '"Structural indicators" monitor whether the legislative, policy and regulatory frameworks of a State or government (at all levels) provide an environment that encourages realisation of human rights. "Process indicators" monitor the action taken to realise human rights; for example, the allocation of resources to services for disadvantaged individuals and groups. "Outcome indicators" monitor actual access to water and sanitation services; for example, whether households have access to a latrine or whether water is of adequate quality.'

150 ibid 18.

151 See further <www.sdg6monitoring.org/home> accessed 11 June 2018.

monitoring methodologies developed thereunder are likely to set robust and informed standards for measuring compliance with and realisation of the right. Target 6.1 has a single associated indicator relating to the 'proportion of population using safely managed drinking water services'. Guidance published by UN-Water elaborates further upon use of this indicator, advising, for example, that 'this indicator can be disaggregated by service level: no service, basic services and safely managed services'.[152] It also includes detailed guidance on the particular testing to occur in household surveys at each of three steps of progressive monitoring of Indicator 6.1.1.[153] Similarly, Target 6.2 is also measured against a single indicator relating to the 'proportion of population using safely managed sanitation services, including a hand-washing facility with soap and water'. UN-Water guidance on Indicator 6.2.1 elaborates on the meaning of 'improved sanitation facilities' and 'handwashing facilities', and advises on disaggregation by service level and on the data to be gleaned from household surveys and from service providers at each step of progressive monitoring.[154] In the case of both indicators, data received annually from national officials will be compiled by WHO and UNICEF, which will together act as the responsible custodian.[155] Of course, integrated monitoring for SDG 6 covers the entire range of targets relevant to realisation of the right to water and sanitation as set out under General Comment No. 15, including water quality and wastewater management, water use and scarcity, water resources management, water-related ecosystems, international cooperation and stakeholder participation.[156]

Other multilateral organisations, such as the European Union,[157] have also developed sets of indicators for monitoring compliance with and realisation of SDG 6, which will similarly inform and hasten development of monitoring standards for the right to water and sanitation. In January 2017, the UNESCO International Hydrological Programme (IHP) launched its Water Information Network System (WINS), which aims to provide UNESCO Member States with an open source, open access, web-based information platform to serve as a global reference for decision makers and stakeholders on water-related issues at all levels.[158] It consists of three main components, providing:

[152] UN-Water (n 101) 5.

[153] ibid.

[154] ibid 7.

[155] The WHO/UNICEF Joint Monitoring Programme has published its first report using these newly developed indicators. See WHO/UNICEF JMP, 'Progress on drinking water, sanitation and hygiene: 2017 update and SDG baselines' (12 July 2017) <https://data.unicef.org/wp-content/uploads/2017/07/JMP-2017-report-launch-version_0.pdf> accessed 11 June 2018.

[156] Respectively, SDG Targets 6.3, 6.4, 6.5, 6.6, 6.a and 6.b

[157] See EU Eurostat, 'EU SDG Indicator Set' (28 April 2017) <http://ec.europa.eu/eurostat/documents/276524/7736915/EU-SDG-indicator-set-with-cover-note-170531.pdf> accessed 11 June 2018.

[158] See further <http://en.unesco.org/ihp-wins> accessed 11 June 2018.

1. Geo-referenced data (GIS) on the state of water resources at global, regional, national and local level, allowing users to visualise and generate maps;
2. A platform for interdisciplinary collaboration and knowledge sharing among water-related stakeholders (e.g. databases, reports, graphs, tables, videos, and webinars), and
3. A platform for water-related stakeholders to build social networks and interrelations (i.e. discussion groups).

Significantly, the UNESCO-IHP WINS initiative is a response from the IHP Secretariat to a request from UNESCO Member States to 'provide support to Member States to build their institutional capacities, human resources and a sound basis in science capacity for the monitoring and implementation of Sustainable Development Goal 6 (SDG 6) and other water-related goals'.[159]

Also relevant to monitoring implementation of the human right to water and sanitation is guidance developed by UNECE and WHO on target setting and reporting[160] under the auspices of the 1999 UNECE Protocol on Water and Health,[161] which imposes obligations upon States parties in relation to the provision of universal access to adequate supplies of wholesome drinking water.[162] Recognising that the Protocol 'is a powerful tool to promote and operationalize the achievement of the 2030 Agenda' and that 'the Protocol's provisions and principles fully align with SDG 6', the UNECE/WHO guidance gathers together case studies showcasing good practices and lessons learned in order 'to assist efforts by Parties to the Protocol and other States to effectively shape their target-setting processes'.[163] The guidance showcases best practice in relation to, *inter alia*, institutional arrangements, baseline analysis and prioritisation of issues, development of targets and their financial and economic implications, public involvement in target setting, publication and promotion of targets, development of programmes of measures and action plans for implementation and review and assessment of progress and reporting.

7.3.6 *Procedural Governance Standards*

Effective implementation of the right to water and sanitation clearly involves adherence to a suite of procedural standards widely regarded as inherent to its realisation. In addition to the specific provisions of global and regional human rights instruments

159 UNESCO Press Release, 25 January 2017.

160 UNECE/WHO, 'Collection of good practices and lessons learned on target setting and reporting under the Protocol on Water and Health' (UN 2016).

161 UN Doc (n 68). See further UNECE/WHO, 'A Healthy Link: The Protocol on Water and Health and the Sustainable Development Goals' (November 2016) UN Doc ECE/INF/NONE/2016/16 <www.unece.org/fileadmin/DAM/env/water/mop4/Informal_doc/1623151_E_FinalWEB_rev.pdf> accessed 11 June 2018.

162 Protocol Articles 4(2)(a) and 6(1)(a).

163 UNECE/WHO (n 160) iii.

which might be considered to support the right, all such instruments would now be interpreted and applied so as to require that States generally facilitate a participative approach in respect of projects or policies that might impact on human rights. Such an approach requires the adoption of procedures by which interested groups, or individuals or communities likely to be affected by such projects or policies, can receive and access relevant information, meaningfully participate in decision making and, if necessary, have access to some appropriate means of legal recourse.[164] Such a participatory approach to guaranteeing human rights would equally apply to projects or policies which might impact on the availability of water resources, particularly where this might arise by virtue of environmental risk, as participatory rights are now central to environmental law frameworks at both the national and international levels. Procedural and participative rights are a very significant element of the normative content of the human right to water as set out in General Comment No. 15.[165] Indeed, the requirement for States parties to the ICESCR to ensure a participatory and transparent process for the adoption and implementation of a national water strategy and plan of action is included among the non-derogable 'core obligations' of States under General Comment No. 15.[166]

Such a requirement was highlighted, prior to the present discourse on the human right to water, in the 2001 *Ogoni* case, where water pollution was a central issue. The African Commission on Human and Peoples' Rights gave a broad participative reading to Article 24 of the African Charter on Human and Peoples' Rights, which acknowledges all peoples' right to 'a general satisfactory environment favourable to their development', to include specific procedural guarantees concerning the carrying out of environmental and social impact assessment.[167] Such procedural requirements, which correlate closely with the procedural and informational requirements of the human right to water as set out under General Comment No. 15, would equally apply under existing regional human rights instruments to any major project or policy initiative which threatened the quality or availability of water supply or sanitation services. Similarly, the Inter-American Commission on Human Rights has, in the context of Article 11 of the 1988 Additional Protocol guaranteeing the right to a healthy environment, repeatedly recommended the adoption of domestic legislation providing for meaningful and effective participatory mechanisms for indigenous peoples in the adoption of political, economic and social decisions

164 See generally, Cullet and Gowlland-Gaultieri (n 53).

165 See, for example, General Comment No. 15 (n 4) paras 12(c)(iv), 16(a), 24, 37(f), 48, 55 and 56.

166 ibid para 37(f); General Comment No. 15 para 40 describes the core obligations set out in para 37 as 'non-derogable'.

167 See Cullet and Gowlland-Gualtieri (n 53) 313–14, citing Communication No. 155/96, *The Social and Economic Rights Action Center and the Center for Social and Economic Rights v. Nigeria*, African Commission on Human and Peoples' Rights, 30th Ordinary Session (13–27 October 2001) para 53; See Chapter 5 of this volume by Louis Kotzé and Anel du Plessis relating to the African Charter on Human and Peoples Rights.

that affect their interests.[168] The European Court of Human Rights has taken a broadly similar approach in its interpretation and application of relevant provisions of the European Convention on Human Rights.[169]

These procedural requirements appear even more universally accepted and applied when one considers that broad informational and participatory rights are generally also included under regional and global environmental instruments. The requirement for public participation in international environmental law is exemplified by the 1998 UNECE Aarhus Convention,[170] and such participation requirements are also central to the carrying out of an adequate environmental impact assessment (EIA) consistent with the standards established under international law.[171] More generally, in the field of sustainable development all seminal instruments purport to establish participatory standards which apply not only to States but also to international organisations, including MDBs. Participatory rights are absolutely central to Chapter 18 of Agenda 21 on freshwater resources.[172] Therefore, the accumulated practice of regional human rights enforcement bodies strongly suggests that the CESCR's General Comment No. 15 largely involves a codification of existing State obligations under general international human rights law and general international environmental and sustainable development law, rather than an attempt at the progressive development of participatory principles applying to matters of access

168 See Chapter X to the Second Report on the Situation of Human Rights in Peru, Inter-American Commission on Human Rights; Chapter IX to the Report on the Situation of Human Rights in Ecuador, Inter-American Commission on Human Rights OEA/Ser.L/V/II.96 doc. 10 rev. 1 (Recommendations) (24 April 1997); Case 7615 (Brazil), Inter-American Commission on Human Rights, 1984–1985 Annual Report 24 OEA/Ser.L/V/II.66 doc. 10 rev. 1 (1985), the *Yanomami* case; See Cullet and Gowlland-Gaultieri, ibid 314–15; See further *Awas Tingni Mayagna (Sumo) Indigenous Community v Nicaragua*, Judgment of 31 August 2001, IACHR (Ser. C), No. 79 (2001); See Chapter 4 of this volume by Evadne Grant relating to the American Convention on Human Rights.

169 European Convention for the Protection of Human Rights and Fundamental Freedoms (Rome 1950), 213 UNTS 221. See, for example, *Guerra and Others v Italy* (1998) 26 European Human Rights Reports 357; *Zander v Sweden* (1993) 18 European Human Rights Reports 175.

170 Convention on Access to Information, Public Participation in Decision-Making and Access to Justice in Environmental Matters (Aarhus, 25 June 1998), 38 ILM 517 (1999). See Chapter 6 of this volume by Aine Ryall relating to the Aarhus Convention.

171 See, for example, arts 2(2), 2(6), 3(8) and 4(2) of the 1991 UNECE Convention on Environmental Impact Assessment in a Transboundary Context (Espoo, 25 February 1991) 30 ILM 800 (1991); See also the Protocol on Strategic Environmental Assessment (Kiev, 21 May 2003); a general requirement for EIA in respect of major projects impacting on shared transboundary freshwaters was recognised by the International Court of Justice in the *Pulp Mills* case, *Pulp Mills on the River Uruguay (Argentina v Uruguay)*, Judgment, 20 April 2010 paras 119–21; See further, O McIntyre, 'The Proceduralization and Growing Maturity of International Water Law: *Case concerning Pulp Mills on the River Uruguay (Argentina v. Uruguay)*' (2010) 22(3) Journal of Environmental Law 475–97; O McIntyre, 'The World Court's Emphasis on Procedural Rules in the Recent *Pulp Mills* Case: Contributing to the Progressive and Coherent Development of International Water Law' (2011) 4(2) Water Alternatives 124–44.

172 Agenda 21 (Rio de Janeiro, 13 June 1992) UN Doc A/CONF.151/26 (Vols I, II and III) (1992); See Cullet and Gowlland-Gaultieri (n 53) 305.

to water. Such practice also provides a rich source of continually evolving standards regarding adequate and effective public participation and procedural engagement. Notably, the Aarhus Convention regime has established a 'clearing-house', which showcases good practice in terms of national legislative implementation of the rights created under the Convention,[173] while the Aarhus Convention Compliance Committee maintains a detailed record of requests, submissions, communications and referrals received from the Parties, the public and the Secretariat, as well as decisions on compliance and the details of their implementation.[174] Of course, this focus on procedural obligations arising from diverse sources enjoying varying degrees of legal authority further intimates that the human right to water and sanitation can usefully be understood as a 'creature of global administrative law'.[175]

7.4 CONCLUSION

Irrespective of the formal legal nature or status of the putative human right(s) to water and sanitation, a comprehensive framework of normative standards is emerging which informs almost every aspect of the right's implementation and realisation. Thus, the human rights discourse surrounding the imperative of universal access to adequate water and sanitation services would appear to be having a significant progressive effect. This discourse lends added urgency to efforts in pursuit of this worthy aim, but also creates a unified set of broad objectives around which the various water-related activities of a wide and diverse range of actors, public and private, national and international, can coalesce in a wide-ranging consensual global effort. In this way, the decentred, hybrid elaboration of diverse types of right to water-related standards appears to fall within the rubric of global or transnational governance, comprising an intricate mix of public and private normative mechanisms interacting in a complex manner in a dynamic regulatory setting. This complex mix of rules and standards adopted by both State and non-State actors, and the interaction between such rules and standards, may be explained by the phenomenon of 'global administrative law', an analytical approach employed to address the rapidly changing realities of transnational regulation, which increasingly involves, *inter alia*, various forms of industry self-regulation, hybrid forms of private-private and public-private regulation, network governance by State officials and governance by intergovernmental organizations with direct or indirect regulatory powers.[176] Not only does this eclectic mix of normative standards exert a voluntary compliance pull on a range of key actors

173 See <https://aarhusclearinghouse.unece.org> accessed 11 June 2018.

174 See <www.unece.org/env/pp/cc.html> accessed 11 June 2018. See in particular Chapter 6 of this volume by Aine Ryall.

175 See generally McIntyre (n 115).

176 See B Kingsbury, 'Global Environmental Governance as Administration: Implications for International Law' in D Bodansky, J Brunnée and E Hey (eds), *The Oxford Handbook of International Environmental Law* (OUP 2007) 63–84.

involved in the provision or regulation of water and sanitation services, it can also play a significant role in the progressive evolutionary development of formal, legally-binding standards at the national level, both legislative and judicial.[177]

[177] See, for example, J McNally, 'Incorporating Voluntary Standards into National Law: An Overview of the Scandinavian Experience' in L Leonard and MA Gonzalez-Perez (eds), *Beyond the UN Global Compact: Institutions and Regulations* (Emerald 2015) 67–92.

8

Standards in the Procedural Rights of Multilateral Environmental Agreements

Lara Ognibene and Angela Kariuki

8.1 INTRODUCTION

A number of multilateral environmental agreements (MEAs) recognise the link between the environment and human health and well-being. However, only a few of these refer to human rights explicitly. Nonetheless, their treatment of human life, health, and other concerns protected by human rights may increase our understanding of the development of rights standards relating to the environment. These agreements recognise and address the effect of environmental harm on human beings, as well as set out obligations on states to prevent such harm. Moreover, a number of these environmental agreements today incorporate procedural environmental rights,[1] and some MEAs include provisions regarding civil liability and compensation for damage caused by environmental degradation, particularly in the context of pollution. In this chapter we consider the ongoing and gradual development of the standards relating to procedural rights obligations of states within MEAs.

Section 8.2 examines the development of procedural rights in MEAs. It discusses the way in which international consensus developed regarding the importance of procedural rights in decision and policy making relating to the environment. Section 8.3 maps out, by way of examples, the procedural rights elements in a variety of MEAs to provide an overview of their coverage and application. In Section 8.4, an analysis and comment on the factors that affect the development of standards within procedural rights in MEAs is provided. This is to better understand their scope and the processes that are affecting their gradual development. We conclude that the development of standards in procedural rights in MEAs is in its nascent stages, but growing gradually nonetheless. As a general rule, while such provisions can help spur action, taken on their own they do not presently guarantee the promotion and protection of procedural rights in environmental matters.

[1] For the purposes of this chapter, the terms 'procedural rights' and 'participatory rights' will be regarded as being synonymous.

8.2 THE DEVELOPMENT OF THE LAW OF PROCEDURAL RIGHTS IN MEAS

It is important from the outset to make a clear distinction between the intended functions of human rights instruments and MEAs respectively. On one hand, as has been stressed in preceding chapters, international human rights instruments have generally not been drafted with a view to protecting the environment.[2] On the other hand, the term 'right', which is a key component in human rights instruments, is typically not explicitly referred to within MEAs. International human rights instruments are generally more relevant to environmental problems insofar as existing rights – usually the rights to life, private life, health, water, and property – are infringed by environmental nuisances. That said, procedural rights can still be found within specific provisions of numerous MEAs, even though MEAs are generally not regarded as human rights instruments.

While human rights instruments were not generally drafted with the purpose of protecting the environment, their development as a result of international consensus between states, 'General Comments' and the work of regional human rights bodies is that they do nonetheless invariably impose procedural obligations on states in relation to environmental protection. These obligations include duties to: (a) assess environmental impacts and make environmental information public; (b) facilitate public participation in environmental decision making, including by protecting the rights of expression and association; and (c) provide access to remedies for harm.[3]

Another important difference between human rights instruments and MEAs is the timescale of their development. Whereas human rights instruments in the contemporary sense developed from the end of World War II onwards, the first globally applicable MEAs were agreed in the 1970s and 1980s. There have been fewer human rights treaties adopted than environmental agreements, and most of those that have been concluded have been at the regional level.[4]

The later development of awareness of concern for the environment and the resultant development of MEAs meant that, until the 1990s, procedural rights in environmental matters had only really been dealt with at the domestic level and had not been debated or considered at length in international environmental law and governance. However, many environmental agreements do make clear that they are aimed at protecting human beings as well as the environment per se. For example,

2 See Chapters 1, 2, 3, and 4 of this volume by Stephen Turner, Sumudu Attapatu, Karen Morrow, and Evadne Grant, respectively; while the universal human rights treaties do not refer to a specific right to a safe and healthy environment, the UN human rights treaty bodies all recognise the intrinsic link between the environment and the realization of a range of human rights, such as the right to life, health, food, water, and housing. International courts have also recognised the extraterritorial application of all the main human rights treaties.

3 John Knox, 'Mapping Report of Independent Expert on Human Rights and the Environment' UN Doc A/HRC/25/53 (2014).

4 Dinah Shelton, 'Multilateral Treaties on Environment Adopted between 1991 and 2001' (2002) 32 Environmental Policy and Law 70.

the United Nations Convention to Combat Desertification in Those Countries Experiencing Serious Drought and/or Desertification, Particularly in Africa (UNCCD)[5] affirms that human beings in affected or threatened areas are at the centre of concerns to combat desertification and mitigate the effects of drought.[6] It is from this concern for human beings and the links between human welfare and the protection of the environment that procedural rights within MEAs are ultimately derived.

The concern for human beings that is seen within a significant number of international instruments relating to the environment, including treaties, international resolutions, and declarations, has elucidated certain aspects of the nexus between human rights and the environment. The Rio Declaration on Environment and Development,[7] for example, emphasises the need to integrate environmental protection and development in order to achieve sustainable development and allow for a healthy and productive life in harmony with nature.[8] MEAs, by including provisions related to public access to information, public participation in decision-making proceedings, and access to the review of procedures (access to justice), also illustrate the links between human rights and the environment by replicating human rights language and human rights-styled mechanisms within the context of environmental protection. Additionally, some recently concluded international policies and instruments, such as the 2030 Agenda for Sustainable Development and its Seventeen Sustainable Development Goals, endorse procedural rights.[9]

8.2.1 *Rio Declaration*

As the Rio Declaration has been so influential, specific consideration will be given to the role that it has played in the development of procedural rights within MEAs. The 1992 Conference on Environment and Development in Rio de Janeiro formulated the link between human rights and environmental protection largely in procedural terms. The Rio Declaration further illustrates the link between human rights, dignity, and the environment. It provides in Principle 1 that 'human beings are at the centre of concerns for sustainable development. They are entitled to a healthy and productive life in harmony with nature.'[10]

[5] United Nations Convention to Combat Desertification in Countries Experiencing Serious Drought and/or Desertification, Particularly in Africa (adopted 14 October 1994, entered into force 26 December 1996) 1954 UNTS 3 (UNCCD).

[6] ibid Preamble.

[7] United Nations Conference on Environment and Development, 'Rio Declaration on Environment and Development' (June 1992) UN Doc A/CONF 151/5/Rev.1 (UNCED).

[8] ibid Principle 1.

[9] United Nations, 'Transforming Our World: The 2030 Agenda for Sustainable Development' <www.un.org/sustainabledevelopment/development-agenda/> accessed 29 May 2018.

[10] UNCED (n 7) Principle 1.

Principle 10 of the 1992 Rio Declaration states that:

> Environmental issues are best handled with the participation of all concerned citizens, at the relevant level. At the national level, each individual shall have appropriate access to information concerning the environment that is held by public authorities, including information on hazardous materials and activities in their communities, and the opportunity to participate in decision-making processes. States shall facilitate and encourage public awareness and participation by making information widely available. Effective access to judicial and administrative proceedings, including redress and remedy, shall be provided.

Although Principle 10 on participatory and procedural rights is not legally binding, over 150 governments have endorsed it as fundamental to good environmental governance. Furthermore, nonbinding declarations or resolutions adopted by states or intergovernmental organisations may be evidence of existing international law, or they may acquire binding legal character as elements of a treaty-based regulatory regime, or constitute a subsequent agreement between the parties regarding the interpretation of an MEA or the application of its provisions.[11]

Public participation is also emphasised in Agenda 21, the nonbinding, voluntarily implemented action plan emanating from the Rio Conference. The Preamble to Chapter 23 states:

> One of the fundamental prerequisites for the achievement of sustainable development is broad public participation in decision-making. Furthermore, in the more specific context of environment and development, the need for new forms of participation has emerged. This includes the need of individuals, groups, and organizations to participate in environmental impact assessment procedures and to know about and participate in decisions, particularly those that potentially affect the communities in which they live and work. Individuals, groups and organizations should have access to information relevant to environment and development held by national authorities, including information on products and activities that have or are likely to have a significant impact on the environment, and information on environmental protection measures.

Chapter 23 proclaims that individuals, groups, and organisations should have access to information relevant to the environment and development, held by national authorities, including information on products and activities that have or are likely to have a significant impact on the environment, and information on environmental protection matters. Agenda 21 also calls on governments and legislators to establish judicial and administrative procedures for legal redress and remedy for actions affecting the environment that may be unlawful or infringe on rights under the law, and to provide access to individuals, groups, and organisations with a recognised legal interest.[12]

11 Convention on the Law of Treaties (Vienna) 23 May 1969 (entered into force 27 January 1980) (1969) 8 ILM 679 (1969 Vienna Convention) art 31.

12 UNCED (n 7) Agenda 21, Section I – Social and Economic Dimensions para 8.18.

Since Rio, global and regional treaties adopted in the fields of human rights and environmental protection have included provisions specific to the rights contained in Principle 10. The language used by different instruments is far from being homogeneous. Sometimes public participation is used in a broad sense to designate the recommended openness of authorities towards individuals and groups of individuals, and includes the right to information rather than separately guaranteeing it.

Some MEAs also contain substantive rights to a particular environmental quality while others focus on remedies for environmental harm. For example, the Cancun Agreements, adopted by the UN Framework Convention on Climate Change Conference of the Parties in 2010, quote language from a 2009 Human Rights Council resolution recognising that 'the adverse effects of climate change have a range of direct and indirect implications for the effective enjoyment of human rights'.[13]

Generally, global and regional water resource agreements since the Rio Conference, although focusing primarily on interstate management and utilisation of freshwaters, contain at least some reference to public information, participation, or remedies. This growing trend is illustrated in particular by the European water management conventions, namely the Convention on the Protection of the Marine Environment of the Baltic Sea Area[14] and its Protocol on Water and Health,[15] that have provisions covering public information, as well as broader rights related to public participation.[16]

8.2.2 *Rio+20*

The Rio+20 outcome document, 'The Future We Want', built on the Rio Declaration and set out a common vision aimed at 'ensuring the promotion of an economically, socially and environmentally sustainable future for our planet and for present and future generations'.[17] Importantly, it made explicit reference to the need for human rights protection, including the right to development set out in Principle

[13] The Cancun Agreements: Outcome of the work of the Ad Hoc Working Group on Long-term Cooperative Action under the Convention, UN Doc FCCC/CP/2010/7/Add.1, at 2 (2011) (quoting Human Rights Council Resolution 10/4, 25 March 2009, UN Doc A/HRC/RES/10/4).

[14] United Nations Economic Commission for Europe Convention on the Protection and Use of Transboundary Watercourses and International Lakes (entered into force 6 October 1996) (1992) 1936 UNTS 269.

[15] Protocol on Water and Health to the 1992 Convention on the Protection and Use of Transboundary Watercourses and International Lakes (entered into force 4 August 2005) (1999) 2331 UNTS 202.

[16] Jona Razzaque, 'Public Participation in Water Governance' in J Dellapenna and J Gupta (eds), *The Evolution of Law and Politics of Water* (Springer 2009) 361.

[17] United Nations Conference on Sustainable Development Rio+20 Outcome 'The Future We Want' (June 2012) Section 1 ara 1 <www.un.org/disabilities/documents/rio20_outcome_document_complete.pdf> accessed 29 May 2018.

3 of the 1992 Rio Declaration, and to intergenerational equity.[18] As part of it, states recognised that 'opportunities for people to influence their lives and future, participate in decision-making and voice their concerns are fundamental for sustainable development'.[19]

8.3 AN OUTLINE OF PROCEDURAL RIGHTS WITHIN MEAS

Many MEAs include obligations regarding disclosure of environmental information and public participation in decision making. Several of these obligations require states to take actions vis-à-vis members of the public, although the obligations may be owed to the other state parties to the agreement as a matter of law. These provisions may be especially relevant because the obligations may correspond in some respects to recognised human rights. A duty in an MEA to provide information to affected members of the public, for example, may correspond to a right to information recognised in human rights instruments. Many agreements set out obligations to provide information to the public and to ensure participation in decision making. Some also include provisions on access to remedies for environmental harm.

This section outlines specific procedural rights-oriented obligations assumed by states under MEAs. In doing so, and very much through examples rather than exhaustive listing, it maps their application and the development of standards associated with them.

8.3.1 *Access to Information*

Various MEAs guarantee the provision of access to information in relation to environmental matters.

8.3.1.1 Public and Interested Public

The UN Framework Convention on Climate Change (UNFCCC)[20] contains procedural obligations to individuals as well as to other parties. Article 6 requests parties to promote and facilitate at the national and, as appropriate, subregional, and regional levels, and in accordance with national laws and regulations as well as their respective capacities, public access to information on climate change and its effects.[21] Article 12 of the UNFCCC requires parties to include in national communications various kinds of information, including the following:

[18] ibid Section II C para 39.
[19] ibid para 13.
[20] United Nations Framework Convention on Climate Change (entered into force 21 March 1994) (1992) 1771 UNTS 107.
[21] ibid art 6(a)(ii).

1. (a) A national inventory of anthropogenic emissions by sources and removals by sinks of all greenhouse gases … (b) A general description of steps taken or envisaged by the Party to implement the Convention
2. Each developed country Party and each other Party included in Annex I shall incorporate in its communication the following elements of information: (a) A detailed description of the policies and measures that it was adopted to implement its commitment under Article 4 … ; and (b) A specific estimate of the effects that the policies and measures referred to in subparagraph (a) immediately above will have on anthropogenic emissions by its sources and removals by its sinks of greenhouse gases.[22]

According to Article 7 of the Kyoto Protocol, 'each Party included in Annex I shall incorporate in its national communication, submitted under Article 12 of the Convention, the supplementary information necessary to demonstrate compliance with its commitments under this Protocol'.[23] The public should also be informed about issues relating to climate change that include: emission trading and activities related to other flexibility mechanisms under the Kyoto Protocol; investment in green technology projects; financing of such projects; technology transfer; protecting carbon sinks and reservoirs of greenhouse gases; and other important matters.

The 1998 Rotterdam Convention on the Prior Informed Consent Procedure for Certain Hazardous Chemicals and Pesticides in International Trade[24] requires that Parties that are subject to the prior informed consent of importing states 'ensure, to the extent practicable, that the public has appropriate access to information on chemical handling and accident management and on alternatives that are safer for human health or the environment to the chemicals listed.'[25]

Meanwhile, the Stockholm Convention on Persistent Organic Pollutants (Stockholm Convention) requires that Parties, within their capabilities, promote and facilitate provision to the public of all available information on persistent organic pollutants and that the information is kept up to date.[26] It also recommends that Parties can provide such information through the use of safety data sheets, reports, mass media, and other means of communication, as well as by establishing information centres at national and regional levels.[27]

Article 9 of the Convention on the Transboundary Effects of Industrial Accidents requires parties to 'ensure that adequate information is given to the public in the

[22] ibid art 12.

[23] Protocol to the United Nations Framework Convention on Climate Change (entered into force 16 February 2005) (1997) 37 ILM 22 (Kyoto Protocol) art 7(2).

[24] Rotterdam Convention on Prior Informed Consent Procedure for Certain Hazardous Chemicals and Pesticides in International Trade (entered into force 24 February 2004) (1998) 38 ILM 1.

[25] ibid art 15(2).

[26] Convention on Persistent Organic Pollutants (entered into force 17 May 2004) (2001) 40 ILM 532 (Stockholm Convention); UN Doc UNEP/POPS/CONF/4 arts 10 (1)(b)10(2).

[27] ibid art 10(4).

areas capable of being affected by an industrial accident arising out of a hazardous activity'.[28]

The UNCCD[29] has various provisions related to access to information. For example, it states that Parties shall, as appropriate, ensure that the collection, analysis, and exchange of information addresses the needs of local communities, and that local communities are involved in these activities.[30] It also requires that Parties, as appropriate, exchange and make full openly and promptly available information from all publicly available sources relevant to combating desertification and mitigating the effects of drought.[31]

The objective of the Minamata Convention on Mercury,[32] delineated in Article 1, is to safeguard human health and the environment from the negative effects of mercury exposure through reducing emissions and releases of mercury into the atmosphere, land, or water. The Convention states that each Party shall, within its capabilities, promote and facilitate the provision to the public of available information on, among other things, the health and environmental effects of mercury and mercury compounds; alternatives to mercury and mercury compounds; scientific, technical, economic, and legal information concerning mercury and mercury compounds, including toxicological, eco-toxicological, and safety information; the results of its research, development, and monitoring activities required by the Convention; and activities to meet its obligations under the Convention.[33]

An obligation to inform is anticipated in Annex II of the Protocol on Environmental Protection on the Conservation of Antarctic Fauna and Flora.[34] According to Article 6, the Parties shall prepare and make available information setting forth and providing lists of Specially Protected Species and relevant protected Areas to all those persons present or intending to enter the Antarctic Treaty area with a view to ensuring that such persons understand and observe the provisions of the Annex.[35] A parallel provision is inserted in Annex V of the Protocol, on Area Protection and Management, according to which each Party shall make available information setting forth, *inter alia*, the location of protected areas and of historic monuments and sites, as well as the management plans, with a view to ensuring that all persons visiting or proposing to visit Antarctica understand and observe the provisions of the Annex.[36]

[28] Convention on the Transboundary Effects of Industrial Accidents (entered into force 19 April 2000) (1992) 31 LLM 1333; 2105 UNTS 457 (Espoo Convention) art 9.

[29] UNCCD (n 5).

[30] UNCCD (n 5), art 16(b).

[31] ibid.

[32] Minamata Convention on Mercury (entered into force 16 August 2017) (2013) CN560.2014. TREATIES-XXVII.17 (Minamata Convention).

[33] ibid art 18(1).

[34] Protocol to the Antarctic Treaty on Environmental Protection (entered into force 14 January 1998) (1991) 30 ILM (Madrid Protocol).

[35] ibid Annex II art 6.

[36] ibid Annex V art 9.

At a regional level, the African Convention on the Conservation of Nature and Natural Resources of 1968, revised in 2003 and adopted in March 2017, explicitly acknowledges 'the right of all peoples to a satisfactory environment favorable to their development' and a corresponding duty of states to ensure the enjoyment of that right.[37] It provides for procedural rights, requiring parties to ensure public access to information, public participation in decision making, and access to justice in matters related to the environment and natural resources.[38] It also requires Parties to take measures to protect rights of local communities, including intellectual property rights, to require that access to indigenous knowledge be subject to prior informed consent, and to enable active participation by local communities in planning and managing natural resources upon which those communities depend.[39]

8.3.1.2 Member States

Parties to the 1991 Protocol on Environmental Protection to the Antarctic Treaty are to cooperate by, *inter alia*: promoting the protection of the Antarctic environment; assisting with environmental impact assessments; sharing information; and exercising jurisdiction over areas adjacent to the Antarctic Treaty area.[40] The 1992 Protocol on Civil Liability to the Convention on the Transboundary Effects of Industrial Accidents[41] states that, without prejudice to existing international obligations, the parties shall provide for access to information, with due regard to the legitimate interest of the person holding the information, in order to promote the objective of the protocol.[42]

Article 204 of the United Nations Convention on the Law of the Sea (UNCLOS)[43] requires states to 'keep under surveillance the effects of any activities which they permit or in which they engage in order to determine whether these activities are likely to pollute the marine environment'. They must publish the results of this surveillance or make them available to all states.[44]

37 African Convention on the Conservation of Nature and Natural Resources (entered into force 7 March 2017) 11 July 2003 (2003 Revised African Nature Convention) art 3.

38 ibid art 16.

39 ibid art 17.

40 Madrid Protocol art 6.

41 UN Economic Commission for Europe (UNECE) Protocol on Civil Liability and Compensation for Damage caused by the Transboundary Effects of Industrial Accidents on Transboundary Waters to the Convention on the Protection and Use of Transboundary Watercourses and International Lakes and to the 1992 Convention on the Transboundary Effects of Industrial Accidents (adopted 21 May 2003) UN Doc MP/WAT/2000/1 (UNECE Protocol on Civil Liability) art 8.

42 ibid art 8(5).

43 United Nations Convention on the Law of the Sea (entered into force 16 November 1994) (1982) 21 ILM 1261 (Montego Bay) 1833 UNTS 3 (UNCLOS) art 235(2).

44 ibid art 5.

8.3.2 Public Participation

Despite references in MEAs, there is currently less support for a right to participation in environmental decision making than for access to information. Nonetheless, some agreements specifically set out a duty to provide opportunity for public participation or to consult the public, while a number of MEAs provide for public participation only in very general terms.

The Stockholm Convention, for instance, requires Parties, within their capabilities, to promote and facilitate 'public participation in addressing persistent organic pollutants and their health and environmental effects and in developing adequate responses, including opportunities for providing input at the national level regarding implementation of the Convention'.[45] It also requires Parties to consult, where appropriate, their national stakeholders in order to facilitate developing, implementing, and updating their implementation plans under the Convention.[46]

Article 4(1)(i) of the UNFCCC, meanwhile, requires Parties to promote and cooperate in education, training, and public awareness of climate change, and encourage participation in the process, including participation by non-governmental organisations.

The Convention on Biological Diversity (CBD)[47] refers in its preamble to the general lack of information and knowledge regarding biological diversity and affirms the need for the full participation of women at all levels of policy making and implementation. It requires that Parties, where appropriate, allow for public participation during environmental impact assessment.[48] Article 8(j) calls for the participation of indigenous and local peoples in decisions about sharing their knowledge, innovations, and practices concerning conservation and sustainable use of biological diversity.[49] Meanwhile, the CBD's Cartagena Protocol requires Parties, in accordance with their respective laws and regulations, to consult the public in the decision-making process regarding living modified organisms.[50]

The UNCCD contains numerous provisions that relate to procedural rights to participation, including in the Preamble and Articles 10(2)(e), 13(1)(b), 14(2)(19), and 25. In its Preamble, the UNCCD stresses, *inter alia*, the importance of ensuring the full participation of both men and women at all levels in programmes to combat desertification and mitigate the effects of drought. Article 3(a) and (c) begins by recognising that there is a need to associate civil society with the actions of the state. Article 5(d) calls on affected state Parties to promote awareness and facilitate the participation of local populations in efforts to combat desertification and mitigate the effects of drought. The Convention goes furthest among recent MEAs in calling for

45 Stockholm Convention (n 26) art 10 (1)(d).
46 ibid art 7(2).
47 Convention on Biological Diversity (entered into force 29 December 1993) 1760 UNTS 79 (CBD).
48 ibid art 14(1)(a).
49 ibid art 8(j).
50 Protocol on Biosafety (entered into force 11 September 2003) (Cartagena Protocol) art 23(2).

public participation, embedding the issue throughout the agreement. The agreement calls for an integrated commitment of all actors: national governments, scientific institutions, local communities and authorities, and non-governmental organisations, as well as international partners, both bilateral and multilateral.[51]

Regarding action programmes, scientific and technical cooperation, and supporting measures, the UNCCD obliges state Parties to:

> prepare, make public and implement national action programmes, utilising and building, to the extent possible, on existing relevant successful plans and programmes, and subregional and regional action programmes, as the central element of the strategy to combat desertification and mitigate the effects of drought. Such programmes shall be updated through a continuing participatory process...[52]

Again on national action programmes, state Parties shall 'provide for effective participation at the local, national and regional levels of non-governmental organisations and local populations, both women and men, particularly resource users, including farmers and pastoralists and their representative organizations, in policy planning, decision-making, and implementation and review of national action programmes'.[53]

The UNFCCC requests Parties to promote and facilitate at the national and, as appropriate, subregional and regional levels, and in accordance with national laws and regulations as well as with their respective capacities, public participation in addressing climate change and its effects and developing adequate responses.[54] It also calls on Parties to encourage the widest participation in promoting education, training, and public awareness related to climate change.[55]

At the regional level, the European Convention on the Transboundary Effects of Industrial Accidents requires that Parties give the public in the areas capable of being affected an opportunity to participate in relevant procedures regarding prevention and preparedness measures. The Party of origin must ensure that the public of the affected Party is afforded an opportunity to participate, equivalent to that given to the public of the Party of origin.[56]

8.3.3 *Access to Justice*

The Protocol of 1992 to amend the International Convention on Civil Liability for Oil Pollution Damage refers to the need to ensure that adequate compensation is

51 UNCCD (n 5) arts 13(1)(b), 14(2), 19, and 25.
52 ibid art 9(1).
53 ibid art 10 (2f).
54 UNFCCC (n 20) art 6(a)(iii).
55 ibid art 4(1)(i).
56 Espoo Convention (n 28) art 2(6).

available to persons who suffer damage caused by pollution resulting from the escape or discharge of oil from a ship.[57] The Convention provides that owners, with some exceptions, shall be liable for any pollution damage caused by the ship, regardless of fault.[58] The Convention creates fault amounts based on units of account of tonnage of a ship, and provides that owners shall not be entitled to limit their liability under the Convention if it is proved that the pollution damage resulted from their personal act or omission, or was committed with the intent to cause such damage, or was committed recklessly and with knowledge that such damage would probably result.[59] In addition, the Convention allows for claims against insurers or other persons providing financial security.[60] The International Convention on the Establishment of an International Fund for Compensation for Oil Pollution Damage (1992) was also established to provide compensation for victims who do not obtain adequate compensation under the Civil Liability Convention.[61]

The Protocol to amend the 1963 Convention on Civil Liability for Nuclear Damage sets out a strict liability regime for operators of nuclear installations.[62] Jurisdiction over actions under the Convention lies only with the courts of the party within whose territory the nuclear incident occurred.[63] The Convention sets out that the right of compensation under the Convention shall be extinguished with respect to loss of life and personal injury after thirty years from the date of the nuclear incident.[64] In the event that damage to be compensated exceeds the maximum amount available under the Convention, priority in the distribution of the compensation shall be given to claims in respect of loss of life or personal injury.[65]

UNCLOS provides that states shall ensure that recourse is available in accordance with their legal systems for prompt and adequate compensation or other relief for damage caused by pollution of the marine environment by natural or juridical persons under their jurisdiction.[66]

57 Protocol of 1992 to amend the International Convention on Civil Liability for Oil Pollution Damage of 29 November 1969 (entered into force 3 May 1996). Amended by Protocol 2000 (entered into force 1 November 2003) 1956 UNTS 255 (Civil Liability Convention) preamble.

58 ibid art III.

59 ibid art V.

60 ibid art VII.

61 International Convention on the Establishment of an International Fund for Compensation for Oil Pollution Damage (entered into force 16 October 1978) (1971) 1110 UNTS 57 art (2)(a).

62 International Atomic Energy Agency, Protocol to amend the 1963 Convention on Civil Liability for Nuclear Damage (12 September 1997) <www.iaea.org/Publications/Documents/Conventions/protamend.html accessed 29 May 2018. Reference to the 1997 Vienna Convention includes the consolidated text of the 1963 Vienna Convention on Civil Liability for Nuclear Damage as amended by the 1997 Protocol, preamble and art II.

63 ibid art XI.

64 ibid art VI.

65 ibid art VII.

66 UNCLOS (n 43), art 235(2).

At the regional level, a number of agreements specify that access to information and public participation in decision making concerning a range of environmental issues should be supplemented by appropriate access to judicial and administrative review of relevant decisions.[67] For example, the European Convention on the Transboundary Effects of Industrial Accidents requires that Parties provide access to administrative and judicial proceedings to real and potential victims of transboundary industrial accidents. Parties must provide legal remedies to transboundary victims that are equivalent to those available to persons within their own jurisdiction.[68]

8.3.4 *Environmental Impact Assessments*

A special form of procedural protection, unique to environmental law, is the environmental impact assessment (EIA), which has been linked to the rights to information and public participation. The right to participate in the environmental assessment procedure extends beyond the formal obedience of procedural requirements. It requires the meaningful realisation of the right to be heard and the right to have opinions taken into account in decisions concerning the environment and affecting the lives of people. This mechanism has been provided for in many MEAs such as UNCLOS and the CBD, as well as human rights agreements such as the International Labour Organisation Convention No. 169 concerning Indigenous and Tribal Peoples.[69] UNCLOS also provides that when 'States have reasonable grounds for believing that planned activities under their jurisdiction or control may cause substantial pollution of or significant and harmful changes to the marine environment, they shall, as far as practicable, assess the potential effects of such activities on the marine environment and shall communicate the results of such assessments'.[70]

The UN Economic Commission for Europe's Convention on Environmental Impact Assessment in a Transboundary Context (Espoo Convention) exclusively addresses the procedural requirements of environmental impact assessments, including the requirement of public participation in the assessment process.[71]

67 See, for example, the Protocol on Water and Health to the 1992 Convention on the Protection and Use of Transboundary Watercourses and International Lakes (entered into force 4 August 2005) (1999) 38 ILM 1708 (1999 Health Protocol); the Nordic Convention on the Protection of the Environment (entered into force 5 October 1976) (1974) 13 ILM 511 (1974 Nordic Environmental Protection Convention); Convention on Civil Liability for Damage Resulting from Activities Dangerous to the Environment (not in force) (1993) 32 ILM 1228 (1993 Lugano Convention); and the Protocol to the International Convention on the Establishment of an International Fund for Compensation for Oil Pollution Damage (entered into force 3 March 2005) 92FUND/A 8/4 Annex I 748.

68 Espoo Convention (n 28) Accidents art 9(3).

69 ILO Convention concerning Indigenous and Tribal Peoples in Independent Countries (in force 5 September 1991) (1989) 28383 UNTS 664 art 7.

70 UNCLOS (n 43) art 206.

71 Espoo Convention (n 28) art 2.

The Espoo Convention requires each Party to take the necessary legal, administrative, or other measures to, *inter alia*, establish an EIA procedure that permits public participation.[72] The Convention also provides that the Party of origin shall give an opportunity to the public in the areas likely to be affected to participate in relevant EIA procedures regarding proposed activities.[73] Concerned Parties shall ensure that the public of the affected Party in the areas likely to be affected be informed of, and be provided with possibilities for making comments or objections on the proposed activity, and for the transmittal of these comments or objections to the competent authority of the Party of origin, either directly to this authority or, where appropriate, through the Party of origin.[74] The EIA documentation, with relevant information, shall be distributed to the public for comments, and the comments shall be taken into account in the final decision for the proposed activity.

The Espoo Convention states that Parties shall take all appropriate and effective measures to prevent, reduce, and control significant adverse transboundary environmental impact from proposed activities.[75] The Convention requires Parties to undertake an EIA prior to a decision to authorise or undertake a proposed activity listed in Appendix I that is likely to cause a significant adverse transboundary impact.[76] Harmful transboundary 'effects' are defined as, *inter alia*, any effect caused by a proposed activity on the environment including human health and safety, and also 'includes effects on cultural heritage or socio-economic conditions resulting from alterations to those factors'.[77]

The above discussion has shown that MEAs focus mainly on setting out the rights and duties of states vis-à-vis one another, and while they rarely contain explicit provisions on human rights as such, they are relevant to human rights obligations. Among other reasons, these obligations relate to members of the public, which can help to inform related human rights. In addition, the great majority of these agreements are intended to protect interests that are identified in human rights instruments as substantive human rights, including human life, health, and property. What follows is comment and analysis relating to the development of standards within the procedural rights in MEAs.

8.4 COMMENT AND ANALYSIS ON THE DEVELOPMENT OF STANDARDS WITHIN THE PROCEDURAL RIGHTS OF MEAS

This section considers the different factors that affect the development of standards within procedural rights in MEAs. It does this by considering the issue of

72 ibid art 2(2).
73 ibid art 2(6).
74 ibid art 3(8).
75 ibid preamble and art 2.
76 ibid art 2(3).
77 ibid art 1(vii).

compliance mechanisms, the role of international organisations, national action plans (NAPs), the use of high standards for high-risk activities, and the problems relating to imprecision in procedural obligations. It illustrates these aspects by focusing on certain MEAs that provide examples of the issues being examined.

8.4.1 *Compliance Mechanisms*

The first factor to be considered is the nature of the compliance mechanisms within MEAs. These are limited in their effectiveness when compared to those of international human rights regimes. Moreover, no specifically focused international environmental court exists. The central institutions for MEAs are meetings of the parties, whose primary task is to evaluate the implementation and evolution of the treaty regime. Implementation or compliance committees created under MEAs usually consist of government representatives rather than independent experts and take a political rather than a strictly legal approach to compliance.[78] In some cases, small secretariats are created, but they lack broad competence over compliance matters. Most of the MEAs' compliance mechanisms (with a few exceptions) accept submissions only from parties about their own non-compliance or against another party. The latter happens very rarely because parties want to maintain good diplomatic relationships.[79] Individual or civil society complaints are generally not allowed.

The successful efforts to allow the public to bring non-compliance to the attention of the Aarhus Convention Compliance Committee have been replicated in the Protocol on Water and Health to the Convention on the Protection and Use of the Transboundary Watercourses and International Lakes.[80] Other MEAs do not allow communications from the public. In most MEAs, the triggers of the compliance procedure can be submissions by one party against another party, by the Secretariat, or by a party in respect to itself (self-reporting), but only the third is common. Party-to-party submissions are rare and unusual.[81] Communications from the public can be a valuable channel of information about parties' non-compliance.

78 Daniel Bodansky, 'Climate Change and Human Rights: Unpacking the Issues' (2010) 38 Georgia Journal for International and Comparative Law 511.

79 Svitlana Kravchenko, 'The Aarhus Convention and Innovations in Compliance with Multilateral Environmental Agreements' (2007) 18 Colorado Journal of International Environmental Law and Policy 10.

80 UN Economic And Social Council, Economic Commission for Europe, Meeting of the Parties to the Convention on the Protection and Use of Transboundary Watercourses and International Lakes, Protocol on Water and Health to the 1992 Convention on the Protection and Use of Transboundary Watercourses and International Lakes, UN Doc MP WAT/2000/1 (18 October 1999) <www.unece.org/env/documents/2000/wat/mp.wat.2000.1.e.pdf> accessed 30 May 2018. See Chapter 6 of this volume by Aine Ryall related to the Aarhus Convention.

81 Svitlana Kravchenko, 'Procedural Rights as a Crucial Tool to Combat Climate Change' (2010) 38(613) Georgia Journal of International and Comparative Law <http://digitalcommons.law.uga.edu/cgi/viewcontent.cgi?article=1135&context=gjicl> accessed 27 October 2016.

Therefore, the general lack of very effective compliance mechanisms within MEAs has meant that, unlike constitutional rights in many countries, and also the rights that are included within certain regional human rights treaties, a body of case law or jurisprudence relating to formal complaints which assists in the development of standards for their procedural rights has not (notwithstanding certain exceptions) developed within international environmental law.

8.4.2 *The Role of International Organisations*

The Rotterdam Convention[82] illustrates the way that specific international organisations can influence the development of standards within an MEA regime. This convention prescribes minimum standards for public access to information, but it does not provide for public participation in any decision-making procedure. Article 15 of the Convention relates to 'implementation' of the convention and, as previously noted, the requirement of the state to make information available to the public is found in Article 15(2). This provision requires that 'appropriate' access be given to information in relation to 'chemical handling and accident management'. While the term 'appropriate' can be interpreted as setting a broad standard, it naturally leaves much open to interpretation, and therefore it would be necessary for each member state or the Convention body itself to set clearer laws or guidelines. The primary purpose of the Rotterdam Convention is to establish Prior Informed Consent procedures between states when there is the potential of a harmful chemical being exported from one state to another. Additionally, the Convention necessitates the exchange of information between states in relation to the chemicals that they deem to be hazardous. For many developing countries, even complying with those primary purposes of the Convention has proved very difficult.[83] Therefore, it is understandable that other requirements of the Convention such as those found in Article 15(2) have also been difficult to achieve. As such, without external assistance the implementation and development of precise standards in relation to Article 15(2) has proved to be a challenge.

Nonetheless, there are other agencies that have supported the work of the Convention and contributed to its development. For example, the Inter-Organisation Programme for the Sound Management of Chemicals was set up in 1995 to strengthen cooperation and increase international coordination in the field of chemical safety.[84] This programme draws on the expertise of a number of different

82 Rotterdam Convention (n 24).

83 Kees Jansen and Milou Dubois, 'Global Pesticide Governance by Disclosure: Prior Informed Consent and the Rotterdam Convention' in Aarti Gupta and Michael Mason (eds), *Transparency in Global Environmental Governance: Critical Perspectives* (MIT Press 2014).

84 The Inter-Organization Programme for the Sound Management of Chemicals <www.unep.org/chemicalsandwaste/partnership/iomc> accessed 21 September 2017.

international organisations. It was in this context that the World Health Organisation and the United Nations Food and Agriculture Organisation developed an international code on the distribution and use of pesticides, which included guidance on the reporting of health and environmental incidents that result from exposure to pesticides.[85] This code creates voluntary standards which can provide useful guidance to parties of the Convention, in particular in relation to Article 6 but also in relation to aspects of Article 15(2).

Another related example is the work of the international community to clarify the obligations of states relating to procedural rights through the Bali Guidelines, which were adopted by the UN Environment Programme in 2010.[86] While they do not solely address procedural rights within MEAs, they require consideration owing to the guidance that they provide to states relating to their own national legislation. They present a set of twenty-six voluntary guidelines that provide general direction to states on promoting 'the effective implementation of their commitments to Principle 10 of the 1992 Rio Declaration on Environment and Development within the framework of their national legislation and processes'. The provisions of the Bali Guidelines are very closely aligned with those in the UN Economic Commission for Europe (UNECE) Convention on Access to Information, Public Participation in Decision-Making, and Access to Justice in Environmental Matters (Aarhus Convention).[87]

Their adoption signalled an important moment in the field of environmental law as they are meant to demonstrate willingness by states to more thoroughly engage the public at all levels to protect and manage the environment and related resources. The Guidelines provide significant detail of procedural rights. Specifically, they elaborate on the practical implications of the terms contained in less specific instruments – such as 'appropriate', 'adequate', 'effective', and 'meaningful' – which are usually used in international environmental instruments to describe the quality of access to information, decision-making processes, and justice the public should be entitled to.[88]

85 World Health Organization and United Nations Food and Agriculture Organization, 'International Code of Conduct on the Distribution and Use of Pesticides – Guidelines on Developing a Reporting System for Health and Environmental Incidents Resulting from Exposure to Pesticide' (2009) <www.fao.org/fileadmin/templates/agphome/documents/Pests_Pesticides/Code/Incidentreporting09.pdf> accessed 2 April 2017.

86 United Nations Environment Programme (2010) Decision SS/XI/5 Part A, Guidelines for the Development of National Legislation on Access to Information, Public Participation, and Access to Justice in Environmental Matters <http://staging.unep.org/civil-society/Portals/24105/documents/Guidelines/GUIDELINES_TO_ACCESS_TO_ENV_INFO_2.pdf> accessed 30 May 2018.

87 UNECE Convention on Access to Information, Public Participation in Decision-Making and Access to Justice in Environmental Matters (entered into force 30 October 2001) (1998) 2161 UNTS 447; 38 ILM 517 (Aarhus Convention).

88 Uzuazo Etemire, 'Insights on the UNEP Bali Guidelines and the Development of Environmental Democratic Rights' (2016) 28 Journal of Environmental Law 399.

8.4.3 National Action Plans and the Promotion of Participatory Rights

The UNCCD[89] provides an illustration of the degree of consistency of standards as they develop within MEA regimes. As noted in Section 8.3.2, this treaty was framed with particular emphasis on the role of public participation in the development of strategies to achieve its aims, therefore it serves as a useful point of reference on rights of participation in an environmental treaty. An examination of its participatory rights shows a range of different practices that have been developed by different states through their National Action Programmes (NAP), which represent the main method through which the convention seeks to achieve its objectives.[90]

There has been evidence of varying standards of consultation being carried out by states.[91] This can, of course, be understandable, as there are a variety of different political, socioeconomic, cultural and technological factors which impact the methods that are adopted in different countries.[92] However, there is also evidence that some members of communities, often those that are more powerful or more influential, have their concerns taken into account whereas the opinions and concerns of other less influential members of a community tend to be marginalised and neglected.[93] Additionally, there is the criticism that the text of the UNCCD is unclear as to the precise extent that local communities should be involved in such processes.[94] Apart from these factors, research shows that within different countries there are variations in terms of the institutional support,[95] political will,[96] funding,[97] and levels of communication between the participants and the authorities.[98]

The main focus of the UNCCD has been to follow a strategy of pursuing Land Degradation Neutrality in accordance with Sustainable Development Goal 15(3).[99] This has resulted in a programme of monitoring and target setting relating to its accomplishment.[100] As such, the further refinement of the processes of participation have not received the same level of attention. While a range of different practices have evolved, there have been attempts by the UNCCD to 'align' the practices of

89 UNCCD (n 5).
90 Lindsay C Stringer, Mark S Reed, Andrew J Dougill, Mary K Seely, and Martin Rokitzki, 'Implementing the UNCCD: Participatory challenges' (2007) 31 Natural Resources Forum 198.
91 ibid.
92 ibid 200.
93 ibid 202.
94 ibid 208.
95 ibid 207.
96 ibid 200.
97 ibid 209.
98 ibid 206.
99 United Nations, 'Sustainable Development Goals' (2015) <https://sustainabledevelopment.un.org/sdg15> accessed 1 April 2017.
100 UNCCD, 'Land Degradation Neutrality: The Target Setting Programme' (2016) The Global Mechanism of the UNCCD <www.unccd.int/Lists/SiteDocumentLibrary/Publications/4_2016_LDN_TS%20_ENG.pdf> accessed 1 April 2017.

member states in the ways that they approach the development of their NAPs to ensure they are consistent with the overall strategy.[101] This alignment does appear to indicate a non-mandatory standardisation of procedures which suggests an attempt to ensure that states engage in broadly similar processes in the way that they organise the participation that they provide for communities, NGOs, and those affected by desertification within their territories.

8.4.4 *Specific High Standards in Relation to High-Risk Activities*

The next area to be considered is the rare instance where an MEA creates high standards within a treaty text itself. It demonstrates that where the political will exists, such standards can be expressly created within international environmental law. The focus here is on the Protocol to the International Convention on Civil Liability for Oil Pollution Damage, which has arguably developed high standards to ensure that adequate compensation or remedy is available to persons who suffer oil pollution damage resulting from maritime casualties involving oil-carrying ships. Its provisions are imposed on all oil tankers – those registered in Party States and also those entering and leaving a port or terminal installation located in the Party State.[102] It is an MEA based on strict liability – shipowners, with some exceptions,[103] shall be liable for any pollution caused, regardless of fault. This means that claimants can receive compensation promptly, without the need for lengthy and costly litigation. In addition, the Convention allows for claims against insurers or other persons providing financial security.[104] The International Convention on the Establishment of an International Fund for Compensation for Oil Pollution Damage was also established to provide compensation for victims who do not obtain adequate compensation under the Civil Liability Convention, i.e. where the limit of compensation available under the Convention is exceeded or where the tanker owner cannot be identified, is uninsured or insolvent.[105] The establishment and evolution of the Fund and Supplementary Fund, which were created to address damage that could not be compensated under the Convention, are illustrations of

101 UNCCD, 'Ten Steps in the Practical Organization of the NAP Alignment Process' <www.unccd.int/Lists/SiteDocumentLibrary/actionProgrammes/Microsoft%20PowerPoint%20-%20NAP%20alignment%20Step%20by%20Step%20Practical%20Organisational%20Guide%20[Compatibility%20Mode].pdf> accessed 30 May 2018 and UNCCD 'Annotations – Steps in the Practical Organization of the NAP Alignment Process' <http://www2.unccd.int/sites/default/files/relevant-links/2017–01/Microsoft%20Word%20-%20Annotations%20to%20Step%20by%20Step%20Practical%20Organisation%20guide_1.pdf> accessed 30 May 2018.

102 Willem Oosterveen, 'Some Recent Developments regarding Liability for Damage Resulting from Oil Pollution – From the Perspective of an EU Member State' (2004A) Environmental Law Review 1.

103 Civil Liability Convention (n 57) art III.

104 ibid art VII.

105 Convention on the Establishment of an International Fund for Compensation for Oil Pollution Damage (entered into force 30 May 1996). Amended by Protocol 2000, (1 November 2003) 1110 UNTS 57 art (2)(a).

situations in which states have moved toward ensuring that victims of oil pollution damage will be fully compensated for their losses, and that the payment of claims will not have to be forgone because limited funds are available.

8.4.5 *Problems Relating to Imprecision in Procedural Obligations*

The final MEA to be considered is the UNFCCC, which assists in illustrating a growing awareness of the dangers of failing to provide specific detail to states relating to their procedural obligations. Article 6 of the UNFCCC requires state parties to 'promote and facilitate at the national and, as appropriate, subregional and regional levels … public access to information on climate change and its effects'.[106] The UNFCCC provides in Article 6 for an active duty to disseminate information and, in Article 4, the passive duty to give information upon request. Article 12 of the UNFCCC requires parties to include in national communications various kinds of information. The public must also be able to find out whether the numbers of a government's commitments in negotiations are credible. For example, before the 14th Conference of Parties (COP14) to the UNFCCC, NGOs in Ukraine discovered that Ukraine's commitment to reduce greenhouse gas emissions by 20 per cent by 2020 did not reflect the reality of the situation, which was greatly influenced by the economic decline that took place after the collapse of the Soviet Union.[107] The NGOs tried to push the government to change its position and to demonstrate greater transparency prior to COP15 in Copenhagen. When they failed to convince Ukraine's government, they made a statement at COP15 providing their analysis of the situation.[108]

Clearly this is an indication of the need for the standardisation of procedures relating to information collection and provision, alongside adequate and standardised auditing, if rights to information are not to be circumvented through inconsistencies in these processes.

8.5 CONCLUSION

This chapter has, albeit briefly, traced the growth of provisions within international environmental law agreements that either create or support procedural environmental rights. While a few MEAs set minimum standards for access to information, public participation, and access to review procedures in environmental matters, others merely require the promotion or facilitation of public

106 UNFCCC (n 20) arts 6(a), 6(a)(ii).

107 Svitlana Kravchenko, 'Procedural Rights as a Crucial Tool to Combat Climate Change' (2010) 38 Georgia Journal of International and Comparative Law, 613.

108 ibid 623; also Climate Action Network, 'Fossil Awards Day 2: World's Shame Rains on Ukraine' (8 December 2009) <www.climatenetwork.org/fossil-of-the-day/fossil-awards-day-2-worlds-shame-rains-ukraine> accessed 30 May 2018.

awareness and participation in a general manner. It has shown that there are a number of factors that affect the development of standards within those environmental rights. These include the limited effectiveness of compliance mechanisms within MEAs; initiatives at the UN level to clarify related state obligations; the challenge of developing consistency of practice within MEA regimes; the role of international organisations with specific expertise; the political will of states relating to particular environmental issues; and awareness of the dangers of failing to provide clarity of standards within MEAs.

The chapter has therefore shown that MEAs do not, in and of themselves, ensure either environmental human rights or environmental protection. Nonetheless, they are relevant to human rights obligations and can help spur additional environmental rights action. This is because a great majority of these agreements are intended to protect interests that are identified in human rights instruments. This therefore means that the development of standards in procedural rights in MEAs is only in the early stages. Moreover, MEAs are often of limited if any utility to individuals. While international human rights regimes and to a limited extent MEAs, approach the notion that individuals have a fundamental right to a quality environment, they are also often out of reach to individuals who would gain from the recognition of environmental rights at the constitutional level. Unlike human rights treaties, most MEAs do not create rights for individuals exercisable against states. The latter normally create rights and obligations only for states.[109] These obligations are enforceable only by other nations and are not enforceable by members of the public unless incorporated into domestic law.

109 The exception being the 1998 Aarhus Convention (n 87).

9

A Stock-Taking of FPIC Standards in International Environmental Law

Jona Razzaque

9.1 INTRODUCTION

In 2007, the United Nations Permanent Forum on Indigenous Issues stated that:

> It is . . . clear that most local and national indigenous peoples' movements have emerged from struggles against policies and actions that have undermined and discriminated against their customary land tenure and resource-management systems, expropriated their lands, extracted their resources without their consent and led to their displacement and dispossession from their territories.[1]

Indigenous peoples' right to access and manage communal lands and natural resources is central to their collective survival. The reference to Prior Informed Consent (PIC) is common in the human rights and environment field.[2] The UN Declaration on the Rights of Indigenous Peoples makes reference to Free, Prior and Informed Consent (FPIC),[3] whereby FPIC represents a normative framework of indigenous peoples' inherent right to freely pursue their social, economic and cultural development and freely dispose of their natural resources. According to the UN Permanent Forum on Indigenous Issues,

> The common understanding of Free Prior and Informed Consent is that consent should be freely given without coercion, intimidation or manipulation (Free); sought sufficiently in advance of final authorization and implementation of activities (Prior); and founded upon an understanding of the full range of issues entailed by the activity or decision in question (Informed).[4]

1 UN 'United Nations Forum Calls for "Free, Prior and Informed Consent" By Indigenous Peoples for Projects on Their Lands, as Two-Week Session Ends' (25 May 2007) Press Release HR/4926 <www.un.org/press/en/2007/hr4926.doc.htm> accessed 15 April 2018.

2 See generally CM Doyle, *Indigenous Peoples, Title to Territory, Rights and Resources: The Transformative Role of Free Prior and Informed Consent* (Routledge 2014).

3 Articles 10, 11(2), 19, 28(1), 29(2), 32(2) Declaration on the Rights of Indigenous Peoples (UNDRIP) UNGA Res 61/295 (13 September 2007).

4 UN Permanent Forum on Indigenous Issues, 'Analysis prepared by the Secretariat of the United Nations Permanent Forum on Indigenous Issues: Economic and Social Development, Environment and Free, Prior and Informed Consent' E/C.19/2011/13 (10 March 2011) para 29.

One of the first issues that has to be considered when discussing FPIC is the different terminology that has been used to define it and its contents. Over the years it has been described as a right,[5] a principle and a standard.[6] One view is that FPIC may be a stand-alone procedural right with respect to advancing the exercise or implementation of the right to self-determination, treaties and other human rights.[7] Another view is that FPIC is a principle that applies to protect human rights and the specific rights of indigenous peoples such as rights to freedom of expression, to participation and self determination.[8] The Special Rapporteur on the rights of indigenous peoples has referred to the core constituent elements of FPIC, 'consent' and 'consultation', as standards themselves.[9] Therefore, for a chapter that has its focus on 'standards' it is necessary to clarify how the terminology will be used in this instance. It is not the purpose of this chapter to attempt to provide definitions of terms, but for present purposes, FPIC will be treated as a principle that contains certain obligations including 'consent' and 'consultation'. This chapter will consider the development of standards relating to those obligations as they have emerged within the different legal regimes where FPIC is applicable.

This leads to another primary issue which is the wide range of legal sources from which FPIC is derived. Unlike some of the other chapters in this book, the law relating to FPIC is not found in one particular treaty. It is therefore necessary to map out the different areas and sources of law from which it is derived. In doing so, the chapter charts a course through international law, international human rights law, international environmental law and national law to show how each area has played its part in the development of FPIC standards. It also refers to the obligations and standards relating to FPIC that have emerged from other sources, such as international financial institutions (IFIs), as well as contributions

5 T Ward, 'The Right to Free, Prior, and Informed Consent: Indigenous Peoples' Participation Rights within International Law' (2011) 10(2) Northwestern Journal of International Human Rights Law 55; Forest Stewardship Council 'FSC Guidelines for the Implementation of the Right to Free, Prior and Informed Consent (FPIC)' (30 October 2012); J Cariño and M Colchester, 'From Dams to Development Justice: Progress with "Free, Prior and Informed Consent" since the World Commission on Dams' (2010) 3(2) Water Alternatives 423–537; A Erueti, S Down and J Ruru, 'International Indigenous Rights, Investment and Sustainability in the Mining Sector' in S Alam, J Bhuiyan and J Razzaque (eds), *International Natural Resources Law, Investment and Sustainability* (Routledge 2017) 310–28.

6 CESCR General Comment No. 21 (21 December 2009); 'Report of the Special Rapporteur James Anaya on the Rights of Indigenous Peoples' (6 July 2012) A/HRC/21/47 para 49; Information Note by the Secretariat of the World Intellectual Property Organization 'International Workshop on Methodologies regarding Free, Prior and Informed Consent and Indigenous Peoples 17–19 January 2005' (10 January 2005) para 2.

7 Permanent Forum on Indigenous People 'Report of the International Workshop on Methodologies regarding Free, Prior and Informed Consent and Indigenous Peoples' (17 February 2005) E/C.19/2005/3 para 16.

8 Human Rights Council 'Report of the Special Rapporteur on the rights of indigenous peoples, Extractive industries and indigenous peoples' (1 July 2013) A/HRC/24/41 8–11.

9 Report of the Special Rapporteur on the rights of indigenous peoples (6 July 2012) A/HRC/21/47 para 49.

to our understanding which are derived from developments at the United Nations and the work of civil society.

The cross-fertilisation of standards from human rights law to environmental law is evident in the key elements of FPIC. The different human rights instruments offer further understanding of the substantive and procedural standards of FPIC,[10] which are closely linked to environmental human rights.[11] Consultation and consent remain the crucial components of an FPIC process. Having considered the originating sources of law and standards related to FPIC, this chapter goes on to examine the scope and application of FPIC standards that have evolved within the biodiversity and the climate change regimes with particular reference to the challenges brought forward by the REDD+ and benefit-sharing arrangements. It argues that the infusion of FPIC into environmental law brings the flavour of human rights law into the environmental regime, and that there is an obligation on the State to implement FPIC standards in environmental law. The chapter illustrates how detailed safeguards agreed at the international level will play an important part in ensuring that FPIC contributes to, rather than undermines, environmental protection.

9.2 DEVELOPMENT OF FPIC: INTERNATIONAL, REGIONAL AND NATIONAL LAW

FPIC stands on a number of principles of international law such as equality and non-discrimination, self-determination, and fundamental freedoms and human rights. In the *Western Sahara* case the International Court of Justice stated in its Advisory Opinion that entry into the territory of an indigenous people required the freely informed consent of that people as evidenced by an agreement.[12] This affirms the importance of consent as the basis of relations between a State and indigenous people.

FPIC integrates the duty to consult and the objective of obtaining consent to give effect to the substantive rights of indigenous people including rights to property, culture, religion and non-discrimination in relation to lands, territories and natural resources; rights to health and physical well-being in relation to a clean and healthy environment; and rights to set and pursue their own priorities for development, including development of natural resources, as part of their fundamental right to self-determination.[13] Several international legal instruments dealing with

10 UN Economic and Social Council Permanent Forum on Indigenous Issues 'Report of the International Workshop on Methodologies regarding Free, Prior and Informed Consent (FPIC) and Indigenous Peoples' (17 February 2005) E/C.19/2005/3; also see A/HRC/12/34, A/HRC/24/41, A/HRC/21/47 (n 8).

11 UN Human Rights Council 'Report of the Independent Expert on the issue of human rights obligations relating to the enjoyment of a safe, clean, healthy and sustainable environment – Mapping Report' (30 December 2013) UN Doc A/HRC/25/53.

12 *Western Sahara* (Advisory Opinion) 1975 ICJ Rep 12. See also M Janis, 'The International Court of Justice: Advisory Opinion on the Western Sahara' (1976) 17 Harvard International Law Journal 609.

13 A/HRC/21/47 (6 July 2012) paras 48–51.

indigenous peoples assist the normative development of FPIC. For instance, the 1989 International Labour Organization (ILO) Indigenous and Tribal Peoples Convention (No. 169) recognises indigenous peoples' 'right to decide their own priorities for the process of development' and 'to exercise control, to the extent possible, over their own economic, social and cultural development'.[14] The Convention requires that States fully consult with indigenous peoples and ensure their informed participation in the context of development, national institutions and programmes, and lands and resources.[15] Article 6 requires that consultation must be undertaken in good faith, in a form appropriate to the circumstances and with the objective of achieving consent. However, the obligation to seek consent, as opposed to consultation, is limited to occasions of relocation.[16] Article 16 states that if relocation of indigenous peoples 'is considered necessary as an exceptional measure, such relocation shall take place only with their free and informed consent'[17] – interestingly, this text does not mention 'prior'.

The UN Committee on the Elimination of All Forms of Racial Discrimination (CERD), in its 1997 General Recommendation No. 23 on Indigenous Peoples, calls upon States to 'ensure that members of indigenous peoples have rights in respect of effective participation in public life and that no decisions directly relating to their rights and interests are taken without their informed consent'.[18] In its 2008 Concluding Observations, CERD recommended that States (in this instance, the government of Russia) must 'seek the free informed consent of indigenous communities and give primary consideration to their special needs prior to granting licences to private companies for economic activities on territories traditionally occupied or used by those communities'.[19]

The UN Committee on Economic Social and Cultural Rights (CESCR) General Comment No. 21 asks States to 'take measures to recognize and protect the rights of indigenous peoples to own, develop, control and use their communal lands, territories and resources, and, where they have been otherwise inhabited or used without their free and informed consent, take steps to return these lands and territories'.[20] Although the word 'prior' is missing in paragraph 36, paragraph 37 dealing with the collective right of the indigenous people to protect their cultural heritage and traditional knowledge specifically mentions FPIC. General Comment No. 21

[14] International Labour Organization (ILO) Indigenous and Tribal Peoples Convention (entered into force 5 September 1991) C169 27 June 1989 art 7

[15] Articles 2, 6, 15 and 17.

[16] Article 16.

[17] Article 16(2).

[18] CERD 'General Comment No. XXIII' on the Rights of Indigenous Peoples (1997) para 4(d).

[19] See 'Concluding observations of the Committee on the Elimination of Racial Discrimination Russian Federation 73rd CERD session' (20 August 2008) UN Doc CERD/C/RUS/CO/19.

[20] Committee on Economic, Social and Cultural Rights 'General Comment No. 21, Right of everyone to take part in cultural life (art 15, para 1(a) of the International Covenant on Economic, Social and Cultural Rights) adopted at the Committee's forty-third session, 2–20 November 2009' UN Doc E/C.12/GC/21 (21 December 2009) para 36.

emphasises that FPIC is inherent in the rights of indigenous peoples, as States are required to respect 'free, prior and informed consent of indigenous peoples in all matters covered by their specific rights'.[21]

While explaining the elements of FPIC, the Permanent Forum on Indigenous Issues explained that information needs to cover a range of aspects:

> The nature, size, pace, reversibility and scope of any proposed project or activity; The reason(s) for or purpose(s) of the project and/or activity; The duration of the above; The locality of areas that will be affected; A preliminary assessment of the likely economic, social, cultural and environmental impact, including potential risks and fair and equitable benefit-sharing in a context that respects the precautionary principle; Personnel likely to be involved in the execution of the proposed project (including indigenous peoples, private sector staff, research institutions, government employees and others); Procedures that the project may entail.[22]

It has urged States and companies to consult and cooperate with indigenous peoples concerned in order to obtain their consent before the approval of any policies, plans and projects affecting their lands or territories and other resources.[23]

The need for meaningful participation, timely information and effective consultation is integrated into several other international instruments, including the UN Sustainable Development Goals.[24] For example, the FAO Voluntary Guidelines on the Responsible Governance emphasise the relevance of 'particular positions and understandings of individual States' in the FPIC process.[25] In addition, following the ILO Convention, the UNDRIP and the World Bank's policies, the FAO Guidelines also apply 'good faith consultation'.[26]

The UNDRIP focuses on the duty and obligation of the State to secure FPIC where its activity or omissions may affect or impact on other substantive rights of indigenous peoples either through the adoption of legislation, authorization of resource exploitation or disposal of hazardous wastes.[27] The UNDRIP calls on States to consult with indigenous peoples through their representative institutions

21 ibid para 37.

22 Permanent Forum on Indigenous Issues 'Report of the International Workshop on Methodologies regarding Free, Prior and Informed Consent and Indigenous Peoples' (17 February 2005) UN Doc E/C.19/2005/3.

23 UN 'As Permanent Forum Continues, Speakers Highlight Need for Indigenous Peoples to Be Fully Involved in Resolving Conflicts over Land, Natural Resources' (17 May 2016) Press Release HR/5304 <www.un.org/press/en/2016/hr5304.doc.htm> accessed 25 April 2018.

24 Goal 17. Also see Indigenous Peoples Major Group 'Policy Brief on Sustainable Development Goals and post 2015 Development Agenda: A Working Draft' <https://sustainabledevelopment.un.org/content/documents/6797IPMG%20Policy%20Brief%20Working%20Draft%202015.pdf> accessed 15 April 2018.

25 FAO 'Voluntary Guidelines on the Responsible Governance of Tenure of Land, Fisheries and Forests in the Context of National Food Security of 2012' para 9.9 <www.fao.org/docrep/016/i2801e/i2801e.pdf> accessed 25 May 2018.

26 ibid para 9.9.

27 UNDRIP (n 3) Articles 10, 11(2), 19, 28(1), 29(2), 30(1), 32(2).

in order to secure their FPIC, 'prior to the approval of any project affecting their lands or territories and other resources, particularly in connection with the development, utilization or exploitation of mineral, water, or other resources'.[28] FPIC is mentioned in relation to the relocation of indigenous peoples from their lands and territories;[29] redress with respect to the appropriation of their cultural, intellectual, religious and spiritual property;[30] before adopting and implementing legislative and administrative measures that affect indigenous peoples;[31] redress for their lands or resources taken without their consent;[32] disposal of hazardous materials in their territories;[33] as well as prior to the approval of development projects affecting their lands or territories or other resources.[34] Following the UNDRIP, for instance, the American Declaration on the Rights of Indigenous People of the Organization of American States (2016) recognises the right to consent in relation to relocation, modification of indigenous peoples' title to lands and resources, development activities and with regard to resource extraction on certain categories of indigenous peoples' lands.[35]

The UNDRIP adds that 'States shall consult and cooperate in good faith with the indigenous peoples concerned through their own representative institutions in order to obtain their free, prior and informed consent before adopting and implementing legislative or administrative measures that may affect them.'[36] Mutual confidence and reciprocal respect are the key to effective consultation.[37] According to the UN Special Rapporteur on Indigenous Peoples' Rights, 'in many instances, consultation procedures are not effective and do not enjoy the confidence of indigenous peoples, because the affected indigenous peoples were not adequately included in the discussions leading to the design and implementation of the consultation procedures'.[38] According to the Special Rapporteur, 'States must duly address the imbalance of power by ensuring arrangements by which indigenous peoples have the financial, technical and other assistance they need, and they must do so without using such assistance to leverage or influence indigenous positions in the consultations.'[39] This is where the essence of cooperation lies.

28 Article 32.
29 Article 10.
30 Article 11(2).
31 Article 19.
32 Article 28(1).
33 Article 29(2).
34 Article 32(2).
35 OAS General Assembly 'American Declaration on the Rights of Indigenous Peoples' (15 June 2016) AG/RES. 2888 (XLVI-O/16)
36 UNDRIP (n 3) Articles 19 and 32(2).
37 'Indigenous and Tribal Peoples' Rights over Their Ancestral lands and natural resources: Norms and jurisprudence of Inter-American Human Rights System. Rights of Participation, Consultation and Consent' ch 9 para 320. <http://cidh.org/countryrep/Indigenous-Lands09/Chap.IX.htm#_ftn106> accessed 25 May 2018.
38 A/HRC/12/34 (15 July 2009) para 51.
39 ibid paras 50–51.

The emphasis is on the State to adopt a precautionary approach that should guide decision making affecting rights over lands and resources and other rights that are instrumental to the survival of indigenous peoples.[40] The Special Rapporteur adds that 'when consent is given, not just freely and on an informed basis, but also on just terms that are protective of indigenous peoples rights, it will fulfil its human rights safeguard role'.[41] Consultation and informed participation are crucial components of a consent process. Such consultation should be undertaken in good faith in order to establish a dialogue to find appropriate solutions in an atmosphere of mutual respect. In addition, States must facilitate the full, equitable and informed participation of indigenous peoples in decisions that concern them, and development or extractive activities should not take place within the territories of indigenous peoples without their FPIC, subject only to narrow exceptions.[42] For example, consent may not be required if States impose limitations on indigenous peoples' substantive rights which are permissible by international human rights law (e.g. restrictions on the right to property).[43] However, any such limitation will have to be necessary and proportionate.[44] Moreover, even when consent is not strictly required, a 'general duty to consult' remains, and States should ensure good faith consultations with indigenous peoples that would affect them, and engage in efforts to reach agreement or consent.[45]

Several cases affirm that consultation is not necessarily consent, and the duty to consult should be carried out in good faith and with the intention of substantially addressing the concerns of indigenous peoples. For example, in the *Poma Poma* case the Human Rights Committee stated that 'participation in the decision-making process must be effective, which requires not mere consultation but the free, prior and informed consent of the members of the community. In addition, the measures must respect the principle of proportionality so as not to endanger the very survival of the community and its members.'[46]

In addition, projects that have a major impact on traditional indigenous territories require the consent of the indigenous peoples.[47] The *Saramaka* case mentions that, in large-scale projects, the state has a duty to consult and obtain FPIC according to

40 A/HRC/21/47 para 52

41 A/HRC/24/41 para 30

42 ibid para 31.

43 ibid para 31.

44 ibid para 32.

45 UNDRIP (n 3) arts 19 and 32 para 2; ILO Convention No 169 (n 14) art 6 paras 2 and 32; also A/HRC/24/41 para 38.

46 Human Rights Committee 'Poma v. Peru, Views adopted on 27 March 2009' Communication No 1457/2006 paras 7.3–7.6. K Göck, 'The Case of Ángela Poma v. Peru before the Human Rights Committee' in A von Bogdandy and R Wolfrum (eds), *Max Planck Yearbook of United Nations Law*, Vol 14, 337–70.

47 *Maya Indigenous Community of the Toledo District v Belize* Case 12.053 (2004) Inter-Am CHR Report No 40/04 OEA/Ser.L/V/II.122 Doc 5 Rev 1 at 727; B McGee, 'The Community Referendum: Participatory Democracy and the Right to Free, Prior and Informed Consent to Development' (2009) 27 Berkeley Journal of International Law 570.

the customs and traditions of the Saramaka people.[48] It echoes the view of the UN Special Rapporteur who stated that FPIC 'is essential for the [protection of] human rights of indigenous peoples in relation to major development projects'.[49] Interestingly, the African Commission on Human and Peoples Rights in the *Endorois* case[50] noted that for '*any development or investment projects* that would have a major impact within the Endorois territory, the State has a duty not only to consult with the community, but also to obtain their free, prior, and informed consent, according to their customs and traditions'.[51]

As for consultation, in *Saramaka* v. *Suriname* (2007)[52] it was held that States must consult with indigenous and tribal peoples, in good faith, in relation to development or investment projects within their territory. The Inter-American Court of Human Rights (IACtHR) added that such consultation must follow 'culturally appropriate procedures and with the objective of reaching an agreement' and 'in accordance with their own traditions, at the early stages of a development or investment plan, not only when the need arises to obtain approval from the community'.[53] In the *Sarayaku* case, the Court held that 'good faith requires the absence of any form of coercion by the state or by agents or third parties acting with its authorization or acquiescence'.[54] In addition, the Court in the *Sarayaku* case cited examples from several domestic laws and affirmed that the State has an obligation to consult, given that this obligation constitutes a general principle of international law.[55] Anaya also argues that the 'widespread acceptance of the norm of consultation demonstrates that it has become part of customary international law'.[56]

Countries such as Australia, Canada, Malaysia, the Philippines and Venezuela have legislation recognising FPIC standards.[57] However, according to Carino and

48 *Saramaka People v Suriname* (Preliminary Objections, Merits, Reparations, and Costs) Inter-American Court of Human Rights Judgment of 28 November 2007 Series C No 172 [134].

49 UN Commission on Human Rights 'Report of the Special Rapporteur on the Situation of Human Rights and Fundamental Freedoms of Indigenous People' (21 January 2003) E/CN.4/2003/90.

50 African Commission on Human and Peoples' Rights Centre for Minority Rights Development (Kenya) and Minority Rights Group International on behalf of *Endorois Welfare Council v. Kenya* (May 2009) 276/03 para 162 and 291 <www.achpr.org/files/sessions/46th/comunications/276.03/achpr46_276_03_eng.pdf> accessed 15 April 2018.

51 ibid (emphasis added).

52 *Saramaka People v Suriname* (Interpretation of the Judgment on Preliminary Objections, Merits, Reparations and Costs) Series C No 185 IHRL 3058 (IACHR 2008) (12 August 2008).

53 ibid [133].

54 *Kichwa Indigenous People of Sarayaku v Ecuador* Inter-American Court of Human Rights Series C No 245 [186] (2012) <www.escr-net.org/sites/default/files/Court%20Decision%20_English_.pdf> accessed 15 April 2018.

55 ibid [164].

56 J Anaya, 'Indigenous Peoples' Participatory Rights in relation to Decisions about Natural Resource Extraction: The More Fundamental Issue of What Rights Indigenous Peoples Have in Land and Resources' (2005) 22(1) Arizona Journal of International and Comparative Law 7.

57 P Tamang, 'An Overview of the Principles of Free, Prior and Informed Consent and Indigenous Peoples in International and Domestic Law and Practices' Presented at the Workshop on Free, Prior and Informed Consent, UN Doc PFII/2004/WS.2/8 17–19 January 2005.

Colchester, there is a 'wide gap' between FPIC standards at the international level and 'national laws, which give the State strong powers to override community concerns and extinguish customary rights, sometimes even without due process, just by invoking the national interest'.[58] These implementation challenges with regards to consent, information exchange, limited resource and good faith consultations are common in both developed and developing countries.[59]

In conclusion, the discussion highlights that, first, effective consultation is the minimum standard which the State must follow and 'consent' remains a higher obligation which is required only in certain situations. A state may be obliged to obtain the peoples' consent (not mere consultation) in certain circumstances. For example, if a project involves the relocation of indigenous peoples, then consent is not just an aspiration, but a requirement.[60] Consent is also required in cases involving the storage or disposal of toxic waste within indigenous lands[61] and large-scale development or investment projects that would have a major impact within the indigenous peoples' territory. However, the concern is that small-scale projects with major impacts may still go ahead without such consent, and there may be uncertainty over what constitutes a large development project.

Second, consultation is treated as a process, while consent is the objective or outcome. Such consultations must be undertaken in good faith and in a culturally appropriate manner. However, vagueness of the term 'good faith' in international law gives rise to concerns regarding the scope, form and outcome of such consultation.[62] In addition, the UN Special Rapporteur stated that 'in all cases in which indigenous peoples' particular interests are affected by a proposed measure, obtaining their consent should, in some degree, be an objective of the consultations . . . this requirement does not provide indigenous peoples with a "veto power", but rather establishes the need to frame consultation procedures in order to make every effort to build consensus on the part of all concerned'.[63] The 'principles of consultation and consent do not bestow on indigenous peoples a right to unilaterally impose their will on States when the latter act legitimately and faithfully in the public interest'.[64] The challenge is to ensure that 'public interest' considerations within investment decisions do not jeopardise the survival of indigenous people. The emphasis is certainly on mutual understanding and consensual decision making.

58 J Cariño and M Colchester (n 5) 431.

59 A Erueti, S Down and J Ruru (n 5) 310–28.

60 UNDRIP (n 3) art 10; ILO Convention No 169 (n 14) art 16(2). There is support for this view in the case laws of the IACtHR: see, for example, *Sawhoyamaxa Indigenous Community v Paraguay* (2006) IACHR Series C No 146.

61 UNDRIP (n 3) art 29 para 2

62 CP Gillette, 'Limitations of the Obligations of Good Faith' (1981) 4 Duke Law Journal 619.

63 Report of the Special Rapporteur James Anaya on the situation of human rights and fundamental freedoms of indigenous people A/HRC/12/34 (15 July 2009). paras 48–49.

64 ibid.

9.3 FPIC OBLIGATIONS DEVELOPED BY INTERNATIONAL FINANCIAL INSTITUTIONS

In 2011, the International Finance Corporation (IFC), a part of the World Bank Group, announced that 'for projects with potential significant adverse impacts on indigenous peoples', the IFC has adopted the principle of 'Free, Prior, and Informed Consent' informed by the UNDRIP.[65] FPIC, with respect to indigenous peoples, has been incorporated into wider international frameworks and standards through its incorporation into the IFC Performance Standard 7[66] and the associated Guidance Note 7.[67] Performance Standard 7, paragraph 1, recognises that 'Indigenous Peoples, as social groups with identities that are distinct from mainstream groups in national societies, are often among the most marginalised and vulnerable segments of the population.' It provides guidance on what should be taken into account in determining which groups are 'indigenous', and adds that the application of FPIC requires at least one of the following circumstances: to be a project that is likely to impact on lands and natural resources subject to indigenous peoples' traditional ownership or customary use; to involve the relocation of indigenous peoples from traditional ownership or customary lands or natural resources; or be likely to have significant impacts on indigenous peoples' critical cultural heritage, or proposed commercial use of their cultural heritage.[68] Along with the design of the process to achieve FPIC, these guidelines underscore the crucial nature of the protection of indigenous knowledge and the involvement of indigenous groups in the consultation process along with the methods of managing mitigation and relocation, the nature and content of support agreements and forms of compensation.[69]

According to Performance Standard 7, FPIC refers to the combination of a mutually accepted and documented process of culturally appropriate negotiation between the company and appropriate institutions representing indigenous peoples, and evidence of agreement between the parties as the outcome of the negotiations. Guidance Note 7 adds that 'FPIC comprises a process and an outcome',[70] and FPIC applies to 'project design, implementation, and expected outcomes related to impacts affecting the communities of Indigenous Peoples'.[71] It requires free, prior

65 IFC 'Performance Standards on Environment and Social Sustainability' (2012) para 32 <www.ifc.org/wps/wcm/connect/115482804a0255db96fbffd1a5d13d27/PS_English_2012_Full-Document.pdf?MOD=AJPERES> accessed 15 April 2018.

66 ibid 'Performance Standard 7 Indigenous Peoples' (1 January 2012).

67 IFC 'Guidance Note 7 Indigenous Peoples. International Finance Corporation's Guidance Notes: Performance Standards on Environmental and Social Sustainability' (1 January 2012) <www.ifc.org/wps/wcm/connect/efdaaa8043649142947696d3e9bda932/Guidance+Notes+to+Performance+Standards+on+Environmental+and+Social+Sustainability.pdf?MOD=AJPERES> accessed 16 July 2018.

68 Performance Standard 7(n 65) paras 13–17.

69 IFC 'Activities Related to Indigenous Peoples' Issues' (January 2014). <www.un.org/esa/socdev/unpfii/documents/2014/ifc.pdf> accessed 15 April 2018.

70 Guidance Note 7 (n 67) para 25.

71 Performance Standard 7 (n 65) para 11.

and informed consultation and participation as well as good faith negotiation.[72] Good faith negotiation supposes that the parties have the will to engage in the process, provide necessary information for informed negotiation, explore the key issues of importance, use procedures mutually acceptable for the negotiation, have an open mind to change from their initial positions, modify their offers when feasible and give sufficient time for decision making.[73] According to Guidance Note 7, FPIC should be understood as a process that permits communities of indigenous peoples to define a 'collective position' in response to a project while recognizing the fact that different and diverging viewpoints may exist within those communities. Therefore, it is not necessary to obtain 'unanimous support from all members of Affected Communities of Indigenous Peoples'.[74]

In addition, the World Bank's Environmental and Social Safeguard Framework (2016) sets out the requirements for obtaining the consent and support of indigenous peoples in development projects that affect them.[75] This framework deals with identification and assessment of environmental and social risks and impacts associated with projects supported by the Bank through investment project financing. Other initiatives, such as the World Bank-commissioned Extractive Industry Review (2003)[76] and World Commission on Dams (2000),[77] have recommended that the World Bank ensures that FPIC of indigenous peoples be obtained in advance of funding large-scale extractive or hydro projects. These decisions, which often concern large-scale projects, have the potential for profoundly detrimental impacts on the identities, cultures and well-being of indigenous peoples. However, instead of FPIC, the World Bank Operational Policy on Indigenous Peoples 'requires the borrower to engage in a process of free, prior, and informed *consultation*'.[78] This has been criticised by the UN Permanent Forum on Indigenous Issues as it expressed concerns regarding the gap between World Bank policy on indigenous peoples (OP 4.10) and the UNDRIP.[79]

72 Guidance Note 7 (n 67) para 25.

73 ibid.

74 Guidance Note (n 67) para 33.

75 International Bank for Reconstruction and Development/The World Bank 'The World Bank Environmental and Social Framework' (2017) <http://pubdocs.worldbank.org/en/837721522762050108/Environmental-and-Social-Framework.pdf> accessed 26 July 2018.

76 World Bank 'Striking a Better Balance: The World Bank Group and Extractive Industries – The Final Report of the Extractive Industries Review' (2004) <http://documents.worldbank.org/curated/en/961241468781797388/Striking-a-better-balance-the-World-Bank-Group-and-extractive-industries-the-final-report-of-the-extractive-industries-review> accessed 17 July 2018.

77 World Commission on Dams, Dams and Development 'A New Framework for Decision Making' (November 2000).

78 Emphasis added. World Bank Operational Manual 'OP 4.10 Indigenous Peoples' (July 2005, revised in April 2013) para 1. <https://policies.worldbank.org/sites/ppf3/PPFDocuments/090224b0822f89d5.pdf> accessed 15 April 2018.

79 Permanent Forum on Indigenous Issues 'Report to the UN Economic and Social Council' (20–31 May 2013) E/2013/43 and E/C.19/2013/25 para 56. <www.un.org/ga/search/view_doc.asp?symbol=E/2013/43> accessed 15 April 2018.

Moreover, the Equator Principles, launched in 2003 and revised in 2013, represent an example for industry standards, focusing on consultation instead of consent and 'good faith negotiation'.[80] The Equator Principles are a voluntary set of standards for determining, assessing and managing social and environmental risk in project financing. They were developed by private sector banks and based upon the environmental and social standards of the IFC. Principle 5 on stakeholder engagement is of particular importance as it deals with informed consultation and participation with affected communities. A loan will not be provided to projects unless the borrower demonstrates 'effective Stakeholder Engagement as an ongoing process in a structured and culturally appropriate manner with Affected Communities and, where relevant, Other Stakeholders. For Projects with potentially significant adverse impacts on Affected Communities, the client will conduct an Informed Consultation and Participation process.'[81] It adds that the borrower will tailor its 'consultation process: to the risks and impacts of the Project; the Project's phase of development; the language preferences of the Affected Communities; their decision-making processes; and the needs of disadvantaged and vulnerable groups. This process should be free from external manipulation, interference, coercion and intimidation'.[82] It must be noted that the impact of the Equator Principles on local people is difficult to prove, and the lack of transparency and discretionary nature of the Principles remain its key weaknesses.[83]

9.4 FPIC STANDARDS THROUGH AN ENVIRONMENTAL LENS

Within multilateral environmental agreements (MEAs),[84] PIC rather than FPIC is widely recognised, and several MEAs mention the need for States to take measures to ensure that PIC is obtained.[85] In addition, while the Aarhus Convention does not explicitly deal with PIC as a precondition to projects with environmental impacts, it sets binding standards for access to information, which is one of the prerequisites of FPIC.[86] On the one hand, FPIC is closely related to environmental protection (e.g.

80 The Equator Principles 'Principle 5: Stakeholder Engagement' (June 2013) <https://equator-principles.com/wp-content/uploads/2017/03/equator_principles_III.pdf> accessed 15 April 2018.

81 ibid.

82 ibid.

83 JM Conley and CA Williams, 'Global Banks as Global Sustainability Regulators?: The Equator Principles' (2011) 33(4) Law & Policy 542–75.

84 See Chapter 8 by Lara Ognibene and Angela Kariuki in this volume which relates to MEAs.

85 For example, Convention on the Control of Transboundary Movements of Hazardous Wastes and their Disposal (1989) 1673 UNTS 126 art 6, Convention on the Prior Informed Consent Procedure for Certain Hazardous Chemicals and Pesticides in International Trade (Rotterdam Convention) (1998) 2244 UNTS 337 art 12, Stockholm Convention on Persistent Organic Pollutants (2001) 2256 UNTS 119 art 3(2)(b). Cartagena Protocol on Biosafety to the Convention on Biological Diversity (2000) 2226 UNTS 208 arts 7–10.

86 Convention on Access to Information, Public Participation in Decision-Making and Access to Justice in Environmental Matters (1998) 2161 UNTS 447; See also Chapter 6 of this volume by Aine Ryall, which relates to the Aarhus Convention.

biodiversity protection, climate change)[87] and protected areas including the designation of national parks and world heritage sites.[88] On the other hand, PIC is recognised in the Convention on Biological Diversity (CBD) work on Access and Benefit Sharing,[89] CBD guidelines on environmental and social impact assessment of activities affecting indigenous peoples' territories and sacred sites,[90] as well as regional standards on access and benefit sharing adopted by the African Union.[91] This section explores the standards that have evolved to give practical meaning to FPIC in the access and benefit sharing activities under the CBD and the Reducing Emissions from Deforestation and forest Degradation (REDD+) activities under the UN Framework Convention on Climate Change (UNFCCC).[92]

9.4.1 *The Biodiversity Convention Regime: From PIC to FPIC*

PIC is essential to the implementation of a number of provisions of the CBD of importance to indigenous and local communities.[93] It is particularly linked to access and benefit sharing and traditional knowledge. A number of countries' national access and benefit sharing laws includes PIC of indigenous and local communities.[94] This section demonstrates that PIC protects collective interests, it is closely linked to traditional knowledge and benefit sharing arrangements and the scope of

87 For example, see UN Special Rapporteur 'Report on Human Rights and Climate Change' A/HRC/10/61 (15 January 2009) para 68; UN HRC 'Report of the Special Rapporteur on the issue of human rights obligations relating to the enjoyment of a safe, clean, healthy and sustainable environment' A/HRC/34/49 (19 January 2017) <http://srenvironment.org/wp-content/uploads/2017/02/A_HRC_34_49-Final.pdf> accessed 15 April 2018.

88 Permanent Forum on Indigenous Issues 'Analysis prepared by the Secretariat of the United Nations Permanent Forum on Indigenous Issues on Economic and Social Development, Environment and Free, Prior and Informed Consent' E/2011/13 (10 March 2011). Paragraph 24 states that 'The Permanent Forum made five recommendations related to environmental conservation and protected areas that included protecting sacred places and ceremonial sites, the need for social impact assessments as well as the recognition of indigenous peoples' free, prior and informed consent before declaring protected areas that may have an impact on indigenous peoples and their communities.' <www.un.org/esa/socdev/unpfii/documents/E_C19_2011_13.pdf> accessed 15 April 2018.

89 Convention on Biological Diversity (1992) 1760 UNTS 79. See CBD Conference of Parties Decision V/26 para 11.

90 COP-7 of the CBD Decision VII/16F Annex: The Akwe: Kon Guidelines for the Conduct of Cultural, Environmental and Social Impact Assessment regarding Developments Proposed to Take Place on, or Which are Likely to Impact on, Sacred Sites and on Lands and Waters Traditionally Occupied or Used by Indigenous and Local Communities.

91 Organization of African Unity 'African Model Legislation for the Protection of the Rights of Local Communities, Farmers and Breeders, and for the Regulation of Access to Biological Resources' (2000) <www.cbd.int/doc/measures/abs/msr-abs-oau-en.pdf> accessed 28 May 2018.

92 UN Framework Convention on Climate Change 1771 UNTS 107.

93 Contribution of the Convention on Biological Diversity and the Principle of Prior and Informed Consent (2005) International Workshop on Free, Prior and Informed Consent and Indigenous Peoples (New York, 17–19 January 2005).

94 JC Medaglia, F Perron-Welch, FK Phillips, 'Overview of National and Regional Measures on Access and Benefit Sharing Challenges and Opportunities in Implementing the Nagoya Protocol' CISDL Biodiversity & Biosafety Law Research Programme (25 June 2014).

PIC is wider as it applies to indigenous as well as local communities.[95] PIC in the CBD includes indigenous and local communities as well as owners of traditional knowledge, and the holders of knowledge, innovation and practices.[96] However, it should be noted that indigenous peoples and local communities do not have the same rights under human rights law.[97] This section argues that FPIC is not yet integrated in its robust form within the biodiversity regime, and the process to apply FPIC is still marred with uncertainties regarding the consent process.

9.4.1.1 PIC and Traditional Knowledge

PIC is a key component of the implementation of Article 8(j) of the CBD, which requires that traditional knowledge of indigenous and local communities be used with 'the approval and involvement of the holders of such knowledge, innovations and practices'/ Furthermore, Article 8(j) requires that benefits arising from the application of traditional knowledge, innovations and practices should be shared equitably with the indigenous communities concerned. The CBD encourages Parties to implement national legislation to protect traditional knowledge, and the key challenge is to set the difference between the PIC process and the 'approval and involvement' process. PIC in relation to access to traditional knowledge can be found in Decision V/16,[98] and later in paragraph 53 of the Akwé: Kon guidelines:[99]

> Where the national legal regime requires prior informed consent of indigenous and local communities, the assessment process should consider whether such prior informed consent has been obtained. Prior informed consent corresponding to various phases of the impact assessment process should consider the rights, knowledge, innovations and practices of indigenous and local communities; the use of appropriate language and process; the allocation of sufficient time and the provision of accurate, factual and legally correct information. Modifications to the initial development proposal will require the additional prior informed consent of the affected indigenous and local communities.

95 UN Special Rapporteur on Human Rights and Biodiversity (2017) (n 87).

96 COP 7 Decision VII/16.

97 DA Posey and G Dutfield, 'Beyond Intellectual Property Rights: Towards Traditional Resource Rights for Indigenous Peoples and Local Communities' (1996) International Development Research Centre, Ottawa, Canada.

98 Access to traditional knowledge, innovations and practices of indigenous and local communities should be subject to prior informed consent or prior informed approval from the holders of such knowledge, innovations and practices. COP 5 Decision V/16 Article 8(j) and Related Provisions (May 2000) para 5; Annex: Programme of the Work on the Implementation of Article 8(j) and related provisions of the CBD. <www.cbd.int/decisions/cop/?m=cop-05> accessed 15 April 2018.

99 Akwé: Kon Voluntary Guidelines for the Conduct of Cultural, Environmental and Social Impact Assessments regarding Developments Proposed to take Place on, or which are Likely to Impact on, Sacred Sites and on Lands and Waters Traditionally Occupied or Used by Indigenous and Local Communities. The Guidelines were adopted at COP7 in 2004; see also Chapter 4 of this volume by Evadné Grant which also discusses the significance of the Akwé Kon Guidelines.

Article 13(1)(b) of the Nagoya Protocol offers a weak version of PIC[100] as it asks the national focal point to provide information to

> applicants seeking access to traditional knowledge associated with genetic resources, where possible, information on procedures for obtaining *prior informed consent or approval and involvement, as appropriate,* of indigenous and local communities and establishing mutually agreed terms including benefit-sharing [emphasis added]

In addition, Article 16(1) of the Nagoya Protocol states that:

> Each Party shall take appropriate, effective and proportionate legislative, administrative or policy measures, as appropriate, to provide that that traditional knowledge associated with genetic resources utilized within their jurisdiction has been accessed in accordance with *prior informed consent* **or** *approval and involvement of indigenous and local communities and that mutually agreed terms have been established,* as required by domestic access and benefit-sharing legislation or regulatory requirements of the other Party where such indigenous and local communities are located. [emphasis added]

The provision of the Nagoya Protocol prioritises the sovereign rights of the member States over their genetic resources as they have the discretion not to require PIC for access to genetic resources (Article 6) or traditional knowledge associated with genetic resources (Article 7). Article 7 of the Protocol aims to ensure that traditional knowledge associated with genetic resources held by the indigenous and local communities is accessed with their PIC or approval and involvement based on mutually agreed terms. The Explanatory Guide argues that '"consent" and "approval" have a similar meaning in the English language and that it is 'reasonable to conclude that the terms "approval" and "consent" have essentially the same meaning when appearing alongside each other in the Nagoya Protocol. The addition of "or approval and involvement" to the term PIC could therefore appear redundant.'[101] At the same time, the Explanatory Guide also accepts that 'there might be a material difference between references to "PIC" and to "approval and involvement"' as PIC has acquired a particular status under international law' and 'the term "approval" ... is rarely employed in international legal instruments, and

100 Protocol on Access to Genetic Resources and the Fair and Equitable Sharing of Benefits Arising from Their Utilization to the 1992 Convention on Biological Diversity UNEP/CBD/COP/DEC/X/1 (29 October 2010). Similar wordings are used in Tkarihwaié:ri Code of Ethical Conduct to Ensure Respect for the Cultural and Intellectual Heritage of Indigenous and Local Communities Relevant to the Conservation and Sustainable Use of Biological Diversity (29 October 2010) UNEP/CBD/COP/DEC/X/42 para 11 <www.cbd.int/traditional/code/ethicalconduct-brochure-en.pdf> accessed 15 April 2018.

101 T Greiber, SP Moreno, M Åhrén, JN Carrasco, EC Kamau, JC Medaglia, MJ Oliva and F Perron-Welch in cooperation with N Ali and C Williams, 'An Explanatory Guide to Nagoya Protocol on Access and Benefit Sharing' (IUCN 2012) 111. <http://cmsdata.iucn.org/downloads/an_explanatory_guide_to_the_nagoya_protocol.pdf> accessed 26 July 2018.

can hardly be referred to as a term of art with specific elements automatically attached to it'.[102] This allows some flexibility to member States to use 'approval and involvement' as defined in their national legislation, thus avoiding the use of PIC standards. In addition, the Preamble of the Nagoya Protocol states that an 'innovative solution' is required when it is not possible to obtain or grant PIC.[103] However, according to the Explanatory Guide to the Nagoya Protocol, if the member State 'does not clearly declare that PIC is not required, it should be assumed that PIC is required'.[104]

A push to expressly include FPIC came in November 2015 when the Ad Hoc Open-ended Inter-sessional Working Group on Article 8 (j) and related provisions considered the draft voluntary guidelines 'to ensure the [free,] prior informed consent [or approval and involvement] of indigenous peoples and local communities'.[105] In this document, 'free' means 'indigenous peoples and local communities are not coerced, pressured, intimidated or manipulated and that their consent is voluntarily given' and should be 'unencumbered by expectations and timelines that are externally imposed'.[106]

> [Free,] prior informed consent [or approval and involvement] should be understood as a continual process building mutually beneficial, ongoing arrangements between users of traditional knowledge and indigenous peoples and local communities, in order to build trust, good relations, mutual understanding, intercultural spaces, knowledge exchanges.[107]

The draft guidelines first highlighted that granting of FPIC without any agreement based on mutually agreed terms will not transfer ownership to the users of traditional knowledge, 'but merely allows temporary use'.[108] Both indigenous and non-indigenous communities need to have benefit-sharing agreements in place. Second, consent has to be sought in advance to access traditional knowledge and 'shall be obtained in good faith with no coercion, intimidation or manipulation'.[109] Third,

102 ibid 111.

103 Also see Nagoya Protocol (n 103) art 10.

104 Greiber et al (n 104).

105 Voluntary guidelines for the development of mechanisms, legislation or other appropriate initiatives to ensure the [free,] prior informed consent [or approval and involvement] of indigenous peoples and local communities for accessing their knowledge, innovations and practices, the fair and equitable sharing of benefits arising from the use and application of such knowledge, innovations and practices relevant for the conservation and sustainable use of biological diversity and for reporting and preventing unlawful appropriation of traditional knowledge. The Ad Hoc Open–Ended Inter-Sessional Working Group on Article 8(j) and Related Provisions of the Convention on Biological Diversity, Ninth meeting, Montreal, Canada, 4–7 November 2015, Agenda item 4 UNEP/CBD/WG8J/REC/9/1 (7 November 2015) <www.cbd.int/recommendations/wg8j/?m=wg8j-09> accessed 15 April 2018.

106 Paragraph 14 of the Draft Guidelines (2015).

107 ibid para 6.

108 ibid para 9.

109 ibid para 17.

'due importance' should be given to customary decision-making processes of indigenous and local communities 'in relation to the procedural and substantive aspects of the consent process'.[110] However, the COP13 (2016) adopted a watered-down version of the draft guidelines that include PIC as well as FPIC or 'approval and involvement', 'depending on national circumstances' reaffirming the sovereign rights (and discretion) of the member States.[111] It is interesting to note that the indigenous people and local communities have the right not to grant consent or approval.[112] Elements of PIC or FPIC or 'approval and involvement' include a 'written application in a manner and language comprehensible to the traditional knowledge holder'.[113] The process and the decision making should be legitimate and culturally appropriate and should take into account 'possible social, cultural and economic impacts'.[114] The indigenous and local communities should have access to adequate and balanced information, and all parties should have 'the same understanding of the information and terms provided'.[115] While the guidelines do not propose a 'one size fits all' approach, PIC or FPIC or 'approval and involvement' remain

> a continual process of building mutually beneficial, ongoing arrangements between users and holders of traditional knowledge of indigenous peoples and local communities, in order to build trust, good relations, mutual understanding, intercultural spaces, knowledge exchanges, create new knowledge and reconciliation and includes the full and effective participation of indigenous peoples and local communities.[116]

9.4.1.2 PIC and Access and Benefit Sharing

Indigenous peoples have the right to share in the benefits arising from activities taking place on their traditional territories, especially in relation to natural resource exploitation. The duty to establish benefit-sharing mechanisms for peoples affected by such activities is set out explicitly in Article 15.2 of ILO Convention No. 169 and

110 ibid para 8.

111 Mo'otz Kuxtal Voluntary Guidelines for the development of mechanisms, legislation or other appropriate initiatives to ensure the 'prior and informed consent', 'free, prior and informed consent' or 'approval and involvement', depending on national circumstances, of indigenous peoples and local communities for accessing their knowledge, innovations and practices, for fair and equitable sharing of benefits arising from the use of their knowledge, innovations and practices relevant for the conservation and sustainable use of biological diversity, and for reporting and preventing unlawful appropriation of traditional knowledge CBD/COP/DEC/XIII/18 (17 December 2016) <www.cbd.int/doc/decisions/cop-13/cop-13-dec-18-en.doc> accessed 26 July 2018.

112 ibid para 7. The guidelines do not apply to traditional knowledge associated with genetic resources under the Nagoya Protocol.

113 ibid para 17.

114 ibid.

115 ibid.

116 ibid paras 8 and 9.

has been reiterated by, *inter alia*, the jurisprudence of the IACtHR and the CERD.[117] According to the Special Rapporteur on Indigenous Peoples:

> Indigenous peoples' right to share in the benefits arising from activities affecting their traditional territories reflects the broad international recognition of the right to indigenous communal ownership, which includes recognition of rights relating to the use, administration and conservation of the natural resources existing in indigenous territories, independent of private or State ownership of those resources.[118]

Anaya has also noted that 'benefit sharing is one of the guarantees required in any case involving limitations on the rights of indigenous communal ownership', and that 'benefit sharing must be understood as equivalent to the right to fair compensation for limitation or deprivation of property, as recognized in various international instruments'.[119] In addition, the Report by the Special Rapporteur on Human Rights and the Environment confirms the crucial nature of FPIC in the context of access and benefit sharing,[120] and adds that any restriction imposed on communal property rights in the territory and the natural resources that have been traditionally used 'may not deny a community's survival as a tribal or indigenous people', and that a State is required 'to conduct assessment, consultation and benefit–sharing and, with respect to projects that would have a major impact, to obtain their free, prior and informed consent'.[121]

PIC is an important element of the CBD provisions on access to genetic resources[122] and the fair and equitable sharing of benefits. PIC is required to 'authorize access to genetic resources; control their subsequent use; and establish the fair and equitable sharing of benefits from their subsequent use'.[123] Article 15 of the CBD recognises the sovereign rights of States over natural resources and, as a result, access to genetic resources is subject to national legislation. It also establishes that access to genetic resources shall be granted on mutually agreed terms and subject to the PIC of the contracting party providing such resources. Both the Bonn Guidelines 2000[124] and

117 Human Rights Council 'Report of the Special Rapporteur on the Situation of Human Rights and Fundamental Freedoms of Indigenous Peoples' (19 July 2010) A/HRC/15/37 para 76 (citing Concluding Observations of the Committee on the Elimination of Racial Discrimination: Ecuador (15 August 2008) UN Doc CERD/C/ECU/CO/19 para 16; *Case of the Saramaka People v. Suriname*, Inter-American Court of Human Rights Series C No 172 (2008) [129]).

118 ibid para 77.

119 ibid.

120 Human Rights Council 'Report of the Special Rapporteur on the Issue of Human Rights Obligations Relating to the Enjoyment of a Safe, Clean, Healthy and Sustainable Environment' A/HRC/34/49 (19 January 2017).

121 ibid para 56.

122 According to Article 15(5) of the CBD, access to genetic resources is made subject to the PIC of the Party providing the genetic resources, *unless otherwise determined by that Party*. Emphasis added.

123 T Greiber et al. (n 104) 8–9.

124 Article 24–40 of the Bonn Guidelines on Access to Genetic Resources and Fair and Equitable Sharing of the Benefits Arising out of Their Utilization (2002) CBD Decision VI/24 <www.cbd.int/doc/publications/cbd-bonn-gdls-en.pdf> accessed 15 April 2018.

the Nagoya Protocol[125] include specific reference to PIC. According to the Nagoya Protocol, in exercising their sovereign rights over genetic resources, member States may decide to require or not to require PIC for access to their genetic resources.[126] The State may 'demand PIC in all cases of access', or 'demand PIC for access to certain types of genetic resources', or 'PIC for access to genetic resources for particular purposes' or 'fully exempt PIC in all cases of access (a Party may also waive PIC but require a notification of access)'.[127] The potential users of access to genetic resources should inform 'those affected and those authorized to make decisions' about 'the potential uses in order to be able to make a fully educated decision'.[128] According to the Explanatory Guide to the Nagoya Protocol,[129]

PIC of access and benefit sharing requires that:

- the provider who makes the genetic resources available gives his/her consent through an affirmative act;
- this decision (affirmative act/consent) is based on information provided by the potential user of the genetic resources; and
- the information is provided prior to the actual decision (affirmative act/consent) that grants access.

Therefore, first, the access requirements, determined by national regulations, may require that PIC (or approval and involvement) can be obtained from the indigenous and local communities for access to genetic resources if the indigenous and local communities have the 'established right to grant access to such resources'.[130] Second, the CBD requires that 'access, where granted, shall be on mutually agreed terms'.[131] If access to genetic resources is subject to PIC, the provider country is under an obligation to issue a permit or its equivalent 'as evidence of the decision to grant prior informed consent and of the establishment of mutually agreed terms'.[132]

The African Union Model Legislation is an example where PIC (not FPIC) is required to access biological resources, community knowledge and technologies, and the importance of consent and consultation is underscored.[133] PIC is defined as the 'complete and accurate information' given by a collector and 'based on that information, the prior acceptance of that collector by the government and the concerned local community or communities to collect biological resources, or

125 Articles 6, 7, 10, 13–17 of the Nagoya Protocol (n 103).
126 CBD (n 95) art 15(5); Nagoya Protocol (n 103) art 6(1).
127 Greiber et al. (n 104) 96.
128 Greiber et al. (n 104) 9.
129 ibid.
130 Nagoya Protocol (n 103) art 6(2).
131 CBD (n 94) Article 15(4).
132 Nagoya Protocol (n 103) art 6(3); Greiber et al. (n 104) 105.
133 OAU Model Law 'Model Legislation for the Protection of the Rights of Communities, Farmers, Breeders and Access to Biological Resources' (2000) <www.cbd.int/doc/measures/abs/msr-abs-oau-en.pdf> accessed 15 April 2018.

indigenous knowledge, or technologies'.[134] This law states that 'any access to any biological resources ... shall be subject to an application for the necessary prior informed consent and written permit' and 'shall be directed to the National Competent Authority unless otherwise explicitly provided for by law'.[135] The Model Law adds that:

> Any access carried out without the prior informed consent of the State and the concerned local community or communities shall be deemed to be invalid and shall be subject to the penalties provided in this legislation or any other legislation that deals with access to biological resources.[136]

The National Competent Authority, subject to conditions, may 'unilaterally withdraw consent and repossess the written permit' – however, any such 'termination or withdrawal of consent shall be done in consultation with the concerned local community or communities'.[137] The local communities have the right to refuse access to their biological resources, innovations, practices, knowledge and technologies where such access will be detrimental to the integrity of their natural or cultural heritage.[138] In addition, local communities have the 'right to withdraw consent or place restrictions on the activities relating to access where such activities are likely to be detrimental to their socioeconomic life, or their natural or cultural heritage'.[139] This legislation applies to 'local and indigenous communities'; however, the Model Law does not define 'indigenous communities', and the definition of 'local communities' does not include indigenous communities.[140]

9.4.2 *Climate Change Convention: FPIC as a Safeguard for REDD+ Projects?*

FPIC establishes the framework for consultations with indigenous peoples relating to project approval and negotiations related to mitigation and adaptation measures. For example, without FPIC, the clean development mechanism may have serious implications for the rights of indigenous people.[141] Citing the importance of compensation, the International Indigenous People's Forum on Climate Change adds that 'compensation measures must cover already damaged and lost lands, resources and livelihoods of Indigenous Peoples due to adverse impacts of climate change, and

134 ibid s 1.
135 ibid s 3.
136 ibid s 5(2).
137 ibid s 14.
138 ibid s 19.
139 ibid s 20.
140 ibid ss 1 and 2.
141 International Indigenous Peoples Forum on Climate Change: Our Proposals to COP21 and Beyond (29 November 2015). <www.forestpeoples.org/sites/fpp/files/news/2015/12/IP%20Political_statement.pdf> accessed 15 April 2018.

must be contingent on FPIC'.[142] Similar concerns were raised by the African Commission's Resolution 153 that urges the African Union to

> ensure that human rights standards safeguards, such as the principle of free, prior and informed consent, be included into any adopted legal text on climate change as preventive measures against forced relocation, unfair dispossession of properties, loss of livelihoods and similar human rights violations.[143]

Indigenous peoples are intrinsically linked to the conservation, management and use of forests.[144] According to the Permanent Forum on Indigenous Issues, FPIC should be central when deciding forest policies and programmes for indigenous peoples.[145] The UNFCCC refers to UNDRIP in Appendix I of COP16[146] that details the safeguards that countries should promote when undertaking activities under REDD+. Although FPIC is not expressly mentioned,[147] Appendix I requires the countries to promote and support 'respect for the knowledge and rights of indigenous peoples and members of local communities' and to ensure 'the full and effective participation of relevant stakeholders, in particular indigenous peoples and local communities'.[148]

REDD+ is about improved protection and management of forests using carbon stocks, and REDD+ readiness activities are already underway with projects being designed and implemented in a number of countries.[149] REDD+ is defined as:

> reducing emissions from deforestation and forest degradation in developing countries; and the role of conservation, sustainable management of forests and enhancement of forest carbon stocks in developing countries.[150]

142 ibid.

143 African Commission 'Resolution 153 on Climate Change and Human Rights and the Need to Study its Impact in Africa' (2009) para 1. <www.achpr.org/sessions/46th/resolutions/153/>. Cited by the UN Rapporteur on Human Rights and the Environment in 'Mapping Human Rights Obligations Relating to the Enjoyment of a Safe, Clean, Healthy and Sustainable Environment: Focus report on human rights and climate change' (June 2014) 41 <www.ohchr.org/Documents/Issues/Environment/MappingReport/ClimateChangemapping15-August.docx> accessed 17 July 2018.

144 Permanent Forum on Indigenous Issues, Report of the Seventh Session E/C.19/2008/13, E/2008/43 paras 44 and 45 <www.un.org/esa/socdev/unpfii/documents/UNPFII_7session_report_advance.pdf> accessed 15 April 2018.

145 ibid.

146 Decision 1/CP.16 'The Cancun Agreements: Outcome of the Work of the Ad Hoc Working Group on Long–Term Cooperative Action under the Convention' <http://unfccc.int/files/land_use_and_climate_change/redd/application/pdf/compilation_redd_decision_booklet_v1.2.pdf> accessed 28 May 2018

147 This supports the criticism that FPIC is not accepted as a core principle of REDD+ by parties to the UNFCCC. WWF Forest and Climate Initiative 'WWF Guide to Building REDD+ Strategies (June 2013)' 34 <www.wwf.de/fileadmin/fm-wwf/Publikationen-PDF/WWF_Guide_to_Building_REDD_Strategies-A_toolkit_for_REDD_practitioners_around_the_Globe.pdf> accessed 15 April 2018.

148 Decision 1/CP.16 paras 69, 72; Appendix I paras 2(a), (c) and (d).

149 For examples, see 'UN-REDD Programme and the REDD programmes in partner countries' <www.un-redd.org/partner-countries> accessed 28 May 2018.

150 UNFCCC Decision 1/CP.13 'Bali Action Plan, 13th session of the Conference of the Parties to the UNFCCC' (2007).

Within forest governance, REDD+ offers a 'political and economic trade off' opportunity between developed and developing countries.[151] While a large number of developing countries have readiness policies to reduce forest-based emissions, problems remain with REDD+-related governance mechanisms, which need to be transparent and inclusive.[152]

One critical concern is the ineffective participation of indigenous peoples and affected communities in the land use decisions that affects the long term sustainability of REDD+ projects. Thus, the Joint FCPF/UN-REDD Programme Guidelines on Stakeholder Engagement for REDD+ Readiness[153] focus on principles for effective participation and consultation, and concrete guidance on planning and implementing such consultations. The Guidelines direct REDD+ countries on how to support effective stakeholder engagement during readiness preparedness for REDD+. According to the Guidelines, the consultation process needs to include 'a broad range of relevant stakeholders at the national and local levels' and must include forest-dependent and vulnerable groups.[154] Any consultation should be transparent and should provide timely access to information as well as dissemination of information in a culturally appropriate way. The aim of such consultation should be to 'facilitate dialogue and exchange of information, and consensus building reflecting broad community support'.[155] It also adds that 'indigenous peoples should have the right to participate through representatives chosen by themselves in accordance with their own procedures and decision-making institutions'.[156] In addition, the consultation process should integrate 'impartial, accessible and fair' grievance and redress mechanisms.[157] As the title of the Guidelines suggests, the focus is consultation and information. For FPIC, it refers to the Guidelines on Free, Prior Informed Consent (FPIC Guidelines)[158]

151 T Cadman and T Maraseni, 'The Governance of REDD+: An Institutional Analysis in the Asia Pacific Region and Beyond' (2011) 55(5) Journal of Environmental Planning and Management 617–35.

152 M Thompson, M Baruah and E Carr, 'Seeing REDD+ as a Project of Environmental Governance' (2011) Environmental Science & Policy 14 (2) 100–10; E Corbera and H Schroeder, 'Governing and implementing REDD+' (2011) Environmental Science & Policy 14(2) 89–99. However, for examples of success stories, see 'External Evaluation of the United Nations Collaborative Programme on Reducing Emissions from Deforestation and Forest Degradation in Developing Countries (the UN -REDD Programme)' Vol I, Final Report (July 2014) <https://wedocs.unep.org/rest/bitstreams/776/retrieve> accessed 15 April 2018.

153 'Joint FCPF/UN-REDD Programme Guidelines on Stakeholder Engagement for REDD+ Readiness with a Focus on the Participation of Indigenous Peoples and Other Forest-Dependent Communities' (20 April 2012). <www.forestcarbonpartnership.org/sites/fcp/files/2013/May2013/Guidelines%20on%20Stakeholder%20Engagement%20April%2020,%202012%20(revision%20of%20March%2025th%20version).pdf> accessed 15 April 2018.

154 ibid para 8.

155 ibid.

156 ibid.

157 ibid.

158 UN-REDD Programme 'Guidelines on Free, Prior Informed Consent' (UNDP January 2013). <www.uncclearn.org/sites/default/files/inventory/un-redd05.pdf> accessed 15 April 2018.

formulated by the UN-REDD programme that assist countries to develop and implement strategies in order to facilitate REDD+ readiness.

The FPIC Guidelines offer a framework to undertake effective consultations and obtain consent as and when appropriate, as determined by the country in consultation with relevant rights holders and consistent with their duties and obligations under international law. The guidelines specify that a 'key component of effective stakeholder engagement and consultation' is FPIC[159] and add that

> FPIC applies to REDD+ regarding potential changes in resource uses that could *significantly impact* the substantive rights of indigenous peoples and, where relevant, other forest dependent communities. Under these circumstances, consistent with international human rights instruments and other treaty obligations, potentially impacted peoples have the right to participate in and *consent to or withhold consent* from a proposed action.[160] [emphasis added]

The FPIC Guidelines note that 'free' refers to a process that is 'self-directed by the community from whom consent is being sought unencumbered by coercion, expectations or timelines that are externally imposed',[161] and consent is the 'the collective decision made by the rights-holders and reached through the customary decision-making processes of the affected peoples or communities'.[162] The FPIC Guidelines offer a checklist to determine whether FPIC is required.[163]

The FPIC Guidelines underscore that, first, the process of FPIC needs to respect the collective right of the indigenous and local community to determine what type of consultation process and decision making is appropriate for them.[164] Consent is based on collective considerations reached through customary processes or through mutually agreed terms.[165] Second, the FPIC Guidelines do not promote a 'blanket application of FPIC' for all forest-dependent communities and state that parties need to 'evaluate the circumstances and nature of the forest-dependent community in question, on a case by case basis, through among others a rights-based analysis, and secure FPIC from communities that share common characteristics with indigenous peoples, and whose underlying substantive rights are significantly implicated'.[166] Third, in order to minimise potential future conflict,[167] the indigenous and local community should be informed about all aspects of project development (e.g. initiating a process, designing a project, developing a project implementation

159 ibid para 8.
160 ibid 18.
161 ibid.
162 ibid 20.
163 ibid 27.
164 ibid 20.
165 ibid 33.
166 ibid 11.
167 For example of such conflicts in Indonesia (Riau, Central Kalimantan) see: www.misereor.org/fileadmin//user_upload/misereor_org/Publications/englisch/documentation-workshop-rights-before-REDD.pdf accessed 28 May 2018.

agreement) as good practice.[168] Fourth, consent is not a one-off process and can be 'given or withheld in phases, over specific periods of time for distinct stages or phases of REDD+'.[169] Thus, 'under certain circumstances, it must be accepted that the project will not proceed and/or that engagement must be ceased if the affected people decide that they do not want to commence or continue with negotiations or if they decide to withhold their consent to the project'.[170] Fifth, rights holders may choose to grant their consent on the basis of certain conditions (e.g. restricted access, benefit sharing). 'If these conditions are not met, the community may review and either reaffirm or refuse consent. This option may be invoked at any stage of programme implementation.'[171] Sixth, FPIC is part of a process that requires monitoring throughout the project. Independent verification of such FPIC process may involve participatory monitoring,[172] which is mutually agreed by all relevant rights holders.[173] At the same time, a grievance mechanism (e.g. at the national, subnational or community level) and the right to legal assistance regarding the consent process are required to ensure that the indigenous and local community have access to remedies including compensation, and that disputes are settled in a timely and proper manner.[174]

It is worth mentioning another UN-REDD guidance on Social and Environmental Principles and Criteria (SEPC) that provides a framework to support countries in developing national approaches to REDD+ safeguards.[175] Criterion 9 of the SEPC asks countries to seek FPIC and 'respect and uphold the decision taken (whether consent is given or withheld)'. The glossary of the SEPC provides that governments must obtain the FPIC of 'directly or indirectly affected indigenous peoples, tribal groups, ethnic minorities and other forest dependent communities'.[176] Moreover, voluntary standards[177] such as the REDD+ Social and Environmental Standards (REDD+ SES) for government-led programmes are developed with support from NGOs such as the Climate, Community and Biodiversity Alliance (CCBA) and CARE International. These standards expand on REDD+ standards listed in Appendix I of the Cancun Agreement,[178] and call for the 'free, prior and informed consent of indigenous peoples and local communities

168 FPIC Guidelines (n 161) 19.
169 ibid 20.
170 ibid 20.
171 ibid 30.
172 ibid 45.
173 ibid 33.
174 ibid 29–30.
175 UN-REDD Programme 'UN-REDD Programme Social and Environmental Principles and Criteria (SEPC)' UN-REDD Programme Eighth Policy Board Meeting, Asuncion, Paraguay UNREDD/PB8/2012/V/1 (25–26 March 2012).
176 UN-REDD SEPC ibid 12.
177 Other international safeguards initiatives include the Strategic Environmental and Social Assessment (SESA) process of the Forest Carbon Partnership Facility (FCPF).
178 Decision 1/CP.16 (n 149).

for any activities affecting their rights to lands, territories, and resources'.[179] These voluntary standards for REDD projects require full and effective participation of project-affected indigenous people and local communities as well as 'consultation and free, prior and informed consent',[180] and are being implemented in several developing countries.[181]

9.5 CONCLUDING COMMENTS

There is no doubt that FPIC is a universally recognised principle integrating consultation and consent. It is a derivative of underlying substantive rights (e.g. the right to self-determination, land and resource rights) and procedural obligations,[182] and requires implementing legislation and process at the national level. It promotes the minimum standard that a State must follow to guarantee the indigenous people's rights. This chapter identifies several concerns including the vagueness of the term 'consultation' and 'consent', weak information provisions, inadequate grievance mechanisms and monitoring that hinder the effective implementation of FPIC. It also underscores the need to incorporate international guidelines into national laws; strengthen national institutions to provide effective consultation, information and remedies to the affected communities; ensure that environmental and social impact assessments are conducted effectively; and endorse monitoring of the FPIC process, including third-party monitoring.

FPIC is required for any decision directly relating to the rights and interests of indigenous people such as natural resource extractions, logging, the establishment of protected areas, construction of dams, resettlement and any other decisions affecting the status of their land rights.[183] FPIC recognises the communal nature of indigenous peoples, and the regional human rights fora have developed considerable jurisprudence on the protection of collective interests through FPIC. The case laws underscore that, at a minimum, all members of a community should be fully

179 REDD+ Social and Environmental Standards, version 2 (10 September 2012) para 1.3 <www.redd-standards.org/standards/redd-social-and-environmental-standards-version-2/5-redd-ses-version-2-english/file> accessed 15 April 2018.

180 ibid Principle 6.

181 For example, Brazil, Ecuador, Indonesia, Nepal and Tanzania. <www.redd-standards.org/> accessed 15 April 2018.

182 For example, information and participation in decision making, access to effective remedies, guarantee reasonable benefits from development activities, obligation to conduct environmental and social impact assessment, etc. 'Individual Report on the Rights of Indigenous Peoples, Report No. 8, Prepared for the Independent Expert on the Issue of Human Rights Obligations Relating to the Enjoyment of a Safe, Clean, Healthy, and Sustainable Environment' (December 2013) <www.ohchr.org/Documents/Issues/Environment/Mappingreport/8.Indigenous-10-April-2014.docx> accessed 7 January 2019.

183 Report of the Special Rapporteur James P. Anaya 'The Situation of Human Rights and Fundamental Freedoms of Indigenous Peoples, Promotion and Protection of all Human Rights, Civil, Political, Economic, Social and Cultural, including the Right to Development' A/HRC/9/9 (11 Aug 2008) ch III paras 34–43.

and accurately informed of the nature and consequences of the process and that they should be provided with an effective opportunity to participate individually or collectively in decision making.[184] In addition, FPIC requires transparency regarding projects on indigenous territories by States and companies in accordance with the customary laws and practices of the respective indigenous peoples.[185] In recent years, a few non-governmental organisations have been involved in creating community protocols,[186] and those promoting FPIC guidelines are targeting specific business sectors such as the extractive industries[187] to develop FPIC standards at the national and international levels.

Indeed, FPIC is not only applicable to indigenous peoples. The discussion on access and benefit sharing and REDD+ underscores that FPIC applies to non-indigenous as well as indigenous peoples. As there is no one definition of 'indigenous people',[188] there is also no consistent definition of 'local community' or 'non-indigenous community'. Local communities may include 'women and marginalised and/or vulnerable groups'.[189] Indigenous peoples have a separate set of rights culminating from UNDRIP, ILO convention 169 and other international human rights instruments. Therefore, the FPIC processes for access and benefit sharing or REDD+ activities need to take into account the different types of law, including customary or traditional practices and statutory law. Any agreement between the project proponent and the indigenous and local communities can be on the basis of customary practices or mutually agreed terms. The FPIC process may appear to be complicated by the difficulty of determining who comprises the relevant community and who speaks for that community.

The evolution of PIC to FPIC in environmental law is not smooth, and is fraught with conceptual as well as implementation challenges. There is reluctance within the biodiversity regime to accept FPIC as the core standard, and as evidenced in the 2016 Mo'otz Kuxtal Guidelines, other forms of approval process offer flexibility to member States to avoid using PIC or FPIC standards. In addition, there is also a need to follow consistent practices so that a lower standard of approval process is not applied to the affected community. Such approval processes applied in the access and benefit sharing projects may not be identical, but should be similar to FPIC processes. It also highlights that a blanket application of FPIC for all communities (i.e. indigenous and non-indigenous) is not possible. This gives the impression that local communities may have a set of rights different from the indigenous population

184 *Kichwa Indigenous People of Sarayaku* (n 54) [211]

185 For example, A/HRC/24/41 (1 July 2013) (n 8); A/HRC/34/49 (19 January 2017).

186 Natural Justice, 'Biocultural Community Protocols: A Toolkit for Community Facilitators' (2012) <www.community-protocols.org/toolkit> accessed 15 April 2018.

187 A Buxton and E Wilson, 'FPIC and the Extractive Industries: A Guide to Applying the Spirit of Free, Prior and Informed Consent in Industrial Projects' International Institute for Environment and Development, London <http://pubs.iied.org/pdfs/16530IIED.pdf> accessed 15 April 2018.

188 UN REDD+ FPIC Guidelines (n 161) 36–40.

189 REDD+ SES Standards (n 182) 8.

at the national level. Thus, the FPIC related guidelines need to clearly set out transparent and inclusive processes to identify 'local communities' and 'indigenous communities', and such process should not be imposed by the State (or the decision makers) in such a way to include or exclude certain indigenous or local communities.

The chapter also highlighted that the good faith criterion[190] has the potential to weaken FPIC standards. On the one hand, the good faith criterion acts as a precondition on the decision makers as they perform their duties and obligations. On the other hand, there is no clear definition of 'good faith' at the international or national level, and good faith is accepted as a guiding principle relating to the manner in which State obligations can be exercised.[191] The application of good faith highlights the need to address the unequal bargaining power generally existing between State or third-party developers and indigenous peoples. In the context of FPIC, such good faith needs to ensure that the project-affected communities can effectively participate in all stages of decision making and have the technical, financial and other means to protect their rights and participate in the decision-making processes. In addition, communities affected by the violation of such good faith obligations should be able to access effective remedies – without such protection, good faith consultation remains weak.

The relevance of strong FPIC processes to safeguard biodiversity and forest resources from external threats is beyond question. At the national level, FPIC standards need to support monitoring and reporting on safeguards throughout the project implementation (e.g. REDD+ and access and benefit sharing projects). It is time for countries to strengthen the transparency and participatory elements of the process and to implement the FPIC safeguards that alleviate social and environmental risks.

190 Good faith implies that 'parties to a transaction to deal honestly and fairly with each other, to represent their motives and purposes truthfully and to refrain from taking unfair advantages'. A D'Amato, 'Good faith' in *Encyclopedia of Public International Law* (1992) 599.

191 AR Ziegler and J Baumgartner, 'Good Faith as a General Principle of (International) Law' in AD Mitchell, M Sornarajah and T Voon (eds), *Good Faith and International Economic Law* (Oxford 2015). S Reinhold, 'Good Faith in International Law' (2013) UCL Journal of Law and Jurisprudence <http://discovery.ucl.ac.uk/1470678/1/2ucljlj40%20-%20good%20faith.pdf> accessed 15 April 2018.

10

Environmental Standards and the Right to Life in India: Regulatory Frameworks and Judicial Enterprise

Gitanjali N. Gill

10.1 INTRODUCTION

India, a nation of 1.34 billion people,[1] has a range of laws and enforcement agencies that respond to a market-driven developing country. There is a strong environmental policy, legislative framework and well-established institutions at both national and state levels. However, India's increasing prosperity has resulted in growing public awareness and a consequential demand for improved environmental quality. Environmental laws and associated standards aim to ensure the maintenance of environmental quality parameters and maintain the ecological balance. The state has also enjoyed the benefits of the transplantation of environmental standards from developed nations and international institutions thereby promoting domestic standards. Powerful ministries, notably the Ministry of Environment, Forest and Climate Change, claim to operate under the aegis of sustainable development. However, the regulatory instruments and normative standards, often piecemeal and sectoral, have failed to encompass the holistic nature of the environment and human well-being. There exists a gap between increasing public demand for environmental protection and the enforcement failure to implement relevant legislation and related rules. It resulted in the establishment of green tribunals that promote environmental governance. Consequently, judicial intervention to protect the environment and ecology assumes enhanced importance. Fortunately, India benefits because of its proactive, imaginative judiciary, particularly concerning environmental protection and through the expansive interpretation of the right to life under Article 21 of the Constitution of India.[2] Any threat to the environment or ecology can lead to the violation of the right to life under Article 21, which attracts judicial intervention. Judicial initiatives focus on conservation, including

[1] United Nations Department of Economic and Social Affairs 'World Population Prospects' (2017) <www.un.org/development/desa/publications/world-population-prospects-the-2017-revision.html> accessed 31 May 2018.

[2] Constitution of India (1950) art 21: 'No person shall be deprived of his life or personal liberty except in accordance with the procedure established by law.'

preservation, maintenance, sustainable utilisation, restoration and enhancement of the natural environment, which are vital for the sustenance of all forms of life.

This chapter traces and evaluates the origin and scope of standards within environmental rights in India through both the regulatory framework and judicial activity. Accordingly, the chapter is divided into three parts. Section 10.2 offers an account of how the Indian judiciary has locked together the Constitution and the environment via public interest litigation (PIL), and reviews how the National Green Tribunal (NGT) has utilised key sections of the Constitution to promote the right to environment. Section 10.3 presents and reviews the process of transplantation of normative standards and the fundamental weakness of the effective application of both imported and domestic standards. It demonstrates both the unusual importance of the Indian judiciary and how a specialist tribunal using in-house expertise provides science-based insights to develop standards that deal with the protection of India's environment and society. Finally, the conclusions are laid out in Section 10.4.

10.2 DEVELOPMENT OF AN ENVIRONMENTAL RIGHT: CONSTITUTIONAL MANDATE AND JUDICIAL INNOVATION

In India, there is no direct legal articulation of the right to environment, neither in the Constitution of India nor in statute law. The proactive judiciary in the 1980s, acting as 'amicus environment', through innovative and creative judicial craftsmanship developed a new, broad-based, people-oriented approach that promoted access to justice and environmental jurisprudence. The use of PIL emerged as a procedural tool 'redressing public injury, enforcing public duty, protecting social, collective, "diffused" rights and interests or vindicating public interest'.[3] Importantly, the interpretation of three Constitutional provisions (Articles 21, 48A and 51A(g)) resulted in a major change to India's environmental landscape.

Significantly, the Indian Supreme Court has articulated an expansive interpretation of Article 21, given that the right to life is a fundamental right. Article 21 of the Indian Constitution reflects the US Supreme Court Justice William Brennan's vision of a living constitution helping to understand and provide an expansive formulation of human dignity.[4] The Indian judiciary's commitment to interpret the Constitution to allow it to progress as a living document from then to now is

[3] SP Sathe, *Judicial Activism in India* (OUP 2002) 217; PN Bhagwati, 'Judicial Activism and Public Interest Litigation' (1984) 23 Columbia Journal of Transnational Law 561; *Kesavananda Bharathi v State of Kerala* (1973) 4 SCC 225; Also see Upendra Baxi, 'Taking Suffering Seriously: Social Action Litigation in the Supreme Court of India' (1985) Third World Legal Studies 107–09. Baxi describes it as 'social action litigation' (SAL) and argued that whereas PIL in the United States has focused on 'civic participation in governmental decision making', the Indian PIL discourse was directed against 'state repression or governmental lawlessness' and was focused primarily to support the rural poor.

[4] William J Brennan, 'The Constitution of United States: Contemporary Ratification' (speech given at Georgetown University as part of its Text and Teaching Symposium) (12 October 1985).

a chronological transformative process that both recognises and benefits the welfare of society. To quote Justice Brennan, 'as we adapt our institutions to the ever-changing conditions of national and international life, those ideals of human dignity – liberty and justice for all individuals – will continue to inspire and guide us because they are entrenched in our Constitution. The Constitution with its Bill of Rights thus has a bright future, as well as a glorious past, for its spirit is inherent in the aspirations of our people.'[5]

Contextualising Brennan's visionary aspiration, the Indian judiciary has interpreted Article 21 of the Constitution of India to allow for the protection of the right of citizens to live a quality of life that reflects human dignity. In *Francis Coralie* v. *Delhi*[6] Justice Bhagwati stated: 'We think that the right to life includes the right to live with human dignity and all that goes along with it, namely, the bare necessities of life such as adequate nutrition, clothing and shelter over the head and facilities for reading, writing, and expressing oneself in diverse forms.'[7] However, the human dignity principle becomes illusionary in the absence of the right to environment. Subsequently, the Supreme Court of India in *Virender Gaur* v. *State of Haryana*[8] observed expansively:

> Article 21 protects the right to life as a fundamental right. Enjoyment of life ... including the right to live with human dignity encompasses within its ambit, the protection and preservation of the environment, ecological balance free from pollution of air and water, sanitation, without which life cannot be enjoyed. Any contra acts or actions would cause environmental pollution. Environmental, ecological, air and water pollution, etc ... should be regarded as amounting to a violation of Article 21. Therefore, a hygienic environment is an integral facet of the right to a healthy life and it would be impossible to live with human dignity without a human and healthy environment.[9]

The Supreme Court has expanded the constitutional provisions identified above by introducing innovative substantive and procedural changes to the traditional judicial process. These changes support those seeking environmental justice who under established procedures would otherwise be unable to access the Court. Substantive changes not only include the right to environment as a part of the right to life,[10] but also the derivative application of principles of international environmental law and strict compliance with regulations and

5 ibid.
6 AIR (1981) SC 746.
7 ibid 753.
8 (1995) 2 SCC 577; also see *Municipal Corporation of Greater Mumbai v Kohinoor CTNL Infrastructure* (2014) 4 SCC 538; *Court on Its Own Motion v Union of India* (2012) (12) SCALE 307; *In re Noise Pollution* AIR (2005) SC 3136.
9 ibid 580–81.
10 *Delhi Jal Board v National Campaign for Dignity and Rights of Sewerage and Allied Workers* (2011) 8 SCC 574; *M C Mehta v Kamal Nath* (2000) 6 SCC 213; *State of Uttranchal v Balwant Singh Chaufal* (2010) 3 SCC 40.

standards.[11] Associated procedural expansion has provided a platform for the implementation of these substantive rights. It includes a broader understanding of *locus standi* (representative and citizen standing),[12] interpreting letters written to the court as petitions, appointing fact-finding commissions and implementing directions as continuing *mandamus*.[13] Thus, the Supreme Court has endorsed the *ratio* that the right to a clean, safe, hygienic, decent, pollution-free and wholesome environment is a legitimate expectation flowing from Article 21.[14]

Further, Article 48A, a directive principle of state policy, mandates the state to protect and improve the environment and safeguard forests and wildlife. The policy prescription has assumed the legal status of imposing an obligation to protect the environment not only on government, but also on courts.[15] Article 51A(g) imposes a fundamental duty on every citizen to protect and improve the natural environment including forests, lakes, rivers and wildlife and to have compassion for living creatures. The social obligation under Article 51A(g) has broadened the meaning of 'citizen' to permit public-spirited citizens, interested institutions and NGOs to file and advance environmental PILs to protect ecology and the environment.[16]

11 The principles include intergenerational equity, precautionary and polluter pays principles, sustainable development. See *Deepak Nitrate v State of Gujarat* (2004) 6 SCC 402; *AP Pollution Control Board v Nayudu I* (1999) 2 SCC 718; *Vellore Citizen Welfare Forum v Union of India* AIR (1996) SC 2715.

12 Representative standing allows any member of the public, acting bona fide, to advance claims against violations of human rights of victims who because of their poverty, disability or socially or economically disadvantaged position could not approach the Court for judicial enforcement of their fundamental rights. NGOs and environmental activists working on behalf of poor and tribal people have entered the courts through the exercise of this procedure. The citizen standing provides a platform to seek redress for a public grievance; this affects society rather than an individual grievance. See generally *Indian Council for Enviro-Legal Action v Union of India* (1996) 3 SCC 21; *In re Judges Transfer Case* AIR (1982) SC 149; *Almrita Patel v Union of India* Writ Petition No. 888 (1996); *M C Mehta v Union of India* AIR (1997) SC 734. These types of actions can be compared and contrasted with the *actio popularis* provisions discussed by Alexandra Aragao in Chapter 11.

13 Gitanjali N Gill, 'Human Rights and the Environment in India: Access through Public Interest Litigation' (2012) 14 Environmental LR 203–04; Michael G Faure and AV Raja, 'Effectiveness of Environmental Public Interest Litigation in India: Determining the Key Variable' (2010) 21 Fordham Environmental LR 225; Lavanya Rajamani, 'Public Interest Litigation in India: Exploring Issues of Access, Participation, Equity, Effectiveness and Sustainability' (2007) 19(3) Journal of Environmental Law 293; Geetanjoy Sahu, 'Implications of Indian Supreme Court's Innovation for Environmental Jurisprudence' (2008) 4(1) Law, Environmental and Development Journal 375; Shyam Divan and Armin Rosencranz, *Environmental Law and Policy in India* (OUP 2001) 133; Jona Razzaque, *Public Interest Environmental Litigation in India, Pakistan, and Bangladesh* (Kluwer Law International 2004).

14 *Hindustan Zinc Limited v Rajasthan Electricity* (2015) 12 SCC611; *Occupational Health and Safety Association v Union of India* (2014) 3 SCC 547; *M.K. Balakrishnan (1) v Union of India* (2009) 5 SCC 507; *TN Godavaraman Thirumulpad (87) v Union of India* (2006) 1 SCC 1; *M.C. Mehta v Union of India* (2004) 6 SCC 588; *Hinch Lal Tiwari v Kamala Devi* (2001) 6 SCC 496; *Subhash Kumar v State of Bihar* (1991) 1 SCC 598.

15 *MC Mehta v Kamal Nath* (1998) 9 SCC 589; *Intellectual Forum v State of Himachal Pradesh* (2006) 3 SCC 549.

16 *Centre for Environmental Law v Union of India* (2013) SCC Online SC 345; *MC Mehta v Union of India* (2004) 12 SCC 118.

In addition, Article 47 makes improvement of public health a primary duty of the State to fulfil its Constitutional obligations under Article 21.[17] None of this can be achieved without controlling environmental pollution and preserving the environment while recognising that materialistic resources are limited and claimants are many.[18]

Thus, the judicial lexicon of interpretation preserved the link between life and environment and successfully placed the right to life and human dignity within environmental discourse. The 'collaborative approach, procedural flexibility, judicially supervised interim orders and forward- looking relief'[19] by and large received strong public support and acquired social legitimacy. It is a 'testament to Indian democracy'[20] in recognising and addressing popular distrust of government and its inaction.

However, environmental PIL is not without critics. Concerns such as the rapidly increasing number of petitions, expensive and delayed disposal of petitions, complex technical and scientific issues, inconsistent approaches by the courts based upon individual judicial preferences, unrealistic directions and the issue of creeping jurisdiction have created doubts about the effectiveness of PIL in environmental matters. It has been suggested that the Court is guilty of populism as well as adventurism, thereby in violation of the doctrine of separation of powers.[21] The court, however, has denied any such usurpation. In its pronouncements, it has justified its actions either under a statutory provision or as an aspect of its inherent power.[22]

Within this context, the foundations for an environmental court were laid by the Supreme Court seeking an informed judicial forum that advances a distinctively green jurisprudence.[23] Accordingly, the Indian Parliament passed the National

[17] *Vincent Panikulangara v Union of India* (1987) 2 SCC 165; *S Jagannath v Union of India* (1997) 2 SCC 87.

[18] *Javed v State of Haryana* AIR 2003 SC 3057; *Unnikrishnan, J P v State of AP* (1993) 1 SCC 645.

[19] Rajamani (n 13).

[20] ibid 12.

[21] Varun Gauri, 'Public Interest Litigation in India: Overreaching or Underachieving?' (2009) Number 5109 Policy Research Working Paper, The World Bank 4; Shubhankar Dam, 'Law-Making beyond Lawmakers: Understanding the Little Right and the Great Wrong (Analysing the Legitimacy of the Nature of Judicial Law-Making in India's Constitutional Dynamic)'(2005) 13 Tulane Journal of International and Comparative Law 109; BN Srikrishna, 'Judicial Activism – Judges as Social Engineers: Skinning a Cat' (2005) 8 Supreme Court Cases Journal 3; Ashok H Desai and S Muralidhar, 'Public Interest Litigation: Potential and Problems' in BN Kirpal, Ashok H Desai, G Subramanium, R Dhavan and R Ramachandran (eds), *Supreme But Not Infallible: Essays in Honour of the Supreme Court of India* (OUP 2000); Upendra Baxi, 'How Not to Judge the Judges: Notes towards Evaluation of the Judicial Role' (1983) 25 Journal of the Indian Law Institute 211.

[22] Sahu (n 13) 391; Also, the approach of the Indian courts can be compared and contrasted with those of other jurisdictions. See, for example, Chapter 13 by Nathan Cooper relating to South Africa.

[23] The Law Commission of India was influenced by decisions of the Supreme Court of India that in dicta advocated the establishment of environment courts. The judgments in *AP Pollution Control Board v MV Nayudu* 1999(2) SCC 718 and 2001(2) SCC 62, *MC Mehta v Union of India* AIR 1987 SC 965 and *Indian Council for Enviro-Legal Action v Union of India* 1996(3) SCC 212 recommended the

Green Tribunal Act (NGT) in June 2010.[24] The NGT was established as a specialised environmental court providing effective and expeditious disposal of cases relating to environmental protection, conservation of forests and other natural resources, including enforcement of environmental legal rights, giving relief and compensation for damages to persons and property and for matters connected or incidental. Any 'aggrieved person' can seek relief from the Tribunal.[25] Following the dicta of the Supreme Court, the NGT recognised the right to environment as a part of the right to life, and in *M/S Sterlite Industries Ltd v Tamil Nadu Pollution Control Board*[26] stated:

> Article 21 of the Constitution of India . . . is interpreted to include in the right to life the right to a clean and decent environment. It is in the form of right to protect the environment, as by protecting environment alone can we provide a decent and clean environment to the citizenry. The most vital necessities, namely air, water and soil having regard to the right to life under Article 21 cannot be permitted to be misused or polluted to reduce the quality of life of others. Risk of harm to the environment or to human health is to be decided in public interest.[27]

10.3 THE RELATIONSHIP OF ENVIRONMENTAL STANDARDS WITHIN ENVIRONMENTAL RIGHTS

10.3.1 *Regulatory Framework*

A clean and safe environment can enhance the quality of life. It reduces mortality and morbidity, promotes healthier lifestyles and improves the lives of women, children and the elderly. It is a social good. According to a 2016 UNEP Report, 'investing in a healthy environment is investing in the health and well-being of current and future generations . . . Investments in preserving, improving or restoring environmental quality can bring out positive interactions and be catalytic, avoiding contradictions among sector strategies and delivering multiple benefits across all goals for enhanced well-being and quality of life.'[28]

establishment of environmental courts, which would have the benefit of expert advice from environmental scientists and technically qualified persons, as part of the judicial process.

24 The Gazette of India (No 19 of 2010). The NGT was established on 18 October 2010 and became operational on 5 May 2011 with New Delhi as the principal bench and four regional benches in Bhopal, Chennai, Pune and Kolkata.

25 An 'aggrieved person' has been given a liberal interpretation to include any person whether that person is a resident of that area or not, and whether the individual is aggrieved and/or injured or not. See s 18(2) National Green Tribunal Act 2010, and cases: *Amit Maru v MoEF* (Judgment 1 October 2014); *Goa Foundation v Union of India* (Judgment 18 July 2013).

26 Judgment 8 August 2013; also see *Sher Singh v State of Himachal Pradesh* (Judgment 4 February 2014).

27 ibid para 113.

28 United Nations Environment Programme Thematic Report 'Healthy Environment, Healthy People', Ministerial Policy Review 2nd session of the United Nations Environment Assembly, Nairobi (23–27 May 2016) 14.

Environmental standards are legal limits placed to regulate the concentration of pollutants that can be released into the environment without causing harm to human health and the environment. They constitute a combination of science (measuring risk) and policy (judging safety).[29] The science provides verifiable scientific evidence of 'substances, its exposure and likely effects on public health, risk, exposure and damage to the environment'.[30] Policy includes normative prescriptions that require balancing of 'consideration of society's attitude to risk, achievability, costs and benefits to the environment and society, economic growth and wider issues such as sustainability'.[31]

The Indian regulatory paradigm provides a comprehensive framework of laws, rules and standards and a developed institutional structure. In India, the preferred approach of the regulators involves command and control measures for controlling pollution despite the increased recognition for the use of economic and fiscal policy instruments for the control of pollution since 1990.[32]

The creation of environmental standards is but the first step, thereafter comes the process of monitoring, inspection, compliance and enforcement. The 2006 Indian National Environmental Policy[33] acknowledges that the development of environmental standards cannot be universal. It can be argued that countries should set standards in terms of their national priorities, policy objectives and resources.

29 William W Lowrance, Of Acceptable Risk: Science and the Determination of Safety (William Kaufmann Inc 1976). Lowrance states, 'Determining safety, then, involves two extremely different kinds of activities ... Measuring risk – measuring the probability and severity of harm – is an empirical, scientific activity; Judging safety – judging the acceptability of risks – is a normative, political activity.' (75–76). Also see US National Research Council of the National Academy of Sciences (NAS/NRC) Report *Risk Assessment in the Federal Government: Managing the Process* (The National Academies Press 1983) ('Red Book'). According to the Red Book, the standard-setting exercise involves two aspects – risk assessment ('the characterization of the potential adverse health effects of human exposures to environmental hazards' 18) based on scientific evidence and analysis; and risk management ('an agency decision-making process that entails consideration of political, social, economic, and engineering information with risk-related information to develop, analyse, and compare regulatory options and to select the appropriate regulatory response to a potential chronic health hazard' 18–19) based on value judgments.

30 See SNIFFER 'Environmental Legislation and Human Health – Guidance for Assessing Risk' (2007) 7 <www.sepa.org.uk/media/28984/assessment-of-environmental-legislative-and-associated-guidance-requirements-for-protection-of-human-health.pdf> accessed 15 September 2017.

31 ibid; see also Cary Coglianese and Gary E Marchant, 'Shifting Sands: The Limits of Science in Setting Risk Standards' (2004) 152 (4) University of Pennsylvania Law Review 1255–360.

32 The research suggests that the use of fiscal incentives (including tax concessions, pollution taxes or marketable pollution permits) has been rather limited and there appear to be no serious attempts in India to use the same. Natural resource management is carried out through allocations from central (for example, programmes of the Ministry of Environment and Forests and the Ministry of Agriculture) and state budgets. See Debesh Chakraborty and Kakali Mukhoopadhyay, *Water Pollution and Abatement Policy in India: A Study from an Economic Perspective* (Springer Netherlands 2014) 144–45; MN Murty and Surender Kumar, 'Water Pollution in India: An Economic Appraisal' India Infrastructure Report Water: Policy and Performance for Sustainable Development (2011) 290–93; S Kumar and S Managi, *The Economics of Sustainable Development: The Case of India* (Springer 2009) 45.

33 <www.moef.nic.in/public-information/policy-statements> accessed 18 August 2017.

The environmental standards in India refer both to ambient standards[34] as well as emission standards.[35] The framework of laws is regularly revisited to determine if standards are furthering national environmental policy. Normally it is the shared responsibility of the regulatory authorities – Ministry of Environment, Forest and Climate Change (MoEF&CC), Central Pollution Control Board (CPCB) and State Pollution Control Boards (SPCB) – to oversee the development and implementation of standards. The MoEF&CC is the nodal agency at the federal level responsible for adopting and publishing the ambient quality and minimum national emission standards. These national standards are drafted by the CPCB, an apex central body positioned under MoEF&CC, responsible for the prevention, control or abatement of pollution under the many environmental laws.[36] The SPCB at the state level usually adopts the national level minimum standards. However, the SPCB has the authority to develop, set and apply location-specific stringent standards.[37] The SPCB relies on the CPCB's 'Guidelines for Development of Location Specific Stringent Standards' document to ensure sustainability of the required

34 ibid 43–44. The ambient standards are the acceptable levels of specified environmental quality parameters at different categories of locations (residential, industrial, environmentally sensitive zones and others). Specific considerations for setting ambient standards in each category of location include the reductions in potential aggregate health risks (morbidity and mortality combined in a single measure) to the exposed population; the risk to sensitive, valuable ecosystems and man-made assets; and the likely societal costs of achieving the proposed ambient standard.

35 ibid. Emission standards are the permissible levels of discharges of specified waste streams by different classes of activities. Emissions standards for each class of activity need to be set based on general availability of the required technologies, the feasibility of achieving the applicable environmental quality standards at the location (specific or category) concerned with the proposed emissions standards, and the likely unit costs of meeting the proposed standard. The MoEF&CC provides minimum national standards for emissions to air and water for over 100 industries/activities ranging from high emitting industries to localised sources.

36 For example, the development of emission standards for industrial sectors is set out under the Air (Prevention and Control of Pollution) Act (1981) and further built upon in the Environment (Protection) Act (1986). Currently, the Peer and Core Group Committee (P&CGC) is an expert body within the CPCB playing a key role in the setting of emission standards. The standards recommended by the P&CGC are then considered by the MoEF&CC and the Environment Minister. If the Environment Minister is content, the standards are placed on the MoEF&CC website for public consultation (30–60 days). The responses from stakeholders (including industry, academia, NGOs) are taken into consideration by the MoEF&CC Expert Committee. Once approved and final, the standards are published in the in the Gazette of India and CPCB website. For a detailed discussion, see Shakti Sustainable Energy Foundation, 'A Review of the Process of Setting Industry-Specific Emission Standards in India' (2016) <http://shaktifoundation.in/report/review-process-setting-industry-specific-emission-standards-india/> accessed 12 December 2017.

37 For example, s 17(1)(g) of the Air (Prevention and Control of Pollution) Act (1981): 'To lay down, in consultation with the Central Board and having regard to the standards for the quality of air laid down by the Central Board, standards for emission of air pollutants into the atmosphere from industrial plants and automobiles or for the discharge of any air pollutant into the atmosphere from any other source whatsoever not being a ship or an aircraft: provided that different standards for emission may be laid down under this clause for different industrial plants having regard to the quantity and composition of emission of air pollutants into the atmosphere from such industrial plants.'

environmental quality of that location.[38] The guidance document states that a review of best available technologies (BAT) in the world will facilitate the maximum reduction in pollution achievable at the tail end. Often the availability and cost of such technologies may be prohibitive but BAT in the Indian scenario may be interpreted as the best demonstrated technology elsewhere and practicable. This is helpful for India to align itself with current international best practice such as World Health Organisation (WHO) Guidelines, US Environmental Protection Agency (USEPA) and EU limits and practices to protect life, public health and environment.[39]

For example, the ambient air quality standards include initiatives developed in consonance with global best practice and are in keeping with the latest advancements in technology and research based upon uniform conformity of standards in both residential and industrial areas. The ambient air quality standards set by the Central Pollution Control Board (CPCB) provide for maximum pollutant loads in the air and guide regulators on the environmental quality that ought to be maintained in the atmosphere for a healthy living and safe environment.[40] India's Air Quality Index (AQI), launched in 2015 for ten cities,[41] monitors the ambient concentration values of air pollutants and their likely health impacts (known as health breakpoints). Air Quality subindexes and health breakpoints have evolved for eight pollutants (PM_{10}, $PM_{2.5}$, NO_2, SO_2, CO, O_3, NH_3 and Pb) for which short-term (up to twenty-four hours) National Ambient Air Quality standards are prescribed.[42] The setting of AQI is a welcome initiative to inform people about daily air quality and health advisories.[43]

38 PROBES/127/2008–2009 <http://cpcb.nic.in/Publications_Dtls.php?msgid=2> accessed 10 December 2017.

39 For example, WHO 'Air Quality Guidelines for Particulate Matter, Ozone, Nitrogen Dioxide and Sulphur Dioxide: Global Update' (2005); <http://ec.europa.eu/environment/air/quality/standards.htm> accessed 10 July 2017; USEPA National Primary Water Drinking Standard (EPA 816 F-02-13 July 2002); Directive 2001/81/EC of the European Parliament and of the Council of 23 October 2001 on national emission ceilings for certain atmospheric pollutants [2001] OJ L309 (National Emission Ceilings Directive).

40 There are twelve critical pollutants (PM_{10}, $PM_{2.5}$, NO_2, SO_2, CO, O_3, NH_3, Pb, Ni, As, Benzo(a) pyrene and Benzene) whose maximum permissible concentration limit is prescribed to be uniformly applied across India <www.cpcb.nic.in/National_Ambient_Air_Quality_Standards.php> accessed 18 April 2017.

41 Delhi, Agra, Kanpur, Lucknow, Varanasi, Faridabad, Ahmedabad, Chennai, Bangalore and Hyderabad.

42 <http://safar.tropmet.res.in/index.php?menu_id=1> and <http://aqicn.org/map/india/> accessed 14 May 2017.

43 The Centre for Science and Environment, a public interest and research advocacy organisation, welcomed the launch and stated 'it is cautioning them about possible health consequences. This can help build public awareness as well as public support for hard decisions needed to get cleaner air.' <www.dnaindia.com/india/report-india-s-first-air-quality-index-launched-will-monitor-pollution-levels-across-country-2075189> accessed 12 April 2017.

Noise is a non-visible pollutant contaminating the air with high decibel intensity.[44] Realising the need to control and regulate noise levels, standards have been prescribed for ambient air, based on area classification, construction work, loudspeakers and firecrackers.[45] The WHO guidelines for community noise provided the lead and direction regarding noise standards and regulations.[46]

In the automotive sector, emission standards since 2000 aim to regulate the output of air pollutants from internal combustion engine equipment, including motor vehicles, and include fuel specifications details.[47] These are based on the European Union regulatory pathway. Nationwide implementation of BS IV (equivalent to Euro IV exhaust emission norms) standards for new vehicles came into effect on 1 April 2017, followed by BS VI (equivalent to the present Euro VI norms) emission standards for all major on-road vehicle categories in India from 1 April 2020.[48]

Similarly, the provision and maintenance of clean drinking water is vital to people's health, communities and the economy. A 2010 United Nations General Assembly Resolution explicitly recognised the human right to water and sanitation and acknowledged the right to safe and clean drinking water and sanitation as a human right essential for the full enjoyment of life and all human rights.[49] The Bureau of Indian Standards (BIS)[50] has specified standards for safe drinking water for human consumption and cooking purposes. It includes water supplied by pipes or any other means for human consumption by any supplier. The standard prescribes desirable and permissible limits, test methods and sampling procedure for ascertaining the suitability of water for drinking purposes. Water is categorised as unfit for human consumption if it is bacteriologically, virologically or biologically contaminated. Similarly, if the presence of

44 s 2(a) of the Air (Prevention and Control of Pollution) Act 1981 and s 2(b) of the Environment (Protection) Act 1986.

45 The Noise Pollution (Regulation and Control) Rules 2000; also see <www.cpcb.nic.in/Noise_Standards.php> accessed 23 April 2017.

46 BB Lindvall, T Schwela, 'World Health Organization: Cluster of Sustainable Development and Healthy Environment' Department for Protection of the Human Environment, Occupational and Environment Health (Geneva 1999); Guidelines for Community Noise and the European Environmental Noise Directive 2002/49/EC <http://ec.europa.eu/environment/noise/directive_en.htm> accessed 10 October 2017.

47 Fuel types include diesel, gasoline and hydrogen.

48 'Euro VI fuel to be in metros before 2020: Nitin Gadkari' *The Economic Times* <http://economictimes.indiatimes.com/news/economy/policy/euro-vi-fuel-to-be-in-metros-before-2020-nitin-gadkari/articleshow/51076348.cms> accessed 10 May 2017; The International Council on Clean Transportation (April 2016) <www.theicct.org/sites/default/files/publications/India%20BS%20VI%20Policy%20Update%20vF.pdf> accessed 10 May 2017.

49 UNGA Res 64/292 'The human right to water and sanitation' (28 July 2010) A/RES/64/292 ; also see Committee on Economic, Social and Cultural Rights 2002 'Comment Number 15 Right to Water'; see Chapter 7 by Owen McIntyre which specifically addresses the right to water.

50 BIS is a national standard body for the harmonious development of activities of standardization, marking and quality certification of goods. See Bureau of Indian Standards <www.bis.org.in/bis_overview.asp> accessed 20 May 2017.

organoleptic and physical characteristics, undesirable chemical and toxic compounds, radioactive substances and pesticide residues are beyond the permissible and desirable limit, it makes water unfit for drinking purposes.[51] The standards have been formulated taking into consideration the EU Directives relating to the quality of water intended for human consumption (80/778/EEC)[52] and Council Directive 98/83/EC, the USEPA national primary water drinking standard (EPA 816 F-02–13 July 2002) and WHO Guidelines for Drinking Water Quality (second edition) and supporting information.[53]

The process of developing environmental standards at global, regional and national levels is complex and results differ between countries and regions, with standards derived, expressed, monitored, and implemented differently. However, the pervasive use of 'legal transplants'[54] in a globalised world helps improve the content and design of the national environmental laws of the receiving nations. This is typically helpful for legal systems where environmental law is at an embryonic stage or is slow to respond to environmental crises. Prestige, cost saving, international harmonisation and modernisation are all important motivations for relying on legal transplants to develop environmental law and governance.[55] The complex and uncertain risks with shared environmental externalities make it desirable for nations to import good practice rules or principles into their legal system. Drawing on the

51 ibid.

52 Repealed by Directive 98/83/EC.

53 Additionally, to restore and maintain the wholesomeness of water bodies and ensure water quality monitoring, guidelines have been framed for surface and ground water quality status. Ground water is an essential and vital component of the life support system. The ground water resources are utilized for drinking, irrigation and industrial purposes. The Uniform Protocol on Water Quality Monitoring Order 2005 and Guidelines for Water Quality Management helps in determination of natural freshwater qualities, determination of long-term trends in the levels of critical water quality indicators in freshwater resources and determination of the fluxes of organic matter, suspended solids, nutrients, toxic chemicals and other pollutants, see <http://wqaa.gov.in/Content/uniform_wq_monitoring.aspx>. The CPCB follows the United Nations Global Environmental Monitoring System (GEMS) <http://web.unep.org/gemswater/who-we-are/overview> accessed 25 May 2018. The MoEF&CC and three major central institutions – Central Water Commission, Central Ground Water Board and Central Ground Water Authority – are responsible for ground water management.

54 The academic discourse on legal transplantation reveals fundamental differences over transplant existence and its feasibility. See Alan Watson, *Legal Transplant* (University of Georgia Press, 1993); Pierre Legrand, 'The Impossibility of "Legal Transplants"' (1997) 4 Maastricht Journal of European and Comparative Law 111; O Kahn-Freund, 'On Uses and Misuses of Comparative Law' (1974) 37 Modern Law Review 1; E Orucu, 'Family Trees for Legal Systems: Towards a Contemporary Approach' in MV Hoecke (ed), *Epistemology and Methodology of Comparative Law* (Hart 2004) 359–75; Jan M Smits, 'A European Private Law as a Mixed Legal System' (1998) 5 Maastricht Journal of European and Comparative Law 328.

55 Alan Watson, 'Aspects of Reception of Law' (1996) 44 American Journal of Comparative Law 335; Michele Graziadei, 'Transplants and Receptions' in John Jackson, Máximo Langer and Peter Tillers (eds), *Crime, Procedure and Evidence in a Comparative and International Context: Essays in Honour of Professor Damaska* (Hart Publishing 2008) 458; John Jupp, 'Legal Transplants As Tools for Post-Conflict Criminal Law Reform: Justification and Evaluation' (2014) (3)1 Cambridge Journal of International and Comparative Law 389–91.

laws of the shared ecological system helps in addressing environmental challenges and enhances the ability to tailor mitigation and adaptation actions at the national level.[56]

India has benefitted through legal transplants by developing environmental standards that otherwise would have been challenging and slow to activate due to underdeveloped coordination and synergies between existing regulatory institutions, its processes including human and technical capacity constraints. However, it does not imply that the legal transplants have been a 'copy-paste',[57] 'cross-pollination'[58] or a simple 'mimicry'[59] exercise. The setting of standards is based upon the relative experience of other countries and being successful 'can satisfy that demand and the authority of a new law is less likely to be questioned if it has been borrowed from a foreign country where it has been successfully applied'.[60] However, successful legal transplantation is subject to genuine technical differences with respect to different aspects of environment (air, water or noise) or different receptors (humans, flora or fauna). Local and national parameters such as pollution levels, empirical data and epidemiological studies relating to risk to health or environment, availability of pollution control technology and cleaner technology, geographical scope, technical methodology, legal context and nature of socioeconomic assessments are critical parts of the environmental standard-setting process.[61] It is an exercise based on approximation and not absolute targets.[62] Thus, a prior application of an evaluative local technical parameter test is fundamental to determine the prospect of its success or failure from the problem formulation stage to its execution. In fact, it is not the 'process' but the 'value' of the environmental standard that assumes priority provided it emerges from a 'trusted regime that is clear and auditable and capable of achieving its objectives. The more positive the projected outcomes of the law relative to these criteria, the greater the justification for developing it by legal transplant.'[63]

56 Louis Kotzé and Caiphas Soyapi, 'Transnational Environmental Law: The Birth of a Contemporary Analytical Perspective' in Douglas Fisher (ed), *Research Handbook on Fundamental Concepts of Environmental Law* (Edward Elgar Publishing 2016) 95; Johnathan B Wiener, 'Something Borrowed for Something Blue: Legal Transplants and Evolution of Global Environmental Law' (2000/2001) 27 Ecology Law Quarterly 1295–372; Louis J Kotzé, *Global Environmental Governance* (Edward Elgar Publishing 2012) 282.

57 ibid Kotzé and Soyapi 94.

58 ibid.

59 Gregory Shaffer and Daniel Bodansky, 'Transnationalism, Unilateralism, and International Law' (2011) 1(1) Transnational Environmental Law 33.

60 Jupp (n 55) 389.

61 Andrew Farmer, Robert Lee, Stefania Loutseti, Kieron Stanley, Jacqui Warinton and Paul Whitehouse, 'Setting Environmental Standards within a Socioeconomic context' in Mark Crane, Peter Matthiessen, Dawn Stretton Maycock, Graham Merrington and Paul Whitehouse (eds), *Derivation and Use of Environmental Quality and Human Health Standards for Chemical Substances in Water and Soil* (CRC Press 2009) 1, 5–29.

62 Anil Agarwal, *Slow Murder: The Deadly Story of Vehicular Pollution in India* (Centre for Science and Environment 1996) 51.

63 Jupp (n 55) 406.

The setting of India's standards is moderately stringent compared with international practices or the European regulatory framework. For instance, the formulation and implementation of progressive automotive emission standards in India have generally lagged behind equivalent EU standards by about five years in major cities and ten years nationwide due to local contextual and technical concerns.[64] A 2016 study[65] reviewed the emission standards development process for three key industrial sectors in India (thermal power, iron and steel and brick kiln industries) and stated 'it is not clear, at least for these sectors, if international standards were considered; at least they do not appear to have been used as a benchmark for best practice in most instances'.[66]

The effective state implementation of environmental standards also remains disappointingly low. For instance, in 2015 an environmental health research study found that about 55 per cent of the population (660 million Indians) lived in areas where the fine particulate matter air pollutant (PM 2.5) exceeded the national standard. Nearly half of these people resided in areas where pollution levels were more than twice the standard.[67] There are factors that contribute to the implementation gap and poor environmental governance. These include inadequate information and understanding of assessment of risks and consideration of risk management alternatives, insufficient coordination between the CPCB and SPCBs, slack performance of inadequately funded statutory bodies and enforcement agencies to enforce comprehensive standard compliance, multi-layered corruption, political interference and a lack of will to tackle ensconced industrial and commercial interests, significant human and technical capacity constraints, limited public participation and absence of regulatory powers to impose fine or penalties.[68] A damning report commissioned by the MoEF&CC[69] condemns the regulatory agencies dealing with environmental matters by stating:

> The state – arbitrary, opaque, suspiciously tardy or in-express-mode at different times, along with insensitivity – has failed to perform ... the administrative machineries in

64 The International Council on Clean Transportation 'India Bharat Stage VI Emission Standards' (ICCT Policy Update 2 April 2016).

65 Shakti Foundation (n 36).

66 ibid 23.

67 Rohini Pande, Robert Rosenbaum and Kevin Rowe, 'Closing India's Implementation Gap on Pollution Control' (*Fair Observer*, 24 August 2015) <www.fairobserver.com/region/central_south_asia/closing-indias-implementation-gap-on-pollution-control-79201/> accessed 10 December 2017.

68 Shripad Dharmadhikary, 'Setting Environmental Standards: Comparing Processes in Thermal Power Plants in India, US, and EU', Economic and Political Weekly (13 May 2017); South Asian Human Rights Documentation Centre, *Human Rights and Humanitarian Law: Developments in Indian and International Law* (OUP 2008) 423; OECD Report 2006 'Environmental Compliance and Enforcement in India: Rapid Assessment' www.oecd.org/env/outreach/37838061.pdf accessed 18 January 2017; Shyam Divan and Armin Rosencranz, *Environmental Law and Policy in India* (OUP 2001) 2–3.

69 High Level Committee on Forest and Environment Related Laws Report (MoEF&CC) (2014) <http://envfor.nic.in/sites/default/files/press- releases/Final_Report_of_ HLC.pdf> accessed 12 June 2016.

> the Government in the domain of Environment & Forests at all the levels, authorized to administer by Parliament's statutory mandate, appear to have abdicated their responsibilities . . . the legislations are weak, monitoring is weaker, and enforcement is weakest . . . the institutional failures include lack of enforcement, flawed regulatory regime, poor management of resources, inadequate use of technology; absence of a credible, effective enforcement machinery; governance constraints in management; policy gaps; disincentives to environmental conservation, and so on.[70]

The recognition of a right to an environment under Article 21 does not necessarily result in its enforceability and execution.[71] According to the 2016 WHO Urban Ambient Air Pollution database,[72] India has sixteen of the world's thirty most polluted cities. The levels of ultra-fine particles of less than 2.5 microns (PM2.5s) – which can cause fatal damage to heart and lungs – are highest in India. In relation to water, India has the highest number of people globally without safe water. Nearly 76 million people have no access to a safe water supply. Approximately 140,000 Indian children die annually from diarrhoea.[73] A report by the Comptroller and Auditor General (CAG) of India in its Performance Audit of Water Pollution in India (2011–2012)[74] states that 'water pollution has not been adequately addressed in any policy in India, both at the central and the State level . . . provisions for a generation of resources for prevention of pollution, treatment of polluted water and ecological restoration of polluted water bodies are not adequate . . . MoEF&CC/CPCB and the States failed to carry out comprehensive identification and quantification of human activities which impact water quality and the different sources which affect water quality. No agency in the country has assessed the risks of polluted water in rivers/lakes/ground water to health and environment.'[75] The position remains unchanged. In 2015, 62 per cent of untreated sewage was discharged directly into water bodies.[76] Eighty per cent of India's surface water is polluted, leading to an increasing likelihood of vector-borne diseases: cholera, dysentery, jaundice and diarrhoea.[77]

70 ibid 8, 22.

71 Alexandre Charles Kiss and Dinah Shelton, *International Environmental Law* (UNEP 2003) 393; Lavanya Rajamani, 'The Increasing Currency and Relevance of Rights-Based Perspectives in the International Negotiations on Climate Change' (2010) 22(3) Journal of Environmental Law 395; Douglas Korsah-Brown, 'Environment, human rights and mining conflicts in Ghana' in Lyuba Zarsky (ed), *Human Rights and the Environment* (Earthscan 2002) 81.

72 <www.who.int/phe/health_topics/outdoorair/databases/cities/en/> accessed 21 October 2016.

73 WaterAid, 'Water: At What Cost? The State of the World's Water' (*Water Aid*, 2016) <www.wateraid.org/news/news/water-at-what-cost-our-latest-report-reveals-the-state-of-the-worlds-water> accessed 21 December 2016.

74 <www.environmental-auditing.org/portals/0/auditfiles/india_f_eng_water-pollution-in-india.pdf> accessed 26 July 2016.

75 ibid 7,16 and 28.

76 CPCB Bulletin, 1 (July 2016) 6.

77 Sushimi Deyl, '80% of India's surface water may be polluted, report by international body says' (*The Times of India*, Mumbai, 28 June 2015) <http://timesofindia.indiatimes.com/home/environ

10.3.2 *Judicial Enterprise*

The state's failure to effectively address environmental degradation has resulted in the increased public standing of the judiciary because of its innovative efforts to protect health, ecology and the environment. There is increased judicial responsibility to undertake appropriate action via Article 21 of the Constitution. In *M.C. Mehta* v. *Union of India*[78] the Supreme Court observed:

> If this Court finds that the authorities had not taken action required of them by law and that their inaction is jeopardising the right to life (Article 21) of the citizens of this country or any section thereof, it is the duty of this Court to intervene. If it is found that the respondents [state agencies] are flouting the provisions of law and the directions and orders issued by the lawful authorities, this Court can certainly make appropriate directions to ensure compliance with law and lawful directions made thereunder.[79]

Currently, the NGT plays a major role in developing both environmental jurisprudence and its practical application through the interpretation of Article 21. It has institutionalised the technical content of decision making involving specialised scientific knowledge and advice through its expert members.[80] A major innovation is the NGT's readiness to use their expertise to translate knowledge from synoptic to specific, thereby offering problem-solving solutions that replace absent, weak or ineffective environmental standards and regulations. The underpinning rationale is based on the premise that 'environmental law and policy decisions must be informed by science ... if this could be accomplished, the environmental law and policy world could benefit substantially from the ever-growing body of scientific knowledge'.[81] Jassanoff rightly states 'experts are by definition boundary-crossers whose job it is to link scientific knowledge to matters of social significance: they are the diagnosticians of public problems, the explorers of solutions and the providers of remedies ... it is the experts who translate the claims ... to serve the immediate agenda of policy (decision-making)'.[82]

ment/pollution/80-of-Indias-surface-water-may-be-polluted-report-by-international-body-says/articleshow/47848532.cms> accessed 15 August 2016.

78 (2004) 6 SCC 588; also see *Indian Council for Enviro-Legal Action v Union of India* (1996) 3 SCC 212.

79 ibid 616.

80 The National Green Tribunal (NGT) Act 2010 provides that the technical experts include persons from life sciences, physical sciences, engineering or technology with fifteen years' experience in the relevant field or administrative experience, including five years' practical experience in environmental matters in a reputed national-level institution, or central or state government. Interestingly, there is no room for social scientists with appropriate specialisation or familiarity with environment or occupational risk.

81 Mary Jane Angelo, 'Harnessing the Power of Science in Environmental Law: Why We Should, Why We Don't, and How We Can' (2008) 86 Texas Law Review 1527–73.

82 Sheila Jasanoff, 'Quality Control and Peer-Review in Advisory Science' in Justus Lentsch and Peter Weingart (eds), *The Politics of Scientific Advice: Institutional Design for Quality Assurance* (CUP 2011) 19, 24–25.

The interface between science and law is particularly visible in the NGT, where scientific experts work alongside fellow legally qualified judges as collective environmental decision makers of homologous standing.[83] The engagement of scientific experts, akin to Peter Hass' 'epistemic communities',[84] involves them as constructive science scholars in environmental decision making. Their expertise filters through to improve environmental management via judicious use of scientific knowledge to ensure minimal damage to the environment and protect society's wider interest. The judicial pronouncements of the NGT have on occasion supplanted legislative powers by temporarily occupying the main executive space.

The author was provided in 2014–15 with official research and interview access to all bench members of the NGT. In particular, she reviewed the working relationship between the judicial and scientific bench members in the five Tribunals.[85] Some of their responses are reproduced below.

According to NGT Expert 1:

> Environmental issues are complex. We are dealing with natural systems and future events based upon impacts. In today's world, environmental effects need serious consideration based upon the likely impacts and magnitude. So, if we feel that the activity is injurious to public health and/or environment and violates Article 21, we pass appropriate orders of expanding the scope of rules and regulations by adopting the principle of constructive intuition to give it a wider meaning to attain the primary object and purpose of the Act in question. Such an interpretation would serve the wider public interest in contrast to the private or individual interest.[86]

Expert 2 stated:

> Where there are gaps or limitations in the regulations [environmental standards], the NGT interferes and gives directions to the government to incorporate the same. The Tribunal interprets serious and complex environmental harms both as individual and social centric. The larger interest of the society, public health, and

83 Gitanjali Nain Gill, 'Environmental Justice in India: The National Green Tribunal and Expert Members' (2016) 5(1) Transnational Environmental Law 175, 181. This chapter does not address the challenging issues within the sociology of knowledge, which include the multiple roles of experts vis-à-vis policy creation and its promotion. The relationship of science and policy has generated a body of lively and disparate opinion and literature beyond the limited scope of this chapter

84 Peter M Haas, 'Epistemic Communities' in Daniel Bodansky, Jutta Brunée and Ellen Hey (eds), *Oxford Handbook of International Environmental Law* (OUP 2007) 791, 793. Haas describes distinctive features of 'epistemic communities' as 'networks … often transnational – of knowledge-based experts with an authoritative claim to policy relevant knowledge within their domain of expertise. Their members share knowledge about the causation of … phenomena … and a common set of normative beliefs about what actions will benefit human welfare in such a domain. Members are experts with professional training who enjoy social authority based on their reputation for impartial expertise.'

85 Gitanjali Nain Gill, *Environmental Justice in India: The National Green Tribunal* (Earthscan-Routledge 2017) 148–85.

86 Interview 15 July 2014.

protection and preservation of environment needs to be addressed for the present and future generations under Article 21 of the Constitution.[87]

Expert 3 opined thus:

> Normally we go into the details of technical and scientific aspects of the environmental problem and its impact. We also conduct local inspections at the site and examine the prevailing conditions. We discuss the situation with the people inhabiting in the area. For us, it is important to interfere in situations where the law [standards] is outdated and affects the fundamental right of right to environment.[88]

In a similar vein, judicial members 1 and 3 stated that 'we definitely interfere with the policy. The NGT keeps a check on the regulators to ensure that the laws drafted ensure environmental protection and maintain public welfare, health and environment under Article 21. Where the laws are inadequate or do not address the issues properly, appropriate policy intervention is justifiable.'[89]

These interview accounts from judicial and scientific members describing their decision-making processes, rationales and anticipated outcomes are illustrated by selected NGT case reports that consider the adequacy and implementation of environmental standards. The cases are divided into two heads, (1) risk assessment and (2) nature conservation and management. They identify knowledge and policy gaps reflecting the interconnection between environmental standards and Article 21.

10.3.2.1 Risk Assessment

Risk assessment involves 'evaluation of scientific information on the hazardous properties of environmental agents and on the extent of human exposure to those agents'.[90] It is a four-step process that includes identification of hazard to determine the qualitative nature of the adverse consequence, relationship between levels of exposure and probable adverse consequences, quantification of exposure, and characterizing the risk in probabilistic terms.[91] Risk assessment plays an important role in decision making through the dose-response curve to characterise and quantify risks. The dose-response curve acts as a valuable tool and guides decisions to be made in an informed manner based on risk assessments and associated impacts with the estimated exposure to the pollutants on human health and environment.[92]

87 Interview 14 April 2015.

88 Interview 14 July 2014.

89 Interview 30 March and 8 April 2015. The author was afforded unique academic access to interview NGT bench members. The interviews were conducted in the period 2014–16. All interviews were semi-structured, followed the same set of questions, were recorded and subsequently transcribed. Individual permission to use recorded material was obtained but on the condition of anonymity.

90 Angelo (n. 80) 1526.

91 ibid 1527.

92 Farmer (n 61) 23 and 24.

For instance, noise pollution is one area where the absence of or weak noise standards and ineffective implementation have resulted in unabated noise levels in urban India. The problem has not been adequately addressed and remedied despite posing a serious threat to the health of people, especially children and the elderly. Depending on its duration and volume, the effects of noise on human health and comfort are divided into four categories, physical effects (hearing defects), physiological effects (increased blood pressure, irregularity of heart rhythms and ulcers), psychological effects (disorders, sleeplessness and going to sleep late, irritability and stress) and finally effects on work performance (reduction of productivity and aural misunderstanding).[93]

In *D. B. Nevatia* v. *State of Maharashtra*[94] the NGT directed the federal government, namely the Ministry of Road Transport and Highways, Government of India, to provide source-specific standards for sirens and multi-tone vehicles within a period of three months from the date of the order for compliance with the ambient air quality standards under the Noise Pollution (Regulation and Control Rules) 2000. The standards were to be notified by the State of Maharashtra's Transport Department and Pollution Control Board within one month of the date of notification from the Ministry of Road Transport and Highways. According to the NGT,

> the controversy before us is pertaining to vehicular noise caused by unrestricted use of sirens and multi-tone horns having un-specified standards, being fitted in the ambulances, government and police vehicles ... poses significant noise pollution problems to the residents and violates their right to life. A large number of the public are also exposed to high levels of noise which have adverse impacts on their health and wellbeing and violates their right to a healthy environment, guaranteed under Article 21 of the Indian Constitution.[95]

The standards were issued on 31 July 2014 but were not implemented effectively at the time of registration of the vehicles. The NGT in March 2016 directed the adoption of a consultative process to resolve the ongoing matter in the larger interest of public.[96]

The federal government, via the MoEF&CC, drafted reduced threshold noise standards at airports in the wake of the order passed by the NGT in the case of *Indian Spinal Injuries Hospital* v. *Union of India*.[97] The Indian spinal injuries hospital along with residents near the Delhi international airport expressed concern over aeroplane noise violations and their impact on health. The engine thrust caused

93 Lindvall (n 46).

94 National Green Tribunal, Principal Bench, New Delhi 9 January 2013.

95 ibid para 7.

96 Sadaf Modak, 'Setting Standards for Vehicle Horns: NGT Issues Orders to Government Authorities' *The Indian Express* (Mumbai, 22 February 2016) <http://indianexpress.com/article/cities/mumbai/setting-standards-for-vehicle-horns-ngt-issues-order-to-govt-authorities/> accessed 10 June 2016.

97 National Green Tribunal, Principal Bench, New Delhi 27 January 2016; Nikhil M Ghanekar, 'Threshold Noise Levels at Airports Reduced' (*DNA India*, 14 October 2016) <www.dnaindia.com/india/report-threshold-noise-levels-at-airports-reduced-2263843> accessed 17 November 2016.

anxiety to patients and people living near the airport and resulted in lack of sleep and a distraction to doctors performing surgery in the hospital.

The deteriorating air quality[98] in India's capital Delhi is a threat to the city's inhabitants, particularly to infants, children and the elderly. The World Health Organisation, in its 2016 report entitled 'Ambient Air Pollution: A Global Assessment of Exposure and Burden of Diseases',[99] stated that with very high levels of particulate matter measuring 10 microns or less, Delhi is among the most polluted cities in the world. In November 2016, in the case of *Vardhman Kaushik* v. *Union of India*,[100] the NGT declared Delhi's air pollution as an 'environmental emergency' situation due to the ineffective implementation of the air quality standards by the regulatory authorities. The air quality standards grossly exceeded the limits, the violation being nearly twenty times in excess, thus having a serious impact on public health. For instance, the standard norms for PM10 is 100 μg/m3, and for PM2.5 60 μg/m3. These values were violated to the extent of PM10 as 1690 μg/m3 and PM2.5 as 885 μg/m3 in November 2016. The NGT expressed grave concern over the inability of the regulatory authorities to implement air quality standards and observed:

> The basic and fundamental question that arises for consideration of this Tribunal is whether the state government can provide any justification acceptable scientifically in law as to why the people of Delhi should be exposed to such severe pollution and have endlessly suffered from one disease or the other. The Hon'ble Supreme Court of India decades back had declared that Article 21 of Constitution of India has to be expanded so as to include right to decent and clean environment as a fundamental right ... The State can hardly raise a defence particularly of its inability to enforce laws on an environmental front. The State owes a constitutional duty to protect public health and to provide at least clean air for its citizens to breathe. The principle of inter-generational equity does not support any development even if it is carried under the doctrine of sustainable development where the next generation would be exposed to the worst environmental and ecological environment. The children of today have a right to breathe clean air and play in the playground rather than be ordered to be shut down in their respective homes ... It appears that to attain the prescribed standards as of now would be a dream difficult to achieve as of today.[101]

98 There are seven major contributors to air pollution in Delhi. These are: construction activity and carriage of construction material, burning of municipal solid waste and other waste, burning of agriculture residue, vehicular pollution, dust on the roads, industrial and power house emission including fly-ash and emissions from hot-mix plants and stone crushers. The transport sector contributes nearly 23 per cent of the air pollution. It is estimated that 66 per cent of the vehicular pollution results from diesel vehicles.

99 World Health Organisation, 'Ambient Air Pollution: A Global Assessment of Exposure and Burden of Disease' (2016) <http://who.int/phe/publications/air-pollution-global-assessment/en/> accessed 20 September 2016.

100 National Green Tribunal, Principle Bench, New Delhi 10 November 2016.

101 ibid 8, 9, 10.

Air pollution caused by burning of used tyres in open spaces in an unauthorised and unscientific manner is toxic, mutagenic and hazardous.[102] It affects the environment and human health. The NGT in *Asim Sarode* v. *State of Maharashtra*[103] directed the regulatory authorities to urgently develop regulations and guidelines to ensure environmentally sound disposal practices of the used tyres based on the available toxicological and eco-toxicological risks and associated consequences of an unsafe activity.

Risk assessment thus reviews actions that directly impact the health of the community and environment and thereby run contrary to Article 21. In *Manoj Misra* v. *Union of India*[104] the Tribunal stated:

> The health of the public is a matter which ought to find absolute priority in the agenda of proper governance by the State. Right to health is a part of the right to life guaranteed by Article 21 of the Constitution of India. Where the planning processes are left to the government and to the public bodies, it is inherent that overriding considerations of public health and danger to life must be issues to which top priority consideration is bestowed. Where there is a failure in this regard, the courts will have to step in. Nothing can be more fundamental than the issue of public safety and public health.[105]

10.3.2.2 Nature Conservation and Management

The recognition and consideration of nature conservation and management is within the NGT's mandate. The Supreme Court has determined that the conservation and protection of nature and inanimate objects by adopting an eco-centric approach is an inextricable part of life.[106] This logic is based on the premise that nature has an impact on human well-being, as it is the life support system of planet earth. Human life depends on the conservation of the environment including biodiversity, the degradation of which affects the right to life under Article 21. The NGT, in its judgment in *Tribunal on its Own Motion* v. *Secretary of State*,[107] recognised this approach by stating:

102 ELaw, 'Health impacts of open burning of used (scrap) tires and potential solutions (science memo)' <www.elaw.org/content/health-impacts-open-burning-used-scrap-tires-and-potential-solutions-science-memo> accessed 24 April 2018.

103 National Green Tribunal, Western Zone Bench, Pune 6 September 2014.

104 National Green Tribunal, Principal Bench, New Delhi 13 January 2015.

105 ibid para 53.

106 In *Intellectual Forum, Tirupathi v State of A.P* AIR 2006 SC 1350 the Supreme Court of India recognised 'all human beings have a fundamental right to a healthy environment commensurate with their well-being . . . ensuring that natural resources are conserved and preserved in such a way that present as well as the future generation are aware of them equally' (para 84).

107 National Green Tribunal, Central Zone Bench, Bhopal 4 April 2014. The NGT followed the Supreme Court rationale in the case of *Centre for Environment Law WWF-1 v Union of India* (2013) 8 SCC 234.

> Anthropocentrism is always human interest focussed thinking that non-human has only instrumental value to humans, in other words, humans take precedence and human responsibilities to non-humans are based on benefits to humans. Eco-centrism is nature-centred, where humans are part of nature and non-humans have intrinsic value. In other words, human interest does not take automatic precedence and humans have obligations to non-humans independently of human interest. Eco-centrism is, therefore, life-centred, nature-centred where nature includes both humans and non-humans. Article 21 of the Constitution of India protects not only the human rights but also casts an obligation on human beings to protect and preserve a species becoming extinct, conservation and protection of environment is an inseparable part of right to life.[108]

The following NGT cases identify the appropriateness and feasibility of the nature conservation and management approach in environmental law by updating legal standards through scientific knowledge to protect the environment against harmful anthropogenic activities. One example is a wetland ecosystem. In *Forward Foundation* v. *State of Karnataka*[109] the NGT stated:

> Wetlands are amongst the most productive ecosystems on the earth . . . they are also ecologically sensitive and adaptive systems. 'Free' services provided by wetlands are often taken for granted, but they can easily be lost as wetlands are altered or degraded in a watershed . . . Ecosystem goods provided by the wetlands mainly include: water for irrigation; fisheries; non-timber forest products; water supply; pollutant removal, flood attenuation, groundwater recharge, shoreline protection, wildlife habitat and recreation . . . Various services provided by wetlands include carbon cycle/ carbon sequestration: swamps, mangroves, peat lands, mires and marshes play an important role in carbon cycle . . . Wetlands provide . . . one of the most ecologically and economically important ecosystems on earth.[110]

In this case, the NGT allowed an application filed by an NGO, the Forward Foundation, interested in the restoration of ecologically sensitive wetland, specifically in the State of Karnataka. The principal grievance related to commercial projects, including the creation of a special economic zone park, hotels, residential apartments and a mall, which were being developed by the respondents on the wetlands and catchment areas of the water bodies – the Agara and the Bellandur Lakes. The construction adversely affected the environment, ecology, and particularly the water bodies and their biodiversity, and impacted the water supply to the city of Bengaluru (Bangalore), thereby violating Article 21 of the Constitution. The entire ecosystem was exposed to a severe threat of environmental degradation and consequential damage.

108 ibid 256. Also see *Sudeip Shrivastava v State of Chattisgarh* Judgment 24 March 2014; *Charudatt P Koli v M/s Sea Lord Containers* National Green Tribunal (Western Zone Bench), Pune 18 December 2015.

109 National Green Tribunal, Principle Bench, New Delhi 7 May 2015.

110 ibid paras 56–58.

Interestingly, the NGT ordered a revised minimum distance from water bodies as a buffer zone, thereby creating a standard different from the statutory Wetland Rules 2010. The NGT directed that a distance of 75 metres from the periphery of the water body be maintained as a green belt and buffer zone for all the existing water bodies, i.e. lakes and wetlands. This buffer/green zone would be treated as a no construction zone for all intents and purposes, including restrictions on any kind of encroachment, poaching or any permanent construction. According to the NGT, the 50 metres distance prescription under the Wetland Rules 2010 suffered from an inbuilt contradiction, legal infirmity, and was without any scientific justification. The NGT stayed the construction of projects, ordered demolition and imposed heavy penalties.

In a subsequent case, *Anand Arya* v. *Union of India*,[111] the NGT Tribunal promoted India's wetlands by directing the Central Wetlands Regulatory Authority, responsible for identification and conservation of wetlands, to meet regularly and ensure that wetlands in all states are identified and notified at the earliest possible time.

Again, in *Biodiversity Management Committee* v. *Union of India*[112] the NGT directed the government to formulate guidelines in consultation with the local communities relating to uncertain baseline data about biodiversity resources and traditional knowledge, and to establish a benefit sharing formula arising from utilisation of natural resources to people and communities. Plants and other biological resources are used by traditional communities for a variety of purposes, particularly in health care, food and in many household utilities. A participatory approach elicits and makes visible diverse local realities, priorities, categories and indicators that contribute towards protecting the life, livelihood and culture of the traditional communities, and promotes conservation of natural resources.[113]

Thus, the proposed participatory guidelines offer a pathway to the stakeholders to regenerate the degraded forests and biodiversity to which human well-being and life are intimately linked under Article 21. To that extent, employing participatory management can provide feedback to update regulatory efforts as information increases and helps in a better decision-making process through detailed analyses of the management of complex ecosystems.

The review of the NGT decisions shows that environmental protection and nature conservation and management have been given the status of a fundamental right and brought under Article 21 of the Constitution of India. Judgments reflect scientific input and not only respond to the issues between the parties, but may also offer policy advice or requirements that have application far beyond the courtroom door.

[111] National Green Tribunal, Principal Bench, New Delhi 22 July 2016.

[112] National Green Tribunal, Central Zone Bench, Bhopal 4 May 2016.

[113] See also *J R Chicham v State of Madhya Pradesh* National Green Tribunal, Central Zone Bench (Bhopal May 2014); *Narmada Khand Swabhiman Sewa v State of Madhya Pradesh* National Green Tribunal, Central Zone Bench (Bhopal 1 October 2014).

10.4 ENVIRONMENTAL STANDARDS: CHALLENGES

Framing regulations with robust environmental standards is crucial to anticipate and address responses and ensure effective implementation. As stated earlier, the setting of India's standards is moderately stringent compared with international practice. Issues of techno-economic feasibility of the standards and the availability of required abatement technologies may be prohibitive.[114] Resources (skills and manpower) of pollution control boards involved in the process are strained, thereby impacting the process of development of environmental standards, and ultimately the environmental standards themselves.[115]

Further, the application and enforcement of environmental standards are limited. The reasons include a lack of enforcement by pollution control boards, a lack of understanding regarding the risks associated with exceeding environmental standards, clarity of process, a lack of suitable expertise and failure to comply with the obligation regarding environmental monitoring.[116] For example, despite the ground-breaking decisions of the NGT, the issue of the implementation of its decisions and orders remains a major challenge. While parties are heard and decisions are made within the Tribunal, on occasions the directions of the Tribunal are far-reaching and require the active participation and positive responses of numerous third parties. It is at this point that the hostility of potentially affected groups, organisations, corporations, politicians, ministries and agencies results in delay, indifference, refusal or lack of resources. Powerful players seek to frustrate sensitive decisions of the NGT by limiting its reach and impact. In *Vardhman Kaushik* v. *Union of India*[117] the NGT observed:

> The authorities, departments and the state governments have not even initiated the process for compliance of the (earlier) directions. With the increasing pollutants in the air, life of residents in the NCR [National Capital Region], Delhi is becoming more and more vulnerable to various diseases and the greatest sufferer of these pollutants are young children of today and India's tomorrow. The slackness and casual attitude of the authorities of the state Government is exhibited from the very fact that the air pollution is increasing and has reached to an alarming level which would make it difficult for the people of Delhi even to breathe freely much less fresh air.[118]

Recent work provides statistical evidence demonstrating a dominant pattern of a tight group of 'repeat players' being plaintiffs regularly bringing actions before the Tribunal against the appropriate regulatory authorities.[119] It identifies the parties

114 Shakti Foundation (n 36).
115 ibid.
116 See Pande and Dharmidakry (n 67 and 68) for further details.
117 See *Vardhman Kaushik* (n 100).
118 ibid para 2.
119 Gill (n 85) 194–97.

to environmental disputes by analysing some 1,130 cases decided by the National Green Tribunal between July 2011 and September 2015. The most active plaintiffs were NGOs, social activists and public-spirited citizens who between them brought 47.2 per cent of all cases. The MoEF&CC was the defendant in 284 cases, out of which some 203 cases, 71.5 per cent, were brought by NGOs. Additionally, state governments along with pollution control boards were defendants in 341 cases, out of which 135 cases, 39.6 per cent, were brought by NGOs et al. The MoEF&CC's, state governments' and pollution control boards' frequent appearances as defendants before the NGT suggest a repeated failure on the part of regulatory authorities to undertake their statutory environmental protection duties. The regulatory framework has been unable to deliver due to

> a knee-jerk attitude in governance, flabby decision-making processes, ad hoc and piecemeal environmental governance practices ... the lasting impression has remained that the Acts and the appurtenant legal instruments have really served only the purpose of a venal administration, at the Centre and the States, to meet rent-seeking propensity at all levels.[120]

10.5 CONCLUSION

India's population is gargantuan, as are its internal problems that reflect poverty, social inequality, geographical size, bureaucratic inefficiency or indifference and endemic corruption. The tripartite relationship of checks and balances between Parliament, the Executive and the Judiciary, entrenched in Western common law constitutionalism and bequeathed to newly independent India in 1947, continues to experience limited success. The cumbersome, multi-party legislature[121] that meets infrequently is linked to executive and 'bureaucratic inactivity and apathy; sometimes excesses that cause the problem and sometimes the problem is caused by the ostrich-like reaction of the executive'.[122] This inefficient and ineffective relationship has disturbed the inherited constitutional balance and placed the judiciary in the position of *primus inter pares* reaching to find environmental solutions within the legal framework.

Judicial space has become the first and ultimate forum to resolve environmental conflicts because of the failure of regulatory agencies. The broad 'representative and citizen standing' in environmental PIL and liberal 'aggrieved party' standing as interpreted by the NGT have promoted a transformative process being polycentric, participatory and democratic to protect and improve the environment and ecology under Article 21 of the Constitution. The constitutional mandate of Articles 48A and 51A(g) establishing a duty of the state and every citizen to protect and improve the

120 HLC Report (n 69) 8.

121 'Democracy in India: The Do-Nothing Lok Sabha' (*The Economist*, Asia section 17 December 2016) 47.

122 *Swaraj Abhiyan v Union of India* (2016) 7 SCC 498 at 510 (J Madan Lokur).

environment has promoted dynamism and provided the opportunity to victims and protectors of environmental degradation to access justice in a participatory manner.

Environmental standards exist in India having either been 'transplanted' or developed by the State and its agencies. The pervasive challenge is that of effective monitoring, inspection, compliance and enforcement of these standards. It is at these crucial points involving the active participation of ministries and regulatory agencies that flaws and failures occur. However, India's experience has fostered a supplementary stream of law and legal regulation emanating from the responsible judiciary, especially the NGT through its imaginative and dynamic interpretation and application of the right to life and environment based on Article 21 of the Constitution.

Thus, the mantle of environmental protection and the creation, promotion and enforcement of standards has fallen upon the judiciary particularly on the NGT. Decisions are increasingly more than simply adjudicatory. The reliance of the judiciary on scientific expertise to assess risk, and nature conservation and management reflects the critical importance of the question of appropriateness of environmental standards and its implications for human health and environmental protection under Article 21. The judicial approach not only promotes outcomes that foster improved standards but also encourages regulatory authorities to involve stakeholders in standard setting processes. These judicial decisions are based on ecological, technological and scientific resource knowledge that either formulates policies or assists regulatory agencies with the implementation of these policies, thereby adopting both a problem-solving and policy creation approach (either mandatory or advisory).

Judicial activism in India is not pejorative: it reflects realism, guardianship, welfare and social responsibility. Former Chief Justice of England and Wales Lord Woolf expressed his appreciation of the proactive approach of Indian judiciary by stating, '... court was to perform its essential role in Indian society, it had no option but adopt the course it did and I congratulate it for the courage it has shown.'[123]

Subsequently, Justice Kirby in his Hamlyn lecture stated that, '... the accretions of power to the judiciary ... have come about as a result of failures and inadequacies in law-making by the other branches and departments of the government. Constitutional power hates vacuum. Where it exists, in the form of silence, confusion or uncertainty about the law, it is natural that those affected, despairing of solutions from the other law-making organs of the government, will sometimes approach the judicial branch for what is in effect a new rule. They will seek a new law that responds quickly to their particular problem. In India ... judicial activism is not viewed as one of condemnation. So, urgent and numerous are the needs of that society that anything else would be regarded by many-including many judges and lawyers-as an abdication of the final court's essential Constitutional role.'[124]

[123] Justice Michael Kirby, *Judicial Activism: Authority, Principle and Policy in the Judicial Method* (The Hamlyn Lectures Fifty-Fifth Series, Sweet and Maxwell 2004) 39.

[124] ibid 38, 65 and 66.

11

Environmental Standards in the Portuguese Constitution

Alexandra Aragão

11.1 INTRODUCTION

The Portuguese Constitution[1] provides an example of the standards of environmental protection that have developed at the constitutional level within a country that is a member of the European Union (EU). Therefore, their examination assists us in our understanding of environmental provisions in a constitution where regional law also applies. Their operation in practice shows that despite their relatively high level of detail, they only gain normative force[2] and operability when they are elaborated at the infra-constitutional level.[3] It is there that they are given practical meaning through the assignation of tasks, the listing of illegal activities, the fixing of quantitative thresholds, the setting of deadlines, the establishment of monitoring schemes and the provision of sanctions. Therefore, this chapter focuses on those developments, and as such can be contrasted with certain other chapters of the book in which judicial activism plays a more prominent role in the development of such standards. This chapter also looks at the way that some of the environmental provisions of the constitution are of specific interest on their own merit, as they represent novel types of obligations within the field of environmental constitutionalism through which new standards are emerging.

To examine the development of standards associated with the environmental provisions of the Portuguese Constitution, this chapter firstly examines the provisions themselves within their historical context. It then goes on to consider the relationship that they have had on the development of infra-constitutional standards. It places the standards that correspond with the constitutional provisions into three categories: those areas where the legislation responds directly to the requirements of EU law; those instances where Portuguese standards go further than EU law (what is sometimes known as the 'gold plating' of EU law); and also

[1] Constitution of the Portuguese Republic (2005 7th revision) (Portuguese Constitution).

[2] Catherine Thibierge (ed), *La Force Normative: Naissance d'un Concept* (LGDJ 2009) 33–53.

[3] On the impact of environmental-related constitutional provisions on the creation of legislation and national policy making see Stephen J Turner, *A Substantive Environmental Right: An Examination of Legal Obligations of Decision-Makers towards the Environment* (Kluwer Law International 2009).

those standards which do not respond to EU law and can be seen as national autonomous initiatives. It is in the latter two categories in particular that specific standards of environmental protection related to the provisions of the national constitution can be clearly identified.

11.2 THE PORTUGUESE CONSTITUTION AND ITS PROVISIONS RELATING TO THE ENVIRONMENT

In 1976, in the aftermath of the non-violent revolution that put an end to the fascist regime and paved the way for democratic government, the new Portuguese Constitution was promulgated.[4] Even though other countries had used provisions in their national constitutions for the protection of the environment before this time, the Portuguese Constitution became the first to create a specific environmental right. The 1976 constitution has been subject to revision, and the current constitution contains a number of provisions that relate to environmental protection. However, the most prominent is Art. 66, which reads as follows:

Article 66 – Environment and quality of life

1. Everyone has the right to a healthy and ecologically balanced human living environment and the duty to defend it.
2. In order to ensure the right to the environment within an overall framework of sustainable development, the State, acting via appropriate bodies and with the involvement and participation of citizens, is charged with:
   (a) Preventing and controlling pollution and its effects and the harmful forms of erosion;
   (b) Conducting and promoting town and country planning with a view to a correct location of activities, balanced social and economic development and the enhancement of the landscape;
   (c) Creating and developing natural and recreational reserves and parks and classifying and protecting landscapes and places, in such a way as to guarantee the conservation of nature and the preservation of cultural values and assets that are of historic or artistic interest;
   (d) Promoting the rational use of natural resources, while safeguarding their ability to renew themselves and ecological stability, with respect for the principle of inter-generational solidarity;
   (e) In cooperation with local authorities, promoting the environmental quality of rural settlements and urban life, particularly on the architectural level and as regards the protection of historic zones;

[4] The preamble of the Portuguese Constitution reflects quite clearly the euphoric spirit of experiencing freedom for the first time in forty years. 'On the 25th of April 1974 the Armed Forces Movement crowned the long resistance and reflected the deepest feelings of the Portuguese people by overthrowing the fascist regime.'

(f) Promoting the integration of environmental objectives into the various policies of different sectors;
(g) Promoting environmental education and respect for environmental values and assets;
(h) Ensuring that the fiscal policy renders development compatible with the protection of the environment and the quality of life.

The right clearly denotes a qualitative standard that everyone is entitled to a human environment that is 'healthy and ecologically balanced'.[5] The Constitutional Court has not been called upon to adjudicate on the precise meaning of this standard of environmental protection, as responsibility for determining standards of environmental protection has been left to the government through legislation and regulation. It can be noted that the Constitutional Court does have the authority to review legislation to ensure that it is consistent with the constitution, but this mechanism has not been utilised in relation to the environment.[6] It can also be noted that Art. 66 provides a range of responsibilities that the government must fulfil to ensure 'the right to environment within an overall framework of sustainable development'.[7] It would be reasonable to infer that, to ensure the environmental right in Art. 66(1), the government has the responsibility *inter alia* to create legislation and regulation which includes standards within the areas listed in Art. 66(2)(a–h). This is especially the case when Art. 66 is read in conjunction with Art. 9 of the constitution, which details the 'fundamental tasks of the State' and which confirms that the State must protect and enhance the Portuguese people's cultural heritage, defend nature and the environment, preserve natural resources and ensure correct town and country planning.[8]

There are a number of points that relate to these provisions and their relationship to the development of standards. Firstly, it appears that the authors of the constitution had a broad understanding of what is meant by 'a healthy and ecologically balanced environment'.[9] The provisions in Art. 66 refer to anthropocentric concerns such as 'preventing and controlling pollution',[10] as well much broader concerns such as 'developing natural and recreational reserves',[11] 'the conservation of nature',[12] 'the rational use of natural resources'[13] and 'ecological stability'.[14] Therefore,

5 Portuguese Constitution art 66(1). Besides the classic personal rights, freedoms and guarantees, the Constitution establishes a long list of economic, social and cultural rights and duties. See José Casalta Nabais, *O Dever Fundamental de Pagar Impostos – Contributo para a Compreensão Constitucional do Estado Fiscal Contemporâneo* (Almedina 2015).
6 ibid. See art 278 on *ex ante* review of constitutionality, art 280 on *ex post* concrete review of constitutionality and art 281 *ex post* abstract review of constitutionality.
7 ibid art 66(2) (a–h).
8 ibid art 9(e).
9 ibid art 66(1).
10 ibid art 66(2)(a).
11 ibid art 66(2)(c).
12 ibid.
13 ibid art 66(2)(d).
14 ibid art 66(2)(d).

the requirement for the government to create legislation and regulation and the relevant associated standards would appear to extend to a broad and possibly eco-centric interpretation of what is understood to comprise a 'healthy and ecologically balanced human living environment'. This appears to be reinforced by the broad responsibilities that the State has under Art. 9 (e), which can be regarded as creating a duty to protect all aspects of the environment.

Secondly, the scope of the provision places a responsibility on the government within a range of different sectors. This is made clear through the requirement that it work 'via appropriate bodies' and 'within an overall framework of sustainable development' to ensure the purposes of the provision.[15] In this vein, Art. 66(2) also refers to 'town and country planning',[16] 'balanced social and economic development',[17] 'architectural' and 'historic zones'[18] and 'promoting the integration of environmental objectives into the various policies with a sectoral scope'.[19] As such, there appears to be a responsibility on the government to integrate the protection of the environment into a broad and diverse range of activities across its administration to ensure that the rights enjoyed by citizens are realised. If legislative and regulatory standards are a logical corollary to achieve those objectives, the government is constitutionally mandated to adopt them accordingly.

What is particularly notable, and innovative within the Portuguese Constitution is that the government is required under Art. 66(2)(f) to ensure that fiscal policy is 'compatible with the protection of the environment and the quality of life'. This indicates that any legislative and regulatory standards developed in relation to fiscal policy, must be consistent with the overall requirement of Art. 66. This provision is analysed in further detail in Section 11.3.

Thirdly, it can be argued that the standards that are developed under the constitution are irreversible through the principle of non-regression.[20] In other words, abrogation of standards of environmental protection or their replacement by less effective ones can potentially be considered to be unlawful and in violation of the level of environmental protection that has developed under Art. 66.

Fourthly, there are no specific provisions within the Portuguese Constitution that detail environmental procedural rights, although Art. 66(2) does make reference to the 'involvement and participation of citizens'. The constitution does contain in Art. 48 more generic provisions relating to access to information and participation in

15 ibid art 66(2).
16 ibid art 66(2)(b).
17 ibid.
18 ibid art 66(2)(e).
19 ibid art 66(2)(f).
20 Michel Prieur and Gonzalo Sozzo, *Le Principe de Non Régression en Droit de l'environnement* (Bruylant 2012) 28–29.

decision making.[21] There are also generic provisions relating to access to justice that are found in Art. 20, which provides all citizens with the guarantee of 'access to the law and the courts in order to defend those of his rights and interests that are protected by the law'.[22] Portugal is, however, a party to the Aarhus Convention[23] and also a member of the EU, and as such is required to comply with the standards of procedural environmental rights that are developing under that treaty and through EU law.[24]

However, in terms of procedural rights, what is notable is that the Portuguese Constitution provides two other mechanisms through which justice can be sought. These are the right to submit complaints to an ombudsman,[25] and also the right of *actio popularis*.[26] The latter is of particular interest within the context of this analysis as there are very few constitutions that provide for this type of litigation (although it is common among Portuguese-speaking jurisdictions),[27] and therefore Section 11.3 of this chapter considers its effectiveness and the standards that have developed in relation to it. Additionally, Art. 281 allows any norm to be challenged in the Constitutional Court by a competent organ (the President of the Republic; the President of the Parliament; the Prime Minister; the Ombudsman; the Attorney General; one tenth of the Deputies[28]), and the Court can declare a norm unconstitutional from the outset (*ex tunc*).[29]

However, in spite of the availability of these mechanisms, litigation has not been used to any great extent in relation to constitutional issues with regard to the environment in Portugal. It is possible that one key reason relates to the general inefficiency of the Portuguese judicial system. The 2016 EU Justice Scoreboard

21 Portuguese Constitution art 48. 'Participation in public life: 1. Every citizen has the right to take part in political life and the direction of the country's public affairs, either directly or via freely elected representatives. 2. Every citizen has the right to be given objective clarifications about acts of the State and of other public entities and to be informed by the Government and other authorities about the management of public affairs.'

22 ibid art 20(1).

23 Convention on Access to Information, Public Participation in Decision-Making and Access to Justice in Environmental Matters (adopted 25 June 1998, entered into force 30 October 2001) 2161 UNTS 447 (Aarhus Convention).

24 See Chapter 6 by Aine Ryall of this volume relating to the Aarhus Convention.

25 Portuguese Constitution art 23.

26 ibid art 53(3).

27 *Actio popularis* is common to several Portuguese-speaking countries and regions: Constitution of the Federative Republic of Brazil (1988 rev 2017) art 5(LXXIII) <www.constituteproject.org/constitution/Brazil_2017?lang=en> accessed 15 July 2018; Constitution of the Republic of Angola (2010) art 74 <www.constituteproject.org/constitution/Angola_2010?lang=en> accessed 15 July 2018; Constitution of the Republic of Cape Verde (1980 rev 1992) art 58 <www.constituteproject.org/constitution/Cape_Verde_1992?lang=en> accessed 15 July 2018; Constitution of the Republic of Mozambique (2004 rev 2007) art 81 <www.constituteproject.org/constitution/Mozambique_2007> accessed 15 July 2018; in Macao, The Basic Law of the Macao Special Administrative Region of the People's Republic of China art 36 <www.wipo.int/edocs/lexdocs/laws/en/mo/mo019en.pdf> accessed 15 July 2018.

28 Portuguese Constitution art 281.

29 ibid arts 280 and 281(3).

reveals certain practical constraints that affect the use of the Portuguese justice system. The time needed to resolve a case in Portugal in 2010 was around 1,100 days while in seventeen European countries it was less than 200 days. The number of pending cases in the first instance per 100 inhabitants was fifteen, while in twelve European countries it was around two.[30] In the 2016 Flash Eurobarometer survey, on the issue of 'Perceived independence of the national justice systems in the EU among the general public', Portugal suffers from a critically negative image.[31] Fifty-nine per cent of the respondents in Portugal considered that there was very much interference or pressure from economic or other interests in the justice system (the European average was 37 per cent). Concerning the status and independence of the judiciary, 41 per cent of the respondents considered that judicial independence is not guaranteed in Portugal (where the European average was 22 per cent).

Therefore, while the courts have not played such an active role in the development of standards associated with environmental rights in the constitution, the legislature has. In fact, it has been the legislature and the executive that have taken the leading role in developing standards. Therefore the following section will focus primarily on the way that this process has taken place.

11.3 THE DEVELOPMENT OF STANDARDS RELATING TO THE ENVIRONMENTAL PROVISIONS OF THE PORTUGUESE CONSTITUTION

The immediate point to make when considering the development of standards relating to the provisions of the national constitution is that Portugal, as a member of the EU, is subject to the regulations and directives that are derived from the EU, and many of those obligations overlap with the obligations that the Portuguese government has under its own national constitution. Therefore, it can be argued that where laws and standards have been enacted for the protection of the environment, they are in fact elaborations of the Portuguese government's compliance with EU law rather than specific measures taken to comply with the Portuguese constitution. However, even where EU environmental law is applicable there are certain instances in which the Portuguese government has gone further than the requirements of the particular regulation or directive concerned, and where that has happened, it is possible that those measures and standards can be attributable to provisions of the constitution. Additionally, as has already been alluded to, there are certain aspects of the Portuguese Constitution that create particular obligations

30 In 2012 the score improved to 850 days. There are no data for 2013 and 2014. European Commission, 'Effective Justice' (*Europa*) <http://ec.europa.eu/justice/effective-justice/files/justice_scoreboard_2016_en.pdf> accessed 15 July 2018.

31 EU Open Data Portal, 'Flash Eurobarometer 435: Perceived Independence of the National Justice Systems in the EU among the General Public' (*Europa*, April 2016) <http://data.europa.eu/euodp/en/data/dataset/S2116_435_ENG> accessed 15 July 2018.

upon the Portuguese government relating to the environment which do not overlap with EU law, and therefore it is of particular interest to consider them, to understand what associated standards of environmental protection have developed.

Therefore, this section will consider each of the aforementioned categories of environmental law and standards in turn with a view to understanding their relationship with the national constitution.

11.3.1 Portuguese Environmental Standards That Correspond with EU Law

There are many areas of law and standards which fall into the first category because EU environmental law is so far reaching, therefore, this section will just provide a summary. Such examples include water quality standards which correspond to the Water Framework Directive,[32] standards relating to the quality of bathing water which correspond to the EU Bathing Water Directive[33] and standards relating to environmental procedural rights which are required to correspond with the EU and Portugal's obligations under the Aarhus Convention.[34] Other examples include air pollution,[35] climate change,[36] biodiversity loss,[37] chemical risk and control[38] and genetically modified organisms.[39] Therefore, while the standards developed under these laws arguably comply with the requirements of the constitution, they are also responsive to EU law, and therefore it would be difficult to attribute them solely to the constitution.

11.3.2 Portuguese Environmental Standards That Go Further Than EU Law – 'Gold Plating'

In the second category, there are a number of areas of legislation where the Portuguese government has developed more stringent standards than those required

32 Directive 2000/60/EC of the European Parliament and of the Council of 23 October Establishing a Framework for Community Action in the Field of Water Policy [2000] OJ L327/1.

33 Directive 2006/7/EC of the European Parliament and of the Council of 15 February 2006 concerning the Management of Bathing Water Quality and Repealing Directive 76/160/EEC [2006] OJ L64/37.

34 Aarhus Convention (n 23).

35 Directive 2008/50/EC of the European Parliament and of the Council of 21 May 2008 on Ambient Air Quality and Cleaner Air for Europe [2008] OJ L152/1.

36 Directive 2009/29/EC of the European Parliament and of the Council of 23 April 2009 amending Directive 2003/87/EC so as to Improve and Extend the Greenhouse Gas Emission Allowance Trading Scheme of the Community [2009] OJ L140/63.

37 Council Directive 92/43/EEC of 21 May 1992 on the Conservation of Natural Habitats and of Wild Fauna and Flora [1992] OJ L206/7.

38 Directive 2012/18/EU of the European Parliament and of the Council of 4 July 2012 on the Control of Major-Accident Hazards Involving Dangerous Substances, Amending and Subsequently Repealing Council Directive 96/82/EC Text with EEA Relevance [2012] OJ L197/1.

39 Directive (EU) 2015/412 of the European Parliament and of the Council of 11 March 2015 Amending Directive 2001/18/EC as Regards the Possibility for the Member States to Restrict or Prohibit the Cultivation of Genetically Modified Organisms (GMOs) in their Territory [2015] OJ L68/1.

by EU law (sometimes known as the 'gold plating of EU law'), and in certain instances there is evidence that this is due to the influence of the constitution.

The first example concerns the law relating to environmental impact assessments (EIA). Under the EIA Directive, the results of an assessment need only to 'be taken into consideration[40] in the final decision relating to a development. However, in Portugal the recommendations of an EIA are binding on that final decision where significantly adverse environmental impacts are identified. In fact, the law stipulates that if adverse impacts are significant and they cannot be avoided, reduced or remedied, the development cannot be authorised.[41] In such cases, other public interests such as tourism and industrial or urban development cannot override the protection of the environment. Furthermore, if an authorization is illegally issued, the administrative act is null and void,[42] and those civil servants involved can be criminally liable, facing a potential custodial sentence of up to three years.[43]

These rules are much stricter than those required by EU law and respond to the requirements of the constitution.[44] The correlation between the wording used in the preamble of the current Law on Environmental Impact Assessment[45] and the constitution[46] is quite clear in showing that the purpose of the law is to meet the constitutional goals. The preamble states that the main objective is to reinforce 'the effectiveness, robustness and coherence of this fundamental instrument of preventive environmental protection and sustainable development policy', which corresponds with the wording found in Art. 66 of the constitution.[47]

In spite of the strength of the law relating to EIAs in Portugal, social and economic factors still have a major influence in the decision making of certain types of projects

40 Directive 2011/92/EU of the European Parliament and of the Council of 13 December 2011 on the Assessment of the Effects of Certain Public and Private Projects on the Environment [2012] OJ L26/1, art 8. The Directive 2014/52/EU of the European Parliament and of the Council of 16 April 2014 amending Directive 2011/92/EU on the Assessment of the Effects of Certain Public and Private Projects on the Environment [2014] OJ L124/1 adds an important adverb of manner: 'the results of consultations and the information gathered pursuant to articles 5 to 7 shall be *duly* taken into account in the development consent procedure' (emphasis added).

41 Decree-Law No 151-B/2013 of 31 October art 22.

42 ibid.

43 Criminal Code (approved in 2010) on Violation of Town Planning Rules art 278-A.

44 Practical application of stricter national rules sometimes faces challenges and constraints. See Alexandra Aragão 'The Impact of EC Environmental Law on Portuguese Law' in Richard Macrory (ed), *Reflections on 30 Years of EU Environmental Law: A High Level of Protection?* (Europa Law 2006) 505–13.

45 Decree-Law 151-B/2013 of 31 October. Last paragraph of the preamble: 'In short, the system now introduced, complemented by the ongoing revision or elaboration of the various existing and planned legislation and regulatory documents, will lead to a change and harmonization of procedures and practices in EIAs, Effectiveness, robustness and coherence of this fundamental instrument of preventive environmental protection and sustainable development policy.'

46 Portuguese Constitution art 66(2) and (2)(a): 'In order to ensure the right to the environment within an overall framework of sustainable development, the State, acting via appropriate bodies and with the involvement and participation of citizens, is charged with preventing and controlling pollution and its effects and the harmful forms of erosion.'

47 ibid §6 of the preamble *in fine*.

which are categorised as having significant environmental impacts. This is the case with developments that are categorised as Projects of National Interest (PNI).[48] The legal regime for PNIs was created in 2005,[49] and it was specifically designed to streamline and promote large investment projects in spite of their environmental impacts.[50] Although the regime does provide environmental safeguards, once the PNI categorization is attached to a project by the government, administrative organs are under pressure to accept significant environmental impacts due to the economic and political factors related to the development.

The PNIs are not foreseen in the constitution and reflect a cyclical preference for short-term economic prosperity over more sustainable and long-term development. Therefore, in practice, the application of the PNI is not entirely in conformity with the level of environmental protection intended by the Constitution. This has not been challenged, although the Constitutional Court would have the competence to determine such an issue.[51]

The second example refers to industrial emissions. Within the EU, the approach of the relevant law is to prompt industry to employ state of the art technology, minimise pollution and reduce energy consumption along with certain emissions and waste. This is done through an integrated approach using concepts such as emission limit values, environmental quality standards and best available techniques.[52]

In Portugal, in addition to transposing Directive 2010/75/EU, the national legislator has introduced supplementary requirements to put in place a strategy to favour innovation and industrial symbiosis. The concepts of eco-efficiency, responsible business area and eco-innovation[53] contribute to this purpose. According to Portuguese law, eco-innovation 'means any form of innovation which allows or aims at demonstrable significant progress towards achieving the objective of sustainable development by reducing environmental impacts and increasing resilience to environmental pressures or by using natural resources in a more efficient and responsible way'.[54] 'Eco-efficiency' means a strategy of action leading to the

[48] Resolution 95/2005 of the Council of Ministers of 24 May, applicable to investment projects greater than 25 million. In 2011, it was enlarged to projects greater than 10 million. In some conditions it can be applied to smaller projects, according to Decree-Law no 76/2011 of 20 June.

[49] ibid.

[50] The majority of the PNI projects are developments within the tourist industry carried out in natural sensitive areas.

[51] Portuguese Constitution arts 280 and 281, respectively, on concrete and abstract review of constitutionality and legality.

[52] Directive 2010/75/EU of the European Parliament and of the Council of 24 November 2010 on Industrial Emissions (Integrated Pollution Prevention and Control) [2010] OJ L334/17, art 3(5), (6) and (10).

[53] The concept of eco-innovation is the only one that can be found in EU law. The Eco-innovation initiative was part of the 'EU's Entrepreneurship and Innovation Programme (EIP) set up to support innovation among SMEs and to improve their competitiveness'. It was launched in 2008, see European Commission, 'Eco-Innovation: When Business Meets the Environment' (*European Commission*, 8 January 2015) <http://ec.europa.eu/environment/eco-innovation/> accessed 15 July 2015.

[54] Decree Law 169/2012 of 1 August on Creating a Responsible Industry System, amended in 2015 art 2(h).

provision of competitive goods and services that meet human needs while simultaneously reducing progressively the negative environmental impacts and the resource intensity throughout the product life cycle.[55] Finally, a responsible business area (or a multipolar responsible business area) refers to a business centre or a set of business centres located in the same territorial areas, or functionally linked together and managed by the same management entity.[56] The final aim of the whole system is to 'prevent risks and inconveniences arising from the operation of industrial establishments with a view to safeguarding public and workers' health, the safety of persons and goods, safety and health at work, the quality of the environment and a correct spatial planning, within a framework of sustainable development and corporate social responsibility'.[57] In addition to respecting the emission limit values, observing the environmental quality standards and implementing the best available technologies, the industrial operators are also required to cooperate symbiotically and to invest in eco-innovation to provide eco-efficiency.

These concepts are another result of the constitutional duty to integrate environmental objectives into sectoral policies and arguably demonstrate a certain standard in terms of policy making.[58] It can be highlighted that industrial innovation is a constitutional goal. Article 100 states that the objectives of the industrial policy shall be:

(a) The increase of industrial production within an overall framework of the modernisation and adjustment of social and economic interests and the international integration of the Portuguese economy;
(b) The strengthening of industrial and technological innovation;
(c) The increase of the competitiveness and productivity of industrial enterprises.[59]

As a consequence, the integration of environmental objectives into industrial policy leads directly to eco-innovation. With this example too, Portugal went further than EU law required and arguably set higher standards of environmental policy integration, which can be attributed to specific provisions within the constitution.

There are a number of other examples. In some cases, national transposition has increased the strength of protection beyond the minimum mandatory extent; an example is publicity law. While EU law requires that it be made illegal to advertise products or services that encourage behaviour prejudicial to the protection of the environment on the television,[60] in Portugal the same prohibition is applicable to

55 ibid art 2(g).
56 ibid art 2(dd) and (ee).
57 ibid art 2(2)(a).
58 Portuguese Constitution art 66(2)(f).
59 ibid art 100.
60 Council Directive 89/552/EEC of 3 October 1989 on the Coordination of Certain Provisions Laid Down by Law, Regulation or Administrative Action in Member States concerning the Pursuit of Television Broadcasting Activities [1989] OJ L298/23, art 12.

any advertising medium.[61] Furthermore in Portugal, the law specifically relating to motor vehicle advertising has been made even more robust as any images, ideas or suggestions of vehicle use that could be harmful for the environment are proscribed.[62] It can be seen that the government adopted these measures as part of its obligations under the Constitution. Article 7 of the Publicity Law states that 'advertising which, by its form, object or purpose, offends the fundamental values, principles and institutions constitutionally consecrated is prohibited'. Another example would be publicity which shows someone using diving devices to destroy underwater ecosystems, or preferring disposable to reusable products or using noisy products in the wild; none of these restrictions exists in the corresponding EU law.[63]

A final example relates to the transposition of the EU directive on Access to Environmental Information.[64] In the process of transposition, the Portuguese Parliament chose to enlarge the generous conditions of access to information, to all information held by public authorities.[65] This is an effect of the so-called principle of open administration, present both in the law on access to administrative and environmental information[66] and in the Code of Administrative Procedure,[67] which follow Article 48 of the Constitution on 'participation in public life'.

11.3.3 *Environmental Standards Directly Attributable to the National Constitution*

There are some aspects of environmental law that are not within EU competence. One such area is town and country planning.[68] From a legislative point of view, it involves the development of laws and standards that are designed to achieve the most appropriate location of activities (both industrial and leisure) while taking into account natural resources and the protection of the environment to ensure balanced social and economic development. As detailed above, the constitution requires that the government conduct and promote town planning 'with a view to a correct location of activities, balanced social and economic

61 The Advertising Code (approved by Decree-Law 330/90 of 23 October, entered into force 17 March 2010, amended for the last time in 2014) art 7.

62 ibid art 22(a).

63 Directive 2005/29/EC of the European Parliament and of the Council of 11 May 2005 concerning Unfair Business-to-Consumer Commercial Practices in the Internal Market and Amending Council Directive 84/450/EEC, Directives 97/7/EC, 98/27/EC and 2002/65/EC of the European Parliament and of the Council (Unfair Commercial Practices Directive) [2005] OJ L149/22.

64 Directive 2003/4/EC of the European Parliament and of the Council of 28 January 2003 on Public Access to Environmental Information and Repealing Council Directive 90/313/EEC [2003] OJ L41/26.

65 Environmental Information Law 26/2016 of 22 August.

66 ibid art 2.

67 Law 4/2015 of 7 January art 17.

68 Portuguese Constitution arts 9(e), 66(2)(b) and (c).

development and the enhancement of the landscape'.[69] Therefore, the infra-constitutional standards that have developed can be directly attributed to the constitution.

The best example is the law establishing the general rules of public policy on soil, territorial planning and urbanism.[70] This law clearly fulfils the constitutional duty to integrate environmental protection and territorial planning. It includes a range of goals relating to a wide breadth of aspects of the environment including soil quality, biomass production, carbon sinks, biodiversity reserves, erosion, greenhouse gas emissions, conservation, coastlines and reservoirs.[71] What is also interesting is that it appears to grant the environment priority over other economic, social and cultural functions.[72]

As previously mentioned, a very innovative environmental provision of the constitution is the requirement under Art. 66(2)(h) that the government ensures 'that the fiscal policy renders development compatible with the protection of the environment and the quality of life'. In accordance with this provision, 2015 saw important green fiscal reform[73] take place under the slogan 'taxing more what we burn and less what we earn'.[74] This led to a paradigm shift that was based on the assumption that increasing taxation on pollution and resource degradation would trigger several benefits. The expectation was that it would allow a decrease in taxation on labour, reduce external energy dependency, induce more sustainable production and consumption patterns, promote an efficient use of resources, foster entrepreneurship and job creation, diversify sources of income and reinforce the neutrality of the tax system[75].

The fiscal measures[76] adopted include the following: incentives for bike sharing, car sharing and public transport;[77] tax incentives for end-of-life vehicle renovation;[78] VAT reduction on electric vehicles;[79] tax on lightweight plastic bags;[80] increase in

69 ibid art 66(2)(b).
70 Law 31/2014 of 30 May.
71 ibid art 2(a), (d), (e), (h), (i), (j) and (k).
72 ibid art 2(b), (c), (f), (g), (l), (m) and (n).
73 Regulated by the Law 82-D/2014 of 31 December.
74 Government of Portugal, 'Green Taxation Reform: Taxing More What we Burn and Less What we Learn' (*Crescimento Verde*) <www.crescimentoverde.gov.pt/wp-content/uploads/2014/10/ReformaFiscalidadeVerde_GreenTaxReform_emagazine.pdf> accessed 15 July 2018.
75 ibid 11.
76 ibid 12–15.
77 Law 82-D / 2014 of 31 December art 59b on the green tax reform allows the deduction of 110 per cent of the expenses on car sharing and 140 per cent on bike sharing. Art 59c grants a 120 per cent deduction of the expenses on bicycle fleets.
78 Decree-Law 39/2010 of April 26 as amended in 2014 art 53a establishing the legal regime of electric mobility exempts the conversion of vehicles with internal combustion engines into electric vehicles from the payment of any fee.
79 Law 82-D/2014 of 31 December art 30 on the green tax reform establishes a new contribution on light plastic bags produced, imported or purchased in Portugal.
80 Decree-Law 178/2006 of 5 September, amended for the last time in 2013 art 58. The framework waste law gradually increases the waste management tax applicable to land-filling activities.

the waste management fee to discourage landfilling of municipal waste;[81] reductions in the real estate tax to benefit environmentally beneficial uses of property (production of renewable energy, waste water treatment, waste management, agriculture) or adoption of voluntary territorial planning (plans for the prevention of forest fires);[82] the revision of the water management fee;[83] a tax benefit on the income tax for ENGOs;[84] and a carbon tax applicable to sectors not included in the European Emissions Trading Scheme.[85]

In the case of private individuals, the law grants the possibility of earmarking a small percentage of the VAT that they pay to go to environmental non-governmental organizations or environmental public interest bodies.[86] Legal persons promoting environmental public interest goals are granted an exemption from tax on revenue. Additionally, expenses incurred by companies to meet the costs of repairing environmental damage are tax deductible.[87]

In this regard, it might be possible to argue that the constitution has created a qualitative standard that the government must meet in relation to its fiscal policy. It is difficult to discern precisely what that standard is apart from the broad requirement that the government measures must lead to 'development compatible with the protection of the environment and the quality of life'. Having said this, the response of the government has been to develop a precise range of legislative measures that have set specific requirements that respond directly to that qualitative standard.

In relation to environmental education, the constitutional provision in Art. 66(2)(g) requires the promotion of 'environmental education and respect for environmental values and assets'. It does not create a standard as such, but puts forward a policy goal that must be integrated within the government's programme of work. However, in pursuing this goal it is possible that certain standards have been set by the measures that the government has instituted. In 2014, the Framework Law on the Environment established the principle of environmental education as a core principle of public policy by providing for 'environmental education, which requires educational policies aimed at environmental awareness, supporting education for sustainable development and providing citizens with environmental skills in a continuous process, which promotes participatory citizenship and calls for accountability, in particular through volunteering and environmental patronage, with a view to protecting and improving the environment in all its human

81 Decree-Law 215/89 of July 1 art 44 a and b on the Tax Benefits Statute establishes a reduction of 15 per cent to 50 per cent reduction in the municipal tax rate on real estate.

82 Law 82-D/2014 of 31 December art 59d on the green tax reform creates tax incentives for good forest management.

83 Several articles of the Decree-Law 97/2008 of 11 June on the economic and financial regime of water resources are amended.

84 Law 35/98 of July 18 art 14 on non-governmental environmental organizations.

85 Decree-Law 73/2010 of June 21 art 92-A on the Code of Special Taxes on Consumption.

86 Decree-Law 442-A/88 of November 30, last modified by Law 41/2016 of December 28 art 78-F(2b).

87 Decree-Law 442-B/88 of November 30, last modified by Decree-Law 22/2017 of February 22 art 40.

dimension'.[88] This statement of intent certainly appears to create qualitative standards for the type of education that should be developed. Also, it must be noted that the relationship between environmental education and citizens' duties is clarified through the same law which states that 'the right to the environment is inextricably linked to the duty to protect it, to preserve it and to respect it, so as to ensure long-term sustainable development, especially for future generations'.[89]

On 8 June 2017, the National Strategy for Environmental Education for the period up to 2020 was approved by the Council of Ministers. It sets out the themes that have priority for environmental education as being: decarbonizing society (climate, energy efficiency, sustainable mobility), the circular economy (dematerialization, collaborative economy and sustainable consumption, product conception and efficient use of resources, waste valuation), valuing the territory (ordination of the territory, coast, water, nature and biodiversity). Each of these themes corresponds to paragraphs of Article 66 of the constitution on the right and duty to protect the environment. In this way, the National Strategy for Environmental Education itself is a manifestation of the constitutional duty to promote environmental education. It is the first time that any government has adopted such a strategic document, and it is likely to contribute to the further development of specific standards in terms of environmental education that correspond with the constitution.

Finally in this section, consideration will be given to the specific standards relating to procedural rights. Following an amendment to the Constitution, in 1997[90] the citizen's right to initiate a legislative procedure was regulated by law. The current law regulating this right of direct democracy[91] requires a minimum of 35,000 signatures of registered voters to begin the procedure. There are no restrictions relating to the subjects that can be addressed by citizens' legislation, provided that the proposal respects the Constitution and does not involve an increase in expenditure or a decrease in public budget revenues for that financial year. In 2015, a popular initiative in favour of the recognition of the dignity of 'non-human animals' was presented to Parliament. It resulted in a new law, enacted a few months later, that established a system to control wandering animals while forbidding and detailing penalties for their indiscriminate killing.[92]

In terms of access to justice, the constitution states that 'everyone is guaranteed access to the law and to the courts to defend their rights and legally protected interests, and justice may not be denied for insufficient economic means'.[93] Even

88 Law 19/2014 of the 14 April art 4(d).

89 ibid art 8(1).

90 Constitutional Law 1/97 of September 20, the Fourth Constitutional Revision.

91 Law 17/2003 of 4 June, amended in 2012.

92 Bill 976/XII (*Assembleia da República*) <www.parlamento.pt/ActividadeParlamentar/Paginas/DetalheIniciativa.aspx?BID=39568> accessed 15 July 2018.

93 Portuguese Constitution art 20. More recently, the Framework Law on the Environment Law 19/2014 of 14 April art 7 reaffirms that 'everyone shall have the right to full and effective protection of their rights and legally protected interests in the environment'.

though the State has a formal duty to protect environmental interests, and despite the role of the public prosecutor,[94] the State is unable to resolve all environmental conflicts. The result has been the emergence of actions for representation of diffuse interests,[95] or *actio popularis,* which are a response to the inability of public authorities to always effectively protect the environment.

Actio popularis was first included in the Portuguese Constitution forty years ago.[96] Yet, it was only in 1989, after the second constitutional amendment, that the environment became one of the diffuse interests protected by it.[97] The constitution is clear that 'everyone is granted the right of *actio popularis,* including the right to apply for compensation for injuries, in the cases and under the terms provided for by the law, either personally or via associations for the defence of the interests in question, in particular to: (a) promote the prevention, cessation or judicial prosecution of offences against public health, consumer rights, the quality of life, the preservation of the environment and cultural heritage'.[98]

Six years later, in 1995, Parliament enacted the first law on *actio popularis*[99] establishing a detailed legal regime.[100] Now, legal standing is granted to anyone, 'regardless of whether they do or do not have a direct interest in the demand'.[101] The author will represent 'in his own initiative and with no need for a mandate or express consent, all the other holders of rights or interests who have not exercised the right to opt-out'.[102] As defined, the *actio popularis* legal regime is clearly committed to triggering real effects and going further than merely being a symbolic law. This is why the exercise of the right to *actio popularis* does not require the payment of any

94 The public prosecutor represents those that do not have a voice, such as disabled persons or absent persons and as a spokesman for trans-individual interests. Under its statutes, Law 47/86 of 15 October, amended for the last time in 2011 art 3e it is bound 'to assume, as provided for by the law, the defence of collective and diffuse interests'.

95 The concept of 'diffuse interests' is not completely strange to European Union Law. Since 2004 it has been present in the preamble of Directive 2004/35/CE of the European Parliament and of the Council of 21 April 2004 on Environmental Liability with Regard to the Prevention and Remedying of Environmental Damage [2004] OJ L143/56: 'persons adversely affected or likely to be adversely affected by environmental damage should be entitled to ask the competent authority to take action. Environmental protection is, however, a *diffuse interest* on behalf of which individuals will not always act or will not be in a position to act' (emphasis added).

96 Constitutions including *actio popularis* (n 27).

97 Constitutional Law 1/89 of July 8, the Second Constitutional Revision.

98 Portuguese Constitution art 52(3).

99 Law 83/95 of 31 August amended for the last time in 2015.

100 The judgment issued by the Supreme Court of Conflicts in 2010 synthesises the value of actio popularis: 'the main contribution of popular action was to overcome the shortcomings of a judicial protection of the values referred to in article 52, paragraph 3 of the CRP and to extend the legitimacy to defend these values, using the notion of diffuse interest.

The novelty that the figure of diffuse interest brings to judicial protection is to provide a guardianship in a supra-individual perspective and not only based on the defence of subjective legal positions, hence, as it was stated in paragraph 2 of article 9 of the CPTA, such action may be brought "independently of (the author) having a personal interest in the claim."' (Case 23/09 Judgment of 29 September 2010).

101 Law on *Actio Popularis* art 2, no 2.

102 ibid art 14.

prior court costs,[103] it can assume any form (civil, administrative or criminal) and is granted not only to individuals but also to associations.[104] In terms of the evidence required, the law states that 'evidence collection can be made at the instigation of the judge, regardless of the extent of the evidence presented by the parties themselves'.[105]

As such, it is clear that as a result of specific provisions within the constitution, standards relating to access to justice have developed. The cases that have been heard using the *actio popularis* provision have mainly been instigated by non-governmental organizations and less frequently by citizens and companies. Despite the fact that litigants are not subject to court fees, *actio popularis* cases still occur infrequently. As a result, in 2015 the law relating to *actio popularis* was amended to strengthen the powers of the public prosecutor. Now the public prosecutor has powers of representation and procedural intervention, and may also substitute the original author if they withdraw from the proceedings or behave in a way which is detrimental to the diffuse interests at stake.

Two recent cases have been selected to illustrate the approach that the courts have taken in *actio popularis* cases. Firstly, a case concerning a decision on road construction was made in June 2015, by the Southern Central Administrative Court, which declared that the mere existence of an NGO is sufficient for it to have legal standing.[106] The case concerned the decision to cut down cork oak trees to build a high-speed road through countryside on the east coast of Portugal. Despite the recognition of legal standing, the substantive arguments in the case were not accepted by the court and the road construction ultimately went ahead.

Secondly, in January 2016, the Supreme Administrative Court recognised the legal standing based on *actio popularis* of a local NGO from the island of Madeira. The case concerned an appeal against a decision of the Municipality of Santa Cruz to approve the licensing of several new private constructions (villas and apartment buildings) in a rural cliff-top area. Standing was recognised based on the sole fact

[103] ibid art 20 no 1.

[104] Law 35/98 of 18 July (amended in 2014) on Environmental Non-Governmental Organizations art 10 declares that:

The NGO, regardless of having or not direct interest in the claim, are entitled to:

(a) propose legal actions necessary for prevention, correction, suspension and termination of acts or omissions by public or private entities that are or could be a cause of environmental degradation;
(b) initiate, under the law, legal action to enforce civil liability in respect of the acts and omissions mentioned in the above paragraph;
(c) ask for judicial review of administrative acts and regulations that violate the laws for protection of the environment;
(d) complain, accuse or act as civil parts in criminal proceedings for crimes against the environment and follow processes of administrative offense, when required, with memorials, technical advice, examination suggestions or other evidence gathering initiative until the case is ready for a final decision.

[105] Law on Actio Popularis art 17.

[106] Case 8199/11 Judgment of June 2015.

that 'the legal provisions that protect the environment are being or have been violated by the Municipality'.[107] The court declared that the broad constitutional concept of environment includes not only norms protecting the natural environment *stricto sensu*, but also norms on house construction, urban architecture, territorial planning or public domain.[108] This allowed the court to recognise the arguments of the plaintiff association in relation to the disregard of procedural rules (various opinions of public authorities had not been requested) without them having to refer to specific environmental damage.

Although there has not been a considerable amount of litigation concerning the provisions in the constitution relating to the environment, these cases illustrate the willingness of the courts to engage with such issues, and the judgements further assist our understanding of the 'standards' of protection that can be associated with those provisions.

11.4 CONCLUSION

It can be said that a nation can develop its constitution in two ways: 'intentionally' and 'reactively'. Where a State develops the law relating to its constitutional environmental mandate intentionally, it is through the purposeful and systematic adoption and implementation of laws that create the conditions for the fulfilment of the constitution. Legal norms generate the framework conditions that are indispensable for the protection of the environment.

Where a State develops its laws reactively, it is through conflict and dispute resolution on a case-by-case basis. It can be argued that where courts are relied upon in this way to put the constitution into effect, it is a second-best option as the judiciary decide individual cases and are not in the best position to take a holistic view of the wider challenges at stake.

In Portugal, creation of legislation is the primary method in which the actual standards of environmental protection that are represented in the constitution are given clarity and substance. In this sense, the legislative branch of government acts as the *longa manus* of the constitution. The environmental provisions are given clarity as the legislation determines precisely what aspects of the environment are protected and the extent to which that protection is provided; they are also given substance through legal mechanisms that can be brought to bear in the event of non-compliance.

However, neither the constitutional provisions nor the laws themselves that relate to environmental protection operate like prophecies; they are not magic formulae that self-fulfil simply through enactment. They still, as in all jurisdictions, require active commitment from the relevant executive and judicial branches of

107 Case 1362/12 Judgment of January 2016 1.
108 ibid.

government to ensure that their purposes are properly fulfilled. Notwithstanding the argument that relying on the courts to put into effect the constitution is a second-best option, it also has to be said that the lack of judicial leadership in Portugal in terms of environmental protection may be a consequence of the real and perceived deficiencies of the national courts.

This chapter has also shown examples of innovative provisions that expand our understanding of the development of standards within environmental constitutionalism. This is because, in certain instances, the standards that have been developed, as a result of the constitution, go beyond that which is expected from EU law. For example, this is seen in Portuguese law relating to EIAs and industrial emissions. As such, it shows that even where a powerful regional organization such as the EU provides strong leadership in the development of environmental standards, a national constitution can influence the development of standards by pushing them to a higher level than that required under the regional treaty.

Probably of even greater significance are those innovative aspects of the Portuguese constitution which extend environmental protection within the sphere of business and industry. This is seen specifically through the extensive nature of the provisions of Art. 66, which have meant that constitutional standards have developed in relation to areas such as environmental education[109] and fiscal policy.[110] This has shed light on an expanded understanding of the Portuguese government's constitutional duties relating to the environment. In accordance with this, as the government is required to 'promote the integration of objectives into sectoral policies', this has led to environmental standards being developed and applied within a range of sectors under the aegis of Art. 66.

It is possible therefore that the Portuguese constitution is providing useful precedents in these times. The expansive range of provisions within Art. 66 also corresponds with a contemporary understanding of environmental protection which can be characterised by the integration of environmental concerns into all aspects of business, industry and development.

109 Portuguese Constitution art 66(g).
110 ibid art 66(h).

12

The Argentine Constitution and Its Relationship with Environmental Standards

Silvia Nonna

12.1 INTRODUCTION

The aim of this chapter is to examine the relationship between the environmental provisions of the Argentine Constitution[1] and standards of environmental protection. The Argentine Constitution is of particular interest as it specifically requires the government to create legislation that will provide for 'minimum standards' of environmental protection. Therefore this chapter seeks to consider those provisions within the context of the tensions and realities that confront the development and enforcement of environmental protection in the country.

The chapter will provide a brief description of the way that environmental law has developed at the local, regional and national levels in order that the constitutional provisions can be seen within their proper context. It will then provide an understanding of the national Constitution itself, and in particular its requirement that the government establishes 'minimum standards' of environmental protection. Following that, it will proceed with an overview of the incumbent legislation that provides for those minimum standards with a view to highlighting any possible inconsistencies, omissions and areas of overlap. It will then continue with further analysis which considers the issues that may affect the successful enforcement of those standards.

In addition, the standard of environmental protection related to Art. 41 of the 1994 Constitution will be considered in the light of certain cases. This analysis assists in demonstrating the challenges of applying the environmental mandate within the Constitution to the administrative oversight of business and industry.

12.2 BACKGROUND – THE DEVELOPMENT OF ENVIRONMENTAL LAW IN ARGENTINA

To understand the relationship that the Argentine Constitution has with the development of standards of environmental protection, it is necessary to consider the

[1] Constitution of the Argentine Nation, 1994 (Argentine Constitution). (See the Appendix to this chapter).

different stages of development of environmental law that the nation has experienced, the governmental organization of the country and also the manner in which legislation functions on the national and provincial levels. This provides the context that the constitutional provisions are integrally linked to and also the background to some of the tensions that influence the effectiveness of their implementation.

Argentina is a federal republic, consisting of twenty-three provinces along with the autonomous city of Buenos Aires. Four stages can be identified in the evolution of its environmental law. These are: firstly, a period from the late 1800s during which natural resources started to be regulated; secondly, a period that commenced in 1972 in which regulation of the environment in the contemporary sense can be said to have commenced; thirdly, a period following the signing of the Federal Environmental Pact in 1993[2] that paved the way for the right of people to a healthy environment through a new constitutional mandate in 1994; and finally the fourth stage starting in 2002, in which the minimum standards acts were enacted by Congress pursuant to the amended Constitution. This section will consider the first two stages and the third and fourth will be considered in subsequent sections.

The first stage involved the regulation of natural resources between the end of the nineteenth century and the last quarter of twentieth century. Regulation was framed through national laws that provinces could choose to adopt. Thus, the provinces had the option to adopt and enforce environmental law of the time. Legislation passed during that period regulated natural resources such as water, air, flora, fauna, protected areas, soil and the subsoil.

As for the second stage which started in 1972, two main categories of legal development occurred. These were the adoption of international environmental treaties[3] and the development of environmental provincial regulation. The Earth

[2] National Environmental Policy (Law No 25.675) annex II.

[3] Agreement on the Prevention of Sea Pollution by Dumping Waste and Other Materials (Law No 21.947) (1979) ratifies the Convention on the Prevention of Marine Pollution by Dumping of Wastes and other Matter (entered into force 24 March 2006) 1046 UNTS 484; Approval of an International Convention for the Prevention of Pollution from Ships (Law No 24.089) ratifies the International Convention for the Prevention of Pollution from Ships (entered into force 2 October 1983) 1340 UNTS 61 (MARPOL 73/78); Approval of the Vienna Convention for the Protection of the Ozone Layer (Law No 23.724) ratifies the Vienna Convention for the Protection of the Ozone Layer (entered into force 22 September 1988) 1513 UNTS 293; Approval of the Montreal Protocol on Substances that Deplete the Ozone Layer (Law No 23.778) ratifies the Montreal Protocol on Substances that Deplete the Ozone Layer (entered into force 1 January 1989) 1522 UNTS 3; Amendment of the Montreal Protocol Relating to Substances that Deplete the Ozone Layer (Law No 24.167) and Approval of the Amendment to the Montreal Protocol on Substances that Deplete the Ozone Layer (Law No 24.418) approved amendments to the Montreal Protocol on Substances that Deplete the Ozone Layer (entered into force 1 January 1989) 1522 UNTS 3; Approval of the United Nations Framework Convention on Climate Change (Law No 24.295) ratifies the United Nations Framework Convention on Climate Change (entered into force 21 March 1994) 1771 UNTS 107; Approval of the Convention on International Trade in Endangered Species of Wild Fauna and Flora (Law No 22.344) ratifies the Convention on International Trade in Endangered Species of Wild Fauna and Flora (entered into force 1 July 1975) 993 UNTS 243 (CITES); Approval of the Convention on

Summit in 1992[4] was a key driver in the development of environmental law in Argentina and many other Latin American countries. Its influence led most countries in South America to set up ministries to regulate and govern environmental issues. Even so, in Argentina during the 1970s environmental control was entrusted to the Health Authority, and that responsibility was later transferred to the Social Development Authority. It was not until January 2016 that the Ministry of Environment and Sustainable Development was created.[5]

With regards to the development of environmental regulation at the provincial level, the provinces soon integrated the concept of environmental protection; provincial constitutions were amended and local environmental regulations were passed. In 1993, the Federal Environmental Pact[6] was signed by all of the provinces as well as the national authority. It had the objective of simplifying the many existing rules and the complex relationships that the federal government had with the provinces in relation to environmental protection. The pact paved the way for the next major step that Argentina was going to take, which was the amendment of the national Constitution itself.

The original national Constitution of 1853 understandably made no mention of the environment as significant concern for the environment only began in the 1960s. However, prior to 1994, s. 33 of the former Constitution, which included 'not enumerated' or 'implied' rights, had been used for the protection of the environment by giving expression to the right to health and dignity of people.[7] Following the Earth Summit in 1992,[8] numerous countries began to amend their national constitutions to include provisions related to the protection of the environment. In 1993,

Wetlands of International Importance (Law No 23.919) ratifies the Convention on Wetlands of International Importance Especially as Waterfowl Habitat (entered into force 21 December 1975) 996 UNTS 245; Approval of the Convention on the Fight Against Desertification in Countries Affected by Severe Drought or Desertification (Law No 24.701) ratifies the United Nations Convention to Combat Desertification in Countries Experiencing Serious Drought and/or Desertification, Particularly in Africa (entered into force 26 December 1996) 1954 UNTS 3; Approval of the Basel Convention (Law No 23.922) ratifies the Basel Convention on the Control of Transboundary Movements of Hazardous Wastes and their Disposal (adopted 22 March 1989, entered into force 5 May 1992) 1673 UNTS 57 (Basel Convention); Approval of the Rotterdam Convention (Law No 25.278) ratifies the Rotterdam Convention on the Prior Informed Consent Procedure for Certain Hazardous Chemicals and Pesticides in International Trade (entered into force 24 February 2004) 2244 UNTS 337; Approval of the Stockholm Convention (Law No 26.011) ratifies the Stockholm Convention on Persistent Organic Pollutants (entered into force 17 May 2004) 2256 UNTS 119.

4 United Nations, 'Conference on Environment and Development' (Rio de Janeiro, Brazil, 3–14 June 1992) (Earth Summit).

5 President Mauricio Macri signed an Executive Order creating the Ministry of Environment and Sustainable Development within the first month of being in office: Law of Ministries (Decree 13/2015) as amended by Law of Ministries (Decree 223/2016).

6 Law No 25.675 (n 2).

7 Argentine Constitution s 33 – 'The declarations, rights and guarantees which the Constitution enumerates shall not be construed as a denial of other rights and guarantees not enumerated, but arising from the principle of sovereignty of the people and from the republican form of government.'

8 United Nations General Assembly 'Report of the United Nations Conference on Environment and Development' (12 August 1992) UN Doc A/CONF.151/26 (Vol 1).

Congress passed Act 24.309,[9] which put forward the need to make a constitutional amendment.[10] Congress established the subject areas that would be debated for that purpose and also proposed a series of basic clauses and open clauses; the latter included the environment. During the constitutional amendment process,[11] the right to preservation of the environment was highlighted as a third generation human right, and this ultimately led to the inclusion of Section 41 which specifically provides for the protection of the environment.

12.3 CONSTITUTIONAL PROTECTION OF THE ENVIRONMENT

Section 41 of the 1994 Constitution provides the right to a 'healthy and well balanced environment'. Amongst its stated objectives and obligations, it incorporates the concept of sustainable development. In its first paragraph it recognises that citizens have a right to an environment that meets a certain standard. It defines this as being one that is 'a healthy and balanced environment fit for human development in order that productive activities shall meet present needs without endangering those of future generations'. The integral use of language that corresponds with key components of the concept of sustainable development can be interpreted to mean that the required standard of environmental protection must be taken into account in any decision where 'development' of a community is concerned.[12]

As well as creating a right for citizens, s. 41 also creates a number of duties for individuals and the government. Consistent with the 'polluter pays' principle, it creates an obligation to repair damage as a priority by restoring the environment to its prior condition. This obligation needed to be given effect by statute and as such was incorporated in the General Environment Act in 2002.[13] Additionally, in the second paragraph it states that the authorities have a duty to defend the environment, to control the rational use of natural resources, to preserve the natural and cultural heritage and to preserve biological diversity. The last part of the second paragraph imposes a duty on the authorities to provide for environmental education and information to guarantee the participation of the nation's citizens in environmental decision making.

Probably most importantly for the purposes of this chapter is paragraph three, which states that it is the nation's responsibility to 'regulate the minimum protection standards'

9 National Constitution: Declaration of the Need for Its Reform (Law No 24.309).

10 The 1994 amendment to the Constitution of Argentina was significant. It was adopted on 22 August 1994 by a Constitutional Assembly that was held in the cities of Santa Fe (Santa Fe Province) and Paraná (Entre Ríos Province). Among other modifications, the amendment included third and fourth generation rights, rules for the defense of democracy and constitutionality and the creation of new administrative bodies.

11 Sessions were held in the capitals of those neighbouring provinces from 25 May 1994 until the approval of the constitutional amendment on 22 August 1994.

12 Daniel Alberto Sabsay, 'Constitution and Environment in relation to Sustainable Development' (2003) 21(1) Pace Environmental Law Review 155, 156; (See the Appendix to this chapter.)

13 Law No 25.675 (n 2).

for the environment. This means that it is the responsibility of the national congress to issue regulations containing minimum standards for environmental protection. This legislation becomes mandatory and applicable to all provinces so that all citizens, regardless of their place of residence or origin, enjoy the same guaranteed minimum standards; however, provincial authorities may enact complementary and even more stringent or detailed regulations if they wish. Section 12.4 provides more detail relating to the way that these 'minimum protection standards' have been developed through statute.

The fourth paragraph prohibits the introduction of dangerous and radioactive waste into the nation's territory. These standards had already been developing at the legislative level through hazardous waste legislation,[14] following the adoption of the Basel Convention.[15] The Act includes in its annexes I and II the corresponding annexes of the Basel Convention. However, it must be noted that radioactive waste is excluded from the scope of the Basel convention, and therefore the scope of protection provided under the Constitution goes further than that provided under the treaty.

It can be noted that the setting of minimum standards at the federal level has raised some issues regarding the relationship between the federal and provincial governments. Ultimately the federal government must establish the general guidelines and coordinate the national environmental policy through COFEMA (Federal Council of Environment);[16] the execution and implementation of this policy must be carried out by the provinces and municipalities. The Supreme Court Justice Horacio Rosatti has stated that Argentina's federal system reflects not only the practical advantages provided by a decentralised management system, but also the need to respect regional differences and local traditions.[17] All the same, it is clear that the standards of

14 The hazardous waste regime in Argentina regulates and controls industrial waste generation, treatment, transport and final disposal. It establishes comprehensive control on the life cycle of wastes, through the supervision of all the actors involved, linked by a unique document: the 'manifest'. It has been established through legislation which includes: Hazardous Waste – Generation, Handling, Transport and Treatment – Standards (Law No 24.051); Hazardous Waste: Approval of the Basel Convention (1991) (n 3); and the Dangerous Residues Law (Law No 24.051).

15 Basel Convention (n 3). In response to a public outcry following the discovery in the 1980s in Africa and other parts of the developing world of deposits of toxic wastes imported from abroad.

16 Law No 25.675 (n 2) arts 2(J), 23–24.

Art 2: Objectives

(j) Establish a federal interjurisdictional coordination system for the implementation of national and regional environmental policies.

Art 23: The Federal Environmental System is established with the aim of developing the coordination of environmental policy, for the achievement of sustainable development, between the national government, provincial governments and the City of Buenos Aires. It will be implemented through the Federal Environment Council (COFEMA).

Art 24: The Executive Power will propose to the Assembly of the Federal Council of Environment the dictating of recommendations or resolutions, as appropriate, in accordance with the Constitutive Act of that federal body, for the effective validity and effective application of the laws of minimum budgets, the complementary provincial, and its regulations in the different jurisdictions.

17 Horacio D Rosatti, *Constitutional Environmental Law* (Rubinzal-Culzoni Editores 2007).

environmental protection that are provided in practice can be affected by the manner in which individual provincial governments implement national law and policy. As such, it has also become clear that as environmental protection affects so many areas of government policy,[18] more work needs to be done at the federal and provincial levels to achieve greater clarity, effectiveness and efficiency.

12.4 THE MINIMUM STANDARDS ACTS

This section will provide details and analysis of the minimum standards legislation that the National Congress has passed to comply with section 41 of the 1994 Constitution. Since 2002, Congress has enacted eleven minimum standards acts which cover a wide range of specific environmental issues. The Acts referred to below, together with the local 'complementary' procedural rules and regulations, constitute the modern framework for environmental protection in Argentina.

12.4.1 *Integrated Management of Industrial Waste Act (2002)*[19]

This legislation was intended to replace the hazardous waste regime. To date, the Act has not been effectively implemented, despite being in force. The intention was to replace the categorization by lists (as under the Basel Convention) with a risk-based system. In practice, the previous legislation, Act 24.051,[20] is enforced and coexists with the new regime. This leads to a permanent and dangerous confusion in a sector that should be clearly regulated.

12.4.2 *Polychlorinated Biphenyls (PCBs) Management and Disposal Act (2002)*[21]

This Act was passed in response to public pressure related to PCB leaks from transformers and other power transmission and distribution equipment. Its aim is to control PCB-associated operations through the decontamination or elimination of equipment that contains PCBs, the elimination of used PCBs, the prohibition of entry into the country of PCBs as well as the prohibition of their production and trade. The Act also led to the creation of the Integrated National Registry of PCB Owners, whereby PCB manufacturers, traders and owners need to be centrally registered.[22]

[18] Juan Rodrigo Walsh, 'La Politica Ambiental Argentina – Pasado, Presente y Perspectivas para un Modelo de Desarrollo Sustentable' (Argentinian Environmental Policy – The Past, the Present and Perspectives for a new Model of Sustainable Development) 127 March/April/May Forensic Synthesis: Journal of the San Isidro Bar Association 8. <www.casi.com.ar/sites/default/files/sf-127-r.pdf> accessed 25 July 2018.

[19] Comprehensive Management of Industrial Waste and Service Activities (Law No 25.612).

[20] Law 24.051 (n 14).

[21] Management of PCBs (Law No 25.670).

[22] ibid art 4.

12.4.3 The General Environment Act (2002)[23]

The General Environment Act established the national environmental policy, and shortly after being enacted it constituted the basis for several judicial decisions. Fundamentally, it established the basic institutional structure through which specific laws should be enacted, construed and applied. It establishes clear objectives, contains guiding and priority principles and outlines national environmental policy instruments.

The Act is particularly important as it defines the concept of 'minimum standards' that are referred to in Article 41 of the Constitution as being 'every regulation that grants uniform or common environmental protection for all the national territory, with the objective of imposing necessary conditions to guarantee environmental protection'.[24] It establishes that the regulation of basic standards shall describe 'the necessary conditions to guarantee the dynamic of the ecological systems, maintain their capacity to recharge and, in general, guarantee environmental preservation and sustainable development'.[25]

The Act considers the 'environment' in its widest sense, taking into consideration sustainable management, the preservation and protection of biological diversity and the effective implementation of sustainable development. The inclusion of principles in the Act also warrant attention. Accordingly, it establishes the following as principles of national environmental policy: congruence, prevention, precaution, progressivity, responsibility, intergenerational equity, sustainability, subsidiarity, solidarity and cooperation.[26]

It details the tools required to achieve the objectives of the national environmental policy in the context of the above-mentioned principles. As such, it enumerates and then develops in individual chapters different instruments such as: environmental land planning, environmental impact assessment, systems of control over the development of anthropic activities, environmental education, environmental information systems and an economic regime for the promotion of sustainable development.[27]

The Act consolidates a federal environmental system to coordinate environmental policy and to make decisions at different levels of government. As such, it formalises the status of the Federal Environmental Council as an inter-federal agency with a statutory duty to ensure debate and coordination among the various provincial environmental agencies with the federal environmental authorities.[28]

With regard to citizen participation, the Act provides for participation of the community and civil society in decision-making processes.[29] It focuses on the right

23 Law No 25.675 (n 2).
24 ibid art 6.
25 ibid.
26 ibid art 4.
27 ibid art 8.
28 Law No 25.675 (n 2) art 25(1).
29 ibid arts 16–21.

of every person to be heard in a decision-making process, and also on the right of access to justice.[30] Participation is especially guaranteed through environmental impact assessment procedures and land order procedures.[31] Therefore, authorities are required to institutionalise consultation processes and public hearings prior to the authorization of activities that may cause negative impacts on the environment.

12.4.4 *Water Environmental Management Regime Act (2003)*[32]

The aim of this Act is to establish the minimum standards of environmental protection for the preservation of water and its rational use. It provides that the national authority has the responsibility to determine acceptable limits of contamination, make directions for the recharging of aquifers, make environmental standards for water quality and prepare a national plan for the rational use of water.[33]

The Act is in force, although its operation at the administrative level is minimal. However, it has been applied in certain cases, including the Mendoza case,[34] which is referred to in more detail in Section 12.5.5.2.

12.4.5 *Environmental Public Information Act (2004)*[35]

This Act establishes minimum standards relating to the right of access to environmental information.[36] It focuses on the development of systematised, simple, quick and easily comprehensible mechanisms to allow access to information at no cost.[37]

These procedural aspects were developed through a resolution adopted by COFEMA,[38] which approved a flow chart and indicated the methods to be used to request information. The law places an obligation upon the appropriate agency to ensure that rapid access to information is facilitated.

12.4.6 *Integrated Management of Household Waste Act (2004)*[39]

This Act of basic harmonised standards formalises the common principles and objectives that are applied to the adequate management of domiciliary wastes for

30 ibid arts 19–20.
31 ibid art 21.
32 Regime of Environmental Management of Waters (Law No 25.688).
33 ibid art 7.
34 *Mendoza Beatriz Silvia and Others v Estado Nacional and Others* (M 1569 XL) (Corte Suprema de Justicia de la Nación, 20 June 2006).
35 Regime of Free Access to Public Environmental Information (Law No 25.831).
36 ibid art 1.
37 ibid art 3.
38 Resolución COFEMA N° 110/2005 (15 December 2005) 'Procedimiento para el acceso a información pública ambiental' (Procedure for Access to Public Environmental Information).
39 Household Waste Management (Law No 25.916).

the whole country,[40] and it also provides a legal framework for several projects and programmes that were already in place in certain provinces and cities.

The Act establishes minimum and common standards to protect people, their quality of life and also the environment itself. Its overall objectives are to achieve an adequate and rational management of domestic waste, promote its valorization, minimise its negative impacts and further its minimization. It includes details of the fines and sanctions available to the authorities in carrying out their responsibilities.[41]

12.4.7 *Protection of Native Forests Act (2007)*[42]

This Act establishes minimum standards for the protection of native forests. It requires that all provinces establish land use plans for native forests with categories of forest protection according to their relative importance for conservation.[43]

The Act has been a key focal point for native forest conservation, galvanizing public opinion and civil society. This is because native forests have been viewed not only as natural resources to be preserved, but also as providers of environmental services.[44]

The issue of minimum standards relating to native forests is a complex issue due to the technical difficulties involved and the variety of interests that need to be taken into account. However, it has become innovative because it includes the possible use of economic instruments owing to the environmental services that are provided.[45] As such, integrated approaches are being developed contemplating not only environmental dimensions, but economic and social ones too.

12.4.8 *Control of Grassland Burning Activities Act (2009)*[46]

This Act regulates grassland burning. It establishes the guidelines that must be respected when grassland and vegetable waste burning activities are carried out, with the aim of ensuring the adequacy and preparation of the land for subsequent use.

40 ibid art 1.
41 ibid arts 26–32.
42 Environmental Protection of Native Forests (Law No 26.331).
43 ibid art 4.
44 ibid art 5. Environmental services are those tangible or intangible benefits generated by native forest ecosystems which are necessary for the preservation of the natural and biological system as a whole and to ensure quality of life to all inhabitants of the Nation that benefit from the native forests. Among others, the environmental services that native forests provide to society are: hydric regulation; preservation of biodiversity; fixing of gas emissions producing a greenhouse effect; contribution to diversification and beautification of the landscape; defense of the cultural identity.
45 ibid.
46 Law of Minimum Budgets of Environmental Protection for Control of Burning Activities (Law No 26.552).

The principal aim of the Act is the prevention of a range of different types of damage to the environment, which include those relating to natural resources, cultural resources, health and public security.

Grassland burning is fundamentally a local issue, and therefore local regulation should be sufficient to control poor practices. In this respect, as a minimum standard, the Act establishes that every burning activity must be duly authorised by the competent local authority.[47]

12.4.9 *Protection of Glaciers and Periglacial Environment Act* (2010)[48]

This Act establishes minimum standards for the protection of glaciers and the periglacial environment 'with the object to preserve them as strategic reserves of water resources for human consumption; for agriculture and as water providers for the recharge of hydrographical basins; for biodiversity protection; as a source of scientific information and as tourist attractions'.[49] Additionally it makes clear that 'glaciers constitute goods of public character'.[50]

In terms of the specific administrative responsibilities that the government has, it states the need to elaborate a national inventory of glaciers,[51] although these have not yet been presented or made public. It also includes the prohibition of certain activities for their general protection.[52] However, these measures may prove insufficient if other actions, such as climate change, cause further glacial retreat.

The Act is not yet in force owing to a legal challenge which seeks to exclude certain activities such as mining from its scope.[53]

12.4.10 *Prevention of Forest and Brush Fires Act* (2013)[54]

This Act has the objective of setting up a comprehensive management system by national and provincial authorities to prevent forest and brush fires. Its scope is broader than that established by earlier legislation found in the Control of Grassland Burning Activities Act (2009).[55]

47 ibid art 13.

48 Regime of Minimum Budgets for the Preservation of Glaciers and the Environment Periglacial (Law No 26.639).

49 ibid art 1.

50 ibid.

51 ibid arts 3–4.

52 ibid art 6.

53 *Barrick Exploraciones Argentinas SA y otro v Estado Nacional s/acción declarativa de inconstitucionalidad* (Corte Suprema de Justicia de la Nación, 3 July 2012).

54 Fire Management (Law No 26.815) (*Información Legislativa*, 2013) <http://servicios.infoleg.gob.ar/infolegInternet/anexos/205000–209999/207401/texact.htm> accessed 8 May 2018.

55 Law No 26.552 (n 46).

It includes a more comprehensive institutional framework for the National Plan for Fire Management.[56] The framework involves the National Parks Administration,[57] the National Environmental Authority[58] and provincial authorities.[59]

Forest fires are a problem in some provinces, they are recurrent at certain times of the year. The issue does arguably deserve minimum standards, however, financing preventative measures is always an obstacle to effective implementation.

12.4.11 *Management of Empty Containers of Phytosanitary Products Act (2016)*[60]

This Act regulates the integral management of empty phytosanitary product containers.[61] Its objectives are to ensure that these containers are not employed in applications that may involve risks to human health or the environment, to improve management efficiency, and also to streamline the administrative procedure for the registration and authorization of traders, users, operators and applicators. A dual and complementary application of minimum standards is foreseen between the national Ministry of Agriculture and the national Ministry of Environment; each ministry undertaking specific functions that will need to be carefully coordinated with the objective of achieving 'sustainable agriculture'.[62]

12.4.12 *Analysis of the Minimum Standards Acts*

In general, all the Acts mentioned above aim to create frameworks to integrate principles of national policies into law and establish the main instruments for their enforcement. However, not all those acts are self-sufficient; in other words, they cannot be enforced without other complementary legislation. Most require regulatory frameworks and technical norms to be applicable. Indeed, the lack of this kind of legislation currently undermines the effectiveness of the minimum standards legislation.

Furthermore, for environmental management to be effective, the enforcement of environmental legislation by administrative bodies and agencies is crucial. Human,

56 Law No 26.815 (n 54) art 24(b); see Maria C Dentoni, 'Argentine National Fire Management Plan' 7.4 Fire Situation in Argentina (*Food and Agriculture Organization of the United Nations*) <www.fao.org/docrep/006/AD653E/ad653e01.htm#TopOfPage> accessed 25 July 2018.

57 National Parks of Argentina (*Parques Nacionales de Argentina*) <www.parquesnacionales.gob.ar/> accessed 25 July 2018.

58 Ministry of the Environment and Sustainable Development (*Argentina.gob.ar*) <www.argentina.gob.ar/ambiente> accessed 25 July 2018.

59 Provincial environmental authorities of the twenty-three Argentine provinces and of the city of Buenos Aires.

60 Phytosanitary Products (Law No 27.279).

61 ibid art 1.

62 ibid art 14.

technical and financial resources are needed to ensure their efficient implementation. The commitment at the highest levels of government is also not as strong as it should be and, as such, allocated funds are never sufficient.

The eleven minimum standards acts identify duties and obligations and new functions for local environmental agencies in coherence with the federal environmental system.

The duties and powers of the administrative bodies tasked with the enforcement of environmental legislation have increased. Unfortunately, in most cases this has not been accompanied by the necessary human, technical and financial resources to facilitate effective enforcement. Despite the positive aspects brought by the environmental legislation mentioned, the experience gained during recent decades leads to the conclusion that the challenge, at least for Argentina and most Latin American countries, is to strengthen capabilities to provide effective and efficient environmental law enforcement.

12.5 ENVIRONMENTAL LITIGATION UNDER THE ARGENTINE CONSTITUTION

Under s. 43 of the Constitution, all persons may file a summary proceeding to protect constitutional rights (provided there is no other regular legal remedy) if the public authorities infringe, limit or threaten, by act or omission, the rights and guarantees contained in the Constitution. This part of the chapter analyses the standard of environmental protection that has been afforded through such actions.

There has been a clear evolution that is reflected by the court judgments issued after the 1994 constitutional amendment regarding the enforcement of the right to live in a clean and healthy environment as stated in s. 41. However, as has been noted in Section 12.2, prior to the advent of the right to a healthy environment, other provisions of the Constitution had been used to protect environmental concerns. Therefore, to fully trace the evolution of standards of protection in constitutional litigation related to the environment, attention must be divided between those cases heard before the 1994 amendment and those heard after it.

12.5.1 *Cases Pre-1994*

12.5.1.1 Barracas Slaughterhouses Case (1887)

The earliest such case is that of the *Barracas slaughterhouses – Saladeristas Podestá*,[63] which dates back to 1887. In this instance a decision was made based on implicit constitutional rights that were derived primarily from the right to life and

[63] *Saladeristas Podestá, Bertam, Anderson, Ferrer y otros v Provincia de Buenos Aires* (La Corte Suprema de Justicis de la Nación, 14 May 1887).

the right to health. The Supreme Court ordered the province of Buenos Aires to suspend the operation of slaughterhouses and ordered them to adopt urgent hygienic and public health measures prohibiting the discharge of liquid waste into the Riachuelo River.

12.5.1.2 Kattan y Otros v. Gobierno Nacional (1983)

A subsequent case that set a trend in the environmental arena, specifically with regard to those entitled to make environmental claims, was *Kattan, Alberto E. and others* v. *National Government – Executive Power* (1983).[64] This action was based on the assertion that authorised hunting could threaten the well-being of a species as well as alter the environment in which it lived. The claimant, Alberto Kattan, a law professor, requested the suspension of certain permits 'until there are definite studies on the environmental and faunistic impacts that such hunting may cause'.[65] Based on implied rights guaranteed by Article 33 of the Argentine Constitution,[66] the claim was filed specifically against the executive authorizations granting Japanese companies the right to fish fourteen skunk dolphins. Federal Judge Oscar Garzón Funes recognised the standing of a Buenos Aires City citizen to file a claim by virtue of the diffuse interests and constitutional implied rights.[67] As such, this case extended the right to bring such legal actions to the population in general and the decision became a landmark in the development of Argentine environmental law. In terms of standards, it can be seen as a landmark case in relation to the 'standard' of protection conferred through the right of 'access to justice' within Argentine constitutionalism.

12.5.1.3 Bustos y Otros v. Fabricaciones Militares (1986)

Two years after Kattan's claim, Bustos Miguel and others filed a claim against a military factory requesting a suspension of activities that were causing severe illnesses in a particular neighborhood.[68] The factory concerned was producing sulphuric acid, the fumes of which were causing severe impacts to the health of the neighbouring community as well as damaging their properties. The judgment concluded that 'although it could be said that the activity is developed in order to

64 *Kattan, Alberto E y otros v Gobierno Nacional – Poder Ejecutivo* (Juzgado Nacional de la Instancia en lo Contencioso-Administrativo Federal Nro 2 (J N Fed Contencioso Administrativo) (No. 2 10 May 1983).

65 ibid.

66 Argentine Constitution s 33 protected human rights and principles on the basis of the Roman law concept that citizens have a duty to protect the '*domino public*'. See John E Bonine, 'Standing to Sue: The First Step in Access to Justice' II B *(Law Mercer.edu)* <http://www2.law.mercer.edu/elaw/standingtalk.html> acceessed 26 July 2018.

67 *Kattan* (n 64).

68 *Bustos and Others v Fabricaciones Militares* (Juzgado Federla de Primera Instancia de La Plata, 30 December 1986).

satisfy public interest it has to be suspended because it is harming the life, health and physical integrity of the people'.[69] The judges based their decision on national laws and regulations, but additionally cited s. 33 of the Argentine Constitution and the American Convention on Human Rights to justify the factory closure.[70]

12.5.2 *Cases Post-1994*

1994 heralded the advent of the explicit environmental right within the national Constitution and coincided with a period in which new opinions relating to collective and individual protection of the environment had started to become more readily accepted. These views had an influence on the standard of environmental protection available under s. 41.

12.5.2.1 Quevedo Miguel Ángel y Otros c/ Aguas Cordobesas S.A. Amparo (2002)

In 2002, in the case *Quevedo Miguel Ángel y otros c/ Aguas Cordobesas S.A. Amparo*[71] a judge in the city of Córdoba determined that provision of clean water is a basic service that forms part of public health policy, which is consistent with international treaties that were contemplated in the 1994 Constitution. The judge also found that it was applicable both to the individual and the collective health of the population. Therefore, suspending the service for lack of payment was a violation of section 42 of the 1994 Constitution.[72]

12.5.2.2 Mendoza, Beatriz et al. v. Estado Nacional et al. Matanza Riachuelo (2006)

The *Mendoza Beatriz et al.* v. *National State et al. Matanza Riachuelo* case,[73] and particularly the role that the National Supreme Court of Justice played in it, have had a major impact on the development of environmental rights in Argentina.

69 ibid.

70 American Convention on Human Rights 'Pact of San José, Costa Rica' (entered into force 18 July 1978) 1144 UNTS 123. International human rights instrument adopted in Costa Rica on 22 November 1969.

71 *Quevedo Miguel Ángel y otros c/ Aguas Cordobesas SA Amparo* (Sentence 260) (Juzgado de 1st Inst. y 51 Nom Civil y Com de Córdoba, 5 April 2002).

72 Argentine Constitution s 42. See complete text in Appendix. As regards consumption, consumers and users of goods and services have the right to the protection of their health, safety and economic interest; to adequate and truthful information, to freedom of choice and equitable and reliable treatment; see also Chapter 7 of this volume by Owen McIntyre relating to the right to water and sanitation.

73 *Mendoza, Beatriz Silvia y otros v Estado Nacional y otros s/daños y perjuicios* (daños derivados de la contaminación ambiental del Río Matanza – Riachuelo) (M.1569.XL) (Corte Suprema de Justicia de la Nación, 20 June 2006).

The Matanza-Riachuelo River flows for approximately 64 kilometres, from the District of La Matanza to the shores of La Boca. It became known as one of the most polluted rivers in the world as large quantities of industrial waste and untreated sewage had been discharged into it over many years. According to the 2010 National Census, over 6 million people reside in the vicinity of the basin.[74] This resulted in environmental problems impacting the health and lives of thousands of inhabitants, especially those from the most vulnerable social groups, who often lacked basic services such as clean drinking water, sanitation, health services and decent housing. Additionally it must be noted that the region includes areas of significant ecological value that require protection.

In 2004, a group of people that lived in the basin filed a claim before the National Supreme Court against the national government, Buenos Aires Province, the Autonomous City of Buenos Aires and forty-four companies. They claimed compensation for the damage suffered as a result of the pollution and requested that the Court issue an order to halt the offending operations. They also sought a court order for the environment to be restored. Certain NGOs, in filing as third parties, stated that specific economic, social and cultural rights had been directly affected. In particular they argued that the right to health, comprised of access to safe drinking water, adequate sanitary conditions and a healthy environment, had been seriously compromised.

In 2006, the Court issued a judgment which required the national government, Buenos Aires Province and the Autonomous City of Buenos Aires to undertake the work necessary to improve the quality of life of the inhabitants related to the management of the basin, to remedy the ecological components of the basin and to prevent further contamination.[75]

The court's interventionist approach led to the establishment of the Matanza-Riachuelo Basin Authority (ACUMAR),[76] which was charged with following a programme of measures to:

(a) produce and disseminate public information;
(b) control industrial pollution;

[74] Instituto Nacional de Estadistica y Censos: República Argentina, '2010 Census' (*Indec*, 2010) <www.indec.gov.ar/nivel4_default.asp?id_tema_1=2&id_tema_2=41&id_tema_3=135> accessed 7 May 2018.

[75] ibid. For further information: Autoridad De Cuenca Matanza Riachuelo, 'Causa Digitalizada' (*Acumar*) <www.acumar.gob.ar/causa-mendoza/causa-digitalizada/> accessed 8 May 2018.

[76] The lawsuit led to the establishment of a new river basin authority (ACUMAR), an inter-jurisdictional body created by the Law of the Cuenca Matanza Riachuelo (Law No 26.168) (*Información Legislativa*, 2006) <http://servicios.infoleg.gob.ar/infolegInternet/anexos/120000-124999/122769/norma.htm> accessed 25 July 2018. It put in place clean-up, restoration and regional environmental health plans. It is comprised of authorities of the National Executive Power, Buenos Aires Province and Autonomous City of Buenos Aires. It is in charge of the execution of the Integral Plan of Environmental Sanitation of the Matanza Riachuelo Basin. For more details and information on the state of the basin, water quality and general updated data: see Autoridad De Cuenca Matanza Riachuelo, 'Home Page' (*Acumar*) <www.acumar.gov.ar> accessed 5 May 2018.

(c) sanitise refuse sites;
(d) extend water-works, sewers and storm water drainage;
(e) undertake an emergency sanitation plan; and
(f) adopt an (international) measurement system to evaluate the degree of accomplishment of the objectives.

The overall objective of the intervention programme has been the improvement of the inhabitants' quality of life, and as such it required that specific sanitation programmes be adopted to meet the needs of the river basin population. It also demanded an emergency health plan and the integration of public health-related components into the planned clean-up itself.

Additionally, the court created a collegial body composed of the National Ombudsman and those non-governmental organizations (NGO)[77] that became involved as third parties in the case, with the aim of strengthening and facilitating citizen participation, especially in certain aspects of the judgment such as compliance.

The decision changed the manner of policy making by giving ACUMAR the responsibility to act as the single governing authority for the river basin and to facilitate its recovery and improvement. This initiative was taken to simplify decision making and applicable regulation, and also to improve the policing of polluting activities. National, provincial and local governments had previously had powers relating to the basin, and a single authority with its own unified regulation was needed to avoid confusion and the means for polluters to evade oversight and control.[78]

However, in spite of the intervention of the Supreme Court in this case, it has to be noted the situation in practice has been a different story. ACUMAR has been seriously criticised for the minimal progress that has been made in carrying out its functions.[79] While some clean-up operations have been carried out, the underlying

77 Asociación Ciudadana por los Derechos Humanos (Citizen Association for Human Rights), Asociación de Vecinos de la Boca (Neighborhood Association of La Boca), Centro de Estudios Legales y Sociales (Center for Legal and Social Studies), Fundación Ambiente y Recursos Naturales (Environment and Natural Resources), Fundación Greenpeace Argentina (Greenpeace Foundation Argentina).

78 Silvia Nonna, 'Presentation' (Environment Day Seminar, 8 June 2015). Argentina and its various jurisdictions suffer from 'normative inflation' and 'regulatory creep'. Because there are many different rules of different levels regulating the same issue, sometimes they overlap, sometimes they become incoherent or they are not clear enough, neither for those who have to implement nor those who have to enforce them. And they end up becoming a problem for those who want to fulfill them and give the defaulters the perfect excuse not to follow them. Furthermore, regulations generally create unnecessary bureaucracy that, as is well known, does not contribute to an improved environmental quality or enforcement ratio.

79 Ricardo A Gutiérrez and Lucas Christel, 'Environmental Rights and Water Issues in Argentina' (Congress of the Latin American Studies Association, San Francisco, USA, 23–26 May 2012) <www.unsam.edu.ar/profesores/ricardogutierrez/LASA%202012%20Gutiérrez%20&%20Christel%20Paper.pdf> accessed 25 September 2017.

problem of changing the practices of the polluting industries has not been solved, and at the time of writing, levels of pollution and incidences of unhealthy living conditions remain extremely high.[80]

Since the *Mendoza* case the Supreme Court has made other judgments which further illustrate the standard of environmental protection that can be expected as a natural consequence of the provisions of section 41 of the 1994 Constitution. Three recent cases are worth considering.

12.5.2.3 Asociación Argentina de Abogados Ambientalistas de la Patagonia c/Santa Cruz, Provincia de y Otro s/Amparo Ambiental (2016)

In the case of *Asociación Argentina de Abogados Ambientalistas de la Patagonia c/ Santa Cruz, Provincia de y Otro s/Amparo Ambiental* (2016),[81] the Supreme Court allowed a petition made by an association of environmental lawyers which ultimately asserted the standard of certain substantive and procedural environmental rights. It ordered the government to provide information about the construction works planned within a project designed to develop hydroelectric resources in the Santa Cruz River. The court requested information regarding compliance with the requirement that public hearings be held in accordance with the General Environmental Act.[82]

The court deemed it necessary to ensure that any environmental impact assessment had been properly carried out both in terms of public participation and the applicable science related to water, flora, fauna, landscape and existing and future populations. The court later jointly convened a public hearing on 21 July 2017 with the Ministry of the Environment to hear comments on the environmental impact report submitted by the Ministry of Energy.

12.5.2.4 Fundación Ciudadanos Independientes c/San Juan, Provincia de, Estado Nacional y Otros s/Acción Ambiental Meramente Declarativa (2016)

In the case of *Fundación Ciudadanos Independientes c/San Juan, Provincia de, Estado Nacional y Otros s/Acción Ambiental Meramente Declarativa* (2016),[83] the Supreme Court requested that the Province of San Juan compile a report regarding the existence and scope of possible leaks of cyanide and heavy metals from a mine. The court also required disclosure as to whether the population had received

80 Daniel Gutman, 'Argentina's Never-Ending Environmental Disaster' (*Inter Press Service: News Agency*, 11 February 2017) <www.ipsnews.net/2017/02/argentinas-never-ending-environmental-disaster/> accessed 25 September 2017.

81 *Asociación Argentina de Abogados Ambientalistas de la Patagonia v Santa Cruz, Provincia de y Otro s/ Amparo Ambiental* (Corte Suprema de Justicia de la Nación, 21 December 2016).

82 Law No 25.675 (n 2).

83 *Fundación Ciudadanos Independientes v San Juan, Provincia de, Estado Nacional y Otros s/Acción Ambiental Meramente Declarativa* (Corte Suprema de Justicia de la Nación, 20 September 2016).

information about the scope of the leaks and their possible consequences. The court based its decision on the grounds that it was the custodian of constitutional rights and guarantees, and also under Art. 32 of the General Environmental Act,[84] which provides that the court must take all necessary measures regarding any detrimental environmental actions during the process in order to protect the 'general interest'.[85]

12.6 ADDRESSING CONSTITUTIONAL 'STANDARDS' OF ENVIRONMENTAL PROTECTION

It is clear from the aforementioned discussions relating to the minimum standards legislation and the interventions by the courts related to s. 41 of the Constitution that the issues of the standards of environmental protection in practice are closely tied to the efficiency and effectiveness of the administration of environmental law at the local, provincial and national levels. In this respect, significant headway has been made recently to improve the institutional structures that administer environmental law in the country. It would be fair to say that the structures at the national level for the administration of environmental law have until recently been relatively weak. However, in January 2016 the Ministry of the Environment was created, which has elevated the importance of environmental protection within government at the national level.[86] Therefore, slowly the country has taken significant steps in terms of its institutional and legal frameworks to fulfill the environmental provisions enshrined in the Constitution.

Nevertheless, it can be argued that there are still considerable challenges that need to be addressed and associated reforms that need to be undertaken. Within those challenges lie questions related to organizational structures, appropriate goal setting, management efficiency, types of environmental legislation, implementation methods and the integration of transparency and accountability.

This author argues that there are a number of reforms that are particularly necessary to further the improvement of the administration of environmental law in order that the constitutional mandate under s. 41 can be fully realised. It can be argued that COFEMA should be the incumbent body to analyse and plan federal environmental policy. As such, it should be in a position to review existing policy and regulations to enhance their quality and to develop appropriate standards. To achieve its objectives, its functions need to be made clear and a budget should be provided to include full-time staff. Additionally, in terms of bureaucratic oversight related to the environment, the administration needs to be self-governing, independent of politics and run by appropriately trained professionals.

[84] Law No 25.675 (n 2) art 32.
[85] Such intervention bears similarities to that of the Indian courts. See Chapter 10 of this volume by Gita Gill relating to the Indian Constitution.
[86] Decree 13/2015 (n 5).

In terms of the appropriate methods to be used, it can be argued that the challenge is to achieve a balance between a 'command and control' system and a voluntary compliance system; in other words a dual system that includes 'sticks' and 'carrots'. The use of incentives can be a more effective way for the administration and the various regulated sectors to work together to achieve specific environmental goals. As such, Argentina could benefit from greater use of economic incentives. There is already evidence of such approaches being adopted. For example, the Native Forest Protection Regime (as noted above) includes the potential for the use of payments for environmental services.[87]

Argentina and its various jurisdictions suffer from 'normative inflation' and 'regulatory creep'.[88] There can be many rules at different levels regulating the same issue which leads to unnecessary duplication. It also means that sometimes the applicable rules and regulations are unclear or incoherent, which provides an obstacle to those tasked with enforcing them. This, of course, provides an excuse for those causing harm to the environment. Therefore, research is currently underway[89] to analyse the levels of inconsistency between federal and provincial laws and how the minimum standards function in practice. This analysis is necessary to provide recommendations for legislative and administrative reform that can assist in the accomplishment of the government's mandate under s. 41 of the national Constitution.

12.7 CONCLUSION

In 1994, with the amendment of the national Constitution, Argentina mandated the government to adopt minimum standards for the protection of the environment. Under this mandate, minimum standards legislation was adopted to provide adequate levels of environmental protection. Additionally, both before and after the inclusion of the environmental provision in the national Constitution, there have been numerous cases where provisions of the Constitution have been used to justify

87 Law No 26.331 (n 42) (n 13).

88 Nonna (n 78).

89 University of Buenos Aires, 'A Normative and Jurisprudential Analysis of the New Competency Scheme in Environment Matters. Contributions to Twenty Years of the Reform of the National Constitution: UBACyT Projects' (*Facultad de Derecho*, 31 July 2016) <www.derecho.uba.ar/investigacion/inv_proyectos_vigentes_ubacyt_2014_nonna.php> accessed 7 May 2018.

At the University of Buenos Aires a group of scholars and researchers is currently working within the framework of a research project to find out the reasons and bring possible solutions to the weak implementation of minimum standards and trying to identify incoherence of regulation in force within the federal environmental system. Research project for UBA programme on science and technology. Integrated group directed by Silvia Nonna. Researchers: Senior: Natalia Waitzman, Lisandro Dellazuana, Lucía De Nicola, Agustina Mazzini, Violeta Radovich. Junior: Leila Cohen Sabba, Laura Gofman, Victoria Bunchicoff, María Elisa Dugo, Mónica Pires. Students: Florencia Azul Rufino Bonomo, Delfina Vila Moret, Cristian De Fazio, Pablo Schlottahuer, Florencia Reissing, Martina Bergamini, Florencia Nocera.

intervention by the courts to require governmental authorities, and in turn business and industry, to ensure that minimum standards of environmental protection are put into practice.

However, what this chapter has also illustrated is that the constitutional mandate and the intervention of the courts alone are insufficient to lead to the levels of environmental protection that the country needs. In other words, the law is only effective when it is coupled with adequate systems of administration and enforcement. There is a range of work that is required of the government, which includes the design of efficient regulatory frameworks, the development of effective monitoring and compliance mechanisms, the integration of effective institutional coordination, the appropriate use of budgeting and expertise and the integration of public participation in the creation of standards themselves. These are some of the components that ultimately can lead to the 'internalization' of this constitutional right and which can lead to it being guaranteed in practice.

Therefore, despite the positive aspects brought by the constitutional mandate and the related minimum standards Acts, the experience gained over the last two decades leads this author to think that the challenge, at least for Argentina and most Latin American countries, lies in the strengthening of administrative and governmental capacity to provide effective and efficient environmental law enforcement. While progress in this sphere has definitely been slow, it can also be said that it is gradually moving in the right direction.

APPENDIX

Relevant Sections of the 1994 National Constitution

Section 31: This Constitution, the laws of the Nation enacted by Congress in pursuance thereof, and treaties with foreign powers, are the supreme law of the Nation; and the authorities of each province are bound thereby, notwithstanding any provision to the contrary included in the provincial laws or constitutions, except for the province of Buenos Aires, the treaties ratified after the Pact of November 11, 1859.

Section 41: All inhabitants are entitled to the right to a healthy and balanced environment fit for human development in order that productive activities shall meet present needs without endangering those of future generations; and shall have the duty to preserve it. As a first priority, environmental damage shall bring about the obligation to repair it according to law.

The authorities shall provide for the protection of this right, the rational use of natural resources, the preservation of natural and cultural heritage and of biological diversity, and shall also provide for environmental information and education.

The Nation shall regulate the minimum protection standards, and the provinces those necessary to reinforce them, without altering their local jurisdictions.

The entry into the national territory of present or potential dangerous wastes, and of radioactive ones, is forbidden.

Section 42: As regards consumption, consumers and users of goods and services have the right to the protection of their health, safety and economic interests; to adequate and truthful information; to freedom of choice and equitable and reliable treatment. The authorities shall provide for the protection of said rights, the education for consumption, the defense of competition against any kind of market distortions, the control of natural and legal monopolies, the control of quality and efficiency of public utilities and the creation of consumer and user associations. Legislation shall establish efficient procedures for conflict prevention and settlement, as well as regulations for national public utilities. Such legislation shall take into account the necessary participation of consumer and user associations and of the interested provinces in the control entities.

Section 43: Any person may file a prompt and summary proceeding regarding constitutional guarantees, provided there is no other legal remedy, against any act or omission of the public authorities or individuals which currently or imminently may damage, limit, modify or threaten rights and guarantees recognised by this Constitution, treaties or laws, with open arbitrariness or illegality. In such case, the judge may declare that the act or omission is based on an unconstitutional rule. This summary proceeding against any form of discrimination and about rights protecting the environment, competition, users and consumers, as well as about rights of general public interest, shall be filed by the damaged party, the ombudsman and the associations which foster such ends registered accordingly (. . .)

Section 121: The provinces reserve to themselves all the powers not delegated to the Federal Government by this Constitution, as well as those powers expressly reserved to themselves by special pacts at the time of their incorporation.

Section 124: last paragraph *in fine*: The provinces have the original dominion over the natural resources existing in their territory.

13

The South African Constitution – Standards of Environmental Protection

Nathan J. Cooper

13.1 INTRODUCTION

Focusing on South Africa, this chapter considers the ways in which constitutionally enshrined rights to a healthy environment and to water have been applied and adjudicated upon. In so doing, the chapter interrogates the degree to which precise standards relating to the procedural and substantive aspects of these rights have been acknowledged by the courts, through legislation, and elsewhere. Inclusion of an environment right and a right to water within domestic constitutions is rare. Furthermore, sufficient clean water is an essential component of a healthy environment. Therefore, both of these rights are considered together here.

In this chapter, standards of environmental protection are understood as being capable of expression in one or more of the following ways. First, standards can be quantitative, meaning that they measure some aspect of the relevant right. For instance, a right to fifty litres of water per person per day would represent a quantitative standard. Second, standards can be qualitative. For example, a right to the highest attainable standard of health, or a right to participation in cultural life,[1] both make claims around quality of life, while eschewing quantifiable measurement. Third, standards can be directional, which is to say that they set the direction of travel towards full realisation. This type of standard is most commonly associated with obligations to progressively realise a particular (quantitative or qualitative) right, as seen for instance in the right of access to adequate housing, in Section 26 of the South African Constitution, where the State is required 'to take reasonable legislative and other measures, within its available resources, to achieve the progressive realisation of the right'.[2]

However, some care must be taken with this typology. Standards relating to the *quality* of air or water for example would still constitute quantitative standards if

[1] See Articles 12 and 15 of the International Covenant on Economic, Social and Cultural Rights (adopted 16 Dec 1966, entered into force 3 January 1976) 993 UNTS 3 (ICESCR).

[2] Constitution of the Republic of South Africa, 10 December 1996; see also ICESCR ibid art 2.

expressed in terms of measurement. Consequently, it is not intended to be rigidly imposed. It can be argued that all three types of standard are present in relation to the environmental right, and the right to water. These are discernible in both legislation and in the interpretation of courts, within several cases.

The 1996 Constitution of the Republic of South Africa contains a substantive environmental right. Section 24 of the Constitution provides that everyone has the right to a healthy environment, and also the right to have the environment protected from pollution and ecological degradation, which promotes conservation and secures ecologically sustainable development.[3] For brevity, this is referred to throughout as the 'environmental right'. Section 27 provides that everyone has a right of access to sufficient water.[4] This is referred to as the 'right to water', except where specific consideration is needed regarding access and sufficiency. Twenty years after adopting these rights, considerable progress has been made in improving people's access to water, and in environmental protection. But serious challenges remain before the provisions of both rights can be consistently and universally enjoyed.

It is argued that while standards relevant to both rights do exist, they suffer variously from a lack of precision and from an absence of adequate contextualisation to ensure that they are calibrated to fulfil the rights which they relate to. Moreover, conceiving of the environmental right and the right to water (and of socioeconomic rights in general) as individual rights risks missing the communal/community dimensions inherent in securing a healthy environment, including access to sufficient water.

13.2 THE LAW: CONSTITUTIONAL AND LEGISLATIVE PROVISIONS ON THE ENVIRONMENTAL RIGHT AND THE RIGHT TO WATER

Chapter 2 of the Constitution, the Bill of Rights, contains a wide array of rights loosely grouped as civil and political rights (*inter alia* equality[5], freedom[6], dignity[7]), socioeconomic rights (health, food, water[8], education[9]) and group rights (cultural, religious and linguistic communities[10]), to use a standard typography.[11] Both the environmental right and the right to water can be understood to be socioeconomic rights (albeit that the environmental right also requires measures to prevent

[3] s 24.
[4] s 27(1).
[5] s 9.
[6] ss 12, 15, 16, 21.
[7] s 10.
[8] s 27.
[9] s 29.
[10] s 31.
[11] Karel Vasak, 'Human Rights: A Thirty-Year Struggle: the Sustained Efforts to give Force of law to the Universal Declaration of Human Rights' *UNESCO Courier* 30:11, Paris: United Nations Education, Scientific and Cultural Organization, November 1977.

pollution and ecological degradation, and to promote conservation and ecologically sustainable development).[12] The inclusion of such socioeconomic rights in the Constitution and the extent of their protection have been matters of some controversy.[13] The State is required to 'respect, protect, promote and fulfill' each of the rights in the Bill of Rights[14]. Yet the socioeconomic rights enshrined in the Constitution are qualified.[15] The environmental right and the right to water are to be realised through 'reasonable legislative and other measures'.[16] Furthermore, the environmental right does not protect against the promotion of 'justifiable economic and social development',[17] while the right to water is placed within the limits of the available resources of the State, to achieve progressive (not immediate) realisation.[18] All rights may be limited only in terms of law of general application, to the extent that the limitation is reasonable and justifiable in an open and democratic society based on human dignity, equality and freedom.[19]

Additionally – and crucially, regarding the interpretation of the rights at issue here – Section 39 of the Constitution (the constitutional interpretation clause) requires that a court, tribunal or forum must consider international law and may consider foreign law when interpreting any legislation and when developing the common law and customary law. This provision means that the scope of, and discourse around, an internationally acknowledged human right to water is particularly pertinent to the domestic constitutional position in South Africa, as is consideration of internationally acknowledged principles pertaining to entitlements to a healthy environment.[20]

In order to provide some context for the right of access to water, a brief overview of the General Household Survey (2016)[21], and the South African Human Rights Commission Report (2016)[22] gives the most recent picture of the nation's access to water for domestic use.

12 Const. South Africa (n 2) s 24(b)(i-iii).

13 See the first and second Constitution Certification judgments in relation to the inclusion and justiciability of socioeconomic rights: re Certification of the Constitution of the Republic of South Africa 1996 (4) SA 744 (CC); Certification of the Constitution of the Republic of South Africa, 1996 (CCT 23/96) [1996] ZACC 26.

14 Const. South Africa (n 2) s 7.

15 s 36.

16 s 24(b), s 27(2).

17 s 24(b)(iii).

18 s 27.

19 s 36.

20 United Nations Conference on Environment and Development, 'Rio Declaration on Environment and Development' (3–14 June 1992) UN Doc A/CONF.151/26 (Vol I) Agenda 21, Chapter 1; National Environmental Management Act 107 of 1998, s 25 (NEMA).

21 'STATS SA' (*Statistics South Africa*) <http://cs2016.statssa.gov.za> accessed 21 March 2018.

22 'Report to access sufficient water and decent sanitation in South Africa: 2014' (*South African Human Rights Commission*) <www.sahrc.org.za/home/21/files/FINAL%204th%20Proof%204%20March%20-%20Water%20%20Sanitation%20low%20res%20(2).pdf> accessed 21 March 2018.

The percentage of households in the Eastern Cape with access to water decreased from 78.5% in 2014 to 74.9% in 2015, making it the province in which households had the poorest access to water in 2015.[23] Access in other provinces in 2015 was as follows: KwaZulu-Natal 84.2%, Mpumalanga 85.5%; Western Cape 99.2%; Free State 96.1%; Gauteng 97.7%; Northern Cape 96.5% and North West 86.1%. Average access nationally in 2015 was approximately 90%. An estimated 45.8% of households had access to piped water in their dwellings in 2014. A further 27% accessed water on site, while 14% relied on communal taps and 2.7% relied on neighbours' taps.[24] With a total population of 52,980,000 in 2015[25] this means that 5,298,000 people lacked access to on-site or off-site piped or tap water in 2015.[26] Of those who received piped water from a municipality, almost 25% experienced interruptions to their piped water supply at least once a month.[27]

The main legislation through which the environmental right and the right to water are promulgated is now briefly considered.

13.2.1 *The Environmental Right*

Section 24 of the South African Constitution provides that:

> Everyone has the right – (a) to an environment that is not harmful to their health or well-being; and (b) to have the environment protected, for the benefit of present and future generations, through reasonable legislative and other measures that – (i) prevent pollution and ecological degradation (ii) promote conservation; and (iii) secure ecologically sustainable development and use of natural resources while promoting justifiable economic and social development.

As such, the right requires further clarification at this point. The definition of 'environment' is broad, encompassing physical, chemical, aesthetic and cultural facets that influence human health and well-being.[28] This in turn infers a broad definition of health – as including physical and psychological integrity[29] – and well-being, which Kotze and du Plessis interpret to mean 'welfare', and as such is intended to cover 'environmental interests which do not necessarily have health implications'.[30]

23 'All percentages from the General Household Survey 2016' (*Statistics South Africa*, 2015) <www.statssa.gov.za/publications/P0318/P03182014.pdf> accessed 28 July 2017 (GHS 2016).
24 ibid.
25 ibid.
26 Author's own calculation based on figure for total population of South Africa in 2016. Note: The total population for 2016 is reported as 55.6 million people. See: 'STATS SA' (*Statistics South Africa*) <http://cs2016.statssa.gov.za> accessed 28 July 2017.
27 GHS 2016 (n 23) 24.4 per cent.
28 *See* NEMA (n 20) s 1(xi).
29 Loretta A Feris and D Tladi, 'Environmental Rights' in Danie Brand and Christof Heyns (eds), *Socio-Economic Rights in South Africa* (Pretoria University Press 2005) 249–66.
30 Louis J Kotze and Anel du Plessis, 'Some Brief Observations on Fifteen Years of Environmental Rights Jurisprudence in South Africa' (2010) 3 (1) Journal of Court Innovation 158, 166.

The environmental right also lists various positive obligations on the part of the State. Reasonable legislative and other measures are required to prevent pollution and ecological degradation, promote conservation and secure ecologically sustainable development and use of natural resources.[31] However, the definition and scope of these obligations – and therefore the degree to which the environmental right incorporates environmental *standards* – is not clear from looking at the Constitution alone. For example, what would constitute reasonable legislative and other measures to prevent pollution, in a diverse polity, simultaneously blighted by unremitting poverty and gifted with huge (mineral and private capital) wealth? Indeed, recourse to the maxim of reasonableness, and the challenges that this brings, is also considered in Section 13.3 in relation to the right to water. In pursuit of greater clarity, consideration will be given first to the relevant legislation, and then to the efforts of the courts (to greater or lesser degrees) to interpret the appropriate scope of the environmental right.

The National Environment Management Act 107 of 1998 (NEMA) is the principal environmental framework law in South African domestic law, regulating all actions, both public and private, which may affect the environment. Given such broad scope, it is clear that not only does NEMA operationalise the environment right in Section 24 of the Constitution, but also that it extends beyond this, to establish generic environmental management principles, institutions and governance mechanisms.[32] Of particular importance to any enquiry into the ability of constitutional provisions (including the environment right, and the right to water) to effect positive change are the requirements of *locus standi*. These delimit which classes of person or group may approach the courts regarding any breach, or threatened breach, of relevant constitutional rights. While the *locus standi* provisions in the South African Constitution are widely regarded to be generous,[33] Section 32 of NEMA expands them further by providing that any person or group of persons may seek appropriate relief in respect of any breach or threatened breach of any provision of the Act, or of any other statutory provision concerned with the protection of the environment or the use of natural resources, *in the interests of the environment*, as well as where a person or group of person's own interests are affected.

Therefore, Section 32(e) is worthy of particular note. While Chapter 1 of NEMA clearly states that 'Environmental Management must place people and their needs at the forefront of its concerns',[34] the above explicit acknowledgement that anyone can seek relief in the interest of protecting the environment makes provision for remedies that transcend solely anthropocentric concerns. Indeed, with reference to

[31] Const. South Africa (n 2) s 24.

[32] See NEMA (n 20) chapters 1, 2 and 3 respectively.

[33] Loretta A Feris, 'Environmental Rights & Locus Standi' in Alexander Paterson and Louis J Kotze (eds), *Environmental Compliance and Enforcement in South Africa: Legal Perspectives* (1st edn, Juta Law 2009).

[34] NEMA (n 20) s 2(2).

the typology of standards already set out, Section 32(e) creates a qualitative standard of access to justice in the interests of the environment. Such an innovative and expansive conferral of legal standing, to support environmental protection, can be seen as a forerunner to more recent innovations, most notably in New Zealand and India, where, respectively, the Whanganui River and the Ganges and Yamuna Rivers now enjoy legal standing in their own right.[35]

13.2.2 *The Right to Water*

Section 27 of the South African Constitution provides for a right of access to sufficient water as follows:

> Section 27(1): Everyone has the right to have access to – (a) health care services, including reproductive health care; (b) *sufficient* food and *water*; (c) social security, including, if they are unable to support themselves and their dependents, appropriate social assistance. (2) The state must take reasonable legislative and other measures, within its available resources, to achieve the progressive realisation of each of these rights. (emphasis added)

As such, the right requires a definition of both 'sufficiency' and 'access'. Neither terms are defined in the Constitution, but sufficient water has been defined in the literature variously as between 20 and 50 litres per day (lpd)[36] and has received legislative definition as 25 lpd (as discussed further below).[37] By eschewing a minimum quantum, the right to water (as framed within the Constitution) represents a qualitative standard for access to water, not a quantitative one (while its qualification of progressive realisation also represents a directional standard, ultimately – but not yet – towards universal access to sufficient water). While the Water Service Regulations do require a specific quantum (25 lpd),[38] arguably this is too small to realise the qualitative standard of sufficiency, and as such, has been the focus of litigation, considered below.

Sufficiency has been described as being dependent on three factors: accessibility, adequate quality and adequate quantity.[39] These factors encompass the five components of the human right to water as interpreted by the Committee on Economic, Social and Cultural Rights, namely that water must be sufficient, safe, acceptable, physically accessible and affordable.[40]

35 See Chapter 16 in this volume relating to the rights of nature by Craig Kaufmann and Linda Sheehan.

36 See Peter H Gleick, 'Basic Water Requirements for Human Activities: Meeting Basic Needs' (1996) 21 (2) Water International 83, 88; Peter H Gleick 'The Human Right to Water' (1998) 1 Water Policy 496.

37 Water Services Act 1997, Water Services Regulations, Regulation 3(b) in GN R 509, Government Gazette of 8 June 2001.

38 ibid.

39 John Scanlon et al. 'Water as a Human Right?' (2004) 51 IUCN Environmental Policy and Law Paper 28.

40 United Nations Committee on Economic, Social and Cultural Rights, 'General Comment 15, The right to water' (Twenty-ninth session 2003) UN Doc E/C.12/2002/11 (2002), reprinted in 'Compilation of General Comments and General Recommendations Adopted by Human Rights

13.2.2.1 The Water Services Act 1997

Key legislation has been promulgated in order to give effect to the right of access to sufficient water. The Water Services Act 108 of 1997 (WSA) is the principal legislative mechanism to actualise the obligations of the State. Section 3 of the WSA provides that:

(1) Everyone has a right of access to basic water supply and basic sanitation.
(2) Every water services institution must take reasonable measures to realize these rights.
(3) Every water services authority must, in its water services development plan, provide for measures to realize these rights.[41]

The WSA aims to provide *inter alia* 'the right of access to basic water supply and the right to basic sanitation necessary to secure sufficient water and an environment not harmful to human health or well-being'.[42] The WSA further addresses the social and ecological purposes of water, respectively, setting 'national standards and norms and standards for tariffs in respect of water services' and aiming 'to promote effective water resource management and conservation'.[43] Basic water supply is defined in the WSA as 'the prescribed minimum standard of water supply services necessary for the reliable supply of a sufficient quantity and quality of water to households including informal households, to support life and personal hygiene'.[44] As mentioned above, the WSA sets the minimum quantity for basic water supply as 25 litres of potable water per person per day (25 lpd), or 6 kilolitres per household per month, accessible within 200 metres. This minimum quota is to be provided free of charge and is designated as Free Basic Water (FBW).[45]

Water services authorities, including municipalities, are charged with a duty 'to consumers or potential consumers in its area of jurisdiction to progressively ensure efficient, affordable, economical and sustainable access to water services'.[46] But there are no explicit provisions within the WSA on how access is to be achieved.

Treaty Bodies' UN Doc. HRI/GEN/1/Rev.6 at 105 (2003), hereafter General Comment 15; See Chapters 2 and 7 in this volume by Sumudu Atapattu and Owen McIntyre, respectively.

41 Not only does s 3 of WSA reiterate the Constitutional right of access to sufficient water, it expands it to include basic sanitation. The approach of including the right to basic sanitation within the right of access to sufficient water was upheld by the South African High Court in *Manqele v Durban Transitional Metropolitan Council* (2002) (6) SA 423 (D&CLD).

42 WSA s 2(a).

43 WSA ss 2(b) and 2(j).

44 WSA s 1.

45 'Free Basic Water Programme 2001' (*Department: Water Affairs and Forestry*): <www.dwaf.gov.za/dir_ws/fbw/> accessed 21 March 2018.

46 WSA s 11(1).

13.2.2.2 The National Water Act 1998

The National Water Act 36 of 1998 (NWA) specifically aims to address the past racial and gender discrimination endured under apartheid in relation to water.[47] It is therefore crucial in implementing the constitutional right to water, as well as Section 24 of the Constitution's provision of a right to a healthy environment. The chief aim of the NWA is the protection of South Africa's water resources, and as such the NWA adds ecological context of the right to water to the primarily social aspects stressed in the WSA, and in so doing makes a conceptual link between the environmental right (Section 24) and the right to water.[48] Section 2 states the purpose of the NWA 'to ensure that the nation's water resources are protected, used, developed, conserved, managed and controlled', taking into account, amongst others, the basic human needs of present and future generations, equitable water access, social and economic development, public interest, growing demand for water, ecosystems and biological diversity, as well as international obligations.[49] This echoes the Brundtland Commission's emphasis on intergenerational and intra-generational equity as intrinsic to the definition of sustainable development.[50] Section 2 can therefore be understood as articulating a vision for *sustainable*[51] use of the country's water resources.

The confluence of the WSA and NWA illustrates the importance of considering the socioeconomic right to water within an environmental context that recognises and responds to competing claims for scarce water resources (including domestic, industrial, human, non-human, present and future). Indeed, the NWA has been described as 'the ecological *grundnorm* to facilitate access to water',[52] setting the parameters within which sufficient water can be realised. However, the Constitution makes no mention of prioritising either the right of access to sufficient water above the 'environment right' or vice versa. Similarly, the NWA receives no explicit authority above that of the WSA. Therefore, there is no legislative justification for limiting the social aspect of the right to water within the constraints of the NWA without acknowledging a corresponding need to view ecological priorities in light of the Constitutional obligation to provide access to sufficient water to every citizen. The differing emphases of these two Acts should not encourage incompatible agendas regarding water resources and water services. The WSA and the NWA must be read in conjunction, with the aim of facilitating access to sufficient water

47 NWA s 2(c). See also Nicolas Faysee, 'Challenges for Fruitful Participation of Smallholders in Large-Scale Water Resource Management Organisations: Selected Case Studies in South Africa' (2004) 43 (1) Agrekon 52–73.

48 Louis Kotze, 'Access to Water in South Africa: Constitutional Perspectives from a Developing Country' (2009) 1 Ymparistojuridiikka, 76.

49 NWA s 2.

50 'The Brundtland Report', World Commission on Environment and Development (WCED), *Our Common Future* (Oxford University Press 1987) 43.

51 See s 2(d) NWA.

52 Kotze (n 48) 79.

for all within the context of present and future ecological sustainability[53]. The imperative of providing sufficient water to citizens now, provides a pragmatic framework within which ecological aspects of *inter alia* sustainability, conservation and biological diversity must be addressed[54]. Regarding standards, however, it is not entirely clear whether and how a quantitative standard in the WSA, such as 25 lpd Free Basic Water, will complement (compete with) qualitative or directional standards such as protecting aquatic and associated ecosystems and their biological diversity, or promoting equitable access to water, within this pragmatic framework.[55]

At a more practical level, the NWA also defines types of water use,[56] provides for a hierarchy of water management institutions, and sets out the responsibility of the Department of Water Affairs (DWA) (formerly the Department for Water Affairs and Forestry) for all aspects of the Act's implementation. Provision is made to establish Catchment Management Agencies (CMAs) to develop strategic plans to meet the NWA objectives in each Water Management Area (WMA).[57] However, it must be noted that since beginning operations, there have been significant concerns raised about the creation, functioning and competence of CMAs, which must be addressed if NWA objectives are to be reliably met.[58] It took until 2008 – a decade from the passing of the NWA – to establish any CMAs, and to date only two CMAs are functioning (Inkomati-Usuthu and Breede-Gouritz).[59] This emphasises the often under-acknowledged, but essential requirement of sound administrative systems if standards – both quantitative and qualitative – are to be met.

Together, the constitutional right of access to sufficient water and its main promulgating legislation (WSA and NWA) have framed the goal of the African National Congress (ANC)[60] to realise access to sufficient water as an individual right. This right should be progressively realised, according to the State's available resources and subject to certain qualifications. Measures to ensure economic imperatives, social development and environmental protection are included in these instruments and recourse to restitution is available where individual rights are violated unreasonably. Ultimately, lack of fulfilment of the right to water, and of socioeconomic rights generally, may be pursued through litigation, some of which will be considered below.

53 ibid.

54 NWA s 2.

55 ibid.

56 NWA s 21.

57 Inkomati-Usuthu CMA <www.inkomaticma.co.za> accessed 21 March 2018.

58 Barbara Schreiner and Barbara van Koppen, 'Catchment Management Agencies for Poverty Eradication in South Africa' (2002) 27 (11–22) Journal of the Physics and Chemistry of the Earth 969, 972.

59 I Gouws, 'The Tragedy of the Water Commons: The Case of the Lower Orange Water Management Area' (2008) 4(1) Journal for Trans-Disciplinary Research in Southern Africa 251, 251.

60 See 'Introduction to the Reconstruction and Development Program' (*African National Congress*) <http://anc.org.za/content/reconstruction-and-development-programme-introduction-rdp> accessed 21 March 2018.

13.3 DEVELOPMENT OF STANDARDS

In this section it is argued that progress around the development of standards of socioeconomic and/or environmental protection can be discerned by focusing on the way in which the courts have adjudicated upon the environmental right, and the right to water.

The first case considered focuses specifically on the right of access to sufficient water. Because of this, the following analysis concentrates not only on the Constitutional Court's interpretation of socioeconomic rights, and specifically the right of access to sufficient water, but also on the interpretation provided by the High Court and the Supreme Court of Appeal. Together, the judgments in this case reveal the scope and limitations of using the right to water to achieve what could be articulated as a crucial standard of environmental protection: access to sufficient water for everyone in South Africa. Of particular importance here is the rejection by the Constitutional Court of the subordinate courts' adoption (or acceptance) of a quantitative standard for sufficient water, in favour of a qualitative one.

13.3.1 Mazibuko

The opening paragraphs of *Mazibuko and Others v City of Johannesburg and Others* (2010)[61] before the Constitutional Court provide an apposite summary of the context for this case:

> Although rain falls everywhere, access to water has long been grossly unequal. This inequality is evident in South Africa. While piped water is plentifully available to mines, industries, some large farms and wealthy families, millions of people, especially women, spend hours laboriously collecting their daily supply of water from streams, pools and distant taps . . . despite the significant improvement in the first fifteen years of democratic government, deep inequality remains and for many the task of obtaining sufficient water for their families remains a tiring daily burden. The achievement of equality, one of the founding values of our Constitution, will not be accomplished while water is abundantly available to the wealthy, but not to the poor.[62]

Mazibuko was first heard in the Witswaterand High Court and was brought by a group of residents from the Phiri area of Soweto, near Johannesburg.[63] It challenged the legality of installing prepayment water meters in light of the constitutional right to sufficient water. Installation was undertaken by the City of Johannesburg and its water company, Johannesburg Water, in response to acute water losses in Soweto as a result of corroded pipes, an inaccurate tariff system (that

61 (3) BCLR 239 (CC).
62 ibid [2].
63 *Mazibuko and Others v City of Johannesburg and others* (Centre on Housing Rights & Evictions as amicus curiae) [2008] JOL 21829 (W), hereafter *Mazibuko* (W).

meant more water was used than was predicted to be necessary) and a 'culture of non-payment' for water services that had 'arisen originally as part of the resistance to apartheid local government'.[64]

The case examined the obligations of the City of Johannesburg and Johannesburg Water regarding access to water and the supply of free water for residents who cannot afford to pay. It was contended that since prepayment water meters, by design, require users to pay for water in advance, access to sufficient water is curtailed if users cannot afford to prepay. Such a situation was commonplace for Phiri residents and was raised as incompatible with the constitutional right of access to sufficient water. The WSA's quantification of sufficient water as a minimum standard of 25 lpd was directly challenged in this case on the basis that what is a sufficient quantity of water depends on the requirements of users in particular social circumstances. For instance, people using waterborne sanitation require a greater volume of water to support life and personal hygiene than those using pit latrines.[65] The decision of the High Court put great emphasis on the need to redress past injustices (as a result of apartheid policies) and the dire social and material state of many Phiri residents, described as 'poor, uneducated, unemployed and ravaged by HIV/AIDS'.[66]

In determining the applicants' grounds, the High Court looked to General Comment Number 15 of the United Nations Committee on Economic, Social and Cultural Rights.[67] Applying the General Comment, the court's view was that 'the State is under an obligation to provide the poor with the necessary water and water facilities on a non-discriminatory basis'.[68]

Moreover, the progressive realisation of the constitutional right of access to sufficient water meant that:

> Retrogressive measures taken by the state are prohibited. If such retrogressive measures are taken, the onus is on the state to prove that such retrogressive measures are justified with reference to the totality of the rights provided for in the Covenant[69]. The state is obliged to respect, protect and fulfil the right to water.[70]

64 *Mazibuko and others v City of Johannesburg and others* [2009] JOL 24351 (CC). Hereafter *Mazibuko* (CC) [166].

65 This is particularly pertinent to the interpretation of sufficient water in the Constitution since s 27 links food and water: 'Everyone has the right to have access to- (b) sufficient food and water.' Also, since sanitation is not listed in s 27 of the Constitution, but is recognised as a right in the Water Services Act (s 3(1)), the volume of water that is sufficient must depend on the type of sanitation system being used.

66 *Mazibuko* (W) (n 63) [5].

67 ibid 106. Under s 39(1)(b), relevant international law must be considered by the court. Therefore, the ICESCR had to be considered here. General Comment 15 is an authoritative but non-binding interpretation of the scope of the ICESCR.

68 *Mazibuko* (W) (n 63) [36].

69 ICESCR (n 1).

70 *Mazibuko* (W) (n 63) [37].

The installation of prepayment meters was held to be just such a retrogressive step, preventing residents from access to sufficient water that they had previously enjoyed (before the prepayment meters, Phiri residents had access to a constant supply of water – despite many accruing arrears as a result).[71] The retrogressive step was taken without adequate justification.

It was held that, given the particular needs of the Phiri community (including the need to use waterborne sewerage), a volume of 50 lpd would be a more appropriate quantification of sufficient water than the statutory 25 lpd limit. Satisfied that the respondent could provide this increased amount 'without restraining its capacity on water and its financial resources'[72]the High Court decided wholly in the applicants' favour.

The City of Johannesburg and Johannesburg Water appealed to the South African Supreme Court of Appeal in February 2009.[73] The quantity amounting to sufficient water for Phiri residents was reduced on appeal to 42 lpd. But the High Court's approach was otherwise upheld, and the City of Johannesburg and Johannesburg Water were directed to formulate a revised water policy accordingly.[74]

Mazibuko in the High Court and Supreme Court of Appeal was heralded as an important milestone in socioeconomic jurisprudence in South Africa[75]. It showed the courts' willingness to push the legislature towards concrete manifestations of constitutional rights and not to allow the 'progressive realization' of these rights to result in unconstitutional policies. The impetus to promote and fulfil the right of access to sufficient water was clearly discernible (particularly in Tsoka J's High Court judgment[76]) in the acceptance of the need for sufficient water to be a quantity that promotes dignity and goes beyond the minimum of Free Basic Water already set.[77] The potential implications of *Mazibuko* for people living in similar situations to the Phiri residents were significant. Both decisions demonstrated the courts' engagement with polycentric matters in order to help realise socioeconomic constitutional rights more quickly and more explicitly than would otherwise be the case. But the environmental implications of *Mazibuko* may have been significant too,

71 *Mazibuko* (W) (n 63) Note: Prior to installation of prepayment meters and the associated improvements made to water pipes as part of the City's water services improvement project in Soweto, 'Operation Gcin'amanzi', water services were poor, but the volume of water available was unlimited (except when affected by intermittent technical problems).

72 *Mazibuko* (W) (n 63) [181].

73 *City of Johannesburg & others v Mazibuko & Others (Centre on Housing Rights & Evictions as amicus curiae)* [2009] JOL 23337 (SCA), hereafter *Mazibuko* (SCA).

74 ibid, Summary. Note: Because the SCA found that 42 lpd was the quantity of sufficient water, not 50 lpd as decided by the High Court, the appeal was upheld.

75 Linda Jansen van Rensberg 'The Right of Access to Adequate Water: Discussion of Mazibuko v The City of Johannesburg Case No 13865/06' (2008) 3 Stellenbosch Law Review 434.

76 See generally *Mazibuko* (W).

77 *Mazibuko* (W) (n 63) [1].

potentially doubling the demand for water from a significant portion of the population in a 'water-stressed' country.[78]

However, in September 2009 the Phiri residents appealed to the Constitutional Court (unhappy with the Supreme Court of Appeal's order to reduce the amount of water deemed to be sufficient from 50 to 42 lpd). This was the first time the Constitutional Court had considered the proper interpretation of the right of access to sufficient water. The orders made by the High Court and Supreme Court of Appeal, respectively, were set aside.

The Constitutional Court held that the City of Johannesburg's Free Basic Water policy was not in conflict with Section 27 of the Constitution or Section 11 of the Water Services Act,[79] and the installation of prepaid water meters was lawful. The Court was satisfied that while the Free Basic Water Policy was flawed, it was consistent with the constitutional right of access to sufficient water.[80] This was particularly so since the City of Johannesburg had continually amended its Free Basic Water Policy during the course of the litigation.[81] Consequently, the applicants' appeal was dismissed, and the installation of prepaid water meters in Phiri was affirmed as compatible with Section 27 of the Constitution.[82]

Following *Government of the Republic of South Africa* v. *Grootboom & Others*[83] the principle of reasonableness was applied to the Constitutional Court's judgment in *Mazibuko* as follows: First, the nature of the right of access to sufficient water was accepted as being one of progressive realization. Second, the actions of the respondents (namely the City of Johannesburg, and Johannesburg Water) in constantly reviewing their Free Basic Water Policy, and by providing on occasion for additional free water allowance as well as relief from other municipal charges, together represent reasonable actions in relation to the constitutional right to water, notwithstanding the respondents' continuing obligation towards progressive realization.[84] The clear implication here is that while the actions and policy of the respondents were deemed reasonable at the time of the judgment, they must not be allowed to solidify into an established standard. Rather, the impetus of progressive realization must engender continual revision.[85]

This application of reasonableness directly contrasts with the alternative, quantitative approach to adjudicating on socioeconomic rights, followed by the lower

78 Michael Kidd, Environmental Law (Juta & Co. Ltd 2008) 64.

79 Water Services Act 1997 (108 of 1997), the duty on the part of the Water Services Authorities to provide access to water services is clearly spelled out in s 11(1).

80 *Mazibuko* (CC) (n 61) [163].

81 ibid.

82 *Mazibuko* (CC) (n 61) [169].

83 2001 (1) SA 46 (CC) [7].

84 *Mazibuko* (CC) (n 61) [168]. See also Nathan Cooper 'After Mazibuko: Exploring the Responses of Communities Excluded from South Africa's Water Experiment' (2017) 61 (1) Journal of African Law 57, 70; David Bilchitz, 'Giving Socio-Economic Rights Teeth: The Minimum Core and Its Importance' (2002) 119 South African Law Journal 489.

85 *Mazibuko* (CC) (n 61) [163].

courts in *Mazibuko*: namely, establishing a minimum core obligation for the State to fulfil. Here, two types of standard appear to be at odds. A minimum core approach to the question of access to sufficient water represents a clear and measurable quantitative standard. By contrast, the reasonableness of measures to progressively realise the same right, subject to available resources, represents a directional standard, pointing the way towards eventual fulfilment. Establishing the minimum quantum of water to be deemed sufficient by reference to international standards and domestic, context-specific evidence would seem an appropriate approach to interpreting the constitutional right to water.[86] So it is important to note the reasons that the Constitutional Court raised to vindicate its continued, deliberate and explicit rejection of a minimum core approach, in favour of reasonableness.

First, a constitutional defence can be made for the Court's approach here. It reflects an impetus to maintain a clear separation of powers and to refrain from encroaching on matters of resource allocation, under the purview of the legislature and executive. Arguably such a 'restrained and focused role for the courts'[87] may help achieve 'appropriate constitutional balance'[88] by avoiding direct incursion into budgetary and policy priorities. This approach to the issue of separation of powers can be contrasted with certain other jurisdictions where the judiciary has been able to sustain more interventionist approaches.[89]

Second, the argument was made that quantifying a minimum core requirement here would detract from the duty imposed on the government to continually review its policies to ensure the progressive realization of the right.[90] Indeed, a situation could be envisaged where a defined minimum quantum of water may impede rights holders from receiving more than this quantum in keeping with the provider's capacity to supply. In order to avoid this, the Court reiterates that it is for government to set the target it wishes to achieve, and for the Courts to submit such a target to the standard of reasonableness.[91]

Third, it was asserted that a jurisprudence of reasonableness encourages a continuous contestation for the content of socioeconomic rights, enabling 'citizens to hold government accountable not only through the ballot box but also, in a different way, through litigation':[92] citizens and the courts combining in a dynamic, collaborative endeavour to negotiate what content the right (to water in this case) should have at any one point in time. Indeed, the product of such litigation, according to O'Regan J, is to foster 'a form of participative democracy'.[93]

86 *Mazibuko* (W) (n 63) [128], [172].
87 *Minister of Health and Others v Treatment Action Campaign and Others* [2002] ZACC 15; 2002 (5) SA 721 (CC); 2002 (10) BCLR 1033 (CC) (hereafter *Treatment Action Campaign No. 2*) [38].
88 *Treatment Action Campaign No. 2* [38].
89 See, for example, Chapter 10 by G N Gill in this volume relating to the Indian courts.
90 *Mazibuko* (CC) (n 61) [67].
91 ibid [70].
92 ibid [71].
93 ibid [160].

The clear implication here is that if the Court instead set an ultimate standard for such rights, the accountability of government would be affected, and citizens' role in the democratic process would be diminished. To this end, the Constitutional Court maintained that litigation regarding the positive obligations of socioeconomic rights was an important element of government accountability, concomitant with the founding provisions of the Constitution, 'to ensure accountability, responsiveness and openness'.[94]

The reasons set forth by the Constitutional Court in *Mazibuko* can be summarised as delivering a constitutionally deferent, pragmatic and conditional judgment that the actions of the water service providers regarding the claimant's right to water had been reasonable.[95] Scholarly disagreement persists around the judgment[96] and its potential consequences for effective water governance. The explicit restatement of reasonableness as the appropriate approach to socioeconomic rights litigation is perhaps understandable in a country with limited resources and manifold social and economic problems, although deeper criticism of the judgment is beyond the scope of this chapter. Nevertheless, the case emphasises the tension at the heart of the justiciability of socioeconomic rights visible in the preceding cases: the pragmatism of progressive realization versus the necessity of immediate fulfilment. To those Phiri residents now denied a quantum of water commensurate with their needs, and necessary for their dignity, their right to water rings hollow.

While the interpretative approach of the Court can be acknowledged for its consistency with preceding judgments and its scrupulous adherence to separation of powers sensibilities, it nevertheless represents an impotent constitutional and judicial response to such a crucial and basic need.[97] It must also raise questions about the degree to which the right to water can be said to have generated standards of environmental and/or socioeconomic protection.

The social repercussions of insufficient water for the residents of Phiri (as well as for others in similar situations) are obvious. But there are doubtless economic and environmental consequences too. It is anticipated that the impact of climate change

[94] Const. South Africa (n 2) s 1(d).

[95] See Chapter 14 by D Marrani and S J Turner in this volume for a discussion of the role of the Constitutional Council in France regarding legislation which is inconsistent with the country's constitutional environmental provisions.

[96] See variously Louis J Kotze, 'Phiri, the Plight of the Poor and the Perils of Climate Change: Time to Rethink Environmental and Socio-Economic Rights in South Africa?' (2010) 1 (2) Journal of Human Rights and the Environment 135–60; Jackie Dugard, 'Can Human Rights Transcend the Commercialization of Water in South Africa? Soweto's Legal Fight for an Equitable Water Policy' (2010) Review of Radical Political Economics 1–20; Linda Jansen van Rensburg, 'The Right of Access to Adequate Water [Discussion of Mazibuko v the City of Johannesburg Case no 13865/06]' (2008) 3 Stellenbosch Law Review 415–35; Patrick Bond and Jackie Dugard, 'The Case of Johannesburg Water: What Really Happened at the Pre-paid "Parish Pump"' (2008) 12(1) Law Democracy and Development 1–28.

[97] See Chapter 10 by Gita N Gill in this volume for discussion of the Indian Judiciary's approach to similar questions.

on communities like Phiri will be serious, since the existing socioeconomic deprivations undermine the material and physical resilience necessary to effectively adapt. As the United Nations Intergovernmental Panel on Climate Change, Adaptation and Vulnerability working group explains:

> Poor communities are especially vulnerable, in particular those concentrated in high-risk areas. They tend to have more limited adaptive capacities and are more dependent on climate sensitive resources, such as local water and food supplies.[98]

Emphasising the social, economic and environmental consequences for people living with insufficient water reminds us that the environmental right and the right to water are inextricably linked. It also reflects the established model of sustainable development as pertaining to environmental, social and economic concerns together.[99]

Sustainable development, as a principle, is generally understood to contain elements of equitable use, including intergenerational equity, and sustainable use, which expressed together integrates economic, social and environmental considerations. As illustrated above, and emphasised by the explicit connection drawn between water and protection of biodiversity in the Johannesburg Declaration on Sustainable Development,[100] it is now broadly acknowledged that access to sufficient water must be achieved in ways that are ecologically sustainable.

Furthermore, the environmental right in Section 24 of the South African Constitution makes an explicit requirement to 'secure ecologically sustainable development', while also referring to the requirement, well recognised in relation to sustainable development, that present *and* future generations are to benefit from the right. In short, the right to water and the environmental right should go hand in hand with sustainable development.

As the following case of *BP Southern Africa* makes clear, sustainable development has become widely regarded as 'the fundamental building block' in determining important environmental legal norms in the country.

Triangulating access to water within social, economic and environmental considerations offers a distinctive approach to water governance; one that could be conceived of as representing a standard of environmental protection, with inevitable socioeconomic interlinkages. But the lack of clarity regarding each of the elements of sustainable development has led some to question how such distinctiveness may provide a substantive means by which to progress the reform agenda which

98 C Vogel and P Reid, Vulnerability, Adaptive Capacity, Coping and Adaptation: A Conceptual Framework in R E Schulze (ed), Climate Change and Water Resources in Southern Africa: Studies on Scenarios, Impacts, Vulnerabilities and Adaptation, WRC Report no 1430/1/05 (Water Research Commission 2005) 351–58.

99 World Summit on Sustainable Development, 'Plan of Implementation' (4 September 2002). Available at <www.un-documents.net/jburgpln.htm> accessed 21 March 2018.

100 'Johannesburg Declaration on Sustainable Development' 20 September 2002 UNGA A.Conf/199/20. Available at <www.un-documents.net/jburgdec.htm> accessed 21 March 2018.

surrounds it.[101] Without such substance, sustainable development risks being a hollow concept. Indeed, Fitzmaurice warns that 'the continuing reliance on clichéd and worn out definitions should be abandoned and the concept (or principle) of sustainable development must acquire a tangible and concrete content'.[102]

As an overarching goal of the international community and an increasingly recognised (if non-binding) principle of international law, sustainable development is likely to continue to feature in the rhetoric around operationalizing the right to water and the environmental right. However, as the brief consideration of the concept and application of sustainable development above suggests, too often aspirations towards sustainability are insufficiently developed or robust to be effective. Worst still, without a serious and sustained challenge to human behaviour targeted at preventing pollution and ecological degradation, reducing water consumption and generally 'treading more lightly' on the planet, sustainable development risks being an 'ideological palliative' that helps us 'rationalize our continuing encroachments upon the planet'.[103]

13.3.2 BP Southern Africa (Pty) Ltd *v.* MEC for Agriculture, Conservation and Land Affairs[104]

The case arose from a decision of the Gauteng Provincial Department of Agriculture, Conservation, Environment and Land Affairs (the 'Department'), to refuse an application by BP Southern Africa to build a new petrol/gas filling station. The reasons informing the Department's decision encompassed environmental concerns (including the potential for a filling station on the site to contaminate the water table through seepage), and socioeconomic concerns regarding the desirability of an additional filling station within three kilometres of two existing stations.[105]

The applicant argued that the Department's mandate was limited to environmental considerations. But, relying on the environmental right and the relevant sections of NEMA, the Department contended that their mandate extended across consideration of socioeconomic as well as environmental issues. Importantly here, in relation to identifying standards of environmental protection, the Court affirmed the Department's mandate and confirmed the necessity of including socioeconomic

101 Nathan Cooper and Duncan French, The Right to Water in South Africa: Constitutional Managerialism and a Call for Pluralism in Elena Blanco and Jona Razzaque (eds), *Natural Resources and the Green Economy: Redefining the Challenges for People, States and Corporations* (Martinus Nijhoff 2012) 111, 118.

102 Malgosia Fitzmaurice, *Contemporary Issues in International Environmental Law* (Edward Elgar 2009) 108.

103 Benjamin J Richardson, 'A Damp Squib: Environmental Law from a Human Evolutionary Perspective' (2011) 7 (3) Comparative Research in Law & Political Economy. Research Paper No. 8 31.

104 2004 (5) SA 124 (WLD).

105 ibid 8.

factors in interpreting the environmental right, and people's relationship with the environment. The application was dismissed. Furthermore, the case affirmed the importance of sustainable development (encompassing intergenerational equity and sustainable use of resources) as a guiding principle in constitutional jurisprudence:

> Pure economic principles will no longer determine, in an unbridled fashion, whether a development is acceptable. Development, which may be regarded as economically and financially sound, will, in future, be balanced by its environmental impact, taking coherent cognizance of the principle of intergenerational equity and sustainable use of resources in order to arrive at an integrated management of the environment, sustainable development and socio-economic concerns. By elevating the environment to a fundamental justiciable human right, South Africa has irreversibly embarked on a road, which will lead to the goal of attaining a protected environment by an integrated approach, which takes into consideration, *inter alia*, socio-economic concerns and principles.[106]

As described above, a constitutionally embedded commitment to sustainable development may represent a qualitative standard of environmental protection, capable of determining decisions that span socioeconomic and environmental issues, and thereby operationalizing the environmental right. However, as also noted above, failure to connect quantitative standards to substantive aspects of the environmental right, coupled with the more general observation that sustainable development lacks robust normativity, beyond the need to balance (or to take into account) economic, social, and environmental issue, suggests that sustainable development may be of limited practical use as a standard of environmental protection. In other words, without quantitative standards guiding how an appropriate balance may be struck, sustainable development risks lacking the necessary conceptual coherence to function as an effective (and predictable) standard of environmental protection.

One further brief illustration of the lack of interpretation around the substantive aspects of the environmental right – and therefore the limits of the standards of protection that the environmental right represents – can be found in the case of *HTF Developers (Pty) Ltd* v. *Minister of Environmental Affairs and Tourism and Others*.[107] Case facts will be omitted for the sake of brevity. But, the court's interpretation of the scope and application of Section 24(a) exemplifies the limitations of seeking to use constitutional rights as environmental standards without sufficient substantive definition.

In *HTF Developers*, the court offered some interpretation of Section 24(a) of the Constitution, which states that everyone has a right to an environment not harmful to their health or well-being. Here the court asserted that the term 'well-being' is

106 ibid paras B–D at 144.

107 2006 (5) SA 512 (T).

'manifestly incapable of precise definition',[108] before remarking that the same term 'is critically important in that it defines for the environmental authorities the constitutional objectives of their task'.[109] This tension between the need to define the contents of such a fundamental constitutional provision (in order to measure progress made towards its fulfilment), and the inconstant, permutable nature of the term, suggests that the capacity of the environmental right to provide clear standards of environmental protection is limited. Not only does the indeterminate content of 'well-being' hamper the promulgation of quantitative standards, but it may also undermine clarification of qualitative and/or directional standards. If 'well-being' is incapable of precise description, then claims to (progressively) realise well-being are weakened by the same imprecision of aspiration.[110]

But once again, a minimum core approach to the interpretation of this right offers a way to avoid such semantic pitfalls. Just as 'sufficient water' could be defined as a minimum quantum, determined with reference to international standards and context-specific evidence,[111] so too could the term 'well-being' receive a minimum core definition. This would constitute at least a minimum (quantitative) standard for environmental authorities to fulfil in pursuance of their constitutional objectives.

While it may be the case that defining 'well-being' is more complicated than defining 'sufficient water',[112] a minimum core definition has the benefit of setting a standard without laying claim to a conclusive definition. Moreover, such a minimum core could be revisited and 'ratcheted up' towards more expansive understandings of well-being in due course.

13.3.3 Earthlife Africa Johannesburg *v.* Minister of Environmental Affairs[113]

Most recently, and of particular importance to the task of identifying standards of environmental protection, is the case of *Earthlife Africa Johannesburg* v. *Minister of Environmental Affairs*.[114] Although here again, the dearth of substantive content to the environmental right limits the degree to which the jurisprudence around Section 24 can meaningfully be interpreted to incorporate environmental standards.

[108] ibid para 18.

[109] ibid.

[110] It should be noted that the rights in s 24 are to be met through reasonable legislative and other measures, but that there is no provision for 'progressive realisation' within the State's 'available resources' (as is the case in s 27). Therefore, in contrast to the right to water, the environmental right should be fulfilled immediately, rather than gradually. However, requiring measures taken to be *reasonable* does suggest that s 24 will also need to be realised progressively.

[111] See previous discussion in this chapter of *Mazibuko* at Section 13.3.1.

[112] Louis J Kotze and Anel du Plessis, 'Some Brief Observations on Fifteen Years of Environmental Rights Jurisprudence in South Africa' (2010) 3 (1) Journal of Court Innovation 158–76, 167.

[113] *Earthlife Africa Johannesburg v Minister of Environmental Affairs and Others* (65662/16) [2017] ZAGPPHC 58; [2017] 2 All SA 519 (GP) (8 March 2017).

[114] ibid.

This case concerned an application to construct a coal-fired power station in Limpopo Province, which was identified as a strategic infrastructure project, intended to address the significant energy challenges that the country faces. Section 24 of NEMA requires that such applications must obtain environmental authorization before they may commence. The Chief Director of the Department of Environmental Affairs is the competent authority to grant environmental authorization. Thabametsi Power Company was granted this in February 2015. The applicant, Earthlife Africa – a non-profit organization founded to mobilise civil society around environmental issues – appealed to the Minister of Environmental Affairs (first respondent) against the granting of the environmental authorization, arguing that a thorough environmental impact assessment (EIA), to include a climate change impact assessment, had not been undertaken before the authorization was granted (contrary to Section 24(1) NEMA). However, the Minister upheld the authorization, while also requiring Thabametsi to conduct a more extensive EIA as an additional condition.

Earthlife sought review of the decision to grant the environmental authorization and the appeal decision of the Minister, arguing that it was unlawful, irrational and unreasonable for the Chief Director and the Minister to grant the environmental authorization without the appropriate EIA in place.[115] The High Court accepted the applicant's contention that when interpreted in light of the environmental right, and of South Africa's international obligations to mitigate climate change, Section 24(1) of NEMA makes a climate change impact assessment a mandatory prerequisite before consideration of an environmental authorization. This is despite the absence of any provision within domestic legislation, regulations or policies which expressly requires a climate change impact assessment to be performed. The Court held that such an absence does not mean that there is no duty to consider climate change as a 'relevant factor'.[116] Furthermore, the Court's interpretation of the environmental right, and its application upon the decisions of the Chief Director and the Minister, explicitly connected sustainable development to intergenerational equity within the environmental right,[117] in order that measures to protect the environment are for the benefit of present *and* future generations. The Court's analysis clearly inferred that because 'climate change poses a significant risk to sustainable development in South Africa', and because the principle of sustainable development includes intergenerational equity, 'adequate consideration of climate change' must be made in order to evaluate 'short-term needs' against 'long-term consequences' (meaning concern for the present generation and for future generations).[118]

Not only does the case represent the first climate change litigation in South Africa, it goes some way towards giving the substance to the environmental right, so badly

115 Earthlife (n 113) [8]–[10].
116 ibid [88]. See also NEMA (n 20) s 24(1)(b).
117 NEMA (n 20) s 24(b).
118 Earthlife (n 113) [82].

needed if the environmental right is to provide robust standards of environmental protection.[119] But this judgment should also be seen primarily as clarifying procedural aspects of the environmental right. As such, the decision does infer a procedural standard: that climate change impact assessments, where applicable, are necessary.[120] But requiring a climate change impact assessment will not automatically create a standard for environmental protection that prevents pollution, promotes conservation and secures sustainable development for present and future generations. There remains a distinct absence of substantive obligations that, in the context of this case, could help determine whether or not construction of such a coal-fired power station should go ahead, even after the necessary procedures have been followed. In short, what is 'justifiable economic and social development'[121] in the face of pollution, ecological degradation and the manifold future consequences of climate change? Arguably a much clearer, more coherent, and perhaps ultimately braver interpretation of the substance of the environmental right is necessary if standards stemming from this right are going to provide effective environmental protection.

13.4 CONCLUSIONS

Standards for socioeconomic rights protection are evident in the constitutional right to water and from the legislation and litigation that has followed it. The right of access to sufficient water, pursued through reasonable measures, within the available resources of the State, clearly provides a directional standard which points to the ultimate destination (or qualitative standard) of universal access to sufficient water. The WSA adds a further, quantitative standard, albeit one that has been seriously questioned as to its suitability. The justiciability of the right to water also implies that access to justice forms part of the standard for socioeconomic rights protection required under the constitution.

However, perhaps the most important – and arguably the most problematic – standard is that of 'reasonableness' on the part of the State, as interpreted by the Constitutional Court. As has been argued, developing a standard of reasonableness, rather than adopting a minimum core approach to the right to water, has meant that for many people, whose daily experience is one of living with insufficient water, progress towards realising the right has been frustrated. Furthermore, failure to thoroughly interrogate the potential environmental consequences of universal access to sufficient water, particularly in light of

119 The judgment has not been appealed.

120 Note: Whether such a procedural standard should be characterised as a qualitative standard – since it designates the necessity of a specific state of affairs – or quantitative – requiring a measurable/trackable process, is a moot point. But this does not detract from the fact that a standard can be inferred here.

121 Const. South Africa (n 2) s 24(b)(iii).

the requirement of 'ecologically sustainable development' set out in the environmental right, risks dividing the right to water from the right to a healthy environment. Such division can only make the fulfilment of both rights more difficult.

Similarly, standards of environmental protection are discernible within the environmental right, its promulgating legislation and from the limited associated litigation. These include procedural standards regarding due diligence (as seen in relation to environment impact assessment); qualitative standards around health and well-being (severely limited by a lack of quantitative bench marks or normative content); as well as a standard of securing ecologically sustainable development (as discussed above).

While standards of environmental and socioeconomic protection are discernible in legislation, and through judicial interpretation, they are significantly limited, not least by the courts' rejection of a minimum core approach to sufficient water, and by its reticence to identify clearer substantive obligations around the environmental right. Also, interpretation of both constitutional rights has been constrained by a failure to connect and to integrate socioeconomic rights and environmental protection. As Wynberg and Fig remind us:

> Rights to food, healthcare and water are inextricably woven together with the realisation of environmental rights.[122]

Indeed, the interwoven quality of socioeconomic and environmental concerns has been recently and powerfully articulated in the Oslo Manifesto for Ecological Law and Governance. The Manifesto criticises the 'anthropocentric, fragmented and reductionist characteristics' of mainstream environmental law, which ignores or otherwise fails to confront socioeconomic and ecological interdependency.[123] In response, the Manifesto calls for the reimagination of every area of law, in order to create legal systems which promote ecological integrity, and which therefore are calibrated towards 'intra-/intergenerational and interspecies justice'.[124]

Crucial to this endeavour is the existential insight that we are all one: that no human story, no human right, ever floats free of the dirty earth that grounds it, the mineral water that feeds it, or the air that gives it breath. And so the integrity of all of us – ecological integrity – must become an essential part of the reimaginary enterprise. As legal scholars, this insight, if taken seriously, has the potential to

122 Rachel Wynberg and David Fig, 'Realising Environmental Rights: Civil Action, Leverage Rights, and Litigation' in Malcom Langford, Ben Cousins, Jackie Dugard and Tshepo Madlingozi (eds), *Symbols or Substance: Socio-Economic Rights Strategies in South Africa* (Cambridge, 2013) 5.

123 'Oslo Manifesto for Ecological Law and Governance', adopted at the IUCN WCEL Ethics Specialist Group Workshop, IUCN Academy of Environmental Law Colloquium, University of Oslo, 21 June 2016. Available at <www.elga.world/oslo-manifesto/> accessed 10 November 2017.

124 ibid.

launch us on to a new trajectory of jurisprudence that interweaves social, economic and environmental rights, and infuses each with a normative arc that bends towards ecological integrity. Practically, and in the context of South Africa, this must surely mean clarification of the relationship between the environmental right and other human rights, including the right of access to sufficient water.

14

The French Charter of the Environment and Standards of Environmental Protection

David Marrani and Stephen J. Turner

14.1 INTRODUCTION

As a legal initiative, the French Charter of the Environment (the Charter) makes a significant contribution to the field of environmental rights. The French State has shown a particular commitment to the Charter not only through its inclusion in the national constitution, but through the legal mechanisms that facilitate its practical use as a method of maintaining and setting standards relating to the protection of the environment. This is seen especially in the legal processes that are available to challenge the constitutionality of draft and existing legislation. It is also seen in the manner in which the administrative courts are able to turn to certain Charter provisions as the bases for decision making in environmentally related matters. These processes raise questions relating to the standards of environmental protection that the Charter provides and how the issue of risk relating to the environment is handled through the legislature and the courts.

This chapter proceeds by explaining the evolution of the Charter itself, before considering the factors that affect its use in the development of standards. It then examines the way that the Charter has been operationalised in practice through the decisions of the Constitutional Council and the administrative courts. In doing so it highlights the varying status of different provisions within the Charter itself, how individual citizens are able to rely upon it, the manner in which the Charter provisions are given effect through the different forums of decision making and how a balance is struck in relation to giving effect to the Charter on the one hand and maintaining the principle of separation of powers on the other. All of these factors affect the ultimate standards of environmental protection that the Charter confers on the population living in French territory.

14.2 THE EVOLUTION OF THE CHARTER

The 2004 Charter for the environment was adopted and incorporated into the French Fifth Republic Constitution in 2005.[1] The method used to incorporate the

[1] Loi constitutionnelle 2005–205, 1 March 2005 (Loi constitutionnelle relative à la Charte de l'environnement (1)), JORF 2 March 2005, 3697.

Charter into the constitution was to amend the Preamble of the 1958 Constitution and add a reference to the 2004 Charter for the environment.[2] The first paragraph of the Preamble was amended to include the words 'ainsi que les droits et devoirs définis dans la Charte de l'environnement de 2004' (and to the rights and duties as defined in the Charter for the environment of 2004), so the Preamble now reads as follows:

> The French people solemnly proclaim their attachment to the Rights of Man and the principles of national sovereignty as defined by the Declaration of 1789, confirmed and complemented by the 1946 Constitution Preamble, and to the rights and duties as defined in the Charter for the Environment of 2004.[3]

Originally, the purpose of the Charter was generic and this is seen in certain provisions such as Art. 6 relating to the promotion of sustainable development and Art. 8 relating to the integration of environmental concerns into education and training.[4] However, through the incorporation of the Charter into the Constitution, guaranteed rights and duties were created. Those rights and duties have been recognised, firstly in *ex ante* constitutional control, and then in the context of the new *ex post* constitutional control. As such the Charter has become an effective legal tool, a real 'bill of rights', truly setting standards, reinforcing environmental rights and acknowledging emerging environmental human rights.

The text of the charter is relatively comprehensive in comparison to many environmental rights provisions found in national constitutions. It reads as follows:

The French People,
Considering that :
Natural resources and equilibriums have conditioned the emergence of mankind;
The future and very existence of mankind are inextricably linked with its natural environment;

[2] See D Marrani, 'The Second Anniversary of the Constitutionalisation of the French Charter for the Environment: Constitutional and Environmental Implications' (2008) 10 (1) Environmental Law Review 9–27.

[3] The Preamble of the French Constitution 1958 (as amended on 23 July 2008).

[4] Before the incorporation of the Charter in the Constitution, its philosophical principles became a reference for the French department of education. For instance, in 2004, instruction was given from chief education officers to headmasters of primary and secondary educational institutions on the application of article 8 of the Charter to 'generalise the education on the environment for a sustainable development from the academic year 2004'. Circulaire 2004–110, 8 July 2004, BOEN 28, 15 July 2004, 1473 (Généralisation d'une éducation à l'environnement pour un développement durable (EEDD) – rentrée 2004). It has to be noted that this document replaces a previous one, Circulaire 77–300, 29 August 1977, BOEN 31, 9 September 1977, 2507 (Instruction générale sur l'éducation des éleves en matiére d'environnement). The requirement to develop teaching on environmental protection was always present in the curriculum through specific educational programmes (on forests and animals for example), but never on a general basis. This generalisation of environmental education follows the first law adopted in 1976 on environmental protection (Loi n° 76–629 du 10 juillet 1976 relative à la protection de la nature. JORF, 13 July 1976, 4203).

The environment is the common heritage of all mankind;
Mankind exerts ever-increasing influence over the conditions for life and its own evolution;
Biological diversity, the fulfilment of the person and the progress of human societies are affected by certain types of consumption or production and by excessive exploitation of natural resources;
Care must be taken to safeguard the environment along with the other fundamental interests of the Nation;
In order to ensure sustainable development, choices designed to meet the needs of the present generation should not jeopardise the ability of future generations and other peoples to meet their own needs,
Hereby proclaim:

Article 1

Everyone has the right to live in a balanced environment which shows due respect for health.

Article 2

Everyone is under a duty to participate in preserving and enhancing the environment.

Article 3

Everyone shall, within the limits imposed by statute law, prevent possible damage to the environment one may create or, failing that, limit its consequence.

Article 4

Everyone shall contribute to repairing damage one causes to the environment, within the limits imposed by law.

Article 5

Even if scientific knowledge is uncertain where damages occur which could have serious irreversible effects on the environment, public authorities shall within their own domains of competences, apply the precautionary principle through the implementation of procedures for the evaluation of risks, and the adoption of provisional and proportionate measures in order to prevent the damage occurring.

Article 6

Public policies shall promote sustainable development. To this end they shall reconcile the protection and enhancement of the environment with economic development and social progress.

Article 7

Everyone has the right, in the conditions and to the extent provided for by law, to have access to information pertaining to the environment in the possession of public bodies and to participate in the public decision-making process likely to affect the environment.

Article 8

Education and training with regard to the environment shall contribute to the exercising of the rights and duties set out in this Charter.

Article 9

Research and innovation shall contribute to the preservation and development of the environment.

Article 10

This Charter shall inspire France's actions at both European and international levels.[5]

14.3 FACTORS THAT AFFECT THE DEVELOPMENT OF STANDARDS THROUGH THE CHARTER

To understand the way that the Charter has influenced and been involved in the development of environmental standards, it is important to consider four factors that relate to the legal content of the Charter and the way that it operates in practice. These are referred to as the variable values of the different provisions in the Charter, the different types of legal action available under it, the issue of locus standi and the manner in which it is affected by the distribution of powers in French political institutions. The following deals with each of these in turn.

14.3.1 *Variable Values*

The variable values of the rights and duties enshrined in the Charter have received considerable scholarly attention.[6] Some of the rights and duties have political effect but lack clear legal effect. For example, Arts. 8 to 10 contain rights that could be regarded as policy statements which would not provide the basis of litigation.[7] At the other end of the spectrum are those rights that are actionable, such as Art. 1, which states that everyone has the right to live in an environment that is balanced and respects health; it has been declared that this particular right is a *liberté fondamentale* (fundamental freedom).[8]

5 Loi constitutionnelle 2005–205 (n 1) (translation by David Marrani).

6 See D Marrani (n 2); also, N Chahid-Nouraï, 'La Portée de la Charte pour le Juge Ordinaire' (2005) AJDA Chroniques 1175.

7 The primary objective of article 8 is to be a guide for institutions, particularly the French Parliament and Government. The Charter is applied *a priori*, in policy-making processes of the administration. In that sense, it is a philosophical document.

8 See H Groud and S Pugeault, 'Le Droit à l'Environnement, Nouvelle Liberté Fondamentale' (2005) AJDA Jurisprudence 1357. This was already stated by article L. 521–1 of the Code de Justice Administrative.

However, a distinction also has to be made between what is known as a *principe à valeur constitutionnel* (as seen in Art. 5) and an *objectif à valeur constitutionnel* (as seen in paras 6 and 7 of the Preamble and also in Arts. 1 to 7 (Excl. Art. 5)). The difference between the two is important. A principle of constitutional value is directly applicable and can be invoked by individuals before a court, whereas an objective of constitutional value can be imposed on the legislative power but cannot be directly invoked before a court.[9] This difference represents a tension within the Charter itself where it can be seen to act either as a 'guide' for law makers or an 'axe' that can be used in constitutional review.

Following the Rio Declaration in 1992, the precautionary principle was transposed into French law through article L.110–1.1° of the Environmental Code. It states as follows:

> The absence of certainty, based on current scientific and technical knowledge, must not delay the adoption of effective and proportionate measures aiming to prevent a risk of serious and irreversible damage to the environment at an economically acceptable cost.[10]

It is the only principle of constitutional value included in the Charter and is clearly stated as a 'principle' in Art. 5:

> Even if scientific knowledge is uncertain where damages occur which could have serious and irreversible effects on their environment, public authorities shall within their own domains of competences, apply the precautionary principle through the implementation of procedures for the evaluation of risks, and the adoption of provisional and proportionate measures in order to prevent the damage occurring.

The effect of this is that the precautionary principle becomes a duty that is imposed on public authorities in their decision-making processes. In this sense it does create a meaningful standard that is required of public authorities in the way that they make decisions that have the potential to impact upon the environment.

It is quite interesting to note the difference in treatment of the precautionary principle when compared to the prevention principle, which is found in Art. 3 and which is regarded as an objective of constitutional value.[11] It states that:

9 See F Luchaire, 'Brèves Remarques sur une Création du Conseil Constitutionnel: l'Objectif de Valeur Constitutionnelle' (2005) 64 Revue Française de Droit Constitutionnel 675–84; also French National Assembly, *Rapport fait au nom de la Commission des lois constitutionnelles, de la législation et de l'administration générale de la République sur le projet de loi constitutionnelle (N° 992) relatif à la Charte de l'environnement* (National Assembly, May 2004) <www.assemblee-nationale.fr/12/rapports/r1595.asp> accessed 14 July 2018.

10 Since Loi 2002–276 du 27 Février 2002 art. 132 JORF, 28 February 2002 it appears in the first article (Article L.110–1) of the Environment Code, Code de l'Environnement, enshrining the general principles of environmental law (precautionary, prevention, participation). English version <www.legifrance.gouv.fr/Traductions/en-English/Legifrance-translations> accessed 30 September 2016.

11 Luchaire (n 9) 675–84.

> Everyone shall, within the limits imposed by Statute Law, prevent possible damages to the environment one may create or, failing that, limit their consequences.

It appears to be broader in scope than the precautionary principle as it applies to *everyone*; as such, it blurs the line between public and private obligations. This is also reflected in the objective of Art. 4, which states that:

> Everyone shall contribute to repairing damages one causes to the environment, within the limits imposed by Law.

The objectives of constitutional values (Arts. 3 and 4), responsibility and the prevention principle, are not as explicitly developed as the principle of constitutional value, the precautionary principle in Art. 5. However, this lack of precision appears to be balanced by their more extensive scope of application.

14.3.2 *The Types of Legal Action Available*

As the Charter was originally imagined and designed as a guide for lawmakers, it was supposed to influence and guide legislation and regulation at the national and local levels. It was originally meant to contribute to the 'greening' of bills during their elaboration process. However, it subsequently became a bill of rights that would facilitate constitutional review of future or pre-promulgated statutes.

In this regard, it is important to distinguish between *ex ante* (prior) and *ex post* (after the fact) constitutional review. The 1958 Constitution had originally created solely an *ex ante* control (on pre-promulgated statutes) and only relatively recently has the possibility for *ex post* control (on promulgated statues) been introduced.

The 1958 Constitution set up a Constitutional Council (Council) with mainly political members rather than lawyers.[12] It was not originally supposed to be a supreme court but simply the censor of the legislative power, to check the quality of the legislative process.[13] The Council was created to review the conformity of a statute prior to its promulgation (*ex ante*). Art. 61 of the 1958 Constitution stated that ordinary (statute) laws or international agreements could be scrutinised by the Council after they had been adopted by the French Parliament but before their promulgation (in the case of statute) or their ratification (in the case of international agreements). Initiative for the action was originally given to the President of the Republic, the Prime Minister and the President of the National Assembly and was

[12] There are nine appointed members of the Council including its President, plus all the former Presidents of the Republic. Currently, Valery Giscard d'Estaing, Jacques Chirac and Nicolas Sarkozy are members of the Council, although their proper participation has been very variable.

[13] Since 1958, there has been the introduction of a 'real' constitutional control. This was extended by the revisions of 1971 (with the presentation of a material constitution) and 1976 (extension of control). In 1985, a landmark decision further developed the mission of the Constitutional Council to scrutinise the work of the French Parliament (particularly statute law). See The Constitutional Council, *La loi votée n'exprime la volonté générale « que dans le respect de la constitution »* Const. Décision n° 85–197 DC 23 August 1985.

later extended to sixty deputies or sixty senators to allow the parliamentary opposition to take an active part in the process.

As *ex post* review was the result of a constitutional amendment that occurred in 2008, there was a lack of clarity relating to the way that it can operate in practice. For example, the Council still has not had the opportunity to clarify whether the violation of Arts. 8 to 10 of the Charter can be invoked through *ex post* constitutional control.

However, the Council has had some opportunities to address certain aspects. For example, in 2014, it clarified the constitutional value of the Charter's Preamble by determining that no rights or freedoms were created or guaranteed by those provisions and that they did not provide the basis of *ex post* review.[14] It also confirmed that the first four articles of the 2004 Charter could always be invoked in support of the *ex post* mechanism and that Art. 6 did not create rights or freedoms.[15]

14.3.3 *Locus Standi*

What can be considered as quite radical within the context of the aforementioned discussion is that any individuals involved in legal proceedings have been given the right to initiate an *ex post* review under the new Art. 61–1 of the 1958 Constitution, which states:

> If, during proceedings in progress before a court of law, it is claimed that a legislative provision infringes the rights and freedoms guaranteed by the Constitution, the matter may be referred by the *Conseil d'État* or by the *Cour de Cassation* to the Constitutional Council which shall rule within a determined period.[16]

This opened the possibility for any individual involved in legal proceedings before a court (either administrative or judicial) to contest the legality of a statute on the basis that it might infringe the rights and freedoms guaranteed by the Constitution. There are conditions relating to admissibility: applications must be referred to the Constitutional Council by one of the French Supreme Courts – the Conseil d'Etat as Supreme Court of the administrative court system, or the Cour de cassation, as Supreme Court of the judicial court system. Both courts have the duty of filtering applications to the Constitutional Council. According to Art. 62 of the 1958

[14] Cons. const. Decision 2014–394 QPC, 7 May 2014, *Société Casuca*, JORF 10 May 2014, 7873 <www.conseil-constitutionnel.fr/conseil-constitutionnel/francais/les-decisions/acces-par-date/decisions-depuis-1959/2014/2014–394-qpc/decision-n-2014–394-qpc-du-7-mai-2014.141517.html> accessed 30 September 2016.

[15] ibid. See also Cons. const., Decision 2012–283 QPC, 23 November 2012, *M. Antoine de M.*, JORF 24 November 2012, 18547 <www.conseil-constitutionnel.fr/conseil-constitutionnel/francais/les-decisions/acces-par-date/decisions-depuis-1959/2012/2012–283-qpc/decision-n-2012–283-qpc-du-23-novembre-2012.135146.html> accessed 30 September 2016.

[16] Loi Constitutionnelle de Modernisation des Institutions de la Ve République, JORF 0171, 24 July 2008, 11890 <www.conseil-constitutionnel.fr/conseil-constitutionnel/english/constitution/constitution-of-4-october-1958.25742.html#_Toc308601189> accessed 30 September 2016.

Constitution, if a statute is considered to be unconstitutional by the Council, it will then be repealed.

As Art. 61–1 came into force on 1 March 2010, what has become increasingly important has been the status of French human rights, defined as rights and freedoms guaranteed by the Constitution.[17] Correspondingly, whether the provisions of the 2004 Charter for the environment are also regarded as rights and freedoms for the purpose of Art. 61–1 has become an extremely important issue.

14.4 THE USE OF THE CHARTER AND ITS ROLE IN THE DEVELOPMENT OF STANDARDS OF ENVIRONMENTAL PROTECTION.

This section draws on certain decisions to demonstrate how standards related to the rights and obligations within the Charter are developing in practice. Although the Charter is relatively new, there have been cases that indicate how the Council and the courts have treated environmental standards related to it. Therefore, the analysis focuses on certain factors and certain provisions within the Charter that have had a key influence in this respect. They are the separation of powers and the distribution of decision making, the effect of other constitutional provisions, the standard of protection relating to the precautionary principle and the standard of protection afforded by procedural rights. Each of these aspects is dealt with in turn.

14.4.1 *The Separation of Powers and the Distribution of Decision-Making Relating to Standards*

As previously mentioned, when it comes to the question of legislation itself and whether or not it is consistent with the requirements of the Charter, it is the Constitutional Council that has the responsibility to carry out reviews where necessary. The way that this control operates in practice demonstrates where the responsibilities lie for standard setting relating to legislation in France.

The issue was tested in 2005 when a bill relating to the creation of a maritime register came before the Council for review.[18] The Council mentioned the Charter explicitly in paragraphs 13, 36, 37 and 38 of its decision. Paragraph 37 is probably the

[17] Governmental regulations executing the Loi Organique completing the Constitution in application of Art. 61–1 of the Constitution, provided a starting date of 1 March 2010 for the new *ex post* mechanism. See Loi organique 2009–1523 du 10 décembre 2009 relative à l'application de l'article 61–1 de la Constitution. See also Décret n° 2010–148 du 16 Février 2010 portant application de la Loi Organique n° 2009–1523 du 10 Décembre 2009 Relative à l'Application de l'article 61–1 de la Constitution.

[18] Cons. Const., Decision 2005–514 DC 28 April 2005, *Loi relative à la création du registre international français*, JORF 4 May 2005, 7702. This bill was declared in conformity with the Constitution <www.conseil-constitutionnel.fr/conseil-constitutionnel/francais/les-decisions/acces-par-date/decisions-depuis-1959/2005/2005–514-dc/decision-n-2005–514-dc-du-28-avril-2005.967.html> accessed 30 September 2016.

most important one as it makes the point that the application of Art. 6 had to be left to the discretion of the legislature:

> Considering that following the dispositions of article 6 of the Charter for the Environment of 2004: 'Public policies must promote sustainable development. For this purpose, they conciliate protection and valorisation of the environment, economic development and social progress'; it is a power for the legislature to determine, in the respect of the principle of conciliation laid down by those measures, the terms of its implementation.[19]

This case demonstrates that although certain articles within the Charter can attract constitutional review, the review itself can be limited to procedural aspects relating to the passing of legislation. It demonstrates that whereas the Council was prepared to consider the issue of Art. 6, they ultimately saw it as the legislature's role to make the difficult decisions concerning the compromises that have to be made regarding the economic and environmental demands when making law relating to the implementation of sustainable development. It did not see itself as having the role of making substantive decisions relating to the precise standards of environmental protection that would be required under the government's obligation to promote sustainable development.

The issue of separation of powers features prominently in a number of other chapters in this book where this dilemma involving constitutional, democratic and human rights issues has been treated in various ways by domestic courts throughout the world.[20] The basis upon which this case was decided was reaffirmed in a more recent decision that related to a bill designed to prepare the transition towards a streamlined energy system and to lay down miscellaneous provisions on tariff rates for water and wind turbines.[21] The Council again confirmed that when considering the promotion of sustainable development under Art 6. 'it is for Parliament to determine the manner in which it is to be implemented'.[22]

At the subordinate levels of law making, environmental law in France has always been considered a special branch of administrative law. Its origins are found in the French notion of public order that encompasses *salubrite* (healthiness). Therefore, there are many more cases in the administrative courts than in the judicial courts. The top French administrative court, the Conseil d'Etat, clarified, quite rapidly, the scope of the new environmental constitutional principles and made important progress on the procedures for ensuring that

19 ibid para 17.

20 See, for example, Chapter 10 by Gitanjali Gill relating to the Indian Constitution and Chapter 13 by Nathan Cooper relating to the South African Constitution.

21 Decision No. 2013–666 DC of 11 April 2013 <www.conseil-constitutionnel.fr/conseil-constitutionnel/english/case-law/sample-of-decisions-in-relevant-areas-dc/decision/decision-no-2013–666-dc-of-11-april-2013.136989.html> accessed 18 February 2018.

22 ibid at para 39.

Charter articles which are regularly invoked in the context of litigation are properly considered.

In this context, it is for the legislature to determine the basic principles of environmental protection and to ensure that legislation is consistent with the Charter provisions. Following the creation of legislation, the French administration has the responsibility to implement the principles as defined under the law through the creation of regulations. It is then for the administrative courts to monitor compliance with the regulations. When the regulatory authority creates regulations that are consistent with the statutes, the statutes prevent the administrative court from making any constitutional review, as the administrative court is only supposed to control the legality of administrative acts.

However, there are certain areas where judicial discretion by the administrative courts related to the Charter is possible. The precautionary principle does not require the French Parliament or the executive branch to act specifically for its implementation. It applies directly to the central government and local governments; further elaboration is provided in Section 14.4.2 below.[23] Also in relation to the obligation to promote sustainable development (Art. 6) the administrative judge will verify compliance through the traditional control, called *bilan*, which relates to the striking of a balance between different factors. In other words, the court will consider whether the damage to the environment is or is not excessive, given the expected benefits of a project and the precautions that were taken.[24] It is in these areas that the administrative courts play a role in determining the standards of protection that are applicable under the Charter.

14.4.2 *The Standard of Protection Afforded by the Precautionary Principle*

Considering that the precautionary principle holds special status within the Charter as a principle of constitutional value it is important to consider the manner in which Art. 5 has been treated by the legislative branch of the government and also the Council. A case occurred in 2014 which provides some insight. A bill related to maize cultivation contained a provision stating that 'the cultivation of varieties of genetically modified maize shall be prohibited'.[25] On the one hand, the inclusion of such a provision would appear to indicate that the legislative branch of government could have been influenced by its responsibilities under art. 5 as they had sought to limit any potential for serious harm to the environment in relation to the cultivation of a crop, the safety of which is associated with a degree of scientific uncertainty.

[23] CE, 19 July 2010, *Association du quartier « Les Hauts de Choiseul »* 328687.

[24] CE, 16 April 2010, *Association Alcaly et autres*, 320667 et a.

[25] Decision No. 2014–694 DC of 28 May 2014 para 7 <www.conseil-constitutionnel.fr/conseil-constitutionnel/english/case-law/sample-of-decisions-in-relevant-areas-dc/decision/decision-no-2014–694-dc-of-28-may-2014.141839.html> accessed 18 Feb 2018.

However, the bill was challenged on the basis that the ban on the specific types of maize had no time limit, and as such should be regarded as inconsistent with Art. 5, which states that in the event that such scientific uncertainty exists, *temporary* measures should be implemented. However, the Council found that the provision in the bill was not inconsistent with the Constitution, and as such it appears to have favoured a standard of protection that was higher than that which was argued for by the claimants.

The precautionary principle has been considered by the administrative court in particular in relation to major infrastructure projects. The court has held that it is for the administrative judges to determine whether there is evidence of risk of serious and irreversible impact to the environment or to health, which would justify the application of the precautionary principle. If such risks are present, it must then ensure that the precautionary measures taken are neither insufficient nor excessive having regard, firstly, to the plausibility and gravity of the risk and, secondly, to the importance of the operation.[26]

14.4.3 *The Effect of Other Constitutional Provisions on Standards of Environmental Protection*

Another factor that can affect the standard of environmental protection that is afforded to the environment under the Charter is the effect of other provisions within the Constitution itself. This is illustrated by a Council decision from 2009 that related to a proposed carbon tax.[27] President Sarkozy had promised to introduce a carbon tax; the finance bill concerned allowed for such a tax in Art. 7, but it also included two other provisions (Arts. 9 and 10) which provided exemptions, reductions and refunds under certain circumstances that undermined the effectiveness of Art. 7.[28] The bill itself became the subject of a challenge under the Constitution. On investigation it became clear that 93 per cent of carbon dioxide emissions originating from industries (excluding fuel) would be totally exempt from the tax, and those activities to which the tax would be applicable represented less than half of France's total greenhouse gas emission.[29]

Under French constitutional law, fiscal equality was enshrined in Art. 13 of the 1789 Declaration of the Rights of Man and of the Citizen, which provides

[26] CE 12 April 2013, *Association coordination interrégionale Stop THT et autres*, 342409 et a.

[27] D. Marrani, 'How to End an Attempt to Institute a Carbon Tax: the Conseil Constitutionnel declares that article 7 of the 2010 Budget instituting a carbon tax does not conform to the Constitution of the French Republic' (2011) 13 Env. L. Rev. 50–55; Décision n° 2009–599 DC du 29 Décembre 2009, Loi de finances pour 2010, JORF 31 December 2009, 22995. <www.conseil-constitutionnel.fr/decision//decisions-depuis-1959/2009/2009–599-dc/decision-n-2009–599-dc-du-29-decembre-2009.46804.html> accessed 30 September 2016.

[28] Project de Loi de finances pour 2010, 18 December 2009 <www.senat.fr/petite-loi-ameli/2009–2010/160.html> accessed 17 February 2018.

[29] D Marrani (n 27) 53.

that 'for the maintenance of the public forces, and for administrative expenses, a general tax is indispensable; it must be equally distributed among all citizens, in proportion to their ability to pay'.[30] Therefore, the Council considered the proposed carbon tax in the context of this principle requiring 'equality' in relation to taxation. It found that the exemptions contained in the bill meant that the proposed legislation was not consistent with the principle of equality. Therefore, those particular provisions were also deemed to be contrary to the task of combating climate change.

'Equality' in the sense in which it was applied in this case can be seen in the broader sense as the application of 'equity', or put simply 'fairness' amongst citizens. In dealing with this particular issue the Council relied upon a principle found in the French Constitution, which in contemporary international environmental law finds a parallel in the principle of intragenerational equity.[31] As such, this particular case lays down an important marker in the development of standards of environmental protection by emphasising that where standards relating to environmental protection are proposed or adopted, they must do so in a manner which is fair to all citizens at that time.

14.4.4 *The Standard of Protection Afforded by Procedural Rights*

An area which has involved considerable review is the field of participatory rights. Therefore, the Constitutional Council has been called upon to make determinations related to provisions of draft regulations that have been challenged as not being consistent with the rights and obligations detailed in Art. 7 of the Charter.[32] One example, Decision No. 2012- QPC 262 of 13 July 2012, is a determination made by the Council following a referral by the Conseil d'Etat in which it was claimed that the last sentence of the first subparagraph of Art. L.5125 of the Environmental Code was unconstitutional. The applicant claimed that by not making provision for the participation of the general public in the requirements relating to draft regulations for classified installations (requiring authorisation), the particular sentence concerned violated the principle of participation that is guaranteed under Art. 7 of the Charter. In this particular case the Council decided that the sentence concerned was unconstitutional, and that it was necessary for the law to stipulate that the draft technical regulations concerned should be made public, possibly by electronic means.

30 Declaration of the Rights of Man and of the Citizen (1789) <http://avalon.law.yale.edu/18th_century/rightsof.asp> accessed 14 July 2018.

31 I Vojnovic, 'Intergenerational and Intragenerational Equity Requirements for Sustainability' (1995) 22 (3) *Environmental Conservation* 223–28.

32 Decision No. 2012–269 QPC of 27 July 2012; Decision No. 2012–270 QPC of 27 July 2012; Decision No. 2012–283 QPC of 23 November 2012; Decision 2012–282 QPC of 23 November 2012.

On the other hand, there have been decisions by the Council in which they have determined that the regulations concerned are consistent with the constitution.[33] One example is that related to a claim that the technical standards in building regulations relating to the use of a minimum quantity of wood in new constructions should be subject to public participation requirements under the Charter.[34] The purpose of these regulations was to promote an increase in the production of wood, which would be expected to assist in combating atmospheric pollution.[35] The Council determined that as this technical rule was likely to have 'only an indirect impact on the environment', it was not necessary that the regulation be subject to public participation.[36]

14.5 CONCLUSION

The integration of the Charter of the Environment into the French Constitution in 2005 has had broad implications in relation to the development of standards of environmental protection in France. This has primarily been due to the legal mechanisms that have facilitated the use of the provisions of the Charter to play an active role in steering and providing an element of control in the creation of legislation. In providing a mechanism whereby legislation affecting the environment can be challenged by the Constitutional Council, a framework exists in which proposed and existing laws need to comply with certain standards if they are to be held as consistent with the Charter provisions. However, what this chapter has also shown is that considerable deference is granted to the legislature by the Council when it comes to difficult determinations related to the level of environmental protection that is required under the law.

At the administrative level, the manner in which the precautionary principle and the concept of sustainable development are integrated into decision making through the administrative courts ensures that the Charter provisions are given effect at the local as well as at the national levels.

What is interesting in relation to the integration of the Charter provisions within the systems of government in France is the level of involvement that ordinary citizens can potentially have in the development of standards that relate to the Charter provisions. The extension of constitutional review to allow individual citizens to instigate a challenge to legislation that they believe is inconsistent with the Charter provides considerable scope for citizen participation in lawmaking relating to the environment in a way which is not possible under many other

33 For example: Decision No. 2012–282 QPC of 23 November 2012; Decision No. 2013–308 QPC of 26 April 2013; Decision No. 2013–316 QPC of 24 May 2013;

34 Decision No. 2013–317 QPC of 24 May 2013 relating to paragraph V of Article L. 224–1 of the Environmental Code.

35 ibid para 7.

36 ibid.

jurisdictions. Similarly, the potential to rely on Charter provisions at the level of the administrative courts ensures directly or indirectly that citizens are able to challenge the standard of environmental protection under regulations, and within administrative decision making, to ensure that they, too, are consistent with the constitution.

The full extent to which the mechanisms described in this chapter will be further developed in the future will be interesting to observe. Additionally, the manner in which the Council and the courts interpret the constitutional provisions themselves will require further analysis to understand more fully the precise standards of environmental protection that are conferred under the Charter.

Constitutional developments within national constitutions inevitably influence those of other countries. Future decades will show how far the mechanisms that have been developed under the French constitutional framework influence other countries, especially in the area of challenging the constitutionality of legislation that can affect the environment.

15

The Constitution of Bhutan: A Quantitative Environmental Standard

Stephen J. Turner

15.1 INTRODUCTION

This chapter will consider Art. 5(3) of the Bhutanese constitution, which provides a quantitative environmental standard relating to the level of forest cover that the country is required to maintain.[1] To be precise, it requires the government to ensure that 60 per cent of the land mass of the country is covered by forest for all time. Traditionally, environmental provisions within national constitutions include qualitative standards, with terms such as 'healthy', 'decent' or 'satisfactory' being used to describe the standard of environmental protection being prescribed;[2] therefore, the inclusion of a scientifically ascertainable quantitative standard relating to a specific aspect of the environment is a significant departure from that format. As such, while other chapters in this book seek to determine the different types of 'standards' that have resulted from the promulgation of environmental rights provisions and the precise levels of protection that they afford, this chapter investigates what this quantitative standard means for Bhutan itself in practical terms, and also its potential significance for the international community.

To undertake this investigation it considers the religious, political, social and cultural factors that influenced the creation of the 2008 constitution and which still influence the way that it can be interpreted. It then proceeds to examine the other environmental provisions of the constitution of which Art. 5(3) is a component part. It then analyses the reasoning and practical legal functioning of Art. 5(3) as well as considering the manner in which the Bhutanese government is implementing it through forestry law and policy. Finally, the chapter explores the potential that Art. 5(3) has to influence environmental constitutionalism in other countries and comments on the broader relationship that it has with other developments in the field of global environmental governance.

[1] The Constitution of Bhutan (18 July 2008).

[2] Stephen J Turner, *A Substantive Environmental Right – An Examination of the Legal Obligations of Decision-Makers towards the Environment* (Kluwer Law International 2009) 46–47.

15.2 THE RELIGIOUS, POLITICAL, SOCIAL AND CULTURAL FACTORS AFFECTING THE BHUTANESE CONSTITUTION

The factors that affected the drafting of the 2008 constitution are an important component in understanding its nature and in particular how its environmental provisions will be treated and interpreted in the future. For this purpose, those factors are placed into three categories which are: the role of Buddhism and the policy of 'gross national happiness' (GNH), the political changes and democratisation that have occurred in the country, and the social and cultural norms that are intrinsic to Bhutanese society.

Buddhism is discussed first, as it has been foundational to the history and development of the country, playing an integral role both in the fabric of society and in government itself. That influence can be traced back to medieval times when Buddhist monks fled from neighbouring Tibet and set up monasteries in the region.[3] As has been the case with many countries, there were centuries of power struggles between secular leaders of different principalities; in Bhutan's case, by the seventeenth century a system of leadership had emerged in which the country was jointly ruled by a Buddhist spiritual leader (Je Khenpo) and a secular leader (Druk Desi).[4] As the evolution of the country took place, Buddhism played a central role in government, as political leadership was intertwined with reliance upon the Buddhist Monk Body for theocratic authority and also for the administrative functions that it carried out.[5]

In more recent times, and like some other states in the region, the Bhutanese government has had to make decisions regarding the relationship that religion would have within its political constitution. For example, Thailand in 2007 decided that it would not recognise Buddhism as its national religion even though 95 per cent of its population are Buddhists.[6] Similarly, in Nepal's 2007 interim constitution the country is described as 'secular' to ensure that minority religions are not treated prejudicially, even though the majority of its population are Hindus.[7] In Bhutan's case, the 2008 constitution does not make Buddhism the state religion even though the vast majority of the population are Buddhists. In fact, it clearly separates religion from government,[8] and therefore for the first time it meant that the Central Monk Body ceased to have a formal role in the creation of new legislation.[9] Nevertheless, the constitution does explicitly maintain a strong relationship with Buddhism; Art. 1(13) states that it is the 'spiritual

3 Sarish Sebastian, *Bhutan – A Journey from Tradition to Modernity* (Adroit Publishers 2015) 5.

4 Dhurba Rizal, *The Royal Semi-Authoritarian Democracy of Bhutan* (Lexington Books 2015) 19; Wen-Chen Chang, Li-ann Thio, Kevin Y L Tan and Jiunn-rong Yeh (eds), *Constitutionalism in Asia – Cases and Materials* (Hart Publishing 2014) 107; Sebastian ibid 8.

5 Sebastian (n 3).

6 Chang et al. (n 4) 108.

7 ibid 109.

8 Art 3(3).

9 Chang et al. (n 4) 107.

heritage' of the country,[10] and Art. 9(20) that one of the principles of State policy is that 'the State shall strive to create conditions that will enable the true and sustainable development of a good and compassionate society rooted in Buddhist ethos and universal human values'. As such, it is not surprising that in practical terms Buddhism continues to have a very strong influence on the manner in which the country is governed.[11]

Buddhism has significantly influenced Bhutan's policies towards the environment. The Buddhist tradition has particular reverence for the mountains, streams, rocks and soil alongside a deep respect for all living things. Shera Lhundup states that 'the particular form of Mahayana Buddhism practised in Bhutan is characteristically prohibitive of hunting, fishing or violating any form of life'.[12] As such, the adoption of ecologically friendly policies is an extension of an inherited belief system.[13] This is seen prominently in the ideology of GNH that was introduced by King Jigme Singye Wangchuck in 1972.[14] Priesner states, 'Buddhism is the single most important determinant for ... "Gross National Happiness", the perception of human well-being as the fundamental objective of economic activity.'[15] The pursuit of GNH is an economic policy that provided an alternative set of goals to those sought in the furtherance of maximising Gross Domestic Product (GDP) or Gross National Product (GNP). It can be conceptualised into four constituent pillars, which are: (i) the promotion of equitable and sustainable socioeconomic development, (ii) the preservation and promotion of cultural values, (iii) the conservation of the natural environment and (iv) good governance.[16]

The central role of GNH within the governance of Bhutan led to the Planning Commission being renamed the 'Gross National Happiness Commission' in 2008.[17] This organ of government has the Prime Minister as its chairman, and one of its key tasks is to ensure that 'GNH is embedded firmly into policies and that proper

[10] See Richard W Whitecross 'Separating Religion and Politics? – Buddhism and the Bhutanese Constitution' in Sunil Khilnani, Vikram Raghavan and Arun K Thiruvengadam (eds), *Comparative Constitutionalism in South Asia* (OUP 2013) 133.

[11] For example, in recent years ministers and parliamentarians have made reference to religious beliefs in discussions relating to the use of alcohol and tobacco. See Chang et al. (n 4) 107.

[12] Shera Lhundup, 'The Genesis of Environmental Ethics and Sustaining its Heritage in the Kingdom of Bhutan' (2001–2) 14 Geo Int'l Envtl L Rev 693, 699.

[13] RGOB – Ministry of Agriculture, 'Biodiversity Action Plan for Bhutan' (final draft) (2002) 34 <www.biodiv.be/bhutan/convention-biological-diversity/reports/biodiversity-action-plan-2002/download/en/1/Biodiversity%20Action%20Plan%202002.pdf?action=view> accessed 24 July 2018.

[14] Sebastian (n 3) 69; Chang et al. (n 4) 69.

[15] Stefan Priesner, 'Gross National Happiness: Bhutan's Vision of Development and Its Challenges' in Partha Nath Mukherji and Chandan Sengupta (eds), *Indigineity and Universality in Social Science: A South Asian Response* (Sage Publishers 2004) 212, 223.

[16] ROGB Ministry of Agriculture, 'National Forest Policy' (2011) 3 <www.biodiv.be/bhutan/legal-instruments/policies/national-forest-policy-2011> accessed 24 July 2018; Sebastian (n 3) 70.

[17] Executive Order PM/01/08/895 (24 January 2008). <www.centreforpublicimpact.org/case-study/gross-national-happiness-policy-screening-tool-bhutan/> accessed 24 July 2018.

coordination is undertaken to ensure the implementation of plans and programs'.[18] Additionally, GNH as a 'Principle of State Policy' was incorporated into the national constitution through Art. 9(2), which states that 'the State shall strive to promote those conditions that will enable the pursuit of Gross National Happiness'.[19] The understanding of the assimilation of these principles within the system of government in Bhutan helps to contextualise the role that Art. 5(3) of the constitution has and the manner in which it complements the broader policies that Bhutan has towards the protection of the environment.

The second category of influences on the 2008 constitution have been the political developments in the country. Bhutan moved from being a theocracy to an absolute monarchy in 1907 under the leadership of King Ugyen Wangchuk.[20] This distinctive political history was due in part to the fact that unlike some of its neighbours, Bhutan had not been colonised by the British and became determined to maintain its independence from external influence and coercion.[21] In spite of this, changes that were taking place in other parts of the world gradually affected people's expectations. Therefore, from the middle of the twentieth century the country has seen a gradual process of limited democratisation.

In the 1950s, under the auspices of the Third King Jigme Dorji Wangchuk, serfdom was abolished and a national legislature made up of 130 members was introduced.[22] The king's approach to modernisation was to integrate gradual change, facilitating greater representation of the people of the country, while maintaining the cultural and spiritual heritage of the nation. He stated that 'limited reforms introduced over an extended period under non-crisis conditions were preferable to radical change that would tear apart the social and political fabric of Bhutan's traditional system and lead perhaps to national disintegration'.[23]

This gradual modernisation was combined with a move away from isolationism which saw the country become a member of the United Nations in 1971,[24] and a member of other international institutions such as IFAD, the IMF and the IBRD in the years that followed.[25] Increasingly during the 1980s and 1990s the government came under pressure from groups on the fringes of mainstream society who were dissatisfied with the government's policies and the significant deficit that existed in terms of human rights and democracy.[26] Increased contact

[18] See www.gnhc.gov.bt/about-us/ (last accessed 23 October 2016).

[19] The Constitution of Bhutan (n 1).

[20] Whitecross (n 10) 121.

[21] ibid 116.

[22] Lhundup (n 12) 695.

[23] Leo E Rose, *The Politics of Bhutan* (Cornell University Press 1977) 126.

[24] Lhundup (n 12).

[25] Sebastian (n 3) 11.

[26] Susan Banki, 'The Transformation of Homeland Politics in the Era of Resettlement; Bhutanese Refugees in Nepal and the Diaspora' (2013) 43 Eur Bulletin Himalayan Research 120, 128; Rizal (n 4) 105–12; Ben Saul, 'Cultural Nationalism, Self-Determination, and Human Rights in Bhutan' (2000) 12 Int'l J Refugee L 321–53.

with other countries, combined with a growing middle class,[27] meant that there were new expectations of the government. This undoubtedly influenced King Jigme Singye Wangchuk (The Fourth King of Bhutan) in his 2001 decision that a national constitution should be drafted; this resulted in an extensive consultation process which finally led to its adoption in 2008.[28] The political context that has been briefly described indicates that there are still unanswered questions relating to the way that the constitution will function in the future and the levels of control and accountability that will develop in the different branches of government. This naturally influences the way that the environmental provisions of the constitution will be understood and acted upon in the future.

The final category of influences that affect the way that the constitution takes effect are the social and cultural conditions within Bhutan. Up until the 1960s the country had no paved roads, people generally lived through subsistence farming and transport between settlements was via mule tracks.[29] In terms of health care, up until the 1960s there were just four hospitals, two trained doctors, a few dispensaries and a leper colony.[30] Crucially in terms of understanding the constitution, it is important to take into account the way that Bhutanese society regards political authority. Many of the concepts of democracy that are inherent within western societies, such as challenging authority through legal or political means, are not integral within Bhutanese society. As such, the idea of challenging the monarch or the government on specific issues would not necessarily sit comfortably with many Bhutanese citizens.[31] Therefore, while Bhutanese society has been subject to changing attitudes in recent years, the picture of change that is taking place in Bhutan is one where long-standing cultural values and traditions do still shape and constrain approaches to constitutional rights and the relationship that people have with them.

In summary, when considering the environmental provisions within the constitution, interpretations or assumptions related to development trajectories that may be orthodox by standards of western economies, and which are heavily focused on business and economic performance, may not be readily embraced within Bhutan. As such, scholarship in this field requires a process of analysis that takes into account the political, religious, social and cultural factors that define the values and the type of government that the Bhutanese nation has adopted. This contextual understanding is crucial not only in any analysis of the development of the environmental provisions of the constitution themselves, but also in the understanding of any governmental decision making related to the them.

27 Rizal (n 4) 71.
28 Sebastian (n 3) 112; also Whinnie Bothe, 'The Monarch's Gift: Critical Notes on the Constitutional Process in Bhutan' (2012) 40 Eur Bulletin Himalayan Research 27, 54; Whitecross (n 10) 129 and 141.
29 Lhundup (n 12) 695.
30 Priesner (n 15) 213.
31 Lhundup (n 12) 695.

15.3 THE QUANTITATIVE ENVIRONMENTAL STANDARD WITHIN THE CONSTITUTION

Prior to analysing Art. 5(3) itself, consideration will be given to the broader manner in which the constitution provides for environmental issues. It includes a number of provisions that contain duties for both the government and its citizens to protect the environment.[32] It does not contain a bill of rights or a similarly styled categorisation of its provisions, therefore an understanding of the utility and meaning of particular articles must be drawn primarily from their wording and the relationship that they have with associated provisions in the constitution.

As is usual with national constitutions, it contains the 'right to life',[33] and it includes some provisions which could support procedural claims relating to the environment, such as the right to information[34] and legal aid to secure justice,[35] even though it does not include specific procedural rights relating to environmental matters (such as those relating to access to information, participation in decision making and access to justice) that are found in many other constitutions.[36] Nevertheless, it does make provision for local government administration and requires the state to 'facilitate the direct participation of the people in the development and management of their own social, economic and environmental well-being'.[37]

Art. 5 refers specifically to the protection of the environment. It reads as follows:

1. Every Bhutanese is a trustee of the Kingdom's natural resources and environment for the benefit of the present and future generations and it is the fundamental duty of every citizen to contribute to the protection of the natural environment, conservation of the rich biodiversity of Bhutan and prevention of all forms of ecological degradation including noise, visual and physical pollution through the adoption and support of environment friendly practices and policies.
2. The Royal Government shall:
   (a) Protect, conserve and improve the pristine environment and safeguard the biodiversity of the country;
   (b) Prevent pollution and ecological degradation;
   (c) Secure ecologically balanced sustainable development while promoting justifiable economic and social development; and
   (d) Ensure a safe and healthy environment.
3. The Government shall ensure that, in order to conserve the country's natural resources and to prevent degradation of the ecosystem, a minimum of sixty per cent of Bhutan's total land shall be maintained under forest cover for all time.

32 Arts 5 and 8(2).
33 Art 7(1).
34 Art 7(3).
35 Art 9(6).
36 See Stephen J Turner, *A Global Environmental Right* (Routledge 2014) 24–25.
37 Art 22(1).

4. Parliament may enact environmental legislation to ensure sustainable use of natural resources and maintain intergenerational equity and reaffirm the sovereign rights of the State over its own biological resources.
5. Parliament may, by law, declare any part of the country to be a National Park, Wildlife Reserve, Nature Reserve, Protected Forest, Biosphere Reserve, Critical Watershed and such other categories meriting protection.

Some of these provisions are unremarkable in the sense that they correspond in type and style with those of many other constitutions.[38] In other words, they provide standards that are qualitative or relatively generic in nature. For example, Art. 5(2)(d) refers to the duty of the government to 'ensure a safe and healthy environment'.[39]

What is interesting within the context of the quantitative environmental standard that is found in Art. 5(3) is that Art. 5 itself includes both quantitative and qualitative standards. Therefore, even though specific aspects of the environment such as noise pollution,[40] conservation[41] and physical pollution[42] are all referred to, for those aspects of the environment there is no reference to specific quantitative standards or governmental standard-setting procedures. This would suggest that the Bhutanese government saw appropriate roles for both types of standard; roles that would complement each other rather than compete with each other in the overall accomplishment of the environmental objectives that the constitution sought to achieve.

The requirement under Art. 5(3) that 'Bhutan's total land shall be maintained under forest cover for all time'[43] is a remarkable development within the field of global environmental constitutionalism. In fact, by providing a quantitative rather than a qualitative standard of protection relating to forest cover it bucks the trend in constitutional drafting not just for environmental provisions, but for all types of social, economic and cultural rights, which are normally expressed in qualitative terms. As a novel type of provision within national constitutions it raises certain questions which include those relating to its underlying purpose, its justiciability and also those surrounding the manner in which the government should comply with it.

The provision itself appears to give some of the answers relating to its purpose as it refers to the need to 'conserve the country's natural resources' and the duty to 'prevent degradation of the ecosystem'. The aim of prevention of degradation to ecosystems is consistent with contemporary approaches to environmental management;[44] indeed, there are a number of different 'ecosystem services' that forests

38 See generally J R May and E Daly, *Global Environmental Constitutionalism* (CUP 2014).

39 Art 5(2)d.

40 Arts 5(1) and (2).

41 Art 5(1).

42 Art 5(1) and (2).

43 The Constitution of Bhutan (n 1).

44 World Resources Institute, 'Millennium Ecosystem Assessment (2005). Ecosystems and Human Well-Being: Biodiversity Synthesis' <www.millenniumassessment.org/documents/document.354.aspx.pdf> accessed 19 January 2018.

provide, which include the provisioning of firewood, timber and the resources for natural medicines, the regulation of water absorption which can alleviate the possibility of flooding, acting as a carbon sink and the cultural service of enrichment to a population that is particularly sensitized to nature and the environment. In terms of the requirement to 'conserve the country's natural resource'; such a purpose is entirely consistent with the integration of the principle of intergenerational equity and the need to manage natural resources sustainably.

However, these indications do not clarify why Bhutan chose to adopt the specific standard of 60 per cent forest cover. The answer to that question appears to be based on pre-established forest policy. Following the nationalization of forests in 1969, the government adopted a national forest policy in 1974,[45] within which the government stipulated that it would maintain at least 60 per cent of all land under forest cover and developed a scientific programme for forest management alongside a programme for the restoration of degraded land.[46] It is noteworthy that only two years after the Stockholm Declaration[47] and long before the concept of 'ecosystem services' had been developed within western society,[48] a country should adopt such a far-reaching policy relating to the protection of the environment. As Bhutan's forest policy was further developed in the coming decades, the stipulation of 60 per cent forest cover was maintained; for example, it was reiterated in the Eighth Five Year Plan in 1995,[49] and also in the government's 2002 Biodiversity Action Plan for Bhutan.[50] Therefore, although it represents a significant development in the way in which environmental provisions within national constitutions may be drafted, it did not represent a significant change in Bhutanese forestry policy but a formalisation and continuation of what had previously existed.

With regards to the legal effect of Art. 5(3), it is unlikely that the practical answers will be tested in the near future because Bhutan, according to recent figures, has 70.46 per cent of its land covered by forest.[51] Naturally, there are different definitions

45 T Wangdi, P Lhendup and N Wangdi, 'An Analysis of Forestry Policy, Acts and Rules of Bhutan to Mainstream Climate Change Adaptation. Regional Climate Change Adaptation Knowledge Platform for Asia' (2013) Partner Report Series No. 13. Stockholm Environment Institute, Bangkok <www.weadapt.org/sites/weadapt.org/files/legacy-new/knowledge-base/files/521c8788e61b3bhutan-serie-13-cs5-v7-for-web.pdf> accessed 24 July 2018.

46 ibid 3.

47 United Nations Conference on the Human Environment 1972. UN Doc A/Conf.48/14/Rev.1 (1973).

48 GC Daily, SE Alexander and PR Ehrlich et al., 'Ecosystem Services: Benefits Supplied to Human Societies by Natural Ecosystems' (1997) 2 Issues in Ecology 1–18; R Costanza, R d'Arge, R de Groot et al. 'The Value of the World's Ecosystem Services and Natural Capital' (1997) 387 Nature, 253–60.

49 Royal Government of Bhutan, *Eighth Five Year Plan*, 1998–2003 1. <www.gnhc.gov.bt/wp-content/uploads/2011/04/08fyp.pdf> accessed 5 November 2016.

50 RGOB. Biodiversity Action Plan for Bhutan (2002) (n 15).

51 Purna B Chetri and Kinley Tenzin, *State of Forest Genetic Resources of Bhutan – Country Report* (RNR Research and Development Centre – Royal Government of Bhutan 2012) 1 <www.fao.org/3/a-i3825e/i3825e5.pdf> accessed 24 July 2018.

of what constitutes 'forest';[52] as such some statistics place the figure as high as 72.5 per cent,[53] and there are others that doubt the veracity of this owing to claims of high levels of deforestation in more recent years.[54] Whatever the precise figures actually are, as a result of the levels of forest cover currently published in official statistics, it is unlikely that the government could be subject in the immediate future to constitutional challenge in this regard. It is also possible of course to interpret Art. 5(3) as inviting the exploitation of forest resources until the 60 per cent threshold is reached, thus creating an excuse for environmental degradation rather than representing a high standard of protection. While it is not unfeasible that such an outcome could occur, the evidence to date which is assessed in Section 15.4 indicates that in recent decades the management policy of the Bhutanese government is indeed to maintain a very high level of environmental protection.[55]

15.4 THE JUSTICIABILITY OF ART. 5(3)

While it is unlikely in the near future that the government could face a challenge over its compliance with Art. 5(3), it is still important to consider the issue of potential justiciability, to appreciate the manner in which it could affect decision making. Article 1(11) of the constitution states that 'the Supreme Court shall be the guardian of this Constitution and the final authority on its interpretation'.[56] However, there is no explicit reference in the constitution of a right of citizens to challenge the government in relation to Art. 5(3). There is a right under Art. 7(23) for citizens to take legal proceedings when their fundamental rights under Art. 7 are violated.[57] However, Art. 7 relates to rights such as the right to life,[58] the right to property[59] and the right to information,[60] and does not include specific rights related to the protection of the environment or forestry.

Additionally, Art. 21(18) states that 'every person has the right to approach the courts in matters arising out of the Constitution or other laws subject to section 23 of Article 7'. Furthermore, Art. 21(9) states that 'the Supreme Court may, on its own

52 The definition followed by the RGOB is that adopted by the Global Forest Resources Assessment Report 2000 of the UN FAO which states that they are defined as 'areas where tree crowns cover over 10 per cent of the ground, and cover areas greater than 0.5 hectares'. See Royal Government of Bhutan, Ministry of Agriculture, *Biodiversity Action Plan 2009* (2009) 10 <www.cbd.int/doc/world/bt/bt-nbsap-v3-en.pdf> accessed 24 July 2018.

53 RGOB *Biodiversity Action Plan 2009* ibid 10.

54 B Rai, 'Bhutan's Forests: The Real Picture' (*Kuensal Online*, 2005). <www.kuensalonline.com> accessed 16 August 2016.

55 See especially the *Gedu Plywood Factory* case (n 89).

56 The Constitution of Bhutan (n 1).

57 This is reinforced under the provisions relating to the functioning of the courts and the judiciary. Therefore, art 21(18) states that 'every person has the right to approach the courts in matters arising out of the Constitution or other laws subject to section 23 of Article 7'.

58 Art 7(1)

59 Art 7(9)

60 Art 7(3)

motion or on an application made by the Attorney General or by a party to a case, withdraw any case pending before the High Court involving a substantial question of law of general importance relating to the interpretation of this Constitution and dispose of the case itself'.

The meaning of these provisions was tested in the case of *The Government of Bhutan* v. *Opposition Party* (2011),[61] the first and only constitutional case that has been heard to date by the Supreme Court. The case related to an executive decision to make changes to vehicle taxes without an Act of Parliament. The party in opposition made a claim through the High Court that such a decision was in contravention of Art. 14(1) of the constitution, which states that 'taxes, fees and other forms of levies shall not be imposed or altered except by law'.[62] The claim was successful in the High Court, and on appeal the Supreme Court upheld the decision *inter alia* on the basis that the 'process' that the government had instituted to make the changes was unconstitutional.[63] While the case did not relate to forestry or to environmental matters, important conclusions were made by the Supreme Court in relation to its own authority and also the capacity of the opposition party and citizens to challenge government decision making of a constitutional nature through judicial review.

The High Court concluded *inter alia* that the constitution clearly provided it (at first instance) and the Supreme Court (on final appeal) with the authority to hear judicial review cases on constitutional issues related to decision making by the executive branch of government.[64] It found that ordinary citizens are entitled to bring such cases if they are aggrieved parties, or alternatively through class action suits if they are able to establish *locus standi*.[65] It also found that the opposition party had a special status to bring cases of a constitutional nature owing to its responsibilities under Art. 18(1) of the constitution, which states that it shall 'play a constructive role to ensure that the Government and the ruling party function in accordance with the provisions of this Constitution, provide good governance and strive to promote the national interest and fulfil the aspirations of the people'.[66] As such, the opposition party does not need to show that it is 'aggrieved' or that it had *locus standi* through a specific relationship with the issue concerned. The court held that the opposition party could file such cases as a last resort.[67] In summary it stated that 'filing of petition against the Government by the Opposition Party and individuals who have *locus standi* and a concrete case or controversy must be allowed'.[68]

61 Judgement No. SC (Hung 11–1). <www.judiciary.gov.bt/html/case/Judg/2011/englishj.pdf> accessed 5 November 2016.
62 The Constitution of Bhutan (n 1).
63 Judgement No. SC (Hung 11–1) (n 67) 'Court Findings' [5.7].
64 ibid [5.5] 'Court Findings'. It relied upon arts 7(23), 23(5), 21(9) and 21(18) of the Constitution.
65 ibid [5.1].
66 ibid.
67 ibid.
68 ibid.

Therefore, notwithstanding the lack of a specific provision within the constitution relating to the justiciability of the constitutional obligations of the government, it does appear feasible that, firstly, the party in opposition, and secondly, individuals under specific circumstances might be able to bring constitutional legal action against the government where it appeared to be making decisions that were not consistent with its obligations vis à vis Art. 5(3). The 2011 case also provides an insight into the attitude of the Supreme Court towards its own role. It demonstrates that it is willing to be responsive to claims to ensure that the executive branch of government complies with its constitutional obligations.

A more recent development that may provide an indication of the approach the Bhutanese courts will have relating to Art. 5(3) is the establishment of a 'green bench' within the High Court to resolve disputes on environmental cases.[69] This development is still quite recent, and therefore it is difficult to ascertain what impact it will have. Additionally, in 2016 the Supreme Court announced that it is looking to allow 'public interest litigation' in relation to environmental issues.[70] In announcing this development, the Chief Justice of the Supreme Court of Bhutan, Lyonpo Tshering Wangchuk, stated that this was, in part, a response to the right that citizens have to approach the court on constitutional matters under Art. 21(18) of the constitution.[71] These developments may be partly attributed to the close relationship that Bhutan has had for many years and continues to have with India, which has introduced its own national green tribunal[72] and which has allowed public interest litigation on environmental matters for many years.[73] It remains to be seen whether the influence of India will extend to the manner in which the Bhutanese judiciary interpret and apply the constitution.

Bearing in mind the transition that is gradually taking place politically and socially, it is also uncertain precisely how litigious Bhutanese society may become in the future. It is not culturally routine practice within Bhutanese society to oppose or challenge the government's or the king's authority.[74] However, as the country has gradually modernised in many respects and its citizens become more exposed to influences from other countries, it is possible that knowledge of law and attitudes towards litigation could change. All the same, as a result of the success of the

69 See Irum Ahsan and Gregorio R Bueta, 'Proceedings of the Third Asia Judicial Roundtable on Environmental Justice for Sustainable Development' Colombo, Sri Lanka 8–9 August 2014 (Asian Development Bank, 2014) 11; Pema Seldon, 'Supreme Court to Allow Public Interest Litigation for Environmental Issues' *Business Bhutan* (19 March 2016) 1 and 15.

70 Seldon ibid.

71 ibid.

72 See Chapter 10 of this volume by Gitanjali N Gill, which includes a discussion relating to the work of the National Green Tribunal in India; also Gitanjali N Gill, 'Environmental Justice in India: The National Green Tribunal and Expert Members' (2016) 25 (1) Transnational Environmental Law 175–205.

73 Jona Razzaque, *Public Interest Environmental Litigation in India, Pakistan and Bangladesh* (Kluwer Law International 2004).

74 Lhundup (n 12) 696.

Bhutanese government over the last five decades in maintaining a very high percentage of forest cover in the country, the fledgling nature of the constitution and its environmental provisions, and the lack of a tradition of litigation within Bhutanese society, it is unlikely in at least the foreseeable future that the courts will be requested to hear any cases relating to Art. 5(3).

As the maintenance of 60 per cent of the country's land under forest cover cannot be attributable to litigation or even to the existence of Art. 5(3), Section 15.5 next considers the factors that have led to the country successfully implementing its forest cover policy.

15.5 FOREST MANAGEMENT IN BHUTAN – LAW AND POLICY

As the policy from which Art. 5(3) derives dates back to 1974,[75] it is necessary to consider the development of forest law and policy over at least five decades to understand the extent to which law, policy and practice have led to the maintenance of forest cover in the country at such comparatively high levels. In carrying out this assessment, it is important to bear in mind that Bhutan, like other developing countries, has to take into account a wide range of factors in its approach to forest policy. Those factors include watershed management, poverty reduction, the development of improved transport links, the energy needs of rural communities, housing and construction needs, industry based on forest products, a timber export policy, climate change mitigation and the equitable sharing of benefits from natural resources.

Prior to making this assessment, there is an important caveat that must be taken into account when analysing the significance of Art. 5(3) and Bhutan's forest policy. This is that there is no doubt that Bhutan's forest policy has been aided through the fact that the country has a relatively small population and many of its forests are relatively inaccessible as they exist on steep mountainsides. However, this should not detract from the track record that Bhutan has had in maintaining its forest policy successfully since 1974, when many other countries have recorded severe deforestation during those same decades.[76]

In considering Bhutan's forest law and policy, it is possible to identify specific features that have been prominent since the 1950s. These include the policy of nationalisation, the use of forest management units and national five-year plans, the development of protected areas and programmes of reforestation, and more latterly decentralisation involving the development of community and private forests. This section will consider these approaches with a view to understanding their rationale and effectiveness.

75 Wangdi, Lhendup and Wangdi (n 45).

76 United Nations Food and Agriculture Organization, '2016 State of the World's Forests' (2016) <www.fao.org/3/a-i5850e.pdf> accessed 29 November 2016.

In terms of organisation nationally, the Department of Forests was established in 1952, and this led to more proactive forest management policies.[77] Until the late 1960s forest management was based on traditional and customary rules, and the *Thringzhung Chenmo* ('Mother Act') provided some legal provisions related to the protection of forests and the environment.[78] However, in 1969 the government passed the Forest Act which developed the first national framework to regulate forest resources and which involved nationalisation of all forests in the country.[79] From that point in time all forests came under the overall control and scientific management of the government, with the purpose of ensuring that they could be properly used and protected. However, it was not until 1974 that the government introduced its National Forest Policy (NFP), which introduced further principles that would guide the manner in which forests should be managed, and which included the policy of maintaining 60 per cent of the country under forest cover for all time.[80] Additionally, the NFP placed an emphasis on watershed management and the restoration of denuded forest land,[81] as well as the avoidance of conversion of forest land to other uses and the avoidance of scattered forest habitation.[82]

In terms of putting policy into practice, the NFP was integrated into the five-year plans that Bhutan had instigated in the 1960s to further its economic and social policies and which it still uses throughout its governmental administration to the present day. These plans have facilitated an interventionist approach in which the government ensures that economic development takes place in an environmentally sustainable manner.[83] In terms of legislation, the 1969 Forest Act was repealed in 1995 and replaced by the Forest and Nature Conservation Act (FNCA), which became the main legislative authority for forest governance.[84]

A key component of the government's approach has been to strictly manage those sections of forest that are to be harvested by setting up Forest Management Units (FMU). Currently, about 7 per cent of the country's forests are within FMUs.[85] Each FMU has a management plan[86] to ensure that its use does not damage its ecological productivity.[87] Management plans also make timber available at affordable prices to

77 See RGOB Department of Forests and Parks Services – Ministry of Agriculture and Forests – Royal Government of Bhutan <www.dofps.gov.bt> accessed 24 July 2018.

78 RGOB Ministry of Agriculture – Biodiversity Action Plan 2009 (n 52) 52.

79 RGOB Ministry of Agriculture – National Forest Policy 2011 (n 16) 1.

80 Wangdi, Lhendup and Wangdi (n 45) 3.

81 Department of Forest Services, 'National Forest Policy Review – Bhutan' 57 (*United Nations Food and Agriculture Organization*) <ftp://ftp.fao.org/docrep/fao/005/AC921E/AC921E02.pdf> accessed 25 July 2018.

82 ibid 59.

83 ibid 4; Ministry of Agriculture – Biodiversity Action Plan 2009 (n 52) i.

84 Forest and Nature Conservation Act 1995 (FNCA) <www.nationalcouncil.bt/assets/uploads/docs/acts/2017/Forest-and-Nature-Conservation-Act-of-Bhutan1995_English_1.pdf> accessed 24th February 2019.

85 Purna B Chetri and Kinley Tenzin (n 51) 16.

86 FCNA 1995 (n 84) s 5.

87 RGOB Ministry of Agriculture – Biodiversity Action Plan 2009 (n 52) 35.

local users. Furthermore, an export ban on raw timber has been in place since 1999 to ensure that harvested timber can be made available to Bhutanese citizens.[88] The high level of state control over the timber industry and the priority of protecting the environment is illustrated by the case of the Gedu plywood factory that was financed by a loan from Kuwait.[89] Despite the potential economic benefits of running such a project, the Forest Department limited the number of trees that could be felled to supply the factory to such an extent that it only ran at 15 per cent of its capacity. As a result it was unable to operate in a profitable manner and ultimately had to be closed down.[90]

Integral to the government's forest policy has been the development of protected areas[91] and continual programmes of reforestation. Currently Bhutan's protected areas amount to 51.44 per cent of the country which are made up of wildlife sanctuaries, national parks and nature reserves, as well as one botanic park and seven biological corridors that connect all ten protected areas.[92] The first reforestation programme occurred in 1947.[93] Since that time, five-year plans have been integral to the reforestation of more than 21,500 ha of land.[94]

One side effect of the nationalisation of forests in 1969 was the loss of control and participation in decision making that rural communities traditionally had. Therefore, consistent with international trends towards Community Based Natural Resource Management[95] and decentralisation of control,[96] Bhutan instituted initiatives to create community and private forests which restored a certain degree of local control. The concept of community forests was introduced in the 1980s and was put into a legislative framework in 1995 through the FNCA.[97] As of 2014–15 there were 600 community forests covering 66,934 ha (representing about 1.7 per cent of the area of the country and 2.5 per cent of the forested areas),[98] and which involved 28.3 per cent of rural households.[99] The principle behind community forests is to

88 Purna B Chetri and Kinley Tenzin (n 51) 17.

89 'Gedu Plywood Factory Shut Down' 4 (1) The Bhutan Review Monthly (January 1996) 1 <http://himalaya.socanth.cam.ac.uk/collections/journals/bhutanreview/pdf/TBR_04_01.pdf> accessed 14 November 2016.

90 Stefan Priesner (n 15) 24, 50.

91 FNCA (n 84) s 21.

92 RGOB, Ministry of Agriculture and Forests, 'Summary: Bhutan's State of Parks Report 2016' <www.moaf.gov.bt/summary-of-bhutans-state-of-parks-report-2016-2/> accessed 24 July 2018; Ministry of Agriculture – Biodiversity Action Plan 2009 (n 2009) 32.

93 RGOB National Environment Commission, 'Second National Communication to the UNFCCC' (2011) 40 <http://unfccc.int/resource/docs/natc/snc_bhutan.pdf> accessed 25 July 2018.

94 RGOB Ministry of Agriculture – Biodiversity Action Plan 2009 (n 52) 38.

95 RGOB Ministry of Agriculture – National Forest Policy 2011 (n 16) 13.

96 Bill Buffum, 'Why is There No Tragedy in These Commons? An Analysis of Forest User Groups and Forest Policy in Bhutan' (2012) 4 Sustainability 1448, 1449.

97 FNCA (n 84) s 17.

98 Royal Government of Bhutan, 'SAARC Development Goals – Country Report 2015' 53 <www.gnhc.gov.bt/en/wp-content/uploads/2017/05/SAARC-Development-Goals-Country-Report-2015-1.pdf> accessed 24 July 2018.

99 ibid 53.

enable and empower communities to manage local forests while operating in accordance with specific regulations.[100] The objective is to reduce poverty through increased access to timber and forest produce,[101] and also to contribute to the overall sustainable management of the nation's forests.[102] The policy also has the advantage of creating an interface between large-scale planning and traditional methods of forest management.[103] It has been argued that one of the reasons for the success of Bhutan's community forest programme is that the government is able to supply communities with well-stocked forests rather than degraded forest land, which is often the case in similar schemes in other countries.[104]

Therefore, the legislative and policy approach that the Bhutanese government has adopted to maintain at least 60 per cent of its land mass under forest cover can be characterised by: a value centred approach that fully respects the aspect of the environment concerned in its own right, a recognition of the benefits of the resource as a provider of ecosystem services, the adoption of strict government control through legislation and administration, a commitment where necessary to put ecological protection before the pursuit of profit and also the beneficial involvement and participation of communities in the management and use of the resource.

Having examined Art. 5(3) from a national perspective, Section 15.6 next considers its relevance in the international context. Therefore, it will assess the influence that it may have and how it may provide a perspective from which other aspects of global environmental constitutionalism and global environmental governance may be viewed.

15.6 BHUTAN'S QUANTITATIVE ENVIRONMENTAL STANDARD WITHIN THE GLOBAL CONTEXT

It is important to consider Art. 5(3) within the global context for two reasons. Firstly, its success, or to be more precise the success of the policy that it represents, means that there may be lessons to be learned by other states or indeed by the international community. Secondly, it is important to consider Art. 5(3) within the context of other developments that are taking place internationally to gauge the extent to which it corresponds with trends within global environmental constitutionalism and global environmental governance.

To carry out an analysis of Art. 5(3) within the global context, this section considers specific aspects of its character and the manner in which it functions in practice. The four specific aspects considered are: (i) the inclusion of a quantitative

100 The Forest and Nature Conservation Rules 2000 (RGOB) <www.moaf.gov.bt/download/Legislations/#wpfb-cat-4> accessed 14 November 2016).

101 Ministry of Agriculture – Biodiversity Action Plan 2009 (n 52) 36.

102 Royal Government of Bhutan, 'SAARC Development Goals – Country Report 2015' (n 98) 52.

103 Ministry of Agriculture – National Forest Policy 2011 (n 16) 14.

104 Buffum (n 96) 1450.

environmental standard within the highest level of law in a national jurisdiction; (ii) the environmental ethos within and through which the provision functions; (iii) the type of regulatory mechanisms through which it operates; and (iv) the status of the interface between the state and the commercial sector within which the provision functions. For each of these elements, this section comments on the extent to which they differ or conform with the practice of other countries. In doing so, it will seek to assess the overall contribution that the provision makes to both global environmental constitutionalism and global environmental governance.

Firstly, in considering the use of quantitative environmental standards within the highest level of law in the country, there is some limited evidence that this approach is developing at the international level. For example, Kenya promulgated a new constitution in 2010 that contains a similar type of standard. The Kenyan example differs to that of Bhutan as its corresponding provision sets a target of forest cover that the country aims to achieve. As such, Art. 69(b) of Kenya's constitution states that the country will work to achieve and maintain 10 per cent of the country under forest cover.[105] Data shows that Kenya has a significant way to go before that target is achieved.[106] However, it appears that in the case of Kenya, like Bhutan, the strength of the provision is in its integration into policy and subordinate law. In Kenya's case this has led to government programmes to increase the level of forest cover incrementally within specific time frames.[107]

Within the wider context of global environmental governance it is possible that the approach of adopting quantitative environmental standards at the highest level of law in a national jurisdiction has gained some traction over the last decade. While Bhutan adopted this standard as a policy in 1974, it is clear that many other states at that time were reluctant to adopt meaningful quantitative standards relating to aspects of the environment, owing to the limitations that this can place upon business and industry and the development of their economies as a whole. However, in recent years the science relating to environmental degradation has become clearer, and an understanding of what are sometimes known as the 'planetary boundaries'[108] has placed greater pressure on states to ensure that business and industry is conducted within specific 'ecological constraints'.[109]

Climate change represents an environmental issue in which the science has gradually become clearer but which has not yet been abated through the initiatives

105 The Constitution of Kenya (27 August 2010).

106 According to figures published by Kenya's Forestry Service in 2014, the country had 6.99 per cent of its land under forest cover. See Kenya Forest Service, 'Second Kenya Forest Service Strategic Plan (Period 2014-17)' (2015) 20 <www.kenyaforestservice.org/documents/KFS%20Vision%202015-17%20FINAL%20%20printed.pdf> accessed 25 July 2018.

107 Kenya Forest Service, Second Kenya Forest Service Strategic Plan ibid 28–29.

108 J Rockström et al., 'A Safe Operating Space for Humanity' (2009) 461 Nature, 472–75.

109 R Costanza et al., *An Introduction to Ecological Economics* (St Lucie Press 1997) 83.

that have been taken through the UNFCCC.[110] This has led certain countries to look more closely at the introduction of specific quantitative environmental standards at the highest legal and policy levels. For example, in 2008 the UK government introduced the Climate Change Act that prescribes that the government must reduce the emission of greenhouse gases by 80 per cent (compared to a 1990 baseline) by 2050.[111] Additionally, the design of the 2015 Paris Agreement provides a framework within which states volunteer specific quantitative targets through what has become known as a system of 'pledge and review'.[112]

Therefore, while the approach that Bhutan has taken through Art. 5(3) may be distinctive in terms of global environmental constitutionalism, it may not be distinctive when seen within the context of global environmental governance generally. As such, it may be that the significance of Art. 5(3) in global terms is not the fact that it is a quantitative rather than a qualitative *constitutional* standard. It may be that it is representative of the policymaking in a number of countries to adopt a quantitative standard at a national level relating to a particular aspect of environmental protection.

Secondly, in considering the environmental ethos of the country, it is difficult to draw direct comparisons to Bhutan as its decision-making culture relating to the environment is distinctive and heavily influenced by Buddhism and the concept of GNH.[113] Clearly these factors have had a considerable impact upon the manner in which the Bhutanese have been successful in protecting the environment. What is interesting is that the belief system within Bhutanese culture, which entails an understanding of the intrinsic value of nature and ecosystems, predates the understanding which is gradually developing in more developed economies of the value of nature and ecosystems.[114] What the Bhutanese example demonstrates is that an intrinsic understanding is crucial if decisions are to be made which are, on the face of it, counter-intuitive to the normal instincts that drive decision making relating to economic development. In more developed countries such an intrinsic system of beliefs is more likely to take place through education and science than through religion or culture; however, it appears that it is an important component in being able to successfully adopt a provision such as Art. 5(3).

It may also be that government initiatives within countries such as the United Kingdom, to measure indicators of 'well-being' as well as those relating to economic

110 International Panel on Climate Change, *Climate Change 2014 Synthesis Report Summary for Policy Makers* (2014) 2 <www.ipcc.ch/pdf/assessment-report/ar5/syr/AR5_SYR_FINAL_SPM.pdf> accessed 30 November 2016.

111 The Climate Change Act 2008 <www.legislation.gov.uk/ukpga/2008/27/contents> accessed 25 July 2018.

112 United Nations Framework Convention on Climate Change – Paris Agreement (adopted 12 December 2015, entered into force 4 November 2016) <http://unfccc.int/files/essential_background/convention/application/pdf/english_paris_agreement.pdf> accessed 30 November 2016.

113 ROGB Ministry of Agriculture, National Forest Policy 2011 (n 16) 3; Sebastian (n 3) 70; Priesner (n 15) 223.

114 Lhundup (n 12) 699.

performance, are a reflection of a growing awareness outside of Bhutan of the crucial importance that non-financial factors have in determining what counts as 'success' for a society. [115] While it is unlikely that western economies will convert to adopting GNH as a method of calibrating the success of their economies, 'sustainability indices' such as the Environmental Sustainability Index[116] are now being accorded greater credence and influence. The environmental component of such indices has similarities to the environmental component that has long been part of the measure of GNH. In this sense, the approach towards the environment that is inherent within the policy of GNH could be regarded as either being ahead of its time, or one which is gradually influencing other countries.

Thirdly, the level of state control over natural resources within the country has been a significant factor in the implementation of the law and policy related to forest cover in Bhutan. As the country's forests were nationalised in 1969, the state was able to exert considerable control.[117] This approach can be contrasted with western liberalised approaches which emphasise private property rights over natural resources and are often combined with a reluctance to over-regulate. Where there does appear to be a confluence between the two approaches in the case of Bhutan, it is the move away from a highly centralised approach towards the adoption of community forestry which also reflects a shift towards ensuring that the benefits of the natural resources in particular areas are shared with the local populace. These features are consistent with principles that have developed at the international level in recent decades to encourage greater participation in the management of natural resources at the local level and greater benefit sharing from natural resources amongst local communities.

However, the overall state control of forests in Bhutan and the limitation on private property rights related to them has meant that some of the problems such as 'land grabbing' and the issues related to it have been avoided.[118] Additionally, the type of forest governance techniques developed within western democracies that rely on trade standards, market mechanisms and labelling could be regarded as relatively weak when compared to the hard regulation and strict control imposed by the Bhutanese government.[119] Therefore it is in this area too that it is possible that lessons could be learned by the international community from the Bhutanese approach to natural resource management.

115 UK Government – Office of National Statistics, 'Measuring National Well-Being: Personal Well-Being in the UK, 2014 to 2015' (UK Government – Office of National Statistics, 23 September 2015) <www.ons.gov.uk/peoplepopulationandcommunity/wellbeing/bulletins/measuringnationalwellbeing/2015to2016> accessed 1 December 2016.

116 The Environmental Sustainability Index <http://sedac.ciesin.columbia.edu/data/collection/esi/> accessed 20 January 2018.

117 Ministry of Agriculture – National Forest Policy 2011 (n 16) 1.

118 L Cotula, S Vermeulen, R Leonard and J Keeley, 'Land Grab or Development Opportunity? Agricultural Investment and International Land Deals in Africa' (IIED/FAO/IFAD 2009).

119 G Auld, *Constructing Private Governance: The Rise and Evolution of Forest, Coffee, and Fisheries Certification* (Yale University Press 2014) 2.

When it is borne in mind that national constitutions are rarely static and that they are amended on average every nineteen years,[120] it is possible that other states may consider amending their own constitutional provisions in ways that draw upon the Bhutanese experience. This is not to suggest that other countries should necessarily incorporate quantitative environmental standards into their constitutions, but there may be aspects of the Bhutanese approach that could assist other countries in the way that they approach environmental protection from a constitutional perspective.

15.7 CONCLUSION

It is difficult to predict how successful Bhutan will be in the future in protecting its forests from deforestation, and as such whether it will successfully comply with the requirement of Art. 5(3). It is a country that is in transition politically and one that is gradually modernising economically. Therefore, it will undoubtedly face numerous challenges as it seeks to develop its economy while maintaining its culture, its environment and its traditional values.

As a legal provision Art. 5(3) does appear to be justiciable under certain circumstances. Therefore, if the country does begin to suffer from levels of deforestation that take it closer to the 60 per cent threshold, it will be interesting to see whether that provokes litigation, and more importantly how the courts and the government respond to it.

In the narrower sense, the potential influence that Art. 5(3) may have within global environmental constitutionalism is that other countries may now look more seriously at the possible use of quantitative environmental standards within their constitutions, or at least at the highest level of law and policymaking. Such a move would certainly be consistent with a growing scientific understanding of the ways that it is necessary to maintain our ecosystems and live within specific planetary boundaries.[121]

In the broader sense, an examination of Art. 5(3) and the bases upon which Bhutan's national forest policy has been implemented has the potential to influence other countries in relation to certain other aspects of environmental protection. Firstly, the Buddhist understanding of the value of nature challenges the western ethos of evaluating success in economic terms through levels of GDP. It raises the proposition that valuing the economy through alternative methods that incorporate the intrinsic value of the environment may ultimately be more appropriate if the international community is to achieve its objectives such as those included within the Sustainable Development Goals (SDG).[122] Secondly, it challenges some of the mandatory and non-mandatory interventions that are currently in use in other jurisdictions to achieve forest policy goals.

120 Z Elkins, T Ginsbury and J Melton, *The Endurance of National Constitutions* (CUP 2009) 38.
121 Rockström et al. (n 108).
122 United Nations, Sustainable Development Goals <www.un.org/sustainabledevelopment/sustainable-development-goals/> accessed 20 January 2018.

16

The Rights of Nature: Guiding Our Responsibilities through Standards

Craig M. Kauffman and Linda Sheehan

16.1 INTRODUCTION

In different parts of the world, governments at all levels – from international bodies, to nations, to small communities – are recognizing the inherent rights of nature to exist, regenerate its vital cycles, and be restored when damaged. With the increase in 'rights of nature' lawmaking comes the need to develop implementation structures that will advance and track the laws' success in protecting and enhancing environmental well-being. These structures necessarily include standards, including science-based standards that help assess progress toward 'healthy' ecosystems and species populations. This chapter introduces the concept of nature's rights, compares the different ways these rights are expressed in different legal provisions, identifies the nascent standards that are emerging in different contexts, analyses various challenges facing the development of rights of nature standards, and discusses next steps for developing science-based standards for measuring the well-being of nature.

16.2 RECOGNIZING THE INHERENT RIGHTS OF NATURE IN LAW

The idea that nature has inherent rights that must be protected is old and has roots in Western and non-Western thinking.[1] However, rights of nature may not have been expressed in Western legal systems until 2006.[2] Since then, laws and court rulings recognizing nature as a subject with inalienable rights have emerged at various levels of government in Bolivia,[3]

[1] For the history of rights of nature thought in Western and non-Western traditions, see Craig M Kauffman and Pamela L Martin, 'Can Rights of Nature Make Development More Sustainable? Why Some Ecuadorian Lawsuits Succeed and Others Fail' (2017) 92 World Development 130, 131–32.

[2] Tamaqua Borough, Pennsylvania, Ordinance No. 612 2006 <http://files.harmonywithnatureun.org/uploads/upload666.pdf> accessed 09 February 2019.

[3] Plurinational State of Bolivia, Law of the Rights of Mother Earth, Law No. 071 2010 <http://files.harmonywithnatureun.org/uploads/upload656.pdf> accessed 09 February 2019.

Colombia,[4] Ecuador,[5] India,[6] Mexico,[7] New Zealand,[8] and the United States,[9] and are being developed in Argentina, Brazil, Cameroon, Nepal, and elsewhere.[10]

Rights of nature laws are emerging in response to extreme pressure on ecosystems, and on communities that live and rely on them. A 2016 United Nations report notes that 'intensified competition for natural resources in recent decades has led to multiple social and environmental conflicts all over the world'.[11]

For many, the increase in socio-environmental conflict reveals the inadequacy of existing human rights and environmental laws to address pressures on the environment, which humans depend on for survival.[12] Arguing that the well-being and rights of humans are inextricably linked to those of natural ecosystems, communities and governments around the world are adopting legal provisions recognizing the rights of nature and identifying the flaws in governance systems that fail to recognize nature's rights.

Existing rights of nature laws share general normative beliefs regarding the intrinsic value of nature, the need for humans to see themselves as part of nature, and humans' obligation to live in harmony with nature. However, the laws vary in important respects, owing to the unique contexts in which they emerged. Due to space limitations, we focus our discussion on rights of nature laws in three countries where rights of nature jurisprudence has developed furthest (Ecuador, New Zealand, and the United States) as well as soft law

4 Constitutional Court of the Republic of Colombia, Judgment in case T-622 of 2016, Proceeding T-5.016.242, regarding the Atrato River 2016 <http://croo.epimg.net/descargables/2017/05/02/14037e7b5712106cd88b687525dfeb4b.pdf> accessed 16 December 2017; Supreme Court of the Republic of Colombia, Judgment in case STC-4360–2018, Filing no. 11001-22-03-000-2018-00319-01, regarding deforestation in the Amazon rainforest 2018.

5 Republic of Ecuador, Constitution 2008, ch 7 <http://pdba.georgetown.edu/Constitutions/Ecuador/english08.html> accessed 17 December 2017.

6 Judgment by High Court of Uttarakhand at Naintal regarding Writ Petition (PIL) No. 126 of 2014 (2017) <www.yumpu.com/en/document/view/58002817/writ-petition-pil-no126-of-2014> accessed 17 December 2017; Judgment by High Court of Uttarakhand at Naintal regarding Writ Petition (PIL) No. 140 of 2015 (2017) <http://files.harmonywithnatureun.org/uploads/upload662.pdf> accessed 09 February 2019.

7 Constitution of Mexico City 2017 <http://cdmx.gob.mx/storage/app/uploads/public/589/746/ef5/589746ef5f8cc447475176.pdf> accessed 16 December 2017.

8 Te Awa Tupua (Whanganui River Claims Settlement) Act 2017; Te Urewera Act 2014.

9 By mid-2017 at least forty-three US local governments had adopted rights of nature ordinances. Craig Kauffman and Pamela Martin compiled data on these US cases from interviews and searching the records of community rights networks and various news sources.

10 See <http://www.harmonywithnatureun.org/rightsOfNature/> and <https://celdf.org/law-library/international-law-center/> both accessed 16 December 2017.

11 UNGA 'Report of the Special Rapporteur on the Situation of Human Rights Defenders' UN Doc A/71/281 (2016) 13.

12 See UNGA 'Report of the Special Rapporteur on the Issue of Human Rights Obligations Relating to the Enjoyment of a Safe, Clean, Healthy and Sustainable Environment' UN Doc A/HRC/34/49 (2017) 3–10 (finding that human rights depend on biodiversity).

developing at the international level. These cases are representative of the range of rights of nature laws created to date.

16.2.1 *Ecuador*

In 2008, Ecuador became the world's first country to instantiate rights of nature constitutionally. Ecuador's rights of nature provisions were significantly shaped by Ecuadorian Indigenous movements due to their place in President Correa's coalition. Indigenous movements had long protested against neoliberal economic policies and advocated an alternative development approach rooted in Indigenous norms and values.[13] Ecuador's constitution pledges to build a new form of sustainable development based on the Andean Indigenous concept *sumak kawsay* (*buen vivir* in Spanish), which is rooted in the idea of living in harmony with nature.[14] The constitution's preamble 'celebrates' nature, defined as *Pachamama*, a sacred deity revered by Indigenous people in the Andes. It also presents a guiding principle for the new development approach: that humans are part of nature, and thus nature is a vital part of human existence. Ecuador's constitution presents *sumak kawsay* as a set of rights for humans, communities, and nature, and portrays rights of nature as a tool for achieving a post-neoliberal development model.

Ecuador's constitution defines nature broadly, as 'Pachamama, where life is reproduced and occurs'.[15] *Pachamama* is typically translated as 'Mother Earth' in English. The broad definition portrays nature's rights as being inherent to all of the Earth's ecosystems. In this way, Ecuador's rights of nature legal provisions differ from a number of other rights of nature laws, which recognize the rights of specific ecosystems (described below).

Article 71 of Ecuador's constitution introduces both rights and enforcement, recognizing nature's right 'to integral respect for its existence and for the maintenance and regeneration of its life cycles, structure, functions and evolutionary processes. All persons, communities, peoples and nations can call upon public authorities to enforce the rights of nature'. Article 72 addresses restitution, stating that 'nature has the right to be restored. This restoration shall be apart from the obligation of the State and natural persons or legal entities to compensate individuals and communities that depend on affected natural systems'. That is, relief must run back to the injured party, nature, regardless of whether or not harm is also caused to humans.

13 Marc Becker, *Indians and Leftists in the Making of Ecuador's Modern Indigenous Movements* (Duke University Press 2008).

14 Ecuador Constitution (n 5) Preamble. For definitions of sumak kawsay/buen vivir, see Craig Kauffman, *Grassroots Global Governance: Local Watershed Management Experiments and the Evolution of Sustainable Development* (Oxford University Press 2017) 194–95.

15 Ecuador Constitution (n 5) art 71. All English translations throughout the chapter are by Craig Kauffman.

Article 73 establishes the precautionary principle and provides the only indication of minimum standards, or thresholds beyond which nature's rights would be violated:

> The State shall apply preventive and restrictive measures on activities that might lead to the extinction of species, the destruction of ecosystems and the permanent alteration of natural cycles. The introduction of organisms and organic and inorganic material that might definitively alter the nation's genetic assets is forbidden.

16.2.2 *New Zealand*

New Zealand's rights of nature laws also arose in part from indigenous views of humans' relationship to nature. This occurred through the process of resolving long-standing treaty disputes between New Zealand's government and two Māori iwi (tribes) over natural ecosystems. In 2012, the Whanganui Iwi and New Zealand's government signed the Whanganui River Agreement (*Tutohu Whakatupua*) settling all historical Treaty of Waitangi claims of the Whanganui Iwi in relation to the Whanganui River.[16] Legislation implementing the agreement (Te Awa Tupua Act) was passed by Parliament in March 2017.[17] The second law stemmed from the 2013 Deed of Settlement signed by New Zealand's government and the Tūhoe Iwi regarding the forest Te Urewera. New Zealand's Parliament adopted legislation to implement this agreement (the Tūhoe Claims Settlement Act and the Te Urewera Act) in July 2014.[18]

Because of their unique origin, New Zealand's laws define nature and its rights differently than in other countries. These laws only recognize rights of particular ecosystems: the Whanganui River (Te Awa Tupua) and the forest Te Urewera. The laws explicitly define the boundaries of these ecosystems and restrict legal personality to them.

The definition of nature and its rights stem from Māori conceptions of their relationship to nature. Māori iwi trace their ancestral lineage to a common ecosystem, which they view as a living, spiritual being. Since the Māori conceptualize nature as an ancestor rather than property, they do not emphasize the concept of rights, but rather the concept of guardianship resulting from their duty to care for their ancestor.

The Te Awa Tupua Act recognizes the river (Te Awa Tupua) as a legal person with 'all the rights, powers, duties, and liabilities of a legal person'.[19] This reflects the Whanganui Iwi's view that the river is a living entity with intrinsic value that is incapable of being owned in an absolute sense, and it enables the river to have legal

16 Tūtohu Whakatupua 2012 <www.wrmtb.co.nz/new_updates/TuutohuWhakatupuaFinalSigned.pdf> accessed 16 December 2017.

17 Te Awa Tupua Act (n 8).

18 Tūhoe Claims Settlement Act 2014; Te Urewera Act (n 8).

19 Te Awa Tupua Act (n 8) clause 14(1).

standing in its own right. To uphold and protect the river's interests, the settlement requires the appointment of a guardian (Te Pou Tupua) authorized to speak on behalf of Te Awa Tupua and charged with protecting its interests. The guardian body is comprised of one iwi representative and one Crown representative. The appointment of guardians recognizes the inseparability of the people and the river and the responsibilities inherent in that relationship to take care of the river as kin.

The Te Urewera Act similarly recognizes the Tūhoe Iwi's genealogical ties to the forest and their view of the forest as a living spiritual being, named Te Urewera. It also recognizes legal personhood status for Te Urewera, with 'all the rights, powers, duties, and liabilities of a legal person'.[20] Te Urewera is not owned by anyone, but rather owns itself. The Act recognizes Te Urewera's intrinsic value and created the Te Urewera Board to serve as guardian of Te Urewera's interests.

Compared to other rights of nature laws, New Zealand's are more limited in terms of their recognition of nature's rights. Neither law includes a statement of inherent rights. Rather, Te Awa Tupua and Te Urewera are simply declared to be legal persons, like corporations or trusts. This grants them the right of procedural access to New Zealand's political and legal systems. The two ecosystems can own property, incur debts, petition the courts (represented by their guardians), and receive reparations for damages, should a court rule in their favour. However, the laws do not explicitly guarantee the ecosystems' right to maintain their integrity or be restored, much less to flourish, as many local laws do in the United States.

16.2.3 *United States*

Approximately forty municipalities around the United States, from Pittsburgh, Pennsylvania[21] to Santa Monica, California,[22] have passed local laws creating enforceable rights for ecosystems. For example, Pittsburgh's ordinance states:

> Natural communities and ecosystems, including, but not limited to, wetlands, streams, rivers, aquifers, and other water systems, possess inalienable and fundamental rights to exist and flourish within the City of Pittsburgh. Residents of the City shall possess legal standing to enforce those rights on behalf of those natural communities and ecosystems.[23]

The US laws primarily stemmed from environmental lawyers and activists who criticized existing environmental laws for focusing on mitigating harms rather

[20] ibid clause 11.

[21] City of Pittsburgh, Code of Ordinances, Title 6, art 1, ch 618, 'Marcellus Shale Natural Gas Drilling Ordinance' 2010 <https://library.municode.com/pa/pittsburgh/codes/code_of_ordinances?nodeId=COOR_TITSIXCO_ARTIRERIAC_CH618MASHNAGADR> accessed 16 December 2017.

[22] Santa Monica, Santa Monica Municipal Code, Ordinance 2421, ch 4.75 2013 <www.smgov.net/departments/council/agendas/2013/20130409/s20130409_07A1.htm> accessed 16 December 2017.

[23] ibid ch 618.03(b).

than preventing them, and who advocated new laws empowering communities to prevent environmental degradation. Consequently, rights of nature in the United States tend to be linked to community rights. Nature is typically framed as a collection of natural communities whose welfare is necessary for the well-being of human communities. Nature's rights are often expressed through community bills of rights that provide a legal basis for municipal residents to defend their interests against corporations invoking property and other rights to justify environmental degradation.

The rights recognized in many US laws go beyond those listed in Ecuador, Bolivia, and New Zealand. In addition to the right to exist and be fully restored, they also recognize nature's right 'to flourish'. This has important implications for determining where to set the threshold of standards. Humans inevitably impact the ecosystems of which they are a part. Under Ecuador's constitution, human impacts may not violate nature's rights if the system or species population can still regenerate itself (a minimal standard). The distinction is like the difference between breaking your arm (a temporary damage that will heal naturally) and the permanent damage of cutting off your arm.[24] By contrast, the right to flourish switches the emphasis from preventing permanent damage to ensuring some level of well-being for an ecosystem. This would require a more restrictive definition of which human impacts are acceptable, and thus stricter standards based on measurements of the well-being of ecosystems. We analyse this issue further in subsequent sections.

16.2.4 *Activism at the International Level*

At the international level, certain states have attempted to develop international acceptance and soft law relating to the concept of the rights of nature. In 2009, the Bolivian President Evo Morales called on the UN General Assembly to adopt a Universal Declaration of the Rights of Mother Earth (UDRME).[25] The proposal received backing from nine countries, including Ecuador.[26] Bolivia then sponsored the 2010 World People's Conference on Climate Change and the Rights of Mother Earth, where some 35,000 people from 140 countries drafted and approved a citizens' UDRME.[27] It affirms that all components of nature, including humans, have inherent rights, including (but not limited to) the right to life and to exist and the right 'to full and prompt restoration' when rights are violated (Article 2).

24 Kauffman interview with Natalia Greene, Coordinator, Global Alliance for the Rights of Nature (Quito, Ecuador, 30 July 2015).

25 Evo Morales, 'Address by H.E. Mr. Evo Morales Ayma, the President of the Plurinational State of Bolivia', 64th Session of the General Assembly of the United Nations (2009) 2.

26 ALBA-TCP, 'Declaración Especial Por Una Declaración Universal de los Derechos de la Madre Tierra' (Special Declaration for a Universal Declaration for the Rights of Nature) 2009 <https://www.alainet.org/es/active/33808> accessed 16 December 2017.

27 World People's Conference on Climate Change and the Rights of Mother Earth, 'Rights of Mother Earth' (2010) <https://pwccc.wordpress.com/programa/> accessed 16 December 2017.

The UDRME adds that nature's rights, like human rights, 'arise from the same source as existence' (Article 1).

A platform for developing soft law around rights of nature now exists within the UN General Assembly. Since 2009, there have been annual intergovernmental negotiations on constructing a non-anthropocentric understanding of sustainable development rooted in the principle of living in harmony with nature. These negotiations have produced several UN General Assembly resolutions and UN Secretary General reports calling for a new development paradigm that recognizes the rights of nature.[28] In 2015, the United Nations General Assembly requested an expert report on how to develop Earth Jurisprudence (Earth-centred law, policy, and science), and established a worldwide network of experts to develop and lead implementation of the report's recommendations.[29] The UN released the final Expert Report on Earth Jurisprudence in August 2016.[30] Among its conclusions, the report asserts the 'fundamental legal rights of ecosystems and species to exist, thrive and regenerate'.[31] In 2017, the UN General Assembly Dialogue focused on developing strategies for applying Earth Jurisprudence to advance the Sustainable Development Goals.[32] The UN's Harmony with Nature initiative provides an online platform for sharing information, developing partnerships, and coordinating actions to achieve this goal.[33]

Transnational networks of citizens are also pressuring the UN to adopt the UDRME. For example, advocates have developed model fora of international experts (known as 'citizens' tribunals') to hear, consider, and offer conclusions regarding alleged violations of nature's rights, including but not limited to violations of the UDRME.[34] The forum concept was inspired by citizens' tribunals established in the 1960s to investigate and publicize human rights violations.[35] Just as those citizens' tribunals provided social pressure to strengthen international human rights law, the rights of nature fora promote rights of nature law internationally.

16.3 NASCENT RIGHTS OF NATURE STANDARDS

Because rights of nature laws emerged so recently, standards specifying how nature's rights should be interpreted in specific circumstances are in a very early stage of

28 See <http://harmonywithnatureun.org/unDocs/> accessed 09 February 2019.

29 UNGA Res A/RE/S/70/208 (2015) 3–4.

30 UNGA Res A/71/266 (2016).

31 ibid 7.

32 UNGA 'Interactive Dialogue of the General Assembly on Harmony with Nature' (21 April 2017) <http://www.harmonywithnatureun.org/dialogues/> accessed 16 December 2017; UNGA 'Report of the Secretary-General' UN Doc A/72/175 (2017).

33 United Nations, 'Harmony with Nature' <http://www.harmonywithnatureun.org/> accessed 16 December 2017.

34 Global Alliance for the Rights of Nature, 'International Rights of Nature Tribunal' <http://therightsofnature.org/rights-of-nature-tribunal/> accessed 16 December 2017.

35 Cormac Cullinan, 'A Tribunal for Earth: Why It Matters' (Global Alliance for the Rights of Nature, 2005) <http://therightsofnature.org/a-tribunal-for-earth-why-it-matters/> accessed 16 December 2017.

development. Such standards have been slow to develop in part because rights of nature can be controversial and have been impacted by political conflict, as we describe in Section 16.3.1. Nevertheless, early standards are emerging, particularly in Ecuador, and processes are underway in New Zealand and the United States, as described in Sections 16.3.2 and 16.3.3, respectively. These standards are being tested through application in particular circumstances.

16.3.1 *Developing Standards in Ecuador*

In Ecuador, early efforts to craft secondary laws and institutions that could give form to the constitution's rights of nature provisions stalled amid conflict over the government's plans to expand mining.[36] Given the State's priority on exploiting natural systems to fuel social development, Ecuador's National Assembly postponed consideration of rights of nature regulations and did not create the *superintendencia* (autonomous, independent administrative unit) for the environment called for in the constitution.[37] Environmental lawyers and activists drafted a secondary rights of nature law,[38] but decided not to submit it to the National Assembly given the hostile political context and their fear that this would provide an opportunity for legislators to restrict the constitution's rights of nature provisions.[39] Consequently, rights of nature standards initially developed through lawsuits in a highly politicized context.[40]

Articles 72 and 73 of Ecuador's constitution provide some minimum standards necessary to uphold the rights of nature. Any action that *might* lead to the extinction of a species, the destruction of an ecosystem (making it unable to regenerate itself), the permanent alteration of natural cycles, or the alteration of genetic assets (e.g. through the introduction of organic or inorganic material) is considered a violation.[41] The constitution requires the State to prevent an action when there is reason to believe it will likely incur one of the above violations.[42]

Decisions from rights of nature judicial actions indicate how rights of nature standards are evolving in Ecuador. While Ecuador has a civil law system, the lack of secondary laws greatly empowered judges and prompted them to consider judicial precedent when considering rights of nature lawsuits. These lawsuits and associated

36 Kauffman and Martin (n 1) 132–33.

37 Kauffman interview with Patricio Hernandez, Coordinator of Legislative Policy, ECOLEX Corporation (Quito, Ecuador, 3 August 2015).

38 Unpublished draft rights of nature law obtained by Kauffman from its author, Patricio Hernandez.

39 Natalia Green (n 24); Kauffman interview with Esperanza Martínez, President, Acción Ecológica (Quito, Ecuador, 7 August 2015); Kauffman interview with Alberto Acosta, former President of Ecuador's Constituent Assembly (Quito, Ecuador, 13 July 2015); Patricio Hernandez (n 37).

40 Kauffman and Martin (n 1) 130–42 identify thirteen rights of nature lawsuits and explain how rights of nature legal provisions have strengthened through the creation of judicial momentum.

41 Ecuador Constitution (n 5) art 72–73.

42 ibid art 73.

judicial decisions are detailed elsewhere.[43] We summarize here environmental standards and standards of governance that are implied by key rulings.

Several judicial decisions and administrative actions by the Ministry of Environment establish the standard that killing individual members of endangered or protected species constitutes a rights of nature violation. In 2011, pressured by environmental NGOs and scientific teams, the Galapagos district attorney's office and Galapagos National Park sued a fishing crew for violating the rights of sharks by poaching them. In 2015, the Ninth Tribunal Criminal Court in Guayaquil found the captain and crew guilty and sentenced the captain to two years in prison, and each crew member to one year.[44] The verdict also ordered the destruction of the ship.[45] The judge explained the ruling by invoking rights of nature:

> The Constitution of the Republic of Ecuador in its articles 71, 72, 73, 83 numeral 6, 395 numeral 4, 396, 397 final part and 405; establish several precepts, norms and principles that relate to the rights of nature or Pachamama; with the duty of the State to establish mechanisms to achieve the restoration of damage to nature and the adoption of mechanisms to mitigate the harmful consequences of protecting nature and species.[46]

This marked the first time a court upheld the rights of sharks. Similarly, in 2014, the Ministry of Environment won two lawsuits against individuals who killed a condor and a jaguar, both endangered species.[47] The judge in the condor case agreed with the Ministry's argument that Article 73 of Ecuador's constitution requires the State 'to apply preventive and restrictive measures' on activities that might lead to rights of nature violations, including the extinction of species.[48] In both cases, the hunters were sentenced to prison.

Other judgments established that government construction projects cannot impede the ability of ecosystems or species to regenerate. One such decision relates to road construction by Loja's provincial government, which dumped construction debris into the Vilcabamba River, causing the river's flow to increase and change its path. Landowners sued on behalf of the Vilcabamba River to have the river and surrounding ecosystems restored. The Loja Provincial Court of Justice ruled that the claimants did not have to prove damage to themselves to have standing, but only damage to nature, setting an important

43 Kauffman and Martin (n 1) 130–42.

44 Judgment No. 09171-2015-0004, Ninth Court of Criminal Guarantees, Guayas Province, Republic of Ecuador (23 April 2015) 55–59.

45 ibid 58.

46 ibid 54.

47 Judgment No. 2003-2014 – C.T., National Court of Justice, Specialized Chamber of Criminal, Military Criminal, Criminal Police and Transit Cases, Republic of Ecuador (7 September 2014); Kauffman and Martin (n 1) 137.

48 Legal claim filed by Ecuador's Ministry of Environment with the District Attorney's office of Tena, Ecuador, Personal Action No. 0323046 (19 November 2012) 3; Ecuador Constitution (n 5) 22.

standard of governance.[49] In 2011, the judge ruled in favour of the Vilcabamba River and ordered the Provincial Government to restore the river and surrounding ecosystems through measures specified by the Ministry of Environment.[50]

A 2012 judicial ruling in the municipality of Santa Cruz, Galapagos Islands, set the precedent that obstructing the migration and breeding patterns of species violates the rights of nature.[51] This lawsuit involved the municipal government's plans to expand a main boulevard adjacent to a marine reserve area. The construction area constituted a species habitat, and the road crossed a migratory path for marine iguanas and other species. Invoking rights of nature (Articles 71–73), and citing the Vilcabamba case as precedent, the judge ordered that construction be suspended until the municipality conducted an environmental impact assessment that would guarantee that construction was carried out in a way that would protect species habitats, particularly during migration season. The case establishes further precedent regarding the court's duty to protect nature, even above the autonomous rights of decentralized municipalities.

The Santa Cruz lawsuit is one of several where judges have invoked rights of nature in their rulings even when they are not invoked by either claimants or defendants, suggesting a new standard of judicial oversight regarding rights of nature. The principle that courts have an obligation to protect rights of nature despite the interests of claimants and defendants was upheld by Ecuador's Constitutional Court in its 2009 ruling involving the placement of biodigestors by agroindustrial company PRONACA.[52] After citing numerous violations of nature's rights, the court stated:

> It is the obligation of this Court, as guardian of the fulfillment of Constitutional mandates, to materialize the will of constituents expressed in our Fundamental Charter, which grants rights to Nature as part of a legal philosophy of rights, biocentric and non-anthropocentric, so that when there is uncertainty about the scope of the principle and legal provisions in environmental matters, these should be applied in the sense most favorable to the protection of Nature.[53]

The court ruled that, while in one sense the biodigestors were respecting nature by saving energy, the resulting pollution constituted potential violations of the rights of

49 Judgment No. 11121-2011-0010, Provincial Court of Justice, Loja Province, Republic of Ecuador (30 March 2011) 3–4.

50 ibid 5–6.

51 Judgment No. 269 – 2012, Civil and Mercantile Court, Galápagos Province, Republic of Ecuador (28 June 2012).

52 Judgment No. 0567-08-RA, Resolution 567 of the Constitutional Court of Ecuador, Republic of Ecuador (8 December 2009). This approach can be compared and contrasted with that of other constitutional and supreme courts dealing with the environmental rights provisions within national constitutions. See, for example, how Colombia's Constitutional Court invoked environmental rights recognized in Colombia's constitution to justify recognizing legal rights for the Atrato River (n 5); see also Chapter 10 by Gita Gill related to the Indian Constitution and Chapter 13 by Nathan Cooper related to the South African Constitution.

53 Constitutional Court of Ecuador ibid 7.

nature. Consequently, the court allowed the biodigestors to remain, but ordered the creation of a commission to audit and monitor the biodigestors to ensure that the rights of nature would be protected.[54] The court repeatedly cited nature's right to be restored to its ecological state before PRONACA entered the province, implying the standard to be used for measuring future rights of nature violations.[55] Moreover, the court stated that:

> Such restoration must be comprehensive, as a set of measures oriented to recover in a systemic way the conditions, composition and original structure (vegetation, flora, fauna, climate, water, soil and microorganisms) of an ecosystem or natural process affected or degraded by an anthropogenic activity.[56]

Lawsuits and government action against unauthorized mining indicate levels of pollution that constitute violations of rights of nature. In May 2011, Ecuador's Ministry of Interior issued a request to the Twenty-Second Criminal Court of Pichincha to approve precautionary measures against artisanal miners, accusing them of committing 'grave acts violating the constitutional rights of nature' by releasing high levels of toxins into water sources.[57] While the government could have invoked other laws to justify the crackdown, it chose to base its actions on rights of nature laws. The ministry's request argued the State's duty to protect the rights of water ecosystems justified extraordinary measures, including 'the destruction of all items, devices, tools, and other utensils that constitute a serious danger to Nature'.[58]

On 20 May 2011, the court approved the request and ordered the government to control illegal mining to uphold the rights of nature.[59] President Correa immediately ordered a military operation, carried out on 21 May. Nearly 600 soldiers seized and destroyed more than 200 pieces of heavy mining equipment, including those that local miners had rented from third parties.[60] Similar operations were repeated elsewhere.[61] In these cases, the government and the court treated the release of toxins into rivers, produced by the processing of minerals, as a violation of the rights of nature.[62] This suggests an emerging standard, albeit one that is not always enforced. These cases also established a new standard of enforcement based on

54 ibid 8.

55 ibid 8.

56 ibid 8.

57 Petition for Protective Measures sent by Minister of Interior José Serrano to Judge Juan Pablo Hernández Cárdenas of the Twenty-Second Criminal Court, Pichincha Province, Republic of Ecuador (20 May 2011) 1–2.

58 ibid 4.

59 Constitutional Protective Action No. 0016-2011, Twenty-Second Criminal Court, Pichincha Province, Republic of Ecuador (20 May 2011).

60 Erin Daly, 'The Ecuadorian Exemplar: The First Ever Vindications of Constitutional Rights of Nature' (2012) 21 Review of European Community & International Environmental Law 63, 65.

61 Kauffman and Martin (n 1) 137.

62 Petition for Protective Measures (n 57) 1–4; Constitutional Protective Action No. 0016-2011 (n 59) 1–2; Republic of Ecuador National Assembly, Commission of Biodiversity and Natural Resources, Act of Session No. 66 (15 June 2011).

the precautionary principle – that property can be confiscated or destroyed in order to protect nature's rights. As we discuss below, this standard was incorporated in the Penal Code.

A 2015 ruling by Ecuador's Constitutional Court further supports the principle that rights of nature are transversal, meaning that they are connected to and impacted by all other elements of the legal order, and thus must be taken into consideration when creating policy or deciding court cases. Citing Articles 83 and 395 of the constitution, the Court determined that 'all the actions of the State, as well as of individuals, must observe and be in accordance with the rights of nature'.[63]

This ruling involved a case in which the Ministry of Environment sought to remove dozens of shrimp companies from ecological reserves to protect fragile mangrove ecosystems. In 2011, one shrimp company sued to stop the government's action to remove it. The company argued that 'the economic interest of an individual takes precedence over Nature', and that the government's effort constituted an infringement on constitutional rights to property and to work.[64] The Ministry of Environment initially lost, but appealed to the Constitutional Court. The Ministry argued that the lower court's ruling 'violated the constitution' when the judge placed 'the economic interest of an individual above that of Nature ... since the environmental legislation that governs us is oriented around preventing violations of the rights of Nature'. The Ministry asked the Constitutional Court to rule on this 'to establish a precedent that permits [the State] to exercise fully the respect for Nature'.[65]

On 20 May 2015, Ecuador's Constitutional Court ruled that because rights of nature are transversal, they affect all other rights, including property rights. The Court acknowledged that this reflects 'a biocentric vision that prioritizes nature in contrast to the classic anthropocentric conception in which the human being is the centre and measure of all things, and where nature was considered a mere provider of resources'.[66] The Court ruled that by not guaranteeing the rights of nature, the lower courts violated the constitutional right of due process. The Constitutional Court overturned the lower court sentences and ordered the case to be retried in the Provincial Court, but this time considering rights of nature. In doing so, it indicated a procedural standard that courts must consider rights of nature provisions.

In 2014, Ecuador's government codified the standards developing through the courts in a new Penal Code.[67] Chapter Four specifies 'Crimes against the environment and nature, or Pachamama'. Articles 245 through 257 identify various activities

63 Judgment No. 166-15-SEP-CC, Case No. 0507-12-EP, Constitutional Court of Ecuador, Republic of Ecuador (20 May 2015) 12.
64 ibid 2.
65 ibid 4.
66 ibid 10.
67 Código Orgánico Integral Penal (Penal Code, Organic Law) 2014.

that constitute crimes against biodiversity, water, soil, air, and other aspects of nature. Each of these crimes carries a multi-year prison sentence. Notably, Article 551 legalizes the destruction of private property to protect the rights of nature against the above crimes. This codifies the precedent established by the government's actions against unauthorized mining discussed above.

The Penal Code is written such that rights of nature violations occur when 'grave harm' is committed against an ecosystem or species. In 2015, the Ministry of Environment published its standards for determining when a 'grave harm' occurs. The complete list is too long to detail here. In general, the ministry defines 'grave harm' as occurring when: (1) there is a discharge of a contaminant; (2) the discharge causes an 'evident alteration' of the functioning of an ecosystem, and/or this alteration causes damage to flora, fauna, fragile ecosystems, or human health; and (3) 'there is noncompliance with environmental technical requirements for prevention, mitigation and/or contingency of environmental impacts' required by national environmental regulations.[68] Ecuadorian legal experts have criticized this third criterion because it suggests that rights of nature cannot be violated so long as actions adhere to government-approved regulations, creating a loophole that could weaken rights of nature protections.[69]

16.3.2 *Developing Standards in New Zealand*

Since New Zealand's rights of nature laws do not delineate nature's rights other than through the provision of legal personhood status, decisions on how to balance the rights of ecosystems against the rights of other legal persons (e.g. individuals and corporations) in a given situation will likely be made in New Zealand's Environmental Courts. As happened in Ecuador, standards will likely emerge over time as judges make decisions about how conflicts between rights should be managed, with consideration being given to existing law that may potentially impact those standards.

Currently, the hierarchy of rights in the Te Awa Tupua Act is unclear. On one hand, Part 2, clause 16 states that the Act does not limit any existing interests or private property rights in the Whanganui River, including rights to water, wildlife, fish, or other aquatic life. On the other hand, the Act specifies that any public or private actor taking actions that affect the river must 'have particular regard to' the interests of the river and 'recognize and provide for' the values defining the essence of Te Awa Tupua.[70] Clause 13 recognizes four such values, which include treating Te Awa Tupua as a singular, indivisible, and living entity that contains physical and metaphysical elements. Furthermore, clause 15 requires that any person exercising

68 Republic of Ecuador, Official Registry, Second Supplement No. 598 (30 September 2015) 2–5.

69 Kauffman interview with Francisco Bustamante, legal advisor to Ecuador's Constitutional Court and Ministry of Environment (New Orleans, 26 October 2017).

70 Te Awa Tupua Act (n 8) 3.

functions, duties, or powers under relevant statutes, like the Resource Management Act, must recognize and provide for the status of Te Awa Tupua and the four values discussed above. Decision makers must also issue reports documenting how the legal status and values of Te Awa Tupua were provided for, providing transparency to their decision making.

The Act also establishes a watershed management group representing different stakeholders (Te Kōpuka) charged with developing an integrated watershed management plan through a collaborative process. At the time of writing, various stakeholder groups empowered to participate in Te Kōpuka are selecting their representatives in advance of Te Kōpuka being established and its members formally appointed. Importantly, the Te Awa Tupua Act (clause 38) states that should a discrepancy arise between the group's integrated watershed management plan and existing regulation (such as New Zealand's Resource Management Act), existing regulations must be altered to conform with Te Awa Tupua's integrated management plan. This is arguably one of the most important elements of the Act in terms of strengthening the rights of nature.

The hierarchy of rights is handled somewhat differently in the Te Urewera Act. As a national park, Te Urewera was not previously subject to the Resource Management Act, but was governed by special Conservation Department provisions. The Act removes Te Urewera's status as a national park and grants the Te Urewera Board full authority to determine management of the forest.[71] It is charged with doing so according to the interests of Te Urewera as a living, spiritual being. The Te Urewera Board began crafting the forest management plan in 2015, was charged with completing it in three years, and is on track to do so.[72] This plan will presumably contain standards for ensuring the protection of the forest's rights.

16.3.3 *Developing Standards in the United States*

The process of implementing rights of nature laws in the United States closely parallels that of implementing other, 'traditional', conservation laws. For example, stakeholders involved with passing the Santa Monica Sustainability Rights Ordinance (SRO) have worked with the city's Task Force on the Environment, city environment department staff, the City Attorney's office, and the City Council to move SRO implementation forward.[73] Staff and stakeholders have examined different strategies for applying the SRO's language on nature's 'right to flourish',

71 Jacinta Ruru, 'Te Urewera Act 2014' (October 2014) Māori Law Review 16–17.

72 Kauffman interview with Ambassador John Wood, Chief Crown Negotiator for the Tūhoe settlement negotiations and member of the Te Urewera Board (Wellington, New Zealand, 10 August 2016); Kauffman interview with Tamati Kruger, lead Tūhoe negotiator for Tūhoe treaty settlement negotiations and member of the Te Urewera Board (Wellington, New Zealand, 17 August 2016).

73 See, for example, City of Santa Monica Task Force on the Environment, Meeting Minutes (24 October 2016) <www.smgov.net/uploadedFiles/Departments/OSE/Task_Force_on_the_Environment/TFE_2016/TFE_Minutes_10_24_16.pdf> accessed 17 December 2017.

including through significantly heightened greenhouse gas emissions reductions in the city, a city-wide prohibition on new private wells, and institution of regular staff reports ('consistency determinations') to the City Council that assess compliance of significant new development proposals with the SRO. Particular attention has been paid to aquifer health: compliance with the SRO's standard of 'flourishing' would yield a far healthier aquifer than under state law, which is triggered only where damage to groundwater is 'significant and unreasonable'.[74]

16.4 CHALLENGES TO STANDARD SETTING

Rights of nature laws directly challenge the values and assumptions of dominant political and economic systems, which view humans as separate from nature, treat the elements of nature as objects for human exploitation, and prioritize exponential economic growth over ecosystem functioning. As a UN Secretary General report observes, 'striving for infinite growth in a world of finite resources is contradictory'.[75]

Because they challenge the interests of powerful political and economic actors, efforts to implement rights of nature laws can become highly politicized and conflictual.[76] This has hindered the development of standards. The experiences in Bolivia and Ecuador are illustrative. Both countries have strong laws that, if fully implemented, would require industrial extractivism to be curtailed; indeed, this was a major goal of people who crafted the rights of nature legal provisions.[77] Yet, both countries have expanded industrial mining in the name of economic growth. In Bolivia, there has been little if any movement to apply its rights of nature laws. While rights of nature jurisprudence is gradually developing in Ecuador, the process has been slowed by political opposition and limited political will to address the issue.[78]

Ecuador's development of standards through the courts in a highly politicized environment reveals several challenges. First, the politicization of early rights of nature lawsuits prompted judges to focus on navigating the politicized environment rather than on implementing the specifics of the law.[79] Second, many lawyers, judges, and regulators lacked knowledge about what rights of nature entail and how to interpret them to appropriately balance competing rights, particularly property rights.[80] The idea that individual and corporate property rights must be

74 Cal. Water Code § 10721(x).
75 UNGA 'Report of the Secretary-General' UN Doc A/66/302 (15 August 2011) 17.
76 UNGA 'Report on Human Rights Defenders' (n 11).
77 Alberto Acosta (n 39); Natalia Greene (n 24).
78 Kauffman and Martin (n 1).
79 ibid 134. This insight is based on interviews with numerous Ecuadorian judges and lawyers involved in rights of nature lawsuits who requested to remain anonymous. Due to Internal Review Board rules governing human subjects research, their names cannot be disclosed.
80 Kauffman interview with Hugo Echeverria, Ecuadorian lawyer specializing in rights of nature (Quito, 24 September 2015); Kauffman interview with Pablo Piedra, Ecuadorian lawyer specializing in rights of nature (Quito, 8 September 2015); Kauffman interview with Patricio Benalcazar, Deputy for

curtailed in some cases to uphold nature's rights was not only foreign to many judges, but ran counter to their training.[81]

Several judges consequently issued rulings that clearly contradicted the constitution's rights of nature provisions.[82] A prominent example is the lawsuit over the open pit mining project known as Condor-Mirador. The mining company's own environmental impact study acknowledged that the open pit mine would cause impacts listed as rights of nature violations in the constitution. These include the total removal of ecosystems, including the habitats on which endangered endemic species rely, likely causing the extinction of one or more species.[83] Also, contaminating surface and groundwater with heavy metals and toxic products would be catastrophic for surrounding watershed ecosystems.[84] Article 73 of Ecuador's constitution explicitly requires the State to 'apply preventive and restrictive measures on activities that might lead to the extinction of species, the destruction of ecosystems and permanent alteration of natural cycles'.[85] Moreover, the constitution clearly establishes the precautionary principle; activities likely to produce these outcomes must be stopped and redesigned.[86]

Despite the uncontested evidence of rights of nature violations, the judge ruled that the Condor-Mirador project did not violate the rights of nature for two principle reasons, both of which reflect dubious interpretation of the constitution's rights of nature clauses.[87] First, the judge ruled that since the mining project would not affect a protected area, the environmental damage would not violate the rights of nature. However, the constitution clearly states that all nature has rights, not just nature found in protected areas.[88] The judge also argued that civil society's efforts to protect nature constituted a private goal, while Ecuacorriente (the private mining company) was acting in favour of a public interest, namely development. Ruling that the public interest takes precedent over a private interest, the judge ruled against the claimants. Putting aside the inherent weaknesses of this argument, it contradicts the constitutional principle that nature's rights are both independent of societal interests and of equal value.

Human Rights and Rights of Nature, Ecuador's National Ombudsman's Office (Quito, 14 September 2015); Bustamante (n 69).

81 ibid.

82 Several examples are detailed in Kauffman and Martin (n 1) 135–36.

83 Mark Thurber and Gabriel Noboa, *Estudio de impacto ambiental para la fase de explotación a cielo abierto del proyecto minero de Condor Mirador (Environmental impact study for the open pit exploitation phase of the Condor Mirador mining project)* (Walsh Engineers and Scientists 2010) 374.

84 William Sacher, *Revisión crítica parcial del 'estudio de impacto ambiental para la fase de explotación a cielo abierto del proyecto minero de Condor Mirador' de la empresa Ecuacorriente (Partial critical review of the 'environmental impact study for the open pit exploitation phase of the Condor Mirador mining project' of the company Ecuacorriente)* (Acción Ecológica 2011) 16–17.

85 Ecuador Constitution (n 5) 22.

86 ibid.

87 Judgment No. 1711120130317, Case No. 3160, Provincial Court of Pichincha, Republic of Ecuador (20 June 2013) 11–16.

88 Ecuador Constitution (n 5) 3, 5, 22.

Challenges like politicized environments and lack of knowledge among judges and lawyers are also likely to plague rights of nature laws in the United States, New Zealand, and elsewhere. This raises the need for the training of lawyers, judges, and regulators on implementation of rights of nature laws and standards.

Local rights of nature ordinances in the United States face an additional challenge: questions over their legal standing. Several ordinances have faced court challenges by corporations arguing that restrictions on corporate property rights violate state and federal constitutional guarantees of such rights. In 2015, the Western District Court of Pennsylvania found that Grant Township's ordinance overstepped the legislative boundaries of a second-class township.[89] In response, Grant and Highland Townships passed Home Rule Charters to circumvent the preemptive nature of state laws. At the time of writing, lawsuits challenging both Home Rule Charters were ongoing.[90]

16.5 NEXT STEPS: DEFINING AND MEASURING 'HEALTHY' ECOSYSTEMS[91]

As discussed above, a potentially significant difference among rights of nature laws is whether they solely recognize nature's right to exist and regenerate its vital cycles, or whether they appear to go further by recognizing the right to 'flourish'. The right to flourish presents a particular challenge when it comes to developing standards. The minimum standards emerging in Ecuador, such as avoiding species extinction or ensuring that ecosystems can regenerate, are insufficient to guarantee a higher bar like 'flourishing'. Developing standards for measuring when ecosystems flourish has been challenging both because key terms are not yet defined and because the concept is value laden. Lessons in this regard, however, can be drawn from ongoing scientific and policy advancements in defining 'healthy' ecosystems, and in past efforts to define human health.

Current environmental laws often call for 'healthy' ecosystems and species, raising a need for a clear definition of 'healthy' to guide policymakers. Some discussions of what 'healthy' means have occurred as a result. For example, scientists debated the concept of ocean health extensively roughly twenty years ago, in part to help advance a new, spreading concept of 'ecosystem-based management'.[92]

89 *Pennsylvania General Energy Company, LLC v Grant Township*, No. 14-209ERIE, Judgment, Western District Court of Pennsylvania (14 October 2015).

90 CELDF, 'Grant Township, PA, Sues Department of Environmental Protection for Rights Violations' (Community Environmental Legal Defense Fund, 18 May 2017) <https://celdf.org/2017/05/press-release-grant-township-pa-sues-department-environmental-protection-rights-violations> accessed 17 December 2017.

91 Thanks and acknowledgment to Dr. Brock Bernstein for his expert insights into science-based definitions of ecosystem health.

92 For a review of past discussions, see Garry Scrimgeour and Dan Wicklum, 'Aquatic Ecosystem Health and Integrity: Problems and Potential Solutions' (1996) 15 (2) J N Am Benthol Soc 254–61.

Progress has been made more recently in defining healthy streams.[93] However, there remains no agreed-upon definition of 'healthy' ecosystems and species populations more broadly.

Environmental standards today generally consider 'healthy' to be equivalent to 'not too degraded'. In other words, they generally permit degradation to a point just before (and often past) disease or infirmity. For example, US federal Clean Water Act regulations allow pollutant discharges with comparatively little controls as long as they do not have a 'reasonable potential' to violate standards.[94] Similarly, the US federal Endangered Species Act fails to protect the 'health' of species populations; rather, it only activates when species are threatened with extinction.[95]

Such standards (water quality, species abundance) further fail to incorporate a sufficiently meaningful range of variables to make a systemic assessment of 'health', as opposed to degradation. This is in part due to the reductionist nature of their overarching environmental laws, which are focused narrowly on water, species, air, and other factors and media, in light of their development in an era (late 1960s and early 1970s) of comparatively limited modelling or systemic ecological study.

Recent advancements in modelling technology, and better understanding of ecosystem processes and dynamics, now provide a fertile scientific basis to renew discussions around the meaning of 'healthy' ecosystems and species. Notably, in these discussions, not only science but also values must be considered.[96] 'Science can elucidate how the system works [but] values inform us about what's desired. *Without an explicit consideration of values, health is devoid of meaning*'.[97]

One baseline approach to defining 'healthy' ecosystems is to define them as essentially pristine, or unaffected by humans. This approach could be useful for comparison purposes (e.g. in establishing a reference site) and sometimes, in limited geographic areas, as a policy goal. However, it is not broadly applicable as a management goal. Not only can 'pristine' be challenging to define in this human-impacted world, the term also leaves little room for a practical definition of 'healthy' that includes humans as respectful partners of natural systems.[98]

A more pragmatic alternative, and one that incorporates humans into the ecosystems in which we are situated, is to define 'healthy' ecosystems and species

93 See, for example, California Water Quality Monitoring Council, 'Healthy Streams Partnership' <https://mywaterquality.ca.gov/eco_health/streams/index.html> accessed 17 December 2017.

94 40 CFR § 122.44.

95 16 USC ch 35.

96 David Rapport et al. (eds), *Ecosystem Health* (Blackwell Science 1998) 49. Achieving ecosystem health requires decision makers to 'identify the societal goals that are compatible with sustainable life systems, to identify and validate indicators of ecosystem function that are essential to its evolution and perpetuation, and to merge goals (societal values) with biophysical realities'; ibid.

97 ibid 14, 25–26, 42 (emphasis added).

98 See, for example, Fiorenza Micheli et al., 'Ocean Health' in Hance Smith et al. (eds), *Routledge Handbook of Ocean Resources and Management* (Routledge Press 2015) 113.

populations in terms of the quality of the relationships among humans and elements of the natural world. For example, is there sufficient biodiversity (i.e. suite of relationships) within a natural system to ensure that it flourishes, particularly in the face of increasing stress? And is the essence of humans' relationship with nature one of respect for nature's intrinsic well-being, parallel to the respect one would expect to see in healthy human-to-human relationships? Or is that connection instead a one-sided focus on the level of services nature may provide to humans? In nature, a relationship in which one species grows beyond the ability of the system to support it generally dooms the near-term survival chances of that species. Consideration of the system's needs is key to ensure the system – which includes humans – flourishes. This in turn calls for examination not only of mitigation for human actions on the natural world, but also restoration in light of past actions.

Accordingly, instead of measuring ecosystem and species well-being in terms of what humans can take from the natural world for human needs and desires, a definition of 'healthy' grounded in harmonious, thriving relationships requires consideration of what humans give back to nature.[99] Therefore, it is argued that this baseline, holistic approach to defining 'healthy' and developing associated metrics for its measurement must go beyond mitigating human impacts and also focus on repairing the damage humans have done.

16.5.1 *Analogies with Human Health and Well-Being*

When conceptualizing a holistic definition and assessment of environmental health, definitions of human health and well-being provide a useful analogy. The Constitution of the World Health Organization (WHO) defines human health as 'a state of complete physical, mental and social well-being and not merely the absence of disease or infirmity'.[100] While this definition arguably raises more questions than it answers, some useful lessons can be applied toward defining environmental health.

First, the WHO Constitution considers 'health' as the *integration*, or aggregate, of 'physical, mental and social' states.[101] 'Well-being' is the parameter by which each of these states is judged before being integrated into the measure of overall health. Lessons from the growing understanding of human health as a holistic concept, as envisioned by the WHO Constitution, can help inform environmental scientists examining ecosystem health. The idea of aggregating separate components (or 'attributes') into an overall measure of health is familiar to environmental scientists.

99 See, for example, CW Fowler and L Hobbs, 'Are We Asking the Right Questions in Science and Management?' US Dep't of Commerce, NOAA Technical Memorandum NMFS-AFSC-202 (December 2009) 43 (finding that restoration should be a core element of management 'in all habitats').

100 Constitution of the World Health Organization (adopted 22 July 1946, entered into force 7 April 1948) <http://apps.who.int/gb/bd/PDF/bd47/EN/constitution-en.pdf?ua=1> accessed 17 December 2017.

101 ibid 1.

Though the specific components of the WHO definition of human health do not always map neatly onto ecosystems,[102] useful analogies to all three components (physical, mental, and social) exist. The complex web of interactions among humans and natural systems reach beyond simple cause-and-effect, physical impacts. Humans exist in a network of relationships and glean numerous social and mental benefits from interactions with one another[103] and with nature.[104] Further, species and ecosystems harvest related benefits through evolutionary shifts in cognition and consciousness affected in part by human interactions with them. Standards for ensuring environmental health should therefore reflect the fact that the impacts of human actions on nature are more than physical, for both humans and other species.[105]

In sum, human physical, mental, and social well-being – and ultimately, health – can be achieved through care for relationships. As with relationships with other people, humans and nature can begin to achieve mutually enhancing relationships – i.e. health – if humans begin to return to nature as much as (or more than) is received from using it. For example, new laws could require restoration of natural systems at rates that notably exceed that which would simply make the ecosystem whole post-immediate use (a modest goal still rarely achieved), allowing correction of some of the long-term damage humans have caused. Standards measuring the health of ecosystems should consider and report on this balance between use of and return to (or lack of return to) nature.

Another lesson from the analogy with human health is that environmental health should not be measured merely in terms of the 'absence of disease or infirmity'. The WHO Constitution definition guides law and policy to aim for a state of human health that exceeds this low bar. The same should hold true for environmental health. Unfortunately, as touched on above, 'absence of disease or infirmity' is often the default concept for a 'healthy' ecosystem today. Many environmental laws, including in the United States, presume that flourishing ecosystems are a goal only in special circumstances (e.g. US Wild and Scenic Rivers,[106] Outstanding

102 For example, humans' acceptable range of physical conditions tends to be narrower than those under which an ecosystem might be considered healthy, though the reverse can also be true.

103 Recent studies reinforce that cooperation may have shaped the evolution of life on Earth more than competition. Martin A Nowack, 'Why We Help: The Evolution of Cooperation' (July 2012) Scientific American 34–39; David Grinspoon, *Earth in Human Hands* (Grand Central Publishing 2016) 64.

104 Wallace J Nichols, *Blue Mind: The Surprising Science That Shows How Being Near, In, On, or Under Water Can Make You Happier, Healthier, More Connected, and Better at What You Do* (Little, Brown and Co. 2015); CW Fowler et al., 'Pattern-Based Control Rules for Fisheries Management' US Dep't of Commerce, NOAA Technical Memorandum. NMFS-AFSC-268 (January 2014).

105 Mental and social well-being of species merits deeper examination, such as the work being done in cetacean emotional and social intelligence. See, for example, AAAS Annual Meeting, 'Declaration of Rights for Cetaceans: Ethical and Policy Implications of Intelligence' (19 February 2012) <https://aaas.confex.com/aaas/2012/webprogram/Session4617.html> accessed 17 December 2017.

106 16 USC §§ 1271 *et seq*.

National Resource Waters,[107] and national parks). The overwhelming default in US environmental laws, along with others, is avoiding degradation past a set point. Laws and policies that consider the example of the WHO Constitution and aim for environmental health that exceeds the 'absence of disease or infirmity' will lead toward a holistic standard of 'healthy' that can form the baseline for standards under rights of nature laws. This approach is key to achieving the higher goal of thriving ecosystems, a goal essential to human well-being.[108]

16.5.2 *Natural Variability: Temporal and Spatial Fluctuations*

In developing a holistic definition of 'healthy', another consideration is the rate at which the variables considered will naturally change over time. Standards for measuring health and sustainability accordingly may need to also consider a time frame 'consistent with the system's time and space scale'.[109] Ecosystems are dynamic and characterized by a variety of disturbances, as well as by complex, nonlinear interactions that can lead to alternative conditions potentially quite different from the original state. Fluctuations or cycles in status are a normal part of natural system conditions, and not all species can do well at the same place or time due to competing physical and biological requirements.

To incorporate natural variability into metrics of health, some scientists call for consideration of expected change over time when defining and setting standards for ecosystem health.[110] Variations in the expected natural *rate* of change can provide important information on health, and should be tracked and incorporated. For example, extinctions have always occurred over time, and at varying rates. Scientists today point with deep concern to the rate of extinction as compared with the past, with the United Nations' Millennium Ecosystem Assessment reporting that humans may have increased the rate of global extinctions by as much as 1,000 times the 'natural' rate typical over Earth's long-term history.[111] Conversely, human actions that result in a marked drop in the rate of extinctions over time could provide a metric of overall ecosystem and species health. The US Environmental Protection Agency, for example, defines 'healthy watersheds' as having 'natural land cover [which] supports dynamic hydrologic and geomorphologic processes within their natural range of variation.'[112]

[107] 40 CFR § 131.12(a)(3).

[108] Rapport (n 96) 49.

[109] ibid 236.

[110] See, for example, MJ Allen et al., 'Temporal trends in southern California coastal fish populations relative to 30-year trends in oceanic condition' (2004) Southern California Coastal Water Research Project Biennial Report 2003–2004 264–85.

[111] Millennium Ecosystem Assessment Board, 'Living beyond Our Means: Natural Assets and Human Well-Being' (March 2005) 15 <www.millenniumassessment.org/documents/document.429.aspx.pdf> accessed 17 December 2017.

[112] US EPA, 'Healthy Watersheds Protection: What Is a Healthy Watershed?' <www.epa.gov/hwp/basic-information-and-answers-frequent-questions> accessed 17 December 2017.

Though natural variability is an important consideration in defining and assessing ecosystem and species health, care should be taken to avoid using natural cycles and shifts to rationalize or excuse the impacts of destructive human practices.

16.5.3 *'Normal Form and Function' as a Descriptor of Ecosystem Health*

Developing and operationalizing a definition of ecosystem health that encompasses the dynamic nature of ecosystems across multiple spatial and temporal scales – and that considers and provides input to evolving human policies – undeniably presents significant challenges. One starting approach is to define a healthy ecosystem as one that exhibits 'normal form and function',[113] or 'what works in natural systems'.[114] Fowler describes 'sustainability' as 'doing what is possible to ensure that all systems (e.g. ecosystems, evosystems,[115] and fisheries) exhibit normal form and function'.[116] Using an analogous concept of 'intact' structure and function, stream ecologists have made substantial progress in defining 'normal form and function'.[117] However, defining 'normal' can be a noteworthy challenge for more complex natural systems, such as an ocean.

These challenges need not prevent movement forward, however. Defining 'normal' could start with what it is not – for example, *not* merely the 'absence of disease or infirmity', as discussed above. But how high should environmental laws aim above 'absence of disease or infirmity'? This work remains to be done, though progress is being made. For example, stream ecologists have examined a stream system's 'distance from reference state or condition'[118] as one strategy for defining whether a stream is healthy. The 'reference' state of an ecosystem can be measured in part by the ratio of observed versus expected natural conditions. An unstressed

[113] Fowler et al. (n 104) 1.

[114] Fowler and Hobbs (n 99) 12, 26.

[115] As per Fowler et al. (n 104) 1, 'evosystem' refers to the 'coevolutionary web of interactions among species, cooccurring with, and involving, ecological interactions (i.e. the ecosystem)'; see also DP Faith et al., 'Evosystem Services: An Evolutionary Perspective on the Links between Biodiversity and Human Well-Being' (2010) 2 Curr Opin Environ Sustainability 66–74 (providing additional information on the importance of evosystems in management).

[116] Fowler et al. (n 104) 1.

[117] AM Milner et al., 'Detecting Significant Change in Stream Benthic Macroinvertebrate Communities in Wilderness Areas' (2016) 60 Ecological Indicators 524–37; Charles Hawkins et al., 'The Reference Condition: Predicting Benchmarks for Ecological and Water-Quality Assessments' (2010) 29 (1) J N Amer Benthol Soc 312–43.

[118] A reference state is frequently used to benchmark assessments of ecosystem condition, but offers at least two important differences from 'normal form and function' (assuming the reference state is set correctly). First, in practice reference sites or conditions typically capture only a snapshot in time. They thus do not always or necessarily reflect ecosystems' normal range of temporal heterogeneity. Second, reference sites or conditions generally refer only to specific attributes or metrics, rather than the larger and more complete set of ecosystem features encompassed by the more holistic concept of normal form and function. See, for example, Ángel Borja et al., 'The Importance of Setting Targets and Reference Conditions in Assessing Marine Ecosystem Quality' (2012) 12 Ecological Indicators 1–7.

ecosystem should have observed/expected (O/E) ratio close to one – that is, closer to its expected ('normal') structure and function. Stressed ecosystems will have lower ratios, indicating larger deviations from natural (i.e. 'normal' or 'healthy') conditions. Measuring O/E ratios for ecosystems and species – even if the expected natural state is no longer attainable everywhere – can help inform the meaning of 'healthy' for natural systems and provide guidance for restoration and protection.[119]

16.5.4 *Other Attributes of Healthy Ecosystems: Organization, Vigour and Resilience*

Like the WHO's definition of human health, which folded physical, social, and mental well-being into an integrated understanding of human health, scientists propose aggregating the attributes of system organization, vigour, and resilience into a single, comprehensive assessment of ecosystem health.[120] Most ecosystem studies and monitoring activities currently focus on organization, or ecosystem complexity (species richness, intricacy of interactions).[121] Relatively little attention is paid to vigour (the energy, productivity, or activity of a system, as measured by such variables as food web structure, primary production and energy flow)[122] or resilience (the capacity of a system to cope with and bounce back from stress, or 'maintain its structure and pattern of behavior').[123] However, scientists have propounded that a 'healthy' ecosystem is one that 'has the ability to *maintain its structure (organization) and function (vigour) over time in the face of external stress (resilience)*'.[124] In other words, a 'healthy' ecosystem is one that evolves and perpetuates itself within the context of its expected natural life span in the face of external stress.[125]

Evolving scientific paradigms such as these indicate that a more descriptive set of standards would likely include measurements of all three attributes of ecosystem health. Action to test this approach could begin on a pilot basis at this time, while programs to monitor and collect measurements are developed, funded, and

[119] One example in coastal waters is PERSE (Procedure to Establish a Reference State for Ecosystems), which calculates the probability an observed attribute lies outside the determined reference state. A probability close to zero indicates the system is different from normal form and function; see Isabelle Rombouts et al., 'Evaluating Marine Ecosystem Health: Case Studies of Indicators Using Direct Observations and Modelling Methods' (2013) 25 Ecological Indicators 353–65.

[120] Robert Costanza and Michael Mageau, 'What Is a Healthy Ecosystem' (1999) 33 Aquatic Ecology 105, 112 (emphasis added).

[121] Rapport (n 96) 26, 29.

[122] ibid 26, 28.

[123] ibid 26. Measuring resilience could be considered somewhat analogous to stress tests in medicine, though the effort would usually be considerably more challenging for ecosystems; ibid 28–29 (describing example of New Mexico grassland recovery after a severe drought).

[124] Costanza and Mageau (n 120) 105–15 (emphasis added); Rapport (n 96) 232.

[125] Both biodiversity and life history patterns can help describe a system's resilience to stress. Micheli (n 98) 115. High species richness (the number of species in an ecosystem) is an indicator of high ecosystem stability and the ability to withstand disturbances. Conversely, the relative abundance of species (evenness) can signal a disturbance and a state away from normal form and function.

implemented. The first Heinz Center report on US coastal ecosystems similarly identified needed indicators, even though data were lacking or could not be accessed and integrated at a national scale.[126] Rather than being moot, the Heinz Center recommendations helped stimulate a new US EPA program to create periodic national reports on the nation's ecosystems containing the missing information.[127] Similar recommendations on monitoring needs for ecosystem health could spur needed research, particularly in the areas of system vigour and resilience.

Finally, in addition to reporting scientific data and conclusions regarding the three key ecological attributes of organization, vigour, and resilience, standards designed to help with day-to-day decision making will require information on targets, indicators, and thresholds. Targets are 'point[s] of reference on the specific status or amount of benefit that equals goal achievement'.[128] Targets help provide guideposts that indicate success or the need to change course. They can be based on an ideal state,[129] historical status, or 'maximum possible value'.[130]

Indicators represent the 'physical and ecological components and processes that provide effective warning signals for changed conditions in relation to management goals'.[131] While it can be challenging to develop indicators that are broadly representative, easy to measure, and useful for providing early warnings for managers, some suites of indicators are being adopted to measure ecosystem change and health.[132]

Finally, thresholds mark meaningful change points or levels of concern.[133] In one California example, the state spent considerable effort defining expectations and quantitative thresholds for a number of ecoregions.[134] In light of this notable expenditure of effort, participants discussed alternative, 'best professional judgment' (BPJ) approaches, such as Biological Condition Gradient.[135] If carefully and rigorously applied, BPJ approaches could be useful in some circumstances to further guide monitoring and assessment of environmental health.

126 The Heinz Center, *The State of the Nation's Ecosystems* (Cambridge University Press 2002) 17–18.

127 US EPA, 'Report on the Environment' <http://cfpub.epa.gov/roe/index.cfm> accessed 17 December 2017.

128 Micheli (n 98) 118.

129 ibid 119 (discussing derivation options for calculating the 'ideal state').

130 ibid 118.

131 ibid 119–20.

132 ibid 119 (citing the Puget Sound Partnership's indicators for monitoring ecosystem health).

133 ibid 121.

134 Andrew Rehn et al., 'The California Stream Condition Index (CSCI): A New Statewide Biological Scoring Tool for Assessing the Health of Freshwater Streams', SWAMP Technical Memorandum SWAMP-TM-2015-0002 (September 2015) <www.waterboards.ca.gov/water_issues/programs/swamp/bioassessment/docs/csci_tech_memo.pdf> accessed 17 December 2017.

135 E Shumchenia et al., 'A Biological Condition Gradient Model for Historical Assessment of Estuarine Habitat Structure' (2015) 55 Environmental Management 143 <http://cfpub.epa.gov/si/si_public_record_report.cfm?dirEntryId=307134> accessed 17 December 2017.

16.6 CONCLUSION

Formerly considered a radical idea, rights of nature is spreading and becoming increasingly recognized in laws and policies at various levels of government, in nations as diverse as New Zealand, the United States, Colombia, and India. These laws respond to socio-environmental challenges that reveal the inadequacy of previous environmental statutes, which treat nature as a commodity rather than a living system. Rights of nature laws are structured differently than environmental statutes, owing to their emergence in distinct institutional, political, and socio-cultural contexts. While various rights of nature laws share underlying norms regarding the intrinsic value of nature and resulting obligations of humans, they differ in their legal structure, their definition and framing of nature, the rights recognized, and provisions for enhancing enforcement. To highlight these differences, we compared the rights of nature laws in three countries where the laws are most institutionalized: Ecuador, New Zealand, and the United States.

Because Western rights of nature laws are so new (many less than five years old), standards specifying how they should be applied in practice are just beginning to be developed. We analysed the nascent standards emerging in Ecuador, which has proceeded furthest, and described the standard-setting processes just beginning in New Zealand and the United States. We also identified several challenges facing rights of nature standards generally.

One challenge is that the rights recognized differ across legal instruments. An important difference is whether these legal instruments recognize nature's right to flourish, which arguably requires going beyond minimum standards such as avoiding species extinction or the destruction of an ecosystem's ability to regenerate. Developing standards for ensuring nature's right to flourish is complicated by lack of agreement on how to define and measure ecosystem 'health'. Accordingly, we ended the chapter by proposing the consideration of general guidelines for development of science-based standards for measuring the health and well-being of nature. Science can help give a consistent voice to nature's needs, in a way that guides future attempts to reflect those needs and rights in laws around the world.

17

Standards in Subnational Environmental Constitutionalism

James R. May and Erin Daly

17.1 INTRODUCTION

This chapter examines the instantiation of environmental standards in subnational constitutions. Standards in environmental constitutionalism can emanate from subnational sources, including states, provinces, municipalities, and additional meso-levels of governance that exist between the national and local governments.[1] Subnational constitutionalism is worldwide, advancing myriad civil, political, and socioeconomic rights, and often filling gaps in federal systems.[2] Subnational governments around the globe have seen fit to constitutionalize substantive and procedural environmental rights, environmental duties, and sustainable development for present and future generations, often more elaborately than provided for in national constitutions.

Section 17.2 outlines the development of environmental standards in subnational constitutionalism around the globe, with an emphasis on developments in Brazil and the United States. Section 17.4 focuses on judicial roles in developing environmental standards. Section 17.4 addresses the relationship of subnational constitutional provisions to standards and, in particular, the potential for hybridized national and state standards in environmental constitutionalism.

17.2 EXAMPLES OF ENVIRONMENTAL STANDARDS IN SUBNATIONAL CONSTITUTIONALISM

Most examples of environmental standards in subnational constitutionalism are narrative. The leading examples derive from Brazil, the United States, and Iraq, discussed below.

[1] See generally, James R May and Erin Daly, *Global Environmental Constitutionalism* (CUP 2015) ch 7.

[2] Sylvia Ewald, 'State Court Adjudication of Environmental Rights: Lessons from the Adjudication of the Right to Education and the Right to Welfare' (2011) 36 Columbia J Envtl L 413 <http://columbiaenvironmentallaw.org/assets/pdfs/36.2/Ewald.pdf> accessed May 24, 2018.

17.2.1 Brazil

The Brazilian brand of subnational environmental constitutionalism is especially striking.[3] Spurred initially by the Rio Declaration in 1992 (and buttressed by the Rio+20 Conference in 2012), the most ardent examples of subnational environmental constitutionalism occur at the state level in Brazil. The constitutions for all of Brazil's twenty-six states – and the Federal District – promote environmental protection, often in intricate ways. State constitutions delineate extensive governmental functions in the service of substantive environmental rights, including promoting biodiversity and sustainability, protecting species and water quality, advancing conservation and environmental education, and enforcing environmental requirements. The Mato Grasso constitution is typical, touching all corners of environmental constitutionalism by guaranteeing substantive and procedural rights and imposing duties and responsibilities that apply to all for the benefit of present and future generations.

Notably, the constitutions of most Brazilian states and the Federal District embed a substantive right to a quality environment in some form, most commonly to a "balanced" environment.[4] For example, the constitution of the State of Acre provides that "all have the right to an ecologically balanced environment."[5] Amapá's provides that "all have the right to an ecologically balanced environment, which is an asset of common use and essential to a healthy quality of life."[6] Amazonas' says that "all have the right to a balanced environment, essential to a healthy quality of life."[7] Ceará's constitution refers to a "balanced environment" as an "inalienable right."[8] Goiás' constitution guarantees "an ecologically balanced environment."[9] Mato Grosso's says that "all have the right to an ecologically balanced environment."[10] Maranhão's calls a balanced environment "an asset of common use and essential to people's quality of life, imposing to all, and especially the State and the Municipalities, the duty to ensure their preservation and restoration for the benefit of present generations and future."[11] Similar provisions recognizing a substantive right to a balanced environment are found in the constitutions of the States of Bahia, Espírito Santo, Goiás, Maranhão, Minas Gerais, Paraíba, Paraná, Piauí, Rio de Janeiro, Rio Grande do Sul, Rio Grande do Norte, Santa Catarina, Sergipe, and Tocantins, and in the Federal District.[12] A couple of states vary slightly from the "balanced" formulae, including Mato Grosso do Sul, which

3 See (n 1) ch 7 and App. H.
4 See May and Daly (n 1) 211–13.
5 Constitution of Acre art 206.
6 Constitution of Amapá art 310.
7 Constitution of Amazonas art 229.
8 Constitution of Ceará art 259.
9 Constitution of Goiás art 127.
10 Constitution of Mato Grosso art 263.
11 Constitution of Maranhão art 239.
12 See May and Daly (n 1) App. H and accompanying text.

provides that "all have the right to enjoy an environment free of physical and social factors harmful to health."[13]

The constitutions for most Brazilian states express environmental rights in terms of duties and responsibilities that are owed by all for the benefit of present and future generations. For example, Espírito Santo's constitution reads: "All have the right to an ecologically, healthy and balanced environment, and it is incumbent upon them and in particular to the State and the Municipalities, to ensure its preservation, conservation and restoration for the benefit of present and future generations."[14] Likewise, Mato Grasso's constitution imposes a duty on the state, municipalities, and "the community" "to defend and preserve" the environment "for present and future generations," while Acre's says that "both the State and the community shall defend [the environment] and preserve it for present and future generations,"[15] and Amapá's that "both the Government and the community shall have the duty to defend and preserve it for present and future generations."[16]

The constitutions of some Brazilian states specifically elevate the interests of nature. For example, Bahia's says that "it is incumbent upon the State, beyond all powers that are not prohibited by the Federal Constitution, to ... protect the environment and fight pollution in any of its forms, preserving the forests, fauna and flora." It remains to be seen whether provisions such as this create a "right" on behalf of nature.[17]

Most Brazilian states similarly dictate governmental means for implementing substantive environmental rights, including the States of Amazonas, Bahia, Espírito Santo, Goiás, Maranhão, Mato Grosso do Sul, Minas Gerais, Paraíba, Paraná, Piauí, Rio de Janeiro, Rio Grande do Sul, Rio Grande do Norte, Santa Catarina, Sergipe, and Tocantins, and in the Federal District.[18] For example, the constitution of Santa Catarina provides: "It is incumbent upon the State, in the manner prescribed by law, to ... preserve and restore essential ecological processes and provide for the ecological management of species and ecosystems."[19] The Sao Paolo constitution explains that "the granting of the environmental permit, by body or governmental authority, part of a unified system shall be made in compliance with the general criteria laid down by law, and norms and standards set forth by the Government and in accordance with environmental planning and zoning," and goes on to explain the prerequisite of an Environmental Impact Study and report.[20]

It is difficult to assess subnational environmental constitutionalism in Brazil because there have been few reported decisions and little or no scholarship

13 Constitution of Mato Grosso Sol art 222.
14 Constitution of Espírito Santo art 186.
15 Constitution of Mato Grasso art 263.
16 Constitution of Amapá art 310.
17 Constitution of Bahia art 11.
18 See generally, May and Daly (n 1) ch 7.
19 Constitution of Santa Catarina art 182.
20 Constitution of Sao Paolo art 192.

analyzing the effects of these constitutional developments. Suffice to say that there is ample margin to develop standards that would, for example, illuminate the meaning of a "balanced" environment, not to mention one that is "free of" factors harmful to health.

17.2.2 *United States*

Subnational deployment of environmental rights in the United States is instructive because it underscores both the potential and the limitations of developing standards in environmental constitutionalism.[21] While all efforts to amend the US Constitution to recognize environmental rights have failed,[22] states in the United States have a long tradition of constitutionalizing environmental protection. Indeed, constitutional recognition of natural resources and the environment at the subnational level in the United States harkens back almost two centuries, beginning in 1842 with Rhode Island's protection of "all the rights of fishery, and the privileges of the shore"[23] – although this reflects a decidedly anthropocentric perspective.

The State of New York's constitution was perhaps the first in the world to embody environmental constitutionalism – and the first to develop a corresponding "standard" of no degradation – in what is known as its "Forever Wild" mandate from 1894, which provides:

> The lands of the state, now owned or hereafter acquired, constituting the forest preserve as now fixed by law, shall be forever kept as wild forest lands. They shall not be leased, sold or exchanged, or be taken by any corporation, public or private, nor shall the timber thereon be sold, removed or destroyed.[24]

21 See, for example, James R May and William Romanowicz, 'Environmental Rights in State Constitutions', in James R May (ed), *Principles of Constitutional Environmental Law* 305, ABA Section of Environment, Energy, and Resources (Eli Press 2011); Richard O Brooks, "A Constitutional Right to a Healthful Environment" (1991) 16 Vt L Rev 1103–05 (supporting "decentralization" of constitutional provisions that address the environment, observing "state judges [would] ... be more sensitive in weighing the state's values."); Barton H Thompson Jr, "Environmental Policy and State Constitutions: The Potential Role of Substantive Guidance" (1996) Rutgers L J 871(hereinafter Barton, Environmental Policy); Janelle P Eurick, "The Constitutional Right to a Healthy Environment: Enforcing Environmental Protection Through State and Federal Constitutions" (2001) 11 Int'l Legal Persp 185; Barton H Thompson Jr, "The History and Future of Montana's Environmental Provisions" (2003) 64 Mont L Rev 174.

22 See generally, Robin Kundis Craig, "Should There Be a Constitutional Right to a Clean/Healthy Environment?" (2004) 34 Envtl L Rep 11013.

23 Constitution of the State of Rhode Island and Providence Plantations 1842, art I s 17. For a thorough history of the evolution of Rhode Island's Constitution, see Kevin Leitao, "Rhode Island's Forgotten Bill of Rights" (1996) Roger Williams U L Rev 131.

24 New York State Constitution, art XIV s 1 (originally art VII s 7); Nicholas A Robinson, "'Forever Wild': New York's Constitutional Mandates to Enhance the Forest Preserve" (2007) 284 Pace Law Faculty Publications <http://digitalcommons.pace.edu/cgi/viewcontent.cgi?article=1283&context=lawfaculty> accessed May 24, 2018.

In contrast to many subnational environmental provisions, courts in New York have regularly enforced Forever Wild.[25] New York's Constitution also contains a remarkable mandate that every twenty years voters decide whether to hold elections for delegates to convene a convention to amend the state's charter.[26] This opened the opportunity for reform in 2017, including to incorporate environmental rights.[27] Voters in New York, however, voted down the latest attempt to subject the New York Constitution to referendum and reform.[28]

With the potential for a constitutional convention comes the potential reexamination of the role of environmental constitutionalism, including the Forever Wild provision.[29] Some welcome the opportunity for a convention as an opportunity to advance environmental constitutionalism, including instantiating fundamental environmental rights:

> [T]here is a compelling case for amending the New York Constitution to provide for a right to the environment. If not enacted via a convention, the option exists for the legislature to adopt an environmental right to submit to the voters. Either way, New York deserves to recognize the right to the environment.[30]

Others are skeptical, concerned "that a convention would tamper with the 'forever wild' guarantees."[31]

25 See, for example, *Association for Protection of Adirondacks v MacDonald* 170 NE 902 905 (NY 1930) (holding that timber harvesting is inconsistent with the "Forever Wild" portion of New York State Constitution).

26 See NY State Const (n 24) art XIX s 2:

> At the general election to be held … every twentieth year … the question "Shall there be a convention to revise the constitution and amend the same?" shall be submitted to and decided by the electors of the state; and in case a majority of the electors voting thereon shall decide in favor of a convention for such purpose, the electors of every senate district … shall elect three delegates … [who] shall convene … on the first Tuesday of April next ensuing after their election … [and] any proposed constitution … shall be submitted to a vote … not less than six weeks after the adjournment of such convention.

See generally Peter J Galie, *Ordered Liberty: A Constitutional History of New York* (Fordham University Press 1996) (discussing the history and significance of New York's constitution).

27 See James R May, 'Subnational Environmental Constitutionalism and Reform in New York State' (2017) 38 Pace L Rev 121.

28 See (n 24) art XIX s 2; see Peter J Galie and Gerald Benjamin, "Introduction" in Peter J Galie, Christopher Bopst, and Gerald Benjamin (eds), *New York's Broken Constitution: The Governance Crisis and the Path to Renewed Greatness* (SUNY Press 2016) 1–33 (hereinafter New York's Broken Constitution) for a discussion on needed constitutional reform.

29 See New York State Bar Association, Commentary on the New York State Constitution *The Conservation Article in the Constitution Article* XIV 1–6 (2016).

30 Nicholas A Robinson, "Updating New York's Constitutional Environmental Rights" (2017) 38 Pace L Rev 152, 181.

31 ibid 177.

While New York's Forever Wild provision is unique in advancing environmental protection, it is hardly unique in the canon of subnational environmentalism in the United States. Presently, there are at least 207 natural resource or environment-related provisions in 46 state constitutions, addressing 19 different categories of natural resources or the environment, including water, timber, and minerals.[32] They take eleven different forms, including general policy statements, legislative directives, and individual rights to a quality environment.[33] States recognizing environmental protection as an overarching state policy include Louisiana,[34] Michigan,[35] Ohio,[36] South Carolina,[37] and Virginia.[38] Several more address particular environmental concerns, such as access to water, preservation, re-development, sustainability, pollution abatement, climate change, energy reform, or environmental rights.[39] Dozens more contain provisions fairly characterized as recognizing that the state holds state resources in "public trust."[40]

32 See generally, "Environmental and Natural Resources Provisions in State Constitutions" (2002) 22 J Land Res & Envtl L 74. The categories are: (1) public land acquisition, preservation, or management, (2) public ownership of land and other resources, (3) sovereignty, (4) the balance of use and development, (5) school trust doctrine, (6) public trust doctrine, (7) takings or eminent domain, (8) access to water, (9) allocation of water, (10) water development and reclamation, (11) water resource protection, (12) mining and mineral rights, (13) fish and wildlife, (14) fishing rights, (15) hunting and fishing restrictions, (16) rights of way, (17) timber and forest management, (18) nuclear power, and (19) agriculture. ibid 74–75.

33 ibid 75; The other manifestations include provisions respecting (1) legislative protection, (2) agency authority, (3) general financing, (4) taxing authority, (5) bonding authority, (6) funds and trust accounts, (7) educational programs, and (8) private liability.

34 Louisiana Constitution art IX s 1 ("The natural resources of the state including air and water, and the healthful, scenic, historic, and esthetic quality of the environment shall be protected, conserved, and replenished insofar as possible and consistent with the health, safety, and welfare of the people. The legislature shall enact laws to implement this policy.")

35 Michigan Constitution art IV s 51 ("The legislature shall pass suitable laws for the protection and promotion of the public health.")

36 Ohio Constitution art VIII s 2 ("Environmental and related conservation, preservation, and revitalization purposes … are proper public purposes of the state and local governmental entities and are necessary and appropriate means to improve the quality of life and the general and economic well-being of the people of this state.")

37 South Carolina Constitution, art XII s 1 ("The health, welfare, and safety of the lives and property of the people of this State and the conservation of its natural resources are matters of public concern.")

38 Virginia Constitution art XI ("To the end that the people have clean air, pure water, and the use and enjoyment for recreation of adequate public lands, waters, and other natural resources, its public lands … Further it shall be the Commonwealth's policy to protect the atmosphere, lands, and waters from pollution, impairment, or destruction, for the benefit, enjoyment, and general welfare of the people of the Commonwealth.")

39 See May and Daly (n 1) ch 7.

40 See Craig (n 22).

Currently, five states instantiate a substantive right to a quality environment:[41] Hawai'i,[42] Illinois,[43] Massachusetts,[44] Montana,[45] and Pennsylvania.[46] These provisions are independent of state laws that allow citizens to enforce pollution control statutes.[47]

While most of these five provide a "right" to the "environment," the adjectival objective – "clean" or "healthful" or "quality" – differs from state to state. For example, Hawai'i's and Montana's constitutions aim to afford a "clean and healthful environment,"[48] Illinois' "a right to a healthful environment,"[49] Massachusetts' a "right to clean air and water, freedom from excessive and unnecessary noise, and the natural, scenic, historic, and esthetic qualities of their environment,"[50] and Pennsylvania's "a right to clean air, pure water, and to the preservation of the natural, scenic, historic and esthetic values of the environment."[51] Some of these provisions may overlap with nuisance laws or other codes, such as city and local ordinances that limit noise or protect property owners' access to light and air or access to public amenities such as beaches, but the constitutional provisions tend to be much broader in scope and richer in values, whereas the codes tend toward more precise standard setting.

These provisions have been interpreted to require harm to humans. For example, in *Glisson* v. *City of Marion*, the Supreme Court of Illinois explained that "the primary concern of the drafters ... was the effect of pollution on the environment and human health. The right to a 'healthful environment' was therefore not intended to include the protection of endangered and threatened species."[52] Yet Montana's suggests biocentric concerns, choosing both "clean and healthful" over

41 See Mary Ellen Cussack, "Judicial Interpretation of State Constitutional Rights to a Healthful Environment" (1993) 20 BC Envtl Aff L Rev 181 (noting amendments to state constitutions include "those granting citizens the right to a healthful environment; public policy statements concerning preservation of natural resources; financial provisions for environmental programs; and clauses that restrict the environmental prerogatives of state legislatures.") See also, Edith Brown Weiss, "International Environmental Law and Policy" (1998) Aspen Law & Business 416 (identifying Illinois, Hawai'i, California, Florida, Massachusetts, Montana, Pennsylvania, Rhode Island, and Virginia as embedding environmental rights).

42 Hawai'i Constitution art XI s 9.

43 Illinois Constitution art XI s 2.

44 Massachusetts Constitution art XLIX.

45 Montana Constitution art II s 3.

46 Pennsylvania Constitution art I s 27; see generally, Brian P Wilson, "State Constitutional Environmental Rights and Judicial Activism: Is the Big Sky Falling?" (2004) 53 Emory L J 627; see also (n 23), Thompson (2003) 158 (discussing Montana's finding of a fundamental right to a "healthful environment").

47 See, for example, John C Dernbach "Part I – An Interpretive Framework for Article I, Section 27" (1999) 103 Dick L Rev 693 ("Dernbach I") (explaining purpose of provision).

48 Hawai'i Constitution art XI s 9 ("Each person has the right to a clean and healthful environment."); Montana Constitution art II s 3 (guaranteeing "right to clean and healthful environment").

49 See Ill. Const. (n 44) art XI s 2.

50 See Mass. Const. (n 45) art XLIX.

51 See Pa. Const. (n 47) art I s 27.

52 *Glisson v City of Marion* 720 NE 2d 1034 1042 (Ill 1999).

"healthful" out of concern that the latter would permit the environmental degradation of Montana's most environmentally pristine areas so long as the pollution didn't harm human health.[53] The precise amount of harm required to make a showing that the environmental degradation harms humans is generally left to more general requirements of standing doctrine under the applicable state law. In many cases following the more general federal approach, the quantum of harm is not significant, so long as the plaintiff can show that the harm was sufficient to provide him or her with a sufficient stake in the case. For instance, in the Pennsylvania case of *Robinson Township* v. *Commonwealth*, the court inquired whether "the petitioner filing suit has demonstrated aggrievement, by establishing 'a substantial, direct and immediate interest in the outcome of the litigation.'"[54] In the last few decades, the federal standard for standing has become far more stringent, requiring a showing that harm is concrete, particularized, and actual or imminent, and that the harm is fairly traceable to the defendant's conduct and likely to be redressed by a favorable decision.[55] The state court was far more generous in establishing its standard for determining who has a right to sue and upon what showing.

17.2.3 *Iraq*

The Kurdish Regional Constitution of Iraq contains a cavalcade of narrative environmental standards, including individual rights and responsibilities,[56] governmental policies, and sustainability, in a sort of environmental omnibus provision, which provides:

> First: Environmental protection (land, water, air, plants and animals) is a responsibility of all and if anyone causes damage to them, they are responsible to fix it and to be punished by law.
>
> Second: All citizens have a legitimate right for freedom and equality in an appropriate living status, in a social and economical environment which will provide a prosperous and happy life and has a responsibility for protecting the environment and improving it for the present and future generations.
>
> Third: The Regional Government shall take action to mitigate and treat the sources of pollution in the environment, and in regard to this, it strives to develop forests and protect the fields and protect the green zones inside the cities and their outskirts. The Regional Government shall develop, enlarge and construct public parks, natural parks for protecting animals, plants, and natural resources and

53 Montana Constitutional Convention, Vol V, 1971–1972 at 1243–44 (March 1, 1972).

54 *Robinson Township v Commonwealth of Pennsylvania* Pa Sup Ct No J-127A-D-2012 (decided PA Dec 19, 2013) (plurality opinion). See generally, Erin Daly & James R May, 'Robinson Township v. Pennsylvania, A Model for Environmental Constitutionalism' (2015) 21 Widener L Rev 151.

55 See *Lujan v Defenders of Wildlife* 504 US 555, 560–61 (1992).

56 See Michael J Kelly, "The Kurdish Regional Constitution within the Framework of the Iraqi Federal Constitution: A Struggle for Sovereignty, Oil, Ethnic Identity, and the Prospects for a Reverse Supremacy Clause" (2010) 114 Penn St L Rev 784.

prohibit buildings and institutions and the use of machines and instruments in the natural protectorates.[57]

This is notable because it is so environmentally ambitious, although the judicial power of Iraqi Kurdistan has yet to be reformed to provide rule of law or enforcement authority over constitutional rights.

17.3 JUDICIAL ROLE IN DEVELOPING STANDARDS IN SUBNATIONAL ENVIRONMENTAL CONSTITUTIONALISM

Constitutionally enshrined environmental standards at the subnational level are most effective when they are recognized and enforced judicially.[58] To be sure, as Justice Antonio Herman Benjamin has observed: "Logical reasoning suggests that if it is the judge's responsibility to preserve human life, then it must also be up to the judiciary to ensure whatever is necessary to maintain all living beings, ourselves and all others – the foundations of life."[59] Judicial roles are key in developing standards in environmental constitutionalism: "The judiciary is uniquely equipped to secure public and shared rights, to safeguard individual environmental rights and to hold accountable the authorities whose primary responsibility is to environmental protection."[60]

Yet, amid the varied manifestations of constitutionally embedded environmental provisions at the subnational level, one commonality stands out: they are seldom subject to substantive application,[61] leaving them dormant and awaiting clarity through advocacy.[62] This dearth in applicable jurisprudence is likely due to judicial concerns about recognizing and enforcing emerging constitutional features,[63] restraining economic development and property rights, entering what are often seen as political thickets,[64] or providing causes of action that may displace other legislative prerogatives granted to affected persons, such as state citizen suits to enforce state pollution control

57 Kurdistan Region of Iraq Constitution art 57 <http://cabinet.gov.krd> accessed May 24, 2018.

58 For a general discussion of enforcement in this context, see John C Tucker "Constitutional Codification of an Environmental Ethic" (2000) 52 Florida Law Review 299.

59 Antonio Herman Benjamin, "We, the Judges, and the Environment" (2012) 29 Pace Envtl L Rev 582, 583.

60 Benjamin de Zavala "An Institute for Enhancing Effective Environmental Adjudication" (2010) 3 Journal of Court Innovation 2, 10.

61 See, for example, *Sierra Club v Department of Transport* 167 P3d 292, 313 n28 (HAW 2007) (explaining that "although this court has cited this amendment as support for our approach to standing in environmental cases . . . we have not directly interpreted the text of the amendment.")

62 Constitutional provisions referred to from hereon may be found in the Appendix.

63 Robert A McLaren, "Environmental Protection Based on State Constitutional Law: A Call for Reinterpretation" 12 (1990) U Haw L R 149.

64 The obstacles to enforcing state constitutional environmental rights are strikingly similar to those that afflict enforcement of environmental rights provisions in national constitutions worldwide. See generally, James R May and Erin Daly "Vindicating Fundamental Environmental Rights Worldwide" (2009) 11 Or Rev Int'l L 365–439.

requirements.[65] To be sure, the lack of standards embedded in the constitutional provisions discourages invocation and application. Indeed, another explanation for the dearth of judicial implementation may simply be because litigants and their lawyers are not aware of the potential power of the environmental provisions or of the opportunities that are available to litigants to fill in the textual gaps with instructive standards.

Often, subnational constitutional environmental rights are under-enforced because courts have not found them to be self-executing. A constitutional provision is self-executing if it is "a sufficient rule by means of which the right given may be enjoyed and protected, or the duty imposed may be enforced; and it is not self-executing when it merely indicates principles, without laying down rules by means of which those principles may be given the force of law."[66] Thus, a constitutional provision that *is* self-executing requires nothing more from the legislature before a court can apply it in a relevant case. A constitutional provision that *is not* self-executing requires implementing legislation to be enforced.

In the United States, few state constitutions make clear whether constitutionally embedded fundamental environmental rights are self-executing. Montana's, Pennsylvania's, and Rhode Island's constitutions, for example, are silent about whether their environmental rights are self-executing. Constitutions from other states explicitly require subsequent legislative or judicial action. The environmental rights provisions embedded in Hawai'i's and Illinois's constitutions, for example, are enforceable by "any person ... through appropriate legal proceedings, subject to reasonable limitations and regulation as provided by law."[67] Massachusetts' environmental rights provision seems to assume judicial action without requiring intervening legislative action.[68]

The constitutions of some states in the United States contain a parallel provision that imposes a duty upon the state to enact laws to protect the environment, which suggests to some that corresponding environmental rights provisions are not self-executing. For instance, Rhode Island's constitution provides (with emphasis added) that "it shall be *the duty* of the general assembly to provide for the conservation of the air, land, water, plant, animal, mineral and other natural resources of the state,"[69] and Michigan's that the "legislature *shall provide* for the protection of the air, water and other natural resources of the state from pollution, impairment and destruction."[70] Some see the mandatory "*shall*" as requiring legislative action to effectuate

[65] See generally May, "The Availability of State Environmental Citizen Suits" (2004) 18 Nat Resources & Env't 53.

[66] *Davis v Burke* 179 US 399 (1900).

[67] Hawai'i Constitution, art XI s 9; Illinois Constitution, art XI s 2.

[68] See Mass. Const. (n 45) art XCVII ("The general court shall have the power to enact legislation necessary or expedient to protect such rights.")

[69] Rhode Island Constitution, art I s 17 (emphasis added).

[70] Michigan Constitution, art IV s 52 (emphasis added).

constitutional environmental rights.[71] Others see these provisions as merely invoking "moral force"[72] that does not create a separately enforceable environmental right.[73]

Most state court decisions have found constitutionally embedded provisions in state constitutions *not* to be self-enforcing. For example, in *Enos* v. *Secretary of Environmental Affairs*,[74] the Supreme Judicial Court of Massachusetts held that the constitutional right to clean air and water does not afford an independent means to challenge an agency's decision to grant a permit to operate a sewage treatment plant under the Massachusetts Environmental Policy Act.[75] And in *Commonwealth* v. *Blair*,[76] a state court held that the same right to clean air and water does not provide a cognizable cause of action to gain access to water supply in violation of the Commonwealth's Watershed Protection Act: "The judge correctly rejected the argument that the Commonwealth is duty-bound to acquire interests related to the protection of drinking water."[77]

Moreover, state courts in the United States have held that even state attorneys general could not enforce environmental rights provisions absent implementing legislation.[78] The leading case is *Commonwealth* v. *National Gettysburg Battlefield Tower, Inc.*, in which the Supreme Court of Pennsylvania held that the state's attorney general could not enforce the state's environmental rights provision without further grant of authority from the state legislature.[79] The court reasoned that the provision did not grant the attorney general an unbridled and undefined authority to enforce a vague constitutional mandate to "natural, scenic, historic and esthetic values,"[80] thus exposing individual property owners to enforcement consequences.[81] Likewise, in *State* v. *General Development Corp.*,[82] a court in Florida held that the state attorney could not enforce Florida's constitutional "policy . . . to conserve and protect its natural resources and scenic beauty"[83] to prosecute unauthorized canal

71 A E Dick Howard, State Constitutions and the Environment (1972) 58 (2) Virginia Law Review 193, 199.

72 ibid.

73 Howard (n 73) 200; see Mclaren (n 64) 133.

74 *Laurien Enos & others v Secretary of Environmental Affairs* 731 NE 2d 525 (MASS 2000).

75 ibid at 532.

76 *Commonwealth v Blair* 805 NE 2d 1011,1018 (MASS App Ct 2004).

77 ibid at 1018.

78 Some argue that such judicial reluctance is anathema to the core ideas these provisions were designed to promote. See, for example; McLaren (n 64) 135.

79 *Commonwealth v National Gettysburg Battlefield Tower Inc* 454 Pa 193 205 311 A2d 588 594–95 (PA1973).

80 ibid.

81 ibid; see also *Community College of Delaware County v Fox* 342 A2d 468 482 (PA Commonwealth Ct 1975), in which the court noted that "while [Pennsylvania's environmental rights clause] may impose an obligation upon the Commonwealth to consider the propriety of preserving land as open space, it cannot legally operate to expand the powers of a statutory agency, nor can it expand the statutory powers of the [state agency] as a practical matter here."

82 *State v General Development Corp* 448 So 2d 1074 (FLA Dist Ct App), *aff'd*, 469 So 2d 1381 (Fla. 1985); see McLaren (n 64) 134.

83 Florida Constitution art II s 7; see McLaren (n 64) 134.

construction except under the auspices of "the legislature's enactment of over twenty specific general laws that have explicitly given a state attorney the authority to independently initiate civil suits on behalf of the state in other areas concerning the health, safety, and welfare of Florida's citizens and environment."[84]

Some courts have recently found subnational environmental rights provisions to be self-executing. Leading cases emanate from the supreme courts in Pennsylvania and Hawai'i. First, the development of subnational constitutionalism in the State of Pennsylvania in the United States suggests a potential for the development of standards going forward. The story here begins in 1971 with one of the world's first constitutional incorporations of environmental rights and trust responsibilities – article I, section 27 of Pennsylvania's constitution, which provides:[85]

> The people have a right to clean air, pure water, and to the preservation of the natural, scenic, historic and esthetic values of the environment. Pennsylvania's public natural resources are the common property of all the people, including generations yet to come. As trustee of these resources, the Commonwealth shall conserve and maintain them for the benefit of all the people.

Section 27 was enacted based on "the mischief to be remedied and the object to be attained," namely, to address environmental degradation in the state by promoting individual environmental rights and requiring governmental authorities to hold natural resources in public trust.[86]

This provision lay dormant for more than forty years, however, interpreted *not* to be self-executing and actionable in the absence of legislative implementation, and involving a three-part balancing test announced in *Payne* v. *Kassab* that did not hew to constitutional text.[87]

In 2013, in *Robinson Township* v. *Commonwealth of Pennsylvania*, however, a plurality of the Pennsylvania Supreme Court found major aspects of a state oil and gas law designed to facilitate the development of "shale gas" to contravene section 27.[88] In rejecting the rationale in *Payne* v. *Kassab*, the plurality held that the environmental rights in section 27 are "on par with, and enforceable to the same extent as, any other right reserved to the people in Article I."[89]

84 See *State v Gen Dev* (n 84) at 1080.

85 See Pa. Const. (n 47) article I section 27.

86 See *Robinson Township v Commonwealth* 83 A3d 901 999–1000 (PA 2013).

87 See *Payne v Kassab* 312 A.2d 86 (PA Commw Ct 1973), *aff'd* 361 A.2d 263 (PA 1976).

88 See *Robinson v Commonwealth* (n 88), 83 A3d 901 999–1000 (PA 2013); For commentary, see for example, John C Dernbach, James R May, and Kenneth T Kristl, "Robinson Township v Commonwealth of Pennsylvania: Examination and Implications"'(2015) 67 Rutgers L Rev 1169; Erin Daly and James R May, "Robinson Township: A Model for Environmental Constitutionalism"'(2015) 21 Widener L Rev 151; John C Dernbach, "The Potential Meanings of a Constitutional Public Trust" (2015) 45 Envtl L 463; Kenneth T Kristl, "The Devil Is in the Details: Articulating Practical Principles for Implementing the Duties in Pennsylvania's Environmental Rights Amendment" (2016) 28 Geo Envtl L Rev 589.

89 ibid 953–54.

That the section 27 rationale commanded only a plurality diminished its precedential effect, however, but not for long. In 2017, a majority of the Supreme Court in *Pennsylvania Environmental Defense Foundation* v. *Commonwealth of Pennsylvania* (hereinafter *PEDF*) decided that the section 27 is self-executing and warrants no further legislative action to be enforceable.[90] In *PEDF*, the court ruled that the state has a constitutional obligation to manage state lands as a trustee, including in granting licenses for oil and gas development.[91] The Court also held that the "constitutional language controls how the Commonwealth may dispose of any proceeds generated from the sale of its public natural resources."[92]

Article 27 – much like many provisions that provide such rights – vests two rights in the people of the state. The first right is a substantive right to clean air, pure water, and to the preservation of the natural, scenic, historic, and esthetic values of the environment. The second right is as a beneficiary of a public trust held by the state to preserve and maintain the state's natural resources.

Second, in the 2017 case *In Re Application of Maui Electric Company*, the Supreme Court of Hawai'i held that the Hawai'i constitution's explicit right to a healthy environment is a protectable property interest under that state's due process clause.[93] Hawai'i's Constitution guarantees each person "the right to a clean and healthful environment, as defined by laws relating to environmental quality."[94] It also provides that "no person shall be deprived of life, liberty or property without due process of law."[95] Sierra Club argued that a Power Purchase Agreement that the state's public utility commission had issued to a utility to operate a fossil fuel burning electric power station does not comport with the state's statutory goal to convert to 100 percent renewable energy by 2045, and that they were entitled to a hearing to determine their rights. The court agreed, holding that the constitutional environmental right created the kind of interest (specifically, a property interest) that triggered a hearing under the due process clause. As the court explained:

> The petitioners asserted a protectable property interest in a clean and healthful environment as defined by environmental regulations; that the agency decision adversely affected this interest; and that a due process hearing was required given the importance of the interest, the risk of an erroneous deprivation, and the governmental interests involved.[96]

90 John C Dernbach, Kenneth T Kristl and James R May, 'Pennsylvania Environmental Defense Foundation v. Commonwealth of Pennsylvania: Recognition of Environmental Rights for Pennsylvania Citizens' (2018) 70 Rutgers U L Rev.

91 161 A.3d 911, 916 (PA 2017).

92 ibid.

93 In *Re Application of Maui Electric Company (Sierra Club) v Public Utility Commission of Hawai'i*, SCWC-15-0000640 (Supreme Court of Hawai'i 2017).

94 See Haw. Const. (n 43) art XI s 9.

95 ibid art I s 5.

96 ibid.

The Court also held that the Sierra Club possesses constitutional standing to challenge the permit because the injury to its members is fairly traceable to greenhouse gas emissions.

While neither *PEDF* nor *Maui Electric* offer much in the way of standards, they do kick the door wide open for developing them. Finding the right to be self-executing, *PEDF* invites judicial interpretation of what it means to have a right to "clean water" and so on, and sets implicit if not explicit limits – as a surrogate for standards – for the government's disposition of resources extracted from state lands, in the least. In *Maui Electric*, the court's standard is procedural: the state must provide a due process hearing prior to the deprivation of a constitutionally guaranteed right to a healthy environment. While that process does not dictate the standard to be used in determining whether a constitutional deprivation would take place, it at least guarantees a conversation about it.

While outliers, these courts are not alone in engaging constitutional environmental rights. The Supreme Court of Alaska recently read that state's "public interest" constitutional standard for resource development to require that courts take a hard look at whether state agencies adequately considered the cumulative environmental impacts of oil and gas leases.[97] And the Supreme Court of Montana has subjected that state's environmental rights provision to strict scrutiny,[98] although it has since been reluctant to enforce it.[99]

17.4 HYBRIDIZING STATE AND FEDERAL STANDARDS IN ENVIRONMENTAL CONSTITUTIONALISM

Environmental standards can also be promoted by hybridizing federal and state constitutional prerogatives. For example, ten out of the twenty-eight states of India (Tamil Nadu, Karnataka, Andhra Pradesh, Gujarat, Rajasthan, Maharashtra, Madhya Pradesh, West Bengal, Kerala, and Orissa) "are implementing major wind energy programmes" under the aegis of the federal constitution.[100] At times, the allocation of responsibility for the environment between the local and the national can give rise to political tensions and even military activity when the local and national goals are at odds, or when the revenues produced by exploitation of natural resources have to be equitably shared, as evidenced in negotiations regarding a draft constitution for Kurdistan;[101] most often, however, constitutional environmental provisions can also promote intergovernmental cooperation.

97 *Sullivan v Resisting Environmental Destruction on Indigenous Lands* 311 P3d 625 (AK 2013).

98 *Montana Environmental Information Center v Department of Environmental Quality* 988 P2d 1236 (MONT 1999).

99 See, for example, *Northern Plains Resource Council v Montana Board of Land Commissioners* 288 P3d 169 (MONT 2012).

100 Kirsten Jörgensen, "Climate Initiatives at the Subnational Level of the Indian States and Their Interplay with Federal Policies" (March 16–19, 2011) ISA Annual Convention Montreal.

101 See Kelly (n 57) 764.

Moreover, states that make up the Ethiopian federation (Afar, Amhara, Benishangul-Gumuz, Gambella, Harari, Oromia, Southern Nations, Nationalities, and Peoples' Regional State (SNNPRS), Somali, and Tigray), "share the ... environmental policy objectives" reflected in the national constitution.[102]

Other federal constitutions explicitly delegate the development of environmental standards to subnational entities, including Spain, Germany, and the Netherlands.[103] The federal Canadian Constitution "contains explicit language granting *exclusive* regulatory authority over subnational forest policy to the provinces ... [and that] this is a significant state of affairs since the Canadian provinces actually own or otherwise control 84 percent of the nation's forests."[104] Indeed, the Constitution of Canada provides in pertinent part:

> In each province, the legislature may exclusively make laws in relation to: (a) exploration for non-renewable natural resources in the province; (b) development, conservation and management of non-renewable natural resources and forestry resources in the province, including laws in relation to the rate of primary production therefrom. [105]

A similar pattern has emerged in Argentina, where the Province of Córdoba's constitutional environmental rights preceded those that followed at the national level.[106] Thus, subnational environmental constitutionalism can contribute to the normalization of environmental constitutionalism in a country and can goad activity at the national level.

17.5 CONCLUSION

The variety of subnational constitutional provisions aimed at protecting all facets of the environment in myriad ways, the textual and jurisprudential developments discussed above – and most recently evidenced by the *PEDF* and *Maui Electric* decisions in the United States – suggest that subnational environmental constitutionalism holds enormous potential. It has the potential to achieve the dual goals of advancing human rights and environmental protection at a subsidiary level, afford enormous potential for innovation, and provide additional sources of standards.

102 Tsegaye Regassa, "Sub-National Constitutions in Ethiopia: Towards Entrenching Constitutionalism at State Level" (2009) 2 Mizan Law Review 1.

103 Hans Bruyninckx, *Sustainable Development and Subnational Governments: Policy-Making and Multi-Level Interactions* (Palgrave Macmillan 2002) 109–15, 121–25, 132–34.

104 Blace Hudson, "What Kind of Constitutional Design Is Optimal for Environmental Governance?" (*Environmental Law Professor Blog*, February 6, 2012) <http://lawprofessors.typepad.com/environmental_law/2012/02/what-kind-of-constitutional-design-is-optimal-for-environmental-governance.html> accessed May 25, 2018.

105 See Canada Constitution VI Distribution of Legislative Powers 92A(1) English texts of the Constitution Act of 1867 and the Act of 1892 as amended to the Constitution Act 1999.

106 Maria Antonio Hernandez, *Sub-National Constitution Law in Argentina* (Kluwer Law International 2011) 24; see also Chapter 12 of this volume by Silvia Nonna relating to the Constitution of Argentina.

Subnational environmental constitutionalism offers several advantages to national environmental constitutionalism. Chief among these advantages is subsidiarity, that is, the ability to cater provisions to fit local needs. Such subsidiarity means that subnational provisions can be written to address local concerns, be justiciable in local courts, and be made enforceable by those with the greatest stake in the outcome. Subsidiarity also invites innovation in drafting and implementation. Indeed, as we have seen, some of the most progressive provisions in global environmental constitutionalism arise at the subnational level. For example, most states in Brazil guarantee a fundamental right to a healthy environment, protect resources important to local or indigenous populations, extoll sustainability as a governmental prerogative, and facilitate public participation in environmental matters. And more importantly, subnational environmental constitutionalism provides additional loci for development of environmental standards.

Subnational constitutional courts also have several advantages over national constitutional courts or tribunals. First, they have more freedom to experiment because the reach of their decisions is not as broad; they can function, as American lore says, as "laboratories" of governance.[107] Second, their familiarity with the terrain in question allows them to draw conclusions suited to the geography, history, and culture of the local environment, as was evident in the *Robinson Township* case. Third, they can at once fill gaps in the national system (as environmental constitutionalism does in the United States) or goad the national government into action as might have happened in Argentina. And, as a practical matter, it is often faster and less expensive to pursue a claim all the way to the top of the state judicial hierarchy than to the national one.

And yet, like national constitutions, those at the subnational level may be more ambitious than practical and more sweeping than precise. They are little more likely to entail precise standards either in ends or means than their counterparts at the national level. This leaves open opportunities for litigants to invoke their aspirational provisions in the particular circumstances of individual cases, to encourage the courts charged with vindicating those rights and values to fill the gaps in with more clearly articulated standards.

107 *New State Ice Co v Liebmann* 285 US 262 311 (1932).

18

Conclusion: Analysing the Development of Standards in the Field of Environmental Rights

Stephen J. Turner

18.1 INTRODUCTION

The introduction to this book referred to some of the challenges that have always faced the development of environmental rights and which played an important part in the academic debate surrounding their acceptance. The question of whether they could provide anything other than hortatory guidance to states was natural and still has relevance.[1] This issue has been played out by the problems of applying environmental rights in practice. For example, the difficulty that the European Court of Human Rights (ECtHR) experienced in the case of *Hatton* v. *UK (2003)*[2] in determining whether certain noise levels represented a violation of Art. 8 demonstrated how complex such determinations can be. Similarly, varying standards within the field of procedural rights experienced by different groups of citizens within the same state,[3] or the difficulties in clarifying precisely what standards should be applied at the regional level,[4] illustrate some of the challenges in putting procedural environmental rights into practice.

Having said this, environmental rights have clearly become an important component of many national constitutions and human rights treaty regimes. As such, research related to the precise levels of protection that they should represent is warranted. Each chapter of this book has sought to address this question from the perspective of a specific regime or from the perspective of a type of right, such as the right to water, rights of nature, free prior and informed consent (FPIC) and those present in

[1] S Douglas-Scott, 'Environmental Rights in the European Union – Participatory Democracy or Democratic Deficit' in A Boyle and MA Anderson (eds), *Human Rights Approaches to Environmental Protection* (Oxford University Press 1996) 110; Louis Henkin, *The Age of Rights* (Columbia University Press 1990) 27.

[2] *Hatton and Others v the United Kingdom* [GC] no. 36022/97 ECHR 2003-VIII (para 97).

[3] Lindsay C Stringer, Mark S Reed, Andrew J Dougill, Mary K Seely and Martin Rokitzki, 'Implementing the UNCCD: Participatory challenges' (2007) 31 Natural Resources Forum 198, 202.

[4] Peter Oliver, 'Access to Environmental Information and to Justice in EU Environmental Law: The Aarhus Convention' (2013) 36 (5) Fordham International Law Journal 1423.

multilateral environmental agreements (MEAs). As such, it has mapped out a broad cross-section of the most important types of environmental rights that have developed across the globe.

The purpose of this final chapter will be to draw upon the findings of each of the foregoing chapters to categorise the different types and sources of standards, or emerging standards, that have been evidenced throughout. Such a categorisation assists in providing an understanding of the way that such standards have been developing or failing to develop as the case may be. The chapter then considers what types of research could potentially assist in improving the effectiveness and efficiency of standards in this field as they continue to develop in the future.

18.2 THE DIFFERENT TYPES OF STANDARDS WITHIN THE FIELD OF ENVIRONMENTAL RIGHTS

The survey and analysis of standards within this book has taken into account the terminology used in constitutions and human rights treaties themselves, United Nations (UN) General Comments, guidelines from treaty regimes, guidelines and standards from international organisations, court judgments, determinations from complaint mechanisms and any other evidence that provides an indication of the standard or level of protection that should be provided by those rights that relate to the protection of the environment.

Prior to providing a form of categorisation of the types and sources of standards that have emerged from this research, it is necessary to make certain observations to inform the way that the categorisations can be regarded. The first is that the categories listed here are merely being provided as tools for further analysis, and as such are not intended to be definitive, but open to further development themselves.

The second relates to the use of the term 'standards' itself. The analysis contained in the book has sought to take into account the content of those rights that are used for the protection of the environment and the 'standard' of protection that they ultimately provide. The term 'standard' is therefore used in the generic sense to encapsulate developments which provide detail relating to the level of protection that a regime provides, regardless of whether the authority from which they are derived actually refers to them as a 'standard' as such. Therefore, initiatives such as 'guidelines' have been included as they also provide an indication of the standard of protection that can be expected under a particular regime.

Thirdly, the categorisations provided below generally fall into natural groupings which denote either an *outcome standard*, a *governmental action standard* or a *source* from which the standards are derived. These groupings can be described as follows:

(a) 'Qualitative' and 'quantitative' standards are all *outcome standards* as they denote the outcome in terms of the environment, or a procedure related to the environment, that is expected from a government or its citizens if they comply with the right or duty concerned.

(b) 'Minimum legislative standards', 'standards of enforcement and compliance', 'standards that legislation must comply with' and 'directive standards' all relate to specific standards of *governmental action* that are required if a state is to satisfy its responsibilities under the right or duty.

(c) 'Treaty regimes', 'national and sub-national constitutions', 'legislation and regulations', 'international organisations' and 'courts and complaint mechanisms' can be described as *sources*, as they denote the authority from which particular standards are derived.

What this means is that these categorisations are not all mutually exclusive, as they relate to both the types of standards and their sources. As such, a standard can fall within two or three of the different groupings.

The different categories listed below provide examples (rather than definitive lists) which are drawn from the evidence detailed in this book.

18.2.1 *Qualitative Standards (Outcome Standard)*

These are the most common types of outcome standards to be found in the wording of treaty regimes, national constitutions and sub-national constitutions. They describe the quality that the environment or an aspect of the environment must meet, usually using adjectival language, if it is to comply with the provision concerned. For example, the South African constitution provides that everyone has a right to live in an environment that is 'not harmful to their health or well-being'.[5] Within regional human rights treaties the African Charter of Human and Peoples Rights states that citizens are entitled to live in a 'general satisfactory environment favourable to their development'.[6] Within the Inter-American System the use of the term *vida digna* (dignified life) has arguably become a qualitative standard that is associated with the right to life and the level of protection of the environment that is afforded under it.[7]

Apart from being found within the text of constitutions and human rights treaties, they are provided for by other authorities that provide guidance on those rights that relate to environmental rights. For example, they are seen in general comments

5 Constitution of the Republic of South Africa, 10 December 1996, s 24(a); see Chapter 13 of this volume by Nathan J Cooper.

6 African Charter on Human and Peoples' Rights (Banjul) art 4 (27 June 1981, entered into force 21 October 1986) 21 ILM 59 (1982) art 24; see Chapter 5 of this volume by Louis Kotzé and Anél du Plessis.

7 *Yakye Axa Indigenous Community v Paraguay (Merits, Reparations and Costs)* IACtHR Series C No 125 (17 June 2005) paras 161–64; *Villagrán-Morales v Guatemala (Merits)* IACtHR Ser C No 63 (19 November 1999) para 144; *Sawhoyamaxa Indigenous Community v Paraguay* (Merits Reparations and Costs) IACtHR Ser C No 146 (29 March 2006) para 153; see Chapter 4 of this volume by Evadné Grant.

under the International Covenant on Economic, Social and Cultural Rights (ICESCR).[8] General Comment No. 14 requires water to be 'safe' and 'potable'.[9] Similarly, General Comment No. 15 states that individuals should be free from 'unsafe and toxic water conditions'.[10]

Also, under regimes that provide for participatory rights, levels of consultation have been provided for using qualitative standards. The United Nations Declaration on the Rights of Indigenous Peoples refers to the requirement of consultation with communities to be carried out in 'good faith'.[11]

Qualitative standards can also be found in other contexts, for example in the case of *Lopez Ostra* v. *Spain*, the level of detriment necessary for the admissibility of a claim was stated to be that of 'serious harm' ('des atteintes graves').[12]

18.2.2 *Quantitative Standards (Outcome Standard)*

These are the least common types of standards to be found within the provisions of national constitutions and to date have not been observed at all within the actual texts of regional human rights treaties provisions. The national constitutions that have used them are interesting examples and represent a relatively recent development in the field.

For example, Bhutan promulgated its first national constitution in 2008 and included a provision that the government has a responsibility to maintain 60 per cent of the nation's land under forest cover for all time.[13] Also, Kenya included in its revised 2010 national constitution a provision that made it a requirement of government policy to achieve and then maintain at least 10 per cent of the country's land mass under forest cover.[14] These particular types of constitutional provision may have a distant ancestor in the State of New York's constitution of 1894 which declared that 'the lands of the state, now owned or hereafter acquired, constituting the forest preserve as now fixed by law, shall be forever kept as wild forest lands'.[15] In doing so, it prescribed areas of land that should

8 Annex to UNGA Res. 2200 (XXI) (16 December 1966, in force 3 January 1976) 6 ILM 360 (1967) (ICESCR); see Chapter 2 of this volume by Sumudu Atapattu.

9 UN Committee on Economic Social and Cultural Rights, Doc E/C.12/2000/4 (11 August 2000) para 11; see Chapter 7 of this chapter by Owen Mcintyre.

10 UN Committee on Economic Social and Cultural Rights, Doc E/C.12/2002/11 (20 January 2003) para 37(f).

11 UNGA, 'United Nations Declaration on the Rights of Indigenous Peoples' (2 October 2007) A/RES/61/295 arts 19 and 32(2); see Chapter 9 of this volume by Jona Razzaque.

12 *Lopez Ostra v Spain* no. 16798/90, 9 December 1994, Series A no. 303-C paras 40 and 51; see Chapter 3 of this volume by Karen Morrow.

13 Constitution of Bhutan (18 July 2008); see Chapter 15 of this volume by Stephen J Turner.

14 Constitution of Kenya (27 August 2010) art 69(b); see Chapter 5 of this volume by Louis Kotzé and Anél du Plessis and also Chapter 15 by Stephen J Turner.

15 NY Const art XIV § 1 (originally art VII s 7); see Chapter 17 of this volume by James May and Erin Daly.

remain as 'wild forest lands', and as such set a limitation with some of the characteristics of permanence of the quantifiable standards that are now found in the Bhutanese and Kenyan constitutions.

Quantitative standards are seen more commonly in legislation and regulation that is lower in the hierarchy of laws than national constitutions. However, they are also seen in certain types of guidance that is provided to states (and for non-state actors) in relation to rights such as the right to water. For example, General Comment No. 15 refers to the World Health Organization (WHO) guidelines numerous times to illustrate the quantities and qualities that water supplies should be compliant with. For example, it referred to the fact that in 2000 the WHO estimated that at that time, 1.1 billion persons did not have access to an improved water supply (80 per cent of them rural dwellers) able to provide at least twenty litres of safe water per person a day.[16] Such quantitative references assist in providing measurable benchmarks against which the contents of rights can be developed.

18.2.3 *Minimum Legislative Standards (Governmental Action Standard)*

This type of standard was specifically included in the 2018 Framework Principles contained in the 'Report of the Special Rapporteur on the issue of human rights obligations relating to the enjoyment of a safe, clean, healthy and sustainable environment'.[17] The Framework Principles indicate that for citizens to enjoy a 'safe, clean, healthy and sustainable environment' states are required to 'establish, maintain and enforce effective legal and institutional frameworks'[18] and that 'such frameworks should include substantive environmental standards, including with respect to air quality, the global climate, freshwater quality, marine pollution, waste, toxic substances, protected areas, conservation and biological diversity'.[19]

The Framework Principles are based 'in certain instances on treaties but also on the statements of human rights bodies that have the authority to interpret human rights but not necessarily to issue binding decisions'.[20] This volume has detailed evidence from certain constitutions and regimes containing environmental rights which correspond with key aspects of Framework Principle 11.

16 CESCR 'General Comment No. 15' (n 10) para 1 referring to WHO; The Global Water Supply and Sanitation Assessment 2000 Geneva (2000) 1; see Chapters 2 and 7 of this volume by Sumudu Atapattu and Owen McIntyre, respectively.

17 United Nations Human Rights Council, 'Report of the Special Rapporteur on the issue of human rights obligations relating to the enjoyment of a safe, clean, healthy and sustainable environment.' 37 Sess 19 January 2018. A/HRC/37/59 annex paras 31–33; see Chapter 1 of this volume by Stephen J Turner.

18 A/HRC/37/59 ibid annex para 31.

19 ibid.

20 ibid Main report para 8.

For example, the revised Argentine Constitution of 1994[21] contains a provision which specifically requires the government to create minimum standards of protection through legislation.[22] Thus it states explicitly what is often only inferred in other constitutions. Certain regional human rights treaties also place an explicit obligation on member states to develop associated legislation. For example, the American Convention on Human Rights requires states to adopt 'such legislative or other measures as may be necessary to give effect to those rights'.[23] Also, the Implementation Guide to the Aarhus Convention states that the convention 'provides a "set of minimum standards" that provide a benchmark for states'.[24] In fact, standards developed at a national level can have a symbiotic relationship with human rights treaties themselves in that they inform and aid the development of standards and expectations under a treaty regime.

Such minimum standards also provide a bridge between state obligations vis à vis human rights and those of non-state actors such as corporations. It is at this nexus that states can define more precisely what is required of companies to ensure that they observe and comply with the necessary standards. This means also that such standards become transversal in nature as they can cut across sectors. This cross-sectoral scope is often implicit, but is referred to explicitly in some national constitutions, such as the Portuguese constitution.[25]

18.2.4 Standards of Compliance and Enforcement (Governmental Action Standard)

This type of standard relates to the enforcement of environmental legislation. In some states where standards have been developed through legislation there is limited redress where the levels of enforcement are inadequate, and as such, standards are rendered ineffective. While litigation is an important tool for environmental lawyers, it is an expensive and time-consuming mechanism that can become a blunt instrument if action is required swiftly. It can be rendered nugatory where the standards of enforcement and compliance of environmental legislation are effective.

This is reflected in the work of the Special Rapporteur on the Human Right to a Healthy Environment, as Framework Principle 12 requires that 'states should ensure the effective enforcement of their environmental standards against public

21 The Constitution of the Argentine Nation (as amended 1994); see Chapter 12 of this volume by Silvia Nonna.

22 ibid s 41.

23 American Convention on Human Rights (1969) OAS Treaty Series No 36; 1144 UNTS 123 art 2; see Chapter 4 of this volume by Evadné Grant.

24 United Nations Economic Commission for Europe, The Aarhus Convention: An Implementation Guide (2nd edn 2014) 42; see Chapter 6 of this volume by Áine Ryall.

25 The Constitution of the Portuguese Republic (2 April 1976) art 66(2)(f); see Chapter 11 of this volume by Alexandra Aragao.

and private actors'.[26] The commentary to the provision refers to the requirement that states 'effectively enforce compliance with the standards by preventing, investigating, punishing and redressing violations of the standards by private actors as well as governmental authorities. In particular, States must regulate business enterprises to protect against human rights abuses resulting from environmental harm and to provide remedies for such abuses.'[27]

Standards of compliance can mean that effective monitoring is integrated within a plan of action or strategy. Such monitoring should be set against effective benchmarks to ensure that the assessment of results can trigger remedial action where necessary. For example, General Comment No. 15 stipulates that the strategy and plan of action under the right to water 'should include methods, such as right to water indicators and benchmarks, by which progress can be closely monitored'.[28]

18.2.5 *The Standards That Legislation Must Comply With (Governmental Action Standard)*

This type of standard relates to the quality of legislation that can affect the environment. There have now been numerous cases in which laws have been challenged as being unconstitutional on the basis that they are inconsistent with the environmental provision of a constitution. One of the earliest cases where this occurred was the Hungarian *Protected Forests* case (1994), in which the Constitutional Court struck down amendments to an agricultural land privatization law that would have facilitated the transfer of forests to private ownership.[29] France has shown leadership in this respect as the French national constitution is being used actively to challenge the quality of legislation through reviews by the Constitutional Council.[30] Similarly, at the sub-national level there is evidence of this occurring in the United States.[31] Some national constitutions contain provisions that facilitate challenges to legislation but do not have a history of being used in this way.[32]

The standard that legislation must meet is also seen in regional human rights law such as the *Saramaka* v. *Suriname* case (2007)[33] in which the state's property laws

26 A/HRC/37/59 (n 17); see Chapter 1 of this volume by Stephen J Turner.

27 ibid A/HRC/37/59 annex para 34.

28 CESCR 'General Comment No. 15' (n 10) para 37(f). See further, paras 47, 53 and 54; see Chapters 2 and 7 of this volume by Sumudu Atapattu and Owen McIntyre, respectively.

29 *Magyar Közlöny* case 1994/no 55 1919 (20 May 1994).

30 See, for example, Project de Loi de finances pour 2010, 18 December 2009, Decision No. 2013–317 QPC of 24 May 2013 relating to paragraph V of Article L. 224–1 of the Environmental Code; see Chapter 14 of this volume by David Marrani and Stephen J Turner.

31 See *Robinson Township et al. v Commonwealth of Pennsylvania*, Pa. Sup. Ct, No. J-127A-D-2012 (decided 19 December 2013); see Chapter 17 of this volume by James R May and Erin Daly.

32 See, for example, the Constitution of the Portuguese Republic (n 25) arts 278, 280 and 281.

33 *Saramaka People v Suriname* (Preliminary Objections, Merits, Reparations and Costs) IACtHR Ser C No 172 (28 November 2007).

were found to inadequately reflect the property rights of the Saramaka people, and as such the court ordered the Government of Suriname to take appropriate steps to implement legislative or other measures that would enable the Saramaka people to exercise their rights.[34]

The question with the standard of legislation is the precise test or criteria that determines whether or not legislation is compliant with a constitution or treaty regime. One of the issues that it raises is the question of the 'standard of review', or in other words the level of deference that is granted to a legislative body. This is particularly important when considering the separation of powers and the respective roles of the judiciary and the legislature within democratic government.

18.2.6 Directive Standards (Governmental Action Standard)

This type of standard relates to any other types of actions that states are required to fulfil if they are to realise the environmental right concerned.[35] Therefore, they can relate to the requirement to set up programmes, targets and performance indicators that provide a pathway for the government in their realisation of a particular right. They are required, for example, under general comments such as General Comment No. 15 relating to the right to water, which states that:

> States parties should adopt comprehensive and integrated strategies and programmes to ensure that there is sufficient and safe water for present and future generations. Such strategies and programmes may include: (a) reducing depletion of water resources through unsustainable extraction, diversion and damming; (b) reducing and eliminating contamination of watersheds and water-related ecosystems by substances such as radiation, harmful chemicals and human excreta; (c) monitoring water reserves; (d) ensuring that proposed developments do not interfere with access to adequate water; (e) assessing the impacts of actions that may impinge upon water availability and natural-ecosystems watersheds, such as climate changes, desertification and increased soil salinity, deforestation and loss of biodiversity; (f) increasing the efficient use of water by end-users; (g) reducing water wastage in its distribution; (h) response mechanisms for emergency situations; (i) and establishing competent institutions and appropriate institutional arrangements to carry out the strategies and programmes.[36]

They arguably represent the standard of action required by a government to put in place the necessary pathway towards the realisation of a right.

34 ibid para 63.

35 See Chapter 5 of this volume by Louis Kotzé and Anél du Plessis which refers to 'directive' standards.

36 CESCR 'General Comment No. 15' (n 10) para 28 (footnotes excluded); see Chapters 2 and 7 of this volume by Sumudu Atapattu and Owen McIntyre, respectively.

18.2.7 *Treaty Regimes (Source)*

Treaty regimes sometimes produce guidelines that have the capacity to influence the development of standards or what can be regarded as standards. Examples include the Akwé: Kon Guidelines[37] that were produced by a work programme relating to the provision of the Convention on Biological Diversity[38] requiring parties to 'respect, preserve and maintain knowledge, innovations and practices of indigenous and local communities embodying traditional lifestyles relevant for the conservation and sustainable use of biological diversity and promote their wider application'.[39] They were subsequently adopted at the seventh conference of the parties.[40] While ostensibly these only enjoy the status of 'voluntary guidelines', they are treated with considerable authority. For example, the Inter-American Court of Human Rights when considering environmental and social impact assessments has stated that 'ESIAs must conform to the relevant international standards and best practices.'[41] In a footnote it then describes the Akwé: Kon Guidelines as 'one of the most comprehensive and used standards for ESIAs in the context of indigenous and tribal peoples'.[42]

A number of the different initiatives that have been produced in this vein relate directly to particular MEAs and represent nonbinding guides to member states that assist in the development of legislation, regulations and programmes that would be consistent with their realisation of the treaty objectives. Examples include the voluntary Bonn Guidelines relating to access to genetic resources and benefit sharing developed by the Convention of Biological Diversity,[43] the UN-REDD Programme Social and Environmental Principles and Criteria related to the United Nations Framework Convention on Climate Change[44] and the Aarhus Implementation Guide.[45]

37 Secretariat of the Convention on Biological Diversity, 'Akwé Kon Voluntary Guidelines for the Conduct of Cultural, Environmental and Social Impact Assessment regarding Developments Proposed to Take Place on, or which are Likely to Impact on, Sacred Sites and on Lands and Waters Traditionally Occupied or Used by Indigenous and Local Communities' (CBD Guidelines Series 2004); see Chapters 4 and 9 of this volume by Evadné Grant and Jona Razzaque, respectively.

38 Convention on Biodiversity (Rio de Janeiro) (adopted 5 June 1992, entered into force 29 December 1993) 31 ILM 822.

39 ibid Art. 8(j).

40 Decision Adopted by the Conference of the Parties to the Convention on Biological Diversity (27 February 2004) UNEP/CBD/COP/DEC/VII/16.

41 *Saramaka People v Suriname (Interpretation of the Judgment on Preliminary Objects, Merits, Reparations and Costs)* IACtHR Ser C No 185 (12 August 2008) para 41; see Chapters 4 and 9 of this volume by Evadné Grant and Jona Razzaque, respectively.

42 ibid.

43 Secretariat of the Convention on Biological Diversity, 'Bonn Guidelines on Access to Genetic Resources and Fair and Equitable Sharing of the Benefits Arising out of their Utilization' (2002); see Chapter 9 of this volume by Jona Razzaque.

44 'UN-REDD Programme Social and Environmental Principles and Criteria', UN-REDD Programme Eighth Policy Board Meeting, Asuncion, Paraguay, UNREDD/PB8/2012/V/1 (25–26 March 2012); see Chapter 9 of this volume by Jona Razzaque.

45 UNECE, *Aarhus Convention: An Implementation Guide* (n 24); see Chapter 6 of this volume by Áine Ryall.

Treaty regimes typically have to take into account the fact that member states have different geographies, topographies, natural resource distribution, climate, population, economies and competing pressures on land use in different localities. For this reason it has often been impossible to provide precision related to substantive environmental rights, and as a result even the expectations for procedural rights can be subject to variations. Therefore, in both global and regionally applicable treaties a certain degree of flexibility is incorporated into the treaty obligations. This is seen very clearly within the European Convention of Human Rights regime, where the European Court of Human Rights affords states a 'margin of appreciation' in the way that they interpret and implement their obligations.[46]

This can also mean that in this context it is 'directive' standards that are widely utilised. For example, General Comment No. 14 on the Right to the Highest Attainable Standard of Health provides a series of actions that states are advised to take to ensure that they achieve the requisite standard of protection.[47] It refers to the need for states to

> adopt and implement a national public health strategy and plan of action, on the basis of epidemiological evidence, addressing the health concerns of the whole population; the strategy and plan of action shall be devised, and periodically reviewed, on the basis of a participatory and transparent process; they shall include methods, such as right to health indicators and benchmarks, by which progress can be closely monitored; the process by which the strategy and plan of action are devised, as well as their content, shall give particular attention to all vulnerable or marginalized groups.[48]

18.2.8 National and Sub-National Constitutions (Source)

National and sub-national constitutions that contain environmental rights do inevitably provide broad standards relating to the level of protection that is expected. Terms such as 'healthy', 'safe' or 'clean' are frequently used to describe the standard to which the environment should be maintained.[49] Such terms are often too vague except in the most extreme of cases to provide sufficient clarity as to the precise level of protection that is conferred on the rights holder. They usually require further elaboration from other sources to be given meaningful effect.

46 *Lopez Ostra v Spain* (n 12) para 51; see Chapter 3 of this volume by Karen Morrow.

47 CESCR General Comment No. 14 (n 9); see Chapter 2 of this volume by Sumudu Atapattu.

48 ibid General Comment No. 14 para 43(f).

49 See Stephen J Turner, *A Substantive Environmental Right – An Examination of Decision-Makers towards the Environment* (Kluwer Law International 2009) 44–48; David R Boyd, *The Environmental Rights Revolution – A Global Study of Constitutions, Human Rights, and the Environment* (UBC Press 2012) 47.

18.2.9 *Legislation and Regulation (Source)*

Most states implement the content of the rights in their constitutions through legislation, which will often contain minimum standards or provide the authority for the creation of such standards. As noted above, the Argentine Constitution specifically requires the government to create such legislation.[50] This has resulted in legislation relating to the management of industrial waste,[51] polychlorinated biphenyls (PCBs)[52] and water,[53] amongst other areas.

In many other countries the national constitution itself does not prescribe that the state create minimum standards of protection through legislation; however, governments have created ministries that have the power to create enforceable regulations and standards. For example in India, the government has created the Ministry of Environment Forest and Climate Change, the Central Pollution Control Board and the State Pollution Control Boards to oversee the development and implementation of standards.[54]

In countries that are members of the European Union (EU), standards can be derived both from the EU itself and from the national government. In Portugal, for example, much of the environmental legislation that is required under the national constitution is also required for compliance under EU law; as such, it is often the EU which sets the standards.[55] Therefore, water management law is required to comply with the EU's Water Framework Directive,[56] and the regulation of ambient air quality is required to comply with the EU's Air Quality Directive.[57] However, in certain instances Member States of the EU will go further in their national law than is required under the relevant EU directive; this is commonly known as 'gold plating'. For example, in Portugal, the law relating to environmental impact assessments[58] goes further than that required under the Environmental Assessment Directive,[59] as it requires that the recommendations of an EIA are binding on the final determination made in cases where significant adverse environmental impacts have been identified,[60] whereas under the EU law such recommendations only need to be taken into

50 The Argentine Constitution (n 21) s 41; see Chapter 12 of this volume by Silvia Nonna.

51 Integrated Management of Industrial Waste Act (2002) (Law No 25.612).

52 Management of Polychlorinated biphenyls (PCBs) Management and Disposal Act (2002) (Law No 25.670).

53 The Water Management Regime Act (2003) (Law No 25.688).

54 See Chapter 10 of this volume by Gitanjali N Gill.

55 See Chapter 11 of this volume by Alexandra Aragao.

56 Directive 2000/60/EC of the European Parliament and of the Council of 23 October Establishing a Framework for Community Action in the Field of Water Policy [2000] OJ L327/1.

57 Directive 2008/50/EC of the European Parliament and of the Council of 21 May 2008 on Ambient Air Quality and Cleaner Air for Europe [2008] OJ L152/1.

58 Decree-Law No 151-B/2013 of 31 October 2013 art 22.

59 Directive 2011/92/EU of the European Parliament and of the Council of 13 December 2011 on the Assessment of the Effects of Certain Public and Private Projects on the Environment [2012] OJ L26/1.

60 Decree-Law No 151-B/2013 (n 58) art 22.

consideration.[61] It is possible that the adoption of this stringent standard may have been influenced by the relatively detailed environmental provisions within the Portuguese constitution.[62]

The regulations that government departments institute can have a direct relationship with the environmental provisions of the national constitution. In France, the administrative branches of government create regulations which are required to comply with legislation, which in turn is required to comply with the Charter of the Environment.[63] Therefore, such regulations create standards that should be consistent with the purpose of the constitution on the pain of potential legal challenge.[64]

18.2.10 *International Organisations (Source)*

It has been seen that certain courts and treaty regimes rely on the guidance of international organisations for standards or benchmarks. For example, the WHO produces a range of highly influential guidelines relating to pollutant levels, risk management and public health policy. These include guidelines related to water quality,[65] air quality for particulate matter[66] and indoor air quality.[67] As an example, the WHO Guidelines for Drinking-Water Quality are highly detailed in terms of benchmarks relating to the quantity and quality of water that should be acceptable, and include a range of other benchmarks and indicators such as water safety plans, health-based targets and specific measures that should be taken in times of natural disasters.[68] Such guidelines acquire legitimacy if they are derived from a respected international organization that produces independent responses based on high-quality research.

One of the other major sources of standardisation in the field of environmental rights has been the UN Environment Programme (UNEP, now 'UN Environment'). In 2010 it produced the Bali Guidelines, which were designed to assist countries in filling gaps in national and sub-national legislation with regard to the facilitation of access to information, public participation and access to justice in environmental

61 Directive 2014/52/EU of the European Parliament and of the Council of 16 April 2014 amending Directive 2011/92/EU (n 59) art 8 adds that 'the results of consultations and the information gathered pursuant to articles 5 to 7 shall be duly taken into account in the development consent procedure'.

62 Constitution of the Portuguese Republic (7th revision 2005) art 66; see Chapter 11 of this volume by Alexandra Aragao.

63 Loi constitutionnelle 2005–205, 1 March 2005 (Loi constitutionnelle relative à la Charte de l'environnement (1)), JORF 2 March 2005, 3697.

64 See Chapter 14 of this volume by David Marrani and Stephen J Turner.

65 World Health Organization, *Guidelines for Drinking-Water Quality* (4th edn Incorporating the First Addendum, WHO 2017); see Chapters 2 and 7 of this volume by Sumudu Atapattu and Owen McIntyre, respectively.

66 World Health Organization, *WHO Air Quality Guidelines for Particulate Matter, Ozone, Nitrogen dioxide and Sulfur Dioxide – Global Update 2005 – Summary of Risk Assessment* (WHO 2006).

67 World Health Organization (Europe), *Guidelines for Indoor Air Quality: Selected Pollutants* (WHO 2010).

68 WHO, *Guidelines for Drinking-Water Quality* (n 65).

matters.[69] In 2015, UNEP produced further guidance entitled 'Putting Rio Principle 10 into Action: An Implementation Guide'.[70] Through these initiatives it has standardized approaches that are consistent with the contemporary expectations of states and civil society under Principle 10 of the Rio Declaration.[71]

The World Bank Group and other multilateral development banks are also sources of standards. They generate their own operating policies and procedures related to different types of projects. An example is the International Finance Corporation performance standards, which provide private loan guidelines relating to environment and social sustainability.[72]

While UN organizations or UN-affiliated organizations are often the first port of call when seeking guidelines and standards, some organisations have developed independently of the UN and acquired a significant level of authority. For example, the International Organization for Standardization (ISO)[73] plays a role in the development of certain types of standards that affect environmental rights. These include standards relating to drinking water,[74] waste water services[75] and the management of drinking water distribution networks.[76] The ISO is an independent organization with a membership of 161 national standards bodies,[77] which includes significant representation from business and industry in the development of the standards that it produces. This raises questions relating to the role of private actors in standard-setting procedures that ultimately relate to human rights.[78]

18.2.11 Courts and Complaint Mechanisms (Source)

Courts and complaint mechanisms can have roles to play in the development of standards. At the treaty level, those treaties that include complaint mechanisms have the capacity to play a role in the development of standards relating to the rights that they consider. There has been some limited development in this regard from the treaty bodies of the ICCPR and the ICESCR. For example, in *Angela Poma Poma*

69 UNEP, 'Guidelines for the Development of National Legislation on Access to Information, Public Participation, and Access to Justice in Environmental Matters' (26 February 2010), Decision SS/XI/5 Part A; see Chapter 8 of this volume by Lara Ognibene and Angela Kariuki.

70 UNEP, *Putting Principle 10 into Action: An Implementation Guide* (UNEP 2015).

71 Report of the United Nations Conference on Environment and Development (Rio de Janeiro), 14 June 1992 UN Doc A/CONF. 151/5/Rev.1 (UNCED) Principle 10.

72 International Finance Corporation, 'IFC Performance Standards on Environmental and Social Sustainability' (World Bank Group 2012); see Chapter 9 of this volume by Jona Razzaque.

73 International Organization for Standardization (ISO). <www.iso.org/about-us.html> accessed 12 June 2018; see Chapter 7 of this volume by Owen McIntyre.

74 ISO 24511:2007.

75 ibid.

76 ISO 24518:2015.

77 ISO (n 73).

78 B Morgan, 'Turning off the Tap: Urban Water Service Delivery and the Social Construction of Global Administrative Law' (2006) 17 (1) European Journal of International Law 215, 225.

v. *Peru* (2009),[79] a complaint to the Human Rights Committee (HRC) concerning an assessment of the standard of consultation that had taken place led to a determination that the complainant's right to be properly consulted had been violated.[80] The HRC found that the participation should be 'effective' and that it should not amount to 'mere consultation' but include 'free prior and informed consent' of the community.[81] While such a decision is not binding, it has persuasive character and is therefore highly influential.

The Court of Justice of the European Union has a role to play in enforcing the provisions of the Aarhus Convention. In the cases of *R (Edwards)* v. *Environment Agency* (2013)[82] and *Commission* v. *United Kingdom* (2014)[83] it developed a set of criteria relating to the level of costs that are applicable when citizens seek to access remedies that are covered by the Convention. Similarly, the Aarhus Convention Compliance Committee plays a significant role in developing the standards to which member states are expected to comply in their implementation of the Convention provisions.

At the national level, courts of certain jurisdictions are particularly proactive in the development of standards relating to rights that are used for the protection of the environment. A leading example is that of India, where the courts have traditionally been imaginative, creative and responsive in this respect. That judicial activity has extended to the development of standards through the National Green Tribunal (NGT) and its use of scientific experts to inform the judgments that are delivered.[84] An example of the proactive nature of the NGT is found in the case of *D. B. Nevatia* v. *State of Maharashtra* (2013).[85] In this case, the NGT directed the federal government to provide source-specific noise level standards for sirens and multi-tone vehicles within a period of three months from the judgment.[86]

At the sub-national level there is also some evidence of courts developing certain standards. For example, in the case of *Re Application of Maui Electric Company* (2017)[87] the court construed the provisions of the constitution to signify that the state had an obligation to provide a due process hearing prior to adversely affecting

79 Human Rights Committee, Communication No 1457/2006 Doc CCPR/C/95/D/1457/2006 of March 2009; see Chapter 2 of this volume by Sumudu Atapattu.

80 ibid para 8. It found that there had been violations of art 27 and art 2, para 3 (a), read in conjunction with art 27

81 ibid para 7.6.

82 Case C-260/11 *R (Edwards) v Environment Agency* EU:C:2013:221; see Chapter 6 of this volume by Áine Ryall.

83 Case-C530/11 *Commission v United Kingdom* EU:C:2014:67; see Ryall ibid.

84 GN Gill, 'Environmental Justice in India: The National Green Tribunal and Expert Members' (2016) 5 (1) Transnational Environmental Law 175, 181; see Chapter 10 of this volume by Gitanjali N Gill.

85 National Green Tribunal (New Delhi) Judgment 9 January 2013; see Gill Chapter 10 ibid.

86 ibid NGT para 8.

87 *Re Application of Maui Electric Company (Sierra Club) v. Public Utility Commission of Hawai'i*, SCWC-15–0000640 (Supreme Court of Hawai'i 2017); see Chapter 17 of this volume by James May and Erin Daly.

a citizen's constitutional right to a healthy environment.[88] It therefore made a clear statement relating to the standard of the procedural requirements related to the right.

Naturally, there are questions that relate to the separation of powers when courts intervene to either create or catalyse the elaboration of standards, and this generates important debate.[89]

18.2.12 *Rights of Nature*

For the purpose of this conclusion, rights of nature are given separate mention as the ultimate source of the authority, for the associated standards are the 'rights' of the aspect of the environment concerned, rather than a particular right that humans are entitled to. The non-anthropocentric character of rights of nature and their more recent development means that they are developing in slightly different ways to the more conventional (anthropocentric) types of environmental rights that the majority of this study has been concerned with. Having said this, the evidence surveyed of the nascent standards in this field shows that standards are emerging in court judgments and also in laws.

Individual cases are gradually providing more clarity as to the standard of protection that is required in instances where a right of nature is applicable. For example, in Ecuador the Loja Provincial Court of Justice made such a judgment relating to damage to the Vilacamba River ecosystem resulting from the dumping of waste.[90] It determined that local landowners could sue on behalf of the river and did not need to prove any harm to themselves or their own land, and ordered that the river's ecosystem would have to be restored;[91] as such, both procedural and substantive standards related to the right were further developed.

Additionally, in certain jurisdictions laws are being developed to establish rights of nature and provide broad standards relating to the level of protection that are applicable. For example, Pittsburgh's ordinance states that 'natural communities and ecosystems' have the right to 'exist and flourish'.[92] While such laws do represent sources of generic standards, they clearly require further elaboration, and this is likely to require reliance on research related to associated science and environmental management techniques.[93]

88 The Constitution of Hawai'i art 11 s 9; see May and Daly ibid.

89 See, for example, Loretta Feris, 'Constitutional Environmental Rights: An Under-Utilised Resource' (2008) 24 S Africa Journal of Human Rights 29, 34; see Chapter 13 of this volume by Nathan J Cooper.

90 Judgement No. 11121–2011-0010, Provincial Court of Justice, Loja Province, Republic of Ecuador (30 March 2011) 3–4; see Chapter 16 of this volume by Kauffman and Sheehan.

91 ibid Provincial Court of Justice 5–6; Kauffman and Sheehan ibid.

92 City of Pittsburgh, Ordinance supplementing the Pittsburgh Code, Title Six, Conduct, Article 1 Regulated Rights and actions, by adding Chapter 618 entitled Marcellus Shale Natural Gas Drilling at 618.03(b); see Kauffman and Sheehan ibid.

93 See, for example, Robert Costanza and Michael Mageau, 'What Is a Healthy Ecosystem' (1999) 33 Aquatic Ecology 105; CW Fowler and L Hobbs, 'Are We Asking the Right Questions in Science and

18.2.13 *Other Types of Standards*

The dynamic nature of the developments that have taken place in the field of environmental rights over the last half-century, has shown that new aspects of environmental rights are continually evolving. For example, ensuring protection and freedom of expression for those individuals, sometimes known as 'human rights defenders', who seek to protect their environments and those of the communities in which they live, but who are vulnerable to persecution, physical attack and murder as a result, is a major challenge.[94] As those individuals seek to exercise their rights, there are questions relating to the standard of protection that is available and precisely what the obligations of states and businesses are in this regard.[95]

At the constitutional level, rights that relate to cross-sectoral policy within the field of environmental protection raise questions relating to the standards that those associated policies and laws should represent if they are to be considered to be compliant. For example, in Portugal the national constitution contains a provision which requires 'that the fiscal policy renders development compatible with the protection of the environment and the quality of life'.[96] This is an emerging area within the field of environmental rights which will require greater clarification if it is to prove effective.

18.3 MOVING FORWARD

The fragmented manner in which environmental rights have developed around the world has had a corresponding effect on the way that the standards associated with them have also developed. The global overview is an image of a patchwork of rights and standards, often with variable content, that have developed in different ways as they respond to different types of challenges in practice.

The benefit of the piecemeal development of standards is the avoidance of a 'one size fits all' approach that could potentially be oppressive, inappropriate or unworkable. However, it also means that it can lead to duplication of effort, a certain degree of confusion, *lacunae* in standards in certain areas and a lack of consistency. At worst, what this can mean for those who suffer rights violations, or the threat of them, is that they can be left without protection or redress. Where uncertainty exists, some citizens and organisations have the resources, time, energy and capacity to take the risks involved in bringing test cases to challenge executive branches of government, but many do not.

Management?' NOAA Technical Memorandum NMFS-AFSC-202 (December 2009) 43; see Kauffman and Sheehan ibid.

94 See *Kawas-Fernández v Honduras (Merits, Reparations and Costs)* IACtHR Series C No 196 (3 April 2009) [145–46]; see Chapter 1 of this volume by Stephen J Turner.

95 See 'UN Environment, Promoting Greater Protection for Environmental Defenders – Policy' *(UN Environment)* <https://wedocs.unep.org> accessed 30 July 2018; see Stephen J Turner ibid.

96 Portuguese Constitution (n 25) art 66(2)(h); see Chapter 11 of this volume by Alexandra Aragao.

Overall, this volume has emphasised the importance of the processes that occur once a right has become law. In this sense it has made a distinction between what could be regarded as the primary stage in the development of an environmental right, in other words the moment of promulgation at which the right itself becomes law through a constitution or a treaty, and the secondary stage of development, which can be described as the processes that take place after a right has been promulgated that provide a deeper understanding of its content and the manner in which it should be applied in practice. In shedding light on these areas, this volume has raised a number of questions that relate not just to the standards of protection themselves but also to the processes through which standards develop and how they become recognised in a way that can lead to their practical application. As such, some of the areas that may require further research, analysis and practical development are as follows:

(a) Research relating to the processes that states should implement to develop the minimum substantive environmental standards that are referred to in Principle 11 of the 2018 report by the UN Special Rapporteur of human rights and the environment to realise the right to a 'safe, clean, healthy and sustainable environment';[97]
(b) Research relating to the standards that governmental monitoring, compliance and enforcement mechanisms should meet, as referred to in Principle 12 of the 2018 report by the UN Special Rapporteur of human rights and the environment to realise the right to a 'safe, clean, healthy and sustainable environment';[98]
(c) Research relating to the criteria that can be used to test the standards that legislation that can affect the environment should be consistent with;
(d) Research relating to the standards that procedural environmental rights should meet;
(e) Research relating to the possible ways in which guidelines can be afforded recognition especially at the UN level, when they are developed by actors other than the UN;
(f) Research analysing the most efficient ways to rationalise existing standards from different sources relating to the same subject matter (for example, in such fields as the right to water);
(g) Research to aid in the development of standards that are associated with rights that have either recently emerged or are emerging, such as those that are framed in quantitative terms, those relating to fiscal policy, those relating to human rights defenders and the rights of nature.
(h) Research analysing how communication relating to the development of standards within differing institutions such as scientific, governmental and judicial institutions can be strengthened;

97 UNHRC 'Report of the Special Rapporteur on the issue of human rights obligations relating to the enjoyment of a safe, clean, healthy and sustainable environment' (n 17) Framework Principle 11.
98 ibid Framework Principle 12.

(i) Research focussing on the most efficient methods of developing environmental rights-based standards at the state and national levels within federal systems of government;
(j) Research focussing on the work of tribunals and complaint mechanisms to incorporate an understanding of the most efficient methods of developing and/or applying environmental rights-based standards;
(k) Research considering the most appropriate and efficient methods of incorporating science and technology within the development of environmental rights-based standards.
l) Research considering the manner in which environmental rights-based standards can apply directly to companies through initiatives such as the UN Guiding Principles on Business and Human Rights.[99]

This type of research is of course important to the development of standards within the realm of existing rights that are used for the protection of the environment. However, it also has relevance to any new rights that may emerge in the future. For example, it is possible that at the global level a human right to a healthy environment will be more formally recognised or adopted at some point.[100] If that does occur, then it can be argued that it should do so within a streamlined framework that facilitates the ongoing process for the understanding and development of the standards of protection that relate to it.

While it is not possible to predict precisely what developments will take place in this field in the future, what is certain is that rights that are used for the protection of the environment are continually evolving. As the Special Rapporteur on Human Rights and the Environment emphasised in his final report, 'the relationship between human rights and the environment has countless facets, and our understanding of it will continue to grow for many years to come'.[101] Standards within this field are one of those facets, and the more that we understand of them, the easier it will be to effectively implement and develop environmental rights in the future.

99 UN Human Rights Council, 'Report of the Special Representative of the Secretary-General on the issue of Human Rights and Transnational Corporations and other Business Enterprises, John Ruggie – Guiding Principles on Business and Human Rights: Implementing the United Nations "Protect, Respect and Remedy" Framework' UN Doc A/HRC/17/31 (21 March 2011).

100 See generally John H. Knox and Ramin Pejan (eds), *The Human Right to a Healthy Environment* (CUP 2018).

101 UNHRC 'Report of the Special Rapporteur on the issue of human rights obligations relating to the enjoyment of a safe, clean, healthy and sustainable environment' (n 17) Main report para 10.

Index